ONE DISH MEALS
The Easy Way

Reader's Digest

ONE DISH MEALS
The Easy Way

Published by The Reader's Digest Association Limited
London • New York • Sydney • Cape Town • Montreal

ONE DISH MEALS The Easy Way
was edited and designed by
The Reader's Digest Association
Limited, London.

Printed in Italy

ISBN 0 276 42119 1

Some of the recipes in this book have
been adapted from 'One Dish Meals
The Easy Way', published in 1991
by Reader's Digest, USA.

Front cover *Pot Roast Leg of Lamb with
Port and Redcurrant Glaze comes to the
table surrounded by juicy vegetables and
adorned with a garnish of fresh redcurrants
and fragrant rosemary (see p.70).*

Page 1 *For Lobster Newburg (see p.136),
lobster meat, scallops and tiger prawns are
lightly fried in a creamy sauce and then
baked on a bed of spinach and vegetables.*

Pages 2 and 3 *The finished Lobster
Newburg, served piping hot and slightly
browned from the oven with crusty rolls
and chilled white wine, makes an elegant
meal fit to grace any dinner party table.*

Editor Henrietta Wilkinson
Art Editor Julie Busby

Contributors

Consultant Editor

Pat Alburey

Nutritional Consultant

Anita Bean BSC

Recipes created by

Pat Alburey, Valerie Barrett, Jackie Burrow,
Carole Handslip, Petra Jackson, Angela Kingsbury

**Photography commissioned
for this edition**

Photographers

Martin Brigdale
Amanda Heywood

Home Economists

Berit Vinegrad
Angela Kingsbury

Stylist

Helen Trent

Other photographs from
'One Dish Meals The Easy Way',
published by Reader's Digest USA,
South Africa and Italy.

Contents

SOUPS
16-47

MEAT
48-81

POULTRY AND GAME
82-117

FISH AND SHELLFISH
118-147

VEGETARIAN MEALS
148-173

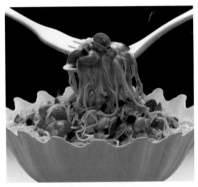

PASTA AND PIZZA
174-203

SALADS
204-233

MICROWAVE MEALS
234-259

QUICK AND EASY
260-285

HOLIDAY MEALS
286-319

MAKE AHEAD AND FREEZE
320-341

Making the most of this book

Cooking is an extremely creative process, a fact that is all too easy to forget during the humdrum process of providing a daily meal. The recipes in this book are designed to inspire both experienced and inexperienced cooks, and they employ fresh ingredients and inventive cooking techniques that will enhance your repertoire of dishes for family and friends.

TWO SIMPLE PRINCIPLES guided the selection of the recipes for this book. Each one had to provide an enjoyable, tasty meal; and each one had to be ready to serve from a single dish or pan. The resulting collection of one-dish meals employs flavours and cooking techniques from around the world. In some, the ingredients are added one after the other to the cooking pot; in others, they are combined just before serving. In all cases, the end result is a complete meal in itself, without the need for extra vegetables or a dessert. Many of the recipes do suggest that a side salad, crusty fresh bread or a selection of pickles would go well with the finished dish, but this is a choice for you to make.

Many of the meals draw on the increasing range of prepared ingredients that are available in shops, especially in the larger supermarkets. Ingredients such as bottled sauces, boneless chicken breasts or cuts of meat, trimmed and ready to stir-fry, can be a boon to the weary cook preparing a meal at the end of a long day. They also encourage the less experienced cook, who can now shop for all the ingredients – fresh, canned, prepared or frozen – to make authentic Italian, Mexican or Chinese meals.

However, it is always best to prepare the ingredients yourself when possible. At the end of each chapter in this book, many of the techniques called for in the recipes are explained and illustrated in easy step-by-step sequence. These can range from boning a fish to building and lighting an effective barbecue, from making dumplings to lining a flan case with filo pastry.

Methods of preparing food have been included so that you have the choice of doing the preparation yourself, rather than relying totally on prepared ingredients. To joint a whole chicken may require a little extra time and effort to do at home, but will cost far less than buying prepared pieces from a supermarket. Similarly, homemade pizza dough will be fresher-tasting and lighter than any you buy from a shop.

How the book is arranged

Some 380 recipes for one-dish meals have been divided into the 11 chapters in this book, according to their basic ingredients. In addition, a number of basic recipes, as well as the techniques that are required for preparing vegetables, are covered in a separate introductory section.

The basic recipes include beef, chicken, fish and vegetable stocks – all of which are salt-free – as well as pancakes and shortcrust pastry. A reliable method of cooking rice and the various cooking times required for different types of rice are also described here.

The main herbs, oils, vinegars, mustards, spices, peppers and seeds are illustrated in the pages that follow.

If you come across any ingredients which are new to you, or which you are not sure how to use, the illustrated Glossary on pp.342-6 will help you to understand them. In these pages you will also find illustrations for the different breads, grains, mushrooms, pulses and shellfish that are called for in the recipes, and which you can find in most of the large supermarkets and delicatessens.

Types of salad and three different dressings are illustrated on pp.232-3, while illustrations of the various types of pasta which you may need appear on p.202.

For further help consult the Index, which lists recipes according to the principal ingredients used in them.

Using the recipes

All the ingredients in the recipes are given in both metric and Imperial measurements. Choose one set or the other to work with, as combining both measurements within a single recipe may create slight discrepancies.

Most of the recipes in this book provide four helpings, and in some cases six. If you are cooking for only two or three, or for a party of eight or 12, simply halve or double the quantity of ingredients accordingly. All the spoon measurements refer to British standard measuring spoons, obtainable from hardware stores or the larger supermarkets.

In some recipes, cross-references appear in brackets in the list of ingredients or in the instructions. These refer to relevant basic recipes, tips on vegetable preparation, and to techniques such as how to fillet a fish.

Getting the balance right

To help you to understand the requirements of a healthy diet, each recipe has been analysed to show you how many calories and how much protein, fat, saturated fat, carbohydrate, added sugar, fibre and sodium are contained in an average serving of the recipe. This information is shown in a chart, as in the following specimen:

Per serving
Calories 498 Protein 39 g
Total fat 18 g (saturated fat 6.8 g)
Carbohydrates 48 g (added sugar 0)
Fibre 4.1 g Sodium 366 mg

Taken from Chicken and Broccoli Salad, p.208.

The figures were analysed using the Comp-Eat 4.0 programme. To help you to use this nutritional analysis effectively, compare the analysis for each recipe with the chart below, which shows the optimum daily amounts per category as suggested by the Department of Health. They are based on the daily needs of adults aged 19-50 who lead a sedentary life. People who are physically active will need more calories and nutrients, while children require relatively fewer calories.

	MEN	WOMEN
Calories	2550	1940
Protein	55.5 g	45 g
Total fat	Less than 94 g	Less than 71 g
Saturated fat	Less than 28 g	Less than 22 g
Carbohydrates	Min. 300 g	Min. 228 g
Added sugar	Max. 64 g	Max. 49 g
Fibre	30 g	30 g
Sodium	1600 mg	1600 mg

Any recipes which use milk have been analysed as if made with semi-skimmed milk, but the recipes can easily be adapted to suit your personal preferences. You can cut back further on the fat content by using low-fat Cheddar instead of the full fat version, or by using a reduced-calorie mayonnaise.

If you are following a salt-free diet, simply omit salt wherever it appears in a recipe, and use one of the homemade stocks suggested on pp.8-9 rather than the packeted cubes, which contain a fair amount of salt. The analysis figures do not take into account any side salad, garnish, extra bread or pickles, chutneys or sauces that you may choose to serve with the meal.

The equipment you need

All the recipes can be cooked using standard kitchen equipment. This includes two saucepans, one of which must be very large; one large, heavy nonstick frying pan, preferably with a lid; a large, flameproof casserole dish; a nonstick wok; a roasting tin; a wire rack; a sieve; a metal colander; a pie dish and a flan dish.

A food processor or blender is called for in certain recipes, but in some cases you can do the same task by hand. Wooden spoons, chopping boards and a set of sharp knives are also needed.

You can adapt some of the above items to do the work of specialised equipment. A roasting tin covered with a wire rack can double for a fish steamer; a frying pan can be used as a paella pan; and a metal colander on top of a saucepan will work as a steamer.

In Holiday Meals, the recipes are suitable for cooking on the most rudimentary equipment – a barbecue, a single ring stove in a caravan, or perhaps a camping stove. Methods of weighing ingredients with makeshift measures are given on p.318.

If you do not own a barbecue, you can adapt these recipes to cook under a pre-heated grill. Position the food 10-15 cm (4-6 in) away from the heat, and watch the food carefully to prevent it scorching. If the food is closer to the source of heat, it will need 5-10 minutes less cooking time.

The recipes in Microwave Meals are specifically for cooking in a microwave oven and not in the conventional way.

Storing and freezing foods safely

Many of the recipes provide an opportunity to use up leftovers, which is useful when you are short of time. In this instance, it is particularly important that the fridge and freezer are in good working order. Maintain the temperature of your fridge at between 0-5°C (32-41°F) and defrost it regularly.

In Make Ahead and Freeze, every recipe incorporates instructions for freezing and thawing the finished dish. However, the dishes work just as well if cooked and served on the same day. If you do cook and freeze the meals ahead, make sure that your freezer displays the 4-star symbol that indicates it is powerful enough to freeze food safely. Ways of preparing food for the freezer and the need for careful thawing and reheating are described on pp.340-1.

Where frozen ingredients are used in the recipes, add them directly from the freezer, particularly in the case of shellfish, to avoid any risk of contamination during thawing. However, when prawns are to be used in a salad thaw them in the shortest possible time in a covered container.

Basic recipes

Stocks

The following recipes for stocks are those used as the basis of the nutritional analysis for all recipes in this book that include stock. If you would rather use a stock cube, adjust the seasoning in the recipe to taste, as stock cubes generally contain a fair amount of salt.

Beef stock

To make 3.4 litres (6 pints)
Preparation time: 20 minutes
Cooking time: 7 hours 30 minutes
Cooling time: 3-4 hours, and overnight to chill

3.2 kg (7 lb) chopped marrow bones
450 g (1 lb) unpeeled onions, wiped
2.7 kg (6 lb) shin of beef, cubed
5 litres (9 pints) water
4 large carrots, peeled and sliced
6 sticks celery, trimmed and sliced
2 leeks, trimmed, sliced and washed
1 whole unpeeled bulb of garlic
Sprig of thyme
2 bay leaves
4 sprigs of parsley
20 black peppercorns
6 allspice berries

1 Preheat the oven to 220°C (425°F, gas mark 7). Put the chopped bones and onions in a roasting tin and brown in the oven for 1½ hours.
2 Transfer the bones and onions to a stockpot or large saucepan, add the beef and 4.5 litres (1 gallon) of the water, then slowly bring to the boil. Add 150 ml (¼ pint) more water, reduce the heat and skim off any scum.

3 In the meantime, pour off any fat from the roasting tin and add the remaining water. Bring the mixture to the boil, stirring well, and boil for about 3 minutes. Strain through a sieve into the saucepan or stockpot, then add all the other ingredients, partially cover and simmer for 5½ hours. Skim off any scum.
4 Strain the stock through a colander lined with a damp, clean muslin or linen cloth into a large bowl, then discard the meat, bones and vegetables. Cover the bowl with a clean cloth, cool for 2 hours, then refrigerate overnight.
5 Discard any solidified fat on the surface of the stock, and keep for up to 3 days in a fridge, or transfer to rigid containers, label and freeze.

Chicken stock

To make 3.4 litres (6 pints)
Preparation time: 20 minutes
Cooking time: 4 hours 30 minutes
Cooling time: 3-4 hours, and overnight to chill

2.7 kg (6 lb) boiling fowl and giblets (except liver), washed and chopped, or chicken drumsticks and wing tips, washed
4.5 litres (1 gallon) water
340 g (12 oz) onions, peeled and quartered
340 g (12 oz) carrots, peeled and sliced
1 whole unpeeled bulb of garlic
4 sticks celery, trimmed and sliced
1 leek, trimmed, sliced and washed
Small branch of lovage
Sprig of thyme
2 bay leaves
2 large sprigs marjoram or oregano
3 whole cloves
20 black peppercorns
2 large pieces mace

1 Put the chicken pieces and giblets into a stockpot or large saucepan and add all but 150 ml (¼ pint) of the water. Bring slowly to

the boil, then add the remaining water, reduce the heat and skim off any scum.
2 Add all the other ingredients, partially cover and simmer for 4 hours, removing any scum that rises to the surface.
3 Immediately after cooking, strain, cool and chill as for beef stock.

The stock will keep for 3 days in the fridge or can be frozen as for beef stock. If you want to make lamb stock, use 2.7 kg (6 lb) scrag end of lamb, cut into pieces. For ham stock, use 900 g (2 lb) bacon hock or knuckle, boned and cut into pieces, and halve the other ingredients.

Fish stock

To make 1.4 litres (2½ pints)
Preparation time: 20 minutes
Cooking time: 40 minutes
Cooling time: 2-3 hours

1.1 kg (2½ lb) white fish trimmings (bones and heads with gills removed), washed
1 small leek, white part only sliced and washed
2 sticks celery, trimmed and thinly sliced
1 medium onion, peeled and thinly sliced
1 small lemon, thinly sliced
Sprig of dill
Sprig of parsley
12 black peppercorns
1 bay leaf
285 ml (½ pint) dry white wine
1.4 litres (2½ pints) water

1 Put all the ingredients in a large, stainless steel or enamel saucepan and bring slowly to the boil.
2 Immediately turn down the heat and skim off any scum on the surface. Partially cover and simmer for 30 minutes.
3 Strain as for beef stock, then use at once or cover and cool for 2-3 hours. Store for 1 day only in the fridge, or freeze as for beef stock.

Vegetable stock

To make 2.6 litres (4½ pints)
Preparation time: 30 minutes
Cooking time: 4 hours 30 minutes
Cooling time: 3-4 hours

....

450 g (1 lb) swede, peeled and diced
450 g (1 lb) carrots, peeled and sliced
450 g (1 lb) onions, peeled and sliced
450 g (1 lb) leeks, trimmed, sliced and washed
1 whole unpeeled bulb of garlic
Small branch of lovage
Sprig of thyme
2 bay leaves
Large sprig of parsley
24 black peppercorns
4 litres (7 pints) water

1 Put all the ingredients in a stockpot or large saucepan and slowly bring to the boil. Reduce the heat, partially cover and simmer for about 4 hours.
2 Strain as for beef stock, after cooking, then cool for 3-4 hours. Store in the fridge for up to 5 days, or freeze as for beef stock.

How to cook rice

Where cooked rice is called for in the recipes in this book, it has been analysed as cooked without salt and by the absorption method.

You can open-freeze any leftover rice you may have (see p.341) and store it in the freezer for up to 6 months. It can be used from frozen wherever cooked rice is called for in a recipe, as can frozen cooked rice, which is available from supermarkets.

You will need 60 g (2 oz) of uncooked rice per person and 1½-3½ times its volume in liquid, depending on the type of rice you use. Pour the rice into a measuring jug to calculate its millilitre (fluid ounce) volume, then empty the jug and measure out the water.

Type of rice	Liquid per volume of rice	Cooking time in minutes
Long-grain white rice	1½ x volume	15
Long-grain brown rice	2 x volume	25-30
Basmati rice	1½ x volume	10
Arborio (risotto) rice	3-3½ x volume	20-40
Wild rice	2 x volume	45-50
Easy-cook white rice	2 x volume	18-20
Easy-cook brown rice	2 x volume	30-35
Easy-cook long-grain and wild rice	2 x volume	18-20

1 Put the rice in a heavy-based saucepan with the required amount of water or stock, and bring to the boil. Stir to separate the grains, then cover and turn the heat down to low.
2 Simmer without lifting the lid for the appropriate cooking time (see above). Check that the rice is tender and that all the liquid has been absorbed. Fluff with a fork and use. (Leave basmati rice to stand in the covered pan off the heat for another 5 minutes.)

How to make shortcrust pastry

These quantities may need to be doubled for some recipes in this book.

To make 300 g (11 oz) pastry
....

⅛ level teaspoon salt
175 g (6 oz) flour
85 g (3 oz) chilled butter or margarine, diced
1 egg, size 2, beaten
2-3 teaspoons cold water

1 Sift flour and salt into a bowl and rub in fat until the mixture resembles fine breadcrumbs.
2 Make a well in the centre of the flour and add the egg and 2 teaspoons of the water. Mix

with a knife to make firm but not dry dough, adding the remaining water if necessary.
3 Turn the dough onto a flat, lightly floured surface and knead gently for 1 minute. Use as required, or refrigerate wrapped in plastic film for up to 2 days.

How to make pancake batter

This method of making and cooking pancakes applies to all the pancake recipes in this book, although the batter ingredients may vary.

To make 8 pancakes, 20 cm (8 in) across
....

115 g (4 oz) plain flour
¼ level teaspoon salt
1 egg, size 2
285 ml (½ pint) milk
30 g (1 oz) butter, melted (optional)

1 Sift the flour and salt into a mixing bowl. Make a well in the centre and gradually stir in the egg with a balloon whisk or wooden spoon, adding a little milk as the mixture thickens, until all the flour and about half the milk are incorporated into a batter.
2 Beat vigorously for 1-2 minutes, then add the remaining milk, and butter, if using. Cover and leave to stand for 30-60 minutes.
3 To cook the pancakes, stir the batter and pour it into a measuring jug. Brush a 20 cm (8 in) nonstick frying pan with vegetable oil, and heat until it gives off a faint blue haze.
4 Pour one-eighth of the batter into the pan, and tip it to coat the bottom. Cook for 1-2 minutes, until lightly browned, then turn over with a palette knife and cook the other side for 1 minute.
5 Turn the pancake onto a plate and cover with greaseproof paper. Make seven more in the same way. Use at once, store in the fridge for 2-3 days in a polythene bag, or freeze.

Making the most of fresh vegetables

Many recipes in this book call for fresh vegetables, some of which need more preparation than just washing and trimming. The ways to strip, peel, chop, blanch, skin and de-seed vegetables are simple techniques which can greatly enhance the presentation of a meal.

THE CAREFUL PREPARATION of vegetables – be they roots, tubers or squashes – is as important as the cooking. Removing the thick, often indigestible parts of vegetables gets rid of any hidden grit, ensures quick and even cooking and improves the appearance of the vegetables before adding them to a dish.

Stripping spinach

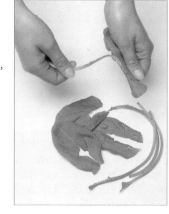

To remove the stalks and thick veins from spinach, fold each leaf in half, hold it firmly and pull off the stalk and vein. Wash the leaves thoroughly in several changes of cold water to remove any grit.

Stringing beans

To remove the string-like fibre along each side of the bean or mangetout, use a small, sharp knife to cut almost through the tip of the pod until it comes into contact with the 'string'. Pull off the string along one side, then repeat along the other side.

Peeling asparagus

Trim the ends of the asparagus spears, then peel the thickest part of the stems with a potato peeler or small sharp knife. This will help the stems to cook as quickly as the tips.

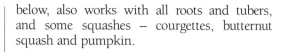

Stripping broccoli

To prevent broccoli florets cooking before the stems, strip off the tough, outer skin of the stalks by inserting a small knife just under the skin at the base of the stalk. Holding the skin firmly, pull it back on itself up to the top of the stalk. Repeat until the stem is completely stripped.

Chopping

Chopping vegetables into dice, cubes or strips greatly improves the appearance of a finished dish, so it is worth taking the time when the recipe calls for special preparation. The technique for dealing with carrots, illustrated below, also works with all roots and tubers, and some squashes – courgettes, butternut squash and pumpkin.

To cut a carrot into strips, cubes and dice

To cut into strips, cut the peeled carrot lengthways into slices about 3 mm (1/8 in) thick. Stack the slices one on top of the other and cut lengthways into fine strips. To cut into dice or cubes, cut across the carrot into slices 6, 13 or 25 mm (1/4, 1/2, or 1 in) thick. Stack the slices one on top of the other and cut lengthways into strips of the same thickness. Cut across the strips into dice or cubes.

Julienne strips

Dice

Cubes

Blanching

Blanching vegetables, by plunging them briefly into boiling water then into cold water to cool them, softens their texture and preserves their colour and flavour. It is important to blanch vegetables before freezing since it stops the activity of enzymes which would destroy their colour and flavour even when frozen. The time depends on the type and size of the vegetable. Spinach needs about 1 minute; broccoli, beans, asparagus and carrots require 2-5 minutes.

Other techniques

The additional techniques illustrated below are ones that are commonly used in this book for the preparation of vegetables.

De-seeding peppers is necessary before slicing them into rings for salads, or cutting them into lengths and strips for stir-fries and casseroles. The tops need to be removed and the central seeds discarded.

Stir-fry strips

1 Slice off the top of the pepper and cut around the inside with a small sharp knife to loosen the core and seeds, then remove and discard them.

2 Rinse the pepper under cold water and dry with kitchen paper. For long strips, cut the pepper in half lengthways, then slice into strips.

3 For shorter strips, cut the pepper into quarters, then slice across each one to make strips.

Salad rings

1 Slice off the top of the pepper and cut around the inside with a small, sharp knife.

2 Cut across the de-seeded pepper in thin slices to make rings.

Grilled peppers are cooked whole, and the seeds removed only after they have been peeled. Grilling gives the peppers a soft texture and sweet musky flavour that is a delicious addition to salads. Do not let the peppers get too dark while grilling, however, or their flavour will spoil. Peel the peppers in a sieve over a bowl in order to catch any juices. You can add the juices to dressings, stews and casseroles. Do not peel the peppers under a cold tap, as you will lose the juices.

To draw out the bitter juices of aubergines, put them in a colander, and stand it over a plate. Sprinkle with tablespoons of salt and leave to stand for 20 minutes. Do this before adding aubergines to stews or casseroles.

To skin and de-seed tomatoes, use a sharp knife to cut out the core from the tops. Put them in a bowl and cover with boiling water, then leave to stand for 1 minute. Drain and peel off the skins, cut in half and remove the seeds with a teaspoon.

Shredding cabbage before cooking it or adding it raw to salads greatly enhances its appearance. You can use this technique to cut hard Dutch white cabbages as well as the looser Savoy type into fine shreds.

Remove the tough outer leaves of the cabbage, then cut it into quarters. Cut out the hard, white, woody core with a large, sharp knife, then cut each quarter into fine shreds. Alternatively shread the quarters in a food processor, if you have one.

Crushing garlic is easy with a garlic crusher, though some people dislike having to clean the crusher afterwards. An alternative is to crush the garlic in a mortar and pestle, or use a large, heavy knife – as garlic is so pungent, it is wise to do this on a separate chopping board.

Crushing garlic

1 Pull away as many cloves of garlic from the main bulb as are needed and peel off the skin.

2 Finely chop the cloves with a large, heavy knife. For roughly crushed garlic, squash the clove under the broad side of a large chopping knife.

Lovage

Coriander

Bay

_Flat-leaf
parsley_

_Curly
parsley_

Chervil

Dill

Fennel

_Bronze
fennel_

Garlic

Herbs, oils, vinegars and mustards

_Although flavourings are usually added to a dish in small quantities, they often have
a significant impact on how it tastes. The way you use them depends entirely on your
personal preferences – and because there are no rules in cooking, the more you experiment
with the wide range of available ingredients, the more interesting the results will be._

ADDING HERBS TO a dish can often be the key
factor for the success of a meal. Fresh
herbs, rather than dried, will always give a
more satisfactory result; while dried herbs may
be stronger, they are not as aromatic.

Growing your own herbs is the best way
to ensure a constant, fresh supply. Herbs
flourish in even the most restricted space – a
window box, or a large herb pot on a window-
sill – but if you have room, grow two or three
plants of each of your favourite herbs at a time.
Then you can pick from the plants in turn and
help them to continue flourishing.

Freezing herbs darkens their colour slightly but will not damage the flavour. Freeze them
loosely packed in plastic bags, then when
frozen transfer them to airtight containers. You
can save on freezer space by crushing the
frozen herbs before storing them.

_**Herbs** of all kinds are sold in larger supermarkets,
either cut or rooted in small pots, or freeze-dried.
A single teaspoon of dried herbs is
equivalent to a tablespoon of fresh._

Drying herbs is a good way of preserving the
delicate leaves, which like shop-bought dried
herbs should be stored in airtight containers
away from the light to preserve their flavour
and colour. They can be kept for 6-12 months,
but after this time they will become musty and
lose their taste.

Pick herbs on a dry but overcast day, and
just before they flower, or they will lose their
flavour. Bunch small-leafed herbs, such as
thyme and tarragon, and tie them with string.
Spread out the bunches in a warm place on a
rack covered with muslin or cheesecloth to
allow the air to circulate, or hang them up.
Herbs with larger leaves, such as sage, mint
and bay, can be dried in the same way, or for
2-3 hours in the oven set at its lowest setting
with the oven door slightly ajar.

Moist herbs, such as parsley, are hard to dry
successfully. Stronger, more robust herbs such
as rosemary, thyme and bay dry fairly well, but
they need a good soaking during cooking or in
a dressing to release their full flavour.

_Golden
marjoram_ _Marjoram_ _Chives_ _Rosemary_

Thyme

Oregano

Basil _Tarragon_

Oils should be kept away from the light, well sealed and in a dry, cool place, as they will deteriorate if exposed to air, bright sunlight or constant heat. It is best to buy more expensive oils – extra virgin olive oil or nut oils – in small quantities and replace them regularly.

Nut oils, such as those pressed from walnuts, hazelnuts or pistachios, are best used sparingly in salad dressings or drizzled over soups or pasta, as a little of their intense flavour goes a long way.

Vinegars come in many regional variations – the different flavours are based on local raw materials. Wine-making regions produce red and white wine vinegars, which lend themselves to flavouring with herbs and are particularly suitable for using in Mediterranean dishes. Cider vinegars come from areas where apples are the main crop, and rice vinegars – a by-product of the paddy fields – are mostly used in Chinese or southeast Asian cooking. Herb-flavoured vinegars such as tarragon and basil add a rich, aromatic flavour to sauces and salad dressings.

Mustards are available in an astonishing range of flavours and textures, most of which are surprisingly mild. Like oils, mustards lose some of their pungency when they are exposed to heat, so they should be added to sauces away from the heat, or to cold salad dressings.

Vinegars such as the coarser distilled and malt vinegars are used for pickling. Red and white wine vinegars are good for cooking, and for using in sauces and salad dressings, while sherry vinegar is often used in marinades. Cider vinegar works well as a substitute for rice vinegar and in salad dressings. Sweet, spicy red rice vinegar is used in seafood sauce, while balsamic and tarragon vinegars give salad dressings a full flavour.

Oils should be stored in a cool, dark cupboard or larder. A basic stock should include two grades of olive oil (one oil for salads, the other for cooking), a bland vegetable or sunflower oil, sesame or toasted sesame oil for stir-fries, and a luxurious nut oil for flavouring salads or pasta. Mild-flavour grapeseed oil is a useful, light oil for salad dressings, while chilli oil spices up marinades.

Mustards come in a variety of flavours, seasoned with white wine, spices and herbs. English mustard and French Dijon mustard are among the hottest varieties; French whole-grain, English honey and the darker German mustard are milder.

13

Ground cinnamon

Cinnamon quills

Cinnamon bark

Root turmeric

Ground turmeric

Whole nutmeg

Ground nutmeg

Mace

Nutmeg with mace coating

Ground cumin

Cumin seeds

Saffron threads

Ground saffron

Allspice berries

Ground allspice

Root ginger

Spices, peppers and seeds

Nutmeg, cloves, cinnamon, pepper, ginger and saffron have been imported to this country for hundreds of years, and used ground or whole, in combinations or singly, to season meat, fish, poultry and vegetables. Such spices can be blended in recognisable seasonings or used according to your own taste, augmented with hot chilli powder and flavourful seeds.

ONCE A PRECIOUS COMMODITY, spices of all types are readily available today, many of them already ground. As with other aromatic flavourings, an open packet of spice will gradually lose its taste, so while ground spices are convenient, a better flavour is achieved by buying whole spices and grinding them yourself before use.

Dry-frying and roasting spices brings out even more flavour and takes only a matter of minutes. Heat the whole spices over a moderate heat in a small pan, shaking or stirring until their colour turns a shade deeper and they give off their new roasted aroma. Take them off the heat before they burn and then grind or crush them in a coffee grinder or with a pestle and mortar.

You can find whole spices in Indian or Chinese food shops, where they are often sold in their original state and are usually cheaper than elsewhere.

Spice mixtures vary according to personal taste, different cultures and traditional uses for them. In Britain, mixed spice – made up of allspice, cloves, nutmeg, and cinnamon or ginger – is mainly used in baking, while the French *quatre epices* – cloves, ground peppercorns, nutmeg and cinnamon or ginger – give patés and other preserved meats their distinctive flavour. *Garam masala*, the base of many Indian curries, consists of up to 20 dry spices in variable quantities, while curry paste (a wet *masala*) generally combines fresh spices such as chilli peppers, garlic, onion and ginger with dried coriander, cumin, cardamom and others. The Chinese five spices – powdered anise, fennel, cloves, cinnamon and anise pepper – flavour pork and other dishes.

Spices add their distinctive flavour to any meal. Star anise is characteristic of Chinese cooking, while cumin and coriander are used in Middle Eastern dishes and in Indian curries. Turmeric, an Asian spice, flavours and colours Indian dishes; it is sometimes misused instead of saffron to give Spanish rice dishes their yellow colouring.

Freeze-dried ginger

Curry powder

Cloves

Coriander seeds

Juniper berries

Cardamom pods

Ground ginger

Root ginger

Ground cloves

Ground coriander

Spice infusions rely on large pieces of spice, which are removed before serving as with bay leaves, or avoided by the diner. Cinnamon is added to custards to infuse, while whole cardamom pods flavour rice.

Saffron, the most expensive of the spices, is highly prized in Spanish cooking. It can be bought as saffron powder, but as this is often adulterated, it is best to buy true saffron threads – each one the stigma of the saffron crocus – and soak them in a little warm water or white wine before use.

Hot spices are ground from peppercorns and chilli peppers. Whole peppercorns (white, black, pink or green) are picked off a vine, while chilli powders are derived from whole red and green chilli peppers which are dried and then ground. Ground chilli pepper comes in differing strengths: cayenne, used to make Tabasco sauce, is very hot, and the many fresh chillies that are available vary widely in strength of flavour.

The seeds are the fieriest part of the chilli, so they are best removed. Keep your hands away from your face and eyes, as the juice of the chillies can cause severe irritation. Make a point of washing your hands as soon as you have finished handling chillies.

Whole seeds, such as those of pumpkins or sunflowers, offer a good source of protein and are high in oils. Either plain or toasted, these make good additions to salads. Poppy seeds are used on top of loaves of bread, in curries, or as a flavouring for hot salad dressings. Celery seeds are a principal ingredient in celery salt.

Seeds such as delicate dill are excellent for flavouring fish, as are the slightly aniseed-tasting fennel seeds. Caraway aids digestion; it is an important constituent of rye bread, and is used in seed cake. Nutty sesame seeds and poppy seeds are widely used in baking.

Green chillies

Annaheim chillies

Mixed pepper-corns

Bird chillies

White pepper

Black pepper

Chilli powder

Scotch bonnet chillies

Paprika

Jalapeño chillies

Caribe chillies

Cayenne

Hot pepper sauce

Sunflower

Fennel

Pumpkin

Black poppy   White poppy   Dill   Caraway   White sesame   Black sesame

Hot peppers such as white and black peppercorns from the pepper vine should be freshly ground in a pepper mill, as ground pepper quickly loses its flavour. Mild paprika is in fact made from dried sweet red peppers, while other ground red peppers vary greatly in strength; the Scotch bonnet chilli from the Caribbean is extremely hot, as are Bird chillies from the East.

SOUPS

Welcoming soup makes a filling, nutritious one-dish meal. Chunky vegetable soups, substantial bowls of pasta in broth and puréed fish bisque are just a few of the wide choice of recipes that follow.

❖

In Lemon Chicken Soup with Coriander Dumplings (left), carrots, celery, onion, chicken pieces and stock combine to make a hearty broth (see p.18).

RICE AND CHICKEN SOUP

Soft grains of nutty brown
rice flavoured with a rich
chicken stock add bulk to this
simple chicken broth. Toasted
flaked almonds provide a
crunchy garnish.

Serves 4
Preparation time: 20 minutes
Cooking time: 35 minutes

30 g (1 oz) butter or margarine
1 tablespoon olive oil
450 g (1 lb) boneless chicken
    breasts, skinned and cut into
    small cubes
1.15 litres (2 pints) chicken stock
    (see p.8)
2 medium carrots, peeled and
    thinly sliced
1 large onion, peeled and
    finely chopped
85 g (3 oz) long-grain brown rice
2 tablespoons chopped
    fresh parsley
¼ level teaspoon salt
Freshly ground black pepper
15 g (½ oz) lightly toasted flaked
    almonds and sprigs of fresh
    parsley to garnish

Per serving
Calories 334 Protein 27 g
Total fat 15 g (saturated fat 6 g)
Carbohydrates 22 g (added sugar 0)
Fibre 2.1 g Sodium 273 mg

1 Melt the butter or margarine
and the oil in a large saucepan
and brown the chicken in it
over a moderate heat for about
10 minutes.

2 Pour in the stock and add
the carrots, onion, rice and
chopped parsley. Season with the
salt and some pepper.

3 Cover the pan and slowly bring
to the boil. Reduce the heat
and simmer gently for about
25 minutes, or until the rice is
tender. Ladle the soup into heated
bowls, garnish with the almonds
and parsley and serve with warm
poppyseed rolls or soda bread.

LEMON CHICKEN SOUP WITH CORIANDER DUMPLINGS

Serves 4
Preparation time: 25 minutes
Cooking time: 55 minutes

30 g (1 oz) butter
1 large onion, peeled and chopped
2 medium carrots, peeled
    and chopped
2 medium sticks celery, chopped
½ level teaspoon ground allspice
1 teaspoon lemon juice
1 tablespoon chopped fresh
    coriander
900 g (2 lb) chicken pieces
1.4 litres (2½ pints) chicken stock
    (see p.8)
½ level teaspoon salt
Freshly ground black pepper

For the dumplings
175 g (6 oz) plain flour
2 level teaspoons baking powder
½ level teaspoon ground cumin
1 tablespoon chopped coriander
Finely grated rind of 1 lemon
¼ level teaspoon salt
Freshly ground black pepper
1 tablespoon lemon juice
30 g (1 oz) butter, melted
6 tablespoons milk
Sprigs of fresh coriander to garnish

Per serving
Calories 514 Protein 42 g
Total fat 21 g (saturated fat 11 g)
Carbohydrates 42 g (added sugar 0)
Fibre 3.4 g Sodium 952 mg

Light, fluffy cumin and
coriander-flavoured dumplings
give this tangy lemon soup a
satisfying substance.

1 Melt the butter in a large
saucepan and gently cook the
onion, carrots and celery in it,
covered, for 10 minutes. Add the
allspice, lemon juice, coriander,
chicken pieces, stock, salt and
some pepper. Bring to the boil,
skimming off any scum from the
surface, then reduce the heat.
Cover and simmer for 30 minutes.

2 Remove the pan from the heat
and lift out the chicken pieces
into a bowl. When cool enough to
handle, take the meat off the bone
and cut it into small pieces,
discarding the skin and bones.

3 Pour the vegetables and the
stock into a food processor and
blend for 20 seconds, or until the
vegetables are finely chopped. Pour
the soup back into the saucepan
and stir in the chicken. Simmer
gently for 5 minutes.

4 Make 12 dumplings (see p.47)
and place them on top of the
soup. Cover and simmer until
light and fluffy. Ladle the soup
and dumplings into heated bowls,
garnish with the coriander
and serve.

CHICKEN SOUP FRANÇAISE

Serves 4
Preparation time: 20 minutes
Cooking time: 25 minutes

1 tablespoon olive oil
1 large onion, peeled and
    coarsely chopped
3 cloves garlic, peeled and
    thinly sliced
1 small red pepper, de-seeded
    and diced
1 small green pepper, de-seeded
    and diced
2 medium courgettes, trimmed,
    halved lengthways and sliced
1 level teaspoon dried marjoram
285 ml (½ pint) passata
1.15 litres (2 pints) chicken stock
    (see p.8)
175 g (6 oz) fresh tagliatelle
450 g (1 lb) boneless chicken
    breasts, skinned and cut into
    small cubes
¼ level teaspoon salt
Freshly ground black pepper

Per serving
Calories 338 Protein 38 g
Total fat 12 g (saturated fat 2.4 g)
Carbohydrates 19 g (added sugar 0)
Fibre 3.3 g Sodium 236 mg

Ribbon pasta and colourful courgettes accompany the chicken – or turkey, if preferred – in this enticing soup. Adding passata (sieved tomatoes) is a quick and easy way of enriching the soup's colour and flavour.

1 Heat the oil in a large saucepan and soften the onion in it. Stir in the garlic and cook for 1 minute more.

2 Mix in the red and green peppers, cover and cook for 5 minutes, stirring occasionally. Add the courgettes and marjoram, cover and cook, stirring occasionally, for 7 minutes, or until the courgettes are just tender.

3 Pour the passata and chicken stock into the saucepan and bring to the boil. Add the tagliatelle and chicken, then reduce the heat. Cover and simmer for 5-8 minutes. Season with the salt and some pepper and serve with Grissini sticks.

A blend of courgettes, peppers and plenty of garlic gives this chicken soup its French character and distinctive flavour.

CHICKEN SUCCOTASH SOUP

To Algonquian-speaking native North Americans, 'succotash' is maize (corn on the cob) and green beans boiled together. This creamy soup combines chicken, beans and sweetcorn.

Serves 4
Preparation time: 20 minutes
Cooking time: 1 hour

1 tablespoon olive oil
1 large onion, peeled and chopped
1.4 kg (3 lb) chicken, cut into eight (see p.115)
1.15 litres (2 pints) chicken stock (see p.8)
Fresh or packet bouquet garni
1 level teaspoon salt
Freshly ground black pepper
425 g (15 oz) cooked lima or butter beans, rinsed and drained
225 g (8 oz) frozen sweetcorn kernels
150 ml (¼ pint) single cream
4 tablespoons chopped fresh parsley

Per serving
Calories 510 Protein 80g
Total fat 23g (saturated fat 8.7g)
Carbohydrates 20g (added sugar 0)
Fibre 6.8g Sodium 685mg

1 Heat the oil in a large saucepan and cook the onion in it over a low heat until softened. Add the chicken pieces, stock and bouquet garni, then season with the salt and some pepper. Bring to the boil, then reduce the heat to low and cook, covered, for 30-40 minutes, until the chicken is tender.

2 Using a slotted spoon, lift the chicken out of the saucepan and put it on a plate. Remove the bouquet garni and skim off all the fat from the surface of the soup. Bring the soup back to the boil and stir in the beans and the sweetcorn. Reduce the heat, cover and cook for 10 minutes.

3 Meanwhile, remove the skin and bones from the chicken and cut the flesh into small pieces.

4 Stir the chicken into the soup and heat through for 5 minutes. Take the soup off the heat and stir in the cream and parsley. Serve in heated soup bowls with slices of toasted granary bread.

CURRIED CHICKEN SOUP

This spicy chicken soup is enriched with either cream or yoghurt to suit your palate. Adjust the amount of curry powder to your taste.

Serves 4
Preparation time: 15 minutes
Cooking time: 45 minutes

450 g (1 lb) boneless chicken breasts, skinned
¼ level teaspoon salt
Freshly ground black pepper
30 g (1 oz) unsalted butter or margarine
1 medium onion, peeled and finely chopped
1 large stick celery, trimmed and sliced
2 medium carrots, peeled and sliced
2 cloves garlic, peeled and crushed
2 level teaspoons medium-hot curry powder
340 g (12 oz) tomatoes, skinned, de-seeded and chopped
1.15 litres (2 pints) chicken stock (see p.8)
1 bay leaf
115 g (4 oz) white long-grain rice
150 ml (¼ pint) single cream or natural yoghurt
Paprika and sprigs of fresh coriander to garnish

Per serving
Calories 404 Protein 39g
Total fat 13g (saturated fat 6.2g)
Carbohydrates 35g (added sugar 0)
Fibre 3g Sodium 229mg

1 Sprinkle the chicken with the salt and some pepper. Melt the butter or margarine in a large saucepan and lightly brown the chicken in it for 2 minutes on each side. Remove the chicken from the pan and set aside.

2 Stir in the onion, celery, carrots and garlic and cook for 2-3 minutes. Mix in the curry powder and cook for 1 minute.

3 Add the tomatoes, stock and bay leaf and bring to the boil. Put the chicken back into the pan and reduce the heat. Cover and simmer for 15-20 minutes, or until the chicken is cooked (see p.117).

4 Remove the chicken from the soup and put it on a plate. Bring the soup back to the boil, then stir in the rice and partially cover the pan. Simmer for 15 minutes, or until the rice is cooked. In the meantime, cut the chicken into small pieces.

5 Remove the bay leaf from the soup, then stir in the chicken and heat through for 2-3 minutes. Take the pan off the heat and stir in the cream or yoghurt. Spoon the soup into heated bowls, garnish with the paprika and coriander, and serve with warm naan bread.

Spicy Chicken and Chilli Soup

Serves 6
Preparation time: 20 minutes
Cooking time: 20 minutes

2 small fresh green chillies,
  de-seeded
4 cloves garlic, peeled
2 tablespoons water
675 g (1½ lb) boneless chicken
  breasts, skinned
1.15 litres (2 pints) chicken stock
  (see p.8)
1 large onion, peeled and
  finely chopped
2 level teaspoons ground cumin
1 bay leaf
1 level teaspoon dried thyme
¼ level teaspoon salt
Freshly ground black pepper
115 g (4 oz) frozen sweetcorn
  kernels
2 tablespoons chopped fresh
  coriander

To garnish
60 g (2 oz) tortilla chips,
  roughly broken
1 medium avocado, halved,
  stoned, peeled and diced
2 spring onions, trimmed
  and sliced

Per serving
Calories 265 Protein 27 g
Total fat 13 g (saturated fat 3.2 g)
Carbohydrates 11 g
(added sugar 0)
Fibre 2.3 g Sodium 191 mg

**The inspiration for this hot
and spicy soup is 'pozole', a
Mexican dish made with corn.**

1 Blend the chillies, garlic and
water in a food processor for
1 minute, or chop the chillies and
garlic and mix with the water.

2 Put the chicken breasts, stock,
onion, cumin, bay leaf, thyme,
salt, some pepper and the chilli
mixture in a large saucepan and
bring to the boil. Reduce the heat,
then cover and simmer for
15 minutes. Lift out the chicken breasts with a slotted
spoon and leave to cool slightly,
then cut into small pieces.

3 Put the pieces of chicken back
into the pan and add the
sweetcorn and coriander. Bring
back to the boil, then simmer for
5 minutes, or until the chicken is
cooked (see p.117). Remove the
bay leaf.

4 Ladle the soup into heated
bowls. Garnish each with a
sprinkling of tortilla chips and
some avocado and spring
onion, then serve.

*Moist chunks of chicken
mingle with aromatic
herbs and spicy chilli
in a broth topped
with avocado.*

TURKEY SOUP WITH PECAN NUTS

Serves 4
Preparation time: 30 minutes
Cooking time: 30 minutes

2 tablespoons olive oil
1 medium onion, peeled
 and chopped
1 stick celery, trimmed and sliced
2 level tablespoons plain flour
1/2 level teaspoon dried sage
Freshly ground black pepper
850 ml (1 1/2 pints) turkey or chicken
 stock (see p.8)
285 ml (1/2 pint) turkey gravy
 or 400 g (14 oz) canned
 chicken soup
1 medium carrot, peeled and diced
60 g (2 oz) fine green beans,
 trimmed and cut into short lengths
1 medium potato, peeled and diced
175 g (6 oz) cooked turkey, diced
60 g (2 oz) shelled pecan
 nuts, halved
1/4 level teaspoon salt
2 tablespoons chopped parsley
150 ml (1/4 pint) single cream
 (optional)

Per serving
Calories 274 Protein 15 g
Total fat 15 g (saturated fat 1.1 g)
Carbohydrates 21 g (added sugar 0)
Fibre 2.3 g Sodium 509 mg

Turkey and pecan nuts team up in this nourishing soup. When you roast a turkey or a large chicken, keep any leftover gravy to make this dish and use the carcass to make stock (see p.8). Walnuts can take the place of pecan nuts, if you prefer.

1 Heat the oil in a large saucepan and fry the onion and celery in it until softened. Stir in the flour, sage and some pepper, and cook, stirring, for 2 minutes.

2 Pour in the turkey stock and turkey gravy, or chicken soup, and bring to the boil, stirring. Mix in the carrot, beans and potato, reduce the heat, cover and simmer for 15 minutes.

3 Stir in the cooked turkey, pecan nuts, salt and some pepper, then simmer for 10 minutes, or until the vegetables are cooked. Sprinkle on the parsley and stir in the cream, if using, then serve.

Pecan nuts offer a contrasting crunch to tender turkey in a soup which makes good use of Sunday lunch leftovers and warms up the coldest autumn and winter days.

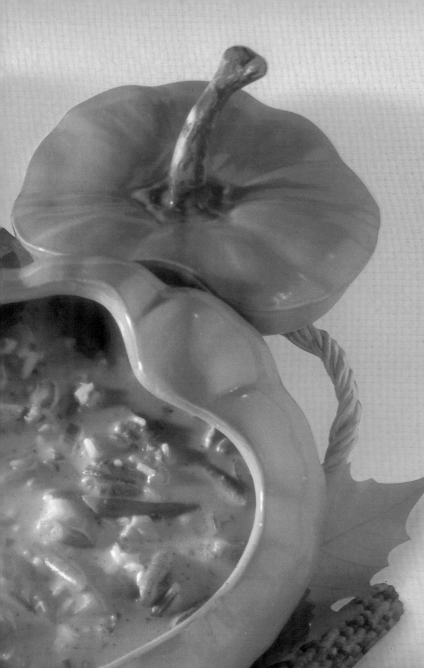

TURKEY, TOMATO AND BARLEY SOUP

Serves 4
Preparation time: 15 minutes
Cooking time: 1 hour

....

2 tablespoons olive oil
450 g (1 lb) boneless turkey, cut into
   small pieces
3 medium sticks celery, trimmed and
   thickly sliced
3 medium carrots, peeled
   and thickly sliced
1 medium onion, peeled
   and chopped
400 g (14 oz) canned chopped
   tomatoes
850 ml (1 ½ pints) chicken stock
   (see p.8)
1 level tablespoon tomato purée
60 g (2 oz) pearl barley
60 g (2 oz) green lentils, cleaned of
   grit and rinsed
1 level teaspoon dried marjoram
1 level teaspoon dried thyme
1 level teaspoon salt
Freshly ground black pepper
2 tablespoons chopped
   fresh parsley
6-8 drops Tabasco (optional)

....

Per serving
Calories 322 Protein 36 g
Total fat 9.8 g (saturated fat 1.2 g)
Carbohydrates 29 g (added sugar 0)
Fibre 31 g Sodium 622 mg

....

Pearl barley and green lentils enrich the texture of this thick soup, while slow and gentle cooking ensures that the vegetables retain their shape and colour. A dash of Tabasco adds a hot touch without disrupting the delicate balance of flavours. You can use boneless chicken instead of the turkey, if you prefer.

1 Heat the oil in a large saucepan, and cook the turkey pieces in it for 5 minutes, stirring.

2 Add the celery, carrots, onion, tomatoes, stock, tomato purée, pearl barley, lentils, marjoram and thyme. Season with the salt and some pepper. Bring to the boil, then reduce the heat. Cover and simmer gently for 50-60 minutes, or until the vegetables and pearl barley are tender.

3 Stir in the parsley and the Tabasco, if using, then serve in heated soup bowls with warm, crusty french bread.

VEGETABLE SOUP WITH TURKEY MEATBALLS

Serves 6
Preparation time: 40 minutes
Cooking time: 30 minutes

340 g (12 oz) minced turkey
30 g (1 oz) Parmesan cheese, grated
1 egg, size 2, lightly beaten
30 g (1 oz) fresh white breadcrumbs
4 tablespoons chopped
    fresh parsley
½ level teaspoon salt

Freshly ground black pepper
1 tablespoon water
2 tablespoons olive oil
2 cloves garlic, peeled and crushed
2 medium courgettes, trimmed,
    halved lengthways and sliced
175 g (6 oz) button mushrooms,
    wiped and sliced
½ level teaspoon dried rosemary

400 g (14 oz) canned
    chopped tomatoes
1 litre (1¾ pints) chicken stock
    (see p.8)
225 g (8 oz) fine green beans, cut
    into short lengths
175 g (6 oz) spaghetti, broken into
    short lengths
225 g (8 oz) cooked cannellini
    beans, rinsed and drained
    (see p.172)

Per serving
Calories 320 Protein 25 g
Total fat 9.7 g (saturated fat 2.6 g)
Carbohydrates 36 g (added sugar 0)
Fibre 7.1 g Sodium 660 mg

The use of pasta in soups is typically Italian, and pasta turns this chunky vegetable soup into a balanced meal. The turkey meatballs are high in protein, low in fat and quick to make. Wet your hands slightly before you shape them – it will prevent the meat sticking.

1 Mix together the minced turkey, Parmesan, egg, breadcrumbs, half the parsley, half the salt, some pepper and the water. Shape the mixture into walnut-sized meatballs, and put them on a plate. Cover and refrigerate.

2 Heat the oil in a large saucepan and cook the garlic in it over a low heat for 1 minute. Mix in the courgettes, mushrooms and rosemary, then cook, stirring occasionally, for a further 10 minutes, or until tender.

3 Add the tomatoes, pour in the stock and stir in the remaining salt. Bring to the boil and then add the green beans and the spaghetti. Partially cover the pan, bring to the boil and cook gently for 8 minutes.

4 Reduce the heat to low, and mix in the meatballs. Cook for 5 minutes, then stir in the cannellini beans and cook for a further 3 minutes, or until the beans are heated through. Season with pepper, sprinkle with the remaining parsley and serve with ciabatta or other Italian bread.

A substantial soup combining courgettes, green beans and mushrooms with delicate turkey and parsley meatballs.

PIGEON SOUP

Pigeon meat deepens the colour of this soup and provides a rich, gamy flavour, which can be heightened with a dash of whisky. The soup is thickened with broth mix, a ready-to-use mixture of pulses, legumes, cereals and rice, sold in health food shops and supermarkets.

Serves 6
Preparation time: 30 minutes
Soaking time for broth mix: 5 hours
Cooking time: 1 hour 30 minutes

60 g (2 oz) butter
1 medium onion, peeled
  and chopped
4 oven-ready pigeons, each
  about 225 g (8 oz)
2 large carrots, peeled and diced
2 large sticks celery, trimmed
  and sliced
1 leek, trimmed, sliced and washed
6 juniper berries, lightly crushed
1 bay leaf
115 g (4 oz) broth mix, soaked and
  boiled for 10 minutes (see p.173)
1.7 litres (3 pints) chicken stock
  (see p.8)
1/2 level teaspoon salt
Freshly ground black pepper
1-2 tablespoons whisky (optional)

Per serving
Calories 310 Protein 22 g
Total fat 17 g (saturated fat 5.5 g)
Carbohydrates 16 g (added sugar 0)
Fibre 3 g Sodium 322 mg

1 Melt the butter in a large, heavy saucepan and cook the onion in it over a moderate heat until softened. Add the pigeons and cook for 10 minutes, turning them frequently until they are well browned all over.

2 Stir in the carrots, celery, leek, juniper berries, bay leaf, broth mix and stock, then bring to the boil. Reduce the heat, partially cover the pan and simmer gently for 1½ hours, or until the pigeons are very tender.

3 Take the soup off the heat and remove and discard the bay leaf. Lift out the pigeons onto a plate and leave them to cool slightly.

4 When the pigeons are cool enough to handle, take all the cooked meat off the bones and cut it into small pieces. Return the meat to the soup and bring back to the boil. Season with the salt and some pepper and stir in the whisky, if using. Ladle the soup into heated soup bowls and serve.

PORK AND EGG NOODLE SOUP

Fresh vegetables, ginger and Chinese egg noodles provide a delicate balance of oriental flavours in this nutritious soup. Groundnut oil comes from peanuts and is suitably light and bland for stir-frying both meat and vegetables.

Serves 4
Preparation time: 45 minutes
Cooking time: 35 minutes

2 tablespoons groundnut oil
450 g (1 lb) boneless shoulder of
  pork, trimmed of fat and cut into
  matchstick strips
1 clove garlic, peeled and crushed
30 g (1 oz) peeled and grated
  root ginger
1.6 litres (2¾ pints) chicken stock
  (see p.8)
450 g (1 lb) fresh spinach, trimmed
  and washed
8 spring onions, trimmed and
  thinly sliced
115 g (4 oz) mangetout, trimmed
  and thinly sliced
225 g (8 oz) oyster mushrooms,
  stalks removed, wiped
  and chopped
225 g (8 oz) Chinese fine
  egg noodles
1 tablespoon soy sauce
1 tablespoon sesame oil
Freshly ground black pepper

1 Heat the groundnut oil in a large saucepan. Stir-fry the pork strips, garlic and ginger in it over a moderate heat for 5 minutes, or until the pork is done (see p.81).

2 Pour in the stock and slowly bring to the boil. Reduce the heat to low, then cover and simmer for 15 minutes.

3 Add the spinach, spring onions, mangetout and mushrooms, and simmer for 10 minutes. Stir in the noodles and cook for a further 5 minutes, or until tender.

4 Add the soy sauce and sesame oil and season with some pepper. Serve the soup from a large, heated tureen or in individual bowls.

Per serving
Calories 529 Protein 36 g
Total fat 24 g (saturated fat 3.3 g)
Carbohydrates 45 g (added sugar 0)
Fibre 8.4 g Sodium 440 mg

HAM AND BUTTER BEAN SOUP

Canned butter beans can replace dried beans in this filling soup. Ask your butcher for a spare ham bone if you lack one.

Serves 4
Preparation time: 15 minutes
Cooking time: 1 hour 30 minutes
Soaking time: 1 hour

225 g (8 oz) dried butter beans, rinsed

1.15 litres (2 pints) water
1 leftover ham bone
1.15 litres (2 pints) ham or vegetable stock (see pp.8-9)
1 large potato, peeled and cut into small cubes
1 large carrot, peeled and sliced
1 stick celery, trimmed and diced
340 g (12 oz) cooked ham, cut into small cubes
115 g (4 oz) fresh spinach, trimmed, washed and shredded

1 tablespoon lemon juice
Freshly ground black pepper
4 spring onions, trimmed and sliced
2 tablespoons chopped fresh parsley

Per serving
Calories 318 Protein 29 g
Total fat 5.8 g (saturated fat 1.9 g)
Carbohydrates 40 g (added sugar 0)
Fibre 14 g Sodium 1085 mg

1 Boil the butter beans in the water for 2 minutes, then take the pan off the heat, cover and leave to stand for 1 hour.

Melting butter beans, potatoes and carrots take on the flavour of ham, while spinach adds a splash of colour.

2 Drain the beans, rinse them and drain again. Return them to the saucepan, add the ham bone and stock and bring them to the boil. Reduce the heat, cover the saucepan and simmer gently for 45 minutes-1 hour, or until the beans are just tender. Remove and discard.

3 Add the potato, carrot and celery to the soup, and then simmer, covered, for 15 minutes. Stir in the ham, spinach and lemon juice, season with some pepper and continue cooking for 10 minutes.

4 Stir in the spring onions and parsley, then serve the soup with some warm crusty bread.

SPICY SAUSAGE AND POTATO SOUP

Serves 4
Preparation time: 15 minutes
Cooking time: 30 minutes

....

1 tablespoon olive oil
30 g (1 oz) butter
1 large onion, peeled and chopped
115 g (4 oz) cooked ham, cut into
   small cubes
225 g (8 oz) pepperoni sausage,
   thinly sliced
450 g (1 lb) jar sauerkraut, rinsed
   and well drained
450 g (1 lb) potatoes, peeled and
   cut into small cubes
850 ml (1½ pints) beef stock
   (see p.8)
1 level teaspoon caraway seeds
   (optional)
Freshly ground black pepper
1 spring onion, trimmed and
   finely chopped

....

Per serving
Calories 433 Protein 15 g
Total fat 29 g (saturated fat 12 g)
Carbohydrates 29 g (added sugar 0)
Fibre 2.6 g Sodium 1516 mg

....

This substantial soup can be livened up by using a touch of beer in place of some of the stock, and by adding extra caraway seeds. If you prefer, substitute 450 g (1lb) of thinly sliced white cabbage for the sauerkraut. Add it to the soup at step 3, after the potatoes have cooked for about 10 minutes, then bring the soup back to the boil before serving.

1 Heat the oil and butter in a large saucepan until sizzling, and then soften the chopped onion in them until brown.

2 Mix in the ham and pepperoni, then brown lightly, stirring occasionally, for 5 minutes. Add the sauerkraut, potatoes, stock and caraway seeds, if using. Season with pepper and bring to the boil.

3 Reduce the heat to moderate, cover, and cook for 15 minutes, or until the potatoes are tender. Ladle the soup into warmed bowls, sprinkle with the spring onion and serve with thick slices of caraway seed or sesame seed bread.

BLACK BEAN SOUP WITH HAM AND SWEET POTATOES

Serves 4
Preparation time: 25 minutes
Cooking time: 40 minutes

....

2 tablespoons olive oil
3 medium red onions, peeled
   and chopped
4 cloves garlic, peeled and crushed
1 large green pepper, de-seeded
   and diced
675 g (1½ lb) sweet potatoes,
   peeled and cut into small cubes
400 g (14 oz) canned chopped
   tomatoes
1 level teaspoon ground cumin
1 level teaspoon ground coriander
½ level teaspoon ground ginger
½ level teaspoon salt
¼ level teaspoon cayenne pepper
1.15 litres (2 pints) ham or chicken
   stock (see p.8)
115 g (4 oz) long-grain white rice
450 g (1 lb) cooked black beans,
   rinsed and drained (see p.172)
225 g (8 oz) cooked ham, cut into
   matchstick strips
2 tablespoons lime juice
8 lime wedges and sprigs of fresh
   coriander to garnish

....

Per serving
Calories 534 Protein 24 g
Total fat 11 g (saturated fat 2.3 g)
Carbohydrates 91 g (added sugar 0)
Fibre 15 g Sodium 1075 mg

....

The last-minute addition of lime juice gives a welcome sharpness to this thick, spicy soup. If you want to reheat the soup the next day, thin it down with a little warm water or tomato juice.

1 Heat the oil in a large saucepan and cook the onions in it until soft. Add the garlic and pepper and cook for another 5 minutes, stirring. Mix in the sweet potatoes and chopped tomatoes, and cook, uncovered, for 3 minutes.

2 Stir in the cumin, coriander, ginger, salt and cayenne pepper. Pour in the stock and bring to the boil, then stir in the rice. Reduce the heat, cover, and simmer for 15-20 minutes, or until the sweet potatoes and rice are just tender.

3 Stir in the black beans and ham and cook for 5 minutes. Add the lime juice, ladle the soup into warmed bowls and garnish with the sprigs of coriander. Serve with the lime wedges and, if you wish, some crusty bread.

In this nourishing winter warmer, the red lentils turn to a rich purée during cooking and absorb the smoky flavour of knackwurst sausages.

LENTIL SOUP WITH KNACKWURST

Serves 4
Preparation time: 15 minutes
Cooking time: 50 minutes

2 tablespoons vegetable oil
3 knackwurst sausages, each
    about 115 g (4 oz), sliced
2 medium carrots, peeled
    and diced
1 medium onion, peeled
    and chopped
1 medium stick celery, trimmed
    and thinly sliced
2 cloves garlic, peeled and crushed
2 tablespoons chopped
    fresh parsley
225 g (8 oz) red lentils, cleaned
    and rinsed (see p.172)
400 g (14 oz) canned chopped
    tomatoes
1 bay leaf
1.15 litres (2 pints) beef stock
    (see p.8)
1/2 level teaspoon salt
Freshly ground black pepper

Per serving
Calories 500 Protein 23 g
Total fat 25 g (saturated fat 8.8 g)
Carbohydrates 49 g (added sugar 0)
Fibre 8.8 g Sodium 811 mg

Lentils make wonderful soups, melting into a thick, substantial soup base that is enriched here with herbs, vegetables and short, thick German sausages. You can use bratwurst or frankfurter sausages in place of knackwurst, or you can vary the flavour and texture of the soup by using a mixture of sausages.

1 Heat the oil in a large saucepan and lightly brown the sausage slices in it for 5 minutes, stirring occasionally. Take them out of the pan and drain on kitchen paper.

2 Pour away all but 1 tablespoon of the fat, then stir in the carrots, onion, celery, garlic and parsley. Fry the vegetables for 5 minutes over a moderate heat.

3 Add the lentils, tomatoes, bay leaf, stock and knackwurst slices. Bring to the boil, then reduce the heat, cover and cook gently for about 40 minutes, or until the lentils are tender. Discard the bay leaf and season with the salt and some pepper. Serve the soup in large, heated soup cups or bowls with sesame bread sticks.

CORN AND BEEF SOUP

Serves 4
Preparation time: 15 minutes
Marinating time: 1 hour
Cooking time: 20 minutes

1 tablespoon light soy sauce
2 tablespoons dry sherry
1/2 level teaspoon soft light
    brown sugar
450 g (1 lb) rump steak, trimmed of
    fat (see p.79), cut into thin strips
1 tablespoon olive oil
1 large onion, peeled and chopped
1 clove garlic, peeled and crushed
225 g (8oz) baby corn, cut into
    small pieces
115 g (4 oz) chestnut mushrooms,
    wiped and sliced
1.15 litres (2 pints) beef stock
    (see p.8)
1 level tablespoon tomato purée
1/4 level teaspoon salt
Freshly ground black pepper
30 g (1 oz) butter, softened
1 level tablespoon plain flour

A sweet and sour marinade of soy sauce, sherry and brown sugar brings out the richness of the beef in this filling soup, and also intensifies its final flavour and colour.

1 Mix the soy sauce with the sherry and brown sugar in a bowl. Stir in the steak strips and leave to marinate for 1 hour.

2 Drain off the marinade and save. Heat the oil in a large saucepan and lightly brown the steak strips in it for 3 minutes. Lift the meat onto a plate, using a slotted spoon, and set aside.

Per serving
Calories 333 Protein 35 g
Total fat 17 g (saturated fat 7.4 g)
Carbohydrates 9.1 g (added sugar 0)
Fibre 1.4 g Sodium 506 mg

3 Add the onion, garlic, corn and mushrooms to the pan and cook for 3 minutes. Stir in the stock, tomato purée, the saved marinade, salt and some pepper. Bring to the boil, reduce the heat, cover and simmer for 10 minutes.

4 Blend the butter with the flour to make a soft paste, then whisk it into the soup. Bring to the boil, stirring, then reduce the heat and stir in the steak strips. Cook for about 3 minutes, until the soup is slightly thick and the steak is heated through. Serve with warm rolls.

Baby corn adds a crispness and juicy sweetness to this rich soup of tender beef and chestnut mushrooms. For extra colour, sprinkle on a tablespoon of chopped fresh parsley.

OXTAIL SOUP

Serves 4
Preparation time: 30 minutes
Chilling time: overnight
Cooking time: 2 hours 15 minutes

1 tablespoon olive oil
1.1-1.4 kg (2½-3 lb) oxtail, cut
   into pieces
1 large onion, peeled
   and chopped
150 ml (¼ pint) ruby port
2 medium carrots, peeled
   and sliced
225 g (8 oz) turnip, peeled
   and diced
2 bay leaves
1 level teaspoon dried thyme
2 cloves garlic, peeled and crushed
1.4 litres (2½ pints) beef stock
2 level tablespoons tomato purée
½ level teaspoon salt
Freshly ground black pepper
225 g (8 oz) small new potatoes,
   scrubbed and halved

Per serving
Calories 704 Protein 65 g
Total fat 35 g (saturated fat 14 g)
Carbohydrates 23 g (added sugar 0)
Fibre 3.5 g Sodium 629 mg

The deep beefy taste of this classic farmhouse broth matures as the soup stands overnight. Some shops sell chopped oxtail in weighed amounts; if you can't find this, look for a tail that is roughly the right weight and ask the butcher to cut it up.

1 Heat the oil in a large stainless steel or enamel saucepan and fry the oxtail until well browned, stirring. Remove from the pan and set aside.

2 Drain all but 1 tablespoon of the fat from the pan, add the onion and cook for 3 minutes. Stir in the port and boil gently for 5 minutes.

3 Return the oxtail to the pan and add the carrots, turnip, bay leaves, thyme, garlic, stock, tomato purée, salt and some pepper. Bring the mixture back to the boil, reduce the heat, cover the pan and simmer for 1½ hours.

Slow-cooked chunks of meat, soft carrots and turnips add body to this traditionally prepared soup.

4 Remove the saucepan from the heat and transfer the oxtail onto a plate, using a slotted spoon. Once the bones are cool enough to handle, remove the meat and return it to the soup.

5 Allow the soup to cool completely, then cover and refrigerate overnight. Next day, skim off the layer of solidified fat from the surface of the soup and remove the bay leaves.

6 Add the potatoes and bring to the boil. Reduce the heat, cover the pan and simmer for 12-15 minutes, or until the potatoes are just soft. Serve with crusty country bread.

Lamb, Barley and Vegetable Broth

Serves 4
Preparation time: 20 minutes
Cooking time: 1 hour 10 minutes

2 tablespoons olive oil
2 large onions, peeled
   and chopped
450 g (1 lb) cooked lamb, diced
1.4 litres (2½ pints) beef or
   chicken stock (see p.8)
450 g (1 lb) swede, peeled
   and cut into small cubes
2 medium carrots, peeled
   and thickly sliced
1 large potato, peeled
   and cut into small cubes
2 sticks celery, trimmed
   and sliced
115 g (4 oz) pearl barley
½ level teaspoon dried thyme
½ level teaspoon salt
Freshly ground black pepper
2 tablespoons chopped fresh
   parsley or chives

This thick, nutritious blend of lamb, swede, carrots, potato and pearl barley is a good way to use up leftover roast meat, and is just as tasty if made with beef.

1 Heat the oil in a large saucepan and cook the onions in it, stirring, until softened. Mix in the lamb and stock and bring to the boil, then reduce the heat and simmer gently for 10 minutes, using a spoon to skim off any foam that rises to the surface.

2 Add the swede, carrots, potato, celery, barley, thyme, salt and some pepper and cook, uncovered, for 45 minutes, or until the barley is tender. Ladle into individual bowls, sprinkle with the parsley or chives and serve with warm wholemeal rolls.

Per serving
Calories 486 Protein 36 g
Total fat 21 g (saturated fat 7.8 g)
Carbohydrates 41 g (added sugar 0)
Fibre 5.5 g Sodium 365 mg

Meatball and Courgette Soup

Serves 4
Preparation time: 45 minutes
Cooking time: 50 minutes

450 g (1 lb) very lean minced beef
1 level teaspoon ground coriander
1 egg, size 3
30 g (1 oz) fresh white
   breadcrumbs
1 small onion, peeled
   and finely chopped
½ level teaspoon salt
Freshly ground black pepper
2 tablespoons olive oil
85 g (3 oz) long-grain white rice
2 spring onions, trimmed
   and finely chopped
2 tablespoons chopped fresh dill
   or 1 teaspoon dried dill
1.4 litres (2½ pints) chicken stock
   (see p.8)
3 medium courgettes, trimmed
   and finely diced
Fresh dill to garnish

Lightly fried minced beef and coriander balls combine with rice, courgettes and fragrant dill in this unusual soup. If you roll the meatballs first and refrigerate them while preparing the other ingredients, they will keep their shape during cooking.

1 Combine the beef with the coriander, egg, breadcrumbs, onion and half the salt and pepper. Divide the mixture into 30 portions, then shape these with wetted hands into small balls. Put on a plate, cover and chill.

2 Heat the oil in a large saucepan and brown half of the meatballs for about 10 minutes, turning them frequently. Remove from the pan and drain on kitchen paper. Repeat with the remaining meatballs.

3 Add the rice, spring onions, dill, stock, the rest of the salt and some pepper and bring to the boil. Reduce the heat to low, cover and cook for 20 minutes.

4 Stir in the courgettes and meatballs and simmer for 8 minutes more, or until the meatballs are cooked through. Ladle the soup into warmed bowls and garnish with the dill.

Per serving
Calories 395 Protein 28 g
Total fat 20 g (saturated fat 6.1 g)
Carbohydrates 28 g (added sugar 0)
Fibre 1.3 g Sodium 405 mg

BOURRIDE

The luxurious texture of this creamy Provençal soup comes from the addition of aïoli, a rich garlic mayonnaise. To make the aïoli in a food processor, blend the garlic and salt with the egg yolks, then, with the processor running, slowly pour in all but 1 tablespoon of the olive oil.

Serves 4
Preparation time: 30 minutes
Cooking time: 15 minutes

2 cloves garlic, peeled and crushed
¼ level teaspoon salt
2 egg yolks, size 2
2 teaspoons lemon juice
285 ml (½ pint) olive oil
1 large leek, trimmed, sliced
   and washed
¼ level teaspoon dried thyme
Thinly pared strip of orange rind
4 halibut steaks, each about
   115 g (4 oz), skinned (see p.145)
340 g (12 oz) whiting fillets, skinned
425 ml (¾ pint) fish stock (see p.8)
1 tablespoon chopped fresh parsley
1 small french stick, cut into 8 slices

Per serving
Calories 1000 Protein 45 g
Total fat 79 g (saturated fat 11 g)
Carbohydrates 28 g (added sugar 0)
Fibre 3.3 g Sodium 624 mg

1 Whisk the garlic, salt, egg yolks and lemon juice in a bowl. Set aside 1 tablespoon of the oil, then gradually whisk a few drops of the remaining oil into the eggs until the mixture begins to thicken. Pour and whisk in the remaining oil until the mayonnaise is thick.

2 Heat the reserved oil in a large, flameproof casserole and fry the leek in it for 3 minutes over a moderate heat. Stir in the thyme and lemon rind, then arrange the halibut and whiting on top of the leek and pour in the stock. Bring to the boil, then reduce the heat and simmer gently for 5 minutes, until the fish is just cooked.

3 Lift the fish and leek onto a heated dish using a slotted spoon, then cover and keep warm. Discard the lemon rind.

4 Whisk the mayonnaise into the fish stock, then stir the soup over a low heat until it is thick enough to lightly coat the back of a spoon. Take care not to overheat the soup or it will curdle.

5 Add the fish and leek to the soup and heat through for 1 minute. Sprinkle with the parsley. Put two slices of bread into each soup plate and spoon the bourride on top. Serve with extra slices of bread.

CRAB AND CALLALLOO SOUP

Serves 4
Preparation time: 10 minutes
Cooking time: 20 minutes

30 g (1 oz) butter
1 medium onion, peeled and
   finely chopped
2 cloves garlic, peeled and crushed
225 g (8 oz) callalloo greens,
   spinach or Swiss chard, washed,
   dried, centre stalks removed and
   leaves roughly shredded
850 ml (1½ pints) chicken stock
   (see p.8)
30 g (1 oz) creamed coconut
1 level teaspoon salt
Freshly ground black pepper
340 g (12 oz) fresh or canned
   white crabmeat, drained
¼ teaspoon Tabasco sauce

Per serving
Calories 197 Protein 18 g
Total fat 13 g (saturated fat 8.6 g)
Carbohydrates 3.4 g (added sugar 0)
Fibre 2.6 g Sodium 1091 mg

A thick, spicy soup from the Caribbean that takes its name from that of the young leaves of the dasheen, or taro, plant used to make it. You can buy callalloo in Afro-Caribbean shops, although fresh spinach, Swiss chard or Chinese pak choi are equally suitable. Creamed coconut is used to sweeten and thicken the soup; this can be bought canned or in a block from specialist grocers and larger supermarkets.

1 Melt the butter in a saucepan and soften the onion and garlic in it over a moderate heat.

2 Mix in the greens and stir-fry for 1-2 minutes until wilted. Stir in the stock, creamed coconut, salt and some pepper. Bring to the boil, then reduce the heat, cover and simmer for 10 minutes.

3 Add the crabmeat and Tabasco sauce and heat through for 5 minutes, stirring gently. Serve with warm soda bread.

SWEETCORN CHOWDER WITH PRAWNS AND RED PEPPERS

Serves 6
Preparation time: 20 minutes
Cooking time: 25 minutes

2 tablespoons olive oil
1 large onion, peeled and
  finely chopped
2 medium red peppers, de-seeded
  and thinly sliced
340 g (12 oz) potatoes, peeled
  and diced
340 g (12 oz) frozen sweetcorn
  kernels
1 bay leaf
1/2 level teaspoon dried marjoram
  or oregano
1/8 level teaspoon freshly grated
  or ground nutmeg
425 ml (3/4 pint) fish or chicken stock
  (see p.8)
425 ml (3/4 pint) milk
Freshly ground black pepper
450 g (1 lb) uncooked prawns,
  peeled and de-veined
150 ml (1/4 pint) single cream
Sprigs of fresh marjoram or oregano
  to garnish

Per serving
Calories 282 Protein 14 g
Total fat 12 g (saturated fat 4.6 g)
Carbohydrates 31 g (added sugar 0)
Fibre 4.6 g Sodium 516 mg

Fish or shellfish are usually the main ingredients of a chowder, which takes its name from the *chaudière* – a stew pot used by the French settlers in the southern states of America to make thick soups.

1 Heat the oil in a large saucepan and soften the onion in it, without browning.

2 Stir in the peppers, potatoes, sweetcorn, bay leaf, marjoram or oregano and nutmeg. Pour in the stock and bring to the boil. Reduce the heat, then cover and simmer for 10-15 minutes, or until the potatoes are cooked.

3 Pour in the milk and season with some pepper. Bring the soup back to the boil and stir in the prawns. Cook for 3-5 minutes over a moderate heat until the prawns turn pink and are cooked through.

4 Remove the bay leaf and stir in the cream, then heat through for 2-3 minutes, taking care not to boil. Pour the chowder into soup bowls, garnish and serve with savoury biscuits.

A rich, stew-like consistency makes a chowder the perfect cold-weather meal. Sweetcorn and potatoes provide the substance, nutmeg the aroma and bright red peppers and prawns a crisp texture.

PRAWN GUMBO

Okra thickens this spicy prawn soup, which is inspired by the traditional gumbo – a Louisiana speciality from the United States that combines French, Spanish, African and American-Indian influences.

Serves 4
Preparation time: 20 minutes
Cooking time: 35 minutes

30 g (1 oz) butter
1 medium red onion, peeled and chopped
1 medium red pepper, de-seeded and chopped
2 level tablespoons plain flour
1 clove garlic, peeled and crushed
1.15 litres (2 pints) fish or chicken stock (see p.8)
2 tablespoons chopped fresh parsley
1 level teaspoon dried thyme
225 g (8 oz) cooked ham, trimmed of fat and diced
400 g (14 oz) canned chopped tomatoes
1/4 level teaspoon cayenne pepper
115 g (4 oz) okra, trimmed and cut into short pieces
340 g (12 oz) cooked rice (see p.9)
450 g (1 lb) large frozen cooked and peeled prawns

1 Melt the butter in a large saucepan and cook the onion and pepper in it over a moderate heat for 5 minutes, taking care not to brown them. Stir in the flour and garlic and cook for 1 minute.

2 Gradually stir in the stock, half of the parsley, the thyme, ham, tomatoes and cayenne pepper. Bring to the boil, stirring, then reduce the heat. Cover and simmer for 10 minutes. Stir in the okra, then cover and simmer for a further 10 minutes.

3 Put the rice in a steamer or metal sieve. Stir the frozen prawns into the soup, then place the steamer, or sieve, of rice on top of the saucepan. Cover and cook for 5-8 minutes, stirring the soup and the rice twice during cooking, or until the prawns and rice are both heated through.

4 Spoon the rice into heated serving bowls and ladle the soup over the top. Sprinkle with the remaining parsley, then serve.

Per serving
Calories 433 Protein 41 g
Total fat 13 g (saturated fat 5.6 g)
Carbohydrates 40 g (added sugar 0)
Fibre 4.8 g Sodium 2563 mg

CRAB AND SCALLOP BISQUE

Crabmeat and scallops form the base of this rich, thick seafood soup. You can use small frozen Queen scallops, thawed and halved, if fresh scallops are unavailable.

Serves 4
Preparation time: 15 minutes
Cooking time: 30 minutes

60 g (2 oz) unsalted butter
60 g (2 oz) long-grain white rice
850 ml (1 1/2 pints) fish stock (see p.8)
150 ml (1/4 pint) dry white wine
225 g (8 oz) fresh or frozen crabmeat, thawed
2 spring onions, trimmed and very finely chopped
2 level teaspoons tomato purée
8 fresh scallops, cleaned and sliced
1/2 level teaspoon salt
Freshly ground black pepper
Sprigs of parsley and grated Gruyère cheese to garnish

1 Melt the butter in a large saucepan and cook the rice in it over a low heat for 2-3 minutes, until shiny. Pour in the fish stock and wine, and add the crabmeat. Cover and simmer gently for 15 minutes, or until the mixture has thickened slightly.

2 Remove the soup from the heat and leave it to cool slightly. Purée it in a blender in two batches until smooth. Rinse the saucepan and pour the soup back into it. Stir in the spring onions and tomato purée, then simmer over a low heat for 5 minutes.

3 Increase the heat until the soup is just bubbling, then stir in the scallops and cook for 3 minutes. Take the pan off the heat and season the bisque with the salt and some pepper. Pour into heated bowls, garnish with the parsley sprigs and Gruyère, and serve.

Per serving
Calories 410 Protein 45 g
Total fat 17 g (saturated fat 9 g)
Carbohydrates 14 g (added sugar 0)
Fibre 0.3 g Sodium 950 mg

SOUPS

CRAB AND BLACK MUSHROOM SOUP

Dried Chinese black mushrooms have a strong, earthy flavour which pairs well with the meaty crab and root ginger in this aromatic soup.

The distinctive flavour of dried Chinese black mushrooms in this rich soup can also be provided by shiitake mushrooms. Both can be found in oriental food stores.

Serves 6
Preparation time: 20 minutes
Cooking time: 20 minutes

30 g (1 oz) dried Chinese black or shiitake mushrooms
200 ml (7 fl oz) boiling water
2 tablespoons olive oil
6 spring onions trimmed and thinly sliced diagonally
1 level tablespoon peeled and grated root ginger
225 g (8 oz) fresh, frozen or canned crabmeat, drained
1.15 litres (2 pints) chicken stock (see p.8)
2 tablespoons soy sauce
1 tablespoon dry sherry
115 g (4 oz) long-grain white rice
115 g (4 oz) frozen peas
1/4 level teaspoon salt
Freshly ground black pepper
2 level tablespoons cornflour
2 eggs, size 2, beaten
1 teaspoon sesame oil

Per serving
Calories 235 Protein 13 g
Total fat 8.4 g (saturated fat 1.4 g)
Carbohydrates 28 g (added sugar 0)
Fibre 1.8 g Sodium 328 mg

1 Soak the mushrooms in the boiling water for 15 minutes, then drain and reserve the soaking water. Slice the mushrooms and discard any stalks.

2 Heat the oil in a large saucepan and stir-fry half the spring onions, the ginger, crabmeat and mushrooms in it for 1 minute. Pour in the stock, soy sauce and sherry and bring to the boil. Stir in the rice and reduce the heat, then cover and simmer for 15 minutes.

3 Strain the soaking water through a sieve lined with kitchen paper, and then pour it into the pan. Add the peas and season with the salt and some pepper. Simmer for 3 minutes.

4 Blend the cornflour with 3 tablespoons of cold water and stir it into the soup. Bring to the boil, stirring, then cook for 1 minute, until the soup thickens.

5 Take the pan off the heat and slowly pour the eggs into the soup. Mix in the sesame oil and pour the soup into heated bowls. Sprinkle with the reserved spring onions and serve with soda bread.

MUSSELS IN WHITE WINE WITH POTATOES

Serves 4
Preparation time: 20 minutes
Cooking time: 30 minutes

200 ml (7 fl oz) dry white wine
1 small onion, peeled and
   finely chopped
1 clove garlic, peeled and crushed
2 tablespoons chopped
   fresh parsley
1 level teaspoon dried thyme
900 g (2 lb) fresh mussels, scrubbed
   and de-bearded (see p.147)
30 g (1 oz) butter
30 g (1 oz) plain flour
570 ml (1 pint) fish stock (see p.8)
¼ level teaspoon salt
Freshly ground black pepper
225 g (8 oz) new potatoes,
   scrubbed and thinly sliced
150 ml (¼ pint) single cream
1 egg yolk, size 2
Garlic croutons (see p.47) and
   1 tablespoon chopped fresh
   parsley to garnish

Per serving
Calories 405 Protein 32 g
Total fat 19 g (saturated fat 9.8 g)
Carbohydrates 18 g (added sugar 0)
Fibre 1.3 g Sodium 883 mg

This rich, stew-like soup has the authentic taste of French provincial cooking. When buying fresh mussels, accept only those with a tightly closed shell.

1 Combine the wine, onion, garlic, parsley and thyme in a large saucepan and bring to the boil, then reduce the heat and simmer for 5 minutes. Add the mussels, cover and cook for a further 5 minutes, shaking from time to time until the mussels open.

2 Line a large colander with kitchen paper and place it over a bowl. Pour the cooked mussels into the colander and discard any that are still closed. Separate the rest from their shells and set them aside; reserve the strained liquid.

Garlic croutons add crunch to this tempting dish of succulent mussels and soft potato slices in a creamy white wine and parsley stock.

3 Rinse the saucepan, then gently melt the butter in it. Stir in the flour and cook, stirring, for 1 minute. Remove from the heat, gradually blend in the stock and the reserved cooking liquid, then season well with the salt and some pepper. Return to the heat, bring to the boil, stirring, and cook for a further 2 minutes.

4 Add the potato slices to the pan, reduce the heat, cover and simmer for 10 minutes, or until the potatoes are just soft.

5 Mix the cream with the egg yolk in a small bowl and stir into the soup. Add the mussels and simmer, stirring, for 3 minutes, taking care not to let the soup boil. Ladle into heated soup bowls, sprinkle with the croutons and parsley and serve with warm french bread.

SAFFRON FISH SOUP

Serves 4
Preparation time: 20 minutes
Cooking time: 35 minutes

1 tablespoon olive oil
1 medium onion, peeled and sliced
1 medium red pepper, de-seeded
   and sliced
1 medium leek, trimmed, sliced
   and washed
850 ml (1½ pints) fish stock
   (see p.8)
¼ level teaspoon chilli powder
60 g (2 oz) orzo or other small
   pasta shapes
285 ml (½ pint) dry white wine
¼ teaspoon saffron threads, soaked
   in 2 tablespoons boiling water
675 g (1½ lb) mixed white fish,
   skinned, boned and cut into cubes
2 scallops, cleaned and diced
¼ level teaspoon salt
Freshly ground black pepper
2 egg yolks, size 3
3 tablespoons double cream
2 tablespoons chopped watercress
   to garnish

Per serving
Calories 393 Protein 39 g
Total fat 14 g (saturated fat 5.1 g)
Carbohydrates 17 g (added sugar 0)
Fibre 2.6 g Sodium 354 mg

Saffron gives its distinctive aromatic flavour and rich golden colour to this luxurious soup. Saffron threads – the laboriously hand-picked, dried stigmas of a variety of crocus – have been prized by cooks since the days of Ancient Greece.

1 Heat the oil in a heavy saucepan and fry the onion, red pepper and leek in it until softened. Add the fish stock, chilli powder and pasta and bring to the boil. Reduce the heat, cover the pan and simmer for 15 minutes.

2 Add the wine, saffron, fish, scallops, salt and some pepper to the pan. Cover once again and simmer for a further 6-8 minutes.

3 Blend the egg yolks with the cream in a small bowl, then stir in 2-3 tablespoons of the hot soup. Add the mixture to the soup and gently heat through, stirring, for 2-3 minutes – do not let it boil or the soup will curdle. Garnish with the watercress and serve with crusty white or brown bread.

FISH AND ASPARAGUS SOUP

Serves 6
Preparation time: 40 minutes
Cooking time: 35 minutes

45 g (1½ oz) unsalted butter
1 clove garlic, peeled and crushed
1 small fennel bulb, trimmed and
   finely chopped, fronds reserved
450 g (1 lb) tomatoes, skinned,
   de-seeded and chopped
225 g (8 oz) asparagus, trimmed
   and chopped, tips reserved
2 level teaspoons tomato purée
1.15 litres (2 pints) fish stock
   (see p.8)
900 g (2 lb) lemon sole
   fillets, skinned
450 g (1 lb) haddock fillets, skinned
285 ml (½ pint) single cream
½ level teaspoon salt
Freshly ground black pepper
2-3 tablespoons soured cream and
   strips of smoked salmon to garnish

Per serving
Calories 336 Protein 38 g
Total fat 18 g (saturated fat 10.6 g)
Carbohydrates 6.4 g (added sugar 0)
Fibre 1.6 g Sodium 478 mg

A thick, savoury blend of fresh lemon sole and haddock with fragrant asparagus and fennel is topped by a garnish of smoked salmon and soured cream.

1 Melt the butter in a saucepan and cook the garlic and chopped fennel in it over a low heat for 5 minutes. Stir in the tomatoes, asparagus stems, tomato purée and the fish stock. Bring to the boil, cover and simmer for 20 minutes.

2 Add the fish fillets to the pan and cook over a low heat for 5 minutes. Remove from the heat and leave to cool slightly. Purée in a blender in two batches.

3 Rinse the saucepan, then pour the soup back into it and stir in the cream. Add the asparagus tips and cook gently, stirring, for about 5 minutes. Stir in the salt and some pepper. Pour into a large, heated tureen, garnish with the soured cream, salmon and reserved fennel fronds and serve.

PEPPERY PARSNIP SOUP

Serves 4
Preparation time: 20 minutes
Cooking time: 30 minutes

30 g (1 oz) butter
1 large onion, peeled and chopped
675 g (1½ lb) parsnips, peeled and chopped
850 ml (1½ pints) vegetable stock (see p.9)
½ level teaspoon salt
2 teaspoons lemon juice
80 g (2¾ oz) peppercorn-coated cream cheese
225 g (8 oz) cooked butter beans, rinsed and drained
2 tablespoons snipped fresh chives

Per serving
Calories 323 Protein 8.1 g
Total fat 18 g (saturated fat 10 g)
Carbohydrates 34 g (added sugar 0)
Fibre 10 g Sodium 382 mg

The unusual addition of peppercorn-coated cream cheese gives the parsnips in this creamy soup a mild peppery flavour. You will need a food processor to make this dish.

1 Melt the butter in a saucepan and cook the onion in it over a moderate heat for 5 minutes. Stir in the parsnips, cover and cook for a further 10 minutes.

2 Pour in the stock, then add the salt and lemon juice. Cover and simmer for 15-20 minutes, or until the parsnips are softened.

3 Leave the soup to cool slightly, then pour it into a food processor and blend it with the cream cheese for 1-2 minutes, until smooth. Return the soup to the saucepan, mix in the butter beans and cook for 5 minutes. Pour the soup into heated bowls, sprinkle with the chives and serve with crostini (see p.47).

GAZPACHO

Serves 4
Preparation time: 20 minutes
Cooking time: 10 minutes
Chilling time: 2 hours

2 large waxy potatoes, peeled and cut into small cubes
225 g (8 oz) stale bread, crusts removed, cubed
285 ml (½ pint) water
4 large ripe tomatoes, skinned, de-seeded and chopped
1 red or yellow pepper, de-seeded and chopped
1 small onion, peeled and chopped
1 cucumber, peeled and chopped
1 clove garlic, peeled
570 ml (1 pint) tomato juice
3 tablespoons red wine vinegar
3 tablespoons olive oil
1 level teaspoon salt
Freshly ground black pepper
1 stick celery, trimmed and chopped
115 g (4 oz) garlic croutons
4 tomatoes, skinned, de-seeded and cut into small dice
1 red pepper, de-seeded and cut into small dice
½ cucumber, peeled, halved, de-seeded and cut into small dice

Per serving
Calories 431 Protein 12 g
Total fat 12 g (saturated fat 1.9 g)
Carbohydrates 73 g (added sugar 0)
Fibre 8.5 g Sodium 1320 mg

This light, cooling Spanish soup is named after one of its main ingredients – soaked bread. Red wine vinegar and garlic croutons give it a sharp bite that refreshes the palate, making it a good choice for a summer's day.

1 Boil the potatoes until tender, then drain and set aside to cool. In the meantime, soak the bread in the water for 5 minutes.

2 Mix the chopped tomatoes, pepper, onion, cucumber, garlic, tomato juice, vinegar, oil, salt and some pepper into the bread.

3 Blend the mixture in batches in a food processor for 2-3 minutes, until smooth. Pour the soup into a bowl and stir in the cooled potato cubes and the celery. Cover and chill in the refrigerator for 2 hours.

4 Garnish the gazpacho with the garlic croutons, diced tomatoes, red pepper and cucumber, and serve with crusty bread.

DOUBLE PEA SOUP

Split peas and green garden peas provide this fresh-tasting soup with a colourful base, and it is enriched with Parmesan cheese and chunks of sausage.

Serves 4
Preparation time: 20 minutes
Cooking time: 1 hour

1 tablespoon olive oil
175 g (6 oz) frankfurters, sliced
1 large onion, peeled and
    finely chopped
2 garlic cloves, peeled and crushed
4 spring onions, trimmed
    and sliced
¼ small iceberg lettuce,
    roughly chopped
2 teaspoons chopped fresh mint
½ level teaspoon ground ginger
725 ml (1¼ pints) water
115 g (4 oz) dried split peas, rinsed
175 g (6 oz) frozen peas
¾ level teaspoon salt
Freshly ground black pepper
45 g (1½ oz) Parmesan
    cheese, grated
Sprigs of fresh mint to garnish

Per serving
Calories 329 Protein 17 g
Total fat 19 g (saturated fat 7 g)
Carbohydrates 24 g (added sugar 0)
Fibre 6.8 g Sodium 920 mg

1 Heat the oil in a large saucepan. Lightly brown the frankfurters in it over a moderate heat for 2-3 minutes, then leave to drain on kitchen paper.

2 Add the onion and garlic to the pan and cook until softened. Stir in the spring onions, lettuce, mint and ginger, then cover the pan and cook for 5 minutes.

3 Pour the water into the pan and add the split peas. Bring to the boil, then reduce the heat. Cover and simmer for 40 minutes, stirring occasionally.

4 Stir in the frozen peas, bring back to the boil and cook for another 5 minutes, or until tender. Take the soup off the heat and leave to cool slightly.

5 Pour the soup into a food processor or blender and purée in separate batches, or pass it through a sieve or vegetable mill, until smooth. Return the soup to the pan, mix in the frankfurters and reheat gently. Season with the salt and some pepper. Pour the soup into heated bowls and sprinkle with the Parmesan. Garnish with the mint and serve with warm crusty rolls.

The hint of mint and ginger contrasts well with the smokiness of frankfurters in this creamy pea soup. A side salad makes a good accompaniment.

White Bean and Cabbage Soup

Serves 4
Preparation time: 20 minutes
Cooking time: 30 minutes

30 g (1 oz) butter
1 large onion, peeled and chopped
2 medium carrots, peeled and sliced
1 medium stick celery, trimmed
    and chopped
2 cloves garlic, peeled and crushed
225 g (8 oz) smoked gammon steak,
    rind removed, diced
1 large potato, peeled and cut
    into cubes
1.15 litres (2 pints) ham or chicken
    stock (see p.8)
1 level teaspoon dried mixed herbs
225 g (8 oz) green cabbage,
    washed, trimmed and
    finely shredded
225 g (8 oz) cooked haricot beans,
    rinsed and drained
Freshly ground black pepper
2 tablespoons Parmesan
    cheese, grated

Per serving
Calories 304 Protein 26 g
Total fat 12 g (saturated fat 7 g)
Carbohydrates 24 g (added sugar 0)
Fibre 7.4 g Sodium 789 mg

Gammon gives this light, tasty soup a delicate smoky flavour, while the beans thicken the texture and offer a good source of fibre. If you use canned haricot beans then this filling soup can be made on the spur of the moment.

1 Melt the butter in a large saucepan and cook the onion, carrots, celery and garlic in it, covered, over a moderate heat for 10 minutes, or until the vegetables are softened but not browned.

2 Increase the heat to high and add the diced gammon. Cook, stirring continuously, until the gammon changes colour.

3 Stir in the potato, stock and herbs and bring to the boil. Reduce the heat, cover and simmer for 15 minutes, then mix in the cabbage and beans.

4 Season the soup with some pepper, then cover and simmer for another 5 minutes, or until the beans are heated through and the cabbage is just cooked.

5 Ladle the soup into heated bowls, sprinkle the Parmesan on top and serve with warmed french bread or some garlic bread.

Pasta and Bean Soup

Serves 4
Preparation time: 10 minutes
Cooking time: 30 minutes

2 tablespoons olive oil
1 medium onion, peeled and
    finely chopped
1 stick celery, trimmed and
    finely chopped
285 ml (1/2 pint) passata (sieved
    tomatoes) or canned
    chopped tomatoes
1 clove garlic, peeled and crushed
3 tablespoons finely chopped
    fresh parsley
1 level teaspoon dried rosemary
340 g (12 oz) cooked haricot beans,
    rinsed and drained
850 ml (1 1/2 pints) beef, chicken or
    vegetable stock (see pp.8-9)
115 g (4 oz) small elbow macaroni
60 g (2 oz) Parmesan
    cheese, grated
1/2 level teaspoon salt
Freshly ground black pepper

Per serving
Calories 331 Protein 16 g
Total fat 13 g (saturated fat 4.1 g)
Carbohydrates 41 g (added sugar 0)
Fibre 8.8 g Sodium 458 mg

Serve this thick, haricot bean soup as a simple but satisfying supper dish. It can be made just as well with cannellini beans.

1 Heat the oil in a large saucepan and cook the onion and celery in it over a moderate heat, stirring occasionally, until softened.

2 Stir in the passata or canned chopped tomatoes, the garlic, 2 tablespoons of parsley and the rosemary, then cover and cook for a further 5 minutes.

3 Add the beans and stock, and bring to a gentle boil. Stir in the macaroni and cook for about 10 minutes, or until the pasta is done, stirring frequently.

4 Stir in all but 2 tablespoons of the Parmesan, the salt and some pepper. Pour the soup into heated bowls, sprinkle with the remaining parsley and the remaining Parmesan and serve with brown soda bread.

Chickpea, Pasta and Spinach Soup

Serves 4
Preparation time: 20 minutes
Cooking time: 30 minutes

2 tablespoons olive oil
1 large onion, peeled and
  finely chopped
1 clove garlic, peeled and crushed
1 level teaspoon dried marjoram
½ level teaspoon dried rosemary
450 g (1 lb) fresh spinach, trimmed
  and washed, or 225 g (8 oz)
  frozen leaf spinach
225 g (8 oz) cooked chickpeas,
  rinsed and drained
1.4 litres (2½ pints) beef
  stock (see p.8)
115 g (4 oz) pasta shells or other
  small pasta shapes
½ level teaspoon salt
Freshly ground black pepper
60 g (2 oz) Parmesan
  cheese, grated
1 tablespoon virgin olive
  oil (optional)

Per serving
Calories 328 Protein 17 g
Total fat 14 g (saturated fat 4.3 g)
Carbohydrates 35 g (added sugar 0)
Fibre 7.8 g Sodium 571 mg

*For an authentic Italian flavour,
serve this soup with a spoonful
of virgin olive oil and a good
helping of freshly grated
Parmesan cheese.*

Chickpeas and pasta absorb
all the fine flavours in this
tasty and quickly made soup,
which provides a filling meal
for a family.

1 Heat the oil in a large saucepan
and brown the onion in it for
about 10 minutes. Stir in the
garlic, marjoram and rosemary
and cook for 2 minutes. Add the
spinach, cover and simmer for a
further 5 minutes.

2 Add the chickpeas and the
stock and bring to the boil.
Mix in the pasta, reduce the
heat and simmer for 10 minutes,
stirring occasionally, until the pasta
is cooked. Season with the salt and
some pepper, then ladle the soup
into heated bowls. Sprinkle
with the Parmesan, pour
over the oil, if using,
and serve with
crusty Italian bread.

Sweet Red Pepper Soup with Ricotta Dumplings

Serves 4
Preparation time: 30 minutes
Cooking time: 40 minutes

2 tablespoons olive oil
1 large onion, peeled and
   thinly sliced
4 cloves garlic, peeled and crushed
1 medium carrot, peeled and
   thinly sliced
1 large potato, peeled and
   thinly sliced
3 large red peppers, de-seeded and
   thinly sliced
400 g (14 oz) canned
   chopped tomatoes
3 fine strips of orange rind
½ level teaspoon ground ginger
285 ml (½ pint) water
Strained juice of 3 large oranges
½ level teaspoon salt
Freshly ground black pepper

For the dumplings
250 g (9 oz) ricotta cheese
1 egg, size 2
1 egg white, size 2
60 g (2 oz) plain flour
½ level teaspoon salt
Freshly ground black pepper
3 tablespoons chopped
   fresh parsley

Per serving
Calories 333 Protein 13 g
Total fat 16 g (saturated fat 5.9 g)
Carbohydrates 36 g (added sugar 0)
Fibre 5.5 g Sodium 382 mg

Freshly squeezed orange juice gives this colourful soup a refreshing zest and fragrant aroma. The ricotta cheese used to make the dumplings can be found in Italian food shops and on the delicatessen counters of most supermarkets.

1 Heat the oil in a large saucepan and cook the onion in it for 5 minutes. Add the garlic, carrot, potato and red peppers, cover and cook gently for 8-10 minutes, or until the peppers are softened.

Sweet red peppers, carrot and tomatoes produce a refreshing soup of vivid colour that makes an attractive contrast to white ricotta dumplings.

2 Stir in the tomatoes, orange rind, ginger, water and half the orange juice. Season with the salt and some pepper. Bring to the boil, then reduce the heat. Cover and simmer for 15 minutes.

3 In the meantime, mix together in a bowl the ricotta, egg, egg white, flour, salt, some pepper and the parsley. Drop about 16 heaped tablespoonfuls of the dumpling mixture into the soup (see p.47) and cook until set. Use a slotted spoon to move the

dumplings onto a heated plate, and then cover and keep them warm until needed.

4 Remove the orange rind, then leave the soup to cool slightly. Purée the soup in a blender or pass it through a sieve; pour it back into the pan, and stir in the remaining orange juice.

5 Heat the soup through without boiling, then pour it into heated bowls. Float the dumplings in the soup and serve with warm rolls.

CREAMY TORTELLINI SOUP

Serves 4
Preparation time: 20 minutes
Cooking time: 20 minutes

3 tablespoons olive oil
1 medium onion, peeled and
    finely chopped
2 cloves garlic, peeled and crushed
1 litre (1¾ pints) chicken or
    vegetable stock (see pp.8-9)
450 g (1 lb) fresh tortellini
225 g (8 oz) frozen peas
2 level tablespoons cornflour
150 ml (¼ pint) soured cream
3 tablespoons chopped
    fresh parsley
Freshly ground black pepper
60 g (2 oz) Parmesan cheese, grated
30 g (1 oz) lightly toasted
    hazelnuts, chopped

Per serving
Calories 474 Protein 20 g
Total fat 33 g (saturated fat 12 g)
Carbohydrates 25 g (added sugar 0)
Fibre 3.2 g Sodium 301 mg

Toasted hazelnuts add the final touch to this simple dish made with tortellini – a pasta stuffed with either spinach and ricotta cheese or with meat. If you prefer, substitute crème fraîche for the soured cream.

1 Heat the olive oil in a large saucepan and cook the onion and garlic in it for 3 minutes, stirring occasionally.

2 Pour in the stock and bring to the boil. Add the tortellini and cook for 10 minutes, then stir in the frozen peas. Bring back to the boil and cook for 5 minutes.

3 Blend the cornflour with the soured cream and stir it into the soup. Add the parsley and season with some pepper. Cook over a low heat for 2 minutes, stirring. Serve the soup, sprinkled with the Parmesan and hazelnuts, with Italian bread.

POTATO AND BACON SOUP

Serves 4
Preparation time: 35 minutes
Cooking time: 45 minutes

1 tablespoon olive oil
225 g (8 oz) smoked back bacon
    rashers, rinds removed
    and reserved
1 large onion, peeled and
    finely chopped
2 small fresh green chillies,
    de-seeded and finely chopped
2 medium sticks celery, trimmed
    and thinly sliced
2 medium carrots, peeled and diced
450 g (1 lb) potatoes, peeled
    and diced
1 level tablespoon plain flour
725 ml (1¼ pints) chicken stock
    (see p.8)
340 g (12 oz) canned sweetcorn
    kernels
¾ level teaspoon salt
Freshly ground black pepper
150 ml (¼ pint) milk
115 g (4 oz) mature Cheddar
    cheese, grated
2 level tablespoons finely snipped
    fresh chives

Per serving
Calories 385 Protein 14 g
Total fat 25 g (saturated fat 11 g)
Carbohydrates 27 g (added sugar 0)
Fibre 3.6 g Sodium 1048 mg

Potatoes and bacon provide this filling winter soup with a subtle smokiness, while fresh green chillies give it its bite.

1 Heat the oil in a large saucepan and fry the bacon rashers and rinds in it over a moderate heat for 8-10 minutes, or until crisp. Remove the pan from the heat, take out the rashers, and drain them on kitchen paper. Discard the rinds, finely chop the bacon and set aside.

2 Reheat the fat in the pan and add the onion, chillies, celery, carrots and potatoes to it. Cook over a moderate heat, stirring, for about 10 minutes, or until the vegetables are softened.

3 Stir in the flour and pour in the stock. Add the sweetcorn, including the juice from the can, the salt and some pepper, then bring to the boil. Reduce the heat, cover and simmer for 20 minutes, or until the vegetables are tender.

4 Stir in the milk and reserved chopped bacon and cook for a further 5 minutes. Ladle the soup into heated bowls, sprinkle with the Cheddar and chives and serve with wholemeal bread.

43

FRENCH ONION SOUP

Slices of garlic bread soak up a delicate, cheese-topped onion broth in this simplest of classic French soups. Gentle, slow frying mellows the flavour of the onions and avoids the bitter taste which develops if they brown too fast.

Serves 4
Preparation time: 15 minutes
Cooking time: 35 minutes

7 tablespoons olive oil
2 cloves garlic, peeled and crushed
900 g (2 lb) onions, peeled and sliced
2 level tablespoons plain flour
2.3 litres (4 pints) chicken stock (see p.8)
225 ml (8 fl oz) red wine
1½ level teaspoons salt
Freshly ground black pepper
16 thick slices french bread
60 g (2 oz) Gruyère cheese, grated

Per serving
Calories 681 Protein 17 g
Total fat 31 g (saturated fat 6.3 g)
Carbohydrates 79 g (added sugar 0)
Fibre 8.7 g Sodium 1412 mg

1 Mix 3 tablespoons of the oil with the garlic, cover and set aside. Heat the remaining oil in a heavy saucepan and very gently fry the onions in it for about 20 minutes, until they are a pale, golden brown. Preheat the oven to 200°C (400°F, gas mark 6).

2 Stir the flour into the onions and then add the stock, wine, salt and some pepper. Bring to the boil, then reduce the heat, cover and simmer for 15 minutes.

3 Meanwhile, brush both sides of each slice of bread with the garlic and oil mixture and put them on a baking tray. Bake in the centre of the oven for 10 minutes, or until crisp.

4 Put two slices of the bread in the bottom of each bowl, then ladle the soup over the top. Sprinkle with the Gruyère and serve with the extra garlic bread.

POTATO AND CHEESE SOUP

Serves 4
Preparation time: 25 minutes
Cooking time: 35 minutes

30 g (1 oz) unsalted butter or margarine
1 large onion, peeled and chopped
450 g (1 lb) potatoes, peeled and diced
2 peppers, 1 green and 1 red, de-seeded and diced
2 cloves garlic, peeled and crushed
1 litre (1¾ pints) chicken stock (see p.8)
1 bay leaf
½ level teaspoon salt
1½ level teaspoons ground cumin
150 ml (¼ pint) natural yoghurt
115 g (4 oz) smoked Cheddar cheese, grated
2 tablespoons chopped fresh coriander leaves
2 spring onions, trimmed and finely sliced
2 small tomatoes, skinned, de-seeded and diced
4 tablespoons croutons (see p.47)

Per serving
Calories 317 Protein 13 g
Total fat 17 g (saturated fat 11 g)
Carbohydrates 30 g (added sugar 0)
Fibre 4.2 g Sodium 539 mg

This rich and warming soup can be varied by using different kinds of cheese each time you make it. Using a food processor or blender speeds up the preparation time, although you can pass the mixture through a sieve or vegetable mill instead.

1 Melt the butter or margarine in a large saucepan and fry the onion in it over a moderate heat until pale golden. Mix in the potatoes, peppers and garlic and continue frying for 5 minutes, stirring occasionally.

2 Pour in the stock and add the bay leaf and salt. Bring to the boil over a high heat, then reduce to a simmer, cover and cook for 20 minutes, or until the potatoes are tender. Remove the bay leaf and leave the soup to cool slightly.

3 Purée the soup with the cumin in a food processor or electric blender – in batches, if necessary – until smooth. Pour the soup into a clean saucepan.

4 Stir in the yoghurt and reheat gently, taking care not to boil. Add half the Cheddar and stir until melted, then ladle the soup into heated bowls. Garnish each one with a sprinkling of the remaining Cheddar, the chopped coriander, spring onions, tomatoes and croutons, and then serve.

Minestrone with Toasted Cheese Slices

Serves 4
Preparation time: 15 minutes
Cooking time: 45 minutes

2 tablespoons olive oil
2 medium onions, peeled
  and chopped
2 medium carrots, peeled and sliced
2 medium sticks celery, trimmed
  and sliced
1 medium leek, trimmed, thinly
  sliced and washed
2 cloves garlic, peeled and crushed
1.7 litres (3 pints) vegetable stock
  (see p.9)
2 level tablespoons tomato purée
115 g (4 oz) green cabbage,
  shredded
400 g (14 oz) canned chopped
  tomatoes
30 g (1 oz) small pasta shapes
  for soups
1 level teaspoon salt
Freshly ground black pepper
8 slices french bread
2 tablespoons pesto sauce
115 g (5 oz) mozzarella cheese, cut
  into 8 slices
30 g (1 oz) Parmesan cheese, grated

Per serving
Calories 565 Protein 24 g
Total fat 22 g (saturated fat 6.8 g)
Carbohydrates 73 g (added sugar 0)
Fibre 9.4 g Sodium 1391 mg

Recipes for this traditional soup vary throughout Italy, but always specify a colourful mix of fresh vegetables with pasta.

1 Heat the oil in a large saucepan and fry the onion in it until just soft. Stir in the carrots, celery, leek and garlic and fry for a further 10 minutes.

For extra flavour, add the Parmesan rind to this soup and remove it before serving.

2 Add the stock, tomato purée, cabbage, tomatoes, pasta shapes, salt and some pepper and bring to the boil. Reduce the heat, cover and simmer for 30 minutes.

3 In the meantime, toast the french bread on both sides, then spread each slice with a little of the pesto sauce. Cover with a slice of the mozzarella, sprinkle with the Parmesan, then put under the grill until the cheeses have melted and browned. Ladle the soup into heated soup bowls, float a slice or two of french bread on top of each one, and then serve.

Making the most of soups

Soup is the ultimate meal in one dish – an infusion of flavours that is produced by a good stock and careful preparation. Soups can be thickened and puréed, frozen and reheated, and served with a wide range of garnishes to suit the simplest or most special occasion.

SOUP CAN BE made from a well-nigh infinite combination of ingredients, from the modest potato to the most exotic fish, and it can be made even more substantial if you add pasta, rice or bread. Few nutrients are lost in the making of soup, since during cooking the goodness is held in the broth. Vitamin C, however, is damaged when exposed to heat, so any green vegetables should be added to soup as late as possible.

Stocks and seasoning

A good-quality stock remains the most important component of a tasty soup. The stock recipes on pp.8 and 9 are saltless; if you choose to use a stock cube, taste the soup first before adding any seasoning recommended in the list of ingredients, and adjust the amount accordingly. Do not be tempted to add any extra salt until you have finished cooking, because the flavour of salt intensifies as the liquid reduces during cooking; what may seem tasteless when the ingredients are first added can quickly become too salty.

You can counteract saltiness by adding potatoes or other root vegetables to the soup and, if necessary, a little more stock or water. If you are on a low-salt diet, omit the salt altogether.

Preparing soups in advance

Apart from fish soups, which are best eaten on the day they are made, most soups can be made the day before and reheated. Meat soups, in particular, will improve in flavour if made in advance, and any excess fat can solidify on the surface and be removed before the soup is reheated. Soups containing starchy foods, like pasta and potatoes, may need to have a little more stock added to them before reheating, and all soups must be brought to a full rolling boil before serving.

How to thicken soups

There are several ways of thickening a soup. Flour can be added at the start of the cooking, before any stock is added, to give it a basic bulk, or a paste of butter and flour combined (known as *beurre manié*) can be whisked into the soup once it is ready to serve. Similarly, instant mashed potato or ground rice can be whisked into a hot soup which is too thin.

Cooking with the lid off allows a soup to evaporate – this helps to thicken it, but its volume will reduce as well. If a soup becomes too thick, you can add stock, or milk, single cream or tomato juice, depending on the type of soup you are making.

Puréeing soups

Blending cooked ingredients with their broth, or puréeing, gives soup a smooth, thick texture. This can be done by hand or in a food processor or electric blender. A blender achieves a finer texture than a food processor. Let the soup cool a little before you purée it, as steam from a boiling hot soup can force the lid off. Puréeing by hand means pushing the cooked ingredients through a vegetable or food

Puréeing through a vegetable mill

Assemble the vegetable mill, and place it over a bowl. Add 2-3 ladlefuls of the soup, then turn the handle until the vegetables are passed through. Discard any remaining coarser pieces, such as pea husks or tomato skins.

Puréeing through a sieve

Place the sieve over a large bowl. Pour 1-2 ladlefuls of soup into the sieve and press it through with the back of a wooden spoon. Add small amounts of soup at a time to make it easier to press through.

mill – a sieve with a fixed blade and handle that pushes the food through, also known as a Mouli-légumes – or a stainless steel or nylon sieve. Do not use a tin sieve, however, as this will react with any acid ingredients and taint the flavour of the soup. Be sure to brush and rinse the sieve thoroughly after use, because particles of food that become clogged in the mesh may encourage germs.

Garnishes and accompaniments

There are many different ways of adding to a soup at the last moment to enliven the flavour, the appearance, or both. Plain soups can be improved with a swirl of cream or yoghurt, or sprinkled with freshly chopped herbs or vegetables (see p.10) or a colourful spice, such as paprika. Ladling soup over toasted bread dates back as far as the Middle Ages, and remains a popular technique, while serving soup with any of the wide variety of breads that are available today adds a welcome contrast in texture and boosts the nutritional value of the meal.

Croutons and crostini Croutons – small cubes of bread fried in butter or oil until crisp – can be added to almost any soup and provide extra flavour and texture. Crostini (or croutes) are slices of bread which are crisped in the oven or toasted under the grill. They may be plain or have a savoury topping. Crostini will keep in an airtight container for 1-2 weeks, or can be frozen for up to 6 months.

Dumplings give substance to a light soup and their high starch content thickens it. They can be made with flour and baking powder, suet, cornmeal or mashed potatoes combined with butter, herbs and spices, eggs or milk. Dumplings should always be added to a gently simmering soup and cooked with the lid on to keep in the steam. This ensures that they are light and fluffy. Never add dumplings to a boiling soup or they will break up.

Making dumplings

1 Sift the dry ingredients into a bowl and mix in any seasoning and herbs. Make a well in the centre and pour in the liquid.

2 Combine all the ingredients with a round-bladed knife to form a fairly soft dough.

3 Roll walnut-sized pieces of dough into balls between lightly wetted or floured hands.

4 When the soup is gently simmering and not boiling, carefully place the dumplings on the surface. Cover and cook for about 10 minutes, or until they are well risen, light and fluffy.

Shaping softer mixtures

Softer dumpling mixtures can be shaped between two metal tablespoons before you add them to the soup.

MEAT

This collection of simmering stews, succulent pot roasts and aromatic stir-fries and pilaffs is inspired by a simple goal: to provide a well-balanced meal based around a cut of meat. You will find meat in all its forms, with a diverse array of vegetables, in recipes that are as suitable for entertaining as they are for feeding the family.

❖

Making the most of meat 78-81

In Roast Pork with Red Cabbage, Apples and Potatoes (left), a brown sugar glaze lends freshly carved meat a hint of sweetness (see p.64).

FRUITED POT ROAST

Tender topside surrounded by sweet potatoes and dried fruits is an excellent alternative to a more traditional meal of roast beef and Yorkshire pudding.

Serves 6
Preparation time: 30 minutes
Cooking time: 2 hours 30 minutes

2 tablespoons olive oil
1.4 kg (3 lb) topside of beef, wiped
1 large onion, peeled and chopped
225 ml (8 fl oz) beef stock
   (see p.8)
½ level teaspoon ground cinnamon
1 bay leaf
2 thinly pared strips orange rind
900 g (2 lb) sweet potatoes, peeled
   and cut into cubes (see p.10)
115 g (4 oz) each ready-to-use
   pitted prunes and dried apricots
60 g (2 oz) large sultanas
½ level teaspoon salt
Freshly ground black pepper
Fresh bay leaves to garnish

Per serving
Calories 516 Protein 46 g
Total fat 20 g (saturated fat 3.5 g)
Carbohydrates 40 g (added sugar 0)
Fibre 2.4 g Sodium 333 mg

1 Preheat the oven to 190°C (375°F, gas mark 5). Heat the oil in a large, flameproof casserole and brown the beef all over for about 10 minutes. Move the beef onto a plate and set aside.

2 Skim all but 2 tablespoons of fat from the casserole. Add the onion to it and cook for about 5 minutes over a moderate heat, or until tender. Stir in the stock, scraping up the browned bits from the bottom of the casserole.

3 Put the beef back into the casserole and add the cinnamon, bay leaf and orange rind. Slowly bring to the boil, cover, and cook in the centre of the oven for 1½ hours, turning the meat every half hour.

4 Stir in the sweet potatoes, prunes, apricots and sultanas, and season with the salt and some pepper. Cover and cook for 45 minutes, or until the beef, potatoes and fruits are tender.

5 Remove the string from around the meat, take out the bay leaf and skim off any excess fat from the cooking juices. Slice the beef and serve it straight from the casserole, or arrange it on a heated serving plate, surrounded by the potatoes and fruit. Spoon the cooking juices over the meat and garnish with the bay leaves.

A touch of cinnamon brings out the fruitiness of apricots, prunes and sultanas in this succulent pot roast.

ROAST BEEF ROYALE

Horseradish sauce adds a tangy flavour to this delicious pot-roasted Sunday joint.

Serves 6
Preparation time: 15 minutes
Cooking time: 1 hour 40 minutes

....

3 tablespoons olive oil
900 g (2 lb) baking potatoes, peeled and cut into large cubes
6 medium carrots, peeled and cut into short pieces
6 medium parsnips, halved widthways and quartered lengthways
2 medium onions, peeled and quartered
1 level teaspoon dried marjoram
½ level teaspoon salt
Freshly ground black pepper
1.1 kg (2½ lb) lean topside of beef
Sprigs of watercress to garnish

For the sauce
150 ml (¼ pint) soured cream
4 level teaspoons finely grated fresh or bottled horseradish
1 tablespoon white wine vinegar
¼ level teaspoon sugar
¼ level teaspoon salt

....

Per serving
Calories 576 Protein 59 g
Total fat 21 g (saturated fat 7.6 g)
Carbohydrates 41 g (added sugar 0)
Fibre 6.9 g Sodium 378 mg

....

1 Preheat the oven to 220°C (425°F, gas mark 7). Put the oil in a large roasting tin and heat in the oven for 30 seconds. Add the potatoes, carrots, parsnips and onions and sprinkle them with the marjoram, half the salt and some pepper. Toss the vegetables in the oil and bake for 10 minutes.

2 Wipe the beef with kitchen paper and sprinkle with the remaining salt and some pepper. Increase the oven temperature to 230°C (450°F, gas mark 8). Arrange the meat in the roasting tin with the vegetables around it.

3 Roast the beef and vegetables, uncovered, for 25 minutes and then reduce the oven temperature to 180°C (350°F, gas mark 4). Turning the meat and vegetables occasionally, cook for 32-36 minutes for rare beef, 40-44 minutes for medium beef or 44-48 minutes for well-done beef. Remove the tin from the oven, cover loosely with foil and leave the meat to rest for 15 minutes before carving.

4 Meanwhile, mix together the soured cream, horseradish, vinegar, sugar and salt, and pour the sauce into a small serving bowl. Arrange the beef and vegetables on a warmed serving dish, garnish with the watercress sprigs and serve with the sauce.

BEEF STROGANOFF WITH PEAS

Strips of steak and green peas dressed in a lively soured cream sauce are served on a bed of pasta in this variant of the classic Russian Stroganoff.

Serves 4
Preparation time: 20 minutes
Cooking time: 30 minutes

....

3 tablespoons olive oil
675 g (1½ lb) sirloin or rump steak, trimmed of fat and cut into thin strips (see p.80)
½ level teaspoon salt
Freshly ground black pepper
1 large onion, peeled and chopped
225 g (8 oz) mushrooms, wiped and thinly sliced
225 g (8 oz) tagliatelle
2 level tablespoons plain flour
285 ml (½ pint) beef stock (see p.8)
225 g (8 oz) frozen peas
150 ml (¼ pint) soured cream or natural yoghurt
2 level tablespoons whole-grain mustard
30 g (1 oz) butter, melted
1 level tablespoon poppy seeds
Sprigs of fresh thyme or rosemary and sautéed, sliced mushrooms to garnish

....

Per serving
Calories 821 Protein 61 g
Total fat 42 g (saturated fat 17 g)
Carbohydrates 58 g (added sugar 0)
Fibre 9.1 g Sodium 422 mg

....

1 Heat 2 tablespoons of the oil in a large frying pan. Add the meat, salt and pepper and brown for 2-3 minutes, stirring, then move the strips onto a plate.

2 Heat the remaining oil in the pan for 1 minute, then soften the onion in it, stirring, over a moderate heat. Add the mushrooms and cook, stirring regularly, for 5 minutes. Put the tagliatelle on to cook (see p.202).

3 Reduce the heat to low, mix the flour into the onions and mushrooms and cook, stirring, for 3 minutes. Increase the heat to moderate, and gradually stir in the stock. Bring to the boil, stirring constantly, then reduce the heat once more and continue stirring until the sauce thickens.

4 Return the strips of beef to the pan, add the peas and cook, uncovered, for 5 minutes, stirring occasionally. Reserve 2 tablespoons of the soured cream, then stir the rest, with the mustard, into the meat mixture. Simmer, stirring continuously, for 1-2 minutes.

5 Drain the pasta, toss it with the melted butter and the poppy seeds and turn onto a heated serving dish. Pour the Stroganoff into the centre, garnish with the reserved soured cream, herbs and mushrooms, and serve.

MARINATED SESAME BEEF STIR-FRY

Serves 4
Preparation time: 40 minutes
Marinating time: 30 minutes
Cooking time: 20 minutes

For the marinade
2 tablespoons soy sauce
2 level tablespoons cornflour
4 tablespoons water
1 tablespoon groundnut oil
1 tablespoon dry sherry
1/2 level teaspoon sugar
675 g (1 1/2 lb) sirloin steak, trimmed
    of fat and cut into thin
    strips (see p.80)

For the sauce
4 tablespoons soy sauce
2 tablespoons dry sherry
1 teaspoon groundnut oil
1/4 teaspoon Tabasco sauce
1 level tablespoon cornflour
4 tablespoons beef stock (see p.8)

For the stir-fry
225 g (8 oz) long-grain white rice
4 tablespoons groundnut oil
30 g (1 oz) peeled and grated
    root ginger
1 clove garlic, peeled and crushed
450 g (1 lb) fresh asparagus,
    trimmed and cut into
    short lengths
115 ml (4 fl oz) beef stock
    (see p.8)
1 tablespoon sesame oil
1-2 teaspoons toasted
    sesame seeds

*Delicate asparagus tips combine
with strips of marinated sirloin
steak on a bed of long-grain rice.
A sprinkling of toasted sesame
seeds adds the final touch.*

**Soy sauce and sherry bring out
the flavours of asparagus and
lean beef in this luxurious
stir-fry. When asparagus is out
of season, use a slightly smaller
amount of frozen asparagus –
let it thaw before cooking.**

1 Combine the soy sauce,
cornflour, water, oil, sherry and
sugar in a large bowl. Add the beef
strips and turn them in the liquid,
then cover the bowl and leave to
marinate for 30 minutes.

Per serving
Calories 756 Protein 55 g
Total fat 35 g (saturated fat 6.9 g)
Carbohydrates 56 g (added sugar 0)
Fibre 3.2 g Sodium 1287 mg

2 In the meantime, prepare the
sauce by mixing the soy sauce,
sherry, oil, Tabasco sauce,
cornflour and stock in a bowl.

3 Put the rice on to cook
(see p.9). Heat 2 tablespoons
of the oil in a large wok or pan
and then stir-fry the beef strips for
2-3 minutes, or until browned.
Place the strips on a plate.

4 Heat the remaining oil in the
wok or pan and stir-fry the
ginger and garlic in it for 1 minute.
Mix in the asparagus and cook
for 1 minute, then pour on the
stock and cook, covered, for
1-2 minutes. Add the beef and
the sauce, and bring to the boil,
stirring. Reduce the heat and
cook for 4-5 minutes, until the
meat is tender and the sauce has
thickened. Stir in the sesame oil.

5 Spoon the rice onto a heated
serving dish, and pour the beef
mixture over the top. Sprinkle
with the sesame seeds and
serve immediately.

52

BRAISED RUMP STEAK

Fresh green beans, celery and soft pieces of swede and potato form a nutritious base for succulent slices of rump steak braised in a spicy beef stock.

Serves 4
Preparation time: 20 minutes
Cooking time: 1 hour 50 minutes

4 medium sticks celery, thickly sliced
1 large onion, peeled and sliced
225 g (8 oz) swede, peeled
   and cut into dice
675 g (1½ lb) top rump of beef, cut
   into 4 slices
¾ level teaspoon salt
Freshly ground black pepper
285 ml (½ pint) beef stock
   (see p.8)
3 tablespoons chilli sauce
1 level teaspoon mustard powder
¾ level teaspoon dried thyme
675 g (1½ lb) waxy potatoes,
   peeled and cut into large chunks
115 g (4 oz) fine green beans,
   trimmed and cut into short pieces
1-2 level teaspoons cornflour
1 tablespoon cold water
3 medium tomatoes, thickly sliced
   and grilled, to garnish (optional)

Per serving
Calories 451 Protein 53 g
Total fat 11 g (saturated fat 4.3 g)
Carbohydrates 37 g (added sugar 0)
Fibre 5.7 g Sodium 528 mg

1 Preheat the oven to 180°C (350°F, gas mark 4). Put the celery, onion and swede into a large, flameproof casserole. Season the slices of beef on both sides with a third of the salt and pepper to taste, then arrange them on top of the vegetables.

2 Combine the stock, chilli sauce, mustard and thyme in a bowl, then pour over the meat and vegetables. Cover and bake in the centre of the oven for 30 minutes.

3 Remove the casserole from the oven and add the potatoes to the meat, covering them with liquid as much as possible. Season with the remaining salt and pepper, cover the casserole and put it back in the oven for 1 hour, adding a little more stock halfway through cooking if the meat and vegetables appear too dry.

4 Stir the beans into the casserole, covering them with liquid, and cook for a further 10-15 minutes, or until the beans are tender.

5 Move the meat from the casserole to a plate and keep warm. Blend the cornflour with the water, stir it into the casserole, then bring to the boil over a moderate heat. Reduce the heat and simmer for 1 minute. Return the meat to the casserole, garnish with the tomato slices and serve.

BEEF AND VEGETABLE PIE

This substantial beef, carrot and mushroom pie with tempting, richly flavoured gravy is an excellent way to use up the leftovers of a weekend roast.

Serves 4
Preparation time: 45 minutes
Cooking time: 30 minutes

2 tablespoons olive oil
30 g (1 oz) butter
225 g (8 oz) carrots, peeled
   and sliced
225 g (8 oz) button onions, peeled
225 g (8 oz) mushrooms, wiped
   and quartered
3 level tablespoons plain flour
½ level teaspoon dried marjoram
Freshly ground black pepper
425 ml (¾ pint) beef stock
   (see p.8)
340 g (12 oz) leftover rare roast
   beef, diced
340 g (12 oz) shortcrust
   pastry (see p.9)
1 egg, size 3, beaten, or milk,
   to glaze

Per serving
Calories 772 Protein 32 g
Total fat 48 g (saturated fat 19 g)
Carbohydrates 58 g (added sugar 0)
Fibre 5.9 g Sodium 471 mg

1 Heat the oil and butter in a large saucepan for 1 minute. Add the carrots and onions and cook until lightly brown – for about 8 minutes. Stir in the mushrooms and cook for 2 minutes.

2 Add the flour, marjoram and some pepper and cook, stirring, for 2 minutes. Gradually mix in the stock and cook, still stirring, for 5 minutes, until the sauce is thickened. Mix in the beef, simmer for 5 minutes, then pour into a large pie dish. Preheat the oven to 220°C (425°F, gas mark 7).

3 On a lightly floured surface, roll the pastry into an oval 2.5 cm (1 in) larger than the pie dish and cut a 1.3 cm (½ in) strip from around the edge of the pastry. Dampen the edge of the pie dish and press the pastry strip onto it. Brush lightly with water and cover the pie with the remaining pastry, pressing the edges together to seal. Trim and flute the pie edge and use the trimmings to make leaves for a central decoration. Brush the pie with the beaten egg or milk and make a small hole in its centre to let out steam during cooking.

4 Place the pie in the centre of the oven and bake it for 30 minutes, until the pastry is golden brown. Serve it at the table with salad and wholemeal bread.

BRAISED BEEFBURGERS

Serves 4
Preparation time: 30 minutes
Cooking time: 50 minutes

85 g (3 oz) wholemeal breadcrumbs
800 g (1¾ lb) lean minced beef
1 egg, size 2, beaten
1 level tablespoon tomato ketchup
2 teaspoons Worcestershire sauce
1 level tablespoon tomato chutney
1 level teaspoon each dried thyme
   and oregano
1 level teaspoon salt
Freshly ground black pepper
2 tablespoons olive oil
1 medium onion, peeled and
   thinly sliced
4 medium carrots, peeled and sliced
2 small parsnips, peeled and diced
115 g (4 oz) baby sweetcorn
2 level teaspoons plain flour
675 g (1½ lb) waxy potatoes,
   peeled and diced
285 ml (½ pint) beef stock
   (see p.8)
Finely chopped fresh parsley
   to garnish

Per serving
Calories 577 Protein 50 g
Total fat 19 g (saturated fat 4.6 g)
Carbohydrates 54 g (added sugar 0)
Fibre 7.8 g Sodium 859 mg

Tasty homemade beefburgers are cooked on a bed of carrots, parsnips and baby sweetcorn in this simple but nutritious family supper.

1 Combine the breadcrumbs, minced beef, egg, ketchup, Worcestershire sauce, chutney, thyme and oregano in a bowl and season with half the salt and a generous amount of pepper. Divide the mixture into eight equal-sized patties.

2 Heat the oil in a large flameproof casserole. Brown the beefburgers on each side then move them to a plate. Add the onion, carrots, parsnips and corn to the casserole and cook over a moderate heat for 2-3 minutes. Stir in the flour and then arrange the beefburgers on top of the vegetables. Place the potatoes around the burgers and pour on the beef stock.

3 Cover the casserole and cook gently for 40-50 minutes, until the beefburgers are cooked and vegetables tender, adding a little more stock if necessary. Once cooked, sprinkle with the chopped parsley and serve.

RUMP STEAK WITH PIZZA SAUCE

A thick tomato sauce seasoned with fragrant oregano brings a taste of Italy to this wholesome platter of steak and vegetables.

Serves 4
Preparation time: 15 minutes
Cooking time: 40 minutes

675 g (1½ lb) medium waxy
   potatoes, peeled
4 tablespoons olive oil
1 clove garlic, peeled and crushed
1 small red chilli, de-seeded and
   finely chopped
675 g (1½ lb) rump steak, trimmed
   of fat, beaten out slightly and cut
   into 4 portions
285 ml (½ pint) passata
   (sieved tomatoes)
225 g (8 oz) fine green beans,
   halved and blanched for
   2 minutes (see p.10)
1 level teaspoon dried oregano
1 tablespoon capers
¼ level teaspoon salt
Freshly ground black pepper
Fresh oregano leaves to garnish

Per serving
Calories 519 Protein 48 g
Total fat 23 g (saturated fat 5.7 g)
Carbohydrates 33 g (added sugar 0)
Fibre 4.9 g Sodium 252 mg

1 Boil the potatoes for 10 minutes, then cool, drain well and cut into slices. Heat half the oil in a large flameproof casserole and gently cook the garlic and chilli in it for 2 minutes. Turn up the heat, add the steak and cook for 2 minutes on each side. Move the steak onto a plate and set aside.

2 Heat the remaining oil in the casserole and fry the potato slices in it for 5 minutes, then lay the steak on top of the potatoes.

3 Mix the passata with the green beans, oregano, capers, salt and some pepper. Pour over the meat, then cover and simmer for 15 minutes, or until the meat is tender but still slightly pink in the centre, shaking the casserole frequently to prevent the potatoes sticking to the bottom. Garnish with the oregano leaves and serve.

CHUNKY BEEF AND ONION COBBLER

Serves 4
Preparation time: 50 minutes
Cooking time: 55 minutes

....

3 tablespoons olive oil
675 g (1½ lb) lean chuck steak,
  cut into cubes (see p.79)
5 large Spanish onions, peeled and
  thinly sliced
2 level teaspoons caster sugar
2 medium carrots, peeled and sliced
850 ml (1½ pints) beef stock
  (see p.8)
400 g (14 oz) canned
  chopped tomatoes
¼ level teaspoon salt

For the scones
275 g (10 oz) plain flour
1½ level teaspoons baking powder
¾ level teaspoon bicarbonate
  of soda
½ level teaspoon salt
70 g (2½ oz) butter or margarine
3 tablespoons chopped
  fresh parsley
175 ml (6 fl oz) buttermilk, milk or
  natural yoghurt

....

Per serving
Calories 834 Protein 59 g
Total fat 36 g (saturated fat 15 g)
Carbohydrates 74 g (added sugar 6 g)
Fibre 6.2 g Sodium 544 mg

A cobbler is a quick and easy version of a pie that has oven-crisp scones as the topping in place of pastry. Cobbler recipes are usually made with sweet fruit, but in this version the scones cover a savoury beef stew.

1 Heat 2 tablespoons of the oil in a large flameproof casserole. Fry the chuck steak in it for about 10 minutes, stirring, until it is browned all over. Add the remaining oil, the onions and sugar to the casserole and cook over a moderate heat for 3 minutes, stirring regularly. Mix in the carrots and cook for a further 3 minutes.

2 Pour in the stock and stir in the tomatoes and salt. Bring to the boil, then reduce the heat, cover and simmer for 40 minutes, until the meat is tender. While it is cooking, preheat the oven to 220°C (425°F, gas mark 7).

3 Make the scones around 15 minutes before the meat is cooked. Sift the flour, baking powder, bicarbonate of soda and salt into a bowl, and rub in the butter or margarine until the mixture resembles fine breadcrumbs. Mix in parsley and buttermilk to form a soft dough.

4 Knead the dough on a lightly floured work surface for a few seconds until smooth. Roll out to 1.3 cm (½ in) thick, then cut out rounds with a 5 cm (2 in) cutter. Knead and roll the trimmings and cut out more rounds. Lay the scones on top of the stew, slightly overlapping each other.

5 Bake for 12-15 minutes, uncovered, in the centre of the heated oven, or until the scones are well risen and golden on top.

Buttery parsley scones soak up the rich gravy around lean chuck steak cubes and tender vegetables.

SPICY BEEF WITH COUSCOUS

Serves 4
Preparation time: 25 minutes
Cooking time: 1 hour 45 minutes

1 tablespoon olive oil
675 g (1½ lb) lean braising steak,
    trimmed of fat and cut into
    cubes (see p.79)
570 ml (1 pint) beef stock (see p.8)
1½ level teaspoons ground
    cinnamon
½ level teaspoon salt
Freshly ground black pepper
225 g (8 oz) medium couscous
4 tablespoons cold water
225 g (8 oz) button onions or
    shallots, peeled
340 g (12 oz) butternut squash,
    peeled, de-seeded and cut into
    small cubes
3 tablespoons balsamic or white
    wine vinegar
1 tablespoon clear honey
225 g (8 oz) ready-to-use pitted
    prunes, halved
225 g (8 oz) cooked chickpeas,
    drained (see p.172)

Per serving
Calories 746 Protein 63 g
Total fat 24 g (saturated fat 8.4 g)
Carbohydrates 74 g (added sugar 5 g)
Fibre 11 g Sodium 283 mg

Couscous and chickpeas are the basis of this substantial stew, and cinnamon, prunes and honey add a touch of the exotic. A quick way to peel button onions and shallots is to steep them in boiling water for 1 minute; when they are cool, the skins should slip off easily.

1 Heat the oil in a very large saucepan (it must be broad and deep enough to hold a large metal sieve), and brown the braising steak in it for 5-8 minutes. Pour in the stock, then season with the cinnamon, salt and some pepper. Bring to the boil, reduce the heat, cover and simmer for 1 hour.

2 Meanwhile, put the couscous in a bowl and sprinkle it with the cold water. Leave to stand for 10 minutes.

3 Stir the onions or shallots, the butternut squash, vinegar and honey into the beef. Bring it back to the boil, then reduce

the heat. Pour the couscous into a large, fine metal sieve and place it over the beef (see p.173). Cover the sieve and saucepan and simmer for 30 minutes, or until the beef and vegetables are tender.

4 Stir the prunes and chickpeas into the stew, then cover and cook for a further 5 minutes. In the meantime, fluff the couscous with a fork and arrange it on a heated serving plate. Spoon the beef over the top and serve.

The couscous becomes light and fluffy when steamed over a pot of simmering beef, butternut squash and button onions.

56

BEEF AND RED WINE STEW

Serves 4
Preparation time: 20 minutes
Cooking time: 1 hour 45 minutes

2 level tablespoons plain flour
½ level teaspoon salt
Freshly ground black pepper
450 g (1 lb) lean braising steak,
  trimmed of fat and cut into
  cubes (see p.79)
2 tablespoons olive oil
1 large onion, peeled and chopped
1 clove garlic, peeled and crushed
225 g (8 oz) button mushrooms,
  wiped
450 g (1 lb) potatoes, peeled and
  cut into cubes
4 medium carrots, peeled and
  thickly sliced
2 medium parsnips, peeled, halved
  and sliced
285 ml (½ pint) beef stock
  (see p.8)
200 ml (7 fl oz) dry red wine
1 bay leaf
2 level teaspoons mixed dried herbs
175 g (6 oz) fresh or frozen button
  brussels sprouts, trimmed
2 tablespoons chopped
  fresh parsley

Per serving
Calories 484 Protein 40 g
Total fat 15 g (saturated fat 4.1 g)
Carbohydrates 41 g (added sugar 0)
Fibre 9.6 g Sodium 346 mg

This rich red wine stew
improves with keeping – if
you make it the day before it is
needed, the flavours will have
time to mix and mature. Use
waxy rather than floury
potatoes, as they hold their
shape during slow cooking.

1 Combine the flour, salt and a
generous amount of pepper in
a large polythene bag. Shake the
meat in it until well coated.

2 Heat the oil in a large, heavy
flameproof casserole and brown
the meat in it for 5-8 minutes. Lift
the meat out of the casserole onto
a plate, and set aside.

3 Add the onion and garlic to
the casserole and cook for
3 minutes. Mix in the mushrooms
and cook for 1 minute more.
Return the meat to the casserole
and stir in the potatoes, carrots,
parsnips, stock, red wine, bay leaf
and mixed dried herbs. Bring to
the boil, then cover the casserole
and simmer for 1¼ hours.

4 Add the brussels sprouts, bring
back to the boil and cook,
covered, for a further 15 minutes,
or until the meat and vegetables
are tender. Remove the bay leaf
and stir in the parsley. Serve
the stew in deep soup plates
with thick slices of granary bread
to mop up the rich gravy.

CHILLI PIE

Serves 4
Preparation time: 30 minutes
Cooking time: 30 minutes

For the pastry case
150 g (5 oz) plain flour
1 level teaspoon baking powder
⅛ level teaspoon salt
85 g (3 oz) cornmeal
2 level teaspoons caster sugar
⅛ level teaspoon cayenne pepper
115 g (4 oz) polyunsaturated
  margarine
1–2 tablespoons chilled water

For the filling
1 tablespoon sunflower oil
1 medium green pepper, de-seeded
  and roughly chopped
4 spring onions, white part only,
  thinly sliced
3 cloves garlic, peeled and
  crushed (see p.11)
2 level teaspoons unsweetened
  cocoa
2 level teaspoons chilli powder
¾ level teaspoon each ground
  cinnamon, coriander and cumin
¼ level teaspoon salt
450 g (1 lb) lean minced beef
400 g (14 oz) canned chopped
  tomatoes
225 g (8 oz) cooked red kidney
  beans, rinsed and drained
115 g (4 oz) frozen sweetcorn
Sprigs of flat-leaf parsley
  to garnish

Dress up this
wholesome variation
on Mexican chilli con carne
with a topping of soured cream,
finely sliced spring onions and
creamy chunks of avocado.

1 Preheat the oven to 180°C
(350°F, gas mark 4). Put
the flour, baking powder, salt,
cornmeal, sugar and cayenne
pepper in a bowl. Rub in the
margarine until the mixture
resembles breadcrumbs, then
add enough of the water to mix
to a firm but not sticky dough.

2 Line a 23 cm (9 in) pie plate
with the pastry (see p.285),
trim the edge and flute it with
your thumb and forefinger. Prick
the pastry case on the bottom
and sides with a fork. Knead and
roll out the trimmings, then cut
out eight small triangles and lay
them on a baking sheet.

Per serving
Calories 859 Protein 41 g
Total fat 35 g (saturated fat 8.6 g)
Carbohydrates 100 g (added sugar 2.5 g)
Fibre 12 g Sodium 864 mg

Tempt your guests with a Mexican touch – a light cornmeal case filled with spicy chilli.

3 Line the pastry case with greaseproof paper, fill it with baking beans and cook in the centre of the oven for 25 minutes. Then remove the greaseproof paper and beans and return the case to the oven for 5 minutes. Meanwhile, cook the pastry triangles for about 10 minutes, until they are crisp and lightly browned. Place the triangles on a wire rack to cool.

4 While the case is baking, heat the oil in a large frying pan and soften the green pepper in it, stirring, for about 5 minutes. Add the spring onions and garlic and cook for 2 minutes, then stir in the cocoa, chilli powder, cinnamon, coriander, cumin and salt. Cook for 1 minute, add the minced beef and cook for 5 minutes more until browned, stirring occasionally.

5 Stir in the tomatoes, beans and corn, and bring the mixture to the boil. Turn down the heat and cook for 10 minutes, until the liquid is slightly reduced. Pour the filling into the hot pastry case, arrange the pastry triangles on top, and garnish with the parsley.

SHEPHERD'S PIE

Serves 4
Preparation time: 20 minutes
Cooking time: 55 minutes

1 tablespoon olive oil
1 medium onion, peeled and chopped
1 medium carrot, peeled and chopped
675 g (1½ lb) lean minced beef
1 level teaspoon dried thyme
2 level tablespoons tomato purée
2 level teaspoons Worcestershire sauce
300 g (11 oz) canned condensed vegetable soup
150 ml (¼ pint) beef stock (see p.8)
Freshly ground black pepper
675 g (1½ lb) potatoes, peeled and halved
60 g (2 oz) Cheddar cheese, grated
1 egg, size 2, beaten
¼ level teaspoon salt

Per serving
Calories 568 Protein 44 g
Total fat 27 g (saturated fat 11 g)
Carbohydrates 38 g (added sugar 0)
Fibre 3.5 g Sodium 779 mg

Shepherd's pie was traditionally made with leftover roast lamb, but this quick and easy version – made with lean minced beef – tastes just as good.

1 Heat the oil in a saucepan and cook the onion and carrot in it for 5 minutes. Stir in the beef and cook for 2-3 minutes, until it changes colour. Add the thyme, tomato purée, Worcestershire sauce, vegetable soup and stock. Season with the pepper, cover and simmer for 40 minutes.

2 In the meantime, boil the potatoes until cooked, drain well and then mash with the cheese, egg, salt and some pepper.

3 Turn the beef mixture into a large, flameproof dish and spread the mashed potato evenly over the top. Decorate with a palette knife or fork, then cook under a moderate grill for about 5 minutes, or until golden brown.

59

BEEF ROULADE

Serves 6
Preparation time: 1 hour
Cooking time: 1 hour 25 minutes

2 tablespoons olive oil
675 g (1½ lb) green cabbage,
    shredded (see p.11)
1 medium onion, peeled
    and chopped
400 g (14 oz) canned peeled
    tomatoes
1 level teaspoon sugar
½ level teaspoon salt
Freshly ground black pepper
285 ml (½ pint) beef stock
    (see p.8)
85 g (3 oz) long-grain white rice
450 g (1 lb) lean minced beef
3 tablespoons fresh white
    breadcrumbs
6 spring onions, trimmed and
    thinly sliced
2 eggs, size 3, lightly beaten
½ level teaspoon ground or freshly
    grated nutmeg
85 g (3 oz) mature Cheddar
    cheese, grated
¼ level teaspoon dried thyme
2 tablespoons chopped
    fresh parsley

Per serving
Calories 381 Protein 25 g
Total fat 21 g (saturated fat 7.4 g)
Carbohydrates 255 g (added sugar 1.3 g)
Fibre 4.6 g Sodium 413 mg

**Long-grain rice and mature
Cheddar make a nutritious
stuffing for a baked roll of
minced beef and breadcrumbs.**

1 Preheat the oven to 180°C
(350°F, gas mark 4). Pour the oil
into a large roasting tin, mix in the
cabbage, onion, tomatoes, sugar,
half the salt and some pepper.
Cover the tin with foil and place it
in the centre of the oven. Cook for
45 minutes, stirring occasionally.

2 Meanwhile, pour the stock into
a saucepan and bring to the
boil. Add the rice and simmer,
covered, for 20 minutes.

3 Mix together the beef,
breadcrumbs, half the spring
onions, eggs and nutmeg in a large
bowl. Season the resulting mixture
with the rest of the salt and some
pepper. Once the rice is cooked,
stir in the remaining spring
onions, the cheese and thyme.

4 Cut a rectangle measuring
30 cm x 25 cm (12 in x 10 in)
from a sheet of baking or waxed
paper. Spread the beef mixture
gently over the paper until it is
evenly covered, then carefully
spoon the rice over the beef,
leaving a 2.5 cm (1 in) border of
uncovered beef all the way around.

5 With the long side of the paper
nearest to you, carefully roll up
the meat and rice mixture like a
swiss roll, peeling away the paper
as you roll. When complete, pinch
the ends to seal in the rice.

6 Remove the cabbage mixture
from the oven and push the
vegetables to the sides of the tin
to make room for the beef roulade.

*A soft and savoury rice filling,
rich with the flavours of beef
stock, complements the light,
crispy minced beef shell and
the slightly sweet stewed
cabbage and tomatoes.*

Carefully lay the roulade down
the centre of the tin using two
fish slices, then return the tin to
the oven. Cook, uncovered, for
40 minutes, or until the meat is
cooked and crisp on the outside.
Serve the roulade thickly sliced
and sprinkled with
the chopped parsley,
accompanied by the
cabbage mixture.

Sancocho

Serves 6
Preparation time: 45 minutes
Cooking time: 1 hour 50 minutes

3 tablespoons olive oil
900 g (2 lb) stewing beef, trimmed
    of fat and cut into cubes
1 large onion, peeled and
    finely chopped
340 g (12 oz) cooked salt beef, cut
    into cubes
60 g (2 oz) yellow split peas, rinsed
    and drained (see p.172)
2.3 litres (4 pints) beef stock
    (see p.8)
1 level teaspoon salt
Freshly ground black pepper
450 g (1 lb) potatoes, peeled and
    thickly sliced
225 g (8 oz) flat field mushrooms,
    wiped and thickly sliced
1 fresh green chilli, de-seeded and
    finely chopped
425 ml (¾ pint) canned
    coconut milk
2 large semi-ripe plantains, peeled
    and thickly sliced
450 g (1 lb) sweet potatoes, peeled
    and thickly sliced

For the dumplings
60 g (2 oz) cornmeal
65 g (2¼ oz) plain flour
1 level teaspoon baking powder
¼ level teaspoon salt
45 g (1½ oz) frozen butter, grated,
    or shredded suet
2 tablespoons cold water
Finely chopped red and green
    chillies or peppers to garnish

Cornmeal dumplings adorn this sumptuous coconut, beef and vegetable stew from Trinidad.

1 Heat the oil in a large flameproof casserole and add the stewing beef. Brown over a moderate heat for 10 minutes, stirring, then transfer the meat to a plate. Add the onion to the casserole and soften over a low heat.

2 Return the browned meat to the casserole and add the salt beef, split peas, stock, salt and some pepper. Bring to the boil, then cover and simmer for 1 hour. Stir in the potatoes, mushrooms, chilli and coconut milk. Bring back to the boil, then cover and simmer for a further 20 minutes.

3 Add the plantains and sweet potatoes to the stew and then make the dumplings (see p.47). Divide the soft, slightly sticky dough into 12 roughly equal pieces and roll each one into a ball.

4 Bring the stew to the boil and add the dumplings. Reduce the heat, cover and simmer gently for 15 minutes, or until the dumplings are puffy and have risen to the surface. Garnish and serve.

Per serving
Calories 782 Protein 54 g
Total fat 31 g (saturated fat 12 g)
Carbohydrates 76 g (added sugar 0)
Fibre 7.6 g Sodium 793 mg

CREAMY PORK AND MUSHROOMS WITH NOODLES

Serves 6
Preparation time: 30 minutes
Cooking time: 40 minutes

15 g (½ oz) dried porcini or
  shiitake mushrooms
425 ml (¾ pint) boiling water
60 g (2 oz) plain flour
½ level teaspoon salt
Freshly ground black pepper
675 g (1½ lb) pork tenderloin,
  trimmed of fat and thinly sliced
3 tablespoons olive oil
8 shallots, peeled, and halved
  if large
340 g (12 oz) fresh mushrooms,
  wiped and quartered
4 tablespoons dry sherry
1 tablespoon chopped fresh
  tarragon, or 1 level teaspoon
  dried tarragon
340 g (12 oz) medium-width
  Chinese egg noodles
340 g (12 oz) sugar snap peas
2 tablespoons lemon juice
4 tablespoons single cream

Per serving
Calories 546 Protein 35 g
Total fat 22 g (saturated fat 5 g)
Carbohydrates 53 g
(added sugar 0)
Fibre 5 g Sodium 364 mg

Dried mushrooms – available in some supermarkets and most health food shops – add a distinctive earthy taste to this dish. If you can't find them, add an extra 60 g (2 oz) of fresh mushrooms and substitute chicken stock for the water.

1 Place the dried mushrooms in a bowl and cover them with the water. Leave to soak for 30 minutes.

2 Meanwhile, put the flour, salt and some pepper in a polythene bag, add the pork slices and shake until they are evenly coated with flour. Heat the oil until very hot in a large, flameproof casserole, and then fry the pork in batches for 5 minutes, or until browned. Put the meat on a plate and leave to one side.

3 Put the shallots and fresh mushrooms in the casserole and cook, stirring, for about 5 minutes, until they begin to soften, adding a little more oil if necessary. Stir in the sherry and cook for 2 minutes, scraping up any browned bits from the bottom of the casserole.

4 Line a sieve with kitchen paper and place it over a bowl. Pour the soaked mushrooms and their liquid into the sieve and leave to

Sherry and tarragon add warm background flavours to a rich cream sauce coating thin strips of lean pork, egg noodles, mushrooms and sugar snap peas.

drain. Place the bowl of mushroom liquid on one side, rinse the mushrooms thoroughly under running water to remove any dirt and, if necessary, cut into slices.

5 Stir the mushrooms and their liquid into the shallot mixture. Add the tarragon and meat and bring to the boil. Reduce the heat,

then cover the pan and simmer for 15 minutes, or until the pork strips are almost tender. In the meantime, cook the noodles (see p.202) and drain well.

6 Add the sugar snap peas and lemon juice to the casserole, then cover and simmer for 10 minutes, or until the peas are just tender. Stir in the cream and noodles and heat through for 2-3 minutes, stirring, then serve.

ITALIAN MEATBALLS

Serves 4
Preparation time: 30 minutes
Cooking time: 15 minutes

- 115 g (4 oz) fresh white breadcrumbs
- 450 g (1 lb) rump steak, trimmed of fat and minced (see p.80)
- 60 g (2 oz) liver sausage, skinned
- 60 g (2 oz) Italian garlic sausage, rind removed, finely chopped
- 3 tablespoons chopped fresh parsley
- 1 clove garlic, peeled and crushed
- 30 g (1 oz) grated Parmesan cheese
- ½ level teaspoon salt
- Freshly ground black pepper
- 1 egg, size 2, beaten
- 2 tablespoons olive oil
- 60 g (2 oz) butter
- 800 g (1¾ lb) spinach, trimmed, washed and blanched (see p.10)
- ¼ level teaspoon freshly grated nutmeg
- 225 g (8 oz) ripe tomatoes, skinned, de-seeded and chopped

Parmesan cheese and garlic sausage bring a flavour of Italy to rich beef meatballs served with buttery spinach and tomato. You can use chuck steak in place of rump steak for the meatballs, if you prefer.

1 Put half the breadcrumbs in a bowl and mix with the steak, liver sausage, garlic sausage, parsley, garlic, Parmesan, salt, some pepper and the egg. Divide the mixture into 12 balls, then roll these in the remaining breadcrumbs. Heat the oil in a large frying pan and fry the meatballs in it for 10-12 minutes, or until they are golden brown.

2 Melt the butter in the pan and stir in the spinach, grated nutmeg and tomatoes. Cook, stirring, for 2 minutes, or until heated through, taking care not to break up the meatballs, then serve with warm granary bread.

Per serving
Calories 620 Protein 48 g
Total fat 36 g (saturated fat 16 g)
Carbohydrates 29 g
(added sugar 0)
Fibre 10 g
Sodium 1146 mg

ROAST PORK WITH RED CABBAGE, APPLES AND POTATOES

Serves 6
Preparation time: 30 minutes
Cooking time: 1 hour 45 minutes

3 tablespoons sunflower oil
2 level tablespoons soft dark
 brown sugar
2 kg (4½ lb) loin of pork, skinned,
 boned and rolled (see p.80)
1 medium onion, peeled
 and finely chopped
450 g (1 lb) red cabbage, trimmed
 and finely shredded (see p.11)
900 g (2 lb) small new potatoes,
 scrubbed
450 g (1 lb) cooking apples, peeled,
 cored and thinly sliced
285 ml (½ pint) red wine
2 tablespoons red wine vinegar
1 level teaspoon salt
Freshly ground black pepper
Sprigs of watercress and wedges
 of red-skinned dessert apples
 to garnish

Per serving
Calories 701 Protein 67 g
Total fat 28 g (saturated fat 8.5 g)
Carbohydrates 39 g (added sugar 5 g)
Fibre 5.7 g Sodium 608 mg

Shredded red cabbage, thinly sliced apples and sweet new potatoes are well matched with lean pork loin in this satisfying Sunday lunch. Most butchers will bone the loin if asked to do so. You will need a very large flameproof casserole or a heavy roasting tin covered with foil.

1 Preheat the oven to 190°C (375°F, gas mark 5). Heat the oil and sugar in a large, flameproof casserole until the sugar dissolves to a caramel, then quickly and evenly coat the pork in it for about 10 minutes, until it is golden brown. Lift the meat onto a plate and keep it warm.

2 Add the onion to the casserole and cook until softened. Mix in the cabbage, potatoes, apples, wine, vinegar, salt and some pepper, then bring to a simmer.

3 Put the pork back in the casserole, cover and cook in the centre of the oven for 1 hour. Remove the lid and cook for a further 30 minutes, or until the pork is cooked (see p.81), adding a little more wine to the cabbage mixture if it is too dry. Remove the string and serve the pork from the casserole, garnished with the watercress and apple wedges.

PORK CHOPS WITH BROAD BEANS

Serves 4
Preparation time: 15 minutes
Cooking time: 50 minutes

2 tablespoons vegetable oil
4 pork spare-rib chops, each about
 225 g (8 oz), trimmed of fat
1 large onion, peeled and
 finely chopped
4 medium carrots, peeled and sliced
2 cloves garlic, peeled and
 crushed (see p.11)
400 g (14 oz) canned chopped
 tomatoes
2 level tablespoons soft dark
 brown sugar
½-1 teaspoon grated orange rind
1 level teaspoon salt
Freshly ground black pepper
340 g (12 oz) frozen baby
 broad beans
Chopped fresh mint and mint sprigs
 to garnish

Per serving
Calories 471 Protein 47 g
Total fat 20 g (saturated fat 6 g)
Carbohydrates 28 g (added sugar 7.5 g)
Fibre 2.7 g Sodium 647 mg

A rich sauce, sharpened with a hint of orange and sweetened with soft brown sugar, keeps the pork moist during baking. You can vary this recipe by using pork loin chops or large pieces of pork tenderloin instead of the fattier spare-rib chops, and by replacing the broad beans with canned flageolet beans.

1 Heat the oil in a flameproof casserole or deep, lidded frying pan and brown the pork chops in it for 5 minutes on each side. Put them on a plate and keep warm.

2 Discard all but 1 tablespoon of the fat from the casserole or pan, then cook the onion in it until softened. Stir in the carrots and garlic and cook for 5 minutes.

3 Mix in the tomatoes, sugar, orange rind, salt and some pepper, then bring to a simmer. Add the pork chops, cover and cook for a further 10 minutes.

4 Stir in the broad beans and bring back to the boil. Cover and cook over a moderate heat for 20 minutes, or until the chops are tender (see p.81). Garnish the pork and vegetables with the chopped mint and mint sprigs, and serve with thick slices of crusty farmhouse bread.

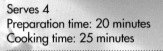

HAM AND SWEET POTATOES IN ORANGE SAUCE

Soft sweet potatoes and crisp florets of broccoli provide a striking contrast of texture in this colourful dish. Canned pineapple chunks can be used in place of the fresh pineapple.

Serves 4
Preparation time: 20 minutes
Cooking time: 25 minutes

2 tablespoons sunflower oil
225 g (8 oz) button onions or shallots, peeled
450 g (1 lb) cooked ham, cut into small cubes (see p.79)
450 g (1 lb) sweet potatoes, peeled, cut into small cubes (see p.10)
425 ml (¾ pint) chicken stock (see p.8)
2 teaspoons grated orange rind
340 g (12 oz) fresh pineapple, skin, core and woody eyes removed, flesh cut into chunks
1 level tablespoon cornflour
Juice of 1 large orange
½ level teaspoon salt
Freshly ground black pepper
340 g (12 oz) fresh broccoli florets

1 Heat the oil in a large, heavy flameproof casserole and cook the onions in it for 5 minutes. Add the ham and sweet potatoes and cook for a further 2 minutes.

Per serving
Calories 392 Protein 27 g
Total fat 14 g (saturated fat 3.2 g)
Carbohydrates 43 g
(added sugar 0)
Fibre 4.6 g
Sodium 1512 mg

2 Mix in the stock, orange rind and pineapple, then cover and simmer for 10 minutes.

3 Blend the cornflour with the orange juice, then add the mixture to the casserole and cook for 1 minute, stirring, until the sauce has thickened. Season with the salt and some pepper.

4 Add the broccoli to the casserole, cover and simmer for 5-10 minutes, or until the vegetables are just tender. Serve the ham and vegetables with thick slices of crusty ciabatta or other Italian bread to mop up the sauce.

Chunks of fresh pineapple and orange juice add an agreeable tartness to the rich sauce in this filling casserole.

CURRIED PORK CHOP BAKE

Serves 4
Preparation time: 15 minutes
Cooking time: 1 hour 45 minutes

4 pork loin chops, each about
   225 g (8 oz), trimmed of fat
1 level teaspoon salt
Freshly ground black pepper
2 tablespoons vegetable oil
2 medium onions, peeled and
   thinly sliced
2 level teaspoons medium-hot
   curry powder
285 ml (½ pint) unsweetened
   apple juice
675 g (1½ lb) potatoes, peeled
   and sliced
4 medium carrots, peeled and
   coarsely grated
225 g (8 oz) white cabbage,
   trimmed and finely shredded
   (see p.11)
Lime wedges and fresh coriander
   leaves to garnish

Per serving
Calories 532 Protein 44 g
Total fat 20 g (saturated fat 6 g)
Carbohydrates 47 g (added sugar 0)
Fibre 6.8 g Sodium 617 mg

Spice up pork chops, shredded cabbage and potatoes with curry powder and apple juice – and turn a simple, wholesome supper into a memorable meal.

1 Preheat the oven to 180°C (350°F, gas mark 4). Season the chops with ¼ teaspoon of the salt and some pepper. Heat the oil in a large, flameproof casserole, and brown the chops in it over a moderate heat for 5 minutes. Lift the chops onto a plate and keep them warm.

2 Discard all but 1 tablespoon of the fat in the casserole, and cook the onions in it until softened. Mix in the curry powder and cook for 1 minute. Pour in 150 ml (¼ pint) of the apple juice, then stir well to loosen any browned bits from the bottom of the casserole.

3 Lay the potatoes on top of the onions. Mix together the carrots and cabbage and scatter them over the potatoes. Sprinkle with the remaining salt and some pepper.

4 Arrange the pork chops on top of the vegetables. Pour in the remaining apple juice, cover and cook in the centre of the oven for 1½ hours, or until the chops and vegetables are tender. Garnish with the lime wedges and fresh coriander leaves, then serve.

PORK AND BROCCOLI STIR-FRY

Serves 4
Preparation time: 30 minutes
Cooking time: 10 minutes

4 tablespoons light soy sauce
3 tablespoons dry sherry
3 teaspoons sesame oil
675 g (1½ lb) boneless pork loin
   or lean shoulder, thinly sliced
1 level tablespoon cornflour
3 tablespoons chicken stock
   (see p.8) or water
2 tablespoons oyster sauce
1 tablespoon black bean sauce
2 tablespoons vegetable or
   peanut oil
6 spring onions, trimmed
   and chopped
1 level tablespoon peeled and
   grated root ginger
2 cloves garlic, peeled and crushed
450 g (1 lb) broccoli, trimmed
   and cut into small florets
225 g (8 oz) baby sweetcorn

Per serving
Calories 433 Protein 43 g
Total fat 24 g (saturated fat 6.3 g)
Carbohydrates 8.8 g (added sugar 0)
Fibre 4.1 g Sodium 1251 mg

Oyster sauce and black bean sauce add a distinctive saltiness and sweetness to this colourful stir-fry of crisp broccoli and tender slices of pork. You can find both sauces in the oriental section of most supermarkets. This stir-fry dish also works well with beef, lamb or chicken; the chicken will take about 2 minutes less to cook.

1 Mix together 2 tablespoons of the soy sauce with 1 tablespoon of the sherry and 1 teaspoon of the sesame oil in a bowl. Stir in the pork slices and leave to marinate for about 20 minutes.

2 Meanwhile, blend the cornflour with the stock or water. Stir in the remaining soy sauce, sherry and sesame oil and add the oyster sauce and black bean sauce. Leave the mixture to one side.

3 Heat the vegetable or peanut oil in a large frying pan or wok and stir-fry the spring onions, ginger and garlic in it for 1 minute. Increase the heat to high and stir-fry the pork for 2-3 minutes, then stir in the broccoli and sweetcorn.

4 Pour over the cornflour sauce and bring it to the boil, stirring. Reduce the heat, cover and simmer for 5 minutes, or until the pork is cooked (see p.81) and the vegetables are just tender. Serve with crusty wholemeal bread.

Pork Medley with Sauerkraut

Serves 4
Preparation time: 20 minutes
Cooking time: 1 hour 5 minutes

- 1 knackwurst or bratwurst, about 115 g (4 oz)
- 2 tablespoons olive oil
- 4 lightly smoked bacon chops, each about 115 g (4 oz), trimmed of fat
- 115 g (4 oz) garlic sausage, cut into thick slices
- 1 medium onion, peeled and thinly sliced
- 2 medium carrots, peeled and thinly sliced
- 450 g (1 lb) sauerkraut, rinsed and drained
- 425 ml (¾ pint) chicken stock (see p.8)
- 115 ml (4 fl oz) dry white wine
- 6 juniper berries (optional)
- 1 level teaspoon caraway seeds
- 1 bay leaf
- 675 g (1½ lb) potatoes, peeled and cut into cubes (see p.10)
- ¼ level teaspoon salt
- Freshly ground black pepper
- 2 dill pickled cucumbers, chopped, and fresh dill to garnish

Per serving
Calories 594 Protein 50 g
Total fat 25 g (saturated fat 8.4 g)
Carbohydrates 39 g (added sugar 0)
Fibre 4.1 g Sodium 2653 mg

Sauerkraut, or 'sour cabbage', is a speciality of Germany and Austria and is also popular in the French regions of Alsace and Lorraine, where it is known as *choucroute*. Juniper berries, an optional addition, give a sharp and spicy background flavour to the dish.

1 Prick the knackwurst or bratwurst all over with a fork. Heat the oil in a large flameproof casserole or frying pan and lightly brown the knackwurst, bacon chops and garlic sausage slices in it for 2-3 minutes. Move them onto a plate and cover, then cook the onion and carrots in the casserole until softened.

2 Add the sauerkraut and cook, stirring, for 1 minute. Pour in the stock and wine, then stir in the juniper berries (if using), caraway seeds, bay leaf and potatoes. Season with the salt and some pepper. Bring the mixture to the boil, then reduce the heat, cover and simmer for 20 minutes.

3 Cut the knackwurst into thick slices and stir them into the casserole. Add the bacon chops and garlic sausage. Spoon the sauerkraut and potatoes over and around the meat, cover and simmer for 20 minutes, or until the potatoes are tender. Remove the bay leaf, garnish and serve.

Slow cooking in a casserole mellows the sharpness of sauerkraut in this smoked meat and cabbage dish based on a traditional recipe from Alsace.

SWEET AND SOUR MEATBALLS WITH RICE

Serves 4
Preparation time: 30 minutes
Cooking time: 45 minutes

225 g (8 oz) lean minced beef
225 g (8 oz) lean minced pork
60 g (2 oz) wholemeal breadcrumbs
1 egg, size 3, lightly beaten
1 small onion, finely chopped
Finely grated rind of 1/2 lemon
Freshly ground black pepper
3 tablespoons olive oil
425 g (15 oz) canned pineapple
   chunks in natural juice
2 tablespoons red wine vinegar
2 tablespoons soy sauce
2 level tablespoons soft light
   brown sugar
2 tablespoons dry sherry
2 level teaspoons peeled and grated
   root ginger
200 ml (7 fl oz) beef stock
   (see p.8)
1 large green pepper, de-seeded
   and chopped
1 large red pepper, de-seeded
   and chopped
2 cloves garlic, peeled and crushed
   (see p.11)
115 g (4 oz) long-grain white rice
340 g (12 oz) mangetout, trimmed
30 g (1 oz) toasted cashew nuts and
   chopped fresh parsley to garnish

Per serving
Calories 542 Protein 34 g
Total fat 23 g (saturated fat 5.5 g)
Carbohydrates 53 g (added sugar 5 g)
Fibre 7.6 g Sodium 620 mg

Beef and pork meatballs combine with rice in a sweet and sour sauce. If you prefer, you can substitute couscous or bulgur wheat for the rice.

1 Mix together the minced beef and pork, the breadcrumbs, egg, onion, lemon rind and some pepper in a bowl. Shape the mixture into about 30 small balls.

2 Heat 1 tablespoon of the oil in a large frying pan, and brown half of the meatballs in it for 5-8 minutes. Remove the meatballs from the pan with a slotted spoon and put them on a large plate. Heat another tablespoon of the oil in the pan and brown the rest of the meatballs in it. Put them on the plate with the first batch, then drain off all the fat in the pan.

3 Pour the juice from the pineapple into a bowl and keep the chunks to one side. Combine the juice with the vinegar, soy sauce, sugar, sherry, ginger and enough stock to make 425 ml (3/4 pint) of liquid, then set aside.

4 Heat the remaining oil in the pan and stir-fry the peppers in it for 2-3 minutes. Add the garlic and cook, stirring, for 2 minutes, then return the meatballs to the pan. Pour in the stock mixture, bring to the boil and stir in the rice. Reduce the heat to low, cover and simmer for 10 minutes.

5 Add the mangetout, cover the pan and simmer for a further 10 minutes, or until the rice and mangetout are tender. Stir in the pineapple chunks and heat for 2-3 minutes. Garnish with the cashew nuts and parsley and serve.

Rich meatballs, tender rice and colourful mangetout and peppers absorb the sweet and sour flavours of pineapple, fresh ginger, sherry and soy sauce.

TOAD-IN-THE-HOLE

A traditional British one-dish meal that wraps golden sausages in a crisp flour batter. Any type of sausage can be used to make this dish.

Serves 4
Preparation time: 45 minutes
Cooking time: 55 minutes

150 g (5 oz) plain flour
1/2 level teaspoon salt
2 eggs, size 3, lightly beaten
175 ml (6 fl oz) milk
60 ml (2 fl oz) water
2 tablespoons vegetable oil
450 g (1 lb) pork sausages
Fresh sage leaves and fried apple rings to garnish (optional)

Per serving
Calories 612 Protein 24 g
Total fat 39 g (saturated fat 13 g)
Carbohydrates 44 g (added sugar 0)
Fibre 1.9 g Sodium 1165 mg

1 Sift the flour and salt into a bowl and make a well in the centre. Pour the beaten eggs into the well, then gradually stir them into the flour with a wooden spoon, adding the milk and water as the mixture thickens.

2 Beat the batter with a wire whisk until smooth and the consistency of unwhipped double cream. Cover and leave to stand for at least 30 minutes.

3 Meanwhile, preheat the oven to 220°C (425°F, gas mark 7). Pour the oil into a roasting tin and heat in the oven for 5 minutes. Remove the tin from the oven and arrange the sausages in it. Cook in the centre of the oven for 10 minutes, or until just golden.

4 Whisk the batter once again, then quickly pour it over the sausages. Return the tin to the oven and cook for 35-40 minutes, or until the batter is well risen, golden brown and crisp. Garnish with the fresh sage leaves and the fried apple rings, if using.

BAKED HAM AND SPINACH GRATIN

In this bubbling, cheese-topped dish, the ham and Cheddar provide plenty of flavouring. There is no need to add salt.

Serves 6
Preparation time: 25 minutes
Cooking time: 55 minutes

550 g (1 1/4 lb) potatoes, peeled and cut into small cubes (see p.10)
30 g (1 oz) butter
1 medium onion, peeled and finely chopped
1 clove garlic, peeled and crushed (see p.11)
30 g (1 oz) plain flour
1 1/2 level teaspoons mustard powder
425 ml (3/4 pint) milk
115 g (4 oz) mature Cheddar cheese, grated
340 g (12 oz) frozen leaf spinach, thawed and drained
450 g (1 lb) cooked ham, cut into small cubes
Fresh watercress to garnish

Per serving
Calories 334 Protein 25 g
Total fat 15 g (saturated fat 8.3 g)
Carbohydrates 25 g (added sugar 0)
Fibre 41 g Sodium 1159 mg

1 Preheat the oven to 190°C (375°F, gas mark 5). Boil the potatoes for 5 minutes, then drain well. Meanwhile, melt the butter in a saucepan and cook the onion in it for 3 minutes. Add the garlic and cook for another 2 minutes.

2 Stir in the flour and mustard powder, then take the pan off the heat. Gradually whisk in the milk and stir over a low heat until the sauce comes to the boil and thickens smoothly. Stir in 85 g (3 oz) of the Cheddar until it has melted, then take the pan off the heat and mix in the spinach.

3 Spoon half of the potato in an even layer in the bottom of a large ovenproof dish. Cover with half of the Cheddar and spinach sauce. Sprinkle the ham on top and cover with the remaining potato. Pour the rest of the sauce over the potato and scatter the remaining Cheddar evenly on top.

4 Cover the dish with greased foil and put it on a baking tray. Bake in the centre of the oven for 30 minutes, then remove the foil and cook for another 15 minutes, or until the sauce is golden and bubbling. Garnish with the watercress and serve.

POT ROAST LEG OF LAMB WITH PORT AND REDCURRANT GLAZE

Serves 6
Preparation time: 40 minutes
Cooking time: 2 hours 45 minutes

1.6-1.8 kg (3½-4 lb) leg of lamb, trimmed of excess fat
1 clove garlic, peeled and cut into slivers
½ teaspoon salt
Freshly ground black pepper
1 tablespoon olive oil
1 long sprig of fresh rosemary
4 medium onions, peeled and quartered
340 ml (12 fl oz) port or red wine
Finely pared rind and juice of 1 medium orange, rind cut into julienne strips (see p.10)
900 g (2 lb) medium new potatoes, scraped or peeled
340 g (12 oz) medium carrots, peeled and cut into thin, diagonal slices
340 g (12 oz) fine green beans, trimmed and cut into short pieces
3 level tablespoons redcurrant jelly
Juice of ½ lemon
175 g (6 oz) fresh or frozen redcurrants, stalks removed
Fresh rosemary and redcurrants to garnish

A thick, richly flavoured glaze of orange, port, redcurrant and lemon gives a luxurious coating to slow-cooked tender lamb.

1 Preheat the oven to 180°C (350°F, gas mark 4). Use a sharp, pointed knife to make small incisions in the lamb. Carefully insert a sliver of garlic into each one, then season the lamb with the salt and some black pepper.

2 Heat the oil in a very large flameproof casserole and brown the lamb in it for 10-15 minutes. Lift the lamb onto a plate and lay the sprig of fresh rosemary on top.

Per serving
Calories 763 Protein 83 g
Total fat 25 g (saturated fat 11 g)
Carbohydrates 45 g (added sugar 4.7 g)
Fibre 8.3 g Sodium 250 mg

3 Fry the onions in the fat in the casserole for 3-4 minutes until lightly browned. Skim off the surplus fat. Add 285 ml (½ pint) of the port or red wine and the orange juice to the onions and bring to the boil. Return the leg of lamb to the casserole and baste it with the port or red wine and orange juice. Cook, covered, in the centre of the oven for 1¼ hours, taking care to baste it frequently.

4 Add the potatoes and carrots to the casserole, arranging them around the lamb. Baste them well with the cooking juices, then cover and cook for 1 hour.

5 Blanch the beans in boiling water for 2 minutes, drain well and add them to the casserole. Cook for 20 minutes, or until the lamb and the vegetables are tender.

6 Lift the lamb from the casserole onto a large, heated serving dish. Lift out the vegetables with a slotted spoon and arrange them around the lamb. Keep it warm.

Slivers of garlic tucked beneath the surface of the meat before cooking add a subtle warmth to lamb roasted with soft onions, juicy carrots, fresh green beans and new potatoes.

7 Bring the cooking juices in the casserole to the boil over a high heat. Skim any remaining fat from the surface, then stir in the redcurrant jelly, lemon juice and orange rind. Continue boiling until the juices are reduced to a heavy glaze that coats the back of a wooden spoon. Stir in the redcurrants and cook for 1-2 minutes, until just softened, then season with black pepper.

8 Stir the remaining port or red wine into the glaze and pour it over the lamb. Before you take the lamb to the table, replace the cooked sprig of rosemary with fresh ones and garnish with the fresh redcurrants.

Serves 4
Preparation time: 1 hour
Cooking time: 1 hour

725 ml (1¼ pints) beef or chicken stock (see p.8)
175 g (6 oz) bulgur wheat
550 g (1¼ lb) aubergines, trimmed and sliced
1 level tablespoon salt
6 tablespoons olive oil
1 large onion, peeled and chopped
2 cloves garlic, peeled and crushed (see p.11)
450 g (1 lb) lean minced lamb
1 level teaspoon each ground ginger, cinnamon and turmeric
2 level teaspoons ground cumin
400 g (14 oz) canned chopped tomatoes
Freshly ground black pepper
60 g (2 oz) pine nuts
2 level tablespoons chopped fresh coriander

Per serving
Calories 649 Protein 33 g
Total fat 39 g (saturated fat 8.1 g)
Carbohydrates 43 g
(added sugar 0)
Fibre 4.5 g Sodium 989 mg

MIDDLE EASTERN BAKE

Bulgur wheat, or cracked wheat, is widely used in Middle Eastern cooking, often as a lighter alternative to rice. Here it is mixed with fresh coriander and pine nuts to make a crispy topping for layers of aubergine and minced lamb seasoned with fragrant spices.

1 Bring the stock to the boil in a large saucepan and then soak the bulgur wheat in it for 30 minutes. Meanwhile, place the aubergines in a large colander, sprinkle them with 2½ teaspoons of the salt and then leave to stand on a plate for 20 minutes.

2 Heat 1 tablespoon of the oil in a second saucepan and fry the onion in it until softened. Add the garlic and lamb and fry, stirring to break up the meat, until it changes colour. Pour off any excess fat, then stir in the ginger, cinnamon, turmeric and cumin and fry for 1 minute. Add the tomatoes, the remaining salt and some pepper, cover and simmer for 20 minutes.

3 In the meantime, bring the bulgur wheat to the boil, then reduce the heat, cover and simmer for 15 minutes, adding some water if needed to stop it from sticking to the pan. Preheat the oven to 200°C (400°F, gas mark 6).

4 Rinse the aubergine slices under cold water and pat them dry with kitchen paper. Heat half the remaining oil in a large frying pan and fry half the aubergine slices on both sides until golden. Drain on kitchen paper, then repeat with the remaining slices.

5 Spread half the lamb mixture in the bottom of a large, shallow ovenproof dish. Cover with the aubergine slices and then spread the remaining lamb over the top.

6 Mix the pine nuts and coriander into the bulgur wheat and spread it over the lamb. Place the dish in the centre of the oven and bake for 30-40 minutes, or until golden and crisp on top, then serve with warm pitta bread.

BOBOTIE

Serves 6
Preparation time: 30 minutes
Cooking time: 1 hour 15 minutes

1 thick slice, about 60 g (2 oz), white bread
225 ml (8 fl oz) milk
2 tablespoons olive oil
2 medium onions, peeled and chopped
1 clove garlic, peeled and crushed (see p.11)
1 level tablespoon mild or hot curry powder
1 level teaspoon turmeric
Finely grated rind of 1 lemon
2 tablespoons lemon juice
1 level teaspoon soft dark brown sugar
½ level teaspoon salt
900 g (2 lb) lean minced lamb
12 blanched almonds, quartered
8 ready-to-use dried apricots, quartered
85 g (3 oz) seedless raisins
1 tablespoon peach or other fruit chutney
Freshly ground black pepper
2 eggs, size 2, beaten
4 bay leaves

Per serving
Calories 540 Protein 41 g
Total fat 26 g (saturated fat 8.6 g)
Carbohydrates 36 g (added sugar 1 g)
Fibre 8.9 g Sodium 481 mg

Cape Malay dishes are among South Africa's oldest and finest specialities. Typical is bobotie – a pungent blend of curried lamb, dried fruit, nuts and spices, baked under an egg and milk topping. You can also use beef or salted cod (see p.146) to make this sweet and spicy dish.

1 Preheat the oven to 180°C (350°F, gas mark 4). Put the bread in a bowl, add 4 tablespoons of the milk and leave to soak.

2 Heat the oil in a large frying pan and soften the onions and garlic in it. Add the curry powder and turmeric, and cook for 1 minute, stirring well.

3 Take the pan off the heat and mix in the lemon rind and juice, sugar, salt, lamb, almonds, apricots, raisins, chutney, soaked bread and some pepper.

4 Spoon the lamb mixture into a lightly greased, shallow ovenproof dish, pressing it down firmly, and level the surface.

5 Lightly whisk the eggs with the remaining milk and pour over the lamb mixture. Float the bay leaves on top, then bake in the centre of the oven for 1¼ hours, or until the topping is set. Remove the bay leaves, and then serve the dish with a green salad and bread as an accompaniment.

LAMB AND ROSEMARY STEW

Serves 4
Preparation time: 35 minutes
Cooking time: 50 minutes

2 tablespoons olive oil
4 lamb chump chops, each about 225 g (8 oz), trimmed of fat
450 g (1 lb) small new potatoes, scrubbed and halved
450 g (1 lb) carrots, peeled and cut into short lengths
2 cloves garlic, peeled and crushed (see p.11)
1 medium onion, peeled and finely chopped
285 ml (½ pint) lamb or beef stock (see p.8)
2 small sprigs of fresh rosemary or 1 level teaspoon dried rosemary
¼ level teaspoon salt
Freshly ground black pepper
225 g (8 oz) fine green beans, trimmed and halved
Sprigs of fresh rosemary to garnish

Per serving
Calories 473 Protein 38 g
Total fat 23 g (saturated fat 8.6 g)
Carbohydrates 31 g (added sugar 0)
Fibre 6.4 g Sodium 261 mg

Fragrant rosemary teams up with lamb in a traditional partnership for this simple stew. It is best to use chump chops of lamb, as they are meatier and juicier than loin chops and can withstand longer cooking.

1 Heat the oil in a large flameproof casserole and brown the lamb in it for 15 minutes over a medium heat. Drain off the excess fat.

2 Add the potatoes, carrots, garlic, onion, stock, rosemary, salt and some pepper, and bring to the boil. Reduce the heat, cover and simmer for 25-30 minutes.

3 Stir in the beans, cover once more and cook for about 8 minutes, or until the lamb and vegetables are tender. Skim off any fat from the surface, garnish with the fresh rosemary and serve.

LAMB PILAFF WITH APRICOTS AND RAISINS

Dried apricots and raisins, plump with tasty cooking juices, add a rich contrast to the savoury chunks of lamb and vegetables.

Serves 4
Preparation time: 20 minutes
Cooking time: 45 minutes

30 g (1 oz) butter
225 g (8 oz) white long-grain rice
1 large onion, peeled and chopped
2 level tablespoons peeled and
  grated root ginger
2 cloves garlic, peeled and
  crushed (see p.11)
570 ml (1 pint) beef stock
  (see p.8)

450 g (1 lb) boneless leg of lamb,
  cut into cubes (see p.80)
1/2 level teaspoon salt
Freshly ground black pepper
2 tablespoons olive oil
2 medium courgettes, trimmed
  and diced (see p.10)
115 g (4 oz) button mushrooms,
  wiped and halved
115 g (4 oz) ready-to-use dried
  apricots, chopped
115 g (4 oz) seedless raisins
2 tablespoons chopped fresh
  parsley to garnish

Per serving
Calories 681 Protein 42 g
Total fat 22 g (saturated fat 8 g)
Carbohydrates 85 g (added sugar 0)
Fibre 10 g Sodium 234 mg

Savoury rice dishes, or pilaffs, are prepared by simmering rice without stirring until all the cooking liquid is absorbed. You can stir this lamb pilaff at the end of cooking to prevent the rice forming a crust, although in the Middle East the crust is considered a delicacy.

1 Melt the butter in a saucepan and fry the rice, onion, 1 tablespoon of the ginger and the garlic in it for 3-4 minutes. Pour in the stock and bring to the boil. Reduce the heat, cover and simmer for 30 minutes, or until most of the liquid has been absorbed by the rice.

2 Meanwhile, season the lamb with the salt and some pepper. Heat 1 tablespoon of the oil in a large frying pan and brown the lamb in it for about 10 minutes, then set aside on a plate lined with kitchen paper.

3 Add the remaining oil to the pan and fry the courgettes and remaining ginger in it for 2 minutes. Stir in the mushrooms and lightly brown for 3 minutes.

4 Mix the apricots, raisins, lamb, courgettes and mushrooms into the rice mixture. Cover and cook, stirring occasionally, for 5 minutes, or until all the liquid has been absorbed and the rice and meat are tender. Sprinkle with the parsley and serve.

LANCASHIRE HOT POT

Serves 4
Preparation time: 40 minutes
Cooking time: 2 hours 20 minutes

8 lamb cutlets, 115 g (4 oz) each,
   trimmed of fat
450 g (1 lb) onions, peeled
   and sliced
4 large carrots, peeled and sliced
1 level teaspoon salt
Freshly ground black pepper
570 ml (1 pint) chicken stock
   (see p.8)
12 live oysters (optional)
900 g (2 lb) potatoes, peeled and
   thinly sliced

Per serving
Calories 469 Protein 38 g
Total fat 14 g (saturated fat 6.2 g)
Carbohydrates 52 g (added sugar 0)
Fibre 6.9 g Sodium 749 mg

During the 19th century when oysters were cheap and plentiful they were often placed beneath the potatoes in a Lancashire hot pot. They add a subtle briny flavour to the dish and remain remarkably tender despite the long cooking time.

Preheat the oven to 180°C (350°F, gas mark 4). Put four of the lamb cutlets in a large, ovenproof casserole and cover them with half the onions and half the carrots. Season with half the salt and some pepper. Repeat with the remaining cutlets, onions and carrots, season with the remaining salt and then add the stock.

2 If using, open the oysters (see p.147), loosen them from their shells and add to the casserole with their juices.

3 Arrange layers of overlapping potato slices on top of the meat, or oysters if using. Cover the pot and cook in the centre of the oven for 2 hours.

4 Increase the oven temperature to 230°C (450°F, gas mark 8). Remove the lid from the casserole and continue cooking for a further 20 minutes, or until the potatoes are brown and crisp, then serve.

Lamb cutlets slowly cooked in tasty chicken stock with carrots, onions and potatoes mellow in this traditional country stew. Sea-fresh oysters make an unusual and luxurious addition to the dish.

LAMB CREOLE WITH CHEESE POLENTA

This sumptuous version of a creole – a tomato and pepper sauce usually made with beef, which is popular in the southern United States – contains corn dumplings and tender lamb.

Serves 6
Preparation time: 1 hour
Cooking time: 2 hours 15 minutes

60 g (2 oz) plain flour
½ level teaspoon salt
Freshly ground black pepper
1.1 kg (2½ lb) meat from leg of lamb, trimmed of fat and cubed (see p.79)
3 tablespoons olive oil
1 large onion, peeled and sliced
2 medium sticks celery, trimmed and thickly sliced
2 medium green peppers, de-seeded and sliced

2 cloves garlic, peeled and crushed (see p.11)
150 ml (¼ pint) beef stock (see p.8)
150 ml (¼ pint) red wine
425 g (15 oz) canned chopped tomatoes
1 level teaspoon soft light brown sugar
½ level teaspoon dried basil
1 level teaspoon each dried thyme and dried oregano
1 bay leaf

For the polenta
425 ml (¾ pint) water
¼ level teaspoon salt
175 g (6 oz) cornmeal (ground maize meal)
30 g (1 oz) butter
115 g (4 oz) Cheddar or Gruyère cheese, grated
1 egg, size 2, lightly beaten
¼ level teaspoon paprika
Fresh bay leaves to garnish

Per serving
Calories 599 Protein 46 g
Total fat 29 g (saturated fat 13 g)
Carbohydrates 35 g (added sugar 1 g)
Fibre 3.6 g Sodium 535 mg

1 Preheat the oven to 180°C (350°F, gas mark 4). Put the flour, salt and pepper in a polythene bag, add the lamb and shake to coat the meat. Heat the oil in a flameproof casserole and brown the meat for 6-7 minutes, then remove and set aside.

2 Add the onion, celery and green peppers to the casserole and sauté for 5 minutes, stirring occasionally. Mix in the garlic, stock, red wine, tomatoes, sugar, basil, thyme, oregano and bay leaf, and bring to the boil. Return the meat to the casserole, cover, and cook in the oven for 1½ hours.

3 In the meantime, to make the polenta, bring the water to the boil in a saucepan with the salt added. Slowly sprinkle in the cornmeal, reduce the heat to low and cook for 10-15 minutes, stirring, until the polenta thickens. Remove from the heat and beat in the butter, cheese and egg. Leave to cool for about 15 minutes.

4 Increase the oven temperature to 200°C (400°F, gas mark 6). Take the casserole out of the oven, skim off any excess fat, discard the bay leaf, and stir. Arrange the polenta in mounds on top and sprinkle with the paprika. Bake in the oven, uncovered, for 25-30 minutes, or until the sauce is bubbling and the polenta is lightly browned. Garnish with bay leaves and serve.

LIVER AND BACON WITH THYME

Serves 4
Preparation time: 15 minutes
Cooking time: 35 minutes

450 g (1 lb) small new potatoes
3 tablespoons olive oil
4 slices lamb's liver, about
 340 g (12 oz), rinsed and wiped
¼ level teaspoon salt
Freshly ground black pepper
1 level teaspoon paprika
30 g (1 oz) butter
85 g (3 oz) unsmoked streaky
 bacon, rinds removed, chopped
1 medium onion, peeled
 and chopped
1 large clove garlic, peeled
 and crushed (see p.11)
1 large dessert apple, cored and
 roughly chopped
400 g (14 oz) canned
 chopped tomatoes
1 small sprig fresh thyme
1 tablespoon Worcestershire sauce
3 tablespoons chopped
 fresh parsley

Per serving
Calories 491 Protein 23 g
Total fat 33 g
(saturated fat 11 g)
Carbohydrates 28 g
(added sugar 0)
Fibre 3.2 g
Sodium 581 mg

Fresh thyme and fragrant apple soften the intense flavours of lamb's liver and bacon in this nutritious and filling dish.

1 Boil the potatoes for 10 minutes, then drain well and cut in half. Heat 2 tablespoons of the oil in a large, heavy frying pan. Fry the potatoes until golden and then transfer to a plate.

2 Season both sides of the liver slices with the salt, some pepper and the paprika. Melt the butter in the frying pan until it is sizzling hot, then brown the liver in it on both sides. Move the liver to a plate and keep warm.

3 Add the remaining oil to the pan and fry the bacon, onion and garlic in it, stirring, until golden brown. Mix in the apple and cook for 2 minutes, then stir in the tomatoes, the thyme and the Worcestershire sauce. Bring to the boil, then reduce the heat and simmer for 3-4 minutes.

4 Stir the potatoes into the sauce and arrange the liver slices on top. Cover and heat through for 3-4 minutes. Season with some more pepper, sprinkle with the parsley and serve from the pan with crusty brown or white bread.

Worcestershire sauce and paprika give a spicy edge to the rich herb and apple sauce.

KIDNEYS WITH MUSHROOMS EN COCOTTE

Fromage frais, a pea purée and mashed potato make a brightly coloured, creamy topping for kidneys and mushrooms in a rich brandy gravy. 'En cocotte' refers to the small, ovenproof dishes, or *cocottes*, in which the individual helpings are served.

Serves 4
Preparation time: 30 minutes
Cooking time: 25 minutes

675 g (1½ lb) potatoes, peeled and quartered
3 tablespoons olive oil
450 g (1 lb) lambs' kidneys, skinned, halved and cored
1 medium onion, peeled and chopped
1 clove garlic, peeled and crushed (see p.11)
225 g (8 oz) button mushrooms, wiped and quartered
4 level teaspoons plain flour
1 level tablespoon tomato purée
225 ml (8 fl oz) chicken stock (see p.8)
2 tablespoons brandy or sherry
½ level teaspoon salt
Freshly ground black pepper
340 g (12 oz) frozen peas
4 tablespoons fromage frais
Sprigs of fresh watercress to garnish

Per serving
Calories 481 Protein 31 g
Total fat 16 g (saturated fat 3.5 g)
Carbohydrates 52 g (added sugar 0)
Fibre 11 g Sodium 524 mg

1 Boil the potatoes until soft. Meanwhile, heat 2 tablespoons of the oil in a heavy frying pan and fry the kidneys in it until sealed all over, then set aside on a plate.

2 Pour the remaining oil into the pan and stir-fry the onion, garlic and mushrooms in it for 3-4 minutes.

3 Add the flour, tomato purée, stock, brandy or sherry, half the salt and some pepper and bring to the boil, stirring until thickened. Return the kidneys to the pan, cover and simmer for about 15 minutes, until tender.

4 In the meantime, boil the peas until cooked, then drain well. Blend the peas in a food processor for 1-2 minutes, or pass them through a sieve, until smooth.

5 Drain and mash the potatoes, then beat in the pea purée, fromage frais, the remaining salt and some pepper. Preheat the grill to high.

6 Spoon the kidney mixture into four cocottes or other individual fireproof dishes, then cover with the potato and pea mixture. Mark the top decoratively with a fork or palette knife and brown under the hot grill. Garnish with the watercress and serve.

STUFFED BRAISED HEARTS

Firm-textured lambs' hearts make full-flavoured cases for this moist sausage stuffing. You will need a darning needle and strong thread to prepare them.

Serves 4
Preparation time: 45 minutes
Cooking time: 2 hours 40 minutes

60 g (2 oz) pork sausage meat
½ level teaspoon chopped fresh thyme
30 g (1 oz) fresh breadcrumbs
1½ level tablespoons chopped fresh parsley
½ small onion, peeled and chopped
½ level teaspoon salt
Freshly ground black pepper
1 egg yolk, size 3
4 lambs' hearts, thoroughly trimmed and washed
2 tablespoons olive oil
12 button onions, peeled
3 medium carrots, peeled and sliced
2 medium sticks celery, trimmed and sliced
2 level tablespoons plain flour
150 ml (¼ pint) red wine
285 ml (½ pint) beef stock (see p.8)
450 g (1 lb) small new potatoes, scrubbed
175 g (6 oz) button mushrooms, wiped

Per serving
Calories 469 Protein 24 g
Total fat 19 g (saturated fat 5.3 g)
Carbohydrates 48 g (added sugar 10 g)
Fibre 7.4 g Sodium 580 mg

1 Preheat the oven to 160°C (325°F, gas mark 3). Meanwhile, mix the sausage meat, thyme, breadcrumbs, 1 teaspoon of the parsley, the onion, half the salt, some pepper and the egg yolk in a bowl. Stuff the hearts with the mixture, then sew up the tops with the needle and thread.

2 Heat the oil in a flameproof casserole and lightly brown the hearts in it, until sealed all over. Move the hearts to a plate, stir in the onions, carrots and celery and fry for 5 minutes.

3 Stir in the flour, then add the wine, stock, the remaining salt and some pepper. Bring to the boil, stirring, then put the hearts back in the casserole, immersing them in the sauce. Cover and cook in the oven for 1½ hours.

4 Take the casserole out of the oven and mix in the potatoes and mushrooms, then return to the oven for 1 hour, or until the hearts are very tender and the vegetables are cooked.

5 Lift the hearts out of the casserole onto a plate with a slotted spoon. Carefully remove the thread, then arrange them on a heated serving dish with the vegetables and sauce. Sprinkle with the remaining parsley and serve with warm crusty bread.

Making the most of meat

Meat – a major source of protein, vitamins and minerals, especially iron – has a valuable role to play in a healthy diet. Knowing how to buy, store and prepare meat will add to the success of the casseroles, stews, pot-roasts, stir-fries and grills in this chapter.

ALTHOUGH MEAT CONTAINS fat, more than half is unsaturated fat and in any case most can be trimmed off before or after cooking. Farmers are breeding beef, lamb and pork to contain less fat, and retailers offer a selection of fat-trimmed joints, steaks and leaner mince.

Buying beef, lamb and pork

Beef should be firm to the touch when you buy it; variations in colour, from bright red to dark red-brown, indicate only how long it has been cut, though meat that is very dark and dry may have been exposed too long. The flesh should be marbled with specks of creamy-coloured fat. A layer of gristle between the muscle and the outer covering of fat may indicate that the meat is from an older animal.

Some people have doubts about eating beef, because of the controversy over BSE – the so-called 'mad cow disease'. The Government's Chief Medical Officer, however, has said that there is no scientific evidence to link BSE with human illness, and that the Government has taken measures to prevent any risk there might have been. People must decide for themselves.

Lamb varies in colour, usually pale pink in young lambs and darkening in older animals. Home-produced lambs have creamy white fat, while fat on imported lamb is firmer. Yellowing fat may be a sign of age. Brittle white fat means that lamb has been frozen too long.

Pork flesh should be firm and smooth with little or no gristle. Younger animals have light pink flesh, while the flesh of older animals

is a deeper pink colour. The flesh of very old animals is darker still and coarsely grained. Any fat surrounding the flesh should be pure white and firm, while small flecks of fat should marble the flesh.

How to keep meat fresh

All fresh meat must be stored in the fridge at 0-5°C (32-41°F). Fresh joints of meat from the butcher can be kept for up to 3 days. Joints should be unwrapped and put on a rack or up-turned saucer, then covered with a large bowl to prevent the meat drying out.

Minced, cubed and sliced meat should be put on a clean plate and covered. It should be used preferably on the day it was bought – and certainly within 24 hours. Uncooked meats should be stored lower in the fridge than

1 *Forerib* ● ●
2 *Sirloin* ● ●
3 *Brisket* ● ●
4 *Thick flank* ● ●
5 *Topside* ● ● ●
6 *Braising steak* ● ●
7 *Rump steak* ●
8 *Sirloin steak* ● ●
9 *Flash fry steak* ● ●
10 *Stewing beef (cubes)* ● ●
11 *Mince (fine)* ●
12 *Mince (coarse)* ●
13 *Fillet steak* ● ●
14 *Silverside* ● ●

Cooking key
● roasting
● pot-roasting and braising
● grilling, barbecuing, frying and stir-frying
● stews and casseroles

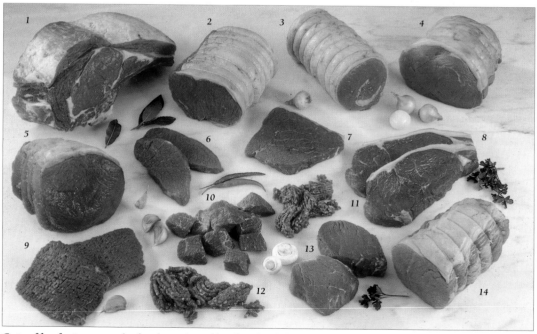

Cuts of beef *suit every style of cooking. A good butcher should be able to provide any cut to order; supermarkets label some cuts by their individual names, but describe others simply as 'beef for braising, stewing or casseroling'. For these purposes, however, cheaper cuts such as chuck and shin, obtainable from your butcher, are just as nourishing.*

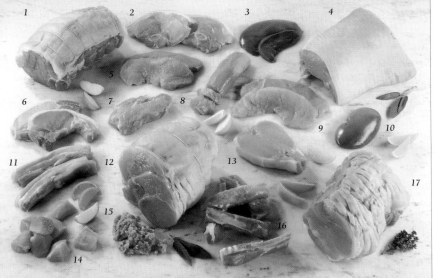

1 Neck end ●●
2 Chump chop ●●●
3 Liver ●●
4 Loin ●●
5 Leg steak ●●
6 Loin chop ●●●
7 Shoulder steak ●●
8 Fillet ●●
9 Escalope ●
10 Kidney ●●
11 Belly slice ●●●
12 Leg ●●
13 Double loin steak ●●●
14 Cubes ●●
15 Mince ●
16 Spare rib ●●
17 Shoulder ●●

Cuts of pork *are usually sold already boned and rolled, but joints on the bone are sometimes available from supermarkets and butchers, and may give your meal extra flavour. If you need a joint of pork, or any other meat, boned out by a butcher, always order well in advance.*

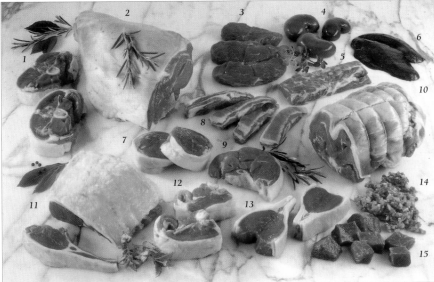

1 Double loin chop ●●
2 Leg ●
3 Leg steak ●
4 Kidney ●●
5 Neck fillet ●●
6 Liver ●●
7 Noisette ●●
8 Breast riblet ●●●
9 Chump chop ●●●
10 Rolled shoulder ●
11 Best end   ●●●
12 Loin chop ●●
13 Valentine steak ●●
14 Mince ●
15 Cubes ●●

Cuts of lamb *present an ever-widening choice. To the traditional choice cuts of loin, leg and shoulder are now added alternatives such as leg steaks, cubes and valentine steaks. Minced meat of all types is usually shaped before cooking, especially for grilling and barbecuing.*

cooked foods, or foods that are eaten raw. Prepacked meat from a supermarket can be stored in its packaging until the 'use-by' date. Controlled atmosphere packs (rigid, plastic containers with a sealed top) should not be opened until you need the meat.

Preparing meat for cooking

Meat can be bought ready-cubed for stewing and casseroling, sliced for braising, or in strips for stir-frying. Although this is a convenience and saves time in preparation, you will find it more economical to prepare the meat yourself. Furthermore, by preparing meat at home you can ensure it is freer of gristle and lower in fat than shop-bought meat. A set of sharp knives, a good-size chopping board and a little extra preparation time are all you need.

Cutting meat into cubes

1 Using a very sharp knife, cut away all visible fat, gristle and other tissue from the meat.

2 For braising cut the meat into large pieces; for stewing cut into long strips, then cut across the grain into neat cubes – small, medium or large, as required.

Homemade mince has a better flavour and texture than any shop-bought mince. You do not need a mincer or food processor to make your own. Mincing the meat with two large, sharp chopping knives (see below) retains more of the meat's juice and gives a better taste. This technique also works for poultry.

Mincing meat by hand

Holding the two knives loosely, and parallel to each other, chop the small cubes of trimmed meat by alternately lifting and dropping the blades as though beating a drum. Chop with the knives until the meat reaches the required texture – coarse, medium or fine. Lift and turn the meat from time to time as you chop.

Cutting meat for stir-frying

Cut the trimmed meat across the grain into slices 6 mm (¼ in) thick. Cut each slice lengthways into thin strips.

Boned, rolled and stuffed joints make impressive all-in-one meals. You can bone and roll a Sunday roast joint and fill it with any of a number of different types of stuffing, then secure the stuffing by tying the joint at intervals with clean, thin string. You can buy a boned joint, do the boning yourself at home (see below), or ask a butcher to do it for you.

Boning, rolling and tying a pork loin

1 Cut away the skin and as much fat as possible from the outside of the loin, leaving a thin, even layer. Turn the loin over and remove any fat and other tissue from the inside.

2 Use a small sharp knife to cut down the sides and under each small rib bone, keeping the knife as close to the bone as possible. When the bones are loose, twist each one free from the spine.

3 Cut deeply between the spine and the flesh until the knife touches the small protruding bones along the vertebrae. Angle the knife to cut over and then under these bones.

4 Once the flesh has been removed from around the vertebrae, cut down the length of the spine to free the meat.

5 Roll the loin up with the fat on the outside and tie it at 2.5 cm (1 in) intervals with clean, thin string. You can use single lengths of string for each tie, or tie a longer piece of string at one end of the loin, then loop it along its length.

Stuffing a roasting joint boosts a meal's nutritional value by adding carbohydrates. Rice, breadcrumbs, bulgur wheat and couscous make excellent bases for roast stuffings, while nuts, herbs, spices, vegetables or dried fruits add extra flavour, colour and texture.

Boning and stuffing breasts of lamb

1 Trim off any excess fat from the skinned lamb breasts, leaving a thin, even layer. With the bones uppermost, slide the knife under the small flap of flesh at the thin end of the breast to loosen it from the bones, then fold it back. Insert the knife between the bones and the flesh, and keeping the blade of the knife close to the bones, work along the length until the bones are free. Repeat with the other breast. These are now ready for rolling and roasting or stuffing.

2 To stuff the boned lamb breasts, lay skin-side down, slightly overlapping, press firmly together and spread the stuffing evenly over the meat.

3 Starting at the narrowest end, roll the breast up like a swiss roll with the stuffing inside.

4 Tie securely with 6-8 pieces of fine, clean string.

Marinating – the technique of soaking meat or poultry in a mixture of ingredients before cooking – is a wonderful way of bringing out its full flavour. The longer the marinating time, the stronger its effect. Overnight marinating produces a prominent flavour, but you will find that even just an hour's marinating will make a noticeable difference to taste.

Marinades can be made from a wide range of ingredients, from simple oil, herb and spice mixtures to more elaborate blends of oils with acid liquids – such as lemon juice, vinegar, wine or sherry – mixed with herbs, spices or other aromatic ingredients such as shallots, onions, garlic or ginger. Acid liquids break down the fibres while the marinade is being absorbed and help to tenderise it.

Use a glass or china bowl for marinating, as metallic dishes react with an acid marinade. Keep the dish or bowl covered while marinating and turn the meat occasionally. Before cooking, wipe the marinated meat with kitchen paper so that it browns successfully when fried, grilled or roasted.

Once you have removed the meat from a marinade, keep the marinade for basting or adding with the meat to the stew or casserole.

How to make sure that meat is properly cooked

Beef and lamb can be safely eaten at any stage of cooking from rare to well done. Pork can be safely eaten as soon as the juices run clear, with no trace of redness, at an internal temperature of at least 73°C (163°F). If you do not possess a meat thermometer, you can check whether meat is done by pressing or pinching it with your fingers: the more yielding the meat, the rarer it is.

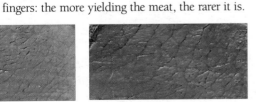

Rare (blood red in the centre)   *Medium (pink to brown meat)*   *Well done (brown meat)*

POULTRY AND GAME

Chicken, turkey, poussins, duck, pheasant, pigeon, rabbit, hare and venison all feature in these varied recipes, incorporated into a wealth of full-flavoured stews, sizzling roasts and warming baked dishes.

❖

Calvados, the French apple liqueur, brings an authentic flavour to Duck Normandy (left) in which flaming burns off the alcohol to leave a mellow, fruity taste (see p.111).

HONEY CHICKEN BREASTS

Oven cooking in honey, lemon and orange makes the chicken in this casserole sweet and tender. Instead of chicken breasts you can use chicken legs, separated into thighs and drumsticks.

Serves 4
Preparation time: 30 minutes
Cooking time: 1 hour 10 minutes

15 g (½ oz) butter
1 tablespoon olive oil
4 boneless chicken breasts, each about 175 g (6 oz), skinned
225 g (8 oz) button onions, peeled
3 medium carrots, peeled and thickly sliced
1 large courgette, trimmed and thickly sliced
Finely grated rind and strained juice of 1 orange and 1 lemon
4 tablespoons clear honey
3 tablespoons Dijon mustard
1 clove garlic, peeled and crushed (see p.11)
1 level tablespoon peeled and grated fresh root ginger
¼ level teaspoon salt
Freshly ground black pepper
225 g (8 oz) easy-cook long-grain and wild rice
Sprigs of watercress and orange rind cut into strips (see p.10) to garnish

1 Preheat the oven to 200°C (400°F, gas mark 6). Heat the butter and oil in a large flameproof casserole and lightly brown the chicken in it for about 3 minutes on each side. Lift the chicken out of the casserole with a slotted spoon and set aside on a plate.

2 Cook the onions, carrots and courgette in the casserole over a moderate heat for 10 minutes.

3 Mix the orange and lemon rinds and juice with the honey, mustard, garlic, ginger, salt and some pepper. Put the chicken back in the casserole and pour in the honey mixture. Bring to the boil, then take the casserole off the heat.

4 Cover the casserole and then put it in the centre of the oven for 50 minutes, basting the chicken frequently with the cooking liquid. After 25 minutes, cook the rice (see p.9).

5 When the chicken is cooked (see p.117) and the rice is done, spoon the chicken and vegetables into the middle of a serving dish. Arrange the rice round the edge, garnish with the watercress and orange rind and serve.

Per serving
Calories 565 Protein 43 g
Total fat 13 g (saturated fat 4.5 g)
Carbohydrates 74 g (added sugar 20 g)
Fibre 3.3 g Sodium 299 mg

RICE-STUFFED CHICKEN

A mixture of long-grain and wild rice enriches the nutty spinach stuffing in this filling chicken meal sufficient for six people. You will need a thin skewer and some clean, thin string to secure the stuffed chicken.

Serves 6
Preparation time: 1 hour
Cooking time: 2 hours

175 g (6 oz) easy-cook long-grain and wild rice cooked (see p.9) and cooled
450 g (1 lb) frozen leaf spinach, cooked, drained and chopped
2 eggs, size 2, lightly beaten
2 tablespoons chopped fresh basil
60 g (2 oz) shelled walnuts, finely chopped
60 g (2 oz) Parmesan cheese, grated
1 clove garlic, peeled and crushed (see p.11)
2.3 kg (5 lb) oven-ready chicken
1 tablespoon olive oil
¼ level teaspoon salt
Freshly ground black pepper
450 g (1 lb) button onions, peeled
450 g (1 lb) carrots, peeled and quartered
Sprigs of fresh basil to garnish

1 Preheat the oven to 180°C (350°F, gas mark 4). Mix the rice with the spinach, eggs, basil, walnuts, Parmesan and garlic.

2 Carefully loosen the skin from the chicken breasts and spread the rice mixture evenly underneath it (see p.117). Fold the wings under the neck and tie the legs together. Put the chicken in a large roasting tin and brush it all over with the oil. Sprinkle with the salt and some pepper.

3 Roast the chicken, uncovered, in the centre of the oven for about 1 hour, basting occasionally with the cooking juices. Add the onions and the carrots to the tin and baste them. Cook for 45 minutes-1 hour, or until the chicken is done (see p.117). If the chicken browns too much, cover loosely with foil.

4 Remove the chicken from the oven, cover with foil and leave to stand for 10 minutes. Lift the the chicken and vegetables onto a heated serving dish, garnish with the fresh basil and serve with a tossed green salad.

Per serving
Calories 670 Protein 72 g
Total fat 27 g (saturated fat 7.7 g)
Carbohydrates 37 g (added sugar 0)
Fibre 6.5 g Sodium 432 mg

CHICKEN JAMBALAYA

Serves 4
Preparation time: 30 minutes
Cooking time: 1 hour

2 tablespoons olive oil
1.6 kg (3½ lb) chicken, cut into
   eight (see p.115) and skinned
¼ level teaspoon salt
Freshly ground black pepper
1 large onion, peeled and chopped
2 medium sticks celery, trimmed
   and sliced
2 green peppers, de-seeded
   and chopped
400 g (14 oz) canned chopped
   tomatoes
2 cloves garlic, peeled and crushed
115 g (4 oz) cooked ham, trimmed
   of fat, and cubed
1 bay leaf
2 level teaspoons paprika
1 tablespoon chopped fresh thyme,
   or 1 level teaspoon dried thyme
4-6 drops Tabasco sauce
225 g (8 oz) long-grain white rice
570 ml (1 pint) chicken stock
   (see p.8)
2 tablespoons chopped fresh
   parsley

Per serving
Calories 701 Protein 73 g
Total fat 23 g (saturated fat 6.2 g)
Carbohydrates 56 g (added sugar 0)
Fibre 4.1 g Sodium 741 mg

This colourful jambalaya stew, based on a Creole recipe, makes a good choice for an informal dinner party. Using cubes of spicy sausage instead of the ham will give it an even hotter taste.

1 Heat the oil in a flameproof casserole and fry the chicken in it for 6-7 minutes until browned. Lift the chicken onto a plate and sprinkle with a little of the salt and some pepper.

2 Skim off all but 2 tablespoons of the fat from the casserole. Add the onion to the casserole and soften, stirring frequently, for about 5 minutes, then add the celery and peppers and cook for another 5 minutes.

3 Stir in the tomatoes, garlic, ham, bay leaf, paprika, thyme, the remaining salt and the Tabasco sauce. Add the chicken pieces and push them under the tomato mixture. Bring to the boil, then reduce the heat to low, cover and simmer for 15 minutes.

4 Stir in the rice and stock, cover and cook for about 25 minutes, or until the chicken is cooked (see p.117) and most of the stock has been absorbed. Take out the bay leaf, sprinkle the chopped parsley over the top of the jambalaya and serve.

Paprika and Tabasco sauce add a piquant spiciness to this chicken, ham and rice stew, adapted from a traditional Provençal jambalaia by early French settlers in the United States.

PORTUGUESE CHICKEN

Serves 4
Preparation time: 40 minutes
Cooking time: 50 minutes

2 tablespoons olive oil
1.6 kg (3½ lb) oven-ready chicken,
    cut into eight (see p.115)
    and skinned
150 ml (¼ pint) port or Madeira
150 ml (¼ pint) dry red wine
400 g (14 oz) canned chopped
    tomatoes
Strained juice of 1 medium orange
450 g (1 lb) small new potatoes,
    scrubbed and quartered
115 g (4 oz) cooked ham, cut into
    small cubes
60 g (2 oz) stuffed green olives,
    halved
450 g (1 lb) curly kale or spring
    greens, trimmed, washed and
    cut into wide strips
12 orange slices to garnish

Per serving
Calories 478 Protein 37 g
Total fat 17 g (saturated fat 3.8 g)
Carbohydrates 29 g (added sugar 0)
Fibre 6.6 g Sodium 887 mg

*Port, red wine, tomatoes and orange make a
deep amber sauce to accompany the
chicken in this casserole inspired by
Portuguese cooking.*

**Savoury stuffed olives and ham
balance the sweetness of the
port or Madeira wine in this
colourful chicken casserole. If
you are short of time, use
chicken legs and thighs instead
of jointing a whole chicken.**

1 Heat the oil in a large frying
pan or shallow flameproof
casserole and lightly brown the
chicken pieces in it for about
10 minutes. Put the chicken on a
plate and set aside. Pour off any
excess fat left in the pan.

2 Pour the port or Madeira and
red wine into the pan or
casserole and bring to the boil.
Stir for 3 minutes, scraping any
browned bits from the bottom of
the pan, then add the tomatoes,
orange juice, potatoes and ham
and bring back to the boil.

3 Put the chicken back
in the pan or casserole,
then reduce the heat. Cover and
simmer, stirring occasionally, for
40 minutes, until the chicken and
the potatoes are tender. Stir in the
olives and kale, cover and cook for
about 10 minutes, or until the
kale is tender.

4 Serve the chicken
on a heated
serving dish, or
from the pan
or casserole,
garnished
with the
orange
slices.

POUSSINS WITH APPLE AND ORANGE

Serves 4
Preparation time: 30 minutes
Cooking time: 1 hour 15 minutes

4 oven-ready poussins, each about
    400 g (14 oz)
675 g (1 1/2 lb) potatoes, peeled
    and thinly sliced
340 g (12 oz) green dessert apples,
    peeled, cored and cut
    into wedges
1 large onion, peeled and
    thinly sliced
1 small bay leaf
3 sprigs parsley
1 medium stick celery, trimmed
    and thinly sliced
Finely grated rind of 1 orange
1/4 level teaspoon each ground
    cloves and allspice
3/4 level teaspoon ground cinnamon
1/2 level teaspoon salt
Freshly ground black pepper
285 ml (1/2 pint) freshly squeezed
    orange juice
1 tablespoon olive oil
2 level tablespoons dry white
    breadcrumbs
1 large orange, cut into wedges,
    and sprigs of watercress
    to garnish

Per serving
Calories 466 Protein 41 g
Total fat 11 g (saturated fat 2.5 g)
Carbohydrates 52 g (added sugar 0)
Fibre 5.2 g Sodium 706 mg

In this aromatic casserole, the delicate flavour of roasted poussins is well matched by the subtle piquancy of cloves, allspice and cinnamon and a rich apple and orange sauce.

1 Preheat the oven to 200°C (400°F, gas mark 6). Cut the poussins down through the back, then open them out and flatten (see p.116). Wash and pat dry with kitchen paper.

2 Put the potatoes, apples and onion in a large, lightly oiled baking dish. Mix in the bay leaf, parsley, celery and orange rind. Sprinkle with the cloves, allspice and cinnamon and season with half the salt and some pepper.

3 Lay the poussins, skin-side up, in the middle of the dish and season with the remaining salt and some pepper. Pour over the orange juice, then brush with the oil and sprinkle with the breadcrumbs. Cook in the oven for 1-1 1/4 hours, or until the poussins are cooked (see p.117), crisp and golden and the vegetables are tender. Take out the bay leaf, garnish and serve.

87

BASIL CHICKEN WITH TOMATOES, CELERIAC AND BARLEY

Serves 4
Preparation time: 20 minutes
Cooking time: 1 hour 15 minutes

1.4 kg (3 lb) oven-ready chicken
   cut into eight (see p.115)
   and skinned
1/2 level teaspoon salt
Freshly ground black pepper
3 tablespoons olive oil
1 large onion, peeled and chopped
2 cloves garlic, peeled and crushed
   (see p.11)
1 small green pepper, de-seeded
   and diced
150 ml (1/4 pint) dry white wine
400 g (14 oz) canned chopped
   tomatoes
150 ml (1/4 pint) chicken stock
   (see p.8)
1/2 level teaspoon dried thyme
1 level tablespoon fresh
   chopped basil
115 g (4 oz) pearl barley
150 g (5 oz) celeriac, peeled
   and diced (see p.10)
1 large courgette, trimmed
   and diced (see p.10)
2 level tablespoons fresh chopped
   basil to garnish

Per serving
Calories 469 Protein 41 g
Total fat 18 g (saturated fat 4 g)
Carbohydrates 31 g (added sugar 0)
Fibre 5.5 g Sodium 462 mg

This substantial, richly flavoured stew combines chicken with aromatic fresh basil and the peppery taste of celeriac – a variety of celery cultivated for its turnip-shaped root. The stew tastes even better if left overnight to mature.

1 Season the chicken pieces with half the salt and some pepper. Heat the oil in a large flameproof casserole and brown the chicken pieces in it for 5 minutes each side. Take the chicken out of the casserole and set aside on a plate.

2 Add the onion, garlic and green pepper to the casserole and cook, stirring, for about 5 minutes, or until softened. Pour in the wine and boil for 1 minute, then return the chicken to the casserole.

3 Stir in the tomatoes, stock, thyme, basil, barley, celeriac, the remaining salt and some pepper. Bring to the boil, then reduce the heat, cover the casserole and simmer for 40-50 minutes until the chicken is almost cooked.

4 Mix in the courgette and cook for a further 5-10 minutes, until just tender. Sprinkle with the basil and serve with warm french bread.

CHICKEN PAPRIKA WITH SPÄTZLE

Paprika – a slightly hot, sweet spice made from certain varieties of sweet red pepper – lends its name and piquant flavour to this Hungarian dish of chicken in a soured cream sauce. Spätzle, which are miniature dumplings widely used in German cuisine, add substance to the sauce.

Serves 4
Preparation time: 20 minutes
Cooking time: 45 minutes

225 g (8 oz) plain flour
1 level teaspoon salt
2 eggs, size 2
3 tablespoons water
1.6 kg (3 1/2 lb) oven-ready chicken,
   cut into eight (see p.115)
   and skinned
Freshly ground black pepper
2 tablespoons vegetable oil
1 large onion, peeled and sliced
2 medium red peppers, de-seeded
   and cut into squares
1 level tablespoon paprika
570 ml (1 pint) chicken stock
   (see p.8)
175 g (6 oz) fresh cauliflower florets
115 g (4 oz) frozen peas
150 ml (1/4 pint) soured cream
Paprika to garnish

Per serving
Calories 674 Protein 58 g
Total fat 26 g (saturated fat 8 g)
Carbohydrates 56 g (added sugar 0)
Fibre 6.7 g Sodium 701 mg

1 Sift the flour and half the salt into a bowl, then work in the eggs with enough of the water to make a firm dough. Lightly knead the dough on a floured board until just smooth, then put it in a polythene bag and refrigerate until needed.

2 Season the chicken with the salt and some pepper. Heat the oil in a large flameproof casserole, and brown the chicken pieces all over for about 6-8 minutes. Remove and drain on kitchen paper.

3 Cook the onion and red peppers in the casserole until they are softened. Stir in the paprika and cook for 1 minute. Pour in the stock, return the chicken to the casserole and bring to the boil. Reduce the heat, cover the casserole and then simmer for 20 minutes or until the chicken is almost cooked (see p.117).

4 Stir in the cauliflower and peas, then bring back to the boil. Remove the dough from the bag and coat it thoroughly with flour. Grate the dough directly into the casserole, stirring all the time. Cover and simmer for about 10 minutes until the spätzle are cooked and the vegetables are tender. Remove from the heat and stir in the soured cream. Sprinkle with paprika and serve.

CHICKEN AND VEGETABLES IN WHITE WINE SAUCE

Serves 4
Preparation time: 25 minutes
Cooking time: 1 hour 15 minutes

1 tablespoon olive oil
60 g (2 oz) streaky bacon, rinds removed, cut into pieces
1.4 kg (3 lb) chicken, cut into eight (see p.115) and skinned
½ level teaspoon salt
285 ml (½ pint) dry white wine
225 g (8 oz) baby onions or shallots, peeled
6 whole cloves
150 ml (¼ pint) dry sherry
2 bay leaves
225 g (8 oz) baby carrots, peeled and trimmed
2 sticks celery, trimmed and sliced
225 g (8 oz) mushrooms, wiped and halved
285 ml (½ pint) chicken stock (see p.8)
Freshly ground black pepper
115 g (4 oz) frozen peas
1 tablespoon chopped fresh parsley
30 g (1 oz) butter, softened
2 level tablespoons plain flour

Per serving
Calories 540 Protein 43 g
Total fat 24 g (saturated fat 9.5 g)
Carbohydrates 18 g (added sugar 0)
Fibre 5.8 g Sodium 698 mg

Parsley, bay leaves and aromatic cloves combine to give a rich fragrance to this light and satisfying kitchen garden stew.

1 Heat the oil in a large saucepan and lightly brown the bacon in it for 5 minutes. Remove from the pan with a slotted spoon, drain on kitchen paper and set aside.

2 Season the chicken portions with the salt, then fry them in the pan – in batches if necessary – for about 10-15 minutes, turning regularly, or until browned on all sides. Transfer to a plate and drain off any excess fat from the pan.

3 Pour the wine into the pan and bring to the boil, stirring and scraping the browned meat juices from the bottom. Turn down the heat and simmer for 5 minutes, or until the wine has reduced by half.

4 Stud two onions or shallots with the cloves, add these to the pan with the sherry and bay leaves, and simmer for 2 minutes. Stir in the carrots, celery, mushrooms, stock, the remaining onions or shallots and the bacon and chicken pieces, and season with pepper.

5 Bring back to the boil, then reduce the heat, cover and simmer for 40 minutes. Stir in the peas and parsley for the last 4 minutes of cooking.

Mushrooms, carrots and tender peas accompany succulent chicken pieces in a sherry-based sauce.

6 Carefully blend the butter with the flour to make a smooth paste, and stir it into the sauce. Cook, stirring, for 3 minutes, or until the sauce thickens slightly. Remove the bay leaves and clove-studded onions or shallots, then serve with warm ciabatta or other Italian bread.

ROAST CHICKEN WITH PRUNE AND NUT STUFFING

Serves 4
Preparation time: 45 minutes
Cooking time: 1 hour 50 minutes

225 g (8 oz) ready-to-use pitted
   prunes, roughly chopped
150 ml (¼ pint) port or red wine
2 tablespoons olive oil
1 large onion, peeled and chopped
1 medium carrot, peeled and
   coarsely grated
3 cloves garlic, peeled and crushed
   (see p.11)
340 g (12 oz) mushrooms, wiped
   and chopped
115 g (4 oz) blanched almonds,
   chopped
400 g (14 oz) curly kale or spinach
   leaves, trimmed, rinsed and
   coarsely shredded
30 g (1 oz) butter
1 tablespoon chopped fresh
   marjoram
175 g (6 oz) fresh white
   breadcrumbs
½ level teaspoon salt
Freshly ground black pepper
2 kg (4½ lb) oven-ready chicken
1 tablespoon olive oil
Fresh celery leaves or
   marjoram to garnish

Per serving
Calories 900
Protein 56 g
Total fat 44 g
(saturated fat 10 g)
Carbohydrates 64 g
(added sugar 0)
Fibre 19 g
Sodium 820 mg

Fruit, chopped nuts and
vegetables make a colourful and
strong-flavoured stuffing for
succulent roast chicken. You
can use either curly kale or
spinach in the stuffing.

1 Soak the prunes in the port or
wine in a small bowl and set
aside. Preheat the oven to 190°C
(375°F, gas mark 5).

2 Heat the oil in a frying pan
and cook the onion, carrot
and garlic in it for 5 minutes,
stirring occasionally. Mix in the
mushrooms and cook for a
further 5 minutes.

3 Add the almonds and the curly
kale or spinach to the pan and
cook for 1 minute. Stir in the
prunes and port or wine, and add
the butter. Cover and simmer for
6-8 minutes, or until the curly kale

or spinach is just tender. Take
the pan off the heat and leave to
cool for 15 minutes. Stir in the
marjoram and the breadcrumbs,
then season with half the salt and
some pepper.

*Prunes soaked in port or red wine add
a rich sweetness to this crunchy
vegetable and nut stuffing.*

4 Rinse the chicken inside and out under a cold tap, then dry well with kitchen paper. Fill the chicken cavity with half the stuffing. Spread a 30.5 cm x 25 cm (12 in x 10 in) piece of foil with butter and spoon the remaining stuffing down the centre. Roll the foil into a sausage shape, then secure the ends tightly and put it in the refrigerator to chill.

5 Put the chicken in a roasting tin, rub it with the oil and season with the remaining salt and some pepper. Roast for 1 hour 30 minutes–1 hour 50 minutes, or until it is cooked (see p.117). Half an hour before the end of cooking, put the foil-wrapped stuffing in the roasting tin with the chicken to heat through.

6 Put the chicken on a heated serving plate, then cover and leave to stand for 15 minutes. Skim off the excess fat from the juices in the roasting tin and discard. Mix the juices with the extra stuffing and arrange in heaped spoonfuls around the chicken. Garnish the chicken and serve with a tomato, cucumber and red onion salad.

Moroccan Braised Chicken

Serves 4
Preparation time: 20 minutes
Cooking time: 1 hour 25 minutes

1.6 kg (3½ lb) oven-ready chicken
1 level teaspoon salt
2 tablespoons olive oil
1 large onion, peeled and chopped
1 level tablespoon peeled and finely chopped root ginger
2 level teaspoons turmeric
1 level teaspoon each ground coriander, cumin, cinnamon and paprika
Freshly ground black pepper
725 ml (1¼ pints) chicken or vegetable stock (see pp.8-9)
3 medium courgettes, trimmed and thickly sliced
1 medium red pepper, de-seeded and roughly chopped
4 medium carrots, peeled and cut into short strips (see p.10)
340 g (12 oz) cooked chickpeas, drained (see p.172)
225 g (8 oz) couscous
30 g (1 oz) pine nuts, lightly toasted (optional)
30 g (1 oz) seedless raisins (optional)
Paprika and fresh bay leaves to garnish

Per serving
Calories 753 Protein 70 g
Total fat 27 g
(saturated fat 5.7 g)
Carbohydrates 61 g
(added sugar 0)
Fibre 7.5 g
Sodium 699 mg

This fragrant chicken dish spices up a Sunday lunch with the flavour of North Africa.

1 Season the chicken inside and out with half of the salt. Tuck the wing tips behind the back and tie the legs together (see p.117).

2 Heat the oil in a very large flameproof casserole and cook the onion and ginger in it until softened. Stir in the turmeric, coriander, cumin, cinnamon, paprika and some pepper, and cook gently for 2 minutes.

3 Add the chicken to the casserole and turn it until it is well coated with the spices. Pour in the stock, add the remaining salt and bring to the boil. Reduce the heat, cover and simmer gently for 45 minutes.

4 Stir in the courgettes, red pepper and carrots, cover and simmer for 30 minutes, or until the chicken is cooked (see p.117). Mix in the chickpeas and simmer, uncovered, for 5 minutes.

5 Put the chicken on a plate and keep warm. Add the couscous to the casserole, cover and leave to stand for 5 minutes, until all of the liquid has been absorbed. Return the chicken to the casserole and sprinkle with the pine nuts and raisins, if using, and a little paprika. Garnish with the bay leaves and serve.

CHICKEN AND PASTA BAKE

Serves 4
Preparation time: 20 minutes
Cooking time: 1 hour 20 minutes

4 chicken legs, each about 340 g
(12 oz), skinned and divided into
drumsticks and thighs
½ level teaspoon salt
Freshly ground black pepper
3 tablespoons olive oil
1 medium leek, trimmed, washed
and chopped
1 stick celery, trimmed and chopped
115 g (4 oz) mushrooms, wiped
and sliced
150 ml (¼ pint) dry white wine
425 ml (¾ pint) chicken stock
(see p.8)
1 level tablespoon chopped fresh
tarragon, or 1 level teaspoon
dried tarragon
1 bay leaf
225 g (8 oz) frozen baby broad
beans or peas
1½ level tablespoons cornflour
150ml (¼ pint) single cream
1 tablespoon lemon juice
2 tablespoons chopped
fresh parsley
60 g (2 oz) unsalted butter
225 g (8 oz) tagliatelle, cooked
and drained (see p.202)
3 tablespoons fresh white
breadcrumbs

**Chicken in creamy tarragon
sauce, a classic French
combination, is enriched with
beans, celery and mushrooms
and baked with pasta ribbons.**

1 Season the chicken with the salt
and some pepper. Heat the oil in
a large frying pan, and brown the
chicken in it for 5 minutes. Put
the chicken pieces on a plate. Add
the leek, celery and mushrooms
to the pan and sauté, stirring,
for 5 minutes. Pour in the wine,
bring to the boil and cook for
1 minute. Stir in the chicken
stock, tarragon and bay leaf,
add the chicken pieces and bring
to the boil. Reduce the heat, cover
and simmer for 25 minutes.

2 Preheat the oven to 200°C
(400°F, gas mark 6). In the
meantime, add the beans or peas
to the chicken. Simmer for
5 minutes, then blend the
cornflour and cream. Add to the
pan and cook, stirring, over a
moderate heat for 5 minutes.
Remove the bay leaf and stir in the
lemon juice and parsley.

3 Melt half the butter in a large,
flameproof dish. Add the pasta,
coating it with the butter, and
spread it evenly across the bottom
of the dish. Spoon the chicken
mixture gently over the top of
the pasta, sprinkle with the
breadcrumbs and dot with the
remaining butter. Place the dish
in the centre of the oven and bake,
uncovered, for 25 minutes, or until
bubbling and lightly browned.
Serve with a mixed salad and
wholemeal bread.

Per serving
Calories 1027 Protein 77 g
Total fat 46 g (saturated fat 18 g)
Carbohydrates 75 g (added sugar 0)
Fibre 5.6 g Sodium 621 mg

*The fresh tastes of baby broad beans and leeks complement the richer,
buttery pasta and a sauce fortified with cream, wine and chicken stock.
A sprinkling of breadcrumbs adds
crunch to the finished dish.*

CHICKEN AND MUSHROOM IN SPICY TOMATO SAUCE

Serves 6
Preparation time: 30 minutes
Cooking time: 40 minutes

2 tablespoons olive oil
4 chicken drumsticks and 4 chicken
 thighs, about 1.4 kg (3 lb)
 in total, skinned
1 medium onion, peeled and
 coarsely chopped
1 clove garlic, peeled and crushed
 (see p.11)
2 medium green peppers, de-seeded
 and sliced
225 g (8 oz) mushrooms, wiped
 and halved
450 ml (16 fl oz) passata (sieved
 tomatoes)
1/4 level teaspoon cayenne pepper
6 thin slices salami, cut into strips
225 g (8 oz) orzo (rice-shaped
 pasta) or long-grain white rice
570 ml (1 pint) chicken stock
 (see p.8)
2 tablespoons chopped
 fresh parsley

Per serving
Calories 502 Protein 44 g
Total fat 21 g (saturated fat 6.4 g)
Carbohydrates 38 g (added sugar 0)
Fibre 3.8 g Sodium 462 mg

Salami and vegetables combine in a zesty sauce for tender chicken. The recipe works best with a hard-textured variety of salami, such as Milano.

1 Heat the oil in a large flameproof casserole. Brown the chicken pieces in it for 6-7 minutes on each side, then remove from the casserole and set aside on a plate.

2 Brown the onion, garlic, peppers and mushrooms in the casserole for 5-10 minutes, stirring, then add the passata, cayenne pepper, salami and chicken. Bring the mixture to the boil, reduce the heat, cover and simmer for 20 minutes.

3 Stir in the orzo or rice and stock, and cover the casserole. Simmer, stirring occasionally, for 15-20 minutes (the full 20 minutes if using rice), until the pasta or rice is tender and the chicken is no longer pink inside. Garnish with parsley and serve accompanied by warm french bread.

Succulent chicken pieces are the main ingredient of this robust stew containing juicy mushrooms, green peppers and rice-shaped orzo pasta.

93

CHICKEN WITH WINE AND MUSHROOMS

This richly flavoured chicken, vegetable and pasta stew is best made with a robust, full-bodied red wine – such as an Italian Chianti or Barolo.

Serves 4
Preparation time: 30 minutes
Cooking time: 50 minutes

2 tablespoons olive oil
4 chicken legs, each about
  225 g (8 oz), skinned (see p.116)
¼ level teaspoon salt
Freshly ground black pepper
1 large onion, peeled and chopped
225 g (8 oz) button mushrooms,
  wiped and halved
2 cloves garlic, peeled and crushed
  (see p.11)
400 g (14 oz) canned tomatoes
115 ml (4 fl oz) passata (sieved
  tomatoes)
225 ml (8 fl oz) red wine
½ level teaspoon dried tarragon
115 g (4 oz) pitted black olives
85 g (3 oz) linguine
Sprigs of fresh watercress to garnish

Per serving
Calories 421 Protein 34 g
Total fat 17 g (saturated fat 3.4 g)
Carbohydrates 24 g (added sugar 0)
Fibre 5.3 g Sodium 945 mg

1 Heat the oil in a large flameproof casserole and fry the chicken legs, two at a time, over a high heat until golden. Move the chicken to a plate and sprinkle with the salt and some pepper.

2 Add the onion to the casserole and sauté it over a moderate heat for 5 minutes. Stir in the mushrooms and garlic, and cook for 3 minutes. Then add the tomatoes, passata, wine, tarragon and olives. Return the chicken to the casserole and bring the stew to the boil. Reduce the heat and simmer, covered, for 15 minutes.

3 Finally, bring the stew back to the boil and stir in the linguine. Cook gently for 8-10 minutes, or until both the linguine and the chicken are done. Garnish with the sprigs of watercress and serve.

CABBAGE AND CARAWAY CHICKEN IN MUSTARD SAUCE

The use of apples in the soured cream and mustard sauce heightens the creamy taste of this aromatic chicken dish.

Serves 4
Preparation time: 15 minutes
Cooking time: 40 minutes

4 boneless chicken breasts, each
  about 175 g (6 oz), skinned
½ level teaspoon salt
Freshly ground black pepper
15 g (½ oz) unsalted butter
1 tablespoon olive oil
1 medium onion, peeled and
  thinly sliced
450 g (1 lb) white cabbage,
  coarsely shredded
1 level teaspoon caraway seeds
2 level teaspoons cornflour
150 ml (¼ pint) milk
570 ml (1 pint) chicken
  stock (see p.8)
2 medium, green dessert apples,
  peeled, cored and thinly sliced
115 g (4 oz) orzo or other very
  small pasta
¾ level tablespoon Dijon mustard
4 tablespoons soured cream
1 tablespoon chopped fresh dill
Sprigs of fresh dill to garnish

Per serving
Calories 428 Protein 38 g
Total fat 15 g (saturated fat 6.4 g)
Carbohydrates 37 g (added sugar 0)
Fibre 6.2 g Sodium 406 mg

1 Season both sides of each chicken breast with the salt and some pepper. Heat the butter and oil in a large flameproof casserole and cook the chicken breasts in it for 2-3 minutes on each side, or until they change colour. Move the chicken to a plate.

2 Add the onion to the casserole and cook, stirring, until softened. Mix in the shredded cabbage and caraway seeds, then cover and cook, stirring occasionally, for 5 minutes.

3 Blend the cornflour with the milk, stir in the stock and pour into the casserole. Add the apples and pasta and bring to the boil. Cook, stirring, for about 2 minutes or until the mixture has thickened slightly. Stir in the mustard, lay the chicken breasts over the vegetables and pasta and cover. Cook gently for about 20 minutes, or until the chicken is done (see p.117).

4 At the last moment, stir in the soured cream and the chopped dill, garnish with the fresh dill and then serve with wholemeal bread.

CHICKEN BREASTS CATALAN

A vibrant blend of French and Spanish influences is evident in this hearty chicken dish flavoured with garlic and basil.

Serves 6
Preparation time: 15 minutes
Cooking time: 45 minutes

6 boneless chicken breasts, each
   about 175 g (6 oz), skinned
½ level teaspoon salt
Freshly ground black pepper
2 tablespoons olive oil
1 large onion, peeled and sliced
1 medium red pepper, de-seeded
   and cut lengthways into
   wide strips
3 cloves garlic, peeled and crushed
   (see p.11)
400 g (14 oz) canned tomatoes,
   juice saved and tomatoes
   quartered
225 ml (8 fl oz) chicken stock
   (see p.8)
1 bay leaf
1 tablespoon finely shredded fresh
   basil, or 1 level teaspoon
   dried basil
150 g (5 oz) long-grain white rice
275 g (10 oz) frozen peas
115 g (4 oz) pitted black olives
Fresh sprig of basil to garnish

Per serving
Calories 407 Protein 44 g
Total fat 13 g (saturated fat 3 g)
Carbohydrates 31 g (added sugar 0)
Fibre 5.8 g Sodium 750 mg

1 Season the chicken breasts with half the salt and some pepper. Heat the oil in a large frying pan for 1 minute, then cook the chicken breasts in it for 3 minutes on each side, or until golden brown. Lift the chicken onto kitchen paper, then cover and set aside.

2 Stir the onion and red pepper into the pan and fry over a moderate heat for 3 minutes. Add the garlic and cook for 2 minutes, then mix in the tomatoes and their juice, the stock, bay leaf, basil and the remaining salt. Season with some more pepper and bring to the boil. Add the rice and reduce the heat. Cover the pan and simmer for 10 minutes.

3 Put the chicken breasts back in the saucepan and spoon the mixture over them. Cover the pan and cook for 10 minutes, then stir in the peas and bring back to the boil. Turn down the heat, cover and continue cooking for 5-10 minutes, or until the chicken is cooked (see p.117) and the rice and peas are tender.

4 Remove the bay leaf, mix in the olives and arrange on a heated serving plate. Garnish with the basil and serve.

The colourful combination of olives, red peppers, basil and tomatoes gives a fresh, Mediterranean flavour to this tempting chicken and rice meal for six.

95

STUFFED CHICKEN ROLLS

Serves 6
Preparation time: 35 minutes
Cooking time: 50 minutes

3 tablespoons olive oil
1 shallot, peeled and
  finely chopped
60 g (2 oz) mushrooms, wiped
  and finely chopped
60 g (2 oz) Parma ham,
  finely chopped
60 g (2 oz) frozen chopped
  spinach, thawed
2 cloves garlic, peeled
  and crushed (see p.11)
30 g (1 oz) fresh white
  breadcrumbs
60 g (2 oz) Parmesan
  cheese, grated
¼ level teaspoon salt
Freshly ground black pepper
6 boneless chicken breast fillets,
  skinned and beaten out thin
2 level tablespoons plain flour
225 g (8 oz) button onions,
  blanched and peeled
340 g (12 oz) fresh tomato and tuna
  sauce or spicy tomato sauce
285 ml (½ pint) chicken stock
  (see p.8)
200 g (7 oz) cooked rice
  (see p.9)
8 slices toasted french bread and
  flat-leaf parsley to garnish

Per serving
Calories 437 Protein 27 g
Total fat 17 g (saturated fat 5 g)
Carbohydrates 48 g (added sugar 0)
Fibre 4.9 g Sodium 825 mg

These stuffed chicken breasts can be made the day before serving, and reheated by bringing the dish to the boil then simmering for 10 minutes. Use ready-prepared tomato and tuna sauce or any other spicy tomato sauce, available from a supermarket or delicatessen.

1 Heat 1 tablespoon of the oil in a large frying pan and cook the shallot and mushrooms in it for 2-3 minutes. Stir in the Parma ham and spinach and cook for 1-2 minutes. Take the pan off the heat, add the garlic, breadcrumbs, Parmesan, salt and some pepper and mix well.

2 Spoon one-sixth of the stuffing onto each chicken breast, then roll up each one and tie with the string. Coat the chicken parcels thoroughly in the flour, shaking off any excess.

3 Heat 1 tablespoon of the oil in a large flameproof casserole and soften the onions in it. Add the remaining oil to the casserole and cook the chicken parcels in it for 5 minutes on each side, until golden brown.

4 Stir in the tomato and tuna sauce and the stock and bring to the boil. Reduce the heat, cover and simmer gently for 30-40 minutes, or until the chicken is cooked (see p.117). Stir in the rice and heat through for 5 minutes.

5 Lift out the chicken and remove the string. Put the chicken back into the casserole, reheat for 2 minutes, then garnish with the french bread and parsley and serve.

Parma ham gives this attractive supper dish a slightly salty flavour, balanced by a tangy tomato and tuna sauce.

QUICK CHICKEN AND DUMPLINGS

Parsley dumplings, cooked in the casserole alongside the chicken and fresh vegetables, put the finishing touch to this satisfying chicken meal.

Serves 4
Preparation time: 25 minutes
Cooking time: 35 minutes

70 g (2½ oz) butter
1 large onion, peeled and chopped
3 cloves garlic, peeled and crushed (see p.11)
675 g (1½ lb) boneless chicken breasts, skinned and cut into cubes
1 level teaspoon mixed dried herbs
425 ml (¾ pint) chicken stock (see p.8)
¼ level teaspoon salt
Freshly ground black pepper
175 g (6 oz) self-raising flour
¾ level teaspoon baking powder
3 tablespoons chopped fresh parsley
175 ml (6 fl oz) milk
340 g (12 oz) frozen mixed vegetables

Per serving
Calories 538 Protein 46 g
Total fat 21 g (saturated fat 12 g)
Carbohydrates 43 g (added sugar 0)
Fibre 2.8 g Sodium 757 mg

1 Melt 30 g (1 oz) of the butter in a large flameproof casserole or saucepan and cook the onion and garlic in it for 5 minutes. Stir in the chicken and cook for 5 minutes, then add the mixed herbs, stock, salt and some pepper. Bring to the boil, then reduce the heat, cover and simmer for 10 minutes.

2 To make the dumplings, sift the flour and the baking powder into a bowl and rub in the remaining butter, until the mixture resembles breadcrumbs. Mix in the parsley, then add enough of the milk to make a soft, slightly sticky dough.

3 Bring the chicken mixture to a gentle boil and stir in the frozen mixed vegetables. Bring back to a gentle boil and cook for 3 minutes.

4 Carefully drop eight rounded tablespoons of the dough onto the top of the gently boiling chicken mixture without letting them touch. Reduce the heat to a simmer, cover, and cook for 12 minutes without lifting the lid so that the dumplings become light and fluffy. Serve the chicken and dumplings from the casserole or in a heated serving dish.

BRAISED CHICKEN WITH SWEET POTATO AND PUMPKIN

You can use a pumpkin or a butternut squash to make this substantial family dish. Either will provide a sweet, buttery flavour and creamy texture to complement the chicken.

Serves 4
Preparation time: 20 minutes
Cooking time: 1 hour

1 tablespoon sunflower oil
1.4 kg (3 lb) chicken, cut into eight (see p.115) and skinned
1 large onion, peeled and thinly sliced
2 cinnamon sticks
1 level teaspoon salt
Freshly ground black pepper
1 clove garlic, peeled and crushed (see p.11)
450 g (1 lb) sweet potatoes, peeled and cut into small cubes
450 g (1 lb) pumpkin or butternut squash, peeled and cut into small cubes
285 ml (½ pint) chicken stock (see p.8)
150 g (5 oz) ready-to-use prunes
Sprigs of fresh flat-leaf parsley to garnish

Per serving
Calories 533 Protein 57 g
Total fat 16 g (saturated fat 4.2 g)
Carbohydrates 43 g (added sugar 0)
Fibre 9 g Sodium 711 mg

1 Heat the oil in a large flameproof casserole and thoroughly brown the chicken pieces in it. Stir in the onion and the cinnamon sticks and cook for 10 minutes.

2 Season with the salt and some pepper. Stir in the garlic, sweet potatoes, pumpkin or butternut squash and the stock, and bring to the boil. Reduce the heat, cover and simmer for about 45 minutes, or until the chicken and vegetables are tender.

3 Stir in the prunes. Heat through for about 5 minutes, until the prunes are plump and soft. Pour the braised chicken into a heated serving dish, garnish with the parsley and serve.

SPICY MEXICAN CHICKEN

Serves 4
Preparation time: 20 minutes
Cooking time: 45 minutes

2 tablespoons olive oil
4 cloves garlic, peeled and
    thinly sliced
675 g (1 1/2 lb) boneless chicken
    breasts, skinned and cut into
    small cubes
1/4 level teaspoon salt
1 level teaspoon chilli powder
400 g (14 oz) canned chopped
    tomatoes
175-225 g (6-8 oz) frozen
    green beans
225 g (8 oz) cooked red kidney
    beans (see p.172)
2 fresh green chillies, de-seeded
    and finely chopped
2-3 level teaspoons unsweetened
    cocoa powder, blended with
    2 tablespoons of boiling water
1/2 level teaspoon ground cinnamon
2-3 level tablespoons finely
    chopped fresh coriander
1 tablespoon fresh lime juice
15 g (1/2 oz) pumpkin seeds
    (optional)
Sprigs fresh coriander or flat-leaf
    parsley to garnish
8 flour tortillas, warmed

Per serving
Calories 516 Protein 46 g
Total fat 20 g (saturated fat 3.5 g)
Carbohydrates 40 g (added sugar 0)
Fibre 2.4 g Sodium 333 mg

Fresh chillies, cinnamon and
a hint of cocoa are contained
in the rich and spicy sauce
with this fiery chicken dish.
Corn chips, soured cream or
sliced avocado can be served
as an accompaniment in place
of the flour tortillas.

1 Heat the oil in a large
flameproof casserole and gently
cook the garlic in it over a low heat
for 1 minute. Stir in the chicken,
add the salt and then cook for
about 15 minutes, until the
chicken pieces are lightly browned.

2 Stir in the chilli powder and
cook for 1 minute, then add
the tomatoes, green beans, kidney
beans, chillies, cocoa mixture,
cinnamon and coriander. Bring
to the boil, and then reduce the
heat to low. Cover and simmer for
about 20-30 minutes, or until
the chicken is cooked (see p.117).

3 Stir in the lime juice and
sprinkle the pumpkin seeds
over the top, if using. Garnish
with the fresh coriander or parsley
and serve with the tortillas.

CHICKEN RISOTTO WITH SPRING VEGETABLES

Serves 4
Preparation time: 20 minutes
Cooking time: 35 minutes

15 g (1/2 oz) butter
1 tablespoon olive oil
450 g (1 lb) boneless chicken
    breasts, skinned and cut
    into cubes
1/2 level teaspoon salt
Freshly ground black pepper
1 medium onion, peeled and
    finely chopped
1 clove garlic, peeled and crushed
    (see p.11)
225 g (8 oz) Arborio (risotto) rice
725 ml (1 1/4 pints) chicken stock
    (see p.8)
115 g (4 oz) sugar snap
    peas, trimmed
6 baby carrots, trimmed, washed
    and halved
1 stick celery, trimmed and sliced
115 g (4 oz) small asparagus spears
400 g (14 oz) canned chopped
    tomatoes
4 tablespoons finely shredded basil
60 g (2 oz) grated Parmesan cheese
Sprigs of fresh basil to garnish

Per serving
Calories 442 Protein 32 g
Total fat 11 g (saturated fat 3.9 g)
Carbohydrates 58 g (added sugar 0)
Fibre 3.7 g Sodium 407 mg

Fresh-tasting vegetables combine
with tender chicken pieces in
this tempting, nutritious risotto.
Arborio rice – a speciality
Italian risotto rice with a creamy
texture when cooked – is sold
in most supermarkets.

1 Heat the butter and oil in a
large, deep, lidded frying pan
or flameproof casserole. Add the
chicken to it and cook, stirring,
for about 5 minutes. Sprinkle with
half the salt and some pepper,
then place the chicken cubes on a
plate and set aside.

2 Add the onion and garlic and
cook until softened. Stir in the
rice and cook for 1 minute, then
pour in the stock and add the
remaining salt and some pepper.
Bring to the boil and then stir in
the sugar snap peas, carrots, celery,
asparagus, tomatoes and basil.
Reduce the heat, cover the pan
and simmer for 10 minutes.

3 Add the chicken pieces,
pushing them well into the rice.
Cover and simmer for a further
10 minutes, or until the rice is
cooked, adding a little more stock
if necessary. Remove from the
heat and stir in two-thirds of the
cheese, sprinkling the rest on top.
Garnish with the sprigs of basil
and serve.

CHICKEN AND BROCCOLI STIR-FRY

Serves 4
Preparation time: 30 minutes
Cooking time: 30 minutes

2 level teaspoons cornflour
4 tablespoons soy sauce
1 tablespoon dry sherry
450 g (1 lb) boneless chicken
  breasts, skinned and cut into
  thin strips
2 tablespoons groundnut oil
2 pieces root ginger, each 2.5 cm
  (1 in), peeled and cut into
  matchstick strips
2 cloves garlic, peeled and crushed
  (see p.11)
450 g (1 lb) broccoli, trimmed
  and cut into small florets, or
  340 g (12 oz) frozen broccoli
  florets, thawed and drained
1 large red pepper, de-seeded
  and cut into long strips
450 ml (16 fl oz) chicken stock
  (see p.8)
85 g (3 oz) farfallini
30 g (1 oz) pine nuts

Per serving
Calories 380 Protein 34 g
Total fat 17 g (saturated fat 1.9 g)
Carbohydrates 24 g (added sugar 0)
Fibre 1.8 g Sodium 953 mg

Broccoli florets and red pepper add colour to this enticing blend of succulent chicken, lightly crisped ginger strips, pine nuts and farfallini.

Ginger, garlic and sherry sauce give this light and lively stir-fry the authentic taste of Chinese cuisine. Make sure that you use fresh root ginger, which has a richness that dried ground ginger cannot provide.

1 Blend the cornflour with the soy sauce and sherry in a bowl, add the chicken strips to the mixture and mix well until evenly coated. Cover and leave to marinate for 10-15 minutes.

2 Heat 1 tablespoon of the oil in a wok or large frying pan, add the ginger and garlic to it and stir-fry over a moderate heat for 2 minutes. Mix in the broccoli and stir-fry for about 3 minutes, then add the pepper and cook for another 3 minutes, or until just softened. Transfer the vegetables to a bowl with a slotted spoon.

3 Heat the remaining oil in the wok or pan, add the chicken strips and stir-fry for 5-6 minutes, or until cooked (see p.117). Add the chicken to the vegetables.

4 Pour the stock into the wok or pan, bring to the boil and then stir in the pasta. Cook over a moderate heat for about 10 minutes, stirring occasionally, until the liquid has been absorbed.

5 Stir the chicken and vegetables into the pasta and add the pine nuts. Heat through for 4-5 minutes, then serve.

CURRIED CHICKEN AND RICE

Serves 4
Preparation time: 30 minutes
Cooking time: 45 minutes

30 g (1 oz) butter or margarine
550 g (1 1/4 lb) boneless chicken
    breasts, skinned and cut into
    strips (see p.116)
1/4 level teaspoon salt
Freshly ground black pepper
1 large onion, peeled and chopped
2 cloves garlic, peeled and crushed
    (see p.11)
85 g (3 oz) mild curry paste
225 g (8 oz) long-grain white rice
425 ml (3/4 pint) chicken stock
    (see p.8)
400 g (14 oz) canned chopped
    tomatoes
340 g (12 oz) cauliflower florets
60 g (2 oz) raisins
115 g (4 oz) frozen peas
150 ml (1/4 pint) natural yoghurt

Per serving
Calories 667 Protein 42 g
Total fat 23 g (saturated fat 6.1 g)
Carbohydrates 78 g (added sugar 0)
Fibre 7 g Sodium 373 mg

Plump raisins and tender peas
add sweetness to this tasty
chicken and vegetable pilaff. It
is flavoured with curry paste,
which cuts back on cooking time
as all the spices are pre-fried.

1 Melt the butter or margarine in
a large flameproof casserole and
cook the chicken strips in it over
a moderate heat for 5 minutes, or
until they are no longer pink.
Move to a plate and season with
the salt and some pepper.

2 Fry the onion and garlic in
the casserole until softened.
Add the curry paste, rice, stock,
tomatoes, cauliflower florets
and raisins, then slowly bring to
the boil. Reduce the heat, cover
the casserole and simmer for
15 minutes, stirring occasionally.

3 Put the chicken back in the
casserole and stir in the peas.
Cover and bring back to the boil,
then reduce the heat and simmer
for 10 minutes, or until the rice is
cooked and the liquid has been
absorbed. Take the casserole off
the heat and stir in the yoghurt,
then serve.

*Cauliflower florets turn this simple pilaff into an eye-catching feast, enriched
with natural yoghurt and served with a selection of sweet fruit chutneys.*

100

CHICKEN LIVER RISOTTO

Peppercorns give a fiery edge to the chicken livers in this creamy risotto. Crush the peppercorns with a pestle and mortar, or put them in a strong polythene bag and use a heavy weight.

Serves 4
Preparation time: 20 minutes
Cooking time: 1 hour 25 minutes

2 tablespoons olive oil
225 g (8 oz) chicken livers, washed, dried, trimmed and chopped
1 large onion, peeled and chopped
2 large carrots, peeled and finely chopped
2 large sticks celery, trimmed and thinly sliced
225 g (8 oz) ripe tomatoes, skinned and chopped
400 g (14 oz) canned chopped tomatoes
225 g (8 oz) arborio (risotto rice)
850 ml (1½ pints) chicken stock (see p.8)
225 g (8 oz) cooked ham, trimmed of fat and diced
2 level teaspoons peppercorns, coarsely crushed
½ level teaspoon salt
1 level teaspoon dried thyme
175 g (6 oz) frozen peas
2 tablespoons chopped fresh parsley

Per serving
Calories 468 Protein 28 g
Total fat 14 g (saturated fat 3.4 g)
Carbohydrates 60 g (added sugar 0)
Fibre 6.6 g Sodium 1021 mg

1 Heat 1 tablespoon of the oil in a large frying pan or wok and lightly brown the chicken livers in it over a moderate heat for about 5 minutes. Put the chicken livers on a plate, cover and set aside.

2 Heat the remaining oil in the pan and fry the onion, carrots and celery in it for 10 minutes, stirring occasionally.

3 Stir in the fresh and canned tomatoes and bring to the boil. Reduce the heat and simmer, stirring frequently, for 15 minutes, or until the mixture is thick. Add the rice to the pan and cook, stirring, for 2 minutes.

4 Pour in a quarter of the stock and bring to the boil. Reduce the heat and simmer, stirring frequently, until all the stock has been absorbed. Repeat, adding a quarter of the stock at a time and making sure all the liquid has been absorbed before adding more. Stir the mixture from time to time to prevent it sticking.

5 When all the stock has been absorbed, mix in the chicken livers, ham, peppercorns, salt, thyme and peas and cook, stirring, for 5 minutes, or until the peas are tender. Sprinkle the parsley over the top and serve.

CHICKEN COBBLER

Light, buttery scones baked over chicken and vegetables in a cheesy sauce make a warming meal and a welcome change from potatoes or rice.

Serves 4
Preparation time: 20 minutes
Cooking time: 20 minutes

2 tablespoons olive oil
2 sticks celery, trimmed and finely diced (see p.10)
1 red pepper, de-seeded and finely diced
225 g (8 oz) courgettes, trimmed and finely diced
4 spring onions, trimmed and finely chopped
2 level tablespoons plain flour
285 ml (½ pint) skimmed milk
150 g (5 oz) mayonnaise
30 g (1 oz) Parmesan cheese, grated
Freshly ground black pepper
340 g (12 oz) cooked chicken or turkey, diced (see p.79)

For the scones
225 g (8 oz) self-raising flour
1 level teaspoon baking powder
¼ level teaspoon salt
15 g (½ oz) butter or margarine
150 ml (¼ pint) milk
Sprigs of fresh parsley to garnish

Per serving
Calories 794 Protein 40 g
Total fat 46 g (saturated fat 8.9 g)
Carbohydrates 59 g (added sugar 0)
Fibre 3.5 g Sodium 888 mg

1 Preheat the oven to 200°C (400°F, gas mark 6). Heat the oil in a large flameproof casserole for 1 minute and stir-fry the celery, red pepper, courgettes and spring onions in it over a moderate heat for about 3 minutes.

2 Mix in the plain flour and cook gently for 1 minute, then gradually pour in the skimmed milk. Cook, stirring, until the mixture has thickened.

3 Take the casserole off the heat and mix in the mayonnaise, two-thirds of the Parmesan and some pepper. Stir in the diced chicken and sprinkle with the remaining Parmesan.

4 Sift the self-raising flour, baking powder and salt into a bowl. Rub in the butter or margarine and mix in the milk to form a soft dough. Knead gently on a lightly floured surface for a few seconds, then roll out to a round 1.3 cm (½ in) thick. Cut into eight wedges and arrange them, evenly spaced, on top of the chicken mixture.

5 Bake for 20 minutes in the centre of the oven, or until the chicken mixture is bubbling, and the scones are well risen and golden brown. Garnish with the parsley and serve.

TURKEY BREASTS WITH ROAST GARLIC PURÉE

Serves 6
Preparation time: 45 minutes
Cooking time: 1 hour 30 minutes

- 1 whole bulb garlic, unpeeled
- 2 tablespoons olive oil
- 1 tablespoon lemon juice
- 30 g (1 oz) finely chopped fresh basil leaves
- 2 turkey breasts, each about 550 g (1¼ lb)
- 340 g (12 oz) fresh Italian or other spicy sausages, casings removed
- 225 g (8 oz) fresh spinach, trimmed, washed and torn into pieces
- 285 ml (½ pint) chicken stock (see p.8)
- 2-3 level teaspoons dried mixed herbs
- 450 g (1 lb) white bread, thickly sliced, toasted and cut into cubes
- ¼ level teaspoon salt
- 2 medium onions, peeled and quartered
- 225 g (8 oz) cherry tomatoes

Per serving
Calories 615 Protein 45 g
Total fat 28 g (saturated fat 10 g)
Carbohydrates 49 g (added sugar 0)
Fibre 5.6 g Sodium 1064 mg

Cherry tomatoes add a welcome juiciness to this meal of turkey, spicy sausage and spinach, and lightly toasted cubes of bread absorb its rich garlic flavour.

Tender breasts of turkey are flavoured with an unexpectedly mild garlic purée, which gives this dish a nutty flavour.

1 Preheat the oven to 200°C (400°F, gas mark 6). Wrap the garlic bulb in foil and bake in the oven for 30-40 minutes, or until the packet feels soft. (If you have a microwave, cook the bulb in just enough water to cover it on High for 2-2½ minutes, depending on the size of the bulb and the output of your microwave oven.) When the garlic is cool enough to handle, squeeze all the pulp out of the skin into a nylon sieve. Press the pulp through the sieve into a bowl, then whisk in 1 tablespoon of the oil, the lemon juice and the basil.

2 Carefully loosen the turkey skin from the flesh to make a large pocket by easing your fingertips under it. Fill the pockets with the garlic purée.

3 Heat a large nonstick frying pan and fry the sausages for about 5 minutes, or until they are no longer pink. Break the sausages into small pieces as they cook. Add the spinach, stock and mixed herbs and then cook, uncovered, for about 5 minutes, or until the spinach has just wilted. Pour the mixture into a large bowl, add the toasted bread cubes, and toss all the contents together.

4 Spread this mixture in the bottom of a large ovenproof dish, then lay the turkey breasts on top, skin-side up. Brush with the remaining oil and sprinkle with the salt. Scatter the onions around the turkey breasts, then cover the dish with foil. Cook in the centre of the oven for 40 minutes.

5 Remove the foil and cook for a further 30-40 minutes, or until the turkey is done (see p.117). Add the cherry tomatoes to the dish, cook for 5-10 minutes more and then serve immediately.

MEXICAN TURKEY PANCAKES

Serves 4
Preparation time: 1 hour
Cooking time: 30 minutes

For the sauce
2 tablespoons olive oil
1 small onion, peeled and
  finely chopped
1 small green chilli, de-seeded
  and finely chopped
1 level teaspoon mild chilli powder
1/2 level teaspoon dried oregano
1/2 level teaspoon ground cumin
800 g (1 3/4 lb) canned chopped
  tomatoes

For the pancakes
115 g (4 oz) plain flour
1 egg, size 3, lightly beaten
285 ml (1/2 pint) milk

For the filling
225 g (8 oz) cooked turkey, diced
225 g (8 oz) cooked red kidney
  beans, rinsed and drained
  (see p.172)

For the topping
115 g (4 oz) Cheddar cheese,
  grated
4 spring onions, trimmed and
  finely chopped

Per serving
Calories 502 Protein 35 g
Total fat 22 g (saturated fat 8.9 g)
Carbohydrates 45 g (added sugar 0)
Fibre 8.8 g Sodium 370 mg

**These hot and spicy turkey
pancakes are reminiscent of
Mexican enchiladas. They can
also be made with flour tortillas
in place of the pancakes and
with a filling of cooked chicken
instead of the turkey.**

1 Heat the oil in a saucepan and
cook the onion in it until
softened. Stir in the chilli, chilli
powder, oregano, cumin and
tomatoes. Bring to the boil, reduce
the heat, cover and simmer for
30 minutes, stirring occasionally.

2 Meanwhile, make eight
pancakes (see p.9) and preheat
the oven to 180°C (350°F, gas
mark 4). Pour one-third of the
tomato sauce into a bowl and mix
in the turkey and kidney beans.
Pour another third of the sauce
into a shallow ovenproof dish.

3 Spread a heaped tablespoon of
the turkey mixture over one
half of a pancake, then fold the
other half of the pancake over the
filling. Fold in half again to form
a triangle, then lay the pancake in
the dish on top of the sauce.
Repeat with the other pancakes,
overlapping them in the dish.

4 Spoon the remaining sauce
over the pancakes, then sprinkle
with the Cheddar and spring
onions. Bake in the centre of the
oven for 20-30 minutes, then serve
with a crisp lettuce salad.

TURKEY AND AUBERGINE PARMIGIANA

**Layers of minced turkey,
pasta and aubergine are
combined with two types of
Italian cheese – Parmesan and
mozzarella. Most supermarkets
and butchers' shops sell minced
turkey, or you can buy skinned,
boned turkey pieces and mince
them yourself (see p.80).**

Serves 4
Preparation time: 35 minutes
Cooking time: 1 hour 10 minutes

1 medium aubergine, trimmed
  and thinly sliced
1 level teaspoon salt
3 tablespoons olive oil
1 large onion, peeled and chopped
1 clove garlic, peeled and crushed
450 g (1 lb) minced turkey
400 g (14 oz) canned tomatoes
3 level tablespoons tomato purée
3/4 level teaspoon dried basil
1/2 level teaspoon dried oregano
Freshly ground black pepper
115 g (4 oz) small pasta shapes
60 g (2 oz) Parmesan cheese, grated
115 g (4 oz) mozzarella cheese,
  grated

Per serving
Calories 538 Protein 51 g
Total fat 25 g (saturated fat 9.4 g)
Carbohydrates 30 g (added sugar 0)
Fibre 4.1 g Sodium 668 mg

1 Sprinkle the aubergine slices
with the salt and then leave
them for 30 minutes to remove
the bitter juices. Meanwhile,
preheat the oven to 180°C (350°F,
gas mark 4).

2 Grease a large baking tray, then
lightly brush the aubergine
slices with two tablespoons of the
oil and arrange them, overlapping
slightly, on the tray. Bake in the
centre of the oven for 5 minutes.

3 Heat the remaining oil in a
large saucepan and cook the
onion and garlic in it until slightly
softened. Stir in the minced turkey
and cook for 10 minutes, or until
the meat is no longer pink.

4 Add the tomatoes, the tomato
purée, basil, oregano and some
pepper. Bring to the boil and cook
for 5 minutes, stirring occasionally
to break up the tomatoes.

5 Spoon one-third of the turkey
mixture into a large, ovenproof
dish. Cover this with one-third of
the pasta and then with one-third
of the aubergine slices. Sprinkle
with one-third of each cheese,
then repeat the layers, ending with
the mozzarella.

6 Cook in the centre of the oven,
uncovered, for 45 minutes,
or until the top is bubbling and
golden, then serve with a mixed
lettuce salad.

TURKEY TETRAZZINI

Serves 4
Preparation time: 35 minutes
Cooking time: 1 hour

30 g (1 oz) butter
1 large onion, peeled and chopped
1 large stick celery, trimmed and thinly sliced
225 g (8 oz) button mushrooms, wiped and thinly sliced
1 litre (1¾ pints) chicken stock (see p.8)
½ level teaspoon each dried thyme and marjoram
175 g (6 oz) fusilli
1 level tablespoon plain flour
285 ml (½ pint) single cream
1 level tablespoon whole-grain mustard
340 g (12 oz) fresh broccoli florets, or frozen broccoli florets, thawed
450 g (1 lb) turkey fillets, cut into strips
¼ level teaspoon salt
Freshly ground black pepper
30 g (1 oz) fresh white breadcrumbs
1 large tomato, sliced
Celery leaves to garnish

Per serving
Calories 544 Protein 39 g
Total fat 23 g (saturated fat 13 g)
Carbohydrates 47 g (added sugar 0)
Fibre 4.7 g Sodium 329 mg

Creamy, oven-baked chicken tetrazzini, a classic American dish created in San Francisco early this century, combines poultry with pasta. This version, made with turkey and broccoli, can be cooked in advance and takes 35-40 minutes to reheat.

1 Preheat the oven to 200°C (400°F, gas mark 6). Melt the butter in a large saucepan and cook the onion and the celery in it over a moderate heat for 5 minutes. Stir in the mushrooms and cook for a further 5 minutes.

2 Pour in the stock, add the thyme and marjoram, and simmer for 3 minutes. Bring to the boil, then stir in the pasta and simmer for 15 minutes.

3 Meanwhile, blend the flour with the cream and mustard until smooth, then stir into the pan. Bring to the boil, stirring.

4 Mix in the broccoli and turkey strips, the salt and some pepper, then simmer for 5 minutes, or until the broccoli is just tender.

5 Spoon the mixture into a large, greased ovenproof dish. Sprinkle with the breadcrumbs and arrange the tomato slices on top. Bake in the centre of the oven for 25-30 minutes, or until golden and crisp. Garnish with the celery leaves and serve.

TURKEY AND BEETROOT HASH

Serves 4
Preparation time: 40 minutes
Cooking time: 30 minutes

60 g (2 oz) unsalted butter or margarine
1 medium onion, peeled and finely chopped
340 g (12 oz) minced turkey
675 g (1½ lb) potatoes, peeled, parboiled for 10 minutes, cooled and grated
225 g (8 oz) cooked beetroot, peeled and diced (see p.10)
1 large courgette, trimmed, coarsely grated and squeezed dry
½ level teaspoon dried sage
½ level teaspoon dried rosemary
1 level teaspoon salt
Freshly ground black pepper
Sprigs of fresh dill to garnish

Per serving
Calories 361 Protein 23 g
Total fat 15 g (saturated fat 8.9 g)
Carbohydrates 37 g (added sugar 0)
Fibre 4 g Sodium 697 mg

You can serve this colourful dish as it is, or with the addition of poached eggs. If the hash breaks as you turn it, just press it back into shape and continue cooking.

1 Heat half the butter or margarine in a nonstick frying pan and cook the onion in it until softened. Add the turkey and cook over a high heat for 3-4 minutes.

2 Transfer the turkey and onion to a large bowl and mix in the grated potatoes, diced beetroot, grated courgette, sage, rosemary, salt and some pepper.

3 Melt the remaining butter or margarine in the pan, then add the turkey and vegetable mixture. Press down well and cook over a moderate heat for about 15 minutes, or until golden and crusty on the bottom.

4 Carefully turn the hash over (see p.284) and cook the other side for 15 minutes, or until the base is golden and crusty and the potatoes are done. Turn out onto a heated serving plate, garnish with the dill and serve with mustard or cranberry sauce.

CHICKEN WITH CORNBREAD CRUST

Serves 4
Preparation time: 45 minutes
Cooking time: 40 minutes

30 g (1 oz) plain flour
1/4 level teaspoon salt
Freshly ground black pepper
450 g (1 lb) boneless chicken
  breasts, skinned and cut
  into cubes
3 tablespoons olive oil
1 medium onion, peeled and
  finely chopped
2 cloves garlic, peeled and crushed
  (see p.11)
1 small carrot, peeled, halved
  lengthways and thinly sliced
400 g (14 oz) canned chopped
  tomatoes
2 medium sticks celery, trimmed
  and chopped
Finely grated rind of 1 orange
1 bay leaf
175 g (6 oz) fresh or frozen fine
  green beans, trimmed and cut into
  short lengths

For the cornbread crust
85 g (3 oz) cornmeal (maize meal)
30 g (1 oz) plain flour
1/2 level teaspoon each sugar
  and salt
1 1/2 level teaspoons baking
  powder
1/4 level teaspoon bicarbonate
  of soda
115 ml (4 fl oz) buttermilk or
  natural yoghurt
1 egg, size 3, lightly beaten
1 tablespoon corn oil
Sprigs of watercress to garnish

Carrot, celery and green beans contribute colour and flavour to this aromatic chicken dish.

1 Sift the flour onto a flat plate and mix in the salt and some pepper. Coat the chicken with the mixture, shaking off the excess. Heat the olive oil in a large flameproof casserole and brown the chicken in it for about 5 minutes. Put the chicken on a plate and set aside.

Per serving
Calories 463 Protein 34 g
Total fat 20 g (saturated fat 3.2 g)
Carbohydrates 38 g (added sugar 0)
Fibre 4.6 g Sodium 800 mg

2 Cook the onion, garlic and carrot in the casserole until softened, then stir in the tomatoes, celery, orange rind and bay leaf. Cook, stirring occasionally, for 5 minutes, or until the liquid is slightly reduced. Return the chicken to the casserole and stir in the fresh beans. Cover and cook for 20-25 minutes, or until the chicken and beans are cooked. (If you are using frozen beans, cook the chicken for 15 minutes before adding the beans.)

3 Meanwhile, preheat the oven to 200°C (400°F, gas mark 6), then make the cornbread crust. Combine the cornmeal, flour, sugar, salt, baking powder and bicarbonate of soda in a bowl. Lightly whisk the buttermilk or yoghurt with the egg and the corn oil and pour them into the cornmeal mixture. Gently blend together to form a slightly lumpy batter, taking care not to mix too much as this will make the crust too heavy.

4 Remove the bay leaf from the chicken. Spoon the crust mix over the chicken, leaving a 2.5 cm (1 in) border round the edge of the dish. Cook in the centre of the oven for 15 minutes, or until the cornbread is golden and springy to the touch. Garnish with the watercress, then serve.

A crisp cornbread crust makes a crunchy topping for tender chicken and vegetables that are subtly scented with orange.

TURKEY LOAF

Serves 6
Preparation time: 20 minutes
Cooking time: 1 hour 20 minutes

2 tablespoons olive oil
675 g (1½ lb) potatoes, peeled and
    thinly sliced
2 medium green peppers, de-seeded
    and thinly sliced
1 medium onion, peeled and
    thinly sliced
¾ level teaspoon salt
Freshly ground black pepper
1 egg, size 2
450 g (1 lb) minced turkey
85 g (3 oz) fine dry breadcrumbs
1 small onion, peeled and
    finely chopped
15 g (½ oz) fresh parsley,
    finely chopped
1 tablespoon Worcestershire sauce
2 medium courgettes, trimmed and
    thinly sliced
400 g (14 oz) canned tomatoes,
    sieved
Fresh basil leaves to garnish

Per serving
Calories 454 Protein 36 g
Total fat 12 g (saturated fat 1.6 g)
Carbohydrates 54 g (added sugar 0)
Fibre 6.8 g Sodium 701 mg

This flavourful, low-fat turkey
loaf is suitable for serving
both as a light supper or as part
of a buffet. For a richer loaf,
use minced pork, beef or veal
in place of the turkey.

1 Preheat the oven to 200°C
(400°F, gas mark 6). Mix the
oil, potatoes, green peppers and
sliced onion in a roasting dish, and
sprinkle with ¼ teaspoon of the
salt and some pepper. Bake in the
centre of the oven for 30 minutes.

2 Beat the egg lightly in a large
bowl, then mix in the minced
turkey, breadcrumbs, chopped
onion, parsley, Worcestershire
sauce, the remaining salt and some
pepper. Line a 20 cm x 13 cm
(8 in x 5 in) loaf tin with
non-toxic plastic film, and press
the turkey mixture firmly into it.

3 Reduce the oven temperature
to 180°C (350°F, gas mark 4).
Take the roasting dish out of the
oven and mix in the courgettes.
Push the vegetables to the sides of
the dish and turn the turkey loaf
out into the middle of it, removing
the plastic film. Pour the sieved
tomatoes over the vegetables.

4 Put in the oven and bake for
40-50 minutes, stirring the
vegetables occasionally, until the
turkey loaf is cooked through and
the vegetables are tender. Garnish
with the basil and serve.

BAKED POUSSINS WITH CHILLI RICE

Serves 4
Preparation time: 35 minutes
Cooking time: 1 hour

4 oven-ready poussins, each about
    400 g (14 oz)
1 tablespoon olive oil
¼ level teaspoon salt
Freshly ground black pepper
200 g (7 oz) frozen or canned
    sweetcorn kernels
200 g (7 oz) canned whole sweet
    red peppers, drained
    and chopped
85 g (3 oz) canned green jalapeño
    chillies, drained and chopped,
    or 2 fresh green chillies,
    de-seeded and chopped
115 g (4 oz) Cheddar cheese,
    grated
400 g (14 oz) cooked long-grain
    white rice (see p.9)
150 ml (¼ pint) soured cream
175 ml (6 fl oz) barbecue sauce
Thinly sliced rings of red pepper
    to garnish

Per serving
Calories 788 Protein 66 g
Total fat 35 g (saturated fat 15 g)
Carbohydrates 55 g (added sugar 0)
Fibre 4 g Sodium 893 mg

Poussins, an attractive choice
for entertaining, are often
prepared by a technique known
as spatchcocking – cutting in
half and laying flat. This makes
it much easier to grill the birds.

1 Preheat the grill to high.
Spatchcock the poussins
(see p.116), then lay them flat in
a large roasting tin, skin-side up.
Brush each one with the oil and
season with the salt and some
pepper. Grill for 5 minutes,
then turn them over and grill for
10 minutes. Turn them again and
grill for a further 5 minutes, or
until the skin is crisp and golden.

2 Meanwhile, preheat the oven
to 200°C (400°F, gas mark 6).
Mix together the sweetcorn,
chopped sweet red peppers,
jalapeño or fresh green chillies,
the Cheddar, rice and soured
cream. Spread the mixture over
the bottom of a large, ovenproof
dish, arrange the poussins on
top, and then spoon the barbecue
sauce over them.

3 Bake, uncovered, in the centre
of the oven for 40 minutes,
or until the poussins are cooked
(see p.117). Garnish with the red
pepper rings and serve with an
avocado and lettuce salad.

COUNTRY-STYLE POUSSINS

Serves 4
Preparation time: 25 minutes
Cooking time: 1 hour 15 minutes

2 tablespoons olive oil
30 g (1 oz) butter
4 oven-ready poussins, each about
    400 g (14 oz)
1 medium onion, peeled and
    finely chopped
2 sticks celery, trimmed
    and chopped
3 medium carrots, peeled
    and chopped
1 clove garlic, peeled and crushed
    (see p.11)
340 g (12 oz) button mushrooms,
    wiped and trimmed
850 ml (1½ pints) chicken stock
    (see p.8)
225 g (8 oz) bulgur wheat
½ level teaspoon salt
Freshly ground black pepper
1 tablespoon chopped fresh sage,
    or 1 teaspoon dried sage
175 g (6 oz) shallots, peeled
225 g (8 oz) drained bottled or
    canned artichoke hearts, cut
    into quarters
Fresh sage leaves to garnish

Per serving
Calories 598 Protein 48 g
Total fat 23 g (saturated fat 8 g)
Carbohydrates 52 g (added sugar 0)
Fibre 4.4 g Sodium 465 mg

A mellow, buttery casserole of poussins baked with bulgur wheat. You can use brown or white long-grain rice instead of the bulgur wheat, and cook the dish in the same way.

1 Heat the oil and butter in a large flameproof casserole, then lightly brown the poussins in it, two at a time, for 5-10 minutes. Take the poussins out of the casserole and set them aside on a plate.

2 Add the onion to the casserole and cook for 5 minutes. Mix in the celery, carrots, garlic and mushrooms and cook, stirring, for another 5 minutes.

3 Add the stock, bulgur wheat, salt, some pepper, the sage and shallots, and return the poussins to the casserole. Bring to the boil, then reduce the heat, cover and simmer for 30-35 minutes.

4 Arrange the artichoke hearts on top of the poussins and cook for a further 10 minutes, or until the poussins are cooked (see p.117) and all the liquid has been absorbed by the bulgur wheat. Garnish with the sage leaves and serve from the casserole.

In this unusual dinner-party dish, bulgur wheat absorbs the cooking juices of the poussins and vegetables and adds its own nutty flavour.

ROAST PHEASANTS WITH WILD RICE, CHESTNUT AND BLUEBERRY STUFFING

A burgundy coloured stuffing of soft fruit and chestnuts gives the pheasants a rich tartness in this festive meal. You will need small wooden or metal skewers.

Serves 4
Preparation time: 40 minutes
Cooking time: 1 hour 20 minutes

- 115 g (4 oz) fresh or frozen peeled chestnuts
- 30 g (1 oz) butter
- 1 medium onion, peeled and finely chopped
- 175 g (6 oz) blueberries or frozen blackcurrants
- 60 g (2 oz) caster sugar
- 175 g (6 oz) cooked wild rice (see p.9)
- 3 tablespoons chopped fresh parsley
- 1/2 level teaspoon salt
- Freshly ground black pepper
- 60 g (2 oz) chilled butter, cut into four slices
- 2 oven-ready pheasants, each 1 kg (2 lb 3 oz), rinsed and dried
- 30 g (1 oz) butter, softened

- 900 g (2 lb) potatoes, peeled and sliced
- 12 button onions, peeled
- 450 g (1 lb) small courgettes, trimmed and quartered lengthways
- 425 ml (3/4 pint) full-bodied red wine
- Celery leaves or small bunches of fresh herbs to garnish

Per serving
Calories 1140 Protein 86 g
Total fat 43 g (saturated fat 20 g)
Carbohydrates 91 g (added sugar 15 g)
Fibre 11 g Sodium 695 mg

1 Preheat the oven to 180°C (350°F, gas mark 4). Put the chestnuts in just enough boiling water to cover them and cook for 6-8 minutes, until tender but not broken up.

2 Meanwhile, melt 30 g (1 oz) butter in a frying pan and soften the chopped onion in it over a moderate heat. Stir in the blueberries or blackcurrants with the sugar, cook for 2-3 minutes, then take the pan off the heat. Drain and chop the chestnuts and add to the mixture, then stir in the rice, parsley, salt and some pepper.

3 Insert a slice of the chilled butter under the skin on both sides of the breast of each pheasant, then fill the cavities with the stuffing. Secure with the skewers, then spread the softened butter all over the pheasants.

4 Arrange both the pheasants diagonally in a large roasting tin, with their breasts to the centre, and cook in the oven for 20 minutes. In the meantime, put the potatoes in a saucepan and cover with water. Bring to the boil, then drain immediately.

5 Increase the oven temperature to 200°C (400°F, gas mark 6). Take the tin out of the oven and turn the pheasants onto their breasts. Baste with the juices in the tin, then arrange the potato slices and button onions around the pheasants and baste again.

Regular basting with butter gives the delicate pheasant skin a deep golden hue, while the courgettes, potato slices and button onions take on a crisp sweetness.

MARINATED POUSSINS WITH APRICOT STUFFING

6 Return the roasting tin to the oven and cook for 20 minutes. Turn the pheasants onto their backs, add the courgettes and baste the pheasants and the vegetables. Roast for a further 20 minutes, then increase the heat to 220°C (425°F, gas mark 7). Baste again and cook for a final 20 minutes, or until the birds are done (see p.117), and the vegetables are golden.

7 Lift the pheasants out of the tin and onto a heated serving platter. Remove the skewers, then spoon the vegetables around the pheasants. Cover and keep hot. Skim off any fat in the tin, taking care to retain the juices, then add the wine. Bring to the boil, stirring and scraping to loosen any browned pieces on the bottom of the tin, and boil rapidly for about 5 minutes, or until reduced by a third. Pour the sauce over the pheasants, or serve separately, then garnish and serve.

Poussins plump with a stuffing of rice, peas and apricots are basted with a glaze of honey and mustard and served with a garnish of fresh mint sprigs.

Serves 4
Preparation time: 30 minutes
Marinating time: 2-3 hours
Cooking time: 1 hour 5 minutes

3 tablespoons each soy sauce, rice wine or dry sherry and olive oil
2 tablespoons each cider vinegar and clear honey
2 level tablespoons Dijon mustard
2 cloves garlic, peeled and crushed (see p.11)
1 tablespoon peeled and grated root ginger
4 oven-ready poussins, each about 400 g (14 oz), rinsed and dried
30 g (1 oz) unsalted butter
1 small onion, peeled and finely chopped
1 stick celery, trimmed and finely chopped
175 g (6 oz) frozen peas

400 g (14 oz) cooked long-grain white rice (see p.9)
6 tablespoons chicken stock (see p.8)
115 g (4 oz) ready-to-use dried apricots, chopped
1/2 level teaspoon each dried thyme and dried sage
1/2 level teaspoon salt
Freshly ground black pepper
150 g (5 oz) apricot jam
Sprigs of fresh mint and parsley to garnish

Per serving
Calories 737 Protein 60 g
Total fat 20 g (saturated fat 8 g)
Carbohydrates 81 g (added sugar 10 g)
Fibre 9.1 g Sodium 486 mg

1 Mix the soy sauce, rice wine or sherry, oil, vinegar, honey, mustard, garlic and ginger in a large bowl, then add the poussins and coat with the mixture. Cover and leave in a cool place for 2-3 hours, or overnight.

2 Preheat the oven to 200°C (400°F, gas mark 6). Heat the butter in a frying pan and gently soften the onion and celery in it, stirring occasionally. Turn off the heat and mix in the peas, rice, stock, apricots, thyme, sage, salt and pepper, then set aside.

3 Drain the poussins, saving the marinade, and pat dry with kitchen paper. Fill the cavity of each one with stuffing, then tie the legs together. Place the poussins breast-side up in a large ovenproof dish.

4 Whisk together the marinade and the apricot jam, then pour over the poussins. Roast in the centre of the oven for 1 hour, basting frequently, until cooked (see p.117). Lift the poussins onto a serving dish and garnish with the mint and parsley. Serve with a crisp green salad and herb bread.

STIR-FRIED DUCK WITH CHINESE NOODLES

Serves 4
Preparation time: 40 minutes
Cooking time: 15 minutes

1 egg white, size 2, lightly beaten
3 tablespoons dry sherry
5 tablespoons vegetable oil
4 level teaspoons cornflour
1/4 level teaspoon salt
450 g (1 lb) boneless duck breasts,
   skinned and cut into thin strips
   (see p.116)
150 ml (1/4 pint) chicken stock
   (see p.8)
3 tablespoons soy sauce
6 spring onions, trimmed and thinly
   sliced diagonally
1 level tablespoon peeled and
   grated root ginger
2 cloves garlic, peeled and crushed
   (see p.11)
115 g (4 oz) button mushrooms,
   wiped and thinly sliced
3 medium carrots, peeled and cut
   into matchstick strips
225 g (8 oz) broccoli florets
1/8 level teaspoon crushed chillies
225 g (8 oz) fine Chinese
   egg noodles
2 tablespoons sesame oil
1 spring onion, trimmed,
   and fresh coriander
   leaves to garnish

Per serving
Calories 662 Protein 34 g
Total fat 36 g (saturated fat 1.7 g)
Carbohydrates 51 g (added sugar 0)
Fibre 4.6 g Sodium 1033 mg

In this colourful stir-fry, soaking the duck in a mixture of egg white and cornflour, a technique known as velveting, protects the delicate flavour and texture of the meat. If you prefer, you can use strips of turkey or chicken breast instead of duck, and asparagus in place of broccoli.

1 Mix together the egg white, 1 tablespoon each of the sherry and vegetable oil, 1 teaspoon of the cornflour and half the salt in a bowl. Add the duck strips, cover and leave to stand for 20 minutes, stirring occasionally.

2 Meanwhile, mix together the stock, soy sauce and the remaining sherry and cornflour in a small bowl and set aside.

3 Heat 3 tablespoons of the remaining vegetable oil in a wok or large frying pan and stir-fry the duck strips in it over a high heat for 3 minutes. Set aside on a plate.

4 Heat the remaining vegetable oil for 1 minute and stir-fry the spring onions, ginger and garlic in it for 30 seconds. Add the mushrooms, carrots, broccoli, crushed chillies and the rest of the salt, and stir-fry for 1 minute. Pour in the stock mixture and bring to the boil. Reduce the heat, cover and simmer for 2 minutes.

5 Meanwhile, cook the egg noodles (see p.202). Put the duck back in the wok or pan and heat through for 2 minutes, then stir in 1 tablespoon of the sesame oil.

6 Drain the noodles and toss with the remaining sesame oil. Arrange the noodles on a large, heated serving dish, and spoon the duck mixture on top. Garnish with the spring onion and coriander leaves and serve immediately with french bread.

Finely sliced spring onions and mushrooms, matchstick strips of carrot and dainty broccoli florets enhance this spicy duck stir-fry.

DUCK NORMANDY

Flambéing the duck pieces with Calvados, the apple liqueur made in Normandy, brings out the gamy flavour in this rich and creamy casserole. Use russets, Cox's or Golden Delicious for the apples in this recipe.

Serves 4
Preparation time: 40 minutes
Cooking time: 1 hour 40 minutes

1.8 kg (4 lb) oven-ready duck, cut into eight (see p.115)
85 ml (3 fl oz) Calvados or brandy
2 medium onions, peeled and chopped
3 cloves garlic, peeled and crushed (see p.11)
3 dessert apples, peeled, cored and sliced
115 ml (4 fl oz) chicken stock (see p.8), or water
550 g (1¼ lb) green cabbage, trimmed and coarsely shredded
1 level teaspoon caraway seeds
½ level teaspoon salt
175 ml (6 fl oz) dry white wine
4 tablespoons lemon juice
450 g (1 lb) small new potatoes, scrubbed
150 ml (¼ pint) single cream
Slices of lemon and apple, and sprigs of fresh thyme to garnish

Per serving
Calories 1177 Protein 29 g
Total fat 94 g (saturated fat 28 g)
Carbohydrates 38 g (added sugar 0)
Fibre 7.6 g Sodium 440 mg

1 Lay the duck pieces skin-side down in a large flameproof casserole, and gently brown over a moderate heat, turning them frequently, for about 15 minutes. Pour off all but 1 tablespoon of the fat from the casserole.

2 Pour the Calvados or brandy over the duck and heat for 30 seconds. Ignite the Calvados with a lighted match, and when the flames have died down, lift the duck onto a plate using a slotted spoon.

3 Soften the onions in the casserole for 5-7 minutes, then add the garlic and cook for 2 minutes. Stir in the apples and the stock or water, and bring to the boil. Reduce the heat and simmer for 15 minutes.

4 Meanwhile, preheat the oven to 190°C (375°F, gas mark 5). Stir the cabbage, caraway seeds, salt, wine, lemon juice, potatoes and duck pieces into the casserole. Cover and cook in the centre of the oven for 40 minutes.

5 Take the casserole out of the oven and stir in the cream. Cover and continue cooking for 20 minutes, or until the duck is tender and golden. Garnish with the slices of lemon and apple and the fresh thyme, and serve.

RABBIT IN MUSTARD SAUCE

A crisp, tangy topping of cheese and breadcrumbs seals in the flavours of rabbit and mustard in this casserole. You can buy jointed, boned and diced rabbit from butchers and supermarkets.

Serves 6
Preparation time: 20 minutes
Marinating time: 1 hour
Cooking time: 1 hour 40 minutes

2 tablespoons whole-grain mustard
1 clove garlic, peeled and crushed (see p.11)
285 ml (½ pint) dry white wine
675 g (1½ lb) diced rabbit meat
1 tablespoon olive oil
1 medium onion, peeled and chopped
3 medium sticks celery, trimmed and sliced
1 level teaspoon dried thyme
2 tablespoons chopped fresh parsley
285 ml (½ pint) chicken stock (see p.8)
½ level teaspoon salt
Freshly ground black pepper
175 g (6 oz) tagliatelle
1 level tablespoon cornflour
150 ml (¼ pint) single cream
30 g (1 oz) fresh white breadcrumbs
60 g (2 oz) Wensleydale or Cheshire cheese, crumbled

Per serving
Calories 413 Protein 32 g
Total fat 15 g (saturated fat 7.2 g)
Carbohydrates 31 g (added sugar 0)
Fibre 1.4 g Sodium 355 mg

1 Mix the mustard with the garlic and wine, then coat the diced rabbit in the mixture. Cover and leave to marinate for 1 hour.

2 Heat the oil in a shallow flameproof casserole and soften the onion and celery in it for 5 minutes.

3 Drain the rabbit, saving the marinade, and stir it into the casserole. Cook for 5 minutes over a moderate heat.

4 Stir in the thyme, half the parsley, the stock, the saved marinade, the salt and some pepper. Cover and simmer gently for 1-1½ hours, or until the rabbit is very tender.

5 Cook the tagliatelle (see p.202) and drain. Blend the cornflour with the cream and stir it into the rabbit. Bring to the boil, stirring, until the sauce thickens slightly, then stir in the cooked tagliatelle.

6 Mix the breadcrumbs with the cheese and the remaining parsley, then sprinkle the mixture over the rabbit and tagliatelle. Brown the dish under a hot grill for about 3 minutes, then serve.

HARE WITH CHESTNUTS AND TAGLIATELLE

Serves 4
Preparation time: 30 minutes
Marinating time: 3 hours
Cooking time: 1 hour 30 minutes

2 tablespoons olive oil
4 tablespoons brandy
10 shallots or button onions, peeled and quartered
900 g (2 lb) hare or rabbit legs, boned and diced
2 rashers streaky bacon, rind removed, cut into small squares
1 level tablespoon plain flour
285 ml (1/2 pint) red wine
2 bay leaves

1 clove garlic, peeled and crushed (see p.11)
Sprig each fresh parsley and thyme
1/4 level teaspoon salt
Freshly ground black pepper
225 g (8 oz) frozen peeled chestnuts
2 short strips orange rind
340 g (12 oz) egg or spinach tagliatelle
60 g (2 oz) Parmesan cheese, finely grated
Chopped fresh parsley to garnish

A brandy and shallot marinade deepens the flavour of the hare in this red wine casserole. Hare is available from good butchers between August and February. They will skin and prepare it for you if asked.

1 Mix 1 tablespoon of oil with the brandy and two of the shallots or button onions in a large bowl. Stir in the hare or rabbit, cover and marinate in the fridge for 3 hours or overnight. Preheat the oven to 160°C (325°F, gas mark 3). Drain and save the marinade, then pat the meat dry with kitchen paper.

2 Heat the remaining oil in a flameproof casserole and fry the bacon and the remaining shallots or onions in it for 3 minutes. Add the hare or rabbit and brown all over for 5 minutes. Add the flour and cook, stirring, for 2 minutes, then add the wine, bay leaves, garlic, parsley, thyme, salt, some pepper and the saved marinade. Bring to the boil, stirring.

3 Remove the casserole from the heat, cover and cook in the centre of the oven for 1 hour, then stir in the frozen chestnuts and the strips of orange rind. Cook for a further 30 minutes, or until the hare and chestnuts are tender.

4 Meanwhile, cook the tagliatelle (see p.202) and drain well. Arrange the pasta on a large heated serving dish and sprinkle with the Parmesan. Remove the bay leaves from the casserole, then spoon the hare or rabbit on top. Garnish with the parsley and serve.

Per serving
Calories 876 Protein 52 g
Total fat 28 g (saturated fat 10 g)
Carbohydrates 89 g (added sugar 0)
Fibre 8.8 g Sodium 535 mg

Chestnuts intensify the gamy flavour of this casserole, while tagliatelle makes a light accompaniment to its rich gravy.

POT-ROAST PIGEON WITH SPLIT PEAS

Small woodpigeons make perfect individual servings in this traditionally English casserole, with bacon, mushrooms, onions and brandy flavouring the thick split-pea sauce. Oven-ready pigeons are available all year round, fresh or frozen, from butchers and supermarkets.

Serves 4
Preparation time: 25 minutes
Cooking time: 1 hour

....

225 g (8 oz) dried green split peas, rinsed and drained
60 g (2 oz) butter
2 tablespoons olive oil
4 oven-ready pigeons, each about 225 g (8 oz)
100 g (3½ oz) streaky bacon, rinds removed, cut into small squares
150 g (5 oz) button onions, peeled
2 sticks celery, trimmed and sliced
115 g (4 oz) mushrooms, wiped and sliced
1 tablespoon brandy
150 ml (¼ pint) dry white wine
285 ml (½ pint) chicken stock (see p.8)
1 tablespoon chopped fresh dill or 1 level teaspoon dried dill
Freshly ground black pepper
Sprigs of fresh dill to garnish

....

1 Preheat the oven to 180°C (350°F, gas mark 4). Put the split peas in a saucepan, cover with water and bring to the boil. Boil for 10 minutes, then drain.

2 Meanwhile, heat the butter and oil in a large flameproof casserole and brown the pigeons, breast-side down, for 5-6 minutes. Take them out of the pan and set aside on a plate.

3 Add the bacon, onions, celery and mushrooms to the casserole and cook for 5 minutes. Stir in the split peas, brandy, wine, stock and dill and bring to the boil. Put the pigeons back in the casserole and push them under the vegetables. Pour in any juices from the plate.

4 Take the casserole off the heat, cover and place in the centre of the oven. Cook for 1 hour, or until the pigeons and peas are very tender. Lift the pigeons out of the casserole with a large fork and put them on a board. Separate the bony back from the rest of each bird with a sharp knife and discard the backs. Return the pigeons to the casserole and reheat for 5 minutes. Garnish with the dill and serve with light rye bread.

....

Per serving
Calories 776 Protein 46 g
Total fat 44 g (saturated fat 13 g)
Carbohydrates 45 g (added sugar 0)
Fibre 9.2 g Sodium 629 mg

....

VENISON CASSEROLE WITH SAUERKRAUT

Marinating and then casseroling brings out the best in venison, which tends to be tougher than most meats. The sauerkraut sharpens the flavour of the dish and gives it a crunchy texture.

Serves 4
Preparation time: 30 minutes
Marinating time: 3 hours
Cooking time: 1 hour 35 minutes

....

2 tablespoons olive oil
450 ml (16 fl oz) strong beer or lager
1 clove garlic, peeled and crushed (see p.11)
8 allspice berries
800 g (1¾ lb) shoulder of venison, trimmed of fat and diced (see p.79)
60 g (2 oz) bacon rashers, rinds removed, chopped
225 g (8 oz) onions, peeled and sliced
1 large carrot, peeled and diced
1 level tablespoon plain flour
¼ level teaspoon salt
Freshly ground black pepper
450 g (1 lb) potatoes, peeled and diced (see p.10)
150 g (5 oz) bratwurst sausages, sliced
225 g (8 oz) sauerkraut, rinsed and drained

....

1 Mix 1 tablespoon of the oil with 4 tablespoons of the beer, the garlic and the allspice berries in a large bowl. Stir in the diced venison, cover and marinate in the fridge for 3 hours or overnight.

2 Preheat the oven to 160°C (325°F, gas mark 3). Drain and save the marinade from the meat, then pat the venison dry with kitchen paper.

3 Heat the remaining oil in a large flameproof casserole and brown the venison and bacon in it for 5 minutes. Stir in the onions and carrot and fry for 3 minutes, then stir in the flour. Pour in the rest of the beer and the saved marinade, then season with the salt and some pepper. Bring to the boil, stirring.

4 Take the casserole off the heat, cover and place in the centre of the oven. Cook for 1 hour, then stir in the potatoes and bratwurst sausages. Cook for 30 minutes more, or until the meat is done and the potatoes are cooked. Spread the sauerkraut over the top of the meat and vegetables, cover and heat through in the oven for 5 minutes, and then serve.

....

Per serving
Calories 742 Protein 71 g
Total fat 33 g (saturated fat 7.3 g)
Carbohydrates 35 g (added sugar 0)
Fibre 3.4 g Sodium 1151 mg

....

Making the most of poultry and game

Poultry, in the form of chicken, turkey and duck, has long been a staple of our diet, and though game was once hard to obtain it is now more readily available. No matter what bird or animal you choose, its versatility presents opportunities for creative one-dish meals.

CHICKEN AND TURKEY meat is lean, tender, and low in fat, which is why these two birds make popular replacements for red meat in the diet. Sunday roasts and festive occasions rely on these versatile birds because they pair well with just about any combination of vegetables, pulses and grains. Game is increasingly available today and the casseroles, stews and pot roasts in this chapter do justice to its rich, robust flavour.

Buying poultry and game

Poultry can be bought fresh, frozen or chilled from supermarkets or butchers. Chicken, poussin, turkey and duck can be bought whole, or (with the exception of poussin) in ready-prepared portions, in strips, cubes or slices of boneless meat, or minced.

Free-range chickens and turkeys are invariably better tasting than mass-produced poultry, although poussins (smaller chickens under 450 g / 1 lb in weight) and some corn-fed chickens often have a good flavour.

Boiling chickens are harder to find, but will give the best depth of flavour to a chicken stock. The flesh is tougher than that of a younger bird and needs long, slow cooking, but retains its flavour. A local butcher might buy in a boiling chicken for you, if asked. Halal butchers always have a supply of fresh boiling fowl, and will clean, chop and skin the birds for you.

All poultry sold in supermarkets is prepacked, generally on polystyrene trays which are wrapped in plastic film, or in controlled atmosphere packs, which are rigid, clear plastic containers with a sealed top. These should not be opened until just before the poultry is cooked, as they are designed to keep the poultry at their freshest.

Unwrapped poultry generally has a better flavour than prepacked joints, and is often fresher. Although many local butchers do sell some of their poultry prepacked, most will also stock a good supply of fresh roasting chickens and chicken portions.

Game can be bought either fresh when it is available (see chart, below), or frozen at other times of the year from butchers and larger supermarkets. Most wild game is hung by the butcher to bring out the flavour, then dressed, ready for cooking.

When game is available

Rabbits and pigeons are available all year. Other game can be shot at fixed seasons, listed below for England and Wales; dates vary in Scotland. Game is available up to ten days after the season's end.

Deer, male (red, fallow, sika)	Aug 1 – Apr 30
Deer, male (roe)	Apr 1 – Oct 31
Deer, female (all species)	Nov 1 – Feb 28
Grouse (red)	Aug 12 – Dec 10
Hare	Aug 1 – Feb 28
Mallard, teal	Sept 1 – Jan 31; (shore Feb 20)
Partridge	Sept 1 – Feb 1
Pheasant	Oct 1 – Feb 1
Snipe	Aug 12 – Jan 31
Woodcock	Oct 1 – Jan 31

When buying frozen game or poultry, check that the wrapping and the meat inside is not damaged in any way, and avoid packaging that is limp, or contains ice crystals with a pink tinge. This is a sign that the game may have already been thawed and then refrozen, which can lead to the growth of bacteria.

Keeping poultry and game fresh

Fresh poultry must be unwrapped and refrigerated, and frozen poultry should be put in the freezer, as soon after purchase as possible. Fresh poultry can be kept for up to two days in a refrigerator, unless the 'use by' date gives a longer period.

All poultry and game should be taken out of its wrapping, where applicable, rinsed under cold running water and dried with kitchen paper. It should then be transferred to a clean plate and covered with foil or a bowl. This allows the air to circulate, but prevents the bird from drying out. Giblets inside turkeys or ducks should be removed and stored separately. Uncooked poultry should always be stored at the bottom of the fridge, away from cooked meats, pies, raw foods and dairy products.

Prewrapped poultry can give off a fairly strong smell, although this should soon disappear after unwrapping. If the smell lingers, return the bird to the butcher or supermarket.

To freeze poultry, make sure it is fresh and has not been frozen before. Freeze it rapidly on the same day you buy it – set the freezer to fast freeze or its lowest temperature a couple of hours beforehand. Cut very large birds into portions, or take the meat off the bone to help it freeze faster.

Thaw poultry and game overnight in the refrigerator, or in a cool place, following any instructions on the wrapping. Open the wrapping slightly to allow the air in to circulate, and cook the poultry as soon as it has thawed.

Preparing poultry and game for cooking

All poultry and game should be thoroughly washed under cold water before cooking. It is especially important to rinse out the cavity area of a bird, checking that it is really clean, especially if you intend to stuff the bird. Pull out any remaining feather tips, and singe off any fine hairs with a lighted match.

Poultry skin should not be eaten by those on a reduced-fat diet and is best removed before casseroling or stir-frying. When roasting chickens or turkeys, leave the skin on to keep the flesh moist, then remove it before eating.

Ducks and geese have a thicker layer of fat just under the skin than chickens and turkeys. Prick the skin thoroughly with a fork or sharp knife before roasting, to let the fat run out. Roast ducks and geese on a wire tray over a roasting tin to catch the dripping fat.

As game is very lean, especially wild game, it needs to be kept moist during cooking. This can be done by barding – pulling strips of pork fat through the flesh with a needle – or by covering the piece of game with thin sheets of pork back fat or bacon.

Marinating brings out the full flavour of poultry and game (see p.81). Remove the skin first so that the marinade can penetrate the flesh. Wine marinades work particularly well with older game birds and boiling chicken, as acid liquids help to tenderise tough flesh.

Jointing a whole bird yourself is a good deal cheaper than buying individual joints, such as leg and thighs, wings, drumsticks and breasts. A variety of white and dark meat from different cuts gives stews and casseroles a richer flavour, and you can use the trimmings to make a stock (see p.8).

You will need a sturdy knife and a strong chopping board to joint a bird. To get the knife through the bone, protect the back of the blade with a cloth and hit it firmly with a kitchen weight or old rolling pin.

Jointing a chicken

1 Cut off the wing tips at the last joint, then lay the chicken on its back on a chopping board. Pull one of the legs away from the body, then use a sharp knife to cut through the skin and flesh to the ball and socket joint. Twist the thigh free and cut right through the flesh to separate the leg from the body. Repeat with the other leg.

2 Hold the chicken firmly upright with the neck end on the board. Use a large, sharp knife to cut halfway down through the ribs to separate the breast and wings from the lower carcass. Pull the breast and lower carcass apart, then cut through the skin at the neck.

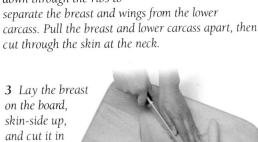

3 Lay the breast on the board, skin-side up, and cut it in half with the knife.

4 Cut each breast in half again, slicing through the flesh just behind the wing. If you prefer, leave the double breast as it is for roasting.

5 Separate the drumstick from the thigh by spreading out each leg and cutting it in half where the thigh bone joins the leg bone.

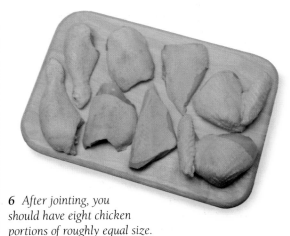

6 After jointing, you should have eight chicken portions of roughly equal size.

Removing the skin is recommended if you want to reduce the fat content. Once a chicken is jointed, it is simple to pull off the skin. You can also skin ready-cut pieces, which is more economical than buying them ready skinned.

Skinning a leg and thigh

1 Starting at the thigh end of the joint, grip the skin firmly and with a good tug, pull it down to the end of the leg.

2 To prevent the leg and thigh expanding apart during cooking, make a small nick in the leg joint between the leg and thigh on the outer edge of the portion.

Boning and cutting flesh into strips yourself is more economical than buying the ready-prepared equivalent. It is a simple operation to take the breast off the bone. All you need are sharp knives and a strong chopping board.

Once you have taken the meat off the bone, it can be minced (see p.80), or cut into strips for stir-frying. If you are preparing turkey breasts or large chicken breasts, cut them in half horizontally before slicing into strips.

To make cutting easier, chill the breasts in the freezer for about 30 minutes, until they are firm but not frozen. This also works for slicing pork loin for stir-fries.

Boning a chicken breast

1 Use a small, sharp knife to cut off the wing tip at the last joint. Pull off the skin over the piece of wing still attached.

2 Insert the knife at the thickest edge of the skinned breast, between the flesh and the bone. Keep the blade very close to the bone and cut the flesh away with small, clean cuts.

Cutting a breast into stir-fry strips

Using a large, sharp knife, cut a boned and skinned chicken breast diagonally across the grain into thin strips. If the breast is very thick, slice it in half horizontally first.

Spatchcocking a poussin

Spatchcocking – opening up and flattening a poussin or small game bird – is a useful technique which is particularly suitable for marinating and barbecuing.

1 Rinse and dry the poussin, then cut off the wing tips with a sharp knife or pair of kitchen scissors. Cut along one side of the backbone.

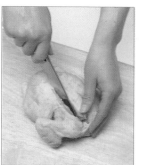

2 Turn the poussin over and cut along the other side of the backbone. Lay the bird breast side up on the board and with the heel of your hand push down firmly on the breast to break the breastbone and flatten the bird.

3 Thread two long metal skewers diagonally through the bird to hold the wings and legs flat.

Stuffing a bird is a simple and popular way of turning roasted or pot-roasted poultry into a more substantial meal. You can fill the cavity or the neck area with a stuffing, or stuff under the skin. Once the bird is stuffed, it should be trussed (see illustration, right) to keep the stuffing in place during cooking.

Breadcrumb, rice or bulgur wheat stuffings mixed with herbs, onion, nuts or other ingredients all work well with poultry. They must always be left to cool completely before being stuffed inside the bird.

Stuffing the neck end

1 Rinse and dry the bird, then fill the neck area with the cold stuffing. Leave a little room for expansion during cooking.

2 Smooth the neck skin over the stuffing to enclose it completely, tucking the flap of skin underneath. Pat the stuffing into shape, then tuck the wing tips underneath the bird to secure the skin. Secure the neck flap of large birds with a fine skewer.

Stuffing under the skin

1 Loosen the skin from the breast by gently inserting the fingertips under the skin at the neck. Push up to the tip of the breastbone on one side, taking care not to split the skin. Repeat on the other side.

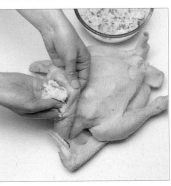

2 Insert the stuffing under the skin in an even layer over the whole breast. When all the stuffing has been used, smooth the outside of the breast into shape. Tuck the neck flap underneath the bird and secure with a fine skewer.

Trussing a chicken

Tuck the legs into the sides of the breast, then tie the drumsticks together with clean, thin string, looping it around the parson's nose, then around the end of the drumsticks.

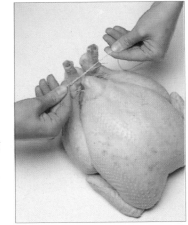

How to check that chicken is cooked

Poultry must be thoroughly cooked to ensure that all bacteria, particularly salmonella and campylobacteria, are destroyed to avoid the risk of food poisoning. Game is not affected in the same way, and is best served very slightly underdone so that the meat is not dry. Quail, however, must be thoroughly cooked.

When stir-frying strips of chicken or other poultry, the colour of the meat changes from pink to white. Strips should be cooked for at least 2-5 minutes, depending on their thickness, before being eaten. Chicken breasts should be cooked for at least 20 minutes, although cooking times vary according to the weight of the meat.

To check that a roasted chicken is cooked, insert a clean skewer into the thickest part of the thigh and watch the juices run. If they are clear in colour, the chicken is ready to eat. If they are slightly pink, it needs further cooking. Leave a roasted bird to stand for 15-20 minutes before carving. This gives the flesh time to re-absorb the juices and firm up, making it easier to carve.

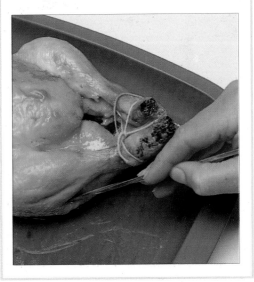

117

FISH AND SHELLFISH

Tender fish steaks, steaming bowls of shellfish, fragrant risottos and nourishing fish pies combine the healthiest of ingredients in the simplest of ways. These recipes offer mouth-watering ideas for cooking an enticing range of seafood, from the homely, such as cod and mackerel, to the more exotic lobster, swordfish and dried salt fish.

❖

Making the most of fish and shellfish 144-7

Portuguese Fish Stew (left) captures all the tasty goodness of halibut, red snapper, baby squid and mussels (see p.121).

MEDITERRANEAN CASSEROLE

Serves 4
Preparation time: 30 minutes
Cooking time: 35 minutes

4 tablespoons olive oil
1 large onion, peeled and sliced
275 g (10 oz) canned baby clams
400 g (14 oz) canned
  chopped tomatoes
285 ml (½ pint) dry white wine
425 ml (¾ pint) fish stock (see p.8)
2 cloves garlic, peeled and chopped
1 bay leaf
1 level teaspoon chopped
  fresh thyme
Finely grated rind of
  ½ small orange
⅛ level teaspoon cayenne pepper
Freshly ground black pepper
1 level teaspoon salt

450 g (1 lb) white fish fillets,
  skinned, boned and cut into cubes
12 fresh mussels, scrubbed and
  de-bearded (see p.147)
2 medium courgettes, trimmed
  and thinly sliced
225 g (8 oz) frozen cooked and
  peeled prawns
1 tablespoon shredded fresh basil
2 tablespoons chopped
  fresh parsley
8 slices french bread, toasted
1 clove garlic, peeled and crushed
  (see p.11)

Per serving
Calories 552 Protein 49 g
Total fat 17 g (saturated fat 2.1 g)
Carbohydrates 44 g (added sugar 0)
Fibre 4 g Sodium 2283 mg

*Crusty french bread brushed with garlic oil
sops up the delicate broth surrounding
mussels, prawns, baby clams,
white fish and courgettes
in this substantial
seafood stew.*

This rich, aromatic dish is based
on bouillabaisse, a classic fish
stew that comes from the area
around Marseilles, in the south of
France. You can use any type of
fish and shellfish, but make sure
there is at least 900 g (2 lb) in all.

1 Heat 2 tablespoons of the oil
in a large, heavy saucepan and
fry the onion in it until softened.
Drain the clams and add the liquid
to the pan with the tomatoes,
wine, stock, chopped garlic, bay
leaf, thyme, orange rind, cayenne,
some black pepper and the salt.
Bring to the boil, reduce the heat,
cover and simmer for 15 minutes.

2 Add the fish, mussels and
courgettes, cover and cook for
8-10 minutes, until the fish is
just opaque and the mussels have
opened. Discard any unopened
mussels and the bay leaf, then
gently stir in the clams, prawns
and basil and heat for 3-4 minutes.
Sprinkle on the parsley.

3 Mix the remaining oil with the
crushed garlic and brush it
over the toasted bread. Divide the
stew between four individual soup
bowls, add two slices of the toasted
bread to each one and serve.

SOUTH CAROLINA FISH RISOTTO

Serves 4
Preparation time: 25 minutes
Cooking time: 45 minutes

1 tablespoon olive oil
115 g (4 oz) unsmoked lean back
   bacon, fat removed, chopped
3 medium sticks celery, trimmed
   and chopped
1 medium green pepper, de-seeded
   and chopped
1 large onion, peeled and chopped
175 g (6 oz) long-grain white rice
400 g (14 oz) canned
   chopped tomatoes
425 ml (3/4 pint) fish or vegetable
   stock (see pp.8-9)
2 tablespoons distilled white vinegar
2 tablespoons balsamic vinegar
1/2 level teaspoon ground cinnamon
1/8 level teaspoon ground cloves
1/4 level teaspoon salt
1/2 teaspoon hot red pepper sauce
675 g (1 1/2 lb) trout fillets, skinned
   and cut into small pieces
Sprigs of fresh parsley to garnish

Lean bacon combines with trout, celery and rice in a hearty dish that is a traditional favourite in the southern United States.

1 Heat the oil in a large shallow flameproof casserole and fry the bacon in it until just crisp. Add the celery, pepper and onion, and sauté until softened.

2 Stir in the rice, tomatoes and stock and bring to the boil. Add the white and balsamic vinegars, cinnamon, cloves, salt and hot pepper sauce. Reduce the heat, cover and simmer for about 15 minutes, stirring occasionally, until the rice is almost cooked.

3 Gently mix in the fish, cover and simmer for 8-10 minutes until the fish flakes easily, and the rice is cooked. Garnish with the parsley sprigs and serve.

Per serving
Calories 489 Protein 50 g
Total fat 14 g (saturated fat 1.5 g)
Carbohydrates 44 g (added sugar 0)
Fibre 3.2 g Sodium 870 mg

PORTUGUESE FISH STEW

Serves 4
Preparation time: 1 hour
Cooking time: 20 minutes

1 medium onion, peeled and
   finely chopped
2 small peppers, 1 red, 1 green,
   de-seeded and finely chopped
340 g (12 oz) ripe tomatoes,
   skinned, de-seeded and chopped
60 g (2 oz) sun-dried tomatoes in
   oil, drained and finely chopped
3 cloves garlic, peeled and crushed
   (see p.11)
1/2 level teaspoon salt
Freshly ground black pepper
6 tablespoons extra virgin olive oil
675 g (1 1/2 lb) halibut steaks,
   skinned, boned and cut into
   large cubes
1 red snapper, about 675 g
   (1 1/2 lb), filleted, skinned and cut
   into large cubes
450 g (1 lb) frozen prepared baby
   squid, thawed, rinsed and
   drained, pouches cut into
   quarters lengthways
225 g (8 oz) frozen cooked mussels
285 ml (1/2 pint) dry white wine
4 tablespoons chopped
   fresh parsley
4 thick slices seeded Spanish pan
   gallego bread, or other close-
   textured bread, cut in half

Generous helpings of halibut and red snapper cooked with mussels, squid, tomatoes and tangy garlic make a full-bodied stew. Fragrant slices of oil-fried bread give an authentic flavour of Portuguese cooking.

1 Combine the onion, peppers, chopped tomatoes, sun-dried tomatoes, garlic, salt and a good amount of pepper in a bowl.

2 Pour 2 tablespoons of the oil into a large flameproof casserole, then spread half the onion mixture evenly over the bottom of it. Arrange the halibut, red snapper, squid and mussels on top, then place the rest of the onion mixture on top of the fish. Add the wine and bring to the boil.

3 Reduce the heat, cover and simmer for 20 minutes, until the fish is just tender, taking care not to allow it to become dry. Sprinkle the parsley over the stew.

4 While the stew is cooking, fry the bread in the remaining olive oil and drain on kitchen paper. Put two pieces of the fried bread into each soup bowl, ladle the stew on top and serve immediately.

Per serving
Calories 839 Protein 92 g
Total fat 35 g (saturated fat 4.2 g)
Carbohydrates 29 g (added sugar 0)
Fibre 3.9 g Sodium 927 mg

PRAWN CLAFOUTI

Fruit baked in batter is a speciality of France's Limousin region, where it is known as *clafouti*. In this savoury version of the dish, succulent prawns are used in place of fruit.

Serves 4
Preparation time: 15 minutes
Standing time: 30 minutes
Cooking time: 35 minutes

For the batter
115 g (4 oz) plain flour
3 eggs, size 3
150 ml (¼ pint) milk
¼ level teaspoon salt
Freshly ground black pepper
⅛ level teaspoon ground nutmeg

30 g (1 oz) butter
340 g (12 oz) large fresh uncooked prawns, peeled and de-veined
1 clove garlic, peeled and crushed (see p.11)
2 tablespoons chopped fresh parsley
225 g (8 oz) canned sweetcorn kernels
115 g (4 oz) bunch watercress, stalks removed, washed
Sprigs of watercress to garnish

Per serving
Calories 347 Protein 19 g
Total fat 14 g (saturated fat 6.1 g)
Carbohydrates 39 g (added sugar 0)
Fibre 4.1 g Sodium 951 mg

1 Preheat the oven to 220°C (425°F, gas mark 7). Put the flour in a bowl and make a well in the centre. In a separate bowl, lightly whisk the eggs and then add the milk, salt, some pepper and the nutmeg. Gradually pour the mixture into the centre of the flour, whisking continuously to make a smooth batter. Cover and leave to stand for 30 minutes.

2 Heat the butter in a frying pan until bubbling, then sauté the prawns in it for 3 minutes, stirring occasionally. Add the garlic and parsley and cook for 2 minutes, or until the prawns turn pink.

3 Cover the bottom of a lightly oiled, shallow, ovenproof dish with the sweetcorn and watercress. Arrange the prawns over the vegetables.

4 Stir the batter and pour it over the prawns. Bake in the oven for about 35 minutes, or until the batter is risen, browned and set in the centre. Garnish with the watercress sprigs and serve with a mixed lettuce salad.

SALMON IN FILO PASTRY

Frozen filo pastry and canned salmon are transformed into an impressive pie, which can also be made with canned tuna and puff or shortcrust pastry.

Serves 4
Preparation time: 35 minutes
Cooking time: 50 minutes

85 g (3 oz) unsalted butter
1 medium onion, peeled and finely chopped
1 small green pepper, de-seeded and finely chopped
2 medium sticks celery, trimmed and finely chopped
3 level tablespoons plain flour
1-2 level tablespoons chopped fresh dill
½ level teaspoon salt
Freshly ground black pepper
425 g (15 oz) canned red or pink salmon, drained, liquid made up to 200 ml (7 fl oz) with fish or vegetable stock (see p.9)
150 ml (¼ pint) milk
1 tablespoon lemon juice
225 g (8 oz) fine asparagus spears, trimmed and cut into short lengths
6 sheets frozen filo pastry, each 34 cm x 19 cm (13½ in x 7½ in), thawed and brushed with 60 g (2 oz) melted butter
Sprigs of dill to garnish

Per serving
Calories 668 Protein 31 g
Total fat 40 g (saturated fat 22 g)
Carbohydrates 49 g (added sugar 0)
Fibre 4.3 g Sodium 1156 mg

1 Melt 30 g (1 oz) of the butter in a saucepan and soften the onion, green pepper and celery in it over a moderate heat. Stir in the flour and cook for 1 minute, then add the dill, salt and some pepper. Gradually stir in the salmon liquid and the milk and bring to the boil, stirring. Reduce the heat and simmer for 3 minutes, or until the mixture is thick. Remove from the heat, cover the surface of the sauce with wet greaseproof paper and set aside for 20 minutes to cool.

2 Preheat the oven to 200°C (400°F, gas mark 6). Stir the lemon juice into the sauce, then remove the skin and bones from the salmon and flake the flesh. Stir the fish into the sauce and pour into a shallow 25 cm x 20 cm (10 in x 8 in) ovenproof dish. Lay the asparagus on top.

3 Arrange two sheets of the pastry, overlapping, on top of the asparagus. Crumple the pastry slightly so that it fits the dish. Repeat with the remaining sheets.

4 Bake in the oven for 20 minutes, then reduce the temperature to 180°C (350°F, gas mark 4). Cook for 10-15 minutes, until the pastry is golden brown and the filling is heated through (cover the top with foil if the pastry browns too fast). Garnish with the dill and serve with a green salad and olive bread.

FISH AND POTATO PIE

Serves 4
Preparation time: 20 minutes
Cooking time: 1 hour 25 minutes

550 g (1¼ lb) potatoes, peeled
   and quartered
30 g (1 oz) butter
1 egg, size 3, lightly beaten
2 tablespoons olive oil
2 peppers, 1 red, 1 green,
   de-seeded and sliced into
   thick rings
3 cloves garlic, peeled and crushed
   (see p.11)
800 g (1¾ lb) canned tomatoes
¼ level teaspoon salt
Freshly ground black pepper
30 g (1 oz) pitted black olives, sliced
450 g (1 lb) cod fillets, skinned,
   boned and cut into small cubes
60 g (2 oz) chopped almonds
6 pitted black olives to garnish

Per serving
Calories 480 Protein 31 g
Total fat 25 g (saturated fat 6.5 g)
Carbohydrates 34 g (added sugar 0)
Fibre 7.5 g Sodium 575 mg

Pitted black olives enrich the flavour of this simple pie of chunky cod and mashed potato, topped with crunchy almonds. You can use leftover mash for the potato case and make both the case and the tomato sauce in advance. Store them separately in the refrigerator until needed.

1 Preheat the oven to 200°C (400°F, gas mark 6). Boil the potatoes until soft, then drain and mash with the butter and half the beaten egg. Spread the potato smoothly over the base and sides of a large pie plate. Using a teaspoon, mark the edge of the potato case into a scalloped

Layers of moist cod and a tangy tomato and pepper sauce fill a case of creamy mashed potato.

pattern. Brush the potato with the remaining beaten egg, then bake in the oven for 15 minutes.

2 Meanwhile, heat the oil in a large frying pan and sauté the peppers and garlic in it, stirring occasionally, for 5 minutes, until the peppers begin to soften. Mix in the tomatoes, salt and some pepper and bring to the boil. Reduce the heat and simmer, uncovered, for 15 minutes, or until the juices are reduced by half. Stir in the sliced olives.

3 Spoon one-third of the mixture into the baked potato case, arrange half the cod on top and cover with half the remaining tomato mixture. Repeat the layers, finishing with the tomato mixture. Sprinkle the chopped almonds over the top.

4 Bake in the centre of the oven for 20-25 minutes, or until the fish flakes easily when tested with a fork. Garnish with the whole olives and serve with slices of farmhouse loaf.

RUSSIAN FISH PIE

Serves 4
Preparation time: 1 hour 45 minutes
Cooking time: 40 minutes

450 g (1 lb) smoked haddock fillet
150 ml (¼ pint) water
150 ml (¼ pint) milk
1 bay leaf
Sprig of fresh parsley
Freshly ground black pepper
115 g (4 oz) frozen, cooked and
   peeled prawns
2 eggs, size 2, hard-boiled, shelled
   and chopped
30 g (1 oz) butter or margarine
30 g (1 oz) plain flour
1 teaspoon lemon juice
⅛ level teaspoon ground nutmeg
2 level tablespoons chopped
   fresh parsley
450 g (1 lb) frozen puff
   pastry, thawed
1 egg, size 3, beaten
Sprig of fresh parsley to garnish

Per serving
Calories 705 Protein 42 g
Total fat 39 g (saturated fat 6 g)
Carbohydrates 49 g (added sugar 0)
Fibre 3.3 g Sodium 1803 mg

This economical version of the traditional Russian dish of *kulebyaka* – a lavish pie containing salmon with rice or semolina and hard-boiled eggs – makes an attractive centrepiece for a dinner party.

1 Cut the haddock into two or three pieces and put it in a saucepan. Pour over the water and milk and add the bay leaf, parsley and some pepper. Bring to the boil, then remove from the heat, cover and leave for 10 minutes.

2 Strain off and reserve the cooking liquid. Skin, bone and flake the fish and put it in a bowl with the prawns and eggs.

3 Melt the butter or margarine in a saucepan, then stir in the flour and cook for 1 minute. Gradually mix in the reserved cooking liquid and bring to the boil, stirring until thickened. Add the lemon juice, nutmeg and parsley and simmer for 1 minute. Mix the sauce gently with the fish, allow to cool, then chill for 1 hour. Meanwhile, preheat the oven to 220°C (425°F, gas mark 7).

4 Roll out the pastry on a floured surface to make a 36 cm (14 in) square, then trim all the edges with a sharp knife. Carefully lift the pastry onto a large baking tray.

5 Spoon the cold fish mixture onto the centre of the pastry and smooth the top. Brush the pastry edges with a little cold water, then lift the two opposite corners of the pastry up and over the fish mixture to meet and overlap slightly in the centre. Repeat with the two remaining

Light puff pastry encloses haddock, prawns and eggs in a nutmeg and parsley sauce.

124

corners, overlapping the first two pieces. Gently press the seams together with a fork and brush the pie with the beaten egg.

6 Bake the pie in the centre of the oven for 40 minutes. If the pastry looks as though it is over-browning, cover it loosely with foil. Serve hot or cold, garnished with a sprig of parsley and accompanied by a green salad.

Serves 4
Preparation time: 30 minutes
Cooking time: 1 hour

225 g (8 oz) smoked haddock or smoked cod fillet
225 g (8 oz) fresh haddock or cod fillet
425 ml (¾ pint) water
1 bay leaf
Sprig of fresh parsley
1 slice of lemon
400 g (14 oz) frozen mixed seafood, thawed and drained
60 g (2 oz) butter
4 spring onions, or 1 shallot or small onion, peeled and finely chopped
30 g (1 oz) plain flour
150 ml (¼ pint) single cream
1 tablespoon capers
2 tablespoons chopped fresh parsley
¼ level teaspoon salt
¼ level teaspoon grated nutmeg
Freshly ground black pepper
600 g (1 lb 5 oz) potatoes, scrubbed and thinly sliced
¼ level teaspoon paprika

SEAFOOD BAKE

A wholesome combination of flaky fish and mixed seafood is cooked in a creamy white sauce and topped with thin potato slices and a dusting of paprika.

1 Preheat the oven to 190°C (375°F, gas mark 5). Put the smoked and unsmoked fish in a saucepan and add the water, bay leaf, sprig of parsley and the lemon slice. Bring to the boil, then cover the pan, remove from the heat and leave to stand for 10 minutes.

2 Strain off the cooking liquid and reserve it, discarding the bay leaf, parsley sprig and lemon slice. Remove and discard the skin and any bones from the fish, then flake the flesh and put it in a large, shallow, ovenproof dish. Arrange the mixed seafood on top.

Per serving
Calories 542 Protein 53 g
Total fat 23 g (saturated fat 13 g)
Carbohydrates 33 g (added sugar 0)
Fibre 2.7 g Sodium 2612 mg

3 Melt 45 g (1½ oz) of the butter in a saucepan and gently fry the spring onions or shallot or onion in it for 2 minutes without browning. Stir in the flour and cook for 1 minute, then gradually stir in the fish cooking liquid. Bring the sauce to the boil, stirring, until it is thick and smooth. Stir in the cream, capers, parsley, salt, the nutmeg and some pepper. Pour over the seafood.

4 Arrange the potatoes on top, then dot with the remaining butter and sprinkle with the paprika. Bake in the centre of the oven for 1 hour, or until the potatoes are browned.

SALMON STEAKS IN FOIL

Serves 4
Preparation time: 20 minutes
Cooking time: 15 minutes

30 g (1 oz) butter, melted
4 large carrots, peeled and
    thinly sliced
225 g (8 oz) Chinese fine egg
    noodles, cooked and drained
    (see p.202)
285 ml (½ pint) single cream
6 spring onions, trimmed
    and chopped
½ level teaspoon salt
Freshly ground black pepper
85 g (3 oz) watercress, trimmed
    and washed
4 salmon steaks, each about
    225 g (8 oz), rinsed and dried
2 tablespoons chopped fresh
    dill or parsley
150 ml (¼ pint) dry white wine
Sprigs of fresh dill and lemon
    wedges to garnish

Per serving
Calories 577 Protein 21 g
Total fat 32 g (saturated fat 14 g)
Carbohydrates 49 g (added sugar 0)
Fibre 5 g Sodium 521 mg

Salmon steaks are wrapped in foil and oven baked – one of the easiest ways to cook fish, giving one of the tastiest results.

1 Preheat the oven to 180°C (350°F, gas mark 4). Cut four sheets of foil, each 51 cm x 30 cm (20 in x 12 in), and brush each sheet on one side with some of the butter. Leave a 5 cm (2 in) border round the edge.

2 Boil the carrots for 5 minutes, then drain and put them in a bowl. Mix in the noodles, the cream, half the spring onions, half the salt and some pepper.

3 Spoon a quarter of the mixture onto the centre of each sheet of foil, then scatter on a quarter of the watercress. Lay the salmon on top and brush with the remaining butter. Sprinkle with the remaining spring onions and salt, the dill and some pepper, then pour a quarter of the wine over each one.

4 Fold the foil over to enclose the salmon and noodles and seal the edges firmly. Lay the packets on a baking tray and cook in the centre of the oven for 15 minutes.

5 Take the packets out of the oven and leave them to stand for 5 minutes. Then open them up and slide the contents onto heated plates. Garnish and serve.

White wine enhances the delicate flavour of this satisfying supper, while the salmon and vegetables remain tender and moist during cooking.

PLAICE AND BROCCOLI BAKE

Tender rolls of plaice stuffed with potato and spring onion are coated in a creamy Cheddar cheese and broccoli sauce.

Serves 4
Preparation time: 30 minutes
Cooking time: 20 minutes

30 g (1 oz) butter
30 g (1 oz) plain flour
425 ml (¾ pint) milk
115 g (4 oz) Cheddar
  cheese, grated
¼ level teaspoon Tabasco sauce
¼ level teaspoon salt
1 tablespoon lemon juice
340 g (12 oz) fresh or frozen
  broccoli florets
675 g (1½ lb) potatoes, cooked,
  drained and mashed
4 spring onions, trimmed
  and chopped
4 double plaice fillets, each about
  175 g (6 oz), skinned
Lemon wedges to garnish

Per serving
Calories 565 Protein 50 g
Total fat 23 g (saturated fat 12 g)
Carbohydrates 42 g (added sugar 0)
Fibre 3 g Sodium 649 mg

1 Preheat the oven to 200°C (400°F, gas mark 6). Melt the butter in a saucepan, mix in the flour and cook, stirring, for 1 minute. Remove from the heat and gradually blend in the milk. Put the pan back on the heat and bring to the boil. Continue to cook, stirring, for 4 minutes, or until the sauce has thickened.

2 Stir in 85 g (3 oz) of the Cheddar, the Tabasco sauce, salt, lemon juice and the fresh broccoli florets. Cook, stirring, for about 4 minutes, or until the Cheddar melts, then cover and take the pan off the heat. (If you are using frozen broccoli florets, add them at this point.)

3 Mix the mashed potato with the spring onions. Lay the plaice fillets on a clean surface and spoon a quarter of the potato mixture onto the head end of each fillet. Roll the fillets up from the head end, and then put them in a large ovenproof dish.

4 Pour the Cheddar and broccoli sauce over the fish and sprinkle with the remaining cheese. Cover with a lid or foil and bake in the oven for 10 minutes. Remove the cover and continue to cook for a further 10 minutes, until the fish is cooked through and the sauce is lightly browned. Garnish with the lemon wedges and serve with crusty brown bread.

HADDOCK FILLETS WITH LEMON AND PARSLEY SAUCE

Lemon and parsley sauce gives a tangy, refreshing taste to this light, summery dish of haddock, courgettes and tomatoes. You can use any firm-fleshed fish fillets.

Serves 4
Preparation time: 20 minutes
Cooking time: 30 minutes

6 tablespoons olive oil
1 medium onion, peeled and
  finely chopped
2 cloves garlic, peeled and
  thinly sliced
225 g (8 oz) long-grain
  white rice
Finely grated rind of 2 lemons
½ level teaspoon salt
570 ml (1 pint) chicken stock
  (see p.8)
2 medium courgettes, trimmed and
  thinly sliced
3 plum tomatoes, coarsely chopped
4 haddock or plaice fillets, each
  about 175 g (6 oz), skinned
4 tablespoons lemon juice
Freshly ground black pepper
4 tablespoons chopped
  fresh parsley

Per serving
Calories 532 Protein 35 g
Total fat 22 g (saturated fat 3.2 g)
Carbohydrates 53 g (added sugar 0)
Fibre 2.3 g Sodium 339 mg

1 Heat 1 tablespoon of the oil in a large, shallow flameproof casserole over a low heat for 1 minute. Add the onion and garlic and cook for 5 minutes.

2 Stir in the rice, lemon rind, salt and stock and bring to the boil. Reduce the heat, cover and simmer gently for 10 minutes. Stir in the courgettes and tomatoes, then cover and cook for 4 minutes.

3 Lay the haddock or plaice fillets on top of the rice mixture and reduce the heat to low. Cover and cook for 10 minutes, or until the fish flakes easily when tested with a fork and all the liquid has been absorbed by the rice. Whisk together the remaining oil, lemon juice, some pepper and the parsley, then pour over the fish and serve.

PLAICE AND TAGLIATELLE FLORENTINE

Serves 4
Preparation time: 30 minutes
Cooking time: 30 minutes

225 g (8 oz) tagliatelle verde
1 tablespoon olive oil
450 g (1 lb) fresh spinach, blanched
  (see p.10) and roughly
  chopped, or 225 g (8 oz) frozen
  leaf spinach, thawed, drained
  and roughly chopped
4 double plaice fillets, each about
  175 g (6 oz), unskinned
½ level teaspoon salt
Freshly ground black pepper
285 ml (½ pint) skimmed milk
60 g (2 oz) butter
4 level tablespoons plain flour
285 ml (½ pint) fish or vegetable
  stock (see pp.8-9)
60 g (2 oz) Gruyère cheese, grated
30 g (1 oz) Parmesan
  cheese, grated
1 level teaspoon Dijon mustard
¼ level teaspoon ground nutmeg

Per serving
Calories 715 Protein 52 g
Total fat 31 g (saturated fat 14 g)
Carbohydrates 60 g (added sugar 0)
Fibre 7.9 g Sodium 945 mg

In French cuisine, the classic dish *à la florentine* – which is named after the city of Florence in northern Italy – combines spinach with a light cheese sauce, and can be made with fish, white meat or eggs. In this variant, ribbons of spinach pasta complement tender plaice fillets.

1 Cook the pasta (see p.202) and drain well. Preheat the oven to 200°C (400°F, gas mark 6). Toss the pasta with the oil in a shallow ovenproof dish, then cover with the chopped spinach.

A rich, creamy Gruyère and Parmesan sauce, lightly browned in the oven, encloses succulent plaice on a bed of fresh spinach.

2 Fold the plaice fillets in half from head to tail with the skin on the inside and lay them in a large frying pan. Season with the salt and some pepper, then pour over the milk. Cover and bring to a simmer over a moderate heat. Cook for 1 minute, then lift the fillets out of the pan with a fish slice, and arrange them on top of the spinach. Save the milk.

3 Melt the butter in a saucepan and stir in the flour over a low heat for 1 minute. Gradually pour in the stock and the saved milk, then bring to the boil and cook for 2-3 minutes, stirring, until thick. Take the pan off the heat.

4 Set aside 2 tablespoons of each cheese, then stir the rest into the sauce. Mix in the mustard and nutmeg. Pour the sauce over the plaice fillets and sprinkle with the reserved cheeses. Bake in the centre of the oven for 20 minutes, until golden brown, then serve.

BRAISED SWORDFISH WITH GINGER

Fresh root ginger adds a subtle spikiness to the full, meaty flavour of this firm saltwater fish. Swordfish, increasingly available from supermarkets and fishmongers, is similar in texture to halibut, which can also be used to make this recipe.

Serves 4
Preparation time: 25 minutes
Cooking time: 30 minutes

285 ml (½ pint) fish stock (see p.8)
150 ml (¼ pint) dry sherry or
    orange juice
4 tablespoons light soy sauce
1 large onion, peeled and
    thinly sliced
2 teaspoons peeled and grated
    fresh root ginger
115 g (4 oz) orzo or other small
    pasta shapes
4 swordfish steaks, each about
    175 g (6 oz)
4 medium carrots, peeled and
    thinly sliced
450 g (1 lb) red or white cabbage,
    finely shredded
½ level teaspoon salt
Freshly ground black pepper

Per serving
Calories 334 Protein 34 g
Total fat 2.4 g (saturated fat 0.4 g)
Carbohydrates 36 g (added sugar 0)
Fibre 6.7 g Sodium 1391 mg

I Put the stock, sherry or orange juice, soy sauce, onion and ginger in a large frying pan and bring to the boil. Reduce the heat, cover and simmer for 5 minutes.

2 Stir in the pasta and bring back to the boil. Cover and cook for 5 minutes. Arrange the swordfish steaks in a single layer on top of the pasta. Reduce the heat, cover and simmer for 5 minutes.

3 Gently turn the fish steaks over with a fish slice or a wide spatula. Scatter the carrots and cabbage on top and season with the salt and some pepper. Cover and simmer for 8-10 minutes, or until the flesh is springy to the touch. Lift the swordfish onto heated plates, toss the vegetables with the pasta and spoon round the fish. Serve with french bread.

MARINATED SWORDFISH STEAKS

Small new potatoes and corn on the cob make a sweet, juicy accompaniment to succulent swordfish steaks in this easy grill. You can marinate the fish at room temperature for just 30 minutes or in a refrigerator for 1-2 hours. Either method ensures that the steaks develop a tangy, citric flavour and aroma.

Serves 4
Preparation time: 20 minutes
Marinating time: 30 minutes
Cooking time: 30 minutes

3 tablespoons olive oil
Finely grated rind and strained
    juice of 1 large lime
1 tablespoon clear honey
1 tablespoon soy sauce
2 level teaspoons dried oregano
¼ level teaspoon salt
¼ teaspoon Tabasco sauce
4 thick swordfish steaks, each about
    175 g (6 oz)
550 g (1¼ lb) small new
    potatoes, scrubbed
4 corn cobs, husks removed
30 g (1 oz) butter, softened

Per serving
Calories 533 Protein 38 g
Total fat 23 g (saturated fat 6.3 g)
Carbohydrates 48 g (added sugar 0)
Fibre 5.9 g Sodium 561 mg

I Mix together 2 tablespoons of the oil, the lime rind and juice, honey, soy sauce, oregano, salt and Tabasco in a large dish. Add the swordfish steaks and coat them thoroughly in the marinade. Cover and then set aside for 30 minutes, basting occasionally.

2 Meanwhile, boil the potatoes until just cooked and drain well. Thread the potatoes onto four metal skewers and brush with the remaining oil.

3 Boil the corn cobs for 5 minutes and drain well. Preheat the grill to high. Lay each cob on a piece of heavy-duty foil and spread with the butter. Lightly wrap the cobs in the foil.

4 Put the corn cobs on the grill rack and cook for 5 minutes, turning halfway through cooking, then set aside and keep warm.

5 Take the swordfish steaks out of the marinade and grill them with the potatoes for about 10 minutes, turning the fish and the potatoes halfway through cooking, until both are browned and cooked through. Serve immediately with the corn cobs.

BAKED STUFFED SALMON

Serves 6
Preparation time: 55 minutes
Cooking time: 40 minutes

115 g (4 oz) cooked long-grain
    rice (see p.9)
1 level tablespoon chopped
    fresh dill
115 g (4 oz) smoked salmon
    trimmings, chopped
60 g (2 oz) pickled dill cucumbers,
    drained and chopped
4 tablespoons soured cream
1.4 kg (3 lb) whole fresh salmon,
    scaled, gutted, washed and
    boned (see p.144)
6 small sprigs of fresh dill
1/4 level teaspoon saffron powder or
    1/2 level teaspoon ground turmeric
2 tablespoons olive oil
1 medium onion, peeled and sliced
2 large peppers, 1 green,
    1 red, de-seeded and sliced
12 pitted black olives
340 g (12 oz) tomatoes, skinned
    and chopped
2 level tablespoons chopped
    fresh parsley
4 tablespoons dry white wine
Sprigs of fresh dill to garnish

Per serving
Calories 501 Protein 41 g
Total fat 27 g (saturated fat 5.4 g)
Carbohydrates 23 g (added sugar 0)
Fibre 3.1 g Sodium 654 mg

**Tender baked salmon are filled
with a mixture of long-grain
rice, chopped smoked salmon
and fresh dill. You can bone the
fish yourself (see p.146) or ask
your fishmonger to do it for you.
You will need a darning needle,
clean thin string and foil.**

1 Preheat the oven to 200°C
(400°F, gas mark 6). Mix the
rice, dill, smoked salmon, pickled
dill cucumber and soured cream,
then fill the salmon with the
mixture. Sew up the opening with
the needle and string and sprinkle
with the saffron or turmeric.

*Saffron-coloured salmon
baked on a colourful
bed of vegetables
makes an eye-
catching dinner
party dish.*

2 Heat the oil in a large frying
pan and soften the onion in it.
Mix in the peppers and cook for
3-4 minutes, then stir in the olives,
tomatoes, parsley and wine and
bring to the boil. After 1 minute,
take the pan off the heat.

3 Line a very large roasting tin
with a sheet of foil large enough
to wrap around the salmon. Pour
the pepper and tomato mixture
into the middle of the foil, then lay
the salmon on top. Fold the foil
over the salmon and seal.

4 Bake in the centre of the oven
for 30-40 minutes, or until
the salmon is cooked but still
moist. Carefully lift the salmon
onto a large heated platter and
remove the string. Spoon the
vegetables and the cooking juices
around the fish, then garnish with
the dill, cut into thick slices and
serve with a green salad.

SALMON SOUFFLÉ

Instant mashed potato flakes turn this tangy salmon soufflé into a substantial meal without affecting its light, puffy texture.

Serves 4
Preparation time: 30 minutes
Cooking time: 50 minutes

15 g (½ oz) fine dried breadcrumbs
30 g (1 oz) unsalted butter
4 large spring onions, trimmed and finely chopped
425 ml (¾ pint) milk
½ level teaspoon salt
Freshly ground black pepper
70 g (2½ oz) instant mashed potato flakes (not granules)
115 g (4 oz) Cheddar cheese, finely grated
6 eggs, size 2, separated
225 g (8 oz) cooked peas
6 drops hot red pepper sauce
425 g (15 oz) canned red salmon, drained, skinned, boned, flaked
⅛ level teaspoon cream of tartar

Per serving
Calories 634 Protein 49 g
Total fat 37 g (saturated fat 16 g)
Carbohydrates 27 g
(added sugar 0)
Fibre 6.9 g Sodium 1493 mg

1 Preheat the oven to 190°C (375°F, gas mark 5). Coat the base and sides of a greased 2.8 litres (5 pints) soufflé dish or straight-sided baking dish with the breadcrumbs. Tap out the excess crumbs and set aside.

2 Melt the butter in a saucepan, and gently soften the spring onions in it for 2-3 minutes. Stir in the milk, salt and some pepper, bring to the boil, then turn off the heat. Quickly stir in the potato flakes until the mixture is thickened.

3 Stir in the Cheddar until melted, then mix in the egg yolks one at a time. Add the peas, red pepper sauce and the salmon, then spoon the mixture into a large bowl.

4 In a separate bowl, whisk the egg whites until foamy, then beat in the cream of tartar until the egg whites hold soft peaks. Fold a quarter of the egg whites into the salmon mixture to loosen it, then gently fold in the rest.

5 Pour the mixture into the soufflé dish and bake in the centre of the oven for 50 minutes, or until puffed, golden brown and softly set. Serve with a green salad and some crusty brown bread.

TROUT STUFFED WITH BULGUR WHEAT

Serves 4
Preparation time: 40 minutes
Cooking time: 20 minutes

2 tablespoons olive oil
1 small onion, peeled and finely chopped
115 g (4 oz) bulgur wheat
725 ml (1¼ pints) fish or vegetable stock (see pp.8-9)
1 level tablespoon each chopped fresh mint and oregano
4 rainbow trout, each about 340 g (12 oz), gutted, cleaned, heads removed and boned (see p.144)
60 g (2 oz) unsalted butter, melted
60 g (2 oz) flaked almonds
Lemon wedges and sprigs of fresh parsley to garnish

Per serving
Calories 672 Protein 59 g
Total fat 38 g (saturated fat 9.7 g)
Carbohydrates 24 g (added sugar 0)
Fibre 2.2 g Sodium 314 mg

The fine texture of bulgur wheat makes a light stuffing for sweet, succulent trout, and fresh mint and oregano scent its delicately nutty flavour. They all work just as well with mackerel or Atlantic char.

1 Heat the oil in a saucepan and soften the onion in it, then mix in the bulgur wheat, stock, mint and oregano. Bring to the boil, reduce the heat, cover and simmer for 10-15 minutes, or until the bulgur wheat is soft. Pour into a sieve, drain and allow to cool.

2 Preheat the oven to 200°C (400°F, gas mark 6). Fill each trout with a quarter of the bulgur mixture, then lay the fish in a greased ovenproof dish. Mix the butter with the almonds and spoon over the trout.

3 Bake in the centre of the oven for 15-20 minutes, or until the fish flakes easily with a fork. Garnish and serve with salad and crusty white bread.

BAKED HERRING ROLLS

Serves 4
Preparation time: 30 minutes
Cooking time: 1 hour

675 g (1½ lb) potatoes, scrubbed
  and thinly sliced
1 medium red onion, peeled and
  thinly sliced
¼ level teaspoon salt
Freshly ground black pepper
425 ml (¾ pint) milk
30 g (1 oz) butter
2 spring onions, trimmed and
  finely sliced
60 g (2 oz) fresh brown or
  white breadcrumbs
Finely grated rind and strained juice
  of ½ lemon
1 level tablespoon chopped
  fresh parsley
1 level teaspoon dried dill weed
4 herrings, each about 175 g
  (6 oz), gutted, cleaned and
  heads and bones removed
  (see p.144)
Sprigs of fresh dill to garnish

Per serving
Calories 529 Protein 33 g
Total fat 24 g (saturated fat 8.3 g)
Carbohydrates 48 g (added sugar 0)
Fibre 3.9 g Sodium 578 mg

A mixture of breadcrumbs, parsley and dill flavoured with tangy lemon makes a light, tasty stuffing for fresh herrings.

1 Preheat the oven to 190°C (375°F, gas mark 5). Grease a large, shallow, ovenproof dish, and arrange the potato and onion slices in the bottom of it in even layers. Stir the salt and some pepper into the milk and pour it over the potatoes. Tightly cover the dish with foil and bake in the centre of the oven for 30 minutes, or until the potatoes are nearly cooked.

2 In the meantime, melt the butter in a saucepan and sauté the spring onions in it for 1 minute. Remove from the heat and stir in the breadcrumbs, lemon rind and juice, parsley, dried dill and some pepper.

3 Lay the herrings flat on a board, skin-side down. Spread the stuffing over each fish, then roll towards the tail. Secure by inserting the small piece of bone attached to the tail into the flesh.

Soft potato slices complement the delicate taste of herring. Rye bread provides a chewy and slightly sour contrast.

4 Remove the dish from the oven and arrange the herrings on top of the potatoes. Bake, covered, for 20 minutes, then uncover and cook for a further 10 minutes, or until lightly browned. Garnish with the fresh dill and serve with pumpernickel or any other dark rye bread.

COD BOULANGÈRE

Mild cod chunks are combined with creamy potato slices and an intriguing parsley, garlic and anchovy sauce. In France the term *à la boulangère* is used for dishes – usually made with lamb – that are cooked in an oven with potatoes and onion. Traditionally, the oven would have been owned by a baker– in French, *boulanger*.

Serves 4
Preparation time: 25 minutes
Cooking time: 1 hour 25 minutes

15 g (½ oz) parsley, chopped
3 cloves garlic, peeled and
    finely chopped
Finely grated rind of 2 lemons
100 g (3½ oz) canned anchovy
    fillets, drained and finely chopped
675 g (1½ lb) potatoes, peeled and
    very thinly sliced
1 medium onion, peeled, thinly
    sliced and separated into rings
Freshly ground black pepper
285 ml (½ pint) single cream or milk
15 g (½ oz) butter
1.1 kg (2½ lb) cod fillets, skinned,
    boned and cut into cubes

Per serving
Calories 585 Protein 58 g
Total fat 24 g (saturated fat 11 g)
Carbohydrates 35 g (added sugar 0)
Fibre 3.5 g Sodium 1785 mg

1 Preheat the oven to 180°C (350°F, gas mark 4). Combine the parsley, garlic, lemon rind and anchovy fillets in a small bowl.

2 Arrange one-third of the sliced potatoes in the bottom of a large, shallow, well-greased ovenproof dish, sprinkle with half the onion rings, then lay one-third of the anchovy mixture over the onion rings and season with some pepper. Repeat with half the remaining potatoes, the remaining onion rings and half the remaining anchovy mixture. Finally, lay the remaining potatoes on the top.

3 Bring the cream or milk to the boil and pour over the potatoes. Dot the surface with the butter, cover with foil, and bake in the centre of the oven for 1 hour, or until the potatoes are almost soft.

4 Remove the dish from the oven, uncover, and arrange the cod on top of the potatoes. Sprinkle with the remaining anchovy mixture, cover once again and return the dish to the oven. Bake for a further 25 minutes, or until the fish flakes easily with a fork, then serve.

PRAWN BAKE

Serves 4
Preparation time: 20 minutes
Cooking time: 1 hour 5 minutes

3 eggs, size 1
425 ml (¾ pint) milk
3 tablespoons dry sherry
2 level tablespoons Dijon mustard
½ level teaspoon salt
¼ level teaspoon ground nutmeg
¼ level teaspoon cayenne pepper
4 medium slices from a large white
    loaf, crusts removed and cut into
    2.5 cm (1 in) squares
30 g (1 oz) butter
1 medium onion, peeled and
    finely chopped
450 g (1 lb) large uncooked prawns,
    peeled and de-veined
225 g (8 oz) cooked peas
15 g (½ oz) fine dry breadcrumbs

Per serving
Calories 367 Protein 26 g
Total fat 15 g (saturated fat 6.9 g)
Carbohydrates 32 g (added sugar 0)
Fibre 5.9 g Sodium 1307 mg

Nutmeg, cayenne pepper and sherry add spice to a satisfying, oven-crisp egg and bread mixture containing succulent prawns and fresh-tasting peas.

1 Preheat the oven to 190°C (375°F, gas mark 5). Whisk together the eggs, milk, sherry, mustard, salt, nutmeg and cayenne pepper in a large bowl. Add the bread, toss well and set aside.

2 Melt the butter in a frying pan and sauté the onion in it until softened. Add the prawns and cook, stirring, for 2-3 minutes or until the prawns turn pink. Tip into the bread and milk mixture, add the peas and stir.

3 Pour into a large, greased soufflé dish and sprinkle the breadcrumbs on top. Bake in the centre of the oven for about 1 hour, or until golden brown and set. Serve with a mixed salad.

PAELLA

Serves 6
Preparation time: 30 minutes
Cooking time: 1 hour

2 tablespoons olive oil
225 g (8 oz) chorizo sausage,
     thickly sliced
1.4 kg (3 lb) oven-ready chicken,
     cut into eight (see p.115)
     and skinned
1 large onion, peeled and chopped
2 large peppers, 1 red, 1 green,
     de-seeded and chopped
2 cloves garlic, peeled and chopped
     (see p.11)
1 level teaspoon paprika
800 g (1¾ lb) canned
     chopped tomatoes
340 g (12 oz) arborio (risotto) rice
½ teaspoon saffron strands, soaked
     in 2 tablespoons of boiling water
850 ml (1½ pints) chicken stock
     (see p.8)
¾ level teaspoon salt
Freshly ground black pepper
225 g (8 oz) frozen peas
12 fresh mussels, well scrubbed
     and de-bearded (see p.147)
340 g (12 oz) frozen cooked and
     peeled prawns, thawed
Lemon wedges and whole prawns
     to garnish

Per serving
Calories 952 Protein 76 g
Total fat 32 g (saturated fat 9.8 g)
Carbohydrates 97 g (added sugar 0)
Fibre 9.5 g Sodium 2206 mg

Chicken, sausage and prawns
are cooked with rice in a classic
one-dish meal named after the
broad, shallow metal pan in
which it is cooked in Spain.
You can cook it in a large, heavy
casserole or frying pan instead.

1 Heat the oil in a large paella
pan or flameproof casserole
and brown the chorizo slices in
it for 2-3 minutes. Move them
to a plate and set aside.

2 Fry the chicken in the casserole
for about 10 minutes until
browned all over, then put it on
the plate with the chorizo. Put
the onion and peppers in the pan
and fry for 10 minutes. Add the
garlic, paprika and tomatoes, and
simmer, uncovered, for 5 minutes.

3 Stir in the rice, saffron mixture,
stock, salt and some pepper,
and bring back to the boil. Add
the chicken, cover and simmer
for 20 minutes over a low heat.

4 Add the peas and the mussels,
burying them in the rice. Cover
the pan and simmer for a further
10 minutes, or until the rice is
cooked, all the liquid has been
absorbed and the mussels are open
(discard any mussels that remain
closed). Stir in the chorizo and
prawns and heat through for
5 minutes. Garnish the paella with
the lemon and prawns and serve.

CAJUN RICE WITH PRAWNS

Serves 4
Preparation time: 15 minutes
Cooking time: 30 minutes

1 tablespoon olive oil
30 g (1 oz) butter
2 cloves garlic, peeled and crushed
     (see p.11)
1 medium onion, peeled
     and chopped
1 medium green pepper de-seeded
     and chopped
1 stick celery, trimmed and chopped
1 small green chilli, de-seeded
     and chopped
2 fresh lime or bay leaves
1 level teaspoon dried thyme
2 level teaspoons paprika
½ level teaspoon salt
¼ level teaspoon cayenne pepper
400 g (14 oz) canned
     chopped tomatoes
425 ml (¾ pint) fish or chicken
     stock (see p.8)
175 g (6 oz) long-grain white rice
175 g (6 oz) small fresh
     okra, trimmed
340 g (12 oz) frozen cooked and
     peeled giant tiger prawns, thawed
Lime wedges to garnish

Per serving
Calories 379 Protein 25 g
Total fat 12 g (saturated fat 5 g)
Carbohydrates 45 g (added sugar 0)
Fibre 5 g Sodium 1705 mg

This Louisiana favourite,
like many southern American
dishes, includes okra, or lady's
fingers, whose unusual texture
pairs well with spicy sauces.
Fresh lime leaves sharpen the
flavour of the rice and prawns;
they can be bought in Asian
shops and some supermarkets.

1 Heat the oil and butter in a
large flameproof casserole or
saucepan. Gently sauté the garlic,
onion, pepper, celery and chilli in
it for 10 minutes, until softened
and just starting to brown.

2 Add the lime or bay leaves,
thyme, paprika, salt, cayenne
pepper and tomatoes, then
pour in the stock and bring the
mixture to the boil. Stir in the rice,
reduce the heat and simmer,
covered, for 5 minutes.

3 Stir the okra into the rice
mixture, cover the pan and
cook for a further 10 minutes.
Then add the prawns and cook,
stirring occasionally, for a further
5-8 minutes, until the rice is
cooked, all the liquid has been
absorbed and the prawns are
heated through. Remove the
lime or bay leaves, garnish with
the lime wedges, and serve.

PRAWNS AND TAGLIATELLE WITH BEER

Serves 4
Preparation time: 20 minutes
Cooking time: 30 minutes

2 tablespoons olive oil
1 large onion, peeled and chopped
2 medium peppers, 1 red, 1 green,
   de-seeded and sliced
225 g (8 oz) mushrooms, wiped
   and sliced
2 cloves garlic, peeled and crushed
   (see p.11)
400 g (14 oz) canned
   chopped tomatoes
285 ml (1/2 pint) lager
1 level tablespoon tomato purée
1 teaspoon chopped fresh thyme
1/2 level teaspoon salt
Freshly ground black pepper
225 g (8 oz) tagliatelle or fettucine
115 g (4 oz) frozen sweetcorn
   kernels
340 g (12 oz) frozen, cooked and
   peeled prawns
Fresh basil leaves to garnish

Per serving
Calories 442 Protein 31 g
Total fat 10 g (saturated fat 1.4 g)
Carbohydrates 56 g (added sugar 0)
Fibre 8.4 g Sodium 1655 mg

Lager beer gives a rather
hearty flavour to this prawn
and tagliatelle combination.
For a more delicate taste, you
can use fish stock or white
wine in place of beer.

1 Heat the oil in a large, heavy
saucepan and fry the onion
and peppers in it over a moderate
heat until softened.

2 Add the mushrooms and
garlic and cook for a further
3 minutes, stirring occasionally.
Stir in the tomatoes, lager, tomato
purée, thyme, salt and some
pepper. Simmer for 12-15 minutes,
stirring occasionally, until the
sauce has thickened slightly.
Meanwhile, cook the pasta
(see p.202) and drain.

3 Add the sweetcorn and prawns
to the tomato sauce and bring
it back to the boil. Reduce the heat
and cook for 4-5 minutes, until
heated through. Gently mix in the
pasta and the fresh basil or parsley.
Pour into a heated serving bowl
and serve with a crisp green salad.

*Tagliatelle, fettucine or any other
flat ribbon pasta goes well with this
prawn, sweetcorn and pepper sauce
distinctively flavoured with lager.*

STIR-FRIED PRAWNS AND SCALLOPS

King or queen scallops are equally suitable for this splendid seafood dish. Stir-frying keeps the prawns and scallops plump and juicy, and also ensures that the mangetout and water chestnuts stay fresh and crisp.

Serves 4
Preparation time: 35 minutes
Cooking time: 15 minutes

5 tablespoons olive oil
600 g (1 lb 5 oz) cooked rice
　(see p.9)
1 large red pepper, de-seeded
　and chopped
1 large carrot, peeled and thinly
　sliced diagonally
225 g (8 oz) canned water
　chestnuts, drained and sliced
115 g (4 oz) mangetout, trimmed
1 level teaspoon sugar
340 g (12 oz) fresh uncooked
　prawns, peeled and de-veined
225 g (8 oz) whole queen scallops,
　or halved large king scallops
3 spring onions, trimmed and
　finely chopped
1 tablespoon peeled and finely
　chopped fresh root ginger
2 tablespoons each soy sauce and
　cider vinegar mixed together

Per serving
Calories 552 Protein 35 g
Total fat 21 g (saturated fat 2.7 g)
Carbohydrates 59 g (added sugar 1.3 g)
Fibre 5.2 g Sodium 825 mg

1 Heat 2 tablespoons of the oil in a large wok or frying pan and stir-fry the rice in it for 2-3 minutes. Spoon the rice into a dish and keep it warm.

2 Heat the remaining oil in the wok or pan over a moderate heat for 1 minute. Stir in the pepper, carrot, chestnuts and mangetout, sprinkle with sugar and stir-fry for 2 minutes, or until the vegetables become glossy.

3 Mix in the prawns and scallops and stir-fry for 3 minutes. Add the spring onions and ginger and stir-fry for 1 minute.

4 Pour in the soy mixture and cook, stirring occasionally, for 1 minute, until the sauce is syrupy, the shellfish is cooked through and the vegetables are still crisp. Mix in the rice and serve immediately.

LOBSTER NEWBURG

A 19th-century New York chef named this method of sautéing chopped lobster in a cream and sherry sauce after a customer, sea captain Ben Wenburg; later it became Lobster Newburg. The sauce suits any blend of seafood.

Serves 4
Preparation time: 45 minutes
Cooking time: 35 minutes

340 g (12 oz) fresh spinach,
　trimmed and washed
900 g (2 lb) potatoes, peeled
175 g (6 oz) frozen mixed
　vegetables, cooked and drained
1 tablespoon olive oil
2 shallots, peeled and
　finely chopped
225 g (8 oz) scallops, cleaned and
　cut into small pieces
150 ml (¼ pint) dry sherry
1 tablespoon brandy (optional)
Meat of 1 lobster, about
　900 g (2 lb), roughly chopped
450 g (1 lb) fresh or frozen cooked
　and peeled tiger prawns
2 level tablespoons cornflour
150 ml (¼ pint) single cream
2 level tablespoons Dijon mustard
1 tablespoon lemon juice
½ level teaspoon salt
Freshly ground black pepper
Paprika and lemon slices to garnish

Per serving
Calories 566 Protein 65 g
Total fat 10 g (saturated fat 1.3 g)
Carbohydrates 44 g (added sugar 0)
Fibre 7.1 g Sodium 2635 mg

1 Preheat the oven to 200°C (400°F, gas mark 6). Blanch the spinach (see p.10) and chop finely. Boil the potatoes until soft, then drain and mash.

2 Spoon the spinach and mixed vegetables into a large, lightly greased gratin dish, then pipe a border of the mashed potato around the edge of the dish. Carefully cover the gratin dish with foil and heat through in the oven for 10 minutes.

3 Heat the oil in a saucepan and sauté the shallots in it until soft, but not brown. Add the scallops and cook for 2-3 minutes until just firm. Pour in the sherry and brandy, if using, and boil gently for 5 minutes until the liquid has reduced by about a quarter. Stir in the lobster meat and prawns.

4 Blend the cornflour with the cream, mustard, lemon juice, salt and some pepper and stir the mixture into the pan. Cook gently for 2-3 minutes, stirring.

5 Take the gratin dish out of the oven, remove the foil and pour the seafood mixture into the centre. Cook in the oven for about 15 minutes, until the potato is lightly browned. Sprinkle with the paprika, then garnish with the lemon slices and serve.

SEAFOOD RISOTTO

Serves 4
Preparation time: 25 minutes
Cooking time: 30 minutes

30 g (1 oz) unsalted butter
   or margarine
2 tablespoons olive oil
2 cloves garlic, peeled and crushed
   (see p.11)
225 g (8 oz) fresh uncooked
   prawns, peeled with tails left on
   and de-veined
8 scallops, cleaned and cut
   into pieces
3 tablespoons chopped
   fresh parsley
1 large onion, peeled and chopped
2 medium sticks celery, trimmed
   and sliced
2 medium carrots, peeled
   and chopped
275 g (10 oz) long-grain white rice
725 ml (1¼ pints) chicken stock
   (see p.8)
400 g (14 oz) canned
   chopped tomatoes
½ level teaspoon salt
225 g (8 oz) asparagus,
   trimmed, and cut into
   short pieces
60 g (2 oz) Parmesan
   cheese, grated
Freshly ground black pepper
1 tablespoon chopped
   fresh parsley to garnish

Per serving
Calories 605 Protein 40 g
Total fat 20 g (saturated fat 8.5 g)
Carbohydrates 69 g (added sugar 0)
Fibre 6 g Sodium 1010 mg

This mouth-watering risotto recipe calls for fresh prawns and scallops, but it can be made just as well with any firm-textured fish – such as salmon or canned tuna, cut into pieces.

1 Heat the butter or margarine and oil in a large flameproof casserole or frying pan and fry the garlic in it for 1 minute. Mix in the prawns, scallops and parsley and cook for 3 minutes. Move the prawns and scallops onto a plate.

2 Add the onion, celery and carrots to the casserole or pan and soften without browning. Stir in the rice, stock, tomatoes and salt and bring to the boil. Reduce the heat to low, cover and simmer for 15 minutes.

3 Arrange the asparagus on top of the rice and cook for about 5 minutes, until the asparagus and the rice are tender.

4 Gently stir in the prawns and scallops and heat through for 3-4 minutes. Mix in the Parmesan and season with some pepper. Serve from the casserole or pan or in a heated serving dish, garnished with the parsley.

Asparagus keeps its delicate flavour and texture when gently simmered on top of the rice and vegetables in this succulent seafood risotto.

RED MULLET AND PARMA HAM

Strong-tasting ham is combined with the delicate flavour of red mullet in this dish from Ancona, on Italy's Adriatic coast.

Serves 4
Preparation time: 20-25 minutes
Marinating time: 2 hours
Cooking time: 25 minutes

4 tablespoons olive oil
Strained juice of 1 lemon
1 clove garlic, peeled and crushed
½ level teaspoon salt
Freshly ground black pepper
4 red mullet, each about 340 g
  (12 oz), scaled, gutted, with head
  and bones removed (see p.144)
2 thick slices Parma ham,
  halved lengthways
675 g (1½ lb) cooked potatoes,
  sliced or diced (see p.10)
2 tablespoons chopped
  fresh parsley
8 pitted black olives, sliced
2 tablespoons fresh white or
  brown breadcrumbs

Per serving
Calories 451 Protein 45 g
Total fat 16 g (saturated fat 2.5 g)
Carbohydrates 33 g (added sugar 0)
Fibre 3.6 g Sodium 887 mg

Marinated red mullet and Parma ham baked with potatoes makes a simple, pleasing lunch.

1 Mix the oil, lemon juice, garlic salt and some pepper in a large, shallow, ovenproof dish. Add the mullet and coat with the mixture. Cover and refrigerate for 2 hours. After 1½ hours, preheat the oven to 180°C (350°F, gas mark 4).

2 Pour off the marinade and reserve, then place a piece of Parma ham between each fish. Mix the potatoes with the parsley and half the marinade and spoon them round the mullet.

3 Sprinkle the olives over the fish, spoon over the remaining marinade and sprinkle with the breadcrumbs. Bake in the oven for 20-25 minutes, or until the mullet are cooked, and then serve.

STUFFED AND GRILLED GREY MULLET

A stuffing of leeks with fruit and nuts adds a lively flavour to the firm-textured fish. If you can't find grey mullet, use trout or salmon in its place.

Serves 6
Preparation time: 20 minutes
Cooking time: 30 minutes

4 tablespoons olive oil
225 g (8 oz) leeks, trimmed, finely
    sliced, washed and drained
Finely grated rind and strained juice
    of 2 lemons
225 g (8 oz) fresh white
    breadcrumbs
3 tablespoons chopped
    fresh parsley
340 g (12 oz) dessert apples,
    peeled, cored and grated
115 g (4 oz) pine nuts
1/2 level teaspoon salt
Freshly ground black pepper
2 eggs, size 2, beaten
2 grey mullet, each about
    1.1 kg (2 1/2 lb), scaled, gutted
    and cleaned (see p.144)

Per serving
Calories 734 Protein 67 g
Total fat 36 g (saturated fat 2.9 g)
Carbohydrates 37 g (added sugar 0)
Fibre 4.6 g Sodium 692 mg

1 Heat 2 tablespoons of the oil in a frying pan and gently fry the leeks in it for 5 minutes. Stir in the lemon rind, half the lemon juice, the breadcrumbs and parsley, and cook for 3 minutes. Add the grated apples and pine nuts. Season with the salt and plenty of black pepper. Take the pan off the heat and allow the mixture to cool slightly.

2 Mix in the beaten eggs to bind the stuffing together, then fill the cavity of each fish with some of the stuffing, pushing it well in. Divide the remaining stuffing into six equal portions and shape each into a neat, round cake.

3 Preheat the grill until it is moderately hot, then line the grill rack with foil. Using a sharp knife, make three or four deep diagonal slashes on both sides of each fish. Brush the remaining oil and lemon juice over both sides of the fish and place them with the stuffing cakes on the grill rack.

4 Cook for 12 minutes, then turn the fish over and cook for another 12 minutes, or until the fish flake easily when tested with a fork. (If the fish tails start to brown too much, cover them with a small piece of foil.) Serve with crusty wholemeal bread and a fresh tomato salad.

MACKEREL STEAMED WITH VEGETABLES

Steaming the mackerel brings out its distinctive flavour. A large roasting tin, preferably enamel, with a wire cooling rack laid either inside or on top makes a suitable steamer. Cover the steamer with a large piece of foil to make it airtight.

Serves 4
Preparation time: 15 minutes
Cooking time: 15 minutes

2 slices of lemon
4 small mackerel, each about
    175 g (6 oz), with heads
    removed, gutted and cleaned
    (see p.144)
Freshly ground black pepper
1 large or 2 small bulbs of fennel,
    about 250 g (9 oz) in all, trimmed,
    halved and thinly sliced, green
    fronds reserved for garnish
450 g (1 lb) potatoes, scrubbed and
    cut into slices
175 g (6 oz) mangetout, trimmed
Lemon wedges to garnish

Per serving
Calories 490 Protein 37 g
Total fat 28 g (saturated fat 6.7 g)
Carbohydrates 23 g (added sugar 0)
Fibre 3.6 g Sodium 242 mg

1 Half fill the roasting tin with water and float the lemon slices in it. Lightly oil the wire rack and place it on the tin, then stand the tin securely on the hob.

2 Season the mackerel inside and outside with pepper, then fill each with sliced fennel. Arrange the potato slices all over the wire rack and place the mackerel on top. Sprinkle any remaining fennel over the fish, and scatter the mangetout round them.

3 Carefully cover the wire rack and the top of the roasting tin with foil, tucking it under the rim. Bring the water to the boil, then reduce the heat and steam for 15 minutes until the fish and vegetables are just cooked. Serve at once, garnished with fennel fronds and lemon wedges.

CURRIED FISH BALLS WITH FETTUCINE

Turmeric, garlic, ginger and paprika flavour these filling fish balls. Creamed coconut cools the effect of the spices; it can be bought dried in blocks or ready to use in cans.

Serves 4
Preparation time: 30 minutes
Chilling time: 1 hour
Cooking time: 25 minutes

550 g (1¼ lb) uncooked minced cod
4 spring onions, trimmed and
    finely chopped
85 g (3 oz) fresh brown or
    white breadcrumbs
1 tablespoon chopped fresh
    coriander or parsley
1 level teaspoon dried oregano
¼ level teaspoon salt
1 egg yolk, size 2, beaten
2 tablespoons olive oil
1 medium onion, peeled and
    finely chopped
1 clove garlic, peeled and
    crushed (see p.11)
1 teaspoon peeled and finely
    chopped fresh root ginger, or
    ¼ level teaspoon ground ginger
¼ level teaspoon turmeric
½ level teaspoon chilli powder
1 level teaspoon paprika
285 ml (½ pint) fish, chicken or
    vegetable stock (see pp.8-9)
2 teaspoons lemon juice

30 g (1 oz) creamed coconut
340 g (12 oz) egg or spinach
    fettucine
150 ml (¼ pint) single cream
Flat-leaf parsley, torn into small
    leaves, or coriander to garnish

Per serving
Calories 687 Protein 39 g
Total fat 23 g (saturated fat 11 g)
Carbohydrates 85 g (added sugar 0)
Fibre 6.3 g Sodium 421 mg

1 Mix the cod, spring onions, breadcrumbs, coriander or parsley, oregano and salt, then bind with the egg yolk. Divide the mixture into 24 and shape into balls. Put the balls on a plate and refrigerate for 1 hour.

2 Heat the oil in a large frying pan and fry the onion in it for 3 minutes over a moderate heat. Stir in the garlic, ginger, turmeric, chilli and paprika and cook for 2 minutes. Add the stock, lemon juice and coconut and bring to the boil, stirring.

3 Stir in the cream and add the fish balls to the pan in a single layer, then reduce the heat. Cover and simmer for 15 minutes, turning the balls once. Meanwhile, cook the fettucine (see p.202).

4 Drain the pasta and arrange it on a heated serving dish. Sprinkle the fish balls with the parsley or coriander, spoon on top of the pasta and serve.

A spicy coconut sauce makes a rich, creamy coating for firm fish balls in this dish inspired by South-east Asian cooking.

STUFFED CALAMARI IN TOMATO SAUCE

Squid pouches filled with a nutty rice stuffing are baked in a fruity tomato, basil and wine sauce. You will need cocktail sticks to secure large squid, but small squid can be threaded onto metal or bamboo skewers.

Serves 6
Preparation time: 35 minutes
Cooking time: 1 hour 25 minutes

4 tablespoons olive oil
1 onion, peeled and finely chopped
1 clove garlic, peeled and crushed
 (see p.11)
1 level tablespoon plain flour
150 ml (¼ pint) dry white wine
900 g (2 lb) ripe tomatoes, skinned
 and roughly chopped, or canned
 chopped tomatoes
150 ml (¼ pint) passata
 (sieved tomatoes)
½ level teaspoon salt
Freshly ground black pepper
2 level teaspoons dried basil
2 level tablespoons chopped
 fresh parsley
900 g (2 lb) large or small prepared
 squid, tentacles chopped
115 g (4 oz) long-grain white rice,
 cooked (see p.9)
4 tablespoons pine nuts
45 g (1½ oz) currants
30 g (1 oz) fine dried breadcrumbs

Per serving
Calories 413 Protein 25 g
Total fat 19 g (saturated fat 1.9 g)
Carbohydrates 35 g (added sugar 0)
Fibre 3.6 g Sodium 505 mg

1 Heat 2 tablespoons of the oil in a saucepan and fry two-thirds of the onion and the garlic in it for 5 minutes. Mix in the flour and cook for 1 minute, then gradually stir in the wine. Bring to the boil.

2 Add the tomatoes, passata, salt, some pepper, basil and parsley. Cover and simmer for 15 minutes.

3 Meanwhile, preheat the oven to 180°C (350°F, gas mark 4). Heat the remaining oil in another saucepan and fry the chopped squid tentacles and the rest of the onion in it for 5 minutes. Stir in the rice, pine nuts and currants.

4 If you are using large squid, stuff them with the rice mixture, then secure the pouches with the cocktail sticks. If you are using small squid, thread the open ends of the pouches three or four at a time onto a metal or bamboo skewer.

5 Arrange the stuffed squid in a large, shallow ovenproof dish and pour the tomato sauce over the top. Sprinkle with the breadcrumbs, and bake in the centre of the oven for 55 minutes, or until the squid is tender. Remove the skewers or cocktail sticks, then serve with a white cabbage salad and pan gallego or other Spanish bread.

HERRING AND APPLE PIE WITH POTATO TOPPING

Serves 4
Preparation time: 20 minutes
Cooking time: 40 minutes

900 g (2 lb) potatoes, peeled
 and quartered
2 tablespoons vegetable oil
1 medium onion, peeled
 and chopped
1 level teaspoon dried sage
340 g (12 oz) green dessert apples,
 peeled, cored and diced
1 level tablespoon plain flour
150 ml (¼ pint) medium dry cider
4 double herring fillets, each about
 70 g (2½ oz), skinned
½ level teaspoon salt
Freshly ground black pepper
2 tablespoons milk
30 g (1 oz) fresh white breadcrumbs
30 g (1 oz) Emmenthal
 cheese, grated
½ level teaspoon paprika
Chopped fresh dill to garnish

Per serving
Calories 893 Protein 48 g
Total fat 52 g (saturated fat 11 g)
Carbohydrates 60 g (added sugar 0)
Fibre 6 g Sodium 513 mg

The sage, cider and apple sauce for this nourishing herring dish is easy to prepare and makes a refreshing contrast to the rich, slightly oily fish. Emmenthal cheese mixed with breadcrumbs gives the potato topping a sweet, crunchy finish, but you can use any cheese of your choice.

1 Boil the potatoes until soft. Preheat the oven to 190°C (375°F, gas mark 5). Meanwhile, heat the oil in a small frying pan and soften the onion in it.

2 Mix in the sage and apples and cook for 2-3 minutes. Stir in the flour and cook for 1 minute, then gradually add the cider. Bring to the boil, stirring until thickened, then pour into a shallow, ovenproof dish and arrange the herring fillets on top.

3 Drain the potatoes and mash them with the salt, some pepper and the milk. Spread the mashed potatoes over the fish.

4 Mix the breadcrumbs with the Emmenthal and scatter over the potatoes. Sprinkle the paprika on top, then bake in the centre of the oven for 30 minutes, or until the top is golden brown. Garnish with the chopped dill and serve with warm, crusty bread.

Baccalà with Polenta

Baccalà, or salted cod, is the traditional Italian fare on religious fast days. This tasty recipe from Vicenza combines the flaked fish with anchovies, cheese and white wine.

Serves 4
Soaking time: 24-48 hours
Preparation time: 30 minutes
Cooking time: 45 minutes

4 anchovy fillets
425 ml (¾ pint) milk
900 g (2 lb) salted cod, soaked
    in cold water (see p.146)
2.8 litres (5 pints) cold water
175 g (6 oz) polenta
½ level teaspoon salt
60 g (2 oz) mature Cheddar
    cheese, grated
60 g (2 oz) butter
1 large onion, peeled and chopped
30 g (1 oz) plain flour
1 clove garlic, peeled and crushed
    (see p.11)
150 ml (¼ pint) dry white wine
Freshly ground black pepper
3 tablespoons chopped
    fresh parsley

Per serving
Calories 784 Protein 88 g
Total fat 25 g (saturated fat 13 g)
Carbohydrates 46 g (added sugar 0)
Fibre 2.8 g Sodium 1803 mg

1 Soak the anchovy fillets in 1 tablespoon of the milk, cover and set aside. Drain the soaked cod, put it in a large saucepan and cover it with 2.3 litres (4 pints) of the cold water. Bring to the boil, change the water and bring to the boil again. Reduce the heat, cover and simmer for 15-20 minutes, until the cod flakes easily when tested with a fork.

2 Meanwhile, preheat the oven to 200°C (400°F, gas mark 6). Pour the remaining water into a saucepan, whisk in the polenta and bring to the boil, stirring. Add the salt and Cheddar. Reduce the heat and stir for 15 minutes more. Then pour the polenta into a greased ovenproof dish, smooth the surface and bake in the centre of the oven for 25 minutes. In the meantime, drain, skin and bone the cod, flake its flesh, then drain and chop the anchovies.

3 Melt the butter in a saucepan and soften the onion in it, without browning. Stir in the flour and garlic and cook for 1 minute. Gradually stir in the wine, the rest of the milk, some pepper and half the parsley. Bring the sauce to the boil, stirring, then reduce the heat and cook for 3 minutes. Gently mix in the cod and anchovies, then pour the mixture over the polenta. Cover and return to the oven for 20 minutes. Sprinkle with the rest of the parsley and serve.

Salted Cod and Potatoes

Preserving fish by drying or salting results in a full flavour and a pleasing, chewy texture. In this recipe, the fish is blended with other ingredients – garlic, olive oil and onions – that are typical of the Basque region of Spain and France.

Serves 4
Soaking time: 24-48 hours
Preparation time: 20 minutes
Cooking time: 40 minutes

675 g (1½ lb) salted cod, soaked in
    cold water (see p.146)
115 ml (4 fl oz) olive oil
2 large onions, peeled and chopped
675 g (1½ lb) potatoes, peeled
    and cut into small cubes
2 cloves garlic, peeled and crushed
    (see p.11)
1 small fresh green chilli, de-seeded
    and finely chopped
1 tablespoon chopped fresh parsley
16 pitted black olives
3 tablespoons white wine vinegar
Freshly ground black pepper
2 eggs, size 2, hard-boiled, shelled
    and sliced
Lemon wedges and sprigs of fresh
    parsley to garnish

Per serving
Calories 693 Protein 63 g
Total fat 35 g (saturated fat 5.5 g)
Carbohydrates 33 g (added sugar 0)
Fibre 4.1 g Sodium 1001 mg

1 Drain the soaked cod then put it in a large saucepan and cover it with 2.3 litres (4 pints) of cold water. Bring to the boil, change the water, and bring to the boil again. Then reduce the heat, cover and cook gently for 15-20 minutes until the fish flakes easily when tested with a fork. Drain, remove and discard any skin and bones, then separate the flesh into coarse flakes and leave to one side.

2 Heat the oil in a large frying pan and fry the onions, potatoes and garlic over a moderate heat for 10 minutes or until they are lightly browned.

3 Stir in the green chilli, chopped parsley, olives, wine vinegar, some pepper and the flaked cod. Cover and cook gently, stirring frequently, for 10 minutes, or until the potatoes are done.

4 Turn into a heated serving dish. Arrange the sliced eggs on top and garnish with the lemon wedges and sprigs of parsley. Serve with a crisp green salad.

AKEE AND SALTED COD

Sweet slices of plantain and creamy akees accompany the salted cod in this tasty, avocado-topped dish.

Serves 4
Preparation time: 25 minutes
Soaking time: 24-48 hours
Cooking time: 50 minutes

675 g (1½ lb) salted cod, soaked in cold water (see p.146)
2 semi-ripe, yellow-skinned plantains
2 tablespoons olive oil
2 cloves garlic, peeled and crushed (see p.11)
1 medium onion, peeled and chopped
1 small green chilli, de-seeded and chopped
½ level teaspoon fresh thyme leaves, or 1½ level teaspoons dried thyme
Freshly ground black pepper
400 g (14 oz) canned tomatoes, drained and chopped
550 g (1¼ lb) canned akees in brine, drained and rinsed
1 small avocado, halved, stoned and peeled, and 1 large tomato, both roughly chopped, to garnish

Per serving
Calories 702 Protein 56 g
Total fat 36 g (saturated fat 2.6 g)
Carbohydrates 37 g (added sugar 0)
Fibre 7 g Sodium 377 mg

Akees – edible parts of the fruits of a tropical tree – give this rich Jamaican dish its creamy texture. They are sold in cans in African-Caribbean shops, but if you can't find them, add shredded callaloo or spinach to the garlic and onion mixture.

1 Drain the soaked cod, place it in a large saucepan and cover with 2.3 litres (4 pints) of cold water. Bring to the boil, change the water and bring to the boil again. Reduce the heat, cover and cook gently for 15-20 minutes until the fish flakes easily when tested with a fork. Drain, remove and discard any skin and bones, then separate the flesh into coarse flakes and set aside.

2 Meanwhile, top and tail the plantains, put them in a large frying pan and cover with water. Bring to the boil, reduce the heat slightly and cook for 15 minutes. Drain, allow to cool, then peel, cut into thick slices and set aside.

3 Heat the oil in a large, shallow, flameproof casserole. Cook the garlic, onion and chilli in it until softened, then stir in the thyme, some black pepper and the tomatoes. Bring to the boil, add the flaked cod and heat for 5 minutes, stirring. Mix in the akees and plantain slices, cover and heat through for 3-5 minutes, then garnish and serve.

Making the most of fish and shellfish

Taste, texture, variety of shape, colour and size – fish and shellfish have all it takes to make interesting one-dish meals. And on top of it all, fresh and saltwater fish and shellfish are among the healthiest foods we can eat, providing essential protein and nutrients.

FISH IS AT its very best when cooked and eaten the same day it is caught. Few have the opportunity to do this – but try at least to cook fish the same day you buy it from the fishmonger or supermarket.

Fresh fish should have bright, sparkling eyes, bright pink gills, very shiny scales and a firm flesh. It should have a pleasant, fresh, salty smell. Ready-prepared fish fillets and steaks should look fresh and translucent, and not milky or dry and yellow round the edges. Duller eyes and skin, or softer flesh, may well indicate that the fish has already been thawed and then refrozen.

Always ask if the fish you are buying has been previously frozen. Shops often display a sign stating that the fish has been frozen and then thawed, but ask if you are not sure.

Take fish home as quickly as possible after buying it. Never leave it in a car, especially in hot weather, for any length of time. Store the fish in a cool place, preferably the fridge, until you use it. If you cannot cook the fish until the next day, wash it under cold running water, and dry it with kitchen paper. Put the fish on a large plate or plastic tray and cover it loosely with foil or plastic film before storing it in the coldest part of the fridge.

Preparing fish for cooking

A fishmonger will usually skin, bone or fillet fish for you, but if you are prepared to do it yourself, the fish will remain fresher longer; the flesh deteriorates faster once it has been taken off the bone. Furthermore, you can then be confident that all the bones have been removed, and you can use the trimmings to make a fish stock (see p.8). Cover any wooden work surfaces or boards with sheets of newspaper before you start work, to prevent them taking on the smell of the fish. This also makes it easy to wrap up and dispose of the entrails when you have finished.

Cleaning and rinsing is essential before cooking. The fins, scales and entrails should be removed, and usually the head is cut off. If the fish is to be cooked whole with the head left on, then snip out the gills with kitchen scissors. Round fish such as trout, mackerel, bass, bream and herring need to be de-scaled and gutted. Flat fish – such as plaice, halibut and sole – are gutted at sea as soon as they are caught to prevent the flesh turning pink; they do not need de-scaling, but they should be washed thoroughly under cold water.

Filleting and skinning at home requires different techniques for round fish and flat fish (see opposite page). Most fish, round and flat, are filleted first, then skinned; one exception is Dover sole, which is skinned first.

It is possible to remove both fillets from one side in one piece to give a double fillet. To do this, make a V-shaped cut behind the head (as for filleting flat fish), then cut down the right or left side where the flesh meets the fins. Insert the tip of the knife under the flesh at the head end and, with short strokes, cut the flesh away from the bones, working right across the fish to the other side.

De-scaling and gutting round fish

1 Wash the fish thoroughly under cold water, then cut off the fins with a pair of kitchen scissors.

2 Put the fish in a large polythene bag or under a sheet of polythene to prevent the scales scattering. Hold the fish firmly by the tail and use a scaling knife, or the back of a small knife, to scrape off the scales, working towards the head.

3 Cut the head off, then cut the fish open along the belly, using a pair of kitchen scissors or a very sharp knife. Pull out the entrails, then wash the fish under cold running water and pat dry with kitchen paper.

4 Remove any black membranes from the flesh inside the fish by sprinkling with salt and rubbing off with kitchen paper.

Filleting flat fish

1 Make a V-shaped cut just behind the head, cutting down to the bones but not through them.

2 With the tail towards you, make a long incision lengthways down the centre of the fish, cutting through the flesh to the bones.

3 Starting at the head end, insert the tip of the knife into the cut and turn the blade so that it lies flat against the bones. With short strokes, cut the flesh away from the bones and remove the fillet.

4 Turn the fish around and remove the second fillet, starting at the tail. Turn the fish over and repeat the process on the other side.

Filleting round fish

1 After de-scaling and cleaning, lay the fish on its side and make a diagonal cut just behind the head, cutting down to the bones but not through them.

2 With the tail towards you, make a deep cut into the flesh right down the centre of the backbone.

3 Keeping the blade of the knife close to the bones, cut away the fillet with short strokes. Repeat the process on the other side.

Skinning a fillet

1 Lay the fillet skin-side down. Hold it firmly at the tail end and make a small, downward cut at the same end through the flesh, until the blade reaches the skin. Turn the knife flat so that the sharp edge is inserted at a slight angle between flesh and skin, pointing towards the head.

2 Using a gentle sawing movement, work the knife towards the head end. The flesh will curl away from the skin as the blade moves along.

Skinning a Dover sole

1 Lay the sole flat on the work surface, black skin up. Make a small, horizontal cut across the skin at the tail end with a small sharp knife. Insert the tip of the knife just under the skin to loosen it.

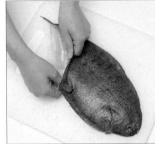

2 Insert your thumb between the skin and the flesh and run it up along one edge of the sole, right up to the head. Repeat along the other edge.

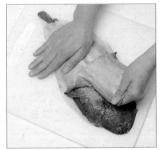

3 Hold the fish firmly by the tail and pull the skin off towards the head. Remove the white skin on the other side in the same way.

Boning and stuffing whole fish is simpler than it sounds. Larger fish, such as salmon, can be boned either from the front (see overleaf) or along the backbone, in order to leave the belly area uncut and free to stuff. In this case, the fish is gutted once the backbone has been removed.

There are various methods of securing the stuffing inside a fish. In the case of the rolled herring (see overleaf), a small piece of bone at the tail is used to hold the herring together. Small cocktail sticks or toothpicks can be used to secure the flesh of a small fish, while larger fish can be sewn up using a clean, large darning needle and some clean, thin string.

Boning and stuffing a salmon

1 Lay the de-scaled, gutted and cleaned salmon on its side and lift up one of the belly flaps. Slide a small, sharp, pointed knife underneath the bones to free them from the flesh on both sides of the backbone.

2 Free the backbone by running the knife along each side of it, taking care not to cut through the skin, then snip off the backbone at each end with kitchen scissors.

3 Fill the salmon with the stuffing, then wrap the belly flaps around the stuffing to enclose it completely, reshaping the fish neatly. Sew the two belly flaps together with a clean, large darning needle and clean, thin string.

Stuffing a herring

1 Open the herring out flat and lay it skin-side up on the work surface. Press firmly along the backbone to completely flatten the fish, then turn it over.

2 Working from the head end, run a thumb underneath the bones on each side of the backbone.

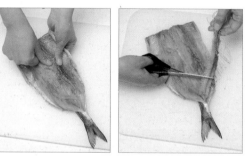

3 Lift the bones away from the flesh in one piece. Cut the backbone off 2.5 cm (1 in) from the tail with kitchen scissors.

4 Spread the stuffing over the herring and roll it up towards the tail (right). Insert the small piece of bone attached to the tail into the flesh to secure (below).

Using dried or salted cod

Methods for preserving fish are as old as the art of fishing itself. Although dried and salted fish lost some popularity with the advent of freezing, preserved fish is still available in some fishmongers, larger supermarkets and Asian and African-Caribbean grocery shops.

The commonest dried fish in this country is salted cod, which is preserved by being left for several weeks between layers of salt. The cod shrinks during the salting process, and – as with all types of preserved fish – it needs to be soaked in cold water before cooking. When buying salted cod, look for fish that is off-white, with a greyish tinge. Yellower fish has been left in the salt too long.

To prepare salted cod, cut the fish into two or three pieces and put them in a large china or glass bowl. Cover with 7.5-10 cm (3-4 in) or more of cold water and leave to soak at least overnight, or for up to 48 hours. Change the water at least four times to rid the fish of as much salt as possible.

To cook, drain off the water and put the cod in a large saucepan. Cover with cold water and bring to the boil, then change the water and bring back to the boil. Cook until the fish flakes easily when tested with a fork.

Buying shellfish

When you buy shellfish, check that it is virtually odourless; any shellfish with a strong smell is not fresh and may be going off. Crabs should feel heavy, and have perfect shells – holes may mean that boiling water has penetrated the shell and made the flesh watery. You can check the freshness of lobster by its tail, which should be springy.

Oysters, mussels and scallops (unless ready-prepared and frozen) should be bought live, while prawns should still be frozen, whether cooked or uncooked. If they are defrosted, it is hard to tell how long they have been thawed, and they may go off rapidly.

As with fish, shellfish should be eaten the day it is bought, and kept as cool as possible beforehand. Seafood mixes available in supermarkets generally have a sell-by date, which should be rigorously followed. Larger supermarkets generally stock frozen shellfish, ranging from scallops and squid to prawns, crab and lobster. These are a good alternative when fresh shellfish is hard to find.

Preparing shellfish for cooking

Prawns generally need to be peeled, although some have their tails left on for the sake of presentation. After peeling, large prawns need to be de-veined – that is, have their black, bitter-tasting intestinal vein removed.

Mussels decay very quickly, and decayed mussels, if cooked, can be the cause of severe food poisoning. It is very important to check that the mussels are all alive before cooking. Any mussels that are open, even slightly, may be dead. If they close when you give them a tap, they can be used. If they do not close, discard them, along with any others that have broken or cracked shells.

Mussels need scrubbing to remove any barnacles, and de-bearding to remove the threadlike beard. If mussels are bought from the fishmonger or supermarket already cleaned and de-bearded, they should still be checked for freshness before cooking. To help free the mussels of any sandy grit, put them into a large bowl after cleaning them and cover them with cold water. Sprinkle a tablespoon of oatmeal or flour into the water, and leave the mussels for 2-3 hours, or overnight, to feed on it and disgorge any grit.

Oysters can be opened by a fishmonger, if you ask. In doing this, however, their juices, which can be used to flavour a sauce, will be lost. It is better to open oysters yourself at home just before you need them for cooking.

To open oysters safely you need a special oyster knife with a protective shield. Never be tempted to use a kitchen knife as it may slip and cause an injury. Oyster knives are not very expensive and can be bought from some fishmongers, good hardware stores and kitchen equipment shops.

Peeling a prawn

1 Hold the body of the prawn firmly and twist off the head.

2 Hold the prawn with the legs upwards and use your thumbs to break the shell away from the body. Then peel it off.

De-veining a prawn

Make a shallow incision along the back of the prawn to expose the intestinal vein, then remove it with a cocktail stick or the tip of a small knife.

Cleaning mussels

1 Put the mussels in a bowlful or sinkful of cold water, and sort them through, discarding any which are already open or which have damaged shells. Use a small knife to scrape off any barnacles.

2 Pull away the 'beards', the thread-like strands on the shells which the mussels use to attach themselves to rocks. Scrub the shells clean under cold running water and rinse in several changes of clean water.

Shucking oysters

1 Hold the oyster, flat-side up, firmly in a cloth, to prevent it slipping and to protect your hands. Insert an oyster knife into the join between the two halves of the shell, in the middle of the straight edge. Slide the knife from end to end along the inside of the top shell to free the muscle, then twist the knife to separate the shell.

2 Gently run the knife under the oyster to loosen it from the bottom shell. Keep the shells in a horizontal position to catch the juices, if needed.

VEGETARIAN MEALS

The choice of vegetables now available all year round makes cooking without meat or poultry an increasing pleasure. These recipes draw inspiration from the cooking traditions of many different countries, putting a wide variety of vegetables, pulses and pastas to good use. Wholesome stews, savoury tarts and moist stuffed peppers are among the mouth-watering delicacies suggested on the following pages.

❖

Stuffed Peppers (left) are filled with a tasty mixture of onion, mushroom, green lentils and rice, flavoured with garlic and oregano (see p.157).

CHEDDAR AND BROCCOLI BREAD PUDDING

Serves 4
Preparation time: 25 minutes
Cooking time: 45 minutes

....

2 tablespoons olive oil
1 onion, peeled and finely chopped
225 g (8 oz) mushrooms, wiped and
   thinly sliced
450 g (1 lb) broccoli, cut into
   small florets
¼ level teaspoon salt
Freshly ground black pepper
8 medium slices wholemeal bread,
   about 340 g (12 oz), crusts
   removed and halved
225 g (8 oz) mature Cheddar
   cheese, grated
3 eggs, size 2
285 ml (½ pint) semi-skimmed milk
2 tomatoes, sliced

....

Per serving
Calories 579 Protein 34 g
Total fat 35 g (saturated fat 16 g)
Carbohydrates 35 g (added sugar 0)
Fibre 6.7 g Sodium 936 mg

....

Any fresh green vegetable – such
as asparagus or fine green beans
– can be used to make this
filling vegetarian supper.

1 Preheat the oven to 190°C
(375°F, gas mark 5). Heat the oil
in a large frying pan and soften the
onion in it. Add the mushrooms
and cook for 2 minutes, then stir
in the broccoli florets, salt and
some pepper. Cover the pan and
simmer for 5 minutes.

2 Lightly butter a large baking
dish, then line it with half the
bread. Spoon half the broccoli
mixture over the bread, then
sprinkle with half the Cheddar.

3 Whisk the eggs with the milk
and pour half into the baking
dish. Add further layers of bread,
broccoli, Cheddar and egg, then
place the tomato slices on top.

4 Cover the dish with foil
and bake in the oven for
20 minutes. Uncover the dish and
cook for a further 15 minutes, until
set and lightly brown. Serve from
the dish with a mixed green salad.

CHEESE AND SWEET PEPPER BAKE

Serves 6
Preparation time: 40 minutes
Cooking time: 45 minutes

....

340 g (12 oz) bulgur wheat
450 ml (16 fl oz) boiling-hot
   vegetable stock (see p.9)
1 tablespoon olive oil
2 large onions, peeled and chopped
2 large peppers, 1 green, 1 red,
   de-seeded and sliced
340 g (12 oz) frozen sweetcorn
   kernels
2 cloves garlic, peeled and crushed
4 tablespoons soy sauce
2 tablespoons dry sherry
Freshly ground black pepper
115 g (4 oz) each Gruyère cheese
   and Emmenthal cheese, grated
570 ml (1 pint) milk
4 eggs, size 2, lightly beaten
1 beefsteak tomato, thinly sliced
2 tablespoons snipped fresh chives

....

Per serving
Calories 502 Protein 23 g
Total fat 17 g (saturated fat 6.7 g)
Carbohydrates 65 g (added sugar 0)
Fibre 4.1 g Sodium 817 mg

....

Bulgur wheat combines with
Gruyère and Emmenthal
cheeses to make a substantial,
slightly crispy topping for a
vegetable bake. Use mature
Cheddar cheese if you want a
more pronounced flavour.

1 Preheat the oven to 160°C
(325°F, gas mark 3). Cover the
bulgur wheat with the stock and
leave for 15 minutes. Meanwhile,
heat the oil in a large frying pan
and soften the onions and peppers
in it for about 5 minutes.

2 Stir in the frozen sweetcorn and
the garlic and fry for 1 minute.
Mix in 1 tablespoon each of the
soy sauce and sherry, then season
well with black pepper. Stir the
rest of the soy sauce and sherry
into the bulgur wheat, and again,
season well with pepper.

3 Lightly grease a large, shallow,
ovenproof dish, then spoon the
onion, pepper and corn mixture
into it. Spread the bulgur wheat
over the top of the vegetables and
sprinkle with the cheeses.

4 Whisk the milk with the eggs,
then pour the mixture over the
cheese. Arrange the tomato slices
on top and bake, uncovered, in the
centre of the oven for 45 minutes,
or until slightly puffy and golden
brown. Sprinkle with the chives,
and serve with a green salad.

ORIENTAL OMELETTE

Serves 4
Preparation time: 30 minutes
Cooking time: 20 minutes

3 tablespoons soy sauce
1 tablespoon dry sherry or rice wine
2 teaspoons sesame oil
225 g (8 oz) firm tofu, cut into small cubes
30 g (1 oz) shiitake mushrooms, soaked in 200 ml (7 fl oz) boiling water
1 level teaspoon cornflour
2 tablespoons vegetable oil
1 medium red pepper, de-seeded and thinly sliced
2 spring onions, trimmed and thinly sliced lengthways
225 g (8 oz) cooked white rice (see p.9)
85 g (3 oz) frozen peas, thawed
85 g (3 oz) beansprouts, rinsed and drained
4 eggs, size 1
3 tablespoons water

Per serving
Calories 355 Protein 17 g
Total fat 19 g (saturated fat 2.3 g)
Carbohydrates 30 g (added sugar 0)
Fibre 4.1 g Sodium 737 mg

An aromatic marinade adds flavour to tofu in this healthy dish.

Compact squares of tofu, shiitake mushrooms and crisp beansprouts provide contrasting tastes and textures in this wholesome omelette with a lively soy-flavoured sauce.

1 Mix the soy sauce and sherry with the sesame oil and coat the tofu in it. Leave to marinate for 20 minutes, turning occasionally.

2 Strain the liquid from the mushrooms through a piece of kitchen paper into a measuring jug. Add the marinade from the tofu and enough water to make 225 ml (8 fl oz), then blend with the cornflour. Pour the mixture into a large frying pan and cook for 2-3 minutes over a moderate heat, stirring, until thickened and clear. Pour the sauce into a serving bowl and keep hot.

3 Slice the mushrooms. Wipe the frying pan with kitchen paper, then heat the vegetable oil for 1 minute. Stir-fry the pepper in it for 2 minutes, then add the spring onions and stir-fry for a further 2 minutes. Add the rice, mushrooms and peas, then scatter the tofu and beansprouts on top.

4 Beat the eggs and water in a bowl until foamy, then pour over the vegetables. Cook over a low heat for about 5 minutes. Lift the edges of the omelette and tilt the pan from time to time to allow all the uncooked egg to set. Serve with the hot sauce, wholemeal bread and a mixed lettuce salad.

151

THREE-CHEESE CALZONES

Serves 4
Preparation time: 1 hour 45 minutes
Cooking time: 30 minutes

....

For the dough
200 ml (7 fl oz) lukewarm water
½ level teaspoon caster sugar
1½ level teaspoons dried yeast
340 g (12 oz) strong plain flour
½ level teaspoon salt
15 g (½ oz) butter

For the filling
1 tablespoon olive oil
1 onion, peeled and chopped
1 small red pepper, de-seeded
    and chopped
1 clove garlic, peeled and crushed
1 tablespoon chopped fresh basil
    or 1 level teaspoon dried basil
340 g (12 oz) broccoli
    florets, chopped
2 tablespoons dry white wine
    or water
225 g (8 oz) ricotta cheese
115 g (4 oz) mozzarella
    cheese, grated
60 g (2 oz) Parmesan
    cheese, grated
1 egg, size 2, beaten
Freshly ground black pepper
Red pepper rings and sprigs of fresh
    marjoram to garnish

....

Per serving
Calories 658 Protein 34 g
Total fat 27 g (saturated fat 14 g)
Carbohydrates 72 g (added sugar 1.3 g)
Fibre 4.1 g Sodium 450 mg

....

Calzone – a filled, folded
pizza – is a speciality of Naples,
in southern Italy. You can make
your own dough or, if you
prefer, use ready-made calzone
dough or a pizza base mix.

1 Make the dough (see p.203).
While it is rising, heat the oil
in a saucepan and soften the onion,
pepper and garlic in it. Mix in the
basil, broccoli and wine or water,
then cover and cook for 5 minutes.
Remove the pan from the heat and
stir in the ricotta, mozzarella, half
the Parmesan, the beaten egg and
some pepper. Cover and set aside.

2 Preheat the oven to 200°C
(400°F, gas mark 6). Knead
the risen dough for 5 minutes,
then divide into four. Roll out each
piece on a lightly floured surface
to form an oval of 20 cm x 15 cm
(8 in x 6 in). Spoon a quarter of
the filling down the centre of each
oval, leaving a 2.5 cm (1 in) space
at each end. Lightly brush the
edges with cold water, then fold
the dough over lengthways to
enclose the filling. Pinch the edges
together, then put the calzones on
a lightly floured baking sheet.

3 Brush with a little cold
water and sprinkle with the
remaining Parmesan. Bake just
above the centre of the oven for
15-20 minutes, until well risen.
Garnish with the red pepper and
marjoram and serve with salad.

*Broccoli, onion, red pepper and basil, bound with a trio of melting cheeses,
make a nutritious and satisfying filling for crisp, light calzone.*

POTATO AND PEPPER GRATIN

Serves 4
Preparation time: 20 minutes
Cooking time: 1 hour 30 minutes

2 tablespoons olive oil
2 medium onions, peeled and
   thinly sliced
2 medium green peppers,
   de-seeded and thinly sliced
900 g (2 lb) potatoes, scrubbed
   or peeled and thinly sliced
225 g (8 oz) mature Cheddar
   cheese, coarsely grated
425 ml (¾ pint) milk
¼ level teaspoon salt
Freshly ground black pepper
¼ level teaspoon nutmeg

Per serving
Calories 475 Protein 21 g
Total fat 27 g (saturated fat 14 g)
Carbohydrates 39 g (added sugar 0)
Fibre 4.9 g Sodium 531 mg

Layers of onions, green peppers and potatoes soften under bubbling Cheddar in this easy gratin dish, which is equally tasty hot or cold. The slicing attachment on a food processor, or a mandolin, will help speed up preparation of the potatoes.

1 Preheat the oven to 180°C (350°F, gas mark 4). Heat the oil in a large frying pan and soften the onions and peppers in it, stirring occasionally.

2 Arrange one-third of the potatoes in a lightly oiled, shallow ovenproof dish, then cover with half the onion and peppers. Repeat the layers, finishing with a layer of potatoes. Sprinkle evenly with the grated Cheddar.

3 Mix the milk with the salt, some pepper and the nutmeg, then carefully pour the mixture over the potatoes. Bake near the top of the oven for 1-1½ hours, or until the potatoes are cooked, most of the milk has been absorbed, and the dish is bubbling and golden brown. Serve with french bread and a crisp green salad.

LATTICE LEEK AND POTATO PIE

A pastry lattice top transforms the classic combination of leek and potatoes into a showpiece.

Serves 6
Preparation time: 1 hour
Cooking time: 40 minutes

For the pastry
225 g (8 oz) plain flour
⅛ level teaspoon salt
115 g (4 oz) butter
60 g (2 oz) Parmesan cheese, grated
⅛ level teaspoon each cayenne
   pepper and mustard powder
1 egg, size 1, beaten
2-3 teaspoons cold water

For the filling
30 g (1 oz) butter
1 tablespoon olive oil
450 g (1 lb) leeks, thinly sliced
   and washed
1 level teaspoon oregano
30 g (1 oz) plain flour
285 ml (½ pint) vegetable stock
   (see p.9)
150 ml (¼ pint) single cream
Freshly ground black pepper
¼ level teaspoon each salt and
   ground nutmeg
Finely grated rind and strained juice
   of ½ lemon
340 g (12 oz) cooked potatoes,
   thinly sliced
2 tablespoons milk to glaze

Per serving
Calories 544 Protein 13 g
Total fat 35 g (saturated fat 19 g)
Carbohydrates 46 g (added sugar 0)
Fibre 4.9 g Sodium 449 mg

1 Make the pastry (see p.9), adding the Parmesan, cayenne and mustard powder before the egg. Wrap and chill the dough.

2 Meanwhile, heat the butter and oil in a large saucepan and soften the leeks in it. Stir in the oregano and flour, then pour in the stock and bring to the boil, stirring, until thick and smooth. Mix in the cream, some pepper, the salt, nutmeg, lemon rind and juice. Remove from the heat, cover and leave to cool for 30 minutes.

3 Preheat the oven to 220°C (425°F, gas mark 7). Take three-quarters of the pastry and roll it out on a lightly floured surface to make an oblong large enough to cover the bottom and sides of a 30 cm x 18 cm (12 in x 7 in) flan tin. Line the tin with the pastry and carefully trim off the excess. Arrange the potato slices in the base of the tin and spread the leek sauce on top.

4 Gently knead the trimmings with the remaining piece of pastry, then roll out to a 30 cm x 15 cm (12 in x 6 in) oblong and cut into 16 thin strips. Brush the edges of the pastry in the tin with cold water, then lay the strips in a lattice pattern on top, pressing the ends onto the pastry edges. Brush with the milk, bake in the centre of the oven for 30-40 minutes and serve.

SEMOLINA GNOCCHI WITH ARTICHOKES

Triangular cheese gnocchi make an aromatic accompaniment to tender Jerusalem artichokes in this warming dish.

Serves 4
Preparation time: 25 minutes
Chilling time: 2 hours
Cooking time: 25 minutes

1 litre (1¾ pints) milk
¼ level teaspoon freshly
   grated nutmeg
115 g (4 oz) fine semolina
130 g (4½ oz) Parmesan
   cheese, grated
2 eggs, size 3, beaten
1 small onion, peeled and quartered
2 small sprigs fresh parsley
4 black peppercorns
1 bay leaf
450 g (1 lb) Jerusalem artichokes,
   peeled and thickly sliced
45 g (1½ oz) butter
30 g (1 oz) plain flour
¼ level teaspoon salt
Freshly ground black pepper

Per serving
Calories 574 Protein 29 g
Total fat 30 g (saturated fat 18 g)
Carbohydrates 51 g (added sugar 0)
Fibre 1.7 g Sodium 759 mg

1 Bring 570 ml (1 pint) of the milk and the nutmeg to the boil in a large saucepan. Pour in the semolina, stirring continuously, and cook for 3-4 minutes or until the mixture is very thick, without letting it stick or burn.

2 Take the pan off the heat and beat in 115 g (4 oz) of the Parmesan and the eggs. Cook, stirring, for 1 minute. Spread the mixture over the base of a lightly oiled 33 cm x 23 cm (13 in x 9 in) tin. Leave to cool, then chill in the fridge for 2 hours.

3 Bring the remaining milk, the onion, parsley, peppercorns and bay leaf to the boil in a saucepan. Remove from the heat, cover and leave to stand. In the meantime, steam the artichokes for about 5 minutes, until just tender, then leave to cool.

4 Preheat the oven to 200°C (400°F, gas mark 6). Melt the butter in a saucepan, stir in the flour and cook for 1 minute. Strain the milk into a jug, then slowly stir it into the pan and bring to the boil, until thickened. Reduce the heat and simmer for 3 minutes, stirring. Mix in the artichokes, salt and some pepper. Pour the mixture into a shallow dish.

5 Cut the chilled semolina into four lengthways and into five widthways, to make 20 pieces. Cut each one into two triangles.

6 Arrange the triangles on top of the sauce, sprinkle with the remaining Parmesan and bake in the centre of the oven for about 25 minutes, or until golden brown. Serve with a crisp green salad.

TOMATO AND AUBERGINE FLAN

Sun-dried tomatoes add a rich piquancy to a savoury flan that is equally tempting hot or cold. You can make your own pastry, or use a ready-prepared flan case if you are short of time.

Serves 4
Preparation time: 1 hour
Cooking time: 50 minutes

300 g (11 oz) shortcrust pastry
   (see p.9)
225 g (8 oz) small aubergines,
   trimmed and sliced
1½ level teaspoons salt
3 tablespoons olive oil
1 medium onion, peeled and
   finely chopped
1 medium green pepper, de-seeded
   and finely chopped
2 cloves garlic, peeled and crushed
2 large plum tomatoes, skinned,
   quartered and de-seeded
60 g (2 oz) sun-dried tomatoes
   in oil, drained and chopped
2 tablespoons shredded fresh basil
3 eggs, size 2
285 ml (½ pint) milk
1 level teaspoon dried basil
Freshly ground black pepper
60 g (2 oz) Parmesan cheese, grated
Sprigs of fresh basil to garnish

Per serving
Calories 623 Protein 19 g
Total fat 42 g (saturated fat 15 g)
Carbohydrates 44 g (added sugar 0)
Fibre 4.7 g Sodium 921 mg

1 Preheat the oven to 200°C (400°F, gas mark 6). Roll out the pastry to a round large enough to line a 25 cm (10 in) flan tin. Fit into the tin, trim the edge, prick all over, then chill for 30 minutes. Bake in the centre of the oven for 10 minutes, then remove and leave to cool.

2 Sprinkle the aubergines with 1 teaspoon of the salt to remove their bitter juices (see p.11). Meanwhile, heat 1 tablespoon of the oil in a frying pan and fry the onion, pepper and garlic in it for about 3 minutes, then set aside on a plate. Add the remaining oil to the pan and lightly brown the aubergines on each side, a few at a time. Drain on kitchen paper.

3 Spread the onion, pepper and garlic mixture over the bottom of the pastry case, then arrange the aubergines and tomatoes on top. Scatter with the sun-dried tomatoes and shredded basil.

4 Put the flan tin on a baking tray. Lightly whisk the eggs with the milk, dried basil, remaining salt, some pepper and the Parmesan, and pour into the pastry case. Reduce the oven temperature to 190°C (375°F, gas mark 5) and bake for 30-40 minutes, until the filling is puffed and set. Garnish with the fresh basil and serve with a green salad and french bread.

CREAMY BEAN PIE

Serves 4
Preparation time: 45 minutes
Cooking time: 25 minutes

900 g (2 lb) potatoes, peeled
  and quartered
1 tablespoon olive oil
5 cloves garlic, peeled and crushed
2 peppers, 1 red, 1 green,
  de-seeded and chopped
2 medium courgettes, trimmed
  and sliced
225 g (8 oz) canned
  chopped tomatoes
¼ level teaspoon salt
Freshly ground black pepper
225 g (8 oz) each cooked
  chickpeas, pinto beans and
  kidney beans, rinsed and
  drained (see p.172)
30 g (1 oz) butter or margarine
2 tablespoons milk
1 egg, size 3, beaten
¼ level teaspoon paprika
Parsley to garnish

Per serving
Calories 495 Protein 21 g
Total fat 14 g (saturated fat 5.5 g)
Carbohydrates 75 g
  (added sugar 0) Fibre 15 g
    Sodium 265 mg

A layer of creamy mashed potatoes dusted with paprika forms the topping for a mix of beans, courgettes and peppers in a tomato-based sauce.

1 Boil the potatoes until just soft, then drain. Meanwhile, heat 2 teaspoons of the oil in a large frying pan and stir-fry half the garlic in it over a moderate heat for 1 minute. Add the peppers and courgettes and sauté for 4 minutes, then stir in three-quarters of the tomatoes. Season with the salt and some pepper, then cook for a further 3 minutes.

2 Preheat the oven to 190°C (375°F, gas mark 5). Blend the chickpeas with the remaining garlic, oil and tomatoes in a food processor until smooth. Add to the pepper and courgette mixture, mix in the pinto beans and kidney beans, then spoon into the bottom of an ovenproof dish.

3 Mash the potatoes with the butter or margarine and the milk. Spread the potatoes over the filling, decorate with a fork, then brush with the beaten egg and sprinkle with the paprika. Place in the centre of the oven and bake for 25 minutes, or until golden brown. Garnish with the parsley and serve.

Pinto beans, kidney beans and chickpeas add substance to this homely pie and offer a good source of fibre and protein.

Serves 4
Preparation time: 30 minutes
Cooking time: 25 minutes
Chilling time: 30 minutes

2 large aubergines, trimmed
  and halved lengthways
60 g (2 oz) couscous
150 ml (¼ pint) boiling vegetable
  stock (see p.9) or water
115 g (4 oz) cooked chickpeas,
  rinsed and drained (see p.172)
175 g (6 oz) cherry tomatoes,
  halved
150 g (5 oz) Greek yoghurt
115 g (4 oz) feta cheese, drained
  and crumbled
60 g (2 oz) raisins
3 tablespoons mayonnaise
3 tablespoons chopped fresh basil
2 tablespoons pine nuts
½ level teaspoon salt
Freshly ground black pepper
2 tablespoons olive oil
1 tablespoon red wine vinegar
Crisp lettuce leaves and tomato
  halves to garnish

Per serving
Calories 523 Protein 13 g
Total fat 40 g (saturated fat 10 g)
Carbohydrates 29 g (added sugar 0)
Fibre 5.3 g Sodium 754 mg

A taste of Greece pervades this unusual combination of pulses, fresh herbs and feta cheese in an aubergine shell.

AUBERGINES WITH RAISIN COUSCOUS

Pine nuts and raisins combine with Greek yoghurt to give the couscous a delicate sweetness in this light summer dish.

1 Preheat the oven to 200°C (400°F, gas mark 6). Prick the aubergines all over with a fork, then place them cut-side down on a baking tray. Cook in the oven for 25 minutes, or until soft.

2 Meanwhile, place the couscous in a large bowl and soak it in the stock or water for 15 minutes, or until all the liquid has been absorbed.

3 Add the chickpeas, tomatoes, yoghurt, feta cheese, raisins, mayonnaise, basil, pine nuts, half the salt and some pepper. Gently mix them into the couscous.

4 Whisk the olive oil, vinegar, the remaining salt and some pepper to make a vinaigrette. Scoop out the flesh of the aubergines, leaving the shell intact. Chop the flesh and mix it with the vinaigrette.

5 Stir the aubergine and dressing into the couscous mixture and then spoon the filling into the aubergine shells. Put the filled shells on a plate or tray, cover and refrigerate for at least 30 minutes. Garnish with the lettuce leaves and tomato halves and serve.

SPICY FRUIT AND NUT MARROW

Serves 4
Preparation time: 20 minutes
Cooking time: 1 hour 30 minutes

2 tablespoons olive oil
225 g (8 oz) onions, peeled
    and chopped
250 g (9 oz) cooking apples,
    peeled, cored and sliced
1/2 level teaspoon each ground
    ginger and ground cumin
1/4 level teaspoon salt
Freshly ground black pepper
225 g (8 oz) frozen peeled
    chestnuts, thawed
115 g (4 oz) ready-to-use pitted
    prunes, quartered
115 g (4 oz) ready-to-use dried
    apricots, quartered
115 g (4 oz) mixed nuts (such as
    cashews, almonds or walnuts)
30 g (1 oz) each sunflower
    and pumpkin seeds
1 marrow, about 1 kg (2 lb 3 oz)

Per serving
Calories 481 Protein 11 g
Total fat 22 g (saturated fat 2.6 g)
Carbohydrates 63 g (added sugar 0)
Fibre 20 g Sodium 161 mg

Prunes, apricots and a variety
of nuts give body to a
nutritious stuffing. Drained,
canned chestnuts or peeled and
cooked fresh chestnuts can be
used in place of frozen nuts.

1 Preheat the oven to 190°C
(375°F, gas mark 5). Heat the
oil in a large saucepan and soften
the onions in it. Add the apples
and cook for 2 minutes, then stir
in the ginger, cumin, salt and
some pepper. Cook for another
2 minutes, then mix in the
chestnuts, prunes, apricots, mixed
nuts and sunflower and pumpkin
seeds, and stir well.

2 Cut the marrow in half
lengthways, scoop out all the
seeds and lay the marrow halves
cut-side up in a roasting tin. Fill
with the fruit and nut mixture,
then cover the tin with foil.

3 Bake in the centre of the oven
for 1¼-1½ hours, or until the
marrow is cooked through and the
stuffing is moist and browned.
Serve hot or cold with a light salad
of frisée lettuce and orange slices.

STUFFED PEPPERS

Using a combination of green,
red and yellow peppers will
add colour to this wholesome,
full-flavoured supper.

Serves 4
Preparation time: 40 minutes
Cooking time: 40 minutes

60 g (2 oz) green lentils, cleaned of
    grit and rinsed
1 litre (1¾ pints) water
30 g (1 oz) sun-dried tomatoes,
    chopped
115 g (4 oz) long-grain brown rice
2 tablespoons olive oil
1 medium onion, peeled and
    finely chopped
1 large clove garlic, peeled
    and crushed
115 g (4 oz) chestnut mushrooms,
    wiped and sliced
1 level teaspoon dried oregano
1 tablespoon chopped fresh parsley
1/4 level teaspoon salt
Freshly ground black pepper
4 large peppers, halved lengthways
    and de-seeded
115 g (4 oz) feta, Lancashire or
    goat's cheese, crumbled
150 ml (1/4 pint) vegetable stock
    (see p.9)
2 tablespoons dry white wine

Per serving
Calories 372 Protein 13 g
Total fat 15 g (saturated fat 5.2 g)
Carbohydrates 48 g (added sugar 0)
Fibre 6.9 g Sodium 560 mg

1 Put the lentils in a saucepan
with the water and boil rapidly
for 10 minutes. Meanwhile, soften
the dried tomatoes in boiling water
for 10 minutes and then drain.

2 Stir the rice into the lentils,
then reduce the heat. Cover
and simmer for 20-30 minutes,
or until the rice and lentils are
tender, then drain well.

3 In the meantime, preheat
the oven to 190°C (375°F,
gas mark 5). Heat the oil in a
large saucepan and soften the
onion. Mix in the garlic and
mushrooms and fry for 2 minutes.
Stir in the softened tomatoes,
the oregano, parsley, salt, some
pepper and the lentils and rice.

4 Fill each of the pepper halves
with the mixture. Put the
peppers in a shallow baking tin
and sprinkle them with the
crumbled cheese.

5 Pour the stock and wine into
the tin and then cover it with
foil. Place in the centre of the oven
and bake for 30 minutes, then
uncover and cook for a further
10 minutes, or until the peppers
are tender and lightly browned.
Serve with a mixed salad.

BEAN AND TOMATO CHILLI

Serves 4
Preparation time: 15 minutes
Cooking time: 30 minutes

1 tablespoon olive oil
1 medium onion, peeled
  and chopped
225 g (8 oz) long-grain brown rice
2 level teaspoons mild or hot
  chilli powder
570 ml (1 pint) vegetable stock
  (see p.9) or water
570 ml (1 pint) passata
  (sieved tomatoes)
200 g (7 oz) canned tomatoes
450 g (1 lb) cooked red kidney
  beans, rinsed and
  drained (see p.172)
225 g (8 oz) canned or frozen
  sweetcorn kernels
225 g (8 oz) green beans, trimmed
  and cut into short lengths
150 ml (¼ pint) soured cream
  or natural yoghurt
85 g (3 oz) mature Cheddar cheese,
  finely grated
60 g (2 oz) pumpkin seeds

Per serving
Calories 748 Protein 31 g
Total fat 27 g (saturated fat 11 g)
Carbohydrates 101 g (added sugar 0)
Fibre 20 g Sodium 386 mg

Soured cream and pumpkin seeds provide a cool and slightly crunchy contrast for this hot, chunky chilli of green beans, kidney beans and sweetcorn.

1 Heat the oil in a large flameproof casserole or saucepan for 1 minute and soften the onion in it over a moderate heat.

2 Stir in the rice and the chilli powder and pour in the stock or water. Bring to the boil, then reduce the heat, cover and simmer gently for 10 minutes.

3 Stir in the passata, tomatoes and their juice, kidney beans, sweetcorn and green beans. Bring back to the boil, then reduce the heat and simmer, stirring occasionally, for 10-15 minutes, until the green beans are tender, the rice is cooked and all the stock has been absorbed.

4 Spoon the soured cream or yoghurt on top of the chilli, sprinkle with the Cheddar and pumpkin seeds and serve.

TOFU STIR-FRY WITH PEANUT SAUCE

Serves 4
Preparation time: 20 minutes
Cooking time: 10 minutes

200 ml (7 fl oz) vegetable stock
  (see p.9)
2 medium carrots, peeled and cut
  into matchstick strips
225 g (8 oz) each green and red
  cabbage, coarsely shredded
450 g (1 lb) firm tofu, rinsed,
  drained and cut into cubes
2 tablespoons olive oil
1 clove garlic, peeled and crushed
1 fresh green chilli, de-seeded
  and chopped (optional)
8 spring onions, trimmed and sliced
  diagonally into short lengths
225 g (8 oz) fresh bean sprouts,
  rinsed and drained
4 level tablespoons smooth
  peanut butter
2 tablespoons soy sauce
1 tablespoon cider vinegar
2 teaspoons granulated sugar
115 g (4 oz) fine Chinese egg
  noodles, cooked and drained
  (see p.202)
Freshly ground black pepper

Per serving
Calories 377 Protein 19 g
Total fat 19 g (saturated fat 2.9 g)
Carbohydrates 34 g (added sugar 2.5 g)
Fibre 8.1 g Sodium 695 mg

Shreds of green and red cabbage are tossed with bean sprouts, carrots, spring onions and protein-packed tofu to create a light, healthy stir-fry. Use firm-textured tofu, as this keeps its neat shape during stir-frying, and for added flavour marinate the cubes in diluted soy sauce and grated fresh root ginger for 20 minutes before cooking.

1 Pour 150 ml (¼ pint) of the stock into a large wok or frying pan and bring to the boil. Add the carrots and green and red cabbage, then cover and cook for 3 minutes.

2 Add the tofu, oil, garlic, chilli, spring onions and bean sprouts. Stir-fry for 2-3 minutes, or until the spring onions and bean sprouts are just tender.

3 Mix the remaining stock with the peanut butter, soy sauce, vinegar and sugar in a small bowl, then stir the mixture into the wok or pan. Add the noodles and some pepper and cook, stirring, for about 2 minutes, until the noodles are heated through and all the vegetables are coated with the sauce. Serve immediately.

PAELLA WITH TOFU

Serves 4
Preparation time: 20 minutes
Cooking time: 50 minutes

2 tablespoons olive oil
1 large onion, peeled and chopped
1 large red pepper, de-seeded
   and chopped
2 cloves garlic, peeled and crushed
400 g (14 oz) canned
   chopped tomatoes
½ level teaspoon salt
1 level teaspoon ground turmeric
½ level teaspoon each dried basil
   and dried thyme
570 ml (1 pint) vegetable stock
   (see p.9)
225 g (8 oz) cooked chickpeas,
   rinsed and drained (see p.172)
225 g (8 oz) long-grain white rice
275 g (10 oz) firm tofu, rinsed,
   drained and cut into cubes
60 g (2 oz) toasted slivered almonds
   and sprigs of fresh thyme and
   oregano to garnish

Per serving
Calories 417 Protein 16 g
Total fat 11 g (saturated fat 1.5 g)
Carbohydrates 67 g (added sugar 0)
Fibre 6.2 g Sodium 293 mg

Leaving the paella to stand once cooked allows the rich aroma and golden colour of the ground turmeric to be fully absorbed by the chickpeas, rice and tofu.

Turmeric gives this fibre-rich meal a mild musky flavour and an attractive colouring. The chickpeas, rice and tofu make a versatile combination for any variations you can think of – fine green beans cut into short lengths, for example, or quartered hard-boiled eggs scattered over the paella just before serving.

1 Heat the oil in a large frying pan and soften the onion, red pepper and garlic in it for 2-3 minutes. Stir in the chopped tomatoes, salt, turmeric and dried basil and thyme, and cook over a moderate heat for 5 minutes.

2 Pour in the stock and mix in the chickpeas, then bring to the boil and stir in the rice. Reduce the heat, cover and simmer gently for 20 minutes, stirring occasionally, until the rice is cooked and most of the liquid has been absorbed.

3 Stir in the tofu and heat through, uncovered, for about 10 minutes. Take the pan off the heat, cover and leave to stand for 10 minutes. Turn into a heated serving dish, garnish with the almonds, thyme and oregano and serve.

LOUISIANA RICE AND BEANS

Serves 4
Preparation time: 20 minutes
Cooking time: 35 minutes

2 tablespoons olive oil
1 large onion, peeled and chopped
1 green pepper, de-seeded
  and chopped
175 g (6 oz) chestnut mushrooms,
  wiped and halved
3 cloves garlic, peeled and crushed
225 g (8 oz) long-grain white rice
400 g (14 oz) canned
  chopped tomatoes
  570 ml (1 pint) vegetable stock
    (see p.9)

1 tablespoon chopped
  fresh marjoram
1/2 level teaspoon salt
Freshly ground black pepper
225 g (8 oz) curly kale or spinach,
  trimmed, washed and shredded
225 g (8 oz) frozen peas
450 g (1 lb) cooked red kidney
  beans, rinsed and drained
  (see p.172)

Per serving
Calories 467 Protein 19 g
Total fat 9.5 g (saturated fat 1.5 g)
Carbohydrates 82 g (added sugar 0)
Fibre 18 g Sodium 332 mg

This satisfying blend of rea
beans and rice is cooked in a
tasty garlic and marjoram stock.
The recipe is inspired by the
thick rice and bean stews that
are a speciality of Louisiana, one
of the southern United States.

1 Heat the oil in a large
flameproof casserole or heavy
saucepan and fry the onion, green
pepper, mushrooms and garlic in it
for 5 minutes, or until softened.

*Curly kale and green peas
add a light, fresh taste
to this hearty
country dish.*

2 Stir in the rice, tomatoes,
stock, marjoram, salt and some
pepper and bring to the boil.
Reduce the heat, cover the pan and
simmer gently for 20 minutes.

3 Add the curly kale or spinach,
peas and beans, stir well and
cook, covered, for 5-10 minutes,
or until all the stock has been
absorbed. Turn into a heated
dish and serve with
french bread.

RICE AND BEANS WITH ITALIAN CHEESE

Serves 4
Preparation time: 20 minutes
Cooking time: 30 minutes

1 tablespoon olive oil
1 large onion, peeled and chopped
2 cloves garlic, peeled and crushed
225 g (8 oz) long-grain white rice
340 g (12 oz) fine green beans, cut
   into short lengths
570 ml (1 pint) vegetable stock
   (see p.9)
175 g (6 oz) Gorgonzola cheese,
   coarsely crumbled
115 ml (4 fl oz) single cream
225 g (8 oz) cooked cannellini
   beans, rinsed and drained
½ level teaspoon salt
Freshly ground black pepper
2 tablespoons chopped
   fresh parsley
1 tablespoon chopped fresh basil

Per serving
Calories 542 Protein 19 g
Total fat 25 g (saturated fat 13 g)
Carbohydrates 65 g (added sugar 0)
Fibre 8 g Sodium 757 mg

Gorgonzola, the classic Italian blue-veined cheese, lends its strong, tangy flavour to this substantial and nutritious dish of rice with green and cannellini beans. If you prefer a milder taste, use a mixture of 60 g (2 oz) grated Parmesan and 115 g (4 oz) shredded mozzarella in place of the Gorgonzola.

1 Heat the oil in a large flameproof casserole or heavy saucepan and fry the onion in it until softened. Stir in the garlic, rice and green beans and cook, stirring, for 1 minute.

2 Pour in the stock and bring the mixture to the boil. Reduce the heat, cover the pan and simmer gently for 20 minutes.

3 Stir the Gorgonzola, cream, cannellini beans, salt and some pepper into the rice mixture. Cook for a further 5 minutes, until the beans are heated through, the rice is cooked and all the stock has been absorbed. Stir in the parsley and basil and serve.

ASPARAGUS AND WALNUT STIR-FRY

Serves 4
Preparation time: 25 minutes
Cooking time: 15 minutes

2 tablespoons groundnut oil
1 level tablespoon peeled
   and grated fresh root ginger
1 clove garlic, peeled and crushed
8 spring onions, trimmed
   and cut into short lengths
340 g (12 oz) asparagus, trimmed
   and cut into short lengths
340 g (12 oz) carrots, peeled
   and cut into matchstick strips
340 g (12 oz) button chestnut
   mushrooms, wiped
225 ml (8 fl oz) vegetable stock
   (see p.9)
2 tablespoons soy sauce
225 g (8 oz) long-grain white rice,
   cooked (see p.9)
2 teaspoons sesame oil
60 g (2 oz) walnuts, chopped and
   lightly toasted

Per serving
Calories 417 Protein 11 g
Total fat 21 g (saturated fat 2.1 g)
Carbohydrates 49 g (added sugar 0)
Fibre 7.5 g Sodium 533 mg

Strips of delicate asparagus, nutty button mushrooms, carrots and spring onions combine with rice and walnuts in a zesty garlic and ginger sauce. When fresh asparagus is not in season, use canned asparagus – simply add the spears to the dish for the final 2 minutes of cooking.

1 Heat the groundnut oil in a wok or very large frying pan and stir-fry the ginger, garlic and spring onions in it for about 30 seconds. Add the asparagus and stir-fry for about 2 minutes.

2 Mix in the carrots and stir-fry for 2 minutes, then add the mushrooms and stir-fry for a further 2 minutes. Pour in the stock and soy sauce, then add the cooked rice. Cover and cook over a moderate heat for 5 minutes, stirring occasionally, until the rice is heated through. Stir in the sesame oil, sprinkle with the walnuts and serve at once.

MUSHROOM AND LENTIL MOUSSAKA

Serves 4
Preparation time: 40 minutes
Standing time: 1 hour
Cooking time: 1 hour

550 g (1 1/4 lb) aubergines,
   trimmed and thinly sliced
2 1/2 level teaspoons salt
4 tablespoons olive oil
1 large onion, peeled and chopped
1 green pepper, de-seeded
   and chopped
2 cloves garlic, peeled and crushed
225 g (8 oz) chestnut mushrooms,
   wiped and sliced
340 g (12 oz) tomatoes, skinned,
   de-seeded and chopped
2 level teaspoons soft light
   brown sugar
1/2 level teaspoon ground cinnamon
Freshly ground black pepper
3 tablespoons chopped
   fresh parsley
2 tablespoons dry white
   wine or water
225 g (8 oz) cooked brown lentils,
   drained (see p.173)
30 g (1 oz) butter
30 g (1 oz) plain flour
285 ml (1/2 pint) milk
2 eggs, size 2, separated
1/4 level teaspoon freshly grated
   or ground nutmeg
115 g (4 oz) Cheddar
   cheese, grated
Chopped fresh parsley to garnish

Aubergines, mushrooms and lentils replace the lamb in this wholesome moussaka, covered with a light soufflé topping. You can make the moussaka the day before you want to serve it and store it in the refrigerator. Make the topping just before you reheat the main dish.

1 Sprinkle the aubergine slices with 2 level teaspoons of the salt (see p.11) and leave for 1 hour. Rinse the slices and pat them dry with kitchen paper.

2 Preheat the oven to 180°C (350°F, gas mark 4). Heat 2 tablespoons of the oil in a large frying pan and fry the aubergine slices in it until lightly browned on both sides. Put them on a plate and set aside.

3 Heat the remaining oil in the pan and cook the onion, green pepper and garlic in it for 5 minutes. Stir in the mushrooms, tomatoes, sugar, cinnamon, 1/4 level teaspoon of the salt, some pepper and the parsley, then pour in the wine or water. Cover and simmer for 10 minutes. Stir in the lentils, then remove from the heat.

Per serving
Calories 522 Protein 22 g
Total fat 35 g (saturated fat 14 g)
Carbohydrates 30 g (added sugar 2.5 g)
Fibre 6.9 g Sodium 819 mg

This rich vegetarian moussaka combines aubergines, olive oil and mushrooms with a creamy soufflé sauce.

4 Arrange half the aubergine slices in the bottom of a large ovenproof dish. Spread the lentil mixture evenly over the top, cover with the remaining aubergine slices, then set aside.

5 Melt the butter in a saucepan, mix in the flour and cook, stirring, for 1 minute. Take the pan off the heat and gradually blend in the milk. Return it to the heat and bring to the boil. Cook, stirring, for 3-5 minutes, or until the sauce thickens.

6 Remove the pan from the heat and beat in the egg yolks. Season the sauce with the remaining salt, some pepper and the nutmeg. Whisk the egg whites until they hold soft peaks. Mix a quarter of the whites into the sauce, then gently fold in the rest.

7 Pour the sauce over the aubergines and sprinkle with the Cheddar. Place in the centre of the oven and bake for 30 minutes. Turn off the oven and leave the moussaka to settle for 10 minutes before serving. Garnish with the parsley, and serve with a crisp lettuce salad and crusty bread.

SPICY LENTILS AND RICE

Serves 4
Preparation time: 15 minutes
Cooking time: 45 minutes

- 2 tablespoons olive oil
- 6 spring onions, trimmed and sliced
- 3 cloves garlic, peeled and coarsely chopped
- 2 medium carrots, peeled and sliced
- 225 g (8 oz) mushrooms, wiped and quartered
- 225 g (8 oz) red lentils, cleaned of grit and rinsed (see p.172)
- 225 g (8 oz) long-grain white rice
- 1 level teaspoon salt
- 1 level teaspoon each ground coriander, cumin, ginger and turmeric
- 1 litre (1¾ pints) vegetable stock (see p.9)
- 225 g (8 oz) curly kale, trimmed, washed and shredded
- 150 ml (¼ pint) low-fat natural yoghurt
- 2 level tablespoons sesame seeds
- Spring onions and carrot strips to garnish (optional)

Per serving
Calories 535 Protein 24 g
Total fat 12 g (saturated fat 2 g)
Carbohydrates 88 g (added sugar 0)
Fibre 11 g Sodium 579 mg

An aromatic blend of coriander, cumin, ginger and turmeric flavours lentils and rice simmered in a tasty vegetable stock. If you want to add crunch, stir in 2-3 tablespoons of unsalted peanuts.

1 Heat the oil in a heavy saucepan and cook the spring onions, garlic, carrots and mushrooms in it for 5 minutes, stirring occasionally.

2 Stir in the lentils, rice, salt, coriander, cumin, ginger, turmeric and stock, and bring to the boil. Reduce the heat, cover and simmer, stirring occasionally, for 30-35 minutes, or until the rice and lentils are cooked and the stock has been absorbed.

3 Stir in the kale, then cover and cook for 2 minutes, or until the kale is slightly wilted. Spoon the yoghurt over the top and sprinkle with the sesame seeds. Garnish with the spring onions and carrot strips, if using, and serve.

LENTIL AND CARROT STEW WITH YOGHURT

Serves 4
Preparation time: 25 minutes
Cooking time: 50 minutes

2 tablespoons olive oil
3 large onions, peeled
  and chopped
225 g (8 oz) green lentils, cleaned
  of grit and rinsed
115 g (4 oz) long-grain brown rice
1.15 litres (2 pints) vegetable stock
  (see p.9)
400 g (14 oz) canned
  chopped tomatoes
3 tablespoons chopped
  fresh parsley
3 cloves garlic, peeled and crushed
1/2 level teaspoon salt
1/2 level teaspoon ground cinnamon
1/4 level teaspoon ground cloves
1/4 level teaspoon cayenne pepper
4 large carrots, peeled
  and chopped
2 sticks celery, trimmed
  and chopped
150 ml (1/4 pint) natural yoghurt
  or soured cream
Cayenne pepper to garnish

Per serving
Calories 433 Protein 20 g
Total fat 9.3 g (saturated fat 1.3 g)
Carbohydrates 72 g (added sugar 0)
Fibre 63 g Sodium 366 mg

Carrots add sweetness and colour to this nutritious and economical winter stew of lentils and rice spiced with cinnamon, cloves and cayenne pepper.

1 Heat the oil in a large flameproof casserole and brown the onions, stirring occasionally. Put half the onions on a plate and leave to one side.

2 Add the lentils and rice to the onions and cook, stirring, for 1 minute. Mix in the vegetable stock, chopped tomatoes, parsley, garlic, salt, cinnamon, cloves and cayenne pepper and simmer gently, uncovered, for 20 minutes. Then add the carrots and celery and cook the stew for a further 20 minutes, or until the rice and carrots are just tender.

3 Scatter the reserved onion over the top of the stew and spoon the yoghurt or soured cream on top. Sprinkle with a little extra cayenne pepper and serve.

CHICKPEA AND TOMATO SPAGHETTI

Spaghetti doused in thick tomato sauce is served with tasty chickpea dumplings, making a satisfying supper.

Serves 4
Preparation time: 45 minutes
Cooking time: 20 minutes

450 g (1 lb) cooked chickpeas,
  rinsed and drained (see p.172)
1 large clove garlic, peeled
1 egg, size 1
1 tablespoon olive oil
30 g (1 oz) fresh white breadcrumbs
30 g (1 oz) grated Parmesan cheese
1/4 level teaspoon salt
Freshly ground black pepper
800 g (1 3/4 lb) canned tomatoes
2 tablespoons tomato purée
340 g (12 oz) spaghetti
175 g (6 oz) frozen peas
Sprig of fresh basil to garnish

Per serving
Calories 605 Protein 30 g
Total fat 12 g (saturated fat 2.9 g)
Carbohydrates 100 g (added sugar 0)
Fibre 1.5 g Sodium 391 mg

1 Put the chickpeas, garlic, egg, oil, breadcrumbs, grated Parmesan, salt and some pepper in a food processor and purée until a smooth paste.

2 Divide the mixture into 16 roughly equal portions and, with wetted hands, shape each portion into a ball.

3 Pour the tomatoes into a wide saucepan or frying pan, add the tomato purée and cook, uncovered, over a moderate heat for 5 minutes, stirring occasionally.

4 Cook the spaghetti (see p.202). In the meantime, carefully add the chickpea balls to the tomato sauce. Bring to the boil, then reduce the heat to low, cover and simmer gently for 10 minutes.

5 Add the peas to the tomato sauce, bring back to the boil, then cover and simmer gently for a further 5 minutes. Drain the spaghetti and put it in a heated serving bowl. Spoon the chickpea balls and sauce over the top and gently toss with the spaghetti. Garnish with the basil and serve.

FALAFEL CASSEROLE

Falafel – lightly spiced chickpea patties – are a staple dish in the Middle East. Here the traditional mixture is fortified with bulgur wheat, egg and breadcrumbs.

Serves 4
Preparation time: 50 minutes
Cooking time: 30 minutes

- 115 g (4 oz) bulgur wheat
- 1 large onion, peeled and quartered
- 1 clove garlic, peeled
- 15 g (1/2 oz) fresh coriander or parsley
- 1 level teaspoon each ground cumin and ground coriander
- 1/4 level teaspoon baking powder
- 1 level teaspoon salt
- 1/8 level teaspoon cayenne pepper
- 225 g (8 oz) cooked chickpeas, rinsed and drained
- 1 egg, size 2, beaten
- 60 g (2 oz) fresh white breadcrumbs
- 675 g (1 1/2 lb) fresh spinach, trimmed and washed
- 6 tablespoons olive oil
- 1 medium onion, peeled and chopped
- 425 ml (3/4 pint) natural yoghurt
- 2 level tablespoons plain flour
- 60 g (2 oz) shelled and skinned unsalted pistachio nuts
- 2 tablespoons chopped fresh coriander or parsley to garnish

Per serving
Calories 472 Protein 25 g
Total fat 14 g (saturated fat 2.5 g)
Carbohydrates 63 g (added sugar 0)
Fibre 11 g Sodium 1070 mg

1 Put the bulgur wheat in a bowl and add just enough cold water to cover it. Leave to soak for 20 minutes, then drain thoroughly, return to the bowl and set aside.

2 In the meantime, put the quartered onion, garlic, fresh coriander or parsley, cumin and ground coriander in a food processor and blend until finely chopped. Add the baking powder, half the salt, the cayenne pepper and chickpeas and blend to a smooth paste. Combine with the egg, breadcrumbs and drained bulgur wheat.

3 Divide this mixture into eight roughly equal portions and, with wetted hands, shape each one into a neat patty.

4 Preheat the oven to 200°C (400°F, gas mark 6). Blanch the spinach (see p.10) and then chop the leaves coarsely.

5 Heat 2 tablespoons of the oil in a large frying pan and soften the onion in it without browning. Add the spinach and the remaining salt and cook for 2 minutes over a high heat, stirring to prevent sticking, until the mixture is dry.

6 Whisk the yoghurt with the flour. Stir it into the spinach mixture, then transfer to a shallow, lightly greased ovenproof dish.

7 Wipe the frying pan clean and heat the remaining oil in it. Lightly brown the falafel on each side for 1-2 minutes, then arrange them on top of the spinach.

8 Bake in the centre of the oven for 15-20 minutes or until the centre of the spinach mixture is lightly set. Sprinkle with the pistachio nuts and chopped coriander or parsley and serve.

A scattering of chopped pistachio nuts adds crunch to chickpea falafel baked with spinach.

CHICKPEA AND VEGETABLE PILAFF

Serves 6
Preparation time: 15 minutes
Cooking time: 35 minutes

2 tablespoons olive oil
1 large onion, peeled and chopped
3 cloves garlic, peeled and crushed
175 g (6 oz) pearl barley
1 level teaspoon each ground
  cinnamon, coriander and cumin
1 level teaspoon salt
Freshly ground black pepper
1.15 litres (2 pints) vegetable stock
  (see p.9)
4 medium carrots, peeled and
  thickly sliced diagonally
2 medium courgettes,
  trimmed and diced
450 g (1 lb) cooked
  chickpeas, rinsed
  and drained
60 g (2 oz) seedless
  raisins
115 g (4 oz)
  unsalted cashew
  nuts or roasted
  peanuts
Fresh flat-leaf
  parsley
  to garnish

Per serving
Calories 397
Protein 13 g
Total fat 16 g
(saturated fat 2.7 g)
Carbohydrates 53 g
(added sugar 0)
Fibre 7.3 g Sodium 348 mg

Traditional Middle Eastern pilaffs consist of rice cooked in a spicy stock with vegetables, fish or meat. This light, nutty variant replaces the rice with chickpeas and pearl barley.

Heat the oil in a large saucepan and gently fry the onion and garlic in it until softened. Stir in the barley, cinnamon, coriander, cumin, salt and some pepper. Pour in the stock and add the carrots and courgettes. Bring the mixture to the boil, then reduce the heat, cover the pan, and gently simmer the stew for 25 minutes.

2 Mix in the chickpeas and raisins and cook for a further 5 minutes, adding a little water if the mixture becomes too dry. Stir in the cashew nuts or peanuts, garnish with the flat-leaf parsley and serve with a green salad and Melba toasts or other crispbreads.

Cinnamon, coriander and cumin provide a warm background flavour for chickpeas and pearl barley.

166

MIXED VEGETABLE CROQUETTES

Three types of crispy potato patty – one made with a zesty caper mixture, another with Cheddar and spring onions and the third with mixed vegetables – are served with coleslaw.

Serves 4
Preparation time: 30 minutes
Chilling time: 1 hour
Cooking time: 10 minutes

675 g (1½ lb) potatoes, cooked, drained and mashed
¼ level teaspoon salt
Freshly ground black pepper
2 eggs, size 2, hard-boiled, shelled and finely chopped
30 g (1 oz) gherkins, drained and finely chopped
1 tablespoon capers, drained
115 g (4 oz) mature Cheddar cheese, finely grated
2 spring onions, trimmed and finely chopped
150 g (5 oz) frozen mixed vegetables, cooked and drained
2 eggs, size 2, beaten
115 g (4 oz) fine fresh white breadcrumbs
1 litre (1¾ pints) vegetable oil for deep-frying
Small bunch of parsley, washed and dried

Per serving
Calories 571 Protein 22 g
Total fat 31 g (saturated fat 7.4 g)
Carbohydrates 54 g (added sugar 0)
Fibre 4.4 g Sodium 696 mg

1 Beat the mashed potatoes with the salt and some pepper, then divide it into three equal portions and put these in separate mixing bowls. Mix the chopped eggs, gherkins and capers into one portion of the mashed potato, the grated cheese and the onions into the second portion, and the mixed vegetables into the third.

2 Divide each mixture into eight pieces. Shape the egg mixture into ovals, the cheese mixture into balls and the vegetable mixture into squares. Put the shaped croquettes on a large platter, cover with non-toxic plastic film and refrigerate for 1 hour.

3 Dip the chilled croquettes in the beaten egg, and then coat them with the breadcrumbs. Refrigerate them again. In the meantime, heat the oil in a deep frying pan to 180°C (350°F). If you do not have a thermometer, test the oil by dropping a small piece of bread into it – if it is the right temperature, the bread should turn brown in 2-3 seconds. Deep-fry the croquettes in batches for 1-2 minutes, or until golden brown. Drain on kitchen paper, then cover and keep hot.

4 Fry the dried parsley in the oil for a few seconds until crisp, then drain on kitchen paper. Garnish the croquettes with the parsley and serve with coleslaw.

RICE AND LENTIL BAPS

Tasty cheese, rice and lentil wedges combine with crispy iceburg lettuce in sesame seed baps. They make an excellent alternative to hamburgers.

Serves 4
Preparation time: 15 minutes
Chilling time: 2 hours
Cooking time: 30 minutes

115 g (4 oz) long-grain white rice
85 g (3 oz) green lentils, cleaned of grit and rinsed
425 ml (¾ pint) vegetable stock (see p.9) or water
4 tablespoons olive oil
1 small red pepper, de-seeded and finely chopped
60 g (2 oz) mature Cheddar cheese, grated
½ level teaspoon salt
Freshly ground black pepper
2 level tablespoons plain flour
2 eggs, size 2, beaten
115 g (4 oz) wholemeal breadcrumbs
4 large sesame seed baps, split and toasted
4 tablespoons mayonnaise
1 small red onion, peeled, thinly sliced and separated into rings
½ small iceberg lettuce, washed and finely shredded
¼ cucumber, sliced

Per serving
Calories 737 Protein 23 g
Total fat 37 g (saturated fat 8.8 g)
Carbohydrates 84 g (added sugar 0)
Fibre 6.4 g Sodium 801 mg

1 Put the rice, lentils and stock or water in a saucepan and bring to the boil. Stir once, then reduce the heat to low. Cover and simmer for 20-25 minutes, until the rice and lentils are cooked (see p.173) and all the liquid has been absorbed.

2 Meanwhile, heat 1 tablespoon of the oil in a frying pan, cook the red pepper in it for 6-8 minutes, and then remove the pan from the heat. Stir in the cooked rice and lentils and the cheese and season with the salt and some pepper. Spread out the mixture on a wetted plate to make a 20 cm (8 in) round, then cover and refrigerate for 2 hours.

3 Cut the chilled rice and lentil cake into quarters. Lightly coat each wedge in the flour, shaking off any excess. Dip the wedges into the egg, then coat evenly with the breadcrumbs. Heat the remaining oil in a large frying pan and fry the wedges in it for 2-3 minutes on each side, or until golden brown. Drain on kitchen paper.

4 Spread the toasted baps with the mayonnaise, then place a rice and lentil wedge on the bottom half of each one. Garnish with the onion, lettuce and cucumber, then cover with the tops of the baps and serve.

ARTICHOKE FRITTATA

Serves 4
Preparation time: 25 minutes
Cooking time: 15 minutes

- 1 tablespoon olive oil
- 1 large onion, peeled and sliced
- 8 eggs, size 3
- 70 g (2½ oz) Parmesan cheese, grated
- 2 tablespoons chopped fresh parsley
- 3 tablespoons single cream
- ¾ level teaspoon salt
- Freshly ground black pepper
- 275 g (10 oz) bottled artichoke hearts in oil, drained and quartered
- 340 g (12 oz) cooked potatoes, cut into small dice
- 30 g (1 oz) butter
- 2 tablespoons snipped fresh chives

Per serving
Calories 450 Protein 25 g
Total fat 31 g (saturated fat 14 g)
Carbohydrates 19 g (added sugar 0)
Fibre 1.8 g Sodium 803 mg

This Italian omelette makes the most of a local speciality – artichoke hearts. These can be found in supermarkets or in Italian food shops.

1 Heat the oil in a large, deep frying pan and lightly brown the onion in it over a moderate heat.

2 Lightly whisk the eggs in a bowl with 60 g (2 oz) of the Parmesan, the parsley, cream, salt and some pepper. Stir in the onion, artichoke hearts and potatoes.

3 Wipe out the pan and then heat the butter in it until sizzling hot. Pour in the egg mixture and cook it over a moderate heat for 10-12 minutes, lifting the edges of the frittata and tilting the pan from time to time to allow any uncooked egg to run underneath.

4 In the meantime, preheat the grill and when the egg is almost set, put the pan under it for 2-3 minutes. Sprinkle the chives and the remaining Parmesan over the frittata and serve immediately with a lettuce salad and some ciabatta, or other Italian bread.

Olive oil, Parmesan cheese and tangy artichoke hearts turn a simple omelette into a mouth-watering Mediterranean treat.

SMOKED CHEESE AND ONION BREAD PUDDING

Serves 4
Preparation time: 20 minutes
Cooking time: 45 minutes

2 tablespoons olive oil
450 g (1 lb) onions, peeled
  and sliced
4 large slices wholemeal bread,
  crusts removed and cut into
  small triangles
4 eggs, size 2
425 ml (¾ pint) milk
Freshly ground black pepper
1 level tablespoon Dijon mustard
115 g (4 oz) coarsely grated mature
  Cheddar cheese
115 g (4 oz) smoked cheese, cut into
  small cubes

Per serving
Calories 526 Protein 29 g
Total fat 33 g (saturated fat 15 g)
Carbohydrates 31 g (added sugar 0)
Fibre 4.7 g Sodium 909 mg

Smoked cheese brings an interesting flavour to this homely cheese and onion bake, although it can be made with plain Cheddar – simply double the amount used.

1 Preheat the oven to 180°C (350°F, gas mark 4). Heat the oil in a large frying pan and soften the onions in it until very tender. Add the bread and toss to mix.

2 Beat the eggs with the milk in a large bowl, then mix in the pepper and mustard. Keep 2 tablespoons of the Cheddar to one side, then stir the remainder with the smoked cheese, into the egg and milk mixture. Gently mix in the onions and bread.

3 Pour the mixture into a lightly oiled, shallow, ovenproof dish and sprinkle with the reserved Cheddar. Place near the top of the oven and bake for 45 minutes, or until risen, golden brown and set in the centre. Serve immediately.

AUBERGINES PARMIGIANA

Layers of melting aubergine are interspersed with tomatoes, onion, basil and mozzarella in this rich Italian dish.

Serves 4
Preparation time: 30 minutes
Standing time: 1 hour
Cooking time: 1 hour

1.1 kg (2½ lb) aubergines, trimmed
  and sliced
1 level tablespoon salt
150 ml (¼ pint) olive oil
1 large onion, peeled and
  finely chopped
675 g (1½ lb) fresh tomatoes,
  skinned, de-seeded and chopped
Freshly ground black pepper
1 tablespoon chopped fresh basil
60 g (2 oz) plain flour
30 g (1 oz) Parmesan cheese, grated
340 g (12 oz) mozzarella
  cheese, sliced
2 tablespoons finely shredded
  fresh basil

Per serving
Calories 747 Protein 30 g
Total fat 60 g (saturated fat 18 g)
Carbohydrates 25 g (added sugar 0)
Fibre 9.4 g Sodium 1351 mg

1 Sprinkle the aubergines with 2½ teaspoons of the salt, and set aside to draw out the bitter juices.

2 Meanwhile, preheat the oven to 180°C (350°F, gas mark 4). Heat 1 tablespoon of the oil in a saucepan and soften the onion in it. Stir in the chopped tomatoes, the remaining salt and some pepper and cook, covered, for 10-15 minutes. Remove the pan from the heat and stir in the basil.

3 Rinse the aubergine slices and drain them well. Pat dry with kitchen paper, then sprinkle with the flour. Heat half the remaining oil in a frying pan and lightly brown the aubergines in batches for 2-3 minutes.

4 Arrange a third of the aubergines over the bottom of a lightly oiled ovenproof dish, then sprinkle with a third of the Parmesan. Layer a third of the mozzarella on top, spacing the slices evenly apart, then spoon over a third of the tomato sauce. Repeat the layers twice.

5 Bake in the centre of the oven for 30 minutes, until lightly browned. Sprinkle with the shredded basil and serve with focaccia or other Italian bread and a lamb's lettuce salad.

TOMATO AND SPINACH TART

Small pasta bows and cottage cheese provide fibre and protein in this healthy vegetable tart. If you are short of time, flute the edge instead of decorating it with pastry leaves.

Serves 4
Preparation time: 30 minutes
Cooking time: 50 minutes

300 g (11 oz) shortcrust pastry
  (see p.9)
2 tablespoons milk to glaze
2 tablespoons olive oil
1 medium onion, peeled and sliced
2 cloves garlic, peeled and crushed
60 g (2 oz) farfallini, or other small
  pasta shapes, cooked and
  drained (see p.202)
225 g (8 oz) cottage
  cheese, drained
2 eggs, size 2, beaten
340 g (12 oz) frozen leaf spinach,
  thawed, well drained
  and chopped
115 g (4 oz) Cheddar
  cheese, grated
½ level teaspoon salt
Freshly ground black pepper
2 tomatoes, sliced

Per serving
Calories 698 Protein 28 g
Total fat 44 g (saturated fat 18 g)
Carbohydrates 51 g (added sugar 0)
Fibre 5.8 g Sodium 1018 mg

1 Preheat the oven to 200°C (400°F, gas mark 6). Roll out the pastry on a floured surface to make a thin round large enough to line a 25 cm (10 in) pie plate. Cover the plate with the pastry and trim the edge. Roll out the trimmings to make decorative leaves, and mark them with a small knife to make veins. Brush the underside of each leaf with cold water, then arrange them, overlapping, around the edge of the lined pie plate. Lightly brush the leaves with the milk and leave in the fridge.

2 Heat the oil in a frying pan and soften the onion in it over a moderate heat. Add the garlic and cook for 1 minute, then remove the pan from the heat and mix in the cooked pasta.

3 Combine the cottage cheese and eggs in a large bowl, then mix in the spinach, Cheddar, pasta mixture, salt and some pepper. Pour the filling into the lined pie plate, smooth it down and bake in the centre of the oven for 30 minutes. Remove the tart from the oven and arrange the tomato slices in an overlapping circle on top. Return to the oven and cook for a further 20 minutes, or until set in the centre.

COURGETTE AND GRUYÈRE QUICHE

Gruyère cheese adds an aromatic touch to a rich, appetising courgette and onion quiche, made with fresh cream.

Serves 4
Preparation time: 40 minutes
Cooking time: 30 minutes

300 g (11 oz) shortcrust pastry
  (see p.9)
2 tablespoons olive oil
1 medium onion, peeled
  and thinly sliced
225 g (8 oz) courgettes, trimmed
  and thinly sliced
115 g (4 oz) Gruyère cheese,
  coarsely grated
200 ml (7 fl oz) single cream
3 eggs, size 3
¼ level teaspoon salt
Freshly ground black pepper

Per serving
Calories 697 Protein 20 g
Total fat 52 g (saturated fat 22 g)
Carbohydrates 40 g (added sugar 0)
Fibre 2 g Sodium 715 mg

1 Preheat the oven to 220°C (425°F, gas mark 7). Roll out the pastry on a lightly floured surface to a round large enough to line a 25 cm (10 in) flan tin. Fit the pastry into the tin, pressing it well into the flutes, and trim the edge. Refrigerate for 20 minutes.

2 Put the lined flan tin on a baking tray and bake in the centre of the oven for 15 minutes. In the meantime, heat the oil in a large frying pan and lightly brown the onion and courgettes over a moderate heat for 5 minutes, stirring continuously. Take the pan off the heat and leave the vegetables to cool slightly.

3 Sprinkle half the Gruyère over the bottom of the pastry case, cover with the courgettes and onion mixture, then sprinkle the remaining Gruyère on the top. Whisk together the cream, eggs, salt and some pepper and pour the mixture into the pastry case.

4 Reduce the oven temperature to 190°C (375°F, gas mark 5) and bake the quiche in the centre of the oven for 20-30 minutes, or until set. Serve hot or cold with light rye bread and a mixed salad.

NUT ROAST

Serves 6
Preparation time: 30 minutes
Cooking time: 1 hour 20 minutes

- 2 tablespoons olive oil
- 2 cloves garlic, peeled and crushed
- 1 medium onion, peeled and chopped
- 2 sticks celery, trimmed and finely chopped
- 225 g (8 oz) red lentils, cooked and drained (see p.173)
- 225 g (8 oz) mixed nuts, finely chopped
- 115 g (4 oz) fresh wholemeal breadcrumbs
- 1/2 level teaspoon salt
- Freshly ground black pepper
- 2 level teaspoons Italian seasoning or mixed herbs
- 1/4 level teaspoon chilli powder
- 4 tablespoons chopped fresh parsley
- 2 eggs, size 2, beaten
- 115 g (4 oz) vegetarian or mature Cheddar
- 150 ml (1/4 pint) passata (sieved tomatoes)
- 15 g (1/2 oz) butter, softened
- 115 g (4 oz) chestnut mushrooms, wiped and thickly sliced

Per serving
Calories 577 Protein 29 g
Total fat 36 g (saturated fat 9.3 g)
Carbohydrates 37 g (added sugar 0)
Fibre 9.8 g Sodium 619 mg

This simple and nutritious nut loaf can be made with any combination of nuts, although using walnuts and Brazils will give the richest flavour.

1 Preheat the oven to 190°C (375°F, gas mark 5). Heat the oil in a small saucepan and sauté the garlic, onion and celery in it until soft. Transfer to a large bowl and mix in the lentils, nuts, breadcrumbs, salt, some pepper, the Italian seasoning or mixed herbs, chilli powder, parsley, eggs, cheese and passata.

2 Take a sheet of nonstick baking paper and line the sides of a 23 cm x 12.5 cm (9 in x 5 in) loaf tin with it. Spread the butter over the bottom of the tin, then add the mushrooms and carefully spoon the lentil and nut mixture on top. Gently press down and smooth the mixture, then cover the tin loosely with foil. Bake in the centre of the oven for 1 hour 20 minutes, or until set.

3 Take the cooked nut loaf out of the oven and carefully turn it out onto a heated serving dish. Remove the baking paper and then serve with a mixed salad.

Tasty chestnut mushrooms decorate the top of this chewy, substantial nut roast.

Making the most of vegetarian cooking

Omitting meat from the diet still leaves a wide range of dishes that you can prepare for strict vegetarians – and which will appeal to meat-eaters too. Fresh ingredients used in imaginative combinations are the secret of a healthy and varied vegetarian regime.

A WELL-ROUNDED vegetarian diet is one that provides appropriate quantities of protein, vitamins and minerals on a daily basis (see p.7). The secret is to combine nutrient-rich ingredients to create balanced meals that supply these essentials, although the recipes can be adjusted as required – for example, soya milk can be substituted for cow's milk.

Finding the required nutrients

Protein sources can be drawn from many different foods, including dairy products, eggs and plant foods, especially cereals, pulses, nuts and seeds. The proteins found in dairy products and eggs contain the eight essential amino acids required by the body. The proteins in plant foods, however, can lack one or two amino acids; for this reason, these foods need to be combined in such a way that all eight amino acids are absorbed in the course of a meal – beans with rice, lentils with pasta and grains with nuts, for example.

Vitamin-rich foods are present in great variety in the meals in this section. Vitamin A is found in dairy products, eggs and brightly coloured fruit and vegetables such as apricots, peppers and carrots. The B vitamins exist in many plant foods; vitamin B_{12} is an exception, being found only in animal products or fortified foods such as soya milk, breakfast cereals or yeast extract. Vitamin C is found in fruit and vegetables, and especially in oranges, strawberries, blackcurrants, broccoli and cabbage. Most meals in this chapter retain their

---

Foods rich in minerals

Iron Whole-grain cereals (bread, pasta, oats, rye and other grains); fortified breakfast cereals; green vegetables; nuts; seeds; dried beans; lentils; soya products.

Calcium Dairy products (milk, cheese and yoghurt); sunflower and sesame seeds; almonds and brazil nuts; very dark green vegetables (spinach, broccoli); tofu; figs; fortified soya milk; beans and lentils.

Zinc Beans and lentils; sunflower, sesame and pumpkin seeds; whole-grain bread and cereals; dairy products; nuts.

---

cooking liquid, and therefore much of their vitamin C. The richest sources of vitamin E are vegetable oils, nuts, seeds and avocados.

Minerals are sometimes in short supply on a vegetarian diet, but they can be found in the food sources listed in the panel above. Avoid eating too much bran or bran-rich foods, as high fibre can hinder the absorption of minerals. Vitamin C enhances the absorption of iron from plant foods, so include citrus fruit, green vegetables or berries in the same meal.

Using pulses and grains

Dried beans, peas and lentils are best cooked from dry. This requires some soaking time in the case of dried beans and some peas. Canned alternatives are available and very

convenient when time is short, but those cooked at home will be less salty and have a better flavour and a firmer texture.

To be kept at their freshest, all pulses and grains should be transferred from their packets into clean, airtight containers. Stored in a cool, dry airy cupboard, whole grains such as rice and barley will keep virtually for ever. Wheat grains – such as bulgur wheat, couscous, semolina, cornmeal and oats – should only be kept for 6-8 months, as should dried pulses. It is a good idea to buy these in small amounts, and make a note of the sell-by date when you transfer them to a storage jar.

Cleaning pulses is important before soaking and cooking. First spread the dried beans, peas or lentils out on a large plate, so that you can remove any discoloured pulses or pieces of grit. Then rinse the sound pulses in a colander under a cold tap, or wash them repeatedly in a bowl until the water becomes clear. Drain well and soak; then precook beans and whole peas, and use lentils and split peas as required.

Soaking pulses such as dried beans and some dried peas is necessary before cooking, as this restores them to their natural size. Remember that soaking doubles their weight, so where a recipe calls for 225 g (8 oz) cooked kidney beans, you will need to soak and cook 115 g (4 oz) dried beans. Canned pulses, on the other hand, will lose weight in rinsing and draining: a 400 g (14 oz) can will provide 225 g (8 oz) cooked beans.

To soak pulses, put them in a large bowl with enough water to come at least 10 cm (4 in) above the beans or peas. Cover and leave for at least 5 hours, or overnight.

When ready to cook the soaked pulses, first thoroughly rinse and drain them. Put them in a large saucepan with 1.7 litres (3 pints) of water for every 225 g (8 oz) soaked beans. Bring to the boil, uncovered, boil briskly for 10 minutes, then rinse and drain the beans and return them to the saucepan. Cover with the same amount of cold water and bring back to the boil. Turn down the heat and partially cover the pan, then simmer very gently for 1-1½ hours, or until tender. The cooking time will vary according to the type of water the beans or dried peas are cooked in – soft water cooks them faster than hard water – and on the age of the bean or pea: those with faded, dull skins, and especially those that are wrinkled, are not fresh.

The nutritional analyses in this book assume that precooked beans and peas added to the recipes are unsalted. If you prefer to add salt, wait until the end of the cooking time. Adding it sooner will toughen them up. Bear in mind that if you are using canned beans, these already contain salt and this will increase the overall salt content of the recipe.

Split lentils and peas need to be cleaned, but can be used in most of these recipes without soaking and precooking. Put them in a saucepan and cover with 850 ml (1½ pints) unsalted water or stock for every 115 g (4 oz) dried split peas or lentils.

Bring to the boil, partially cover, then simmer split peas for 40-60 minutes, red lentils for 20-25 minutes, and green and brown lentils for 25-30 minutes. Since split peas break up during cooking, they are mainly used to thicken soups and stews.

Pulse and grain mixes are combinations of different pulses, and sometimes grains such as couscous or bulgur wheat. These mixes are available in supermarkets and health food shops, where they are generally known as soup or **broth mix**. They need to be soaked and boiled vigorously for 10 minutes, as with dried beans, before being added to a recipe.

Bulgur wheat, a type of cracked wheat, needs to be soaked, but not precooked, before using in salads, falafel or other cooked dishes. Where it is used in a stuffing or pilaff, it can be added without soaking.

Soaking bulgur wheat

Put wheat in a bowl and cover with 285 ml (½ pint) of water for every 115 g (4 oz) wheat. Leave to stand for 20-30 minutes until the bulgur is plump and softened. Tip it into a sieve to drain off any excess water, squeezing dry if necessary.

Falafel is a spicy vegetable dish – a type of Middle Eastern rissole – made from ground chickpeas, or a mixture of chickpeas and soaked bulgur wheat. Round or cake-shaped falafel fried in oil may be served with salads, or used as a filling for pitta bread. Falafel can also be baked in a casserole (see p.165).

Shaping falafel

1 Combine the ingredients for the falafel in a bowl and divide the mixture into eight equal portions (or 16, if making a filling for pitta bread).

2 Take one piece at a time and shape it into a neat, round cake. Flatten it slightly with wetted hands. If you prefer, roll the mixture into balls.

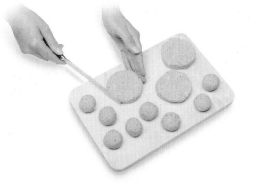

Couscous – which consists of tiny, round grains made from semolina – is used extensively in Middle Eastern cookery. It is traditionally steamed over the meat stew with which it is to be served, suspended in a metal colander or sieve, although it can also steam over gently boiling stock or water. Allow roughly 115 g (4 oz) of couscous per person, and vary the steaming time according to the quantity. Stir large amounts with a fork once or twice.

Steaming couscous

1 Put 225 g (8 oz) of couscous in a bowl and sprinkle with a little cold water to moisten it – about 2 tablespoons per serving. Stir the grains with a fork to make sure they are evenly moist, then leave to stand for 10 minutes.

2 Transfer the couscous to a metal colander or sieve. Place over a stew or gently boiling water, partially cover with a lid and steam for 25-30 minutes, or until the grains are soft and fluffy. Do not let the bottom of the colander or sieve come into contact with the water.

3 Turn the cooked couscous into a warm serving dish and mix it with a fork to break up the lumps. Stir in a little olive oil or a knob of butter, then season with salt and pepper.

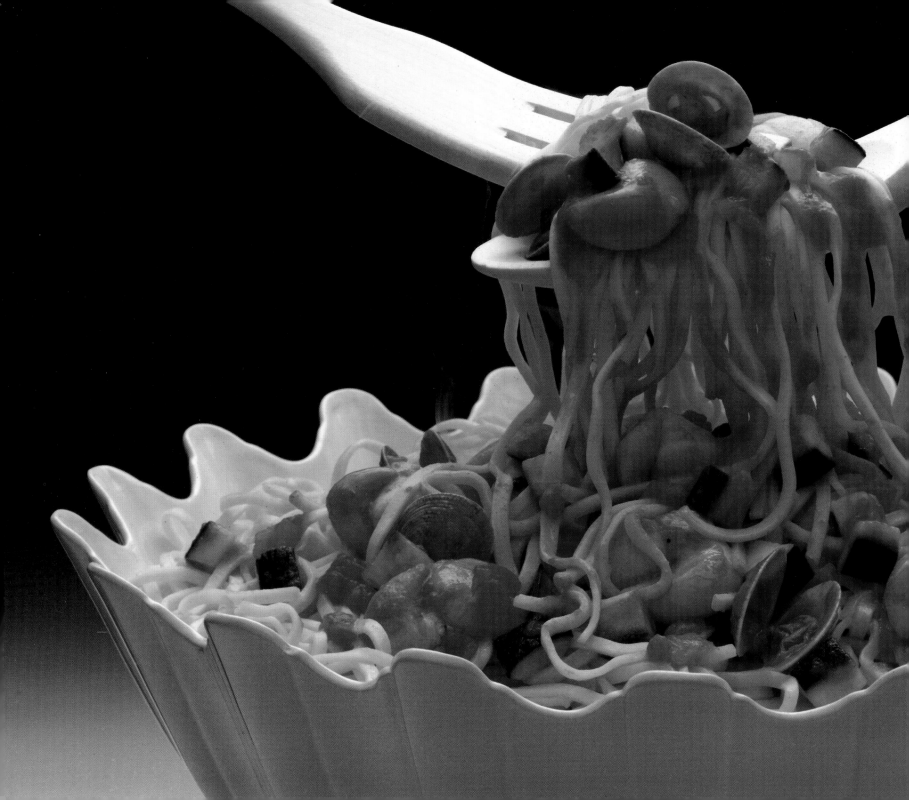

PASTA AND PIZZA

Pasta and pizza can be combined with an almost endless variety of sauces and toppings, making them a favourite basis for substantial all-in-one meals. The pasta and noodle shapes used in these recipes are illustrated on p.202, and a recipe for pizza dough is given on p.203.

❖

Making the most of pasta and pizza 202-3

A thick, spicy topping full of the sea's goodness coats thin ribbon pasta in Seafood and Linguine in Tomato Sauce (left). Fresh clams and prawns or frozen mixed seafood can equally well be used in this recipe (see p.190).

FARFALLE WITH VEAL AND PEPPERS

Serves 4
Preparation time: 25 minutes
Cooking time: 20 minutes

2 level tablespoons plain flour
2 level teaspoons chopped
   fresh tarragon
1 level teaspoon chopped
   fresh marjoram
¼ level teaspoon salt
Freshly ground black pepper
340 g (12 oz) thin veal escalopes,
   cut into strips
2 tablespoons olive oil
4-6 spring onions, trimmed and
   thickly sliced diagonally
2 medium red peppers, de-seeded
   and cut into small squares
225 g (8 oz) farfalle
285 ml (½ pint) beef stock
   (see p.8)
115 ml (4 fl oz) Marsala or dry
   white wine
2 tablespoons double cream
Chopped fresh tarragon to garnish

Per serving
Calories 449 Protein 26 g
Total fat 14 g (saturated fat 4.4 g)
Carbohydrates 54 g (added sugar 0)
Fibre 4.5 g Sodium 233 mg

*Veal, peppers and pasta, a
classic Italian combination,
are the basis of this
colourful meal.*

**Lightly fried strips of veal
combine with spring onions,
red peppers and tarragon to
make a tasty, satisfying sauce
for a bed of bow-tie pasta.**

1 Put the flour, 1 teaspoon of the
tarragon, the marjoram, half
the salt and some pepper into a
polythene bag. Add the veal strips
and gently shake them until they
are evenly coated. Remove the
strips, shake off any excess flour
and leave them to one side.

2 Heat 1 tablespoon of
the oil in a large frying
pan and cook the
spring onions and
peppers in it
over a moderate
heat until
the peppers
are just
softened.
Move
them to
a plate
and set
aside.

3 Cook the pasta (see p.202).
In the meantime, heat the
remaining oil in the pan, add the
veal strips and brown them over
a moderate heat for 5 minutes.
Move them to the plate with the
peppers and onions.

4 Pour the stock and Marsala or
white wine into the pan, add
the remaining tarragon and bring
to the boil, stirring and scraping
up the browned meat juices from
the bottom of the pan. Boil rapidly
for 4-5 minutes, or until the
liquid is reduced by half. Return

the onions, peppers and veal to the
pan, stir in the cream and season
with the remaining salt and some
pepper. Gently heat the sauce for
2-3 minutes, without boiling.

5 Drain the cooked pasta,
turn it into a heated
serving dish and pour
the veal and pepper
sauce on top.
Garnish with the
fresh tarragon and
serve with warm
pugliese or other
Italian bread.

176

Penne with Chunky Meat Sauce

Adding salami or pepperoni gives extra body to the tomato and beef sauce in this dish. You can substitute any other type of pasta for penne and, if pressed for time, use a 375 g (13 oz) jar of tomato sauce in place of the canned tomatoes and the purée.

Serves 4
Preparation time: 20 minutes
Cooking time: 35 minutes

1 tablespoon olive oil
1 large onion, peeled and chopped
2 medium carrots, peeled, halved lengthways and thickly sliced
450 g (1 lb) lean minced beef
115 g (4 oz) piece of Milano salami or pepperoni sausage, cut into small dice
400 g (14 oz) canned tomatoes
2 level tablespoons tomato purée
1/2 level teaspoon salt
Freshly ground black pepper
340 g (12 oz) penne
3 tablespoons chopped fresh flat-leaf parsley
60 g (2 oz) Parmesan cheese, grated
Flat-leaf parsley to garnish

Per serving
Calories 764 Protein 46 g
Total fat 34 g (saturated fat 14 g)
Carbohydrates 74 g (added sugar 0)
Fibre 6.3 g Sodium 1094 mg

1 Heat the oil in a large saucepan and cook the onion and carrots in it until softened. Stir in the beef and cook for 2-3 minutes, until the meat changes colour.

2 Mix the salami or pepperoni, tomatoes, tomato purée, salt and some pepper in with the beef, onion and carrots. Bring the mixture to the boil, reduce the heat, cover the pan and simmer for 20 minutes, stirring occasionally. In the meantime, cook the pasta (see p.202), then drain, return to the saucepan and keep warm. Add the chopped parsley to the sauce and cook for a further 5 minutes.

3 Mix the meat sauce into the pasta and gently heat through for 1-2 minutes. Turn into a warmed serving dish and sprinkle the Parmesan on top. Garnish with the flat-leaf parsley and serve.

Spicy Beef and Spaghetti Pie

A blend of courgettes, carrots and spaghetti forms a case to enclose a savoury beef patty, spiced with garlic, ginger and hot chilli sauce.

Serves 4
Preparation time: 15 minutes
Cooking time: 30 minutes

225 g (8 oz) spaghetti
1 tablespoon olive oil
2 small courgettes, trimmed, halved lengthways and thinly sliced
2 medium carrots, peeled and coarsely grated
550 g (1 1/4 lb) lean minced beef
4-6 spring onions, trimmed and chopped
2 tablespoons chilli sauce
3 tablespoons dry sherry
1 tablespoon soy sauce
1 level tablespoon cornflour
3 cloves garlic, peeled and crushed
1 level teaspoon ground ginger
Blanched carrot and courgette slices and chopped spring onion to garnish

Per serving
Calories 499 Protein 35 g
Total fat 18 g (saturated fat 6.3 g)
Carbohydrates 49 g (added sugar 0)
Fibre 3.7 g Sodium 350 mg

1 Preheat the oven to 200°C (400°F, gas mark 6). Cook the spaghetti (see p.202) and drain.

2 Meanwhile, heat the oil in a large frying pan and cook the courgettes in it for 4-5 minutes, until softened. Remove the pan from the heat, then gently mix in the carrots and spaghetti.

3 Turn this mixture into a lightly greased, shallow, round pie dish and spread it gently and evenly over the bottom and the sides of the dish to form a case.

4 Mix together the beef, spring onions, chilli sauce, sherry, soy sauce, cornflour, garlic and ginger in a large bowl. Carefully spoon the mixture into the spaghetti case and then press it down firmly with the back of a spoon.

5 Cover the dish with foil and place it in the centre of the oven. Bake for 20 minutes, then remove the foil and cook for a further 5 minutes, until the top is lightly browned. Garnish with the carrot and courgette slices and the spring onion, and serve with a tossed green salad.

177

ORIENTAL PORK AND PASTA

Lean pork strips, fresh-tasting vegetables and thin pasta ribbons make an enticing combination. You can use Chinese-style noodles in place of pasta or replace the pork with chicken or turkey, if you prefer.

Serves 4
Preparation time: 20 minutes
Cooking time: 10 minutes

1 clove garlic, peeled and crushed
1 level teaspoon ground ginger
3 tablespoons soy sauce
2 level tablespoons cornflour
450 g (1 lb) pork tenderloin, trimmed
  of fat and cut into long, thin strips
450 ml (16 fl oz) chicken stock
  (see p.8)
1/2 teaspoon hot red pepper sauce
2 teaspoons sesame oil
225 g (8 oz) spaghettini or linguine
2 tablespoons olive oil
1 large carrot, peeled and cut
  into matchstick strips
115 g (4 oz) button mushrooms,
  wiped and sliced
225 g (8 oz) mangetout, trimmed

Per serving
Calories 404 Protein 28 g
Total fat 10 g (saturated fat 2.6 g)
Carbohydrates 53 g (added sugar 0)
Fibre 6.3 g Sodium 818 mg

Carrots and mangetout keep their crunch when stir-fried, and bring a taste of summer to this spicy pork dish.

1 Mix together the garlic, ginger, soy sauce and cornflour in a bowl. Add the pork strips and stir gently to ensure that the meat is well coated. In a separate bowl, mix the chicken stock, red pepper sauce and sesame oil.

2 Cook the spaghettini or linguine (see p.202) and drain well. Meanwhile, heat the olive oil in a wok or large frying pan, add the pork mixture and stir-fry for 5 minutes. Add the carrot and mushrooms and fry for 1 minute, then quickly pour in the stock mixture, bring to the boil and cook for 1 minute, stirring continuously.

3 Mix in the mangetout and cook for a further 2-3 minutes, or until tender. Turn the pasta into a heated serving dish, pour the stir-fried pork and vegetables into the centre and serve immediately.

SPICY PORK AND VEGETABLE SPAGHETTI

Serves 4
Preparation time: 30 minutes
Cooking time: 15 minutes

115 ml (4 fl oz) chicken stock
   (see p.8) or water
3 level tablespoons crunchy
   peanut butter
3 tablespoons soy sauce
2 teaspoons chilli sauce
2 teaspoons sesame oil
1 tablespoon clear honey
1 clove garlic, peeled and chopped
225 g (8 oz) wholemeal spaghetti
2 tablespoons olive oil
450 g (1 lb) pork tenderloin, trimmed
   of fat and cut into long, thin strips
2 large carrots, peeled and cut into
   matchstick strips
2 sticks celery, trimmed and
   finely chopped
175 g (6 oz) sugar snap peas,
   trimmed and blanched
   (see p.10)
4 spring onions, trimmed and
   finely chopped
1 level tablespoon peeled and
   grated fresh root ginger
Finely shredded carrot and spring
   onion to garnish

Per serving
Calories 619 Protein 47 g
Total fat 29 g (saturated fat 7 g)
Carbohydrates 46 g (added sugar 0)
Fibre 6.1 g Sodium 856 mg

A light, spicy and slightly sweet peanut sauce adds bite to this nutritious dish of wholemeal spaghetti with stir-fried pork and vegetables.

1 Put the stock or water in a food processor with the peanut butter, soy sauce, chilli sauce, sesame oil, honey and garlic, and blend until smooth. Leave to one side.

2 Cook the spaghetti (see p.202). Meanwhile, heat the olive oil in a wok or large frying pan and stir-fry the pork in it for 4 minutes over a high heat. Add the carrots and celery and stir-fry for another 4 minutes, then mix in the peas, onions and ginger and cook for a further 4 minutes, or until the pork strips are tender.

3 Drain the spaghetti and turn it into a heated serving bowl. Toss with the pork mixture and the peanut sauce, garnish with the carrot and spring onion and serve.

EGG NOODLES WITH SWEET AND SOUR GAMMON

Serves 4
Preparation time: 30 minutes
Cooking time: 25 minutes

1 level tablespoon cornflour
425 g (15 oz) canned pineapple
   chunks in natural juice, drained
   and juice reserved
2 tablespoons cider vinegar
2 tablespoons soy sauce
1 level tablespoon tomato ketchup
1 tablespoon olive oil
225 g (8 oz) gammon steak,
   trimmed of fat and cut into
   small cubes
1 medium onion, peeled and
   finely sliced
2 large peppers, red and green,
   de-seeded and cut into
   small squares
250 g (9 oz) fine Chinese
   egg noodles
45 g (1½ oz) walnuts, chopped
1 clove garlic, peeled and crushed
3 spring onions, trimmed and
   finely sliced

Per serving
Calories 532 Protein 27 g
Total fat 20 g (saturated fat 2.4 g)
Carbohydrates 66 g (added sugar 0)
Fibre 6.4 g Sodium 1213 mg

Juicy chunks of gammon and pineapple combine with crunchy chopped walnuts and cubes of fresh green and red peppers in a thick sweet and sour sauce.

1 Blend the cornflour with the reserved pineapple juice in a small bowl, then add the vinegar, soy sauce and tomato ketchup.

2 Heat the oil in a wok or large frying pan and stir-fry the gammon and onion in it for 5 minutes over a moderate heat. Add the peppers and stir-fry for another 8 minutes.

3 Cook the noodles (see p.202). Meanwhile, add the walnuts and garlic to the wok or frying pan, reduce the heat to low and stir-fry the mixture for a further 4 minutes. Stir in the cornflour and pineapple juice mixture and the pineapple chunks and bring to the boil, stirring continuously. Reduce the heat again and simmer for about 5 minutes, stirring occasionally, until the sauce is smooth and thick.

4 When the noodles are cooked, drain well and turn onto a heated serving dish. Pour the sweet and sour gammon over the noodles, scatter the spring onion slices on top and serve.

LINGUINE WITH HAM, PEAS AND MUSHROOMS

Serves 4
Preparation time: 15 minutes
Cooking time: 10 minutes

340 g (12 oz) linguine
3 tablespoons olive oil
6 spring onions, trimmed and
  thinly sliced
3 cloves garlic, peeled and crushed
1 teaspoon fresh thyme leaves
  or ½ teaspoon dried thyme
225 g (8 oz) mushrooms, wiped
  and thinly sliced
225 g (8 oz) cooked ham, trimmed
  of fat and cut into thin strips
225 g (8 oz) frozen peas
425 ml (¾ pint) chicken stock
  (see p.8)
¼ level teaspoon salt
Freshly ground black pepper
60 g (2 oz) Parmesan cheese, grated
Sprigs of fresh thyme to garnish

Per serving
Calories 560 Protein 31 g
Total fat 20 g (saturated fat 5.8 g)
Carbohydrates 69 g (added sugar 0)
Fibre 9.7 g Sodium 999 mg

Lean ham cooked with nutty
mushrooms, plump green peas,
spring onions and garlic makes
a hearty topping for a bed of
thin ribbon pasta.

1 Cook the linguine (see p.202).
Meanwhile, heat 1 tablespoon
of the oil in a large frying pan
for 1 minute, then cook the
spring onions and garlic in it for
3 minutes. Add the remaining oil
and the thyme and mushrooms
and cook for a further 3 minutes.

2 Mix in the ham, peas, stock,
salt and some pepper and bring
to the boil. Reduce the heat and
simmer for 3 minutes, or until the
liquid is slightly reduced.

3 Drain the linguine, add it to
the frying pan with the cheese
and toss lightly. Garnish with the
sprigs of thyme and serve.

CHICKEN AND BROCCOLI TAGLIATELLE

**Fresh broccoli florets combine
with spinach pasta in a creamy
herb and chicken sauce. If you
prefer a lower fat content, use
fromage frais in place of single
cream in the sauce.**

Serves 4
Preparation time: 15 minutes
Cooking time: 20 minutes

1 tablespoon olive oil
1 medium onion, peeled
  and chopped
1 medium red pepper, de-seeded
  and cut into thin strips
¼ level teaspoon each dried
  rosemary and dried thyme
225 g (8 oz) tagliatelle verde
340 g (12 oz) broccoli, trimmed
  and divided into small florets
340 g (12 oz) boneless chicken
  breasts (see p.116), skinned and
  cut into thin strips
4 tablespoons dry white wine, dry
  vermouth or water
Freshly ground black pepper
150 ml (¼ pint) single cream
30 g (1 oz) Parmesan cheese, grated
Sprigs of fresh rosemary to garnish

Per serving
Calories 487 Protein 34 g
Total fat 18 g (saturated fat 7.6 g)
Carbohydrates 49 g (added sugar 0)
Fibre 4 g Sodium 173 mg

1 Heat the oil in a large frying
pan for 1 minute and soften the
onion, red pepper, rosemary and
thyme in it, covered, but stirring
occasionally.

2 Meanwhile, cook the tagliatelle
(see p.202), adding the broccoli
florets to the pan for the last
4 minutes of cooking.

3 Increase the heat under the
frying pan to moderately high,
then stir the chicken, wine or
water and some black pepper into
the onion and pepper mixture.
Simmer, stirring, for about
5 minutes, or until the chicken
is cooked (see p.117).

4 Turn down the heat slightly,
stir in the cream and cook for
1-2 minutes, or until heated
through. Cover and keep hot.

5 Drain the tagliatelle and
broccoli and turn them into
a heated serving dish. Pour the
chicken sauce over the top and
sprinkle with the Parmesan.
Garnish with the sprigs of fresh
rosemary and serve.

FUSILLI WITH CHICKEN AND ROAST VEGETABLES

Serves 4
Preparation time: 20 minutes
Cooking time: 25 minutes

450 g (1 lb) boneless chicken
    breasts, cut into small pieces
2 medium green courgettes,
    trimmed and cut into small cubes
450 g (1 lb) yellow courgettes,
    sliced, or butternut squash,
    peeled, de-seeded and cut
    into cubes
2 medium red peppers, de-seeded
    and cut into squares
½ level teaspoon salt
Freshly ground black pepper

½ level teaspoon dried rosemary
    and fennel seeds, crushed
2 cloves garlic, peeled and crushed
3 tablespoons olive oil
4 tablespoons white wine or chicken
    stock (see p.8)
340 g (12 oz) long fusilli
3 tablespoons chopped fresh basil
30 g (1 oz) Parmesan cheese, grated
Sprigs of fresh rosemary to garnish

Per serving
Calories 607 Protein 40 g
Total fat 20 g (saturated fat 5 g)
Carbohydrates 72 g (added sugar 0)
Fibre 5.7 g Sodium 430 mg

Succulent vegetables accompany oven-browned chicken pieces and attractive curly pasta ribbons in a wholesome and satisfying supper.

1 Preheat the oven to 220°C (425°F, gas mark 7). In a large ovenproof dish, mix together the chicken, green courgettes, yellow courgettes or squash, red peppers, salt, some pepper, dried rosemary, fennel seeds, garlic, oil and the wine or stock. Bake in the oven for 20-25 minutes, or until the vegetables and chicken are cooked (see p.117) and lightly browned.

2 Meanwhile, cook the pasta (see p.202) and drain. Mix the pasta, basil and Parmesan into the chicken and vegetables, garnish with the fresh rosemary and serve.

The distinctive, earthy taste of fresh rosemary draws out the flavours of the fragrant basil and fennel sauce and the tasty chunks of chicken and courgette.

181

TAGLIATELLE WITH SPICY CHICKEN SAUCE

Serves 4
Preparation time: 20 minutes
Cooking time: 15 minutes

2 tablespoons olive oil
450 g (1 lb) boneless chicken
   breasts, skinned and cut into strips
450 g (1 lb) yellow courgettes,
   sliced, or butternut squash,
   peeled, de-seeded and sliced
1 red pepper, de-seeded
   and chopped
450 g (1 lb) salsa sauce

2 tablespoons chopped fresh
   coriander
150 ml (¼ pint) chicken stock
   (see p.8)
1 level teaspoon each chilli powder,
   ground cumin and dried oregano
225 g (8 oz) tagliatelle verde
1 avocado, halved, stoned, peeled,
   cut into small cubes and tossed
   with 1 tablespoon lemon juice
60 g (2 oz) Cheddar cheese,
   coarsely grated
Fresh coriander leaves to garnish

Fresh coriander, chilli powder and cumin contribute to the spiciness of this exuberant meal. Mild or hot salsa sauce can be bought in larger supermarkets, or you can use a ready-prepared spicy tomato pasta sauce.

1 Heat the oil in a large frying pan and add the chicken, courgettes or squash and red pepper. Cover and cook for about 8 minutes, stirring occasionally. Mix in the salsa sauce, coriander, stock, chilli powder, cumin and oregano, then cover and cook for 5 minutes, stirring occasionally.

2 Meanwhile, cook the tagliatelle (see p.202) and drain.

3 Gently stir the avocado into the chicken sauce, then add the tagliatelle. Heat through for about 2 minutes, stirring gently, then turn the mixture into a heated serving dish. Sprinkle the Cheddar on top, garnish with the coriander and serve with a lettuce, onion and tomato salad.

Per serving
Calories 591 Protein 39 g
Total fat 25 g (saturated fat 7.6 g)
Carbohydrates 56 g (added sugar 0)
Fibre 5.7 g Sodium 575 mg

Cooling cubes of avocado take the heat out of this colourful combination of spicy tagliatelle, courgettes and chicken.

SPAGHETTI WITH CHICKEN AND WATERCRESS

Serves 4
Preparation time: 20 minutes
Cooking time: 15 minutes

225 g (8 oz) spaghetti
100 g (3½ oz) watercress, trimmed, washed and chopped
60 g (2 oz) pine nuts
60 g (2 oz) Parmesan cheese, grated
2 cloves garlic, peeled and crushed
115 ml (4 fl oz) olive oil
6 tablespoons chicken stock (see p.8)
450 g (1 lb) boneless chicken breasts, skinned and cut into thin strips (see p.116)
340 g (12 oz) whole sweet red peppers, drained and cut into strips
Freshly ground black pepper
Sprigs of watercress to garnish

Per serving
Calories 785 Protein 41 g
Total fat 49 g (saturated fat 9.2 g)
Carbohydrates 48 g (added sugar 0)
Fibre 5.2 g Sodium 314 mg

Pine nuts, widely used in Italian sauces, give body and a mild almond taste to the peppery watercress sauce in this substantial dish. Whole sweet red peppers are sold in jars in supermarkets and delicatessens.

1 Cook the spaghetti (see p.202). Drain well and return the pasta to the saucepan.

2 Meanwhile, put the watercress, pine nuts, half the Parmesan, the garlic, all but 1 tablespoon of the oil and the stock into a food processor. Blend for 1 minute, or until smooth.

3 Heat the remaining oil in a frying pan and fry the chicken strips in it for 3-4 minutes, or until cooked (see p.117).

4 Pour the watercress sauce over the cooked spaghetti, add the chicken and red pepper strips and toss together. Heat through for 3-4 minutes, then pour into a warm serving bowl. Sprinkle with the remaining Parmesan and some pepper, then garnish with the watercress sprigs and serve with warm wholemeal rolls.

CREAMY CHICKEN AND MUSHROOM SPAGHETTI

Serves 4
Preparation time: 15 minutes
Cooking time: 30 minutes

60 g (2 oz) unsalted butter
2 shallots or 1 medium onion, peeled and finely chopped
225 g (8 oz) mushrooms, wiped and sliced
285 ml (½ pint) chicken stock (see p.8)
340 g (12 oz) spaghetti
4 level teaspoons cornflour
150 ml (¼ pint) single cream
175 g (6 oz) frozen peas
275 g (10 oz) cooked chicken, diced
2 level teaspoons whole-grain mustard
¼ level teaspoon salt
Freshly ground black pepper
1 level tablespoon chopped fresh parsley
85 g (3 oz) mature Cheddar cheese, grated

Per serving
Calories 747 Protein 41 g
Total fat 34 g (saturated fat 19 g)
Carbohydrates 74 g (added sugar 0)
Fibre 9.2 g Sodium 467 mg

Button, cup, open or chestnut mushrooms can be used in the rich, nutty sauce that coats the chicken and spaghetti in this warming dish. It is a good recipe for using up chicken left over from a roast.

1 Melt the butter in a large frying pan and soften the shallots or onion in it. Add the mushrooms and cook, stirring occasionally, for 3-4 minutes. Pour in the stock and bring to the boil, then reduce the heat and simmer gently for 5 minutes, stirring occasionally.

2 In the meantime, cook the spaghetti (see p.202). Blend the cornflour with the cream and stir into the stock in the pan. Cook, stirring, for 2-3 minutes, until the sauce is thickened.

3 Mix the peas, chicken, mustard, salt and some pepper into the sauce and bring back to the boil. Reduce the heat and simmer for 5-10 minutes, stirring occasionally. Stir in the parsley.

4 Drain the pasta well and put it into a heated serving bowl. Pour over the sauce and toss with the pasta. Sprinkle with the Cheddar and serve.

TURKEY TAGLIATELLE

Tender strips of turkey mixed with carrots, courgettes and button mushrooms make a colourful, nutritious sauce for a base of ribbon pasta.

Serves 4
Preparation time: 20 minutes
Cooking time: 20 minutes

225 g (8 oz) tagliatelle
2 tablespoons olive oil
450 g (1 lb) turkey or chicken, cut into thin strips
1 onion, peeled and chopped
3 medium carrots, peeled and cut into long, thin strips
115 g (4 oz) button mushrooms, wiped and sliced
2 cloves garlic, peeled and crushed
4 tablespoons white wine
2 medium courgettes, trimmed and cut into long, thin strips
285 ml (1/2 pint) chicken stock (see p.8)
1/2 level teaspoon salt
Freshly ground black pepper
1 level tablespoon cornflour
150 ml (1/4 pint) single cream
3 tablespoons snipped fresh chives or spring onion tops
60 g (2 oz) Parmesan cheese, grated

Per serving
Calories 572 Protein 42 g
Total fat 22 g (saturated fat 9.3 g)
Carbohydrates 53 g (added sugar 0)
Fibre 5.1 g Sodium 487 mg

1 Cook the tagliatelle (see p.202) and drain it well. Meanwhile, heat half the oil in a heavy saucepan and stir-fry the turkey or chicken in it in two batches until it is cooked (see p.117) – this takes around 2 minutes per batch. Transfer to a bowl and set aside.

2 Add the remaining oil to the pan and cook the onion in it until softened. Mix in the carrots, mushrooms and garlic and cook for 2 minutes, then add the wine and cook for a further 3 minutes.

3 Stir in the courgettes, stock, salt and some pepper and bring to the boil. Reduce the heat, cover and simmer gently for 3 minutes.

4 Blend the cornflour with the cream in a cup or small bowl and stir it into the pan. Continue cooking for 2-3 minutes, stirring, until the sauce thickens slightly.

5 Mix the strips of poultry and drained pasta into the vegetables and heat for 2-3 minutes. Pour into a heated serving dish, sprinkle with the chives or spring onion tops and Parmesan and serve.

LINGUINE WITH COURGETTES AND SAUSAGES

Tasty chunks of freshly grilled Mediterranean-style sausage combine with thin courgette slices, cream and pasta ribbons. The recipe also works well with cold cooked turkey or chicken instead of the sausages.

Serves 4
Preparation time: 15 minutes
Cooking time: 15 minutes

225 g (8 oz) linguine or spaghetti
2 tablespoons olive oil
1 onion, peeled and chopped
3 cloves garlic, peeled and crushed
2 medium courgettes, trimmed, sliced lengthways and cut into fine strips
340 g (12 oz) fresh Mediterranean-style sausages, grilled and thickly sliced
150 ml (1/4 pint) single cream
Freshly ground black pepper
115 g (4 oz) mature Cheddar cheese, grated

Per serving
Calories 716 Protein 24 g
Total fat 46 g (saturated fat 21 g)
Carbohydrates 56 g (added sugar 0)
Fibre 3.7 g Sodium 884 mg

1 Cook the linguine (see p.202), drain, return to the saucepan and cover. Meanwhile, heat the oil in a heavy saucepan and fry the onion in it until softened.

2 Add the garlic, courgettes and sliced sausages. Cook for 3 minutes, stirring occasionally. Stir in 6 tablespoons of the cream, season with some of the pepper and heat through thoroughly.

3 Mix the grated Cheddar and remaining cream with the hot pasta, cover and leave to stand for 1 minute. Stir gently and turn onto a heated serving dish. Pour the sausage mixture over the pasta and serve with warm ciabatta or any other Italian bread.

PASTA SHELLS WITH SEAFOOD

Serves 4
Preparation time: 10 minutes
Cooking time: 30 minutes

3 tablespoons olive oil
3 sticks celery, trimmed and
   thinly sliced
2 large cloves garlic, peeled
   and crushed
800 g (1¾ lb) canned
   chopped tomatoes
¼ level teaspoon dried oregano
½ level teaspoon salt
Freshly ground black pepper

225 g (8 oz) pasta shells or
   elbow macaroni
225 g (8 oz) frozen sweetcorn
400 g (14 oz) frozen mixed seafood
115 g (4 oz) frozen peeled prawns
3 tablespoons chopped
   fresh parsley

Per serving
Calories 524 Protein 40 g
Total fat 14 g (saturated fat 1.9 g)
Carbohydrates 64 g (added sugar 0)
Fibre 7 g Sodium 2541 mg

A blend of garlic, oregano and tomatoes draws out the delicate flavours of the seafood in this hearty pasta dish.

This straightforward recipe lends itself to variations – try substituting a firm-fleshed fish for the seafood, or a crisp green vegetable for the corn.

1 Heat the oil in a heavy saucepan and fry the celery and garlic in it for 5 minutes, stirring occasionally. Add the tomatoes, oregano, salt and some pepper and bring to the boil. Reduce the heat, cover the pan and simmer for 15 minutes.

2 In the meantime, cook the pasta (see p.202), then drain well and keep warm.

3 Stir the sweetcorn, seafood and prawns into the tomato sauce and bring back to the boil. Reduce the heat and simmer for 5-7 minutes. Mix in the pasta and parsley, heat gently for 2-3 minutes and serve.

LEMON PRAWNS WITH RIGATONI

Serves 4
Preparation time: 20 minutes
Cooking time: 15 minutes

340 g (12 oz) rigatoni or penne
2 tablespoons olive oil
225 g (8 oz) fresh broccoli florets
1 yellow or red pepper, de-seeded
   and cut into strips
4 spring onions, trimmed
   and chopped
1 tablespoon chopped fresh basil
½ level teaspoon salt
Freshly ground black pepper
340 g (12 oz) uncooked prawns,
   peeled and de-veined, tails left on
Thinly pared rind of half a lemon,
   cut into fine shreds
2 tablespoons lemon juice
1 clove garlic, peeled and crushed
1 level teaspoon peeled and grated
   fresh root ginger
150 ml (¼ pint) single cream

Per serving
Calories 550 Protein 33 g
Total fat 17 g (saturated fat 6 g)
Carbohydrates 69 g (added sugar 0)
Fibre 5 g Sodium 1628 mg

This simple recipe is an excellent choice for supper, especially if you are short of time at the end of a busy day. You can use cooked prawns instead of raw prawns, if you prefer. Add them for the last 2-3 minutes of cooking.

1 Cook the pasta (see p.202) and drain. In the meantime, heat the oil in a large frying pan and add the broccoli, pepper, spring onions, basil, salt and some pepper. Cover and cook for 5 minutes.

2 Stir in the prawns, lemon rind and juice, garlic and ginger, cover again and cook, stirring occasionally, for 5-6 minutes, or until the prawns turn pink.

3 Pour in the cream, then bring to the boil, stirring, for 2 minutes. Mix in the drained pasta and serve.

Lemon rind and juice, fresh root ginger and basil leaves make a fresh-tasting foil for this rich combination of cream, prawns and pasta.

SALMON AND ASPARAGUS WITH PASTA SHELLS

Tender asparagus spears make a refreshing addition to this summery salmon and pasta lunch. Use frozen asparagus if fresh is unavailable – add it to the pan after the pasta has simmered for 10 minutes.

Serves 4
Preparation time: 15 minutes
Cooking time: 25 minutes

30 g (1 oz) butter
1 medium onion, peeled
    and chopped
1 tablespoon medium hot
    curry powder
725 ml (1¼ pints) fish or chicken
    stock (see p.8)
225 g (8 oz) pasta shells or penne
225 g (8 oz) asparagus, trimmed
    and cut into short pieces
150 ml (¼ pint) Greek yoghurt
2 level teaspoons cornflour
400 g (14 oz) canned red salmon,
    drained and flaked
1 red pepper, grilled, de-seeded
    and sliced (see p.11)

Per serving
Calories 493 Protein 32 g
Total fat 19 g (saturated fat 8.3 g)
Carbohydrates 51 g (added sugar 0)
Fibre 4.9 g Sodium 663 mg

1 Heat the butter in a saucepan and soften the onion in it, then add the curry powder and cook, stirring, for 1 minute. Pour in the stock and bring to the boil.

2 Stir in the pasta, then reduce the heat, cover and simmer for 5 minutes. Add the asparagus and simmer for 8 minutes, or until just tender.

3 Blend the yoghurt with the cornflour, then stir into the pasta. Cook, stirring, for a further 2 minutes, then carefully add the salmon and red pepper. Simmer, stirring occasionally, for 2 minutes, until heated through, then serve.

Strips of grilled red pepper add a subtle smokiness to the contrasting flavours of tangy red salmon and delicate fresh asparagus. Greek yoghurt enriches the simple sauce.

Ricotta-stuffed Shells with Caponata Sauce

Caponata, a speciality of Sicily, is a piquant combination of aubergines, capers, olives and anchovies. It is generally served on its own as a cold hors d'oeuvre, but here it makes a zesty pasta sauce.

Serves 4
Preparation time: 45 minutes
Standing time: 1 hour
Cooking time: 30 minutes

For the caponata sauce
225 g (8 oz) aubergines, cut into small dice
1 level tablespoon salt
3 tablespoons olive oil
1 small onion, peeled and thinly sliced
30 g (1 oz) sugar
2 level tablespoons tomato purée
2 tablespoons red wine vinegar
20 g (³⁄₄ oz) canned anchovy fillets, chopped
1 tablespoon capers, chopped
30 g (1 oz) pitted black olives, finely chopped
2 tablespoons each chopped fresh basil and parsley
150 ml (¹⁄₄ pint) chicken stock (see p.8)
Freshly ground black pepper

For the pasta
225 g (8 oz) large pasta shells
340 g (12 oz) broccoli florets, blanched for 3 minutes (see p.10) and chopped

450 g (1 lb) ricotta cheese
2 cloves garlic, peeled and crushed
1 large red pepper, grilled, de-seeded and chopped (see p.11)
1 egg, size 1, lightly beaten
¹⁄₄ level teaspoon salt
Freshly ground black pepper
60 g (2 oz) Parmesan cheese, grated
30 g (1 oz) canned anchovy fillets, drained and halved lengthways
2 tablespoons chopped fresh parsley
2 teaspoons capers
Sprigs of fresh basil to garnish

Per serving
Calories 676   Protein 34 g
Total fat 34 g (saturated fat 13 g)
Carbohydrates 61 g (added sugar 7.5 g)
Fibre 6.3 g   Sodium 1851 mg

1 Place the diced aubergines in a bowl and sprinkle them with the salt. Leave them to one side for 1 hour to draw out the bitter juices and then rinse in a colander, drain and dry well on kitchen paper.

2 Heat the oil in a large saucepan and fry the aubergines and onion in it for 10 minutes, stirring occasionally. Stir in the sugar, tomato purée and vinegar and cook for 1-2 minutes.

The mild flavours of ricotta cheese and broccoli mingle with the sharper tastes of anchovies, capers and olives in these impressive stuffed shells.

3 Mix in the chopped anchovies, chopped capers, olives, basil, parsley, stock and some pepper, then remove the caponata sauce from the heat and set aside.

4 Heat the oven to 180°C (350°F, gas mark 4). Cook the pasta shells (see p.202), drain well and allow to cool. Mix together the broccoli, ricotta, garlic, red pepper, egg, salt, some black pepper and all but 2 tablespoons of the Parmesan in a bowl.

5 Stuff the pasta shells with the broccoli mixture, then arrange the shells in a single layer in a large, greased, ovenproof dish. Pour the caponata sauce over the top and sprinkle with the remaining Parmesan.

6 Bake in the oven for 20-30 minutes, or until bubbling hot and lightly browned. Once cooked, arrange the anchovy fillets on top in a lattice pattern and sprinkle with the parsley. Scatter on the capers, garnish with the basil and serve.

SPAGHETTI WITH PRAWNS AND ASPARAGUS

Serves 4
Preparation time: 15 minutes
Cooking time: 15 minutes

225 g (8 oz) spaghetti
1 tablespoon olive oil
1 medium onion, peeled and sliced
250 g (9 oz) asparagus, cut into short lengths and blanched (see p.10)
225 g (8 oz) canned water chestnuts, drained and sliced
115 g (4 oz) curd cheese
2 level tablespoons Dijon mustard
3 tablespoons dry white wine or vermouth
1/2 level teaspoon salt
Freshly ground black pepper
340 g (12 oz) fresh peeled prawns

Per serving
Calories 397 Protein 27 g
Total fat 9.6 g (saturated fat 3.2 g)
Carbohydrates 51 g (added sugar 0)
Fibre 5.6 g Sodium 410 mg

The creamy curd-cheese sauce in this dish contrasts with the moist prawns and crunchy water chestnuts. Asparagus adds a final touch of colour.

1 Cook the spaghetti (see p.202). Meanwhile, heat the oil in a heavy saucepan and fry the onion in it until softened. Add the asparagus and water chestnuts and cook, stirring, for 1 minute.

2 Reduce the heat and mix in the curd cheese, mustard, wine or vermouth, salt and some pepper. Then stir in the prawns and heat through for 3-4 minutes, taking care not to let the sauce boil.

3 Drain the spaghetti and add it to the sauce, mixing together well. Turn into a large, heated serving bowl, or directly onto four plates, and serve.

Seafood and Linguine in Tomato Sauce

Serves 4
Preparation time: 10 minutes
Cooking time: 20 minutes

1 tablespoon olive oil
1 medium onion, peeled
  and chopped
225 g (8 oz) courgettes, trimmed
  and cut into small cubes
1 level teaspoon chopped
  chillies in oil
800 g (1¾ lb) canned chopped
  tomatoes
2 level teaspoons soft brown sugar
2 teaspoons red wine vinegar
Finely grated rind of 1 orange
½ level teaspoon salt
225 g (8 oz) fresh linguine
  or spaghettini
400 g (14 oz) frozen mixed
  seafood, thawed and drained
275 g (10 oz) canned baby
  clams, drained

Per serving
Calories 467 Protein 44 g
Total fat 7.1 g (saturated fat 0.8 g)
Carbohydrates 59 g (added sugar 2.5 g)
Fibre 4.8 g Sodium 2739 mg

Chopped chillies in oil spice up the tomato sauce in this tangy seafood recipe. If you can't find ready-prepared chillies, then use a chopped fresh green chilli or ½ level teaspoon of chilli powder instead. Packs of frozen mixed seafood can be found in larger supermarkets

1 Heat the oil in a heavy saucepan and soften the onion and courgettes in it for 5 minutes.

2 Stir in the chillies, tomatoes, sugar, vinegar, orange rind and salt and bring to the boil. Reduce the heat and simmer for about 10 minutes, or until the liquid has reduced to a fairly thick sauce.

3 In the meantime, put the linguine on to cook (see p.202). Once the sauce has reduced, stir the seafood and the clams into it and heat through for 3 minutes.

4 Drain the linguine and turn it into a large, heated serving bowl. Pour the sauce on top, then serve with a crisp green salad.

Spicy Baked Crab

Serves 4
Preparation time: 15 minutes
Cooking time: 40 minutes

2 tablespoons olive oil
1 medium onion, peeled
  and chopped
1 level teaspoon ground cumin
2 level tablespoons plain flour
570 ml (1 pint) fish or chicken
  stock (see p.8)
340 g (12 oz) crabmeat
150 ml (¼ pint) soured cream
150 g (5 oz) fresh tagliatelle
115 g (4 oz) frozen sweetcorn
  kernels
225 g (8 oz) frozen broad beans,
  thawed and removed from
  their skins
1 level teaspoon chopped
  chillies in oil
½ level teaspoon salt
30 g (1 oz) tortilla chips, crushed

Per serving
Calories 406 Protein 24 g
Total fat 19 g (saturated fat 6.5 g)
Carbohydrates 38 g (added sugar 0)
Fibre 5.8 g Sodium 897 mg

Crushed tortilla chips make an unusual spicy topping for this dish of baked crabmeat and pasta. Cumin, one of the main spices in curry powder, gives the sauce a warm, pungent flavour.

1 Preheat the oven to 200°C (400°F, gas mark 6). Heat the oil in a heavy saucepan and soften the onion in it. Stir in the cumin and flour and cook for 1 minute.

2 Pour in the stock and bring to the boil, stirring, until the liquid is slightly thick. Mix in the crabmeat, soured cream, tagliatelle, sweetcorn, broad beans, chillies and salt.

3 Bring the mixture back to the boil, then pour it into a shallow ovenproof dish and sprinkle the crushed tortilla chips over the top. Bake in the centre of the oven for 25 minutes, or until crisp and golden brown, then serve.

Spaghettini with Pumpkin Sauce

Serves 4
Preparation time: 15 minutes
Cooking time: 35 minutes

30 g (1 oz) butter
1 large onion, peeled and
  finely chopped
150 ml (¼ pint) vegetable stock
  (see p.9)
900 g (2 lb) pumpkin, peeled,
  de-seeded and finely chopped
340 g (12 oz) spaghettini
¼ level teaspoon freshly
  grated nutmeg
2 tablespoons chopped
  fresh parsley
150 ml (¼ pint) single cream
115 g (4 oz) pecorino
  cheese, grated
Freshly ground black pepper
30 g (1 oz) Parmesan cheese, grated
Chopped parsley to garnish

Per serving
Calories 575 Protein 23 g
Total fat 24 g (saturated fat 14 g)
Carbohydrates 71 g (added sugar 0)
Fibre 5.8 g Sodium 335 mg

Pecorino cheese – a hard, salty sheep's cheese – combines with sweet, creamy pumpkin in this bright, full-flavoured dish. Of the many varieties of pecorino, pecorino romano is the best known. You can buy it from Italian delicatessens and some of the larger supermarkets.

1 Melt the butter in a saucepan, then gently soften the onion in it, covered.

2 Pour in the stock and add the pumpkin. Cover and cook for 25 minutes, or until the pumpkin is soft. Meanwhile, cook the spaghettini (see p.202) and drain well.

3 Stir the nutmeg, parsley, cream, pecorino and pepper into the pumpkin over the heat for 2 minutes. Gently mix in the spaghettini, then pour the mixture into a heated dish. Sprinkle with the Parmesan and parsley and serve.

The sweet, pulpy flesh of cooked pumpkin mixes with cream, nutmeg and grated pecorino cheese to make a piquant but creamy pasta sauce.

CANNELLONI PANCAKES

Serves 4
Preparation time: 1 hour 15 minutes
Cooking time: 25 minutes

For the pancakes
115 g (4 oz) plain flour
1/8 level teaspoon salt
Freshly ground black pepper
2 eggs, size 2, lightly beaten
285 ml (1/2 pint) semi-skimmed milk
1-2 tablespoons vegetable oil
 for frying

For the filling
60 g (2 oz) butter
340 g (12 oz) button mushrooms,
 wiped and sliced
340 g (12 oz) courgettes, trimmed
 and coarsely grated
45 g (1 1/2 oz) pine nuts
6 sun-dried tomatoes in oil, chopped
30 g (1 oz) Parmesan cheese, grated
1/4 level teaspoon salt
Freshly ground black pepper

For the sauce
30 g (1 oz) butter
30 g (1 oz) plain flour
425 ml (3/4 pint) milk
1/4 level teaspoon ground nutmeg
1/4 level teaspoon salt
Freshly ground black pepper
60 g (2 oz) Parmesan cheese, grated
2 tablespoons snipped fresh
 chives to garnish

Per serving
Calories 682 Protein 27 g
Total fat 47 g (saturated fat 20 g)
Carbohydrates 41 g (added sugar 0)
Fibre 3.9 g Sodium 866 mg

In the north of Italy, cannelloni are often made with light pancakes rolled around a savoury filling such as this mushroom, courgette and sun-dried tomato mixture. You can prepare the pancakes a day ahead; when they are cool, store them in a polythene bag or wrapped in foil in the fridge.

1 Sift the flour, salt and some pepper into a bowl and make a well in the centre. Gradually whisk in the beaten eggs and half the milk, then beat to a smooth, thick batter. Mix in the remaining milk, then pour into a jug and leave to stand for 30 minutes.

2 Meanwhile, make the filling. Heat the butter in a large frying pan and stir-fry the mushrooms in it for 3-4 minutes. Mix in the courgettes and cook over a moderate heat for a further 5 minutes, then stir in the pine

Cannelloni pancakes can be filled with any savoury stuffing but pine nuts and sun-dried tomatoes give them an authentic Italian flavour.

nuts and sun-dried tomatoes. Take the pan off the heat and mix in the Parmesan. Season with the salt and some pepper, then set aside and leave to cool.

3 Preheat the oven to 200°C (400°F, gas mark 6). Heat a small frying pan and brush with a little of the oil. Heat until the oil gives off a light haze,

then stir the batter and pour one-eighth of it into the pan. Quickly tilt the pan until the base is evenly coated. Cook for 1-2 minutes, until the top of the batter is set and the underside golden brown. Turn the pancake over and cook the other side for 1 minute, then tip the pancake onto a heated plate and cover with a sheet of kitchen paper. Make seven more pancakes in the same way, stacking them between sheets of kitchen paper.

4 To make the sauce, melt the butter in a small saucepan and stir in the flour. Cook, stirring, for 1 minute over a low heat, then gradually add the milk, nutmeg, salt and some pepper. Simmer for 2-3 minutes, then take the pan off the heat and set aside.

5 Divide the filling between the pancakes, then roll them up and put in a greased, shallow, ovenproof dish. Spoon the sauce on top and sprinkle with the Parmesan. Bake in the centre of the oven for 25 minutes, or until golden brown and heated through. Garnish with the chopped chives and serve with a green salad and ciabatta or other Italian bread.

MACARONI WITH COURGETTES AND RICOTTA CHEESE

Serves 6
Preparation time: 1 hour
Cooking time: 1-1½ hours

....

1 kg (2 lb 3 oz) courgettes, trimmed and coarsely grated
1 level teaspoon salt
30 g (1 oz) butter
2 medium onions, peeled and chopped
200 g (7 oz) elbow macaroni
225 g (8 oz) ricotta cheese
70 g (2½ oz) Parmesan cheese, grated
3 eggs, size 2, lightly beaten
1 tablespoon chopped fresh marjoram, or 1½ level teaspoons dried marjoram
225 ml (8 fl oz) single cream
Freshly ground black pepper
Chopped fresh parsley to garnish

....

Per serving
Calories 420 Protein 20 g
Total fat 24 g (saturated fat 13 g)
Carbohydrates 33 g (added sugar 0)
    Fibre 2.2 g Sodium 593 mg

....

Gentle, slow steaming gives this cheese and vegetable mixture a light texture without losing its rich creaminess. A saucepan with a tightly fitting lid is best for steaming. If you use a stainless steel or thin heatproof plastic bowl, check to see if the filling is cooked after 1 hour.

1 Put the courgettes in a bowl, sprinkle with the salt and leave to stand for 20 minutes. In the meantime, melt the butter in a frying pan and soften the onions in it over a low heat, without browning.

2 Put the courgettes in a colander and squeeze tightly to extract the bitter juices. Add to the pan and cook for about 10 minutes, stirring. Remove from the heat and leave to cool for 15 minutes.

3 Cook the macaroni (see p.202). Meanwhile, put the ricotta and Parmesan in a large bowl and gradually whisk in the eggs. Mix in the marjoram and cream, then set aside. Pour the cooked macaroni into a colander, rinse under cold water and drain well.

4 Mix the onions, courgettes and macaroni into the ricotta mixture. Season with some pepper, then pour the mixture into a large, greased, heatproof mixing bowl or pudding basin and cover tightly with buttered foil.

5 Stand the bowl in a large saucepan and pour enough boiling water into the pan to come halfway up the side of the bowl. Cover the pan with a lid and steam gently for 1-1½ hours, or until firmly set. You may need to top up the water during steaming.

6 Remove the bowl from the saucepan and allow to stand for 10 minutes. Turn out onto a flat serving dish and sprinkle with the chopped parsley. Serve hot or cold with a crisp lettuce and tomato salad and ciabatta or any other type of Italian bread.

RAVIOLI IN HERB AND TOMATO SAUCE

Serves 4
Preparation time: 10 minutes
Cooking time: 20 minutes

2 tablespoons olive oil
1 large onion, peeled and chopped
½ level teaspoon fennel
    seeds, crushed
1 level teaspoon dried basil
2 cloves garlic, peeled and crushed
340 g (12 oz) tomato pasta sauce
60 g (2 oz) pitted black
    olives, sliced
450 g (1 lb) fresh ricotta and
    spinach ravioli
225 g (8 oz) runner or bobby beans,
    trimmed and cut into short lengths
30 g (1 oz) Parmesan cheese,
    grated

Per serving
Calories 395 Protein 15 g
Total fat 20 g (saturated fat 6.5 g)
Carbohydrates 40 g
(added sugar 0)
Fibre 9 g
Sodium 1384 mg

A thick, aromatic sauce coats the al dente ravioli in this quick and easy recipe, which makes the most of the tomato pasta sauces available in delicatessens or large supermarkets. You can use fresh ravioli stuffed with meat in place of the ricotta and spinach variety, if you prefer.

I Heat the oil in a saucepan and cook the onion and fennel seeds in it for about 10 minutes, stirring occasionally. Add the basil, garlic and the tomato sauce, cover and simmer for 5 minutes, then stir in the olives.

2 Cook the ravioli (see p.202) and add the beans for the last 5 minutes of cooking. Drain well.

3 Stir the ravioli and beans into the tomato sauce, then spoon onto warm, individual plates. Sprinkle with the Parmesan and serve with grissini sticks.

The aniseed scent and warm, fragrant taste of crushed fennel seeds refresh the herb and tomato sauce in this straightforward supper dish.

194

PENNE WITH PEPPERS AND MOZZARELLA

Serves 4
Preparation time: 15 minutes
Cooking time: 15 minutes

340 g (12 oz) penne
2 tablespoons olive oil
1 large onion, peeled and
   thinly sliced
3 large peppers, 1 green, 1 red
   and 1 yellow, de-seeded and
   cut into thin strips
½ level teaspoon each dried
   oregano and dried basil
½ level teaspoon salt
Freshly ground black pepper
2 cloves garlic, peeled and crushed
225 g (8 oz) mozzarella
   cheese, grated
30 g (1 oz) Parmesan cheese, grated
Sprigs of fresh oregano to garnish

Per serving
Calories 600 Protein 29 g
Total fat 23 g (saturated fat 10 g)
Carbohydrates 75 g (added sugar 0)
Fibre 7 g Sodium 683 mg

Sweet strips of pepper are tossed with quill-shaped penne in a colourful combination, bound together with melting mozzarella. Red and yellow peppers are slightly sweeter than the green ones, so use all three colours for the best variation in taste. Any pasta shape, such as shells, bows or spirals, can take the place of the penne.

1 Put the penne on to cook (see p.202). Meanwhile, heat the oil in a large frying pan for 1 minute, then sauté the onion, peppers, dried oregano, basil, salt and some pepper in it for about 10 minutes, stirring occasionally, until softened. Mix in the garlic and cook for another 2 minutes.

2 Drain the penne, then put it back in the pan. Stir in the mozzarella, cover and leave to stand for 1-2 minutes, until the cheese has melted. Lightly toss the pepper mixture with the penne.

3 Turn the mixture into a heated serving dish and sprinkle with the Parmesan. Garnish with the fresh oregano and serve.

MACARONI CHEESE

Whole-grain mustard adds a robustness to this hearty family favourite. Cubes of ham, chicken or broccoli florets can all be used to vary the dish.

Serves 4
Preparation time: 30 minutes
Cooking time: 25 minutes

275 g (10 oz) elbow macaroni
60 g (2 oz) butter
60 g (2 oz) plain flour
570 ml (1 pint) milk
285 ml (½ pint) single cream
¼ level teaspoon salt
Freshly ground black pepper
⅛ level teaspoon freshly
   grated nutmeg
1 level tablespoon whole-grain
   mustard
275 g (10 oz) mature Cheddar
   cheese, grated
3 tomatoes, sliced
Sprigs of fresh parsley to garnish

Per serving
Calories 899 Protein 34 g
Total fat 53 g (saturated fat 33 g)
Carbohydrates 75 g (added sugar 0)
Fibre 4.6 g Sodium 825 mg

1 Preheat the oven to 220°C (425°F, gas mark 7) and cook the macaroni (see p.202).

2 Meanwhile, melt the butter in a large saucepan and stir in the flour. Cook over a moderate heat for 1 minute, then gradually mix in the milk, cream, salt, some pepper and the nutmeg. Stir until the sauce comes to the boil and thickens, then reduce the heat and simmer for 2 minutes, stirring.

3 Take the saucepan off the heat and stir in the mustard and three-quarters of the Cheddar, stirring until the cheese melts.

4 Drain the cooked macaroni thoroughly, then mix it into the cheese sauce. Pour the mixture into a shallow ovenproof dish and sprinkle with the remaining Cheddar. Arrange the tomato slices on top, then bake in the centre of the oven for about 25 minutes, or until golden brown and bubbling. Garnish with the parsley sprigs and serve with a lettuce salad and warm granary bread.

FUSILLI WITH BLACK BEANS

Serves 4
Preparation time: 15 minutes
Cooking time: 20 minutes

225 g (8 oz) fusilli or other small
  pasta shapes
2 tablespoons olive oil
1 large onion, peeled and chopped
1 large green pepper, de-seeded
  and chopped
3 cloves garlic, peeled and crushed
340 g (12 oz) tomatoes, de-seeded
  and chopped
340 g (12 oz) cooked black beans,
  rinsed and drained (see p.172)
3 level tablespoons chopped fresh
  coriander or parsley

½ level teaspoon salt
Freshly ground black pepper
1 teaspoon lemon juice
340 g (12 oz) curly kale or spinach,
  trimmed, washed and blanched
  for 2 minutes (see p.10)
225 g (8 oz) Monterey Jack or
  Cheddar cheese, grated

Per serving
Calories 616 Protein 30 g
Total fat 29 g (saturated fat 13 g)
Carbohydrates 63 g (added sugar 0)
Fibre 13 g Sodium 658 mg

Monterey Jack, an American
cheese available in larger stores,
or Cheddar both work well in
this warming pasta dish.

1 Cook the pasta (see p.202).
Meanwhile, heat the oil in
a large frying pan and sauté
the onion and pepper in it for
5 minutes, or until soft. Add the
garlic and cook for 2 minutes.

2 Stir in the tomatoes, beans,
coriander or parsley, salt,
some pepper and the lemon
juice, and simmer for
5 minutes, stirring
occasionally.

3 Roughly chop the kale or
spinach, and stir into the pan.
Continue cooking for 3 minutes.

4 Drain the pasta and add to the
sauce with the grated cheese.
Stir over the heat for 1 minute,
or until the cheese melts, and then
serve straight from the pan.

A light, aromatic coriander, garlic and lemon sauce accompanies this wholesome combination of pasta twirls, black beans and grated cheese.

MUSHROOM AND PEPPERONI PIZZA

Tasty pepperoni, mozzarella and thick mushroom slices come together in this quick, satisfying meal. Pizza bases are available in supermarkets, or make your own at home (see p.203).

Serves 4
Preparation time: 10 minutes
Cooking time: 15 minutes

2 tablespoons olive oil
1 medium onion, peeled and sliced
1 large red pepper, de-seeded and sliced
225 g (8 oz) mushrooms, wiped and thickly sliced
4 pizza bases, each 18 cm (7 in) in diameter
250 g (9 oz) tomato pizza sauce
275 g (10 oz) mozzarella cheese, grated
115 g (4 oz) sliced pepperoni
15 g (½ oz) Parmesan cheese, grated

Per serving
Calories 732 Protein 36 g
Total fat 41 g (saturated fat 17 g)
Carbohydrates 60 g (added sugar 0)
Fibre 7.4 g Sodium 1730 mg

1 Preheat the oven to 230°C (450°F, gas mark 8). Meanwhile, heat the oil in a frying pan and sauté the onion, pepper and mushrooms in it until softened.

2 Lay the pizza bases on two baking trays and spread the tomato sauce evenly over each base. Divide the onion mixture equally between the four pizzas, spreading it out to the edges.

3 Arrange half the mozzarella on the pizzas and then add the pepperoni. Cover with the remaining mozzarella, sprinkle with the Parmesan and place the baking trays in the centre of the oven. Cook for 8-10 minutes, or until the cheese has melted and browned slightly. Serve straight from the oven with a green salad.

197

PIZZA SURPRISE

A shell of light, oven-crisp pizza dough encloses a tasty ham mixture in this healthy variation on the classic Italian dish.

Serves 4
Preparation time: 20 minutes
Cooking time: 20 minutes

400 g (14 oz) fresh spinach leaves, trimmed, washed and blanched for 2 minutes (see p.10)
¼ level teaspoon freshly grated or ground nutmeg
400 g (14 oz) pizza dough (see p.203) or 225 g (8 oz) pizza dough mix, made up as directed on packet
225 g (8 oz) Cheddar cheese, grated
30 g (1 oz) walnuts, roughly chopped
1 red apple, peeled, cored and thinly sliced
115 g (4 oz) cooked ham, chopped
Freshly ground black pepper

Per serving
Calories 589 Protein 31 g
Total fat 28 g (saturated fat 13 g)
Carbohydrates 58 g (added sugar 0)
Fibre 7.4 g Sodium 852 mg

1 Preheat oven to 220°C (425°F, gas mark 7). Roughly chop the spinach, put it in a bowl and toss it with the nutmeg.

2 Divide the pizza dough in half. Roll out one piece on a lightly floured surface to form a circle 28 cm (11 in) across and put it on a greased baking sheet. Sprinkle half the Cheddar over the pizza base, leaving a 2.5 cm (1 in) border all round. Spread the spinach over the cheese and sprinkle with the walnuts, apple and ham. Season well with pepper, then scatter the remaining Cheddar on top.

3 Roll out the remaining dough to form a circle 30.5 cm (12 in) across. Brush the edge of the pizza base with a little water, then cover with the second piece. Press the edges together to seal, marking them with a fork for decoration.

4 Bake in the centre of the oven for 15-20 minutes, or until lightly browned. Cut into quarters and serve with a mixed salad.

Spinach leaves tossed in aromatic nutmeg combine with melted Cheddar cheese, crunchy chopped walnuts, soft juicy slices of sweet red apple and lean pieces of ham, to make the fresh-tasting filling for this unusual stuffed pizza.

PITTA BREAD PIZZA

Serves 4
Preparation time: 20 minutes
Cooking time: 30 minutes

3 tablespoons olive oil
1 large onion, peeled and
  finely chopped
1 large red pepper, de-seeded
  and thinly sliced
½ level teaspoon salt
Freshly ground black pepper
2 level teaspoons dried oregano
225 g (8 oz) mushrooms, wiped
  and thinly sliced
450 g (1 lb) aubergines, trimmed,
  halved and thinly sliced
800 g (1¾ lb) canned
  chopped tomatoes
3 cloves garlic, peeled and crushed
8 pitta breads
225 g (8 oz) mozzarella
  cheese, grated
12 iceberg lettuce leaves

Per serving
Calories 736 Protein 33 g
Total fat 25 g (saturated fat 9 g)
Carbohydrates 102 g (added sugar 0)
Fibre 13 g Sodium 1453 mg

A pitta bread pocket topped
with chopped onion, tomatoes,
mozzarella and thinly sliced
aubergines makes an excellent
improvised pizza.

1 Preheat the oven to 200°C
(400°F, gas mark 6). Heat the oil
in a large frying pan and sauté the
onion, red pepper, salt, some black
pepper and the oregano, stirring
occasionally, for 2 minutes. Add
the mushrooms and aubergines
and cook the mixture for a further
5 minutes, stirring well.

2 Mix in the tomatoes and garlic,
then simmer for 5-8 minutes,
or until the mixture has reduced
by half to make a thick pulp.

3 Put the pitta breads on
baking trays and spread an
equal amount of the aubergine
mixture on each one. Sprinkle
with the mozzarella, then bake
for 10-15 minutes, or until the
cheese has melted. Take four
plates, remove the pitta breads
from the oven and place two on
each plate. Garnish with the
lettuce and serve.

TUNA AND FETA CHEESE PITTAS

Serves 4
Preparation time: 20 minutes
Cooking time: 5 minutes

200 g (7 oz) canned tuna in oil,
  drained and flaked, oil reserved
8 cherry tomatoes, quartered
175 g (6 oz) feta cheese, rinsed
  and cut into small squares
12 pitted black olives
4 large wholemeal pitta breads
4 cos lettuce leaves, washed
  and shredded
Strained juice of ½ lemon
1 tablespoon chopped fresh mint
Freshly ground black pepper

Per serving
Calories 523 Protein 27 g
Total fat 22 g (saturated fat 8.2 g)
Carbohydrates 57 g (added sugar 0)
Fibre 9.7 g Sodium 1479 mg

Savoury tuna, Greek feta cheese
and black olives provide a tangy
stuffing for lightly grilled pitta
breads – ideal for a nutritious,
spur-of-the-moment lunch.

1 Mix together the tuna,
tomatoes, feta and olives
in a bowl. Sprinkle the pitta
breads with a little water, then
heat them under a hot grill for
1 minute on each side until
puffed up. Slit them open along
one side only, and fill each one
with a lettuce leaf and a quarter
of the tuna mixture.

2 Pour the reserved tuna oil
into a jug and whisk in the
lemon juice, mint and some
pepper to make a dressing.
Drizzle the dressing over the
tuna filling inside the pitta
breads and serve with a tossed
green salad.

AUBERGINE AND TOMATO PIZZA

Serves 4
Preparation time: 30 minutes
Cooking time: 30 minutes

130 ml (4½ fl oz) olive oil
225 g (8 oz) aubergines, trimmed
  and thinly sliced
1 shallot, peeled and finely chopped
400 g (14 oz) pizza dough
  (see p.203) or 225 g (8 oz)
  pizza dough mix, made up as
  directed on the packet
340 g (12 oz) tomatoes, skinned
  and sliced
¼ level teaspoon salt
Freshly ground black pepper
2 level tablespoons coarsely
  shredded fresh basil
60 g (2 oz) smoked pork
  sausage, sliced
175 g (6 oz) mozzarella cheese, cut
  into small cubes

Per serving
Calories 708 Protein 22 g
Total fat 45 g (saturated fat 12 g)
Carbohydrates 58 g (added sugar 0)
Fibre 5.1 g Sodium 519 mg

Juicy tomato and aubergine
slices contrast with chewy
mozzarella cheese and smoked
pork sausage in an unusual
rectangular pizza.

1 Heat 2 tablespoons of the oil in
a large frying pan and brown
the aubergine slices in it in four
batches, adding 2 tablespoons of
oil with each batch. Drain the
aubergines on kitchen paper.

2 Heat the remaining oil in the
pan and cook the shallot in it
until softened. Preheat the oven
to 220°C (425°F, gas mark 7).

3 Roll out the pizza dough
on a lightly floured surface
until it is large enough to fit a
33 cm x 23 cm (13 in x 9 in)
pizza tin or baking tray. Fit the
dough into the tin or tray, then
arrange the aubergine slices and
shallot on top. Cover and leave
to stand in a warm place for
15 minutes.

4 Arrange the tomato slices on
top of the pizza and season
with the salt and some pepper.
Sprinkle with the basil and scatter
on the smoked sausage slices
and mozzarella cubes. Bake in the
centre of the oven for 30 minutes,
or until the dough is cooked and
the topping is golden, then serve.

WHOLEMEAL PIZZA

Serves 4
Preparation time: 35 minutes
Cooking time: 30 minutes

115 g (4 oz) each wholemeal flour
  and strong plain white flour
½ level teaspoon salt
1 level teaspoon baking powder
2 teaspoons lemon juice
115 ml (4 fl oz) skimmed milk
5 tablespoons olive oil
115 ml (4 fl oz) passata
  (sieved tomatoes)
2 teaspoons Worcestershire sauce
½ level teaspoon each dried thyme
  and dried oregano
2 cloves garlic, peeled and crushed
2 medium tomatoes, sliced
1 medium onion, peeled and
  finely chopped
115 g (4 oz) button mushrooms,
  wiped and sliced
175 g (6 oz) mature Cheddar
  cheese, grated
30 g (1 oz) Parmesan cheese, grated
65 g (2¼ oz) canned anchovy
  fillets, drained
12 pitted black olives

Per serving
Calories 627 Protein 27 g
Total fat 39 g (saturated fat 14 g)
Carbohydrates 44 g (added sugar 0)
Fibre 5.6 g Sodium 1497 mg

This light, healthy pizza
base made with a blend of
wholemeal and white flours is
a quick and easy alternative to
traditional Italian pizza dough.

1 Preheat the oven to 200°C
(400°F, gas mark 6). Sift both
flours, the salt and baking powder
into a large bowl, tipping in any
bran left in the sieve. Make a well
in the centre of the flour and pour
in the lemon juice, milk and
4 tablespoons of the oil. Mix well
to form a soft dough.

2 Knead the dough on a lightly
floured surface for a few
seconds, until smooth, then roll
out to an oblong large enough to
line a greased 33 cm x 23 cm
(13 in x 9 in) baking tray. Fit the
dough into the tray and prick
lightly all over with a fork.

3 Mix the passata, Worcestershire
sauce, thyme, oregano and
garlic and spread over the dough.
Arrange the tomatoes, onion and
mushrooms on top and sprinkle
with the Cheddar and Parmesan.
Lay the anchovy fillets in a lattice
pattern on top, placing the olives
in the holes in between.

4 Brush with the remaining oil
and cook in the centre of
the oven for 30 minutes, or until
golden and bubbling. Serve with
a tossed green salad.

TORTA RUSTICA

Serves 4
Preparation time: 20 minutes
Cooking time: 35 minutes

400 g (14 oz) pizza dough
    (see p.203) or 225 g (8 oz)
    pizza dough mix, made up
    as directed on packet
400 g (14 oz) fresh spinach leaves,
    trimmed, washed and blanched
    for 2 minutes (see p.10)
225 g (8 oz) ricotta cheese
60 g (2 oz) Parmesan
    cheese, grated
3 eggs, size 2, lightly beaten
3 tablespoons chopped fresh basil
1 clove garlic, peeled and crushed
Freshly ground black pepper
340 g (12 oz) jar whole sweet red
    peppers, drained and cut into
    wide strips
30 g (1 oz) pine nuts
115 g (4 oz) cooked ham, sliced

Per serving
Calories 513 Protein 33 g
Total fat 25 g (saturated fat 9.9 g)
Carbohydrates 42 g
(added sugar 0)
Fibre 7.3 g
Sodium 849 mg

Ricotta and Parmesan cheeses, blended with egg, make a thick, savoury topping; pine nuts add an unmistakable Mediterranean flavour.

Spinach, ham and sweet red peppers make a tasty covering for deep-pan pizza in this satisfying Italian country meal. Always serve pizza piping hot, directly from the oven.

1 Preheat oven to 220°C (425°F, gas mark 7). Roll out the pizza dough on a lightly floured surface to make a circle 30.5 cm (12 in) across, then press it over the bottom and halfway up the sides of a lightly oiled expanding cake tin around 25 cm (10 in) wide.

2 Roughly chop the spinach, put it in a bowl and mix in the ricotta, Parmesan, eggs, basil, garlic and some pepper. Add the red pepper strips and pine nuts.

3 Cover the pizza base with half the ricotta mixture and arrange the ham on top. Spoon the remaining ricotta mixture over the ham. Place the pizza in the centre of the oven and bake for 30 minutes, or until the filling is set and the base is crisp. Cut into quarters and serve with salad.

201

Making the most of pasta and pizza

The Italian flair for one-dish meals is evident in the numerous ways of serving pasta and pizza. Rich in protein, high in carbohydrate and relatively low in calories, pasta is the most adaptable of staples, while pizza bases can be dressed up and down to suit every taste.

IN ITALY, pasta is produced in hundreds of different shapes and sizes, and the variety is having an increasing impact on the selection that is available in British supermarkets and delicatessens. Most types of pasta are sold under their Italian names (see below), which usually describe shape and sometimes size. Generally the suffix *-ini*, as in spaghettini, means thin, while *-oni* indicates thick pasta, as in rigatoni. As well as

the many forms of dried pasta, some fresh pasta is available, most commonly as tagliatelle, ravioli or lasagne. Fresh pasta can be bought from supermarkets, delicatessens and Italian speciality stores.

Pasta that is produced from durum wheat semolina has the best texture, so it is worth checking the label before you buy. Pasta made from other flours tends to become sticky and soft when it is boiled.

Ready-to-use sheets of pasta – such as lasagne or cannelloni tubes – do not need to be cooked in boiling water before being layered or stuffed. While baking, the pasta sheets simply absorb the liquid content of their sauce, which is why it is best to make the sauce for these kinds of dishes slightly thinner than usual.

Cooking times for dried pasta

Allow 60-85 g (2-3 oz) pasta per person

5-6 minutes
Cannelloni
Ditalini

8 minutes
Elbow macaroni

8-10 minutes
Linguine
Lasagne
Spaghettini
Long macaroni
Ziti
Rigatoni

10-12 minutes
Spaghetti
Long fusilli
Tagliatelle ribbons or nests
Trenette
Pasta shapes

12-14 minutes
Penne

Follow packet instructions
Filled pasta

Cooking times for pasta depend on size, shape and freshness, and vary from one brand to another. Dried pasta takes 8-15 minutes to cook, while fresh pasta needs 2-5 minutes. Cook pasta in a large saucepan of boiling water, allowing 1.7 litres (3 pints) of water for every 225 g (8 oz) pasta. Add half a level teaspoon of salt to the water and 2 teaspoons of olive oil to prevent the pasta sticking.

Chinese noodles can be made from wheat flour, rice flour, arrowroot or pea starch. Noodles from the north of China are generally made from wheat, either with or without egg. They come in different thicknesses, and are available both fresh, from Chinese supermarkets, and dried. Do not add salt to the cooking water as Chinese noodles are already salted.

To cook Chinese noodles, bring a large saucepan of water to the boil, allowing 1.7 litres (3 pints) of water for 225 g (8 oz) of noodles. Add the noodles, cover the pan and remove from the heat. Leave fine noodles to stand for 4 minutes and medium noodles for 6 minutes. Drain and shake gently, then serve, or add to stir-fries, soups or casseroles.

RIBBON PASTA

Linguine Trenette

Tagliatelle

SHORT AND TUBULAR PASTA

Ziti

Rigatoni

Cannelloni
Penne

SHAPED PASTA

Farfalle

Macaroni

Fusilli

Conchiglie
Cavatappi

Ditalini

Long fusilli

Orzo Small shells

Long macaroni

LONG PASTA

Stellette

Spaghetti

Lasagne

FILLED PASTA

Wholewheat spaghetti

Ravioli Tortellini

CHINESE EGG NOODLES

Cooking pasta

1 Lower the spaghetti or other pasta into boiling water, pushing it down as it softens. Bring the water back to the boil and reduce heat so that it boils gently. Do not cover. Stir and cook for the recommended time until al dente.

2 As soon as the pasta is cooked, pour it into a large colander – the larger the better as this helps the pasta to drain quickly without cooling. Shake gently to remove the excess water.

3 Pour the drained pasta into a large heated serving bowl. Pour the hot sauce over the top and toss gently with a large spoon and fork.

Making pizza dough

Ready-made bases, fresh or frozen, are available in the larger supermarkets, but for the short time it takes to make your own and for the quality of texture and taste, it is worth making them yourself. The dough needs 1½-2 hours to rise in a warm place, such as in an airing cupboard or near a radiator, or you can rise it in a microwave (see p.259), if you have one. Alternatively, you can make the dough the day before you need it and leave it to rise overnight in the fridge.

Basic pizza dough

To make about 400 g (14 oz) of dough, which is equivalent to two ready-made 23 cm (9 in) pizza bases, you will need:

150 ml (¼ pint) lukewarm water
½ level teaspoon caster sugar
1 level teaspoon dried yeast
225 g (8 oz) strong plain flour
½ level teaspoon salt
30 g (1 oz) butter

Making a pizza base

1 Pour the water into a small bowl and stir in the sugar until dissolved. Sprinkle on the yeast and whisk it in with a fork. Cover and put in a warm place for 10 minutes, until frothy.

2 Sift the flour and salt into a bowl, rub in the butter and make a well in the centre. Stir the yeast liquid, then pour it into the flour and mix to form a soft dough.

3 Knead the dough on a lightly floured surface by folding it towards you, then pushing it down and away with your knuckles. Give the dough a quarter turn and repeat until the dough is silky smooth and elastic, but not sticky.

4 Put the dough in a clean, lightly floured bowl and cover with plastic film. Leave it in a warm place for about 1 hour, or until the dough has doubled in size. If rising slowly overnight, put the bowl in the fridge.

5 Turn the risen dough out onto a lightly floured surface and beat with clenched fists to knock out the air bubbles. Knead again until smooth. Roll the dough out with a rolling pin to a round or oblong, as directed in the recipe.

You can make four individual bases to freeze if you double the quantities. Follow steps 1-5, then divide the dough into four equal pieces and roll out each one to a 20 cm (8 in) round. Place the bases on foil-lined trays and freeze until solid. Remove them from the trays and put them in a rigid container or polythene bag for storing in the freezer.

To cook the bases from frozen, set them on a greased baking tray, spread with a topping, and bake in the centre of the oven, pre-heated to 220°C (425°F, gas mark 7) for 30-35 minutes.

SALADS

Salads can be so much more than lettuce and tomato. Our recipes combine fresh salad ingredients with pasta, rice and pulses – as well as fish, meat and poultry – to provide nutritious light meals.

❖

Making the most of salads 232-3

Tuna fish, anchovies, hard-boiled eggs, olives, tomatoes, potatoes and green beans are packed into Salad Niçoise (left) – a famous summer salad from the sunkissed Mediterranean coast of southern France (see p.223).

CREAMY CHICKEN WALDORF SALAD

Serves 4
Preparation time: 25 minutes

85 g (3 oz) blue cheese, cut
  into cubes
225 ml (8 fl oz) natural yoghurt
150 ml (1/4 pint) buttermilk or
  soured cream
1 level tablespoon caster sugar
1 tablespoon lemon juice
1 tablespoon chopped fresh dill,
  or 1 level teaspoon dried dill
1/8 level teaspoon salt
Freshly ground black pepper
450 g (1 lb) cooked chicken, cut
  into small cubes
175 g (6 oz) sugar snap peas,
  trimmed and blanched for
  3 minutes (see p.10)

2 green dessert apples, washed,
  cored and diced
70 g (2 1/2 oz) watercress, trimmed
  and washed
340 g (12 oz) seedless red grapes,
  washed and dried
3 medium sticks celery, trimmed
  and diced (see p.10)
60 g (2 oz) shelled walnuts,
  roughly chopped
4 slices cinnamon raisin bread,
  lightly toasted and cut into
  small cubes

Per serving
Calories 600 Protein 49 g
Total fat 25 g (saturated fat 7.3 g)
Carbohydrates 47 g (added sugar 0)
Fibre 4.6 g Sodium 589 mg

Chopped apple, celery and
walnuts – the ingredients of
the classic Waldorf salad, first
created at New York's Waldorf-
Astoria hotel – provide the
crunch in this substantial salad.

1 Mash the blue cheese in a large
bowl with a wooden spoon.
Gradually mix in the yoghurt,
buttermilk or soured cream,
sugar, lemon juice, fresh or dried
dill, salt and some pepper to make
a smooth dressing.

2 Mix the chicken, sugar snap
peas, apples, watercress, grapes,
celery, walnuts and bread cubes
into the dressing, until well coated.
Turn the salad into a large bowl
and serve with walnut bread.

*Blue cheese, yoghurt and
buttermilk make up the tart,
creamy dressing which combines
diced chicken, crisp sugar snap peas
and grapes with a Waldorf salad base.*

CURRIED CHICKEN AND RICE SALAD

Serves 4
Preparation time: 20 minutes
Cooking time: 1 hour

450 ml (16 fl oz) chicken stock
(see p.8)
450 g (1 lb) boneless chicken
breasts, skinned
175 g (6 oz) long-grain brown rice
225 g (8 oz) mangetout, trimmed,
halved and blanched (see p.10)
4 large carrots, peeled and grated
4 spring onions, trimmed and
finely chopped
60 g (2 oz) sultanas
310 ml (11 fl oz) low-fat
natural yoghurt
2 level tablespoons mayonnaise
1 level teaspoon mild curry paste
¼ level teaspoon salt
Freshly ground black pepper
6 large cos lettuce leaves, washed
30 g (1 oz) flaked almonds,
lightly toasted

Per serving
Calories 524 Protein 36 g
Total fat 16 g (saturated fat 2.9 g)
Carbohydrates 62 g (added sugar 0)
Fibre 8.8 g Sodium 336 mg

Succulent sultanas counter the spiciness of the curried dressing in this filling rice salad. You can prepare this dish 2-3 hours ahead of time and keep it covered in the refrigerator. Sprinkle on the almonds just before you serve the salad.

1 Pour the stock into a large saucepan and bring to the boil, then reduce the heat. Add the chicken breasts and simmer for 10-15 minutes, or until cooked (see p.117). Put the chicken breasts on a plate and leave to cool for 20 minutes.

2 Pour the stock into a measuring jug and top up with water, if needed, to make 450 ml (16 fl oz). Pour the stock back into the pan and bring to the boil. Stir in the rice, reduce the heat, cover and simmer for 30 minutes, or until the rice is cooked and all the stock has been absorbed. Take the pan off the heat and leave to cool.

3 Cut the cooled chicken breasts into small cubes and put them in a large bowl. Mix in the rice, mangetout, carrots, spring onions and sultanas.

4 Combine the yoghurt with the mayonnaise, curry paste, salt and some pepper in a large bowl. Pour over the chicken and rice mixture and mix gently.

5 Shake the lettuce leaves dry and arrange on a large serving plate. Carefully spoon the salad on top, sprinkle with the toasted almonds and serve.

Chicken and Broccoli Salad

Mango chutney gives a sweet edge to a colourful and spicy salad of firm chicken, fresh broccoli and pasta ribbons.

Serves 4
Preparation time: 20 minutes
Cooking time: 15 minutes

175 g (6 oz) tagliatelle or small
  pasta shapes
340 g (12 oz) small broccoli florets
2 level teaspoons mild or
  hot curry paste
3 level tablespoons mango chutney,
  fruit finely chopped
1 tablespoon white wine vinegar
150 ml (¼ pint) each natural
  yoghurt and soured cream
¼ level teaspoon salt
Freshly ground black pepper
340 g (12 oz) cooked chicken, cut
  into cubes
1 red onion, peeled and
  finely chopped
1 red pepper, de-seeded and cut
  into fine strips
2 tablespoons flaked almonds,
  lightly toasted

1 Cook the pasta (see p.202), adding the broccoli for the last 3 minutes of cooking. Pour into a colander, rinse thoroughly under cold water and drain well.

2 Meanwhile, mix together the curry paste, chutney and vinegar in a small bowl, until smooth. Add the yoghurt, soured cream, salt and some pepper and blend to make the dressing.

3 Put the pasta and broccoli in a large bowl, pour over half the dressing and toss well. Add the chicken, onion, red pepper and the remaining dressing and toss again.

4 Turn the salad onto a serving dish, scatter the toasted almonds over the top and serve.

Per serving
Calories 498 Protein 39 g
Total fat 18 g (saturated fat 6.8 g)
Carbohydrates 48 g (added sugar 0)
Fibre 4.1 g Sodium 366 mg

Chinese Noodle and Chicken Salad

Serves 4
Preparation time: 25 minutes
Cooking time: 10 minutes

175 g (6 oz) Chinese fine
  egg noodles
1 tablespoon toasted sesame oil
115 g (4 oz) smooth peanut butter
115 ml (4 fl oz) water
3 tablespoons soy sauce
2 tablespoons cider vinegar
225 g (8 oz) white cabbage,
  finely shredded (see p.11)
1 red pepper, de-seeded and
  finely sliced
450 g (1 lb) cooked chicken, cut
  into strips
115 g (4 oz) fresh beansprouts,
  rinsed and drained
6 spring onions, trimmed
  and chopped
2 tablespoons roasted peanuts

This refreshing oriental-style salad combines crunchy cabbage and beansprouts with egg noodles and lean chicken strips in a rich peanut butter and soy sauce dressing.

1 Cook the noodles (see p.202), then drain thoroughly, put into a large bowl and mix with 1 teaspoon of the oil.

2 Blend the peanut butter, water, soy sauce, vinegar and the remaining oil in a food processor for 1 minute, or until smooth, to make the dressing.

3 Add the cabbage to the noodles and mix with the dressing. Gently stir in the red pepper, chicken, beansprouts and half the spring onions. Spoon the salad into a clean serving dish, sprinkle with the peanuts and the rest of the spring onions, then serve.

Per serving
Calories 493 Protein 43 g
Total fat 20 g (saturated fat 3.6 g)
Carbohydrates 39 g (added sugar 0)
Fibre 6.7 g Sodium 957 mg

CRUNCHY CHICKEN SALAD

Aromatic fresh basil, a traditional salad herb, forms the basis of an exuberant vinaigrette dressing for this unusual and filling summer dish of diced chicken with tomato and croutons.

Serves 4
Preparation time: 25 minutes
Cooking time: 15 minutes

115 g (4 oz) ciabatta or french
   bread, cut into small cubes
6 tablespoons olive oil
3 tablespoons red wine vinegar
4 level tablespoons chopped
   fresh basil
2 cloves garlic,
   peeled
4 anchovy
   fillets,
   drained

Freshly ground black pepper
340 g (12 oz) cooked chicken,
   diced
900 g (2 lb) tomatoes, skinned,
   de-seeded and cut into cubes
1 large cucumber, peeled and
   cut into small cubes (see p.10)
1 cos lettuce, washed
Sprigs of fresh basil to garnish

Per serving
Calories 477 Protein 31 g
Total fat 28 g (saturated fat 5.1 g)
Carbohydrates 26 g (added sugar 0)
Fibre 6.1 g Sodium 378 mg

1 Preheat the oven to 180°C (350°F, gas mark 4). Spread out the bread cubes on a baking tray and bake in the centre of the oven for 12-15 minutes, or until crisp and pale golden in colour. Remove from the oven and leave to cool.

2 Meanwhile, blend the oil, vinegar, basil, garlic, anchovies and some pepper in a food processor for 30 seconds to make the dressing.

3 Put the croutons, chicken, tomatoes and cucumber in a large bowl, then add the dressing. Toss until well coated and then leave to stand for 5 minutes.

4 Arrange the lettuce leaves on four plates and spoon the salad into the centre. Garnish with the basil sprigs and serve.

Cubes of oven-crisped bread and firm leaves of cos lettuce make a crunchy contrast with succulent tomato, cucumber and tender chicken.

Mediterranean Chicken Salad

Enjoy the full flavour and aroma of Mediterranean herbs in this cooling summer dish.

Serves 4
Preparation time: 1 hour 20 minutes
Chilling time: 2 hours
Cooking time: 20 minutes

340 g (12 oz) aubergine, trimmed, cut into small cubes (see p.10)
1 level tablespoon salt
225 g (8 oz) egg campanelle, fusilli or macaroni spirals

5 tablespoons olive oil
340 g (12 oz) boneless chicken breasts, skinned and cut into thin strips (see p.116)
1 medium onion, peeled and chopped
2 cloves garlic, peeled and crushed
2 sticks celery, trimmed and sliced
1 red pepper, de-seeded and diced
1 tablespoon chopped fresh oregano
1 tablespoon chopped fresh basil

225 g (8 oz) courgettes, trimmed and thinly sliced
175 g (6 oz) plum tomatoes, skinned and chopped
3 tablespoons each water and dry white wine
2 tablespoons red wine vinegar
1 level teaspoon Dijon mustard
3 tablespoons chopped fresh parsley
225 g (8 oz) feta cheese, drained and crumbled, and 12 black olives to garnish

Per serving
Calories 662   Protein 37 g
Total fat 35 g (saturated fat 12 g)
Carbohydrates 52 g (added sugar 0)
    Fibre 6.2 g   Sodium 1142 mg

1 Sprinkle the aubergine cubes with the salt to remove the bitter juices. In the meantime, cook the pasta (see p.202), rinse under cold water and drain well. Put the pasta in a large bowl.

2 Meanwhile, heat 2 tablespoons of the oil in a large frying pan and fry the chicken strips in it for about 5 minutes, or until cooked (see p.117). Put the chicken on a plate and set aside.

3 Add 2 more tablespoons of oil to the pan and fry the onion, garlic, celery, red pepper, oregano and basil in it for 3 minutes, stirring occasionally. Add the aubergine and fry for 5 minutes.

4 Stir in the courgettes and tomatoes and the water and wine and simmer for 10 minutes, or until the vegetables are tender. Meanwhile, whisk the remaining olive oil with the vinegar, mustard and parsley.

5 Mix the vegetables with the pasta, chicken and dressing, then cover and chill for 2 hours, or overnight. Spoon the salad onto a large platter, sprinkle with the crumbled feta and the olives, and serve with ciabatta bread.

Olives and feta cheese provide the finishing touches to this inviting chicken salad, giving it a mild saltiness that complements the flavours of white wine and olive oil.

CHICKEN SALAD WITH PECANS

Serves 4
Preparation time: 20 minutes
Cooking time: 40 minutes

450 ml (16 fl oz) chicken stock
   (see p.8)
450 g (1 lb) boneless chicken
   breasts, skinned
175 g (6 oz) long-grain brown rice
225 g (8 oz) fine green beans,
   trimmed, halved and blanched
   for 3 minutes (see p.10)
60 g (2 oz) pecan nuts,
   lightly toasted
1 large red pepper, de-seeded
   and cut into small squares
4 spring onions, trimmed and
   finely chopped
3 tablespoons sunflower oil
2 teaspoons sesame oil
2 tablespoons white wine vinegar
1 tablespoon orange juice
1/2 level teaspoon dried sage
1/8 level teaspoon caster sugar
1/2 level teaspoon salt
Freshly ground black pepper
Sage leaves and finely shredded
   orange rind to garnish

Per serving
Calories 525 Protein 30 g
Total fat 28 g (saturated fat 2.1 g)
Carbohydrates 41 g (added sugar 0)
Fibre 4 g Sodium 329 mg

A light toasting brings out the distinct walnut-like flavour of pecans, which add a welcome crunchiness to this tender rice and chicken salad. You can toast the pecans under the grill for about 5 minutes, or in a microwave oven (see p.259).

1 Bring the stock to the boil in a saucepan, then add the chicken breasts. Reduce the heat, cover and simmer for 10 minutes, or until the chicken is cooked (see p.117). Lift the chicken onto a plate with a slotted spoon, leave to cool, then cut into small cubes.

2 Meanwhile, pour the stock into a measuring jug and, if necessary, make up to 450 ml (16 fl oz) with water. Return the liquid to the pan and bring it back to the boil. Stir in the rice and simmer over a low heat for 25-30 minutes, or until the rice is cooked and the stock absorbed.

3 Put the rice, chicken, beans, pecans, red pepper and spring onions into a large salad bowl. Whisk together the sunflower and sesame oils, vinegar, orange juice, sage, sugar, salt and some pepper, then pour the dressing over the salad. Toss well, garnish with the sage leaves and shredded orange rind, and serve with mixed grain or walnut bread.

TURKEY AND SPINACH SALAD

Serves 4
Preparation time: 15 minutes
Cooking time: 5 minutes

340 g (12 oz) new potatoes,
   scrubbed and thinly sliced
115 g (4 oz) frozen peas
285 ml (1/2 pint) low-fat
   natural yoghurt
4 tablespoons skimmed milk
1 tablespoon cider vinegar
2 tablespoons chopped fresh dill,
   or 1 level teaspoon dried dill
1/2 level teaspoon salt
Freshly ground black pepper
225 g (8 oz) young spinach leaves,
   washed and dried
225 g (8 oz) mushrooms, wiped
   and thinly sliced
6 large radishes, trimmed and
   thinly sliced
4 spring onions, trimmed and
   thinly sliced
225 g (8 oz) cooked turkey, cut
   into strips (see p.116)
60 g (2 oz) toasted almond flakes
   and radish slices to garnish

Per serving
Calories 316 Protein 29 g
Total fat 12 g (saturated fat 1.9 g)
Carbohydrates 25 g (added sugar 0)
Fibre 8.7 g Sodium 439 mg

Crisp, fresh young spinach goes well with turkey, which tends to be a rather dry meat. The two are combined with a tart but cooling dressing of dill and yoghurt.

1 Gently boil the potatoes and peas together for 5 minutes, then drain well and leave to cool.

2 Whisk together the yoghurt, milk, vinegar, dill, salt and some pepper in a large salad bowl to make the dressing.

3 Mix the potato slices, peas, spinach, mushrooms, radishes, spring onions and turkey into the dressing, until well coated. Turn the salad out onto a serving dish, garnish with the almonds and radish slices and serve.

TURKEY, RICE AND OLIVE SALAD

This delicious summer salad makes the most of leftover turkey. It can also be made with brown rice instead of white.

Serves 4
Preparation time: 30 minutes

1 large clove garlic, peeled and crushed (see p.11)
4 tablespoons olive oil
2 tablespoons white wine vinegar or cider vinegar
1 teaspoon lemon juice
Freshly ground black pepper
450 g (1 lb) cooked turkey breast, cut into strips
225 g (8 oz) long-grain white rice, cooked (see p.9) and cooled
1 large green pepper, de-seeded and diced
115 g (4 oz) pitted black olives, halved
2 large carrots, peeled and coarsely grated
2 sticks celery, trimmed and thinly sliced

Grated carrots add colour and sweetness to this light and nutritious salad.

1 medium red onion, peeled and chopped
60 g (2 oz) salami, sliced thickly and cut into strips
2 teaspoons capers, drained
Lettuce leaves, red onion rings, carrot strips and whole black olives to garnish

Per serving
Calories 605 Protein 41 g
Total fat 25 g (saturated fat 5.7 g)
Carbohydrates 56 g (added sugar 0)
Fibre 5 g Sodium 1002 mg

1 Whisk together the garlic, oil, vinegar, lemon juice and some pepper in a large bowl until smooth to make the dressing.

2 Mix the turkey, rice, green pepper, olives, carrots, celery, onion, salami and capers into the dressing, then cover and leave to stand for 30 minutes.

3 Arrange the lettuce leaves in a serving bowl and spoon the salad on top. Garnish with the onion rings, carrot strips and whole olives and serve with french bread.

TURKEY TABBOULEH

Serves 4
Preparation time: 45 minutes
Chilling time: 1 hour

225 g (8 oz) bulgur wheat
285 ml (1/2 pint) chicken stock
  (see p.8) or hot or boiling water
2 cloves garlic, peeled and crushed
  (see p.11)
2 tablespoons chopped fresh basil
1 tablespoon chopped fresh mint
4 tablespoons olive oil
3 tablespoons red wine vinegar or
  cider vinegar
1/2 level teaspoon salt
Freshly ground black pepper
450 g (1 lb) cooked turkey, diced
2 medium tomatoes, finely chopped
225 g (8 oz) canned sweetcorn
  kernels, drained
4 spring onions, trimmed and
  thinly sliced
Shredded lettuce leaves and sprigs
  of mint to garnish

Per serving
Calories 547 Protein 40 g
Total fat 18 g (saturated fat 3 g)
Carbohydrates 59 g (added sugar 0)
Fibre 2.6 g Sodium 465 mg

The basis of this Middle Eastern salad is bulgur wheat, a cracked wheat that is rich in protein and as versatile as rice. The longer the salad is allowed to chill, the better it will taste.

1 Put the bulgur wheat in a bowl and pour on the stock or water. Leave to soak for 20-30 minutes, or until the grains are tender and all the liquid has been absorbed.

2 Whisk together the garlic, basil, mint, oil, vinegar, salt and some pepper in a small bowl to make the dressing.

3 When the bulgur wheat has cooled down, mix in the turkey, tomatoes, sweetcorn, spring onions and the dressing. Cover and chill in the fridge for at least 1 hour, or overnight.

4 Arrange the lettuce leaves on a serving platter, then spoon the tabbouleh on top. Alternatively, pack the salad into a mould, pressing down well, then turn it out onto a serving platter and surround with the lettuce. Garnish with the mint and serve.

TOMATOES STUFFED WITH RICE AND BLACK-EYED BEANS

Mediterranean sausages add their spiciness to the filling in these full-flavoured beefsteak tomatoes, which are eaten cold.

Serves 4
Preparation time: 20 minutes
Cooking time: 35 minutes

3 tablespoons olive oil
1 onion, peeled and chopped
225 g (8 oz) fresh Mediterranean-
  style sausages, casings removed
2 cloves garlic, peeled and crushed
  (see p.11)
115 g (4 oz) long-grain white rice
285 ml (1/2 pint) chicken stock
  (see p.8)
4 beefsteak tomatoes
2 medium carrots, peeled and
  coarsely grated
225 g (8 oz) cooked black-eyed
  beans, rinsed and drained
  (see p.172)
4 tablespoons chopped
  fresh parsley
2 tablespoons lemon juice
1/2 level teaspoon salt
Freshly ground black pepper
Celery leaves to garnish

Per serving
Calories 415 Protein 14 g
Total fat 18 g (saturated fat 6.5 g)
Carbohydrates 53 g (added sugar 0)
Fibre 3.4 g Sodium 721 mg

1 Heat 1 tablespoon of the oil in a heavy saucepan and fry the onion, sausages and garlic in it for 10 minutes, breaking up the sausages as they cook.

2 Stir in the rice and the stock and bring to the boil. Reduce the heat, cover and simmer for 20-25 minutes, or until the rice is cooked and all the stock has been absorbed.

3 Meanwhile, cut the tops off the tomatoes and scoop out the centres with a teaspoon. Chop up the tomato tops and centres and add them to the rice.

4 Stir the carrots, black-eyed beans, parsley, lemon juice, remaining oil, salt and some pepper into the rice, then leave it to cool.

5 Fill the tomatoes with the cooled rice mixture and arrange them on a serving dish, spooning any remaining rice around the tomatoes. Garnish with the celery leaves and serve.

PENNE AND SMOKED HAM SALAD

Serves 4
Preparation time: 15 minutes
Cooking time: 15 minutes
Standing time: 30 minutes

....

225 g (8 oz) penne
225 g (8 oz) soured cream
150 g (5 oz) mayonnaise
½ level teaspoon salt
Freshly ground black pepper
2 level teaspoons Dijon mustard
2 teaspoons chopped fresh tarragon
1 avocado, halved, stoned, peeled
   and cut into small cubes

340 g (12 oz) thickly sliced smoked
   ham, cut into small cubes
225 g (8 oz) small tomatoes,
   halved
60 g (2 oz) shelled and skinned
   pistachio nuts
225 g (8 oz) baby spinach leaves,
   trimmed and washed

....

Per serving
Calories 857 Protein 30 g
Total fat 61 g (saturated fat 16 g)
Carbohydrates 50 g (added sugar 0)
Fibre 5.7 g Sodium 1669 mg

....

*Fresh-tasting spinach and al dente pasta quills are
major components of this summer salad, enticingly
combined with chopped herbs and smoked ham.*

A sauce of soured cream and mustard adds a tangy flavour to the mix of avocado, nuts, ham and penne – pasta quills – in this satisfying dish. You can use watercress instead of spinach or fresh basil instead of tarragon.

1 Cook the penne (see p.202). Meanwhile, combine the soured cream, mayonnaise, salt, some pepper, mustard and chopped tarragon in a large bowl.

2 Rinse the cooked pasta under cold water and drain well. Toss the pasta in the dressing until thoroughly coated, cover and leave to stand for 30 minutes. Gently mix in the avocado, ham, tomatoes and pistachio nuts.

3 Line a serving dish or four bowls with the spinach leaves. Spoon the pasta mixture over the spinach and serve with warm ciabatta or other Italian bread.

Ham and Sweet Potato Salad

Serves 4
Preparation time: 15 minutes
Cooking time: 15 minutes

450 g (1 lb) sweet potatoes, peeled
   and cut into small dice (see p.10)
115 g (4 oz) cottage cheese
2 level tablespoons mayonnaise
1 level tablespoon Dijon mustard
1/2 level teaspoon caster sugar
1/2 level teaspoon salt
6 tablespoons natural yoghurt
275 g (10 oz) cooked ham, cut into
   matchstick strips
225 g (8 oz) white cabbage,
   finely shredded (see p.11)

Per serving
Calories 341 Protein 20 g
Total fat 17 g (saturated fat 3.9 g)
Carbohydrates 29 g (added sugar 0)
Fibre 4.2 g Sodium 1344 mg

Dijon mustard adds a taste of
France to this substantial ham
salad. Try replacing the sweet
potatoes with new potatoes
when they are in season.

1 Boil the sweet potatoes until just
cooked, then drain thoroughly.
Set aside and leave to cool.

2 Place the cottage cheese,
mayonnaise, mustard, sugar,
salt and yoghurt in an electric
blender and purée until smooth.
Pour the mixture into a large bowl.

3 Gently mix the sweet potatoes,
ham and cabbage into the
dressing, mix well and serve.

Ham and Macaroni with Ricotta Dressing

Serves 4
Preparation time: 10 minutes
Cooking time: 15 minutes
Chilling time: 1 hour

1 tablespoon olive oil
115 g (4 oz) mushrooms, wiped
   and sliced
1 clove garlic, peeled and crushed
   (see p.11)
3 tablespoons chopped
   fresh parsley
115 g (4 oz) ricotta cheese
6 level tablespoons single cream
2 level tablespoons German
   mustard
2 tablespoons balsamic vinegar
1/4 level teaspoon caster sugar
1/4 level teaspoon salt
Freshly ground black pepper
225 g (8 oz) macaroni or small
   pasta shells, cooked (see p.202)
   and drained
225 g (8 oz) frozen mixed
   vegetables (peas, carrots and
   sweetcorn), cooked and drained
275 g (10 oz) cooked smoked ham,
   cut into cubes
      2 tablespoons snipped
      fresh chives

Pasta lengths are combined
with a variety of vegetables in
a cool, creamy ricotta cheese
dressing. Serve chilled for a
summer alfresco lunch.

1 Heat the oil in a large
frying pan and soften the
mushrooms and garlic in it
for 4-5 minutes. Stir in the
parsley, bring to the boil and
boil rapidly until the liquid
released by the mushrooms
has evaporated.

2 Mix together the ricotta,
cream, mustard, vinegar,
sugar, salt and some pepper
in a large salad bowl, then
stir in the macaroni and
mixed vegetables. Add the
mushroom mixture and
ham and mix well. Sprinkle
with the chives, cover the
bowl and chill in the fridge
for 1 hour before serving.

Per serving
Calories 423 Protein 25 g
Total fat 16 g (saturated fat 6.7 g)
Carbohydrates 48 g (added sugar 0)
Fibre 3.5 g Sodium 1085 mg

GERMAN SAUSAGE AND POTATO SALAD

Chunky sausage and potato salad – a classic German combination – is given added zest with a cooked onion, red pepper and mustard dressing.

Serves 4
Preparation time: 15 minutes
Cooking time: 15 minutes

800 g (1¾ lb) new potatoes, cut into small cubes (see p.10)
225 g (8 oz) frozen peas
4 knackwurst or 6 frankfurter sausages
2 tablespoons olive oil
1 small onion, peeled and chopped
1 red pepper, de-seeded and diced
6 tablespoons white wine vinegar
6 tablespoons chicken stock
2 level tablespoons Dijon mustard
½ level teaspoon caraway seeds
½ level teaspoon salt
Freshly ground black pepper
1 level tablespoon chopped fresh dill

1 Boil the potatoes for 7 minutes, then add the peas and boil for a further 3 minutes. Drain well, turn into a large bowl and leave to cool.

2 In the meantime, heat the sausages in a frying pan with a little water for 5 minutes or until the water has evaporated, turning occasionally. Take them out of the pan and slice them thickly on a chopping board. Add the sausages to the potatoes and peas.

3 Heat the oil in the pan and cook the onion and red pepper in it until softened. Add the vinegar, stock, mustard, caraway seeds, salt and some pepper and bring to the boil, stirring.

4 Pour the hot dressing over the potato mixture and toss gently until the mixture is thoroughly coated. Spoon the salad into a serving dish and sprinkle with the dill. Serve warm or cold.

Per serving
Calories 353 Protein 11 g
Total fat 16 g (saturated fat 4.7 g)
Carbohydrates 43 g (added sugar 0)
Fibre 7.8 g Sodium 606 mg

POTATO, BEETROOT AND HAM SALAD

Serves 4
Preparation time: 20 minutes
Cooking time: 15 minutes

450 g (1 lb) waxy potatoes, peeled and cut into small dice (see p.10)
3 medium carrots, peeled and thinly sliced
115 g (4 oz) frozen peas
150 g (5 oz) reduced-calorie mayonnaise
150 ml (¼ pint) Greek yoghurt
4 spring onions, trimmed and finely chopped
2 tablespoons chopped fresh parsley or dill
¼ level teaspoon salt
Freshly ground black pepper
225 g (8 oz) cooked ham, cut into small cubes
175 g (6 oz) cooked beetroot, peeled and cut into small cubes
12 lettuce leaves, rinsed and dried
2 tomatoes, sliced

Per serving
Calories 373 Protein 19 g
Total fat 18 g (saturated fat 3.2 g)
Carbohydrates 36 g (added sugar 0)
Fibre 7.9 g Sodium 1265 mg

Cubes of beetroot lend an attractive pink hue to this substantial dish of potatoes, ham and carrots in a light mayonnaise and yoghurt sauce.

1 Boil the potatoes for 8 minutes, then add the carrots and cook for a further 3 minutes. Stir in the peas and cook for 1 minute, then pour the vegetables into a colander, rinse under cold water and drain.

2 Whisk the mayonnaise and yoghurt together in a large bowl and add the spring onions, parsley or dill, salt and some pepper.

3 Gently mix in the cooked vegetables, the ham and the beetroot until well coated in the dressing. Arrange the lettuce and tomato slices around the edge of a serving plate, spoon the potato salad into the centre and serve.

PRAWN, CORN AND AVOCADO SALAD

Serves 4
Preparation time: 20 minutes
Cooking time: 10 minutes

225 g (8 oz) ditalini or other small
  pasta shapes
450 g (1 lb) uncooked prawns,
  peeled, de-veined, tails left on
2 tablespoons white wine vinegar
  or cider vinegar
2-4 tablespoons chilli sauce
2 tablespoons olive oil
1 tablespoon horseradish sauce
225 g (8 oz) canned sweetcorn
  kernels, drained

60 g (2 oz) radishes, trimmed
  and thinly sliced
2 spring onions, trimmed and
  thinly sliced
1 large avocado, halved, stoned,
  peeled and cut into small dice
1 medium head of radicchio

Per serving
Calories 500 Protein 29 g
Total fat 17 g (saturated fat 2.8 g)
Carbohydrates 60 g (added sugar 0)
Fibre 5.5 g Sodium 371 mg

This unusual spicy salad mixes thimble-shaped pasta pieces with juicy prawns on a bed of radicchio lettuce. If you prefer, use frozen cooked prawns in place of uncooked prawns – just thaw them and add them to the dressing with the pasta.

1 Cook the pasta (see p.202), adding the prawns to the pan for the last 3 minutes of cooking. Then drain, rinse thoroughly under cold water and drain again.

2 Whisk the vinegar, chilli sauce, oil and horseradish sauce in a large bowl to make the dressing. Toss the pasta and prawns in the dressing, then carefully mix in the sweetcorn, radishes, spring onions and avocado.

3 Arrange the radicchio leaves round the sides of a large serving bowl and spoon the salad mixture into the centre. Serve the salad with slices of warm french bread.

Sweetcorn and avocado counter the sharp tastes of radishes, spring onions and a dressing flavoured with chilli and horseradish.

217

TIGER PRAWN AND SUGAR SNAP PEA SALAD

Serves 4
Preparation time: 20 minutes
Cooking time: 15 minutes
Cooling time: 30 minutes

2 tablespoons olive oil
450 g (1 lb) small new potatoes,
    scrubbed and thinly sliced
1 clove garlic, peeled and crushed
    (see p.11)
1 red pepper, de-seeded and cut
    into thin strips
225 g (8 oz) sugar snap
    peas, trimmed
340 g (12 oz) fresh uncooked
    tiger prawns, peeled
    and de-veined
2 sticks celery, trimmed and sliced
150 ml (¼ pint) soured cream
2 level tablespoons mayonnaise
2 level tablespoons natural yoghurt
1 tablespoon lemon juice
2 level teaspoons Dijon mustard
2 tablespoons chopped fresh dill
¼ level teaspoon salt
¼ teaspoon hot red pepper sauce
Sprig of fresh dill to garnish

Per serving
Calories 454 Protein 26 g
Total fat 28 g (saturated fat 7.7 g)
Carbohydrates 26 g (added sugar 0)
Fibre 2.4 g Sodium 1683 mg

Tender prawns, new potatoes
and crunchy sugar snap peas
provide an interesting contrast
of flavours and textures in this
aromatic stir-fry salad.

1 Heat the oil in a large frying
pan or wok and fry the potatoes
and garlic in it for 8 minutes.
Add the red pepper, sugar snap
peas, prawns and celery and
cook, stirring the mixture
occasionally, for 5-8 minutes,
or until the prawns turn pink
and the vegetables are just tender.
Take the pan off the heat, pour
the prawns and vegetables into
a salad bowl and leave to cool
for 30 minutes.

2 Meanwhile, combine the
soured cream, mayonnaise,
yoghurt, lemon juice, mustard,
chopped dill, salt and hot red
pepper sauce in a small bowl.
Pour over the cooled salad and
toss together. Garnish with the
sprig of dill and serve with
warm french bread.

*A lively dressing containing dill and
hot red pepper sauce adds spice to
the freshly cooked prawn mixture.*

MANGO AND PRAWN SALAD WITH FARFALLE

Serves 4
Preparation time: 15 minutes
Cooking time: 15 minutes

225 g (8 oz) farfalle
225 g (8 oz) fine green
   beans, halved
150 ml (¼ pint) low-fat
   natural yoghurt
3 level tablespoons mayonnaise
1 teaspoon mango chutney
   or lime pickle
Finely grated rind of 1 lime
¼ level teaspoon caster sugar
450 g (1 lb) frozen cooked and
   peeled tiger prawns, thawed
   and drained
1 mango, peeled, stoned and cut
   into small pieces
60 g (2 oz) flaked almonds,
   lightly toasted
Lime wedges to garnish

Per serving
Calories 697 Protein 40 g
Total fat 30 g (saturated fat 4.1 g)
Carbohydrates 71 g (added sugar 0.3 g)
Fibre 11 g Sodium 1914 mg

The exotic sweetness of mango complements the sharp, fresh taste of lime in this luxurious salad of prawns, green beans and farfalle – bow-shaped pasta pieces. Use mangetout in place of the green beans, if you prefer.

1 Cook the pasta (see p.202), adding the beans for the last 5 minutes of cooking. Pour into a colander, rinse well under cold water and drain thoroughly.

2 In the meantime, mix the yoghurt, mayonnaise, chutney or lime pickle, lime rind and sugar in a large salad bowl, then stir in the pasta, beans, prawns, mango and half the almonds.

3 Sprinkle the remaining almonds over the salad, garnish with the lime wedges and serve.

RED, WHITE AND GREEN SALAD

Red peppers and green peas are combined with prawns and a nutritious helping of rice to produce a bright and tasty salad.

Serves 4
Preparation time: 20 minutes
Cooking time: 30 minutes
Cooling time: 30 minutes
Standing time: 10 minutes

8 tablespoons olive oil
1 onion, peeled and finely chopped
225 g (8 oz) long-grain white rice
570 ml (1 pint) chicken or fish
   stock (see p.8)
½ level teaspoon salt
Freshly ground black pepper
4 spring onions, trimmed
   and chopped
175 g (6 oz) frozen peas
1 red pepper, grilled, de-seeded
   and sliced
1 tablespoon lemon juice
1 tablespoon red wine vinegar
1 level teaspoon Dijon mustard
2 tablespoons chopped fresh dill
   or parsley
340 g (12 oz) frozen cooked
   and peeled prawns, thawed
   and drained

Per serving
Calories 579 Protein 26 g
Total fat 29 g (saturated fat 4.1 g)
Carbohydrates 57 g (added sugar 0)
Fibre 5.5 g Sodium 1601 mg

1 Heat 2 tablespoons of the oil in a saucepan and soften the onion in it. Stir in the rice, stock, salt and some pepper and bring to the boil. Reduce the heat, cover and cook for 20 minutes.

2 Stir in the spring onions, frozen peas and grilled pepper strips. Cover the pan and cook for 5 minutes, stirring occasionally, until the rice is cooked and all the stock has been absorbed. Take the pan off the heat, pour the mixture into a large bowl and leave to cool for 30 minutes.

3 Meanwhile, whisk together the remaining oil, the lemon juice, vinegar, mustard and dill or parsley in a small bowl. Pour the dressing over the cooled rice, then gently mix in the prawns.

4 Turn the salad into a serving dish, cover and leave to stand for 10 minutes, then serve.

CHILLED PRAWN SALAD WITH ORZO

This attractive prawn jelly, served with rice-shaped pasta pieces – orzo – and dressed in a light, creamy sauce, makes an impressive dinner party dish.

Serves 4
Preparation time: 20 minutes
Chilling time: 3 hours
Cooking time: 10 minutes

4 tablespoons cold water
1 level tablespoon powdered gelatine
175 g (6 oz) reduced-calorie mayonnaise
200 ml (7 fl oz) low-fat natural yoghurt
4 tablespoons lemon juice
1 tablespoon chilli sauce
1/2 level teaspoon salt
1 small onion, peeled and grated
1 stick celery, trimmed and diced
8 pimiento-stuffed olives
400 g (14 oz) frozen, cooked and peeled prawns, thawed and drained
115 g (4 oz) cooked peas
175 g (6 oz) orzo or other small pasta shapes
3 spring onions, trimmed and chopped
Freshly ground black pepper
Finely shredded lettuce leaves and watercress to garnish

Per serving
Calories 445 Protein 33 g
Total fat 16 g (saturated fat 0.7 g)
Carbohydrates 44 g (added sugar 0)
Fibre 4.8 g Sodium 2431 mg

1 Pour the water into a small saucepan and sprinkle the gelatine evenly over the surface. Leave to stand for 5 minutes until the gelatine swells, then stir over a low heat until it has dissolved. Leave to cool slightly.

2 Mix together 150 g (5 oz) of the mayonnaise, 60 ml (2 fl oz) of the yoghurt, the lemon juice, chilli sauce, half the salt, the onion, celery and olives in a large bowl. Mix in the prawns, peas and quickly stir in the gelatine. Pour into a wetted 1 litre (1 3/4 pint) ring mould and gently smooth the surface. Refrigerate for 3-4 hours, or overnight, until set.

3 Cook the pasta (see p.202) and drain. Meanwhile, combine the remaining mayonnaise and yoghurt with the spring onions, the rest of the salt and some pepper in a bowl. Add the pasta and toss until well coated. Cover and chill.

4 Run the tip of a knife around the outer and inner edges of the mould, then dip the mould right up to the rim in very hot water for 5 seconds. Take the mould out of the water, put a serving plate on top of it and turn both upside-down, holding them firmly. Give a sharp shake to free the set prawn mixture, then carefully lift off the ring mould. Mound the pasta in the centre, garnish with the lettuce and watercress and serve.

ROLLMOP HERRING SALAD

Serves 4
Preparation time: 30 minutes
Cooking time: 15 minutes

340 g (12 oz) small new potatoes, scrubbed
150 ml (1/4 pint) soured cream or natural low-fat yoghurt
4 level tablespoons fromage frais or reduced-calorie mayonnaise
2 level tablespoons horseradish sauce
1 level tablespoon chopped fresh dill
Freshly ground black pepper
1/2 iceberg lettuce, separated into leaves
340 g (12 oz) rollmop or other pickled herrings, drained and cut into wide strips
1 red apple, quartered, cored and sliced
115 g (4 oz) cooked beetroot, peeled and sliced
4 eggs, size 2, hard-boiled, shelled and quartered
1 small red onion, peeled and thinly sliced

Per serving
Calories 474 Protein 27 g
Total fat 32 g (saturated fat 11 g)
Carbohydrates 23 g (added sugar 0)
Fibre 2.8 g Sodium 205 mg

Soured cream, fromage frais and horseradish sauce make a lively dressing for this Scandinavian-type salad of pickled herrings, crisp lettuce, beetroot and new potatoes.

1 Boil the potatoes until just tender. Drain and leave to cool. Meanwhile, mix together the soured cream or yoghurt, fromage frais or mayonnaise, horseradish sauce, dill and some pepper in a small bowl to make the dressing.

2 Cut the cooled potatoes into slices and put them in a large bowl. Spoon half the dressing over the potatoes and toss together until lightly coated.

3 Arrange the lettuce leaves on four plates and spoon the potato salad into the centre of each one. Arrange the herrings, apple, beetroot and eggs around the edge of each plate, then sprinkle the onion over the top. Pour the remaining dressing into a small bowl and serve alongside the salad with crusty brown bread.

CREAMY TUNA AND FUSILLI SALAD

In this healthy salad, tuna fish combines with runner beans and tricolore fusilli – spirals of pasta of green, white and red, made with spinach, tomato and plain pasta. For variety, use canned salmon instead of tuna.

Serves 4
Preparation time: 15 minutes
Cooking time: 15 minutes

340 g (12 oz) tricolore fusilli, or other small pasta shapes
225 g (8 oz) bobby or runner beans, cut into short pieces
225 g (8 oz) cooked cannellini beans, rinsed and drained (see p.172)
150 ml (¼ pint) natural yoghurt
3 tablespoons olive oil
3 cloves garlic, peeled
2 teaspoons lemon juice
¼ level teaspoon salt
400 g (14 oz) canned tuna in oil, drained and flaked
1 medium red onion, peeled, halved and thinly sliced
2 tablespoons chopped fresh parsley

Per serving
Calories 768 Protein 40 g
Total fat 34 g (saturated fat 5.8 g)
Carbohydrates 81 g (added sugar 0)
Fibre 9.9 g Sodium 596 mg

1 Cook the pasta (see p.202), adding the green beans for the last 5 minutes of cooking. Rinse well, drain and leave to cool.

2 Meanwhile, put the cannellini beans, yoghurt, oil, garlic, lemon juice and salt in a blender and purée for 1 minute to make the dressing for the salad. Pour into a large bowl.

3 Add the pasta, beans, tuna and onion and toss well. Sprinkle with the parsley and serve with pugliese or any other Italian bread.

Tricolore fusilli mix with red onion slivers and a garlicky white bean sauce in this nutritious, colourful dish.

Tuna and Artichoke Salad

Serves 4
Preparation time: 30 minutes
Cooking time: 10 minutes
Cooling time: 30 minutes

450 g (1 lb) new potatoes,
  scraped and sliced
225 g (8 oz) fine green
  beans, halved
1 small soft lettuce, leaves
  separated, rinsed
  and drained
225 g (8 oz) cherry tomatoes,
  halved
400 g (14 oz) canned tuna in oil,
  drained and flaked
60 g (2 oz) pitted black olives
1 small onion, peeled, halved
  and finely sliced
400 g (14 oz) canned or bottled
  artichoke hearts, drained
  and quartered

2 level tablespoons capers
2 tablespoons red wine or
  tarragon vinegar
2 level teaspoons Dijon mustard
¼ level teaspoon salt
Freshly ground black pepper
6 tablespoons olive oil

Per serving
Calories 604 Protein 30 g
Total fat 44 g (saturated fat 7.3 g)
Carbohydrates 24 g (added sugar 0)
Fibre 4.1 g Sodium 918 mg

*A traditional vinaigrette
dressing flavoured with
Dijon mustard draws out
the tastes of flaked tuna,
green beans and juicy
chunks of tomato. Capers
add a peppery bite.*

Artichoke hearts are a prized salad ingredient in Italy and other southern European countries. They bring a touch of luxury to this fresh-tasting and colourful summer dish.

1 Boil the potatoes for 5 minutes, then add the beans. Continue cooking for 5 minutes, or until both are just tender. Pour into a colander, rinse thoroughly under cold water, then drain well.

2 Line a large shallow bowl with the lettuce leaves. Arrange the potatoes, beans, tomatoes, tuna, olives, onion and artichoke hearts on the lettuce, then scatter the capers over the top.

3 Whisk together the vinegar, mustard, salt and some pepper in a small bowl until smooth. Continue whisking and add the oil in a fine stream, until the dressing thickens slightly. Pour the dressing over the salad, cover and leave to stand in a cool place for 30 minutes. Serve the salad with warm french bread.

CHICKPEA AND CELERY SALAD WITH TUNA

Serves 4
Preparation time: 15 minutes
Standing time: 10-15 minutes

4 tablespoons olive oil
2 tablespoons lemon juice
1 level tablespoon chopped
　fresh oregano
1/4 level teaspoon salt
Freshly ground black pepper
340 g (12 oz) cooked chickpeas,
　rinsed and drained (see p.172)
400 g (14 oz) canned tuna in oil,
　drained and flaked
4 medium celery stalks, trimmed
　and thinly sliced
2 large tomatoes, de-seeded
　and roughly chopped
115 g (4 oz) radishes, washed,
　trimmed and thinly sliced
1 small red onion, peeled and
　thinly sliced
225 g (8 oz) mixed lettuce leaves,
　torn into small pieces
Fresh oregano leaves to garnish

Per serving
Calories 535　Protein 31 g
Total fat 37 g (saturated fat 6.1 g)
Carbohydrates 20 g (added sugar 0)
Fibre 6.6 g　Sodium 577 mg

Celery and radish slices add crunch to a nutritious salad of nutty chickpeas, tomatoes and tasty pieces of tuna on a bed of mixed lettuce leaves.

1 Whisk together the oil, lemon juice, chopped oregano, salt and some pepper in a large bowl, then carefully mix in the chickpeas, tuna, celery, tomatoes, radishes and onion. Stir until well coated.

2 Arrange the lettuce leaves in a large serving dish, spoon the tuna mixture on top and scatter a few whole oregano leaves over the salad. Cover and leave to stand for 10-15 minutes, then serve with warm wholemeal bread.

SALAD NIÇOISE

Serves 4
Preparation time: 45 minutes

1 soft lettuce, washed and dried
225 g (8 oz) small new potatoes,
　cooked, drained, cooled
　and halved
225 g (8 oz) fine green beans,
　trimmed and blanched for
　4 minutes (see p.10)
1 small onion, peeled and very
　thinly sliced
3 medium tomatoes, de-seeded
　and cut into wedges
60 g (2 oz) pitted black olives
50 g (1 3/4 oz) canned anchovy
　fillets, drained and halved
　lengthways
200 g (7 oz) canned tuna in oil,
　drained and flaked
2 eggs, size 2, hard-boiled, shelled
　and cut into quarters
2 tablespoons chopped
　fresh parsley
115 ml (4 fl oz) virgin olive oil
1 tablespoon balsamic vinegar
　or 2 tablespoons
　red wine vinegar
1 clove garlic, peeled and crushed
　(see p.11)
1/4 level teaspoon salt
Freshly ground black pepper

Per serving
Calories 574　Protein 21 g
Total fat 48 g (saturated fat 7.4 g)
Carbohydrates 16 g (added sugar 0)
Fibre 4.4 g　Sodium 1221 mg

This classic salad of tomatoes, tuna, anchovies, black olives and eggs comes from the area around Nice in the south of France, where it is often served as a starter. Some French cooks argue that an authentic salad niçoise is made without boiled vegetables, but many versions of the recipe contain cooked and cooled potatoes and green beans.

1 Arrange the lettuce with its leaves overlapping around the edge of a large salad bowl. Layer the potatoes, beans, onion, tomatoes, olives, half the anchovies, the tuna, eggs and chopped parsley in the centre. Scatter the reserved anchovy fillets over the top of the salad.

2 Whisk together the oil, vinegar, garlic, salt and some pepper, and then pour the dressing over the salad. Serve straight from the bowl with warm crusty bread.

SMOKED HADDOCK AND ORANGE SALAD

Serves 4
Preparation time: 40 minutes
Cooking time: 8 minutes

800 g (1¾ lb) smoked haddock
1 small sprig parsley
6 black peppercorns
1 bay leaf
2 tablespoons lemon juice
150 ml (¼ pint) natural yoghurt
150 g (5 oz) thick mayonnaise
1 small onion peeled and very
   finely chopped
2 level tablespoons chopped
   fresh coriander
½ level teaspoon salt

Freshly ground black pepper
3 large oranges, peeled, pith
   pared off, cut into chunks and
   pips removed
225 g (8 oz) long-grain brown rice,
   cooked (see p.9) and cooled
12 lettuce leaves
2 tablespoons lightly toasted flaked
   almonds to garnish

Per serving
Calories 731 Protein 54 g
Total fat 32 g (saturated fat 4.7 g)
Carbohydrates 60 g (added sugar 0)
Fibre 4.6 g Sodium 2891 mg

Add a touch of luxury to this refreshing salad by stirring 1 tablespoon of cognac and a pinch each of nutmeg and cinnamon into the yoghurt and mayonnaise dressing.

1 Put the haddock in a frying pan with just enough cold water to cover it. Add the parsley, peppercorns, bay leaf and lemon juice and bring to the boil. Reduce the heat, cover and simmer for 5-8 minutes, or until the haddock flakes easily.

2 Drain the haddock, remove and discard the skin and bones, flake the flesh and set aside.

3 Combine the yoghurt and mayonnaise in a large bowl, then stir in the onion, coriander, salt, some pepper, the haddock, orange chunks with any juice, and the rice. Mix well, then cover and leave to stand for 30 minutes.

4 Arrange the lettuce leaves in a large serving dish, or on four plates, then spoon the salad into the centre. Sprinkle with the flaked almonds and serve.

Juicy chunks of orange bring out the flavour of the haddock and add a fruity touch to this unusual rice-based salad.

CRAB AND PASTA SALAD

Serves 4
Preparation time: 30 minutes
Chilling time: 1 hour

225 g (8 oz) elbow macaroni
  or small pasta shells
340 g (12 oz) green beans, trimmed
  and cut into short pieces
3 level tablespoons mayonnaise
225 ml (8 fl oz) low-fat
  natural yoghurt
4 tablespoons chilli sauce
1 teaspoon Worcestershire sauce
2-3 drops hot red pepper sauce
340 g (12 oz) cooked
  crabmeat, flaked
2 medium red peppers, de-seeded
  and finely chopped
8 spring onions, trimmed
  and chopped
225 g (8 oz) mixed lettuce leaves
1/4 cucumber, sliced
2 small tomatoes, sliced

Per serving
Calories 472 Protein 30 g
Total fat 16 g (saturated fat 2.4 g)
Carbohydrates 57 g (added sugar 0)
Fibre 7.8 g Sodium 428 mg

A mixture of spicy sauces gives a refreshing bite to a creamy crab salad that is at its best when well chilled. If you prefer, you can use crabsticks in place of the crabmeat.

1 Cook the pasta (see p.202), adding the beans for the last 4 minutes of cooking. Pour into a colander, rinse under cold water and drain well.

2 Combine the mayonnaise, natural yoghurt, chilli sauce, Worcestershire sauce and hot red pepper sauce in a large bowl.

3 Add the crabmeat, peppers, spring onions, pasta and beans and toss gently in the dressing. Cover and refrigerate for 1 hour.

4 Arrange the lettuce in a salad bowl, stir the chilled crab mixture and spoon it into the middle of the lettuce leaves. Arrange the cucumber and tomato slices on top and serve.

DEVILLED CRAB SALAD

Serves 4
Preparation time: 30 minutes
Cooking time: 5 minutes

225 g (8 oz) asparagus, trimmed
  and cut into short pieces
4 tablespoons olive oil
1 tablespoon lemon juice
1 level tablespoon Dijon mustard
4 drops Tabasco sauce
1/8 level teaspoon cayenne pepper
1/4 level teaspoon salt
Freshly ground black pepper
450 g (1 lb) white crabmeat
225 g (8 oz) baby sweetcorn,
  cooked and drained
2 large peppers, 1 red, 1 green,
  de-seeded and diced
4 spring onions, trimmed
  and thinly sliced
60 g (2 oz) croutons

Per serving
Calories 380 Protein 28 g
Total fat 25 g (saturated fat 4.8 g)
Carbohydrates 13 g (added sugar 0)
Fibre 3 g Sodium 1270 mg

Succulent crabmeat and fresh asparagus are combined with a piquant lemon dressing.

1 Cook the asparagus in boiling water for 5 minutes until just tender, then drain well.

2 Whisk together the olive oil, lemon juice, mustard, Tabasco sauce, cayenne pepper, salt and some black pepper in a salad bowl.

3 Add the asparagus, crabmeat, sweetcorn, red and green peppers and spring onions to the bowl and toss them in the dressing. Sprinkle with the croutons and serve.

225

Spanish Warm Potato Salad

Serves 4
Preparation time: 45 minutes
Cooking time: 15 minutes

675 g (1½ lb) small new potatoes, scrubbed
4 tablespoons each virgin olive oil and sunflower oil
2 tablespoons lemon juice
¼ level teaspoon salt
Freshly ground black pepper
60 g (2 oz) parsley, washed and dried
1 egg, size 2, hard-boiled and shelled
2 large cloves garlic, peeled and crushed (see p.11)
2 large tomatoes, skinned and sliced
3 large peppers, 1 green, 1 red and 1 yellow, grilled, de-seeded and sliced
50 g (1¾ oz) canned anchovy fillets, drained and halved lengthways
200 g (7 oz) canned tuna in oil, drained and flaked
1 small onion, peeled and finely sliced into rings
8 pitted black olives to garnish

Per serving
Calories 618 Protein 22 g
Total fat 43 g (saturated fat 4.7 g)
Carbohydrates 38 g (added sugar 0)
Fibre 6.8 g Sodium 1017 mg

The strong flavours of tuna, onion and anchovies mix with sweet new potatoes and smoky grilled peppers in this warm salad. In Spain, such a salad would be served as part of tapas to whet the appetite, but here it makes an excellent alfresco lunch or supper. You will need a food processor to make the thick garlic and parsley dressing.

1 Boil the potatoes until just soft, then drain, leave to cool slightly and cut in half.

2 Meanwhile, mix the olive and sunflower oils, lemon juice, salt and some pepper in a measuring jug. Blend the parsley, egg and garlic in a food processor for a few seconds, then pour the oil mixture into the processor in a slow, thin stream while the motor is still running.

3 Arrange the tomato slices on a large serving plate and put the peppers, anchovies, tuna, onion rings and potatoes on top. Pour the dressing over the salad, sprinkle with the olives and serve while still warm with pan gallego or other Spanish bread.

Corned Beef with Shredded Mixed Cabbage

Serves 4
Preparation time: 25 minutes
Cooking time: 15 minutes

450 g (1 lb) new potatoes, peeled
115 ml (4 fl oz) each soured cream and natural yoghurt
2 level tablespoons horseradish sauce
2 level teaspoons whole-grain mustard
4 tablespoons cider vinegar
2 level teaspoons caster sugar
½ level teaspoon salt
Freshly ground black pepper
150 g (5 oz) each red and white cabbage, very finely shredded (see p.11)
340 g (12 oz) corned beef, cut into small cubes (see p.79)
2 tablespoons chopped fresh parsley to garnish

Per serving
Calories 369 Protein 28 g
Total fat 17 g (saturated fat 8.1 g)
Carbohydrates 28 g (added sugar 2.5 g)
Fibre 3.8 g Sodium 902 mg

The distinctive taste of corned beef is combined with the crunch of red and white cabbage and tender diced potato in this filling salad. You need to shred the cabbage very finely so that it mixes well with the soured cream and mustard dressing.

1 Boil the potatoes until just soft, then drain and leave to cool slightly. Cut into small cubes and put into a large salad bowl.

2 Meanwhile, combine the soured cream, yoghurt, horseradish sauce, mustard, vinegar, sugar, salt and some pepper in a small bowl to make the dressing.

3 Add the red and white cabbage and the corned beef to the potatoes. Pour the dressing over the top and toss until the beef and vegetables are completely coated. Sprinkle with the parsley and serve from the bowl.

TUNA NOODLE SALAD

The firm flesh of tuna lends itself well to this layered pasta salad. Crinkle-edged trenette adds a stylish touch to the dish, but other flat ribbon pasta, such as tagliatelle, works just as well.

Serves 4
Preparation time: 15 minutes
Cooking time: 15 minutes

225 g (8 oz) trenette or tagliatelle
85 ml (3 fl oz) olive oil
2 tablespoons red wine vinegar
1½ level tablespoons Dijon mustard
1½ tablespoons capers, drained
1½ level teaspoons caster sugar
½ level teaspoon salt
Freshly ground black pepper
200 g (7 oz) canned tuna, drained
    and flaked
225 g (8 oz) runner beans, trimmed,
    sliced and blanched (see p.10)
2 beefsteak tomatoes, sliced
85 g (3 oz) pitted black
    olives, halved
4 tablespoons low-fat
    natural yoghurt
2 level tablespoons mayonnaise

Per serving
Calories 501 Protein 20 g
Total fat 26 g (saturated fat 3.9 g)
Carbohydrates 50 g (added sugar 2 g)
Fibre 5.9 g Sodium 813 mg

1 Cook the pasta (see p.202), then pour into a colander and rinse under cold water. Drain well and leave to cool.

2 Whisk together the oil, vinegar, half the mustard, 1 tablespoon of the capers, the sugar, salt and some pepper in a small bowl to make the dressing. Pour one-third of it into a large mixing bowl, then toss the cooled pasta in it until completely coated.

3 Put half the pasta in the bottom of a large salad bowl, spoon on half the tuna, then arrange half the runner beans, half the tomatoes and a third of the olives in layers on top. Pour over half the remaining dressing. Repeat the layers and finish with the dressing.

4 Mix together the yoghurt, mayonnaise and the rest of the mustard and pour over the top of the salad. Sprinkle with the remaining capers and olives, then serve with warm ciabatta or other Italian bread.

Trenette, with its attractive crinkled edge, divides layers of tangy tuna, runner beans, olives and tomatoes. A clear glass bowl shows off the contrasting bands of colour to the best effect.

227

MINTED PEARL BARLEY WITH PEAS AND CELERY

Serves 4
Preparation time: 35 minutes
Cooking time: 45 minutes
Cooling time: 20 minutes

225 g (8 oz) pearl barley
225 g (8 oz) frozen petits pois
1 small red onion, peeled and
  finely chopped
2 medium sticks celery, trimmed
  and finely diced
4 tablespoons olive oil
2 tablespoons red wine vinegar
1 tablespoon chopped fresh mint
¼ level teaspoon salt
Freshly ground black pepper
340 g (12 oz) Cheddar cheese, cut
  into small cubes
60 g (2 oz) roasted peanuts
  or cashew nuts, chopped

225 g (8 oz) tomatoes, de-seeded
  and cut into small dice (see p.10)
12 lettuce leaves, washed and dried
Finely shredded mint leaves
  to garnish

Per serving
Calories 820 Protein 34 g
Total fat 52 g (saturated fat 22 g)
Carbohydrates 58 g (added sugar 0)
Fibre 10 g Sodium 774 mg

A fresh mint dressing, absorbed
by hot pearl barley, intensifies
the refreshing flavour of this
light, summer salad as it cools.

1 Cook the pearl barley in boiling
water for 40 minutes. Add the
peas, onion and celery, bring back
to the boil and cook for 5 minutes,
then drain and turn into a bowl.

2 Add the oil, vinegar, chopped
mint, salt and some pepper to
the vegetables. Toss them well and
then leave to cool for 20 minutes.

3 Mix the Cheddar, nuts and
tomatoes into the salad.
Arrange the lettuce leaves in
a serving dish and spoon the
mixture into the centre. Garnish
with the shredded mint and serve.

*Cubes of cheese, chopped nuts and
tiny garden peas complement
the chewy texture of
pearl barley in this
minty salad.*

228

THREE-BEAN SALAD

Serves 4
Preparation time: 15 minutes
Cooking time: 10 minutes

225 g (8 oz) frozen baby
   broad beans
225 g (8 oz) frozen fine green beans
5 tablespoons olive oil
2 tablespoons white wine vinegar
1 level tablespoon Dijon mustard
1/4 level teaspoon salt
Freshly ground black pepper
1 clove garlic, peeled and crushed
   (see p.11)
2 tablespoons chopped
   fresh parsley
225 g (8 oz) cooked red kidney
   beans (see p.172), rinsed
   and drained
225 g (8 oz) Gruyère cheese, cut
   into thin strips
115 g (4 oz) radishes, trimmed
   and thinly sliced
1 small red onion, peeled and very
   thinly sliced
Sprigs of fresh parsley to garnish

Per serving
Calories 491 Protein 25 g
Total fat 36 g (saturated fat 14 g)
Carbohydrates 18 g (added sugar 0)
Fibre 5.7 g Sodium 521 mg

The beans used here – broad beans, fine green beans and kidney beans – can be altered to suit the season, your tastes or simply for a change.

1 Boil the broad beans and fine green beans for 6-8 minutes, or until just tender, then rinse under cold water and drain well.

2 Meanwhile, whisk together the oil, vinegar, mustard, salt, some pepper, the garlic and chopped parsley in a salad bowl. Toss the broad beans, fine green beans, kidney beans, Gruyère, radishes and red onion in the dressing, garnish with the parsley and serve with wholemeal bread.

FETA AND MACARONI SALAD

Serves 4
Preparation time: 10 minutes
Cooking time: 10 minutes

340 g (12 oz) macaroni
3 tablespoons roughly chopped
   fresh parsley
4 tablespoons olive oil
2 tablespoons lime or lemon juice
1/4 teaspoon Tabasco sauce
450 g (1 lb) feta cheese, drained
   and cut into small cubes
340 g (12 oz) bottled whole sweet
   red peppers, drained and sliced
60 g (2 oz) pitted black
   olives, halved
Sprigs of fresh parsley to garnish

Per serving
Calories 740 Protein 29 g
Total fat 39 g (saturated fat 18 g)
Carbohydrates 72 g (added sugar 0)
Fibre 6.9 g Sodium 2028 mg

Tangy feta cheese, juicy black olives and sweet red peppers combine with pasta in a piquant parsley dressing.

1 Cook the macaroni (see p.202), then rinse under cold water, drain well and leave to cool for 10 minutes.

2 Meanwhile, blend the parsley, oil, lime or lemon juice and Tabasco sauce in a food processor for 30 seconds, until smooth, to make the dressing.

3 Pour the dressing into a salad bowl and add the macaroni, feta, peppers and olives. Toss thoroughly, then garnish with the sprigs of parsley and serve with granary bread.

VEGETABLE TERRINE

Fresh cream, tasty Cheddar and a sprinkling of nutmeg bring a touch of luxury to this lentil, spinach and pepper paté. It is inspired by the traditional French country dish of terrine, a cooked and chilled preparation that is usually made with fish, meat or poultry.

Serves 4
Preparation time: 40 minutes
Cooking time: 45 minutes
Chilling time: overnight

115 g (4 oz) red lentils
12 medium spinach leaves, blanched (see p.10)
3 peppers, 1 green, 1 red, 1 yellow, de-seeded and diced
1 large carrot, peeled and coarsely grated
3 spring onions, trimmed and thinly sliced
3 eggs, size 3, beaten
150 ml (¼ pint) single cream
150 ml (¼ pint) double cream
⅛ level teaspoon freshly grated nutmeg
115 g (4 oz) mature Cheddar cheese, grated
¼ level teaspoon salt
Freshly ground black pepper

Per serving
Calories 558 Protein 23 g
Total fat 41 g (saturated fat 24 g)
Carbohydrates 26 g (added sugar 0)
Fibre 6.6 g Sodium 467 mg

1 Cook the lentils (see p.173), drain well and set aside in a large bowl. Meanwhile, preheat the oven to 190°C (375°F, gas mark 5).

2 Then grease a nonstick 23 cm x 13 cm (9 in x 5 in) loaf tin and line the sides with eight of the spinach leaves, stem-side inside. Scatter one-third of the diced pepper mixture over the bottom of the tin.

3 Mix the remaining peppers into the lentils with the carrot, spring onions, beaten eggs, single and double cream, the nutmeg, Cheddar, salt and some pepper.

4 Carefully spoon the lentil mixture into the tin and level the surface. Arrange the remaining spinach leaves on top, then cover the top of the tin with foil. Stand in a large roasting tin and pour in enough hot water to come halfway up the sides of the loaf tin.

5 Cook in the centre of the oven for 45 minutes, or until firmly set. Remove the loaf tin from the water, leave to cool, and then chill in the fridge overnight.

6 Turn the terrine out onto a board or serving dish and cut into thick slices. Serve with a tossed green salad and warm, crusty farmhouse bread.

BROCCOLI AND CHEDDAR SALAD

Crunchy chopped walnuts and red pepper in a delicate basil and lemon sauce add a fragrant taste to nutritious broccoli florets, grated cheese and pasta shells in this light cooked salad.

Serves 4
Preparation time: 25 minutes
Cooking time: 10 minutes

225 g (8 oz) conchiglie or other pasta shapes
340 g (12 oz) small broccoli florets
3 spring onions, trimmed and cut into short lengths
4 tablespoons olive oil
1 medium red pepper, de-seeded and diced
60 g (2 oz) walnuts, chopped
1 level teaspoon dried basil
1 level teaspoon caster sugar
¼ level teaspoon salt
Freshly ground black pepper
2 tablespoons cider vinegar
2 tablespoons lemon juice
225 g (8 oz) mature Cheddar cheese, coarsely grated
Fresh basil leaves to garnish

Per serving
Calories 694 Protein 27 g
Total fat 45 g (saturated fat 15 g)
Carbohydrates 49 g (added sugar 1.3 g)
Fibre 4.4 g Sodium 519 mg

1 Cook the pasta (see p.202), adding the broccoli florets for the final 2-3 minutes of cooking. When the pasta and broccoli are just tender, add the spring onions, then immediately remove from the heat and drain thoroughly.

2 Meanwhile, heat 1 tablespoon of the oil in a frying pan and cook the red pepper and walnuts in it for 2-3 minutes. Remove from the heat and stir in the remaining oil, the dried basil, sugar, salt, some pepper, the vinegar and lemon juice, then set aside.

3 Pour the pasta and vegetables into a large serving bowl and add the red pepper mixture and all but 1 tablespoon of the Cheddar. Toss well, then sprinkle with the rest of the cheese and garnish with the basil leaves. Serve warm with ciabatta or other Italian bread.

SUMMER PLATTER

Serves 4
Preparation time: 30 minutes
Cooking time: 15-20 minutes

340 g (12 oz) medium carrots,
 peeled and sliced diagonally
450 g (1 lb) small new potatoes,
 scrubbed and sliced
3 tablespoons lemon juice
2 tablespoons balsamic or
 red wine vinegar
2 level teaspoons Dijon mustard
½ teaspoon salt
Freshly ground black pepper
2 cloves garlic, peeled and crushed
 (see p.11)
15 g (½ oz) chopped fresh basil
115 ml (4 fl oz) olive oil
225 g (8 oz) mixed salad leaves
200 g (7 oz) canned tuna in oil,
 drained and flaked
225 g (8 oz) cooked cannellini
 beans, rinsed and drained
 (see p.172)

*Salami, juicy peppers,
soft cheese and flaky tuna
provide a fascinating
contrast of flavours.*

400 g (14 oz) bottled or canned
 artichoke hearts, drained
 and halved
225 g (8 oz) mozzarella or
 provolone cheese, cut into strips
115 g (4 oz) bottled sweet red
 peppers or antipasto mixed
 peppers, drained
225 g (8 oz) thickly sliced salami,
 cut into strips
115 g (4 oz) pitted black olives
Sprig of fresh marjoram or oregano
 to garnish

Per serving
Calories 1069 Protein 46 g
Total fat 82 g (saturated fat 24 g)
Carbohydrates 41 g (added sugar 0)
Fibre 10 g Sodium 2562 mg

This colourful assortment of meat, fish, cheese and vegetables is an expanded version of the classic Italian *antipasto* (meaning 'before pasta'). The term usually refers to a starter, but this tasty platter is a feast in itself. Serve the dressing separately and allow the diners to help themselves.

1 Steam the carrots and potatoes until just tender, then set aside and leave to cool.

2 Meanwhile, whisk together the lemon juice, vinegar, mustard, salt, some pepper, the garlic, basil and oil to make the dressing. Pour into a serving boat.

3 Cover a large platter with the salad leaves and arrange the carrots, potatoes, tuna, cannellini beans, artichoke hearts, cheese, peppers, salami and olives on top. Garnish with the marjoram or oregano and serve with warm ciabatta or other Italian bread.

Making the most of salads

The abundance of fresh fruit and vegetables available in our shops allows an endless mixing and matching of colour, flavour and texture in salads. Simplicity is the key to creating these colourful and nutritious combinations, while a simple dressing adds the finishing touch.

CRISP LETTUCE LEAVES tossed in a vinaigrette dressing are often all that is needed to accompany some of the rich and filling one-dish meals in this book. However, the increasing range of salad ingredients in our shops means that salads can provide satisfying meals on their own. The wide variety of leafy salad vegetables work particularly well in combinations, such as slightly bitter endive, radicchio or chicory served with sweeter oak leaf, cos, butterhead, Webb's Wonderful or iceberg. Other edible leaves that are easy to find – or grow – are young spinach leaves, lamb's lettuce, dandelion leaves, sorrel, rocket and watercress. Alfalfa and bean sprouts, mustard and cress, and several varieties of cabbage can be bought or grown at home, as can fresh herbs (see p.12). Flowers that can be eaten in salads are harder to find in the shops, and may need to be grown at home. The petals of roses and marigolds and the flower heads of nasturtiums, violets and pansies are all safe to eat and provide an exotic contribution.

Keeping leaves fresh

To keep whole lettuces – and parsley – fresh, rinse upside-down under a cold running tap, as soon after buying them as possible. Shake the lettuce or parsley well to remove the water, then put it into a polythene bag. Swing the bag up and over, holding it by the top corners, and tie together to seal. The lettuce will keep fresh in the bottom of the fridge for up to four days, and parsley for six days.

To refresh limp-looking lettuces, watercress or herbs, plunge them into a bowlful of ice-cold water and dry thoroughly. All salad ingredients should be well dried before combining, or excess water will dilute the dressing. Cover the top of the colander with a plate and shake firmly, or put the leaves in a clean tea cloth and shake gently until the water has gone. Alternatively, shake the leaves dry in a salad basket or spinner, if you have one.

Stoning an avocado

1 Cut the avocado in half lengthways with a sharp stainless steel knife, working the knife around the stone.

2 Twist the two halves in opposite directions to separate them – the stone will remain in one half.

3 Hold the avocado in one hand, protected with a tea cloth. Tap the stone with the blade, then gently twist the knife to free the stone.

Curly endive (frisée)
Radicchio
Oak leaf
Belgian chicory
Cos
Iceberg
Lollo rosso
Soft round
Chinese cabbage
White cabbage
Red cabbage
Mustard and cress
Bean sprouts

Baby spinach
Marigold
Sorrel
Lamb's lettuce
Pansy
Watercress
Rocket
Alfalfa sprouts
Nasturtium

The finishing touch

Most salad dressings fall into three main types – yoghurt or soured cream, vinaigrette, or mayonnaise. The recipes which follow serve four or six and take 5-10 minutes to make.

Lettuce and similar leafy salads should be tossed at the last moment to keep the ingredients crisp. Cabbage salads should be dressed and left to stand for the flavour to be absorbed.

Yoghurt or soured cream dressing is light and creamy and can be used to dress green, leafy salads and grated or chopped vegetables. This dressing can be made entirely with yoghurt or soured cream or, if you prefer a slightly richer taste, use mayonnaise (see recipe, far right). You can use a low-fat or reduced-calorie brand if you wish. Serve the dressing plain, or vary the flavour and texture by adding chopped fresh herbs, chopped spring onions, mustard, watercress, ground cardamom, or freshly grated nutmeg.

Yoghurt and soured cream dressing

To make the dressing you will need:

4 tablespoons Greek yoghurt
6 tablespoons soured cream
2 tablespoons lemon juice
½ level teaspoon caster sugar
1 level teaspoon whole-grain mustard
¼ level teaspoon salt
Freshly ground black pepper

Mix all the ingredients together in a bowl and season with some pepper. Use immediately, or cover and refrigerate for up to 3 hours.

Vinaigrette is a mixture of oil and vinegar, seasoned with salt and pepper and often flavoured with garlic, chopped fresh herbs, or mustard. Make a vinaigrette just before you need it so that the flavour is fresh. For a tart dressing use two parts of oil to one of vinegar, and for a smooth, mild dressing use up to six parts oil to one of vinegar.

A vinaigrette suits just about any type of salad but can be adapted to suit the particular flavour of the salad, or the dish which the salad is accompanying. You can vary the recipe below by using flavoured oils or vinegars (see p.13) or juices such as lemon, lime or orange instead of ordinary vinegar, adding a teaspoon of finely grated fruit rind for extra zest. Cider or sherry vinegar will give a mellower taste. Freshly grated nutmeg, cardamom, cinnamon or allspice will add piquancy, while 1-2 teaspoons of tomato purée will give the vinaigrette a colourful fruitiness.

To make vinaigrette you will need:

½ level teaspoon salt
Freshly ground black pepper
½-1 level teaspoon Dijon mustard
⅛ level teaspoon caster sugar
1 tablespoon red wine or balsamic vinegar
2-5 tablespoons virgin or extra virgin olive oil

1 Stir or whisk together the salt, some pepper, mustard, sugar and vinegar in a bowl, until the salt and sugar dissolve.

2 Gradually whisk in the oil, then mix in the garlic, herbs and any other seasonings.

Mayonnaise is a thick, rich sauce of eggs, oil and vinegar which should be eaten the same day it is made. Note that the Department of Health recommends that the elderly, the sick, babies and toddlers avoid raw, uncooked egg yolk as used in a mayonnaise. Cover and store the mayonnaise in the fridge as soon as you have made it. Try adding a crushed clove of garlic to the egg yolk, or finely chopped fresh herbs, creamed horseradish, tomato purée or Tabasco sauce to the finished mayonnaise.

To make mayonnaise you will need:

1 egg yolk, size 2
¼ level teaspoon salt
½ level teaspoon Dijon mustard
Freshly ground black pepper
1-2 teaspoons lemon juice or white wine vinegar
175 ml (6 fl oz) light olive oil or corn oil
1-2 tablespoons warm water

Mayonnaise

1 Put the egg yolk, salt, mustard and some pepper in a small bowl. Whisk the egg yolk with a stainless steel wire whisk or an electric mixer until slightly lightened in colour, then gradually whisk in the lemon juice or vinegar.

2 Whisking continuously, add a few drops of the oil. When the mayonnaise begins to thicken, pour in the oil in a fine, steady stream. If, halfway through mixing, the mayonnaise becomes very thick, add another teaspoon of lemon juice or vinegar. Add the warm water to adjust the consistency as required.

Vinaigrette

MICROWAVE MEALS

The ease and speed of working with the microwave make it a favourite tool of those who like cooking with a minimum of fuss. These recipes feature traditional, richly flavoured casseroles and soups from around the world, as well as simple suppers from closer to home. They cover a wide range of ingredients and cooking styles, and fully utilise the microwave's strengths in cooking succulent fish and crisp vegetables.

❖

Making the most of the microwave 258-9

Onion, celery, red pepper and croutons provide a tasty, textured filling for fresh fish in Stuffed Fillets of Plaice (left) – an uncomplicated recipe quickly cooked in the microwave, that makes an elegant family supper (see p.251).

BEEF STRIPS WITH CUMIN, CABBAGE AND POTATO

Serves 4
Preparation time: 40 minutes
Cooking time: 25 minutes

3 tablespoons olive oil
450 g (1 lb) sirloin steak, trimmed of
    fat and cut into thin strips
1 large onion, peeled and
    finely chopped
1 clove garlic, peeled
    and crushed (see p.11)
1 level tablespoon cornflour
2 tablespoons water
175 ml (6 fl oz) beef stock
    (see p.8)
1 level teaspoon ground cumin
3/4 level teaspoon dried thyme
1/2 level teaspoon salt
Freshly ground black pepper
450 g (1 lb) green cabbage, washed
    and finely shredded (see p.11)
675 g (1 1/2 lb) potatoes, peeled and
    cut into small dice (see p.10)
Sprigs of fresh thyme and strips of
    red pepper to garnish

Per serving
Calories 486 Protein 37 g
Total fat 21 g (saturated fat 5.6 g)
Carbohydrates 40 g (added sugar 0)
Fibre 6.5 g Sodium 330 mg

Cumin brings a warm and
pungent flavour to this quick
and nutritious combination of
tender strips of steak, chopped
potatoes and shredded cabbage.

1 Pour 1 tablespoon of the oil
into a microwave-safe bowl
and toss the beef strips in it. Cover
(see p.258) and cook on High for
4 minutes, stirring once after
2 minutes. Lift out the beef strips
with a slotted spoon, place on a
plate and leave to one side.

2 Add the remaining oil, onion
and garlic to the microwave-safe
bowl, then cover and cook on
High for 4 minutes, or until the
onion is softened. Carefully blend
the cornflour and water into a
smooth paste and stir it into
the onion mixture. Add the
stock, cumin, dried thyme, salt,
some pepper, the cabbage and
potatoes. Cover and cook on
High for 15 minutes, stirring
every 5 minutes.

3 Mix the beef strips into the
vegetables, cover and heat
through on High for 2 minutes.
Turn the potato mixture into a
large heated serving dish, garnish
with the fresh thyme sprigs and
strips of red pepper and serve.

BEEF AND MACARONI CHILLI

Serves 4
Preparation time: 20 minutes
Cooking time: 30 minutes

1 tablespoon olive oil
1 large onion, peeled and
    finely chopped
2 medium peppers, 1 red, 1 green,
    de-seeded and finely chopped
450 g (1 lb) lean minced beef
1 level tablespoon mild or hot
    chilli powder
115 g (4 oz) button mushrooms,
    wiped and sliced
1/2 level teaspoon salt
Freshly ground black pepper
400 g (14 oz) canned
    chopped tomatoes
175 g (6 oz) elbow macaroni
Thin slices of red chilli and fresh
    coriander leaves to garnish

Per serving
Calories 432 Protein 30 g
Total fat 17 g (saturated fat 6 g)
Carbohydrates 43 g (added sugar 0)
Fibre 5.6 g Sodium 376 mg

This lively and unusual version
of chilli, a classic Mexican dish,
combines short, curved pasta
pieces with minced beef, button
mushrooms and tomatoes.

1 Mix together the olive oil,
onion and peppers in a large,
microwave-safe casserole or bowl.
Cover (see p.258) and cook on
High for 5 minutes, until the
onion is softened, stirring once
after 2 1/2 minutes. Stir in the
minced beef, then cover and cook
on High for 5 minutes, or until
the mince is lightly browned.

2 Mix in the chilli powder,
mushrooms, salt, some
pepper and the tomatoes, then
cover and cook on High for
15 minutes, stirring every
5 minutes. Meanwhile, cook the
macaroni conventionally in a
saucepan (see p.202), drain it
well and add it to the beef
and vegetables.

3 Cover and cook on Medium
for 5 minutes. Garnish with
the red chilli and fresh coriander
and serve with warmed tortillas.

SPANISH MEATBALL STEW

Serves 4
Preparation time: 25 minutes
Cooking time: 45 minutes

450 g (1 lb) lean minced beef
1 egg, size 3
60 g (2 oz) fresh wholemeal
   breadcrumbs
4 cloves garlic, peeled and crushed
   (see p.11)
1/4 level teaspoon salt
Freshly ground black pepper
1/2 level teaspoon each dried basil
   and oregano
2 tablespoons olive oil
1 medium onion, peeled and
   finely chopped
1 medium red pepper, de-seeded
   and finely chopped
400 g (14 oz) canned tomatoes
340 ml (12 fl oz) beef stock
   (see p.8)
2 level tablespoons tomato purée
85 g (3 oz) long-grain white rice
115 g (4 oz) frozen peas
60 g (2 oz) pimiento-stuffed
   green olives

Per serving
Calories 466 Protein 30 g
Total fat 23 g (saturated fat 7.1 g)
Carbohydrates 36 g (added sugar 0)
Fibre 6.1 g Sodium 713 mg

*Green peas and red pepper add a
fresh, slightly sweet taste to a rich
tomato sauce fortified with
nutritious beef stock.*

Lean beef meatballs flavoured
with basil, oregano and garlic
are served with rice and
stuffed olives in this variant
of a traditional Spanish paella.
If you wish, you can use minced
pork or lamb in place of beef,
and pasta instead of rice.

1 Mix together the minced beef,
egg, breadcrumbs, half the
garlic, the salt, some pepper and
the basil and oregano. Divide the
mixture into 16 equal amounts
and shape each one into a ball.

2 Arrange the meatballs evenly
in a preheated browning dish,
or a large, microwave-safe dish.
Cover the dish (see p.258) and
cook on High for 3 minutes, then
turn the dish halfway round in
the microwave and rearrange the
meatballs, moving those in the
centre to the outside. Cover and
then cook on High for 2 minutes,
or until lightly browned.

3 Lift out the meatballs, put
them on a plate and keep them
warm. Mix the oil, onion, red
pepper, the remaining garlic and
some pepper in the dish, cover
and cook on High for 4 minutes,
stirring once after 2 minutes.

4 Add the tomatoes, beef stock,
tomato purée and meatballs.
Cover and cook on High for
5 minutes, stirring once
after 2 1/2 minutes.
Stir in the rice,
cover again and
cook on High
for 3 minutes.

5 Reduce the power to
Medium and cook for a
further 20 minutes, or until
the rice is cooked, stirring
every 5 minutes. Add the peas
and olives and cook on High
for 3 minutes, or until the
peas are cooked and the olives
are heated through.

6 Allow the stew to stand for
5 minutes, then transfer to a
heated serving dish. Serve with
a crisp green salad.

FRUITY CURRIED BEEF

Serves 6
Preparation time: 20 minutes
Cooking time: 35 minutes

1 level tablespoon medium
   curry powder
675 g (1½ lb) lean minced beef
Freshly ground black pepper
225 g (8 oz) onions, peeled and
   thinly sliced
2 tablespoons olive oil
1 level tablespoon plain flour
400 g (14 oz) canned
   chopped tomatoes
1 level teaspoon each ground
   cumin, ground coriander and
   ground turmeric
¼ level teaspoon ground ginger
1 cinnamon stick
200 ml (7 fl oz) fresh orange juice
¼ level teaspoon salt
2 ripe, firm, medium-sized bananas,
   peeled and sliced
2 tablespoons lemon juice
175 g (6 oz) fresh or canned
   pineapple, diced
2 tablespoons fruit chutney
800 g (1¾ lb) cooked long-grain
   rice (see p.9)

Per serving
Calories 489 Protein 27 g
Total fat 16 g (saturated fat 5.1 g)
Carbohydrates 63 g (added sugar 2.5 g)
Fibre 3.8 g Sodium 210 mg

Soft pieces of pineapple and banana combine with spicy beef meatballs in a thick and tasty curry served on a bed of long-grain rice.

1 Mix together the curry powder, minced beef and some pepper in a bowl. Shape the mixture into about 30 small balls with lightly wetted hands and set aside.

2 Mix the onions with the oil in a large microwave-safe bowl and cook, uncovered, on High for 8 minutes, stirring every 2 minutes.

3 Stir in the flour, tomatoes, cumin, coriander, turmeric, ginger, cinnamon stick, orange juice, salt and some pepper.

Cook, uncovered, on High for 5 minutes, or until the sauce comes to the boil. Discard the cinnamon stick, cool slightly, then blend the sauce in a food processor for 1 minute.

4 Pour the sauce back into the bowl and stir in the meatballs. Cover (see p.258) and cook on High for 10 minutes, stirring after 5 minutes. Mix in the bananas, lemon juice, pineapple and chutney, then cover and cook

on High for 2 minutes. Remove from the microwave and leave to stand for 5 minutes.

5 Meanwhile, heat the rice on a large microwave-safe platter for 2 minutes. Pour the curry into the centre of the rice and serve.

Beef meatballs are cooked in a rich sauce spiced with cumin, turmeric, coriander and ginger, and cooled with pineapple and banana.

LAMB AND AUBERGINE GRATIN

Aubergines and lamb give this hearty potato-topped pie a Greek flavour, but you can use lean minced beef in place of the lamb, if you prefer.

Serves 4
Preparation time: 30 minutes
Cooking time: 35 minutes

450 g (1 lb) aubergines, trimmed and halved lengthways
1 level teaspoon salt
450 g (1 lb) potatoes, peeled and evenly sliced
4 tablespoons water
4 tablespoons lamb or beef stock (see p.8)
1 tablespoon olive oil
1 medium onion, peeled and finely chopped
2 cloves garlic, peeled and crushed (see p.11)
675 g (1½ lb) lean minced lamb
½ level teaspoon dried oregano
¼ level teaspoon ground cinnamon
Freshly ground black pepper
340 ml (12 fl oz) passata (sieved tomatoes)
Fresh basil leaves and halved cherry tomatoes to garnish

Per serving
Calories 426 Protein 39 g
Total fat 19 g (saturated fat 7.8 g)
Carbohydrates 26 g (added sugar 0)
Fibre 5.4 g Sodium 435 mg

1 Put the aubergines cut-side up on a plate, sprinkle with the salt and leave to stand for 15 minutes. Meanwhile, put the potato slices in a shallow, microwave-safe dish, sprinkle with the water, then cover (see p.258). Cook on High for 6 minutes, or until the potatoes are just soft. Drain well, then mash with the stock.

2 Rinse the aubergines, pat dry and prick the skins with a fork. Arrange them cut-side up on a microwave-safe plate, cover and soften on High for 5 minutes. Leave to cool slightly, then cut into thin slices and arrange in a large, microwave-safe pie dish.

3 Mix the oil with the onion and garlic in a large, microwave-safe bowl, cover and cook on High for 3 minutes, stirring once after 1 minute. Mix in the lamb, cover and cook on High for 5 minutes, stirring after 3 minutes. Stir in the oregano, cinnamon, some pepper and the passata, then cover and cook on High for 5 minutes.

4 Pour the mixture over the aubergine slices, then spoon the mashed potato around the edge of the dish. Cover and cook on High for 5 minutes. Reduce the power to Medium and cook for 3 minutes more, or until bubbling. Garnish with the basil and tomatoes and serve with a crisp lettuce and cucumber salad.

Cherry tomatoes and fresh basil leaves crown a filling pie that is inspired by a Greek moussaka, but has been adapted for cooking in a microwave oven.

BAKED BEANS WITH GAMMON AND MAPLE SYRUP

Maple syrup mixed with Dijon mustard makes an unusual covering for baked beans and succulent chunks of ham. You can replace the maple syrup with honey, if preferred.

Serves 4
Preparation time: 10 minutes
Cooking time: 20 minutes

450 g (1 lb) rindless gammon steaks, cut into small squares
2 medium carrots, peeled and thickly sliced
5 tablespoons maple syrup
1 level tablespoon Dijon mustard
800 g (1¾ lb) canned baked beans, lightly drained
2 tablespoons tomato ketchup
½ level teaspoon mustard powder
1 level teaspoon chilli powder
30 g (1 oz) fresh white breadcrumbs, lightly toasted
15 g (½ oz) unsalted butter, melted

Per serving
Calories 478 Protein 44 g
Total fat 11 g (saturated fat 4.8 g)
Carbohydrates 55 g (added sugar 30 g)
Fibre 14 g Sodium 2576 mg

1 Put the gammon in the centre of a large microwave dish and arrange the carrots in a single layer round the meat. Mix the syrup with the Dijon mustard and pour over the gammon and carrots.

2 Cover the dish (see p.258) and cook on High for 8 minutes, stirring after 4 minutes.

3 Mix together the baked beans, ketchup, mustard powder and chilli powder, and spoon the mixture evenly over the gammon and carrots. Cover and cook on High for 6 minutes, stirring once after 3 minutes.

4 Use a fork to combine the breadcrumbs and butter, then sprinkle them over the beans. Cook, uncovered, on High for 2 minutes. Leave to stand for 2-3 minutes, then serve with crusty bread rolls and salad.

A sweet-and-savoury dish of gammon and carrots is covered with maple syrup and mustard and topped with a layer of spicy baked beans sprinkled with buttered breadcrumbs.

GAMMON WITH SCALLOPED POTATOES

Sliced potatoes and gammon cubes baked in creamy white sauce are flavoured with red pepper and spring onions, then topped with Parmesan cheese and browned under the grill.

Serves 4
Preparation time: 35 minutes
Cooking time: 35 minutes

550 g (1¼ lb) potatoes, peeled and thinly sliced
175 ml (6 fl oz) chicken stock (see p.8)
2 large spring onions, trimmed and thinly sliced
1 medium red pepper, de-seeded and finely diced
15 g (½ oz) unsalted butter
4 level teaspoons cornflour
175 ml (6 fl oz) double cream
Freshly ground black pepper
340 g (12 oz) thickly sliced baked gammon, cut into small cubes
30 g (1 oz) Parmesan cheese, grated
Small rings of red pepper, spring onion, sliced, and flat-leaf parsley to garnish

Per serving
Calories 533 Protein 32 g
Total fat 32 g (saturated fat 19 g)
Carbohydrates 32 g (added sugar 0)
Fibre 2.9 g Sodium 1083 mg

1 Arrange the potatoes evenly in the bottom of a large microwave-safe dish that will also fit under the grill, and add 115 ml (4 fl oz) of the chicken stock. Cover (see p.258) and cook on High for 10 minutes or until the potatoes are cooked, turning the slices after 5 minutes.

2 Pour off the stock from the potatoes into the remaining stock, and set the potatoes and the stock aside. Put the spring onions, red pepper and butter into the same dish, cover and cook on High for 3 minutes or until the vegetables have softened.

3 Blend the cornflour with the stock, the cream and some black pepper, then stir it into the onion mixture. Cover and cook on High for 3 minutes, stirring after each minute, until the mixture comes to the boil. Gently mix in the cooked potatoes and the gammon cubes and microwave, uncovered, on Medium for 15 minutes, stirring every 5 minutes. Meanwhile, preheat the grill to high.

4 Sprinkle the Parmesan on the gammon and potato mixture and put the dish under the grill to brown. Garnish with the red pepper rings, spring onion slices and parsley, and serve with warm french bread.

PORTUGUESE BEAN STEW

Serves 4
Preparation time: 30 minutes
Cooking time: 30 minutes

1 large onion, peeled and finely chopped
1 medium green pepper, de-seeded and finely chopped
1 clove garlic, peeled and crushed (see p.11)
1 tablespoon olive oil
400 g (14 oz) canned tomatoes
2 medium carrots, peeled and thinly sliced
225 g (8 oz) potatoes, peeled and cut into small cubes
1 bay leaf
60 g (2 oz) pepperoni, finely diced
225 g (8 oz) cooked cannellini beans, rinsed and drained (see p.172)
225 g (8 oz) baby spinach leaves, shredded
225 g (8 oz) honey-roast ham, diced
1 level tablespoon cornflour
3 tablespoons water
Freshly ground black pepper
⅛ level teaspoon cayenne pepper
⅛ level teaspoon salt
3 tablespoons chopped fresh parsley to garnish

Per serving
Calories 339 Protein 22 g
Total fat 14 g (saturated fat 1.7 g)
Carbohydrates 33 g (added sugar 0)
Fibre 9.7 g Sodium 1181 mg

This filling and flavoursome bean stew includes onion, green pepper, garlic, pepperoni and ham, and is highly spiced with fierce cayenne pepper.

1 Mix the onion, green pepper, garlic and olive oil in a large, microwave-safe casserole. Cover (see p.258) and cook on High for 5 minutes, stirring once after 2½ minutes.

2 Mix in the tomatoes, breaking them up with a fork, then add the carrots, potatoes and the bay leaf. Cover and cook on High for 10 minutes, stirring every 3 minutes, until the vegetables begin to soften.

3 Stir in the pepperoni, cannellini beans, spinach and ham. Cover and cook on Medium for 10 minutes, stirring after 5 minutes.

4 Meanwhile, blend the cornflour with the water and stir into the bean mixture. Mix in some black pepper, the cayenne pepper and the salt. Cover and cook on High for 3 minutes, stirring after 1½ minutes, until the mixture boils and thickens. Remove the bay leaf, then sprinkle the parsley over the dish and serve.

SWEET AND SOUR PORK WITH WATER CHESTNUTS

Pineapple, soy sauce, honey and vinegar provide the pork with its sweet and sour flavours in this classic Chinese dish.

Serves 4
Preparation time: 20 minutes
Cooking time: 30 minutes

450 g (1 lb) pork tenderloin, trimmed of fat and cut into strips (see p.80)
425 g (15 oz) canned, unsweetened pineapple chunks, drained and 115 ml (4 fl oz) of the juice saved
3 tablespoons chicken stock (see p.8)
2 tablespoons each soy sauce, clear honey and cider vinegar
2 level tablespoons cornflour
1 medium onion, peeled and coarsely chopped
1 small green pepper, de-seeded and cut into small squares
2 cloves garlic, peeled and crushed (see p.11)

115 g (4 oz) baby carrots, peeled
1 tablespoon sesame oil
115 g (4 oz) small broccoli florets
60 g (2 oz) canned water chestnuts, drained and sliced
675 g (1½ lb) cooked long-grain rice

Per serving
Calories 544 Protein 30 g
Total fat 12 g (saturated fat 3.4 g)
Carbohydrates 84 g (added sugar 10 g)
Fibre 4.4 g Sodium 542 mg

1 Preheat a microwave browning dish, following the maker's instructions. Cook the pork strips in the dish on High for 5 minutes, turning them after 3 minutes, then set aside on a plate.

2 Mix the pineapple juice, stock, soy sauce, honey, vinegar and cornflour in a small microwave-safe bowl, then cook on High for 2 minutes, stirring the sauce every 30 seconds. Cover and set aside.

3 Mix the onion, pepper, garlic, carrots and oil in a microwave-safe bowl, cover (see p.258) and cook on High for 2 minutes. Add the broccoli florets and water chestnuts, then cover and cook on High for 1 minute.

4 Stir in the pork, pineapple pieces and sauce. Cover and cook on Low for 15 minutes, stirring every 5 minutes, until the meat and vegetables are tender. Take the bowl out

Crunchy water chestnuts, crisp broccoli and tender baby carrots accompany strips of pork and succulent pineapple chunks in a delicate sauce.

of the microwave and leave to stand for 5 minutes. Meanwhile, heat the rice in a microwave-safe serving dish on High for about 2 minutes. Pour the pork mixture over the top and, if necessary, reheat for 1-2 minutes on High, then serve.

SMOKED PORK, CABBAGE AND POTATO CASSEROLE

Crisp shredded cabbage and cubes of potato take on a smoky flavour of pork in this filling family dinner. You can use ham, smoked pork sausage or a combination of smoked meats if you prefer.

Serves 4
Preparation time: 20 minutes
Cooking time: 25 minutes

1 medium onion, peeled and finely chopped
1 tablespoon olive oil
450 g (1 lb) white cabbage trimmed and coarsely shredded (see p.11)
1 level teaspoon caraway seeds
450 g (1 lb) potatoes, peeled and cut into cubes (see p.10)
115 ml (4 fl oz) chicken stock (see p.8)
450 g (1 lb) smoked pork loin, cut into 8 slices
1/2 level teaspoon salt
Freshly ground black pepper

Per serving
Calories 406 Protein 41 g
Total fat 16 g (saturated fat 5.3 g)
Carbohydrates 26 g (added sugar 0)
Fibre 5.4 g Sodium 352 mg

1 Mix the onion and oil in a large, microwave-safe casserole and cook on High for 3 minutes, or until the onion is transparent.

2 Mix in the cabbage and caraway seeds and arrange the potatoes around the edge of the dish. Pour in the stock, cover (see p.258) and cook on High for 12 minutes, stirring once after 6 minutes.

3 Take out half the cabbage mixture and keep it to one side. Arrange the pork in a single layer on top of the cabbage in the dish, then spread the remaining cabbage evenly over the pork.

4 Cover and cook on High for 5 minutes. Reduce the power to Medium and cook for a further 5 minutes. Season with the salt and some pepper, then cover and leave to stand for 5 minutes. Serve with a salad of sliced tomato and dill-pickled cucumber.

243

Sausage and Pasta in Napoletana Sauce

Serves 4
Preparation time: 15 minutes
Cooking time: 30 minutes

450 g (1 lb) sweet or spicy
   Italian sausages
1 large onion, peeled and
   finely chopped
1 large green pepper, de-seeded
   and cut into small squares
1 tablespoon olive oil
1/2 level teaspoon fennel
   seeds (optional)

1 level teaspoon dried basil
675 g (1 1/2 lb) fresh Napoletana
   sauce
225 g (8 oz) macaroni, cooked
   and drained (see p.202)
225 g (8 oz) mozzarella cheese
60 g (2 oz) Parmesan
   cheese, grated

Per serving
Calories 1033   Protein 44 g
Total fat 66 g (saturated fat 27 g)
Carbohydrates 70 g (added sugar 0)
Fibre 7.7 g   Sodium 1965 mg

A thin layer of melted mozzarella and Parmesan makes a luxurious topping for macaroni, green pepper and Mediterranean sausage in a thick, tasty sauce.

Tomatoes, onion and fragrant herbs give this dish an authentic flavour of southern Italy. Napoletana sauce, to which the fennel seeds add a distinctive and slightly sweet taste, is just one of many ready-made pasta sauces found in supermarkets.

1 Prick the skin of the sausages with a fork. Put them in a large microwave-safe dish, cover loosely with greaseproof paper, and cook on High for 6 minutes, turning them after 3 minutes. Leave the sausages on a board to cool, then cut them into thick slices.

2 Pour off any fat, then add the onion, pepper and oil to the same dish. Cook on High for 3 minutes, covered (see p.258), stirring once after 1 1/2 minutes. Mix in the fennel seeds, if using, and the basil and Napoletana sauce, then cover and cook on High for 3 minutes, stirring once after 1 1/2 minutes.

3 Add the sausages, macaroni, half the mozzarella and half the Parmesan to the sauce. Cover and cook on Medium for 12 minutes, stirring once after 6 minutes.

4 Sprinkle with the remaining mozzarella and Parmesan and cook on Medium for 1 minute. Take the dish out of the microwave, cover and leave for 5 minutes, then serve with a green salad.

PORK RAGOUT

Serves 4
Preparation time: 25 minutes
Cooking time: 35 minutes

1 tablespoon olive oil
1 large onion, peeled and sliced
1 clove garlic, peeled and crushed
  (see p.11)
3 sticks celery, trimmed and
  finely chopped
2 medium carrots, peeled and sliced
675 g (1½ lb) potatoes, peeled
  and diced (see p.10)
225 g (8 oz) button
  mushrooms, wiped
3 level tablespoons plain flour
150 ml (¼ pint) chicken stock
  (see p.8)
400 g (14 oz) canned
  peeled tomatoes
1 level tablespoon tomato purée
1¼ level teaspoons paprika
½ level teaspoon salt
Freshly ground black pepper
340 g (12 oz) cooked pork, diced
150 g (5 oz) soured cream
2 tablespoons chopped
  fresh parsley

Per serving
Calories 480 Protein 35 g
Total fat 18 g (saturated fat 7.6 g)
Carbohydrates 48 g (added sugar 0)
Fibre 6.9 g Sodium 410 mg

Soft chunks of potato, button mushrooms, carrots and celery provide a rich accompaniment for tasty pieces of pork in this easy, half-hour version of ragout, a thick and flavoursome variety of stew that takes many hours to cook conventionally. The many variations on ragout, originally a French dish, can be made with either meat or fish.

1 Heat the oil in a large microwave-safe casserole on High for 30 seconds. Stir in the onion, garlic, celery, carrots and potatoes, then cover (see p.258) and cook on High for 8 minutes, stirring every 2 minutes.

2 Add the mushrooms, cover and cook on High for 3 minutes, stirring once after 1½ minutes. Sprinkle the flour over the vegetables, then stir and cook on High for 30 seconds. Mix in the stock, tomatoes, tomato purée, 1 teaspoon of the paprika, the salt and some pepper. Cover and cook on High for 12 minutes, stirring every 4 minutes.

3 Add the pork, cover and cook on Medium for 8 minutes, stirring after 4 minutes. Spoon over the soured cream and remaining paprika, then cook on High for 1½ minutes. Sprinkle with the parsley and serve.

CHINESE CHICKEN SOUP

Serves 4
Preparation time: 10 minutes
Cooking time: 20 minutes

1.15 litres (2 pints) chicken stock
  (see p.8)
1 tablespoon soy sauce
1 tablespoon white wine vinegar
1 tablespoon oyster sauce
250 g (9 oz) boneless chicken
  breasts, skinned and thinly sliced
115 g (4 oz) beansprouts, rinsed
  and drained
250 g (9 oz) Chinese fine egg
  noodles, cooked and drained
  (see p.202)
115 g (4 oz) iceberg lettuce,
  trimmed and finely shredded
1 bunch spring onions, trimmed
  and thinly sliced
1 teaspoon sesame oil
2 teaspoons chilli sauce

Per serving
Calories 348 Protein 23 g
Total fat 8.7 g (saturated fat 0.8 g)
Carbohydrates 48 g (added sugar 0)
Fibre 4.8 g Sodium 567 mg

This slightly spicy soup is fortified with soy and oyster sauces and mixed with an intriguing combination of beansprouts, noodles and spring onions. It makes a delightful light lunch or supper, but can also be served – as soups often are in China – to refresh the palate as part of a larger meal.

1 Pour the stock into a large, microwave-safe bowl, cover (see p.258) and cook on High for 8 minutes, or until the stock comes to the boil.

2 Stir in the soy sauce, vinegar, oyster sauce and slices of chicken. Cover and microwave on High for 4 minutes, or until the stock returns to the boil. Mix in the beansprouts and noodles, then cook on High for 2 minutes.

3 Add the lettuce and spring onions and cook on High for 3 minutes. Leave to stand for 2 minutes, then stir in the sesame oil and chilli sauce and serve in warmed bowls.

CHICKEN GUMBO

Okra is the essential vegetable in a gumbo. It provides the dish – a savoury stew, here made with chicken – with its distinctive texture and flavour.

Serves 4
Preparation time: 20 minutes
Cooking time: 30 minutes

30 g (1 oz) butter
1 medium onion, peeled and finely chopped
1 stick celery, trimmed and finely chopped
1 medium green pepper, de-seeded and finely chopped
2 cloves garlic, peeled and crushed (see p.11)
30 g (1 oz) plain flour
400 g (14 oz) canned chopped tomatoes
450 ml (16 fl oz) chicken stock (see p.8)
½ level teaspoon salt
Freshly ground black pepper
225 g (8 oz) small okra, trimmed and sliced
450 g (1 lb) boneless chicken breasts, skinned and cut into small cubes
225 g (8 oz) cooked long-grain white rice
Thin slices of fresh green chilli and celery leaves to garnish

Per serving
Calories 329 Protein 30 g
Total fat 11 g (saturated fat 5.5 g)
Carbohydrates 30 g (added sugar 0)
Fibre 5.3 g Sodium 432 mg

1 Put the butter in a large microwave-safe casserole, cover with a piece of kitchen paper and melt on High in the microwave for 30 seconds. Stir in the onion, celery, green pepper and garlic, cover (see p.258) and cook on High for 5 minutes, or until the vegetables have softened, stirring once after 3 minutes.

2 Mix in the flour and cook on High for 1 minute, then add the chopped tomatoes, stock, salt and some pepper. Cover once again and cook on High for 5 minutes, stirring once after 3 minutes.

3 Mix in the okra and cubed chicken. Cover and cook on High for 12 minutes, stirring every 4 minutes, until the chicken is cooked (see p.117), the okra is tender and the sauce is slightly thickened. Remove the casserole or bowl from the microwave and allow to stand for 5 minutes.

4 Meanwhile, heat the rice in the microwave on High for 3 minutes and then divide it between four heated serving bowls. Ladle the gumbo on top, garnish with the slices of fresh green chilli and celery leaves and serve.

RISOTTO WITH CHICKEN AND MUSHROOMS

Serves 4
Preparation time: 20 minutes
Cooking time: 30 minutes

1 medium onion, peeled and finely chopped
1 medium red pepper, de-seeded and finely chopped
30 g (1 oz) butter
225 g (8 oz) risotto rice
425 g (15 oz) canned chicken broth
115 ml (4 fl oz) dry white wine
175 g (6 oz) mushrooms, wiped and sliced
3 strands saffron, or ¼ level teaspoon turmeric
275 g (10 oz) cooked chicken, cut into strips
60 g (2 oz) frozen petit pois
45 g (1½ oz) Parmesan cheese, grated
½ level teaspoon salt
Freshly ground black pepper
Lemon wedges and freshly snipped chives to garnish

Per serving
Calories 517 Protein 31 g
Total fat 18 g (saturated fat 8.3 g)
Carbohydrates 57 g (added sugar 0)
Fibre 4.4 g Sodium 673 mg

A rich chicken and mushroom sauce made with white wine is the heart of this wholesome risotto. Using one of the many kinds of wild mushroom now available in supermarkets gives the dish an even fuller flavour.

1 Put the onion, pepper and butter in a large, microwave-safe casserole or bowl, then cover (see p.258) and cook on High for 5 minutes, mixing once halfway through cooking. Stir in the rice, cover once more and cook on High for 2 minutes.

2 Add the chicken broth, wine, mushrooms and saffron or turmeric. Mix them in, cover and cook on High for 6 minutes, or until the liquid comes to the boil.

3 Stir well, cover again and cook on Medium for 7 minutes, or until the rice has absorbed almost all the liquid, stirring after 4 minutes. Mix in the chicken and peas, cover once more and cook on Medium for 3 minutes, then leave to stand for 5 minutes.

4 Add the Parmesan and season with the salt and some pepper. Garnish with the lemon wedges and chives and serve.

CHICKEN PAUPIETTES

Serves 4
Preparation time: 40 minutes
Cooking time: 25 minutes

275 g (10 oz) frozen broccoli florets
2 tablespoons water
1 medium carrot, peeled
    and grated
2 level teaspoons Dijon mustard
½ level teaspoon salt
Freshly ground black pepper
85 g (3 oz) mature Cheddar
    cheese, grated
Cocktail sticks to secure paupiettes
4 boneless chicken breasts, each
    about 175 g (6 oz), skinned
    and beaten out thin
1 tablespoon dry sherry
¼ level teaspoon paprika
450 g (1 lb) frozen cooked rice
2 tablespoons chopped
    fresh parsley
225 g (8 oz) button mushrooms,
    wiped and sliced
Watercress to garnish

Per serving
Calories 467 Protein 49 g
Total fat 14 g (saturated fat 6.7 g)
Carbohydrates 37 g (added sugar 0)
Fibre 2.6 g Sodium 529 mg

Button mushrooms and mustard bring out the flavour of tender chicken.

Paupiettes, which are a French speciality, are rolls of meat or fish with a savoury stuffing. In this version of the dish, light parcels of chicken filled with a cheesy vegetable mixture are served on a bed of rice.

1 Put the broccoli in a large, microwave-safe dish. Add the water, cover (see p.258) and cook on High for 7 minutes, turning after 3 minutes. Drain well, leave the broccoli to cool slightly, then chop finely and put in a bowl.

2 Stir in the carrot, mustard, salt, some pepper and 60 g (2 oz) of the Cheddar, and divide into four roughly equal portions.

3 Lay the flattened chicken breasts on a wooden board and spoon a portion of the broccoli mixture across the centre of each one. Fold up the sides of the chicken to enclose the filling, carefully securing the parcel at the top with the cocktail sticks.

4 Arrange the chicken parcels in an even formation in a microwave-safe dish. Sprinkle with the sherry and paprika, then cover and cook on High for 5 minutes, or until the chicken is cooked (see p.117), re-positioning and turning the parcels after 2½ minutes.

5 Remove the parcels from the dish with a slotted spoon and put them on a plate, then cover and keep warm. Add the frozen rice, parsley and mushrooms to the dish, cover once more and cook on High for 7 minutes, stirring the mixture well after 5 minutes.

6 Return the parcels to the dish, arranging them on top of the rice. Sprinkle the remaining Cheddar over the top, cover and cook on High for 2 minutes, or until the cheese has melted. Garnish and serve with a green salad.

TURKEY PICADILLO

Picadillo is the Spanish word for minced meat or a meat and vegetable mixture. Spices and capers turn this simple turkey version into a hearty Mexican meal. You can vary this recipe with beef, pork or chicken and any combination of your favourite vegetables.

Serves 4
Preparation time: 15 minutes
Cooking time: 25 minutes

1 large onion, peeled and finely chopped
1 large green pepper, de-seeded and chopped
2 cloves garlic, peeled and crushed (see p.11)
1 tablespoon olive oil
550 g (1¼ lb) minced turkey
1 level teaspoon chilli powder
1 tablespoon red wine vinegar
1 tablespoon capers, drained

1 level teaspoon dried oregano
½ level teaspoon each ground cinnamon and salt
Freshly ground black pepper
400 g (14 oz) canned chopped tomatoes, drained
225 g (8 oz) cooked red kidney beans, rinsed and drained (see p.172)
60 g (2 oz) raisins
225 g (8 oz) cooked rice (see p.9)
60 g (2 oz) Cheddar cheese, grated
Fresh sprigs of coriander or flat-leaf parsley to garnish

Per serving
Calories 437 Protein 41 g
Total fat 12 g (saturated fat 4.9 g)
Carbohydrates 44 g (added sugar 0)
Fibre 7.2 g Sodium 478 mg

Plump raisins and piquant capers add an unexpected twist to this cheese-topped turkey, rice and bean dish.

1 Mix the onion, pepper, garlic and oil in a large microwave-safe casserole, and cook on High for 3 minutes, stirring once halfway through cooking.

2 Push the vegetables to the centre of the dish and arrange the minced turkey around them. Cover (see p.258) and cook on High for 5 minutes, stirring only the vegetables once halfway through cooking.

3 Mix the turkey into the vegetables, then stir in the chilli, red wine vinegar, capers, oregano, cinnamon, salt and some pepper. Cook, uncovered, on Medium for 1 minute.

4 Mix in the tomatoes, kidney beans, raisins and rice and cook, uncovered, on High for 8 minutes, stirring once after 4 minutes. Spoon onto four plates, sprinkle with the Cheddar, cover and leave to stand for 5 minutes. Garnish and serve with salad.

TURKEY RICE BAKE

Serves 4
Preparation time: 20 minutes
Cooking time: 20 minutes

275 g (10 oz) canned condensed
  cream of mushroom soup
115 ml (4 fl oz) semi-skimmed milk
1 level teaspoon dried sage
1 teaspoon lemon juice
Freshly ground black pepper
225 g (8 oz) cooked rice (see p.9)
450 g (1 lb) cooked turkey, cut
  into dice
450 g (1 lb) broccoli florets,
  blanched (see p.10)
8 spring onions, trimmed and
  thickly sliced
15 g (½ oz) butter, melted
60 g (2 oz) fresh white breadcrumbs
30 g (1 oz) Parmesan cheese, grated

Per serving
Calories 471 Protein 49 g
Total fat 16 g (saturated fat 3.3 g)
Carbohydrates 36 g (added sugar 0)
Fibre 1.3 g Sodium 722 mg

A breadcrumb topping makes a crunchy contrast to the creamy mushroom sauce in this turkey and broccoli bake. This recipe is particularly useful for making the most of Christmas leftovers.

1 Mix the mushroom soup, milk, sage, lemon juice and some pepper in a large, microwave-safe casserole. Set aside 150 ml (¼ pint) of the mixture, then stir the rice and turkey into the casserole. Cover (see p.258) and cook on High for 10 minutes, stirring once after 5 minutes.

2 Arrange the broccoli florets and spring onions on top of the turkey, then spoon the reserved mushroom soup mixture over the vegetables. Cover and cook on High for 8 minutes.

3 Mix the melted butter with the breadcrumbs and Parmesan, then sprinkle over the broccoli and onions. Cook on High for 2 minutes, or brown under a hot grill, and serve.

CREAMED TURKEY WITH SPAGHETTINI

Serves 4
Preparation time: 15 minutes
Cooking time: 15 minutes

275 g (10 oz) spaghettini
1 large red pepper, de-seeded
  and finely chopped
1 clove garlic, peeled and crushed
  (see p.11)
1 tablespoon olive oil
450 g (1 lb) turkey fillets, cut
  into strips
450 g (1 lb) courgettes, trimmed and
  cut into matchstick strips
115 g (4 oz) low-fat cream cheese
¼ level teaspoon each dried thyme
  and marjoram
115 ml (4 fl oz) chicken stock
  (see p.8)
Freshly ground black pepper
30 g (1 oz) Parmesan cheese, grated

Per serving
Calories 541 Protein 41 g
Total fat 19 g (saturated fat 8.7 g)
Carbohydrates 55 g (added sugar 0)
Fibre 4.2 g Sodium 242 mg

Strips of red pepper, courgettes, turkey and fine spaghetti are bound with a herb and cream cheese sauce. Using low-fat cream cheese will produce a thick consistency without piling on the calories.

1 Cook the pasta (see p.202). Meanwhile, combine the red pepper, garlic and oil in a large, microwave-safe casserole and cook, covered (see p.258), on High for 3 minutes, until softened.

2 Mix in the turkey, cover and cook on High for 4 minutes, stirring once after 2 minutes. Add the courgettes, then cover and cook on High for 6 minutes, stirring every 2 minutes. Drain and save the cooking juices.

3 Mix the cream cheese with the thyme, marjoram and some pepper in a small bowl, then gradually blend in the stock and cooking juices until smooth. Pour the mixture over the turkey and vegetables and mix well. Cover and cook on High for 1 minute.

4 Drain the pasta and stir it into the turkey mixture. Mix in the Parmesan, cover and heat through on High for 1-2 minutes, and then serve.

DILL AND LEMON SOLE WITH COURGETTES

Serves 4
Preparation time: 20 minutes
Cooking time: 20 minutes

1 medium onion, peeled and
  finely chopped
2 large cloves garlic, peeled
  and crushed (see p.11)
1 tablespoon olive oil
400 g (14 oz) canned tomatoes,
  drained and chopped
150 ml (¼ pint) fish stock
  (see p.8)
¼ level teaspoon dried thyme
½ level teaspoon dried basil
Freshly ground black pepper
225 g (8 oz) each green and yellow
  courgettes, trimmed and sliced
4 double sole or plaice fillets, each
  about 150 g (5 oz)
2 teaspoons lemon juice
¼ level teaspoon salt
1 level tablespoon chopped
  fresh dill
175 g (6 oz) couscous, cooked
  (see p.173)

Per serving
Calories 310 Protein 33 g
Total fat 7.6 g (saturated fat 1.1 g)
Carbohydrates 29 g (added sugar 0)
Fibre 1.2 g Sodium 347 mg

Fillets from any flat fish work
well in this simple, nutritious
recipe. Single fillets can be
used instead of double ones, if
preferred (see p.145).

1 Mix together the onion, garlic
and oil in a large, shallow
microwave-safe dish. Cook on
High for about 4 minutes, until
the onion is transparent, stirring
once after 2 minutes.

2 Stir in the tomatoes, stock,
thyme, basil and some pepper,
then cover the dish (see p.258)
and cook on High for 3 minutes,
stirring once after 2 minutes. Mix
in the courgettes, cover and cook
on High for 4 minutes, stirring
once after 2 minutes.

3 Sprinkle both sides
of the fish fillets with
the lemon juice, salt and
dill. Fold the fillets in half
from head to tail with the
skin inside.

4 Push the vegetables to the
centre of the dish and arrange
the fish around them with the fold
facing outwards.

5 Cover the dish
and cook on
High for 4 minutes,
or until the fish just
flakes with a fork.

6 Gently push the fish
towards the centre of
the dish, then spoon the
couscous around the
outside. Heat through,
uncovered, on High
for 30 seconds.
Cover and leave
to stand for
2-3 minutes,
then serve.

*Yellow and green courgettes add colour
to tender fillets of sole and fluffy
couscous in this low-calorie meal.*

250

STUFFED FILLETS OF PLAICE

Serves 4
Preparation time: 25 minutes
Cooking time: 15 minutes

30 g (1 oz) butter
1 small onion, peeled and
   finely chopped
2 small sticks celery, trimmed
   and finely chopped
1 small red pepper, de-seeded
   and finely chopped
60 g (2 oz) croutons
115 ml (4 fl oz) chicken or fish
   stock (see p.8)
12 single plaice fillets, each
   about 85 g (3 oz), skinned
450 g (1 lb) frozen chopped
   spinach, thawed and drained
Sprigs of fresh dill and lemon
   twists to garnish

Per serving
Calories 373 Protein 51 g
Total fat 13 g (saturated fat 5.1 g)
Carbohydrates 14 g (added sugar 0)
Fibre 5.5 g Sodium 489 mg

Crunchy croutons and vegetables fill tender rings of plaice on a bed of spinach. You can buy the croutons or make them yourself, and you will need some cocktail sticks to secure the fish rings.

1 Put the butter in a large, shallow microwave-safe dish, cover with kitchen paper and melt on High for 30 seconds. Stir in the onion, celery and red pepper, then cover (see p.258) and cook on High for 3 minutes, or until just softened.

2 Put the croutons in a bowl and stir in the stock and the onion mixture. Shape each plaice fillet into a ring by curling the tail round to the head, with the skin inside, and securing with a cocktail stick.

3 Spread the spinach over the bottom of the dish and arrange the plaice rings on top. Fill the centre of each ring with the crouton mixture and press down gently with a spoon. Cover the dish and cook on High for about 7 minutes, until the fish flakes easily with a fork. Allow to stand for 2 minutes, then garnish with the fresh dill and lemon and serve.

SALMON CAKES IN TARTARE SAUCE

Light fish cakes flavoured with dill and lemon juice are served in a zesty tartare sauce.

Serves 4
Preparation time: 30 minutes
Chilling time: 1 hour
Cooking time: 15 minutes

285 ml (1/2 pint) milk
285 ml (1/2 pint) water
130 g (4 1/2 oz) instant
 mashed potato
1 egg, size 3, lightly beaten
2 spring onions, trimmed and
 finely sliced
1 level teaspoon dried dill
1 tablespoon lemon juice
425 g (15 oz) canned red salmon,
 drained, skinned, boned
 and flaked
1/2 level teaspoon salt
Freshly ground black pepper
60 g (2 oz) fresh white breadcrumbs
1 level teaspoon paprika
4 tablespoons mayonnaise
2 tablespoons natural yoghurt
2 level teaspoons capers,
 finely chopped
2 medium gherkins, finely chopped
1 level teaspoon chopped
 fresh parsley
1 tablespoon tarragon vinegar
Lemon wedges and parsley sprigs
 to garnish

Per serving
Calories 478 Protein 31 g
Total fat 23 g (saturated fat 5.2 g)
Carbohydrates 38 g (added sugar 0)
Fibre 5.2 g Sodium 1482 mg

1 Pour the milk and water into a large, microwave-safe bowl and whisk in the instant mashed potato. Cook on High for 6 minutes, stirring after 3 minutes, then leave to cool slightly.

2 Mix the egg, spring onions, dill, lemon juice, salmon, salt and some pepper into the potato. Divide the mixture into eight and shape each portion into a patty.

3 Mix the breadcrumbs with the paprika on a plate. Coat each salmon cake with the mixture, then place them on a large, flat plate and refrigerate for 1 hour.

4 In the meantime, combine the mayonnaise with the yoghurt, capers, gherkins, parsley and vinegar to make the tartare sauce. Cover and refrigerate.

5 Heat a microwave browning dish on High for 8 minutes, or as instructed by the manufacturer. Cook half the salmon cakes on High for 7 minutes, turning after 4 minutes. Move them from the dish onto a heated serving dish and keep hot, then reheat the browning dish and cook the remaining salmon cakes.

6 Pour the tartare sauce over the salmon cakes, or, if you prefer, serve it separately. Garnish with the lemon wedges and parsley and serve with a green salad.

CONCHIGLIE WITH SMOKED TROUT

Aromatic strips of smoked trout combine with young spinach leaves and delicate shell pasta in a creamy garlic sauce.

Serves 4
Preparation time: 10 minutes
Cooking time: 20 minutes

340 g (12 oz) conchiglie, or other
 small pasta shapes
2.3 litres (4 pints) boiling water
1/2 level teaspoon salt
285 ml (1/2 pint) single cream
1 clove garlic, peeled and crushed
 (see p.11)
115 g (4 oz) smoked trout fillets, cut
 into strips
Freshly ground black pepper
175 g (6 oz) baby spinach leaves
1 tablespoon lemon juice
2 teaspoons chopped fresh dill

Per serving
Calories 490 Protein 20 g
Total fat 16 g (saturated fat 8.5 g)
Carbohydrates 70 g (added sugar 0)
Fibre 6.1 g Sodium 373 mg

1 Put the pasta in a large microwave-safe bowl, then add the boiling water and stir in the salt. Cook on High for 12 minutes, stirring every 3 minutes, until the pasta is just done. Remove from the microwave and leave to stand in the water.

2 Pour the cream into a second microwave-safe bowl. Add the garlic, cover (see p.258) and cook on High for 4 minutes, or until heated through.

3 Drain the pasta, then mix with the hot cream. Stir in the trout and season with some pepper. Cover and cook on High for 2 minutes. Stir in the spinach leaves and lemon juice, then cover and cook on High for 1 minute. Sprinkle with the dill and serve.

JACKET POTATOES STUFFED WITH CRAB AND SPINACH

A light garnish of frisée lettuce and sprigs of dill provides a cool contrast to the warm colours of the stuffed potatoes. A combination of mustard, cayenne pepper and paprika adds spice to the dish.

Hollowed jacket potatoes are filled with a rich, tasty mixture of flaked crabmeat, tender leaf spinach and the soft mashed flesh of the potatoes, making a nutritious light meal.

Serves 4
Preparation time: 10 minutes
Cooking time: 30 minutes

4 baking potatoes, each
    about 225 g (8 oz)
175 g (6 oz) fresh, canned, or
    frozen and thawed crabmeat,
    flaked
225 g (8 oz) frozen leaf spinach,
    thawed, drained and
    squeezed dry
2-3 level tablespoons each low-fat
    natural yoghurt and soured cream
3 level teaspoons tarragon mustard
1/8 level teaspoon cayenne pepper
1/4 level teaspoon paprika
2 tablespoons snipped fresh dill or
    finely chopped spring onion tops
Frisée lettuce leaves and sprigs of
    fresh dill to garnish

Per serving
Calories 262 Protein 16 g
Total fat 5.2 g (saturated fat 1.6 g)
Carbohydrates 40 g (added sugar 0)
Fibre 5.3 g Sodium 220 mg

1 Prick the potatoes all over with a fork, then place them in an evenly spaced formation in the microwave. Cook on High for 13 minutes, turning them halfway through cooking. Leave to stand in the microwave for 5 minutes.

2 Remove the potatoes from the microwave and cut each one in half. Scoop out the flesh into a bowl, leaving a 6 mm (1/4 in) shell.

3 Add the crabmeat, spinach, yoghurt, soured cream, mustard and cayenne to the potato flesh and mix lightly but thoroughly. Fill the shells with the mixture and sprinkle with the paprika.

4 Put the potato shells in a microwave-safe serving dish and cook, uncovered, on High for 5 minutes, or until piping hot. Leave to stand for 5 minutes, then sprinkle with the dill or spring onion tops, garnish with the lettuce and sprigs of dill and serve.

253

MARINER'S STEW

Serves 6
Preparation time: 20 minutes
Cooking time: 20 minutes

....

2 tablespoons olive oil
2 cloves garlic, peeled and crushed
    (see p.11)
1 large onion, peeled and chopped
400 g (14 oz) canned
    chopped tomatoes
225 ml (8 fl oz) fish stock (see p.8)
115 ml (4 fl oz) dry white wine
3 tablespoons chopped
    fresh parsley
1/2 level teaspoon salt
Freshly ground black
    pepper
225 g (8 oz) prepared
    squid, sliced
900 g (2 lb) mixed fish fillets,
    skinned (see p.145) and cut
    into wide pieces
12 large mussels, fresh or
    cooked (see p.147)
6 slices french
    bread, toasted
4 tablespoons thick
    garlic mayonnaise

....

Per serving
Calories 448
Protein 38 g
Total fat 22 g
(saturated fat 3.1 g)
Carbohydrates 21 g
(added sugar 0)
Fibre 2.9 g
Sodium 692 mg

....

*A tasty tomato and garlic sauce
complements the milder flavours
of the fish and seafood.*

**Fresh fish, mussels and squid
served with bread and garlic
mayonnaise make a quick,
refreshing summer supper. You
can use a variety of fresh fish
fillets – choose from cod, plaice,
salmon, trout or haddock.**

I Mix together the oil, garlic and
onion in a large, microwave-safe
bowl, and cook on High for
2 minutes. Stir in the tomatoes,
stock, wine, half the parsley, half
the salt and some pepper.
Cover (see p.258) and
cook on High for
6 minutes.

2 Stir in the squid, fish fillets
and mussels, if using fresh
ones. Cover the bowl and cook
on High for 7 minutes, stirring
once after 3 1/2 minutes.

3 Add the cooked mussels,
if using, then cover the bowl
and heat through on High
for 30 seconds.

4 Season the stew with the
remaining salt and then leave
it to stand for 5 minutes.

5 Put a slice of french bread
in each of six soup dishes.
Ladle the fish stew over the bread
and sprinkle with the remaining
parsley. Top with a spoonful of
mayonnaise and serve.

PRAWN AND FETTUCINE MORNAY

Mornay sauce – a white sauce lightly flavoured with Gruyère cheese – is a favourite of French chefs. Here it is blended with prawns, plump green peas and thin pasta ribbons beneath a crispy crust of breadcrumbs.

Serves 4
Preparation time: 20 minutes
Cooking time: 20 minutes

250 g (9 oz) fettucine
1 tablespoon olive oil
1 clove garlic, peeled and crushed
    (see p.11)
115 ml (4 fl oz) milk
115 ml (4 fl oz) single cream
115 g (4 oz) frozen peas
2 level teaspoons Dijon mustard
60 g (2 oz) Gruyère cheese, grated
450 g (1 lb) frozen cooked and
    peeled prawns, thawed
    and drained
60 g (2 oz) fresh white breadcrumbs
1 tablespoon chopped fresh parsley

Per serving
Calories 546 Protein 41 g
Total fat 18 g (saturated fat 7.7 g)
Carbohydrates 59 g (added sugar 0)
Fibre 5.8 g Sodium 2035 mg

1 Cook the fettucine (see p.202). In the meantime, pour the olive oil into a large microwave-safe casserole dish and heat on High for 1 minute. Add the garlic and cook on High for 2 minutes.

2 Pour in the milk and cream and cook on High for 3 minutes, or until the mixture is boiling. Stir in the peas and microwave on High for another 3 minutes. Mix in the mustard, half the Gruyère and the prawns and cook on High for a further 4 minutes, stirring the mixture once after 2 minutes.

3 Drain the fettucine, mix it into the prawn mixture, cover (see p.258) and cook on High for 4 minutes. Combine the remaining Gruyère and the breadcrumbs and sprinkle over the fettucine. Cook, uncovered, on Medium for 2 minutes or, if you prefer, brown under a hot grill. Sprinkle with the chopped parsley and serve.

SPICY PRAWN AND RICE STEW

Tender prawns combine with tomato, okra and rice in this thick, aromatic stew. You can use either canned or fresh okra.

Serves 4
Preparation time: 20 minutes
Cooking time: 40 minutes

1 large onion, peeled and
    finely chopped
1 medium green pepper, de-seeded
    and finely chopped
1 clove garlic, peeled and crushed
    (see p.11)
1 tablespoon olive oil
400 g (14 oz) canned tomatoes
450 ml (16 fl oz) chicken stock
    (see p.8)
225 g (8 oz) small okra, trimmed
    and sliced
1/2 teaspoon hot red pepper sauce
1/4 level teaspoon dried oregano
175 g (6 oz) long-grain white rice
450 g (1 lb) frozen, cooked and
    peeled prawns, thawed
    and drained
2 tablespoons chopped
    fresh parsley
2 teaspoons lemon juice

Per serving
Calories 360 Protein 32 g
Total fat 6.6 g (saturated fat 1 g)
Carbohydrates 47 g (added sugar 0)
Fibre 5.6 g Sodium 1838 mg

1 Mix the onion, green pepper, garlic and oil together in a large microwave-safe casserole. Cover (see p.258) and cook the mixture on High for 5 minutes, stirring once after 2 1/2 minutes.

2 Add the tomatoes, gently breaking them up with a fork, then stir in the stock, okra, red pepper sauce and oregano. Cover and cook on High for 12 minutes, stirring every 4 minutes, until the okra begins to soften.

3 Add the rice and cook on High for 10 minutes, stirring with a fork after 5 minutes. Mix in the prawns, then cover and cook on High for a further 5 minutes, or until the rice is tender and the prawns are heated through.

4 Leave to stand in the microwave for 5 minutes, then stir in the parsley and lemon juice and serve.

NEW ENGLAND CLAM CHOWDER

This thick and flavoursome shellfish soup is a traditional dish in Newfoundland and the New England region of the United States. Its name is said to come from the French word *chaudière*, meaning 'stew pot'.

Serves 4
Preparation time: 20 minutes
Cooking time: 25 minutes

30 g (1 oz) butter
1 medium onion, peeled and finely chopped
450 g (1 lb) carrots, peeled and diced
2 level tablespoons plain flour
570 ml (1 pint) fish stock (see p.8)
225 g (8 oz) potatoes, peeled and diced
340 g (12 oz) canned clams in brine, drained and chopped
425 ml (¾ pint) milk
½ level teaspoon salt
Freshly ground black pepper
Frozen cooked and peeled prawns, thawed and drained, sprigs of dill and paprika to garnish

Per serving
Calories 315 Protein 20 g
Total fat 9.1 g (saturated fat 5.2 g)
Carbohydrates 39 g (added sugar 0)
Fibre 4.5 g Sodium 1411 mg

1 Put the butter in a large microwave-safe bowl, cover with a sheet of kitchen paper and cook on High for 1 minute. Mix in the onion and carrots, cover (see p.258) and cook on High for 5 minutes, stirring after 2 minutes.

2 Mix in the flour and cook on High for 1 minute. Gradually stir in the stock and then add the potatoes. Cover and cook on High for 8-10 minutes, or until the potatoes are cooked, stirring the mixture once after 4 minutes.

3 Add the clams and milk and season with the salt and some pepper. Cover and cook on High for 4 minutes, or until just beginning to bubble. Reduce the power to Medium and cook for a further 4 minutes.

4 Ladle the soup into heated bowls and garnish with the prawns, dill and a sprinkling of paprika. Serve with chunks of crusty bread.

CHEESE AND TUNA JACKET POTATOES

A well-seasoned, creamy mixture of tuna fish and cheese turns wholesome jacket potatoes into a light, tempting meal.

Serves 4
Preparation time: 25 minutes
Cooking time: 20 minutes

4 large baking potatoes, scrubbed and dried
200 g (7 oz) canned tuna in oil, drained
150 g (5 oz) cottage cheese with chives
½ level teaspoon salt
Freshly ground black pepper
1 level tablespoon mayonnaise
60 g (2 oz) mature Cheddar cheese, grated
⅛ level teaspoon paprika

Per serving
Calories 419 Protein 25 g
Total fat 21 g (saturated fat 6.5 g)
Carbohydrates 35 g (added sugar 0)
Fibre 3.2 g Sodium 485 mg

1 Prick the potatoes all over with a fork. Wrap each one in kitchen paper and microwave on High for 15 minutes, or until softened, turning them over after 7 minutes.

2 Slice off the top of each potato and set aside. Scoop the flesh out of the potatoes and put it into a bowl, reserving the shells. Mash the potato with the tuna, cottage cheese, salt, some pepper and the mayonnaise until well mixed.

3 Fill the potato shells with the tuna mixture, then sprinkle with the Cheddar and paprika. Replace the tops, then arrange the potatoes in a shallow microwave-safe dish. Cook on High for 5 minutes, or until the filling has heated through and the cheese has melted.

ITALIAN POTATO OMELETTE

Serves 4
Preparation time: 15 minutes
Cooking time: 20 minutes

1 medium onion, peeled
  and chopped
1 small red pepper, de-seeded
  and chopped
2 tablespoons olive oil
340 g (12 oz) potatoes, peeled
  and grated
150 g (5 oz) courgettes, trimmed
  and grated

60 g (2 oz) frozen sweetcorn
6 eggs, size 2
¼ level teaspoon salt
Freshly ground black pepper
115 g (4 oz) Cheddar
  cheese, grated
Cucumber slices and sprigs of fresh
  parsley to garnish

Per serving
Calories 415 Protein 22 g
Total fat 27 g (saturated fat 10 g)
Carbohydrates 22 g (added sugar 0)
Fibre 2.9 g Sodium 454 mg

This is a quick and easy variant of a frittata, an Italian omelette that is cooked flat rather than folded double as in the French version of the dish. If you want to make enough to serve six, simply add one or two eggs, increase the amounts of the other ingredients in proportion and adjust the final cooking times upwards, checking every 15-20 seconds.

1 Combine the onion and red pepper with the oil in a 25 cm (10 in) microwave-safe flan dish. Cover (see p.258) and cook on High for 4 minutes, or until the onion is transparent, stirring after 2 minutes.

2 Stir in the potatoes, courgettes and sweetcorn, then cover the dish and cook on High for 8 minutes, or until softened, stirring after 4 minutes.

3 Lightly whisk the eggs with the salt, some pepper and half the Cheddar. Pour over the cooked vegetables and mix well, then cook, uncovered, on Medium for 6 minutes. Sprinkle the remaining Cheddar over the top and leave to stand for 2 minutes. Garnish and serve with warm ciabatta or any other Italian bread and a tossed green salad.

Fresh-tasting courgettes blend with grated potatoes, cheese, red pepper and sweetcorn in this attractive and filling flat omelette.

257

Making the most of the microwave

Microwaves have taken the country by storm – it is estimated that more than six out of ten British homes now contain a microwave oven. The speed of cooking by microwave complements these energy-saving recipes to produce one-dish meals in minutes.

THE BASIC PRINCIPLE of all microwaves is the same – rays of energy penetrate food to a depth of around 3.8 cm (1½ in), starting at the outside edges and moving towards the centre. The food cooks quickly but not always evenly. Microwave ovens vary from one manufacturer to another in terms of power output, size and type of insulation, and the way in which the microwaves are controlled or distributed in the oven. These factors can affect cooking times.

The recipes in this chapter were tested in an 800 W output oven, but will work just as well in lower output ovens. Simply add a little extra cooking time, checking after 20-30 seconds whether the food is ready.

Anyone new to microwave cooking should be familiar both with the manufacturer's manual and with the basic cooking techniques.

Suitable microwave cookware

Round and ring-shaped dishes are the most efficient in a microwave oven, exploiting the microwaves' characteristic of penetrating food from the outside in. If you use square or rectangular dishes, the food in the corners will cook faster than that in the centre.

Although a wide range of equipment has been designed for use in microwaves, any containers which are heatproof – other than those made of metal, or with a metal rim or trim – are microwave-safe.

The size and thickness of cooking dishes affects cooking times. Pyrex baking dishes,

---

Safety tips for microwave cooking

- Handle all food containers with a cloth or kitchen gloves.

- Bamboo items must not be used in a microwave oven – they may catch fire.

- Paper, wood and wicker containers should be used in a microwave for no longer than 2 minutes.

- Never put metal dishes or containers with a metal trim or lid into the microwave: they will cause arcing and can damage the oven's magnetron.

---

bowls and casseroles are particularly useful. Ceramic and pottery containers are thicker, and foods in these will take longer to cook.

To cook the one-dish meals in this chapter, you will need a large casserole dish, a large heatproof mixing bowl, a shallow baking dish or a flan dish. For searing and browning meat and chicken a microwave browning dish is useful; its coating absorbs microwave energy, causing it to become very hot, and when food is pressed onto the hot surface it browns.

Useful cooking techniques

Using a microwave to its full potential is easier if you are aware of some of the techniques that make the most of its qualities.

Standing time should occur once food has been removed from the microwave, or the

---

power has been switched off. This allows for the heat to penetrate evenly, or for the cooking to be completed by the internal heat for another 5-10 minutes, depending on the size and quantity of the food. As a result, the heating and cooking times in some microwave recipes are calculated to include a standing time of about 5-10 minutes to allow for this. This is especially true of denser foods where the microwaves cannot penetrate the centre.

Standing time also ensures that foods do not overcook. If at the end of the standing time the food is still not quite done, continue cooking and check every 20-30 seconds.

With conventional cooking, covering a pan with a lid keeps in the steam, speeds up the cooking time and helps to retain moisture. In microwave cooking, the same principle applies. The dish can be covered with a glass or Pyrex lid – without metal trim – or with microwave-safe plastic film. Make a small gap in the film cover, a technique known as 'venting', to allow some steam to escape.

Venting a stew

1 Pull back one edge of the microwave-safe plastic film covering to make an opening, or prick all over with the tip of a sharp knife.

2 Make the venting hole large enough for a wooden spoon to be inserted through it. This enables you to stir the stew without having to remove the plastic film each time.

Preparing the ingredients

The composition of ingredients themselves makes a difference to cooking times and the cooking techniques that are required. Large, bulky pieces of food take longer to cook than smaller or thinner pieces, for example. It is best to start with all the ingredients at room temperature. Food that has come straight out of the fridge takes longer to heat through.

As the microwaves pass through the food in an irregular pattern, it is essential that foods are prepared properly, positioned correctly and turned or stirred during cooking, even when the oven has a turntable. These factors will ensure that the food cooks evenly.

Ingredients should be cut as close to a standard size as possible. If unevenly cut, the smaller pieces will cook before the larger ones, just as higher, more exposed pieces will cook before flatter ones.

Unevenly shaped foods such as chops or chicken or turkey drumsticks need to be carefully positioned in the dish, and then turned during the cooking time so that the thinner parts do not overcook. The illustration below for chops also applies to other similarly shaped ingredients. Sausages also need to be repositioned during cooking, turned end to end.

How to ensure even cooking

Arrange the chops or drumsticks in a circle evenly spaced apart with the thin ends pointing to the centre. Turn the meat over halfway through cooking, with the thin ends still pointing to the centre.

Saving time with the microwave

The microwave offers many opportunities for saving time. Use the microwave to cook mashed potato quickly. In the microwave, the potatoes hold their shape when cooked and do not become waterlogged while boiling.

Mashing potatoes

Cut the peeled potatoes into small, even-sized pieces and put them in a large, heatproof glass bowl. Add 2-3 tablespoons of cold water, then cover with microwave-safe plastic film. Vent by pricking the cover with a skewer. Cook on High for 6-8 minutes, and stir every 2 minutes. Leave to stand for 5 minutes, then mash well.

Blanching and browning of nuts can be done in the microwave much more quickly and economically than in the conventional way. Bring the nuts to the boil in seconds in the microwave, then remove the skins. The microwave can be used to shell any sort of nuts, and also works well for roasting them.

Blanching almonds

Put the almonds in a small bowl and cover with cold water. Cook on High for 1-2 minutes or until the water boils. Drain, then press the nuts between finger and thumb to pop them out of their skins.

Browning nuts

Spread the blanched nuts in an even layer on a heatproof plate and cook on High, stirring frequently, until roasted to the required colour.

Yeast doughs of all types can be risen in the microwave. If you are making your own pizza bases (see p.203), you can save time by using the microwave to rise the dough.

Rising pizza dough

1 Put the kneaded dough in a bowl, then cover with microwave-safe film. Prick in two or three places with the tip of a skewer or knife to prevent it ballooning. Cook on High for 10 seconds, then leave to stand for 5-10 minutes. Repeat several times until the dough has doubled in size.

2 Remove the plastic film and turn the dough out onto a lightly floured surface. Knead for 1-2 minutes, until smooth, then shape as instructed in the recipe.

QUICK AND EASY

'Fast food' has come to mean a snack eaten on the move, but quickly prepared meals can be filling, nutritious and attractive. These recipes set food on the table in under an hour, most in less than 45 minutes – and some even more quickly. They are suitable for serving as a light lunch for unexpected guests, a satisfying high tea or a last-minute supper.

❖

Making the most of limited cooking time 284-5

Red pepper, carrots, long-grain rice and lean, lightly fried meat make an appetising combination in Pork in Peanut Sauce (left) – a full-flavoured and wholesome stir-fry that you can serve steaming at the table, straight from your wok or frying pan (see p.266).

261

MARINATED STEAK AND VEGETABLES

Serves 4
Preparation time: 20 minutes
Marinating time: 2 hours
Cooking time: 30 minutes

225 g (8 oz) new potatoes,
  scrubbed and thinly sliced
1 large red onion, peeled
  and thickly sliced
2 large peppers, 1 red, 1 green,
  de-seeded and cut into quarters
225 g (8 oz) open-cup
  mushrooms, wiped
550 g (1¼ lb) sirloin steak, cut in
  one thick piece
150 ml (¼ pint) bottled Italian
  salad dressing
Sprig of fresh oregano or
  marjoram to garnish

Per serving
Calories 705
Protein 26 g
Total fat 60 g
(saturated fat 17 g)
Carbohydrates 17 g
(added sugar 0)
Fibre 4 g
Sodium 441 mg

Italian salad dressing makes a simple marinade in this easy recipe that is even quicker if you like your steak quite rare. Grill it for 7-10 minutes for medium rare, 10-12 minutes for medium, or 12-14 minutes for well done.

1 Arrange the potatoes, onion, peppers, mushrooms and steak in separate groups in a large, shallow dish. Pour over the salad dressing, cover and marinate for at least 2 hours, or overnight.

2 Preheat the grill to high. Spread the potatoes in a single layer in a large grill pan and cook under the grill for 10 minutes, turning after 5 minutes.

3 Arrange the onion and peppers on top of the potatoes and grill for 5 minutes. Place the grill rack over the vegetables, then arrange the steak and mushrooms on the rack. Cook for as long as required, basting with the marinade and turning occasionally. Move the mushrooms below the rack when cooked.

4 Cut the steak into thick slices and arrange on a heated serving dish with the vegetables. Garnish with the sprig of oregano or marjoram and serve.

Sizzling steak and juicy peppers, mushrooms, onion and new potatoes are cooked in layers under the grill, saving time and space.

CORNED BEEF AND BROCCOLI HASH

Serves 4
Preparation time: 10 minutes
Cooking time: 30 minutes

4 tablespoons olive oil
1 large onion, peeled and chopped
450 g (1 lb) cooked potatoes, diced
225 g (8 oz) cooked broccoli florets
60 g (2 oz) frozen peas, thawed
340 g (12 oz) corned beef, diced
Freshly ground black pepper
1 tablespoon Worcestershire sauce
Tomato slices and chopped spring
    onion to garnish

Per serving
Calories 418 Protein 28 g
Total fat 24 g (saturated fat 6.2 g)
Carbohydrates 24 g (added sugar 0)
Fibre 3.1 g Sodium 824 mg

Corned beef has a soft, yielding texture and a mild beefy flavour that pairs well with broccoli florets and peas in this tasty fried potato cake.

1 Heat the oil in a large, nonstick frying pan and soften the onion in it over a moderate heat, stirring.

2 Stir in the potatoes and cook for 10 minutes, or until they begin to brown, then mix in the broccoli, peas, corned beef, some pepper and the Worcestershire sauce. Cover the pan and cook for 10 minutes, stirring occasionally.

3 Flatten the mixture with a palette knife or fish slice and cook over a high heat for about 5 minutes, or until the base is crisp and browned. Lift the hash onto a serving plate and cut into wedges. Garnish with the tomato and spring onion, then serve.

QUICK BEEF CHILLI

Serves 4
Preparation time: 10 minutes
Cooking time: 20 minutes

450 g (1 lb) lean minced beef
1 medium onion, peeled and
    finely chopped
1 clove garlic, peeled and crushed
1 medium green pepper, de-seeded
    and chopped
1 level tablespoon chilli seasoning
400 g (14 oz) canned
    chopped tomatoes
425 g (15 oz) canned red kidney
    beans, rinsed and drained
¼ level teaspoon crushed
    chilli flakes
225 g (8 oz) cooked long-grain
    rice (see p.9)
Freshly ground black pepper
4 tablespoons soured cream
Chopped fresh coriander and
    cayenne pepper to garnish

Per serving
Calories 431 Protein 32 g
Total fat 16 g (saturated fat 7.3 g)
Carbohydrates 41 g (added sugar 0)
Fibre 9.5 g Sodium 149 mg

Chilli con carne loses none of its punch in this recipe despite the short time it takes to prepare. Chilli seasoning and crushed chilli provide an instant fiery taste; kidney beans and tomatoes are added to the saucepan straight from the can.

1 Cook the minced beef in a large saucepan over a moderate heat for 5 minutes. Stir in the onion, garlic and green pepper and continue cooking for 5 minutes, stirring occasionally.

2 Mix in the chilli seasoning, tomatoes, kidney beans, chilli flakes, rice and some pepper and bring to the boil, stirring. Reduce the heat, cover and simmer for 10 minutes, or until the rice and beans are heated through and the vegetables are tender.

3 Spoon the chilli into heated serving bowls and top each one with a swirl of soured cream. Garnish with the coriander and a small pinch of cayenne pepper and serve with warmed granary rolls and a green salad.

ITALIAN OMELETTE WITH HAM

Serves 4
Preparation time: 15 minutes
Cooking time: 20 minutes

....

30 g (1 oz) butter
1 medium onion, peeled
   and chopped
1 large red pepper, de-seeded
   and finely diced
1 level teaspoon each dried basil
   and dried oregano
225 g (8 oz) frozen chopped
   spinach, thawed, drained and
   squeezed dry
175 g (6 oz) cooked ham,
   finely diced
5 eggs, size 1
45 g (1½ oz) Parmesan
   cheese, grated
115 ml (4 fl oz) milk
½ level teaspoon salt
⅛ level teaspoon cayenne pepper
225 g (8 oz) cooked long-grain
   white rice (see p.9)

....

Per serving
Calories 383 Protein 26 g
Total fat 21 g (saturated fat 9.9 g)
Carbohydrates 23 g (added sugar 0)
Fibre 3.3 g Sodium 1160 mg

....

Cayenne pepper adds a hint
of spice to this wholesome
flat omelette made with ham,
spinach and long-grain rice. It
is a good way to use up leftover
cooked meat, and is equally
tasty if made with cold turkey.

1 Melt the butter in a large frying
pan and sauté the onion and
red pepper over a moderate heat
until softened. Stir in the basil and
oregano and cook for 1 minute.
Add the spinach and ham and
cook for 2-3 minutes until the
mixture is heated through.

2 Whisk the eggs with 30 g (1 oz)
of the Parmesan, the milk, salt
and cayenne. Pour the mixture
into the frying pan, stir in the rice
and cook for 5 minutes more. In
the meantime, preheat the grill.

3 Sprinkle the remaining
Parmesan over the top of the
omelette, then place the frying pan
under the grill for 3-5 minutes,
or until the omelette is firm and
golden brown. Cut into wedges
and serve with a tossed salad.

SMOKED PORK AND CABBAGE

Serves 4
Preparation time: 15 minutes
Cooking time: 30 minutes

....

2 teaspoons olive oil
1 large onion, peeled and chopped
675 g (1½ lb) shredded
   green cabbage
1 large Granny Smith apple, cored,
   peeled and chopped
4 tablespoons water
225 g (8 oz) tagliatelle
225 g (8 oz) cooked baby
   beetroot, sliced
450 g (1 lb) German smoked pork
   sausage, casing removed,
   thickly sliced
150 ml (¼ pint) soured cream
Freshly ground black pepper
2 tablespoons finely chopped
   fresh dill

....

Per serving
Calories 801 Protein 24 g
Total fat 48 g (saturated fat 19 g)
Carbohydrates 72 g (added sugar 0)
Fibre 11 g Sodium 944 mg

....

The unusual combination of
chunky smoked sausage, baby
beetroot and apple gives this
casserole an authentic German
flavour. Try using sauerkraut
(pickled shredded cabbage)
in place of fresh cabbage.

1 Heat the oil in a large flameproof
casserole for 1 minute and soften
the onion in it over a moderate
heat, stirring frequently. Mix in
the cabbage, apple and water, then
cover and cook for 10 minutes,
stirring occasionally. In the
meantime, put the tagliatelle
on to cook (see p.202).

2 Add the beetroot and sausage
to the casserole, cover and
cook for 8 minutes, or until heated
through. Stir in the soured cream
and season with some pepper.

3 Drain the tagliatelle and mix
into the casserole. Heat through
for 2 minutes, stirring, then
sprinkle with the dill and serve.

GAMMON IN A BUN

Serves 4
Preparation time: 10 minutes
Cooking time: 25 minutes

450 g (1 lb) smoked gammon in one piece, trimmed of fat and cut into thin strips (see pp.79-80)
225 ml (8 fl oz) bottled barbecue sauce
4 medium spring onions, trimmed and finely chopped
225 g (8 oz) frozen green beans, thawed, drained and chopped into short lengths
225 g (8 oz) frozen sweetcorn kernels, thawed and drained
4 large poppyseed rolls or sesame seed buns, split and toasted
Radishes and carrot strips to garnish

Per serving
Calories 423 Protein 39 g
Total fat 10 g (saturated fat 3.3 g)
Carbohydrates 46 g (added sugar 0)
Fibre 5.9 g Sodium 1852 mg

Lightly fried gammon and zesty vegetables served on a roll or bun makes a delightful main-meal sandwich or a tempting substitute for hamburgers at a barbecue.

1 Heat a large nonstick frying pan for 1 minute. Add the gammon strips and stir-fry them over a moderate heat for 8-10 minutes, or until they are just tender.

2 Mix in the barbecue sauce, onions, beans and sweetcorn. Cover the pan, reduce the heat to low and simmer for 15 minutes, stirring occasionally.

3 Put the bottom half of each roll or bun on a heated serving plate, spoon over the barbecue mixture, then cover with the top of the rolls. Garnish with the radishes and carrot strips and serve.

Tasty barbecue sauce brings out the flavours of a colourful mixture of lean smoked gammon strips, juicy kernels of corn, green beans and tangy spring onions.

265

PORK IN PEANUT SAUCE

Serves 4
Preparation time: 30 minutes
Cooking time: 20 minutes

3 tablespoons crunchy peanut butter
4 tablespoons hot water
1 tablespoon white wine vinegar
1 tablespoon soy sauce
1 level tablespoon chopped
    fresh coriander
1 level teaspoon peeled and
    chopped fresh root ginger
2 tablespoons groundnut oil
450 g (1 lb) pork tenderloin, cut
    into strips
1 large red pepper, de-seeded
    and cut into strips
2 medium carrots, peeled and cut
    into thin strips
1 medium onion, peeled and cut
    into eighths
1 clove garlic, peeled and crushed
225 g (8 oz) cooked long-grain
    white rice
2 spring onions, trimmed and
    thinly sliced

Per serving
Calories 625 Protein 24 g
Total fat 48 g (saturated fat 15 g)
Carbohydrates 26 g (added sugar 0)
Fibre 3.3 g Sodium 376 mg

Lean strips of pork combine with crunchy vegetables and long-grain rice in an exuberant peanut butter, ginger, coriander and soy sauce mixture.

1 Whisk together the peanut butter, hot water, vinegar, soy sauce, coriander and ginger. Heat the oil in a wok or large frying pan and stir-fry the pork in it over a high heat for 10 minutes, or until the pork is no longer pink. Remove the pork strips with a slotted spoon and set them aside.

2 Add the red pepper, carrots and onion to the wok or frying pan and stir-fry for 5 minutes. Return the pork to the wok or pan and stir in the garlic and rice.

3 Add the peanut mixture and bring to the boil, stirring. Cook over a moderate heat for 5 minutes, or until the rice is heated through. Garnish with the spring onions and serve with warm mini pitta breads.

PAN-FRIED BEEF AND VEGETABLES

Serves 4
Preparation time: 20 minutes
Cooking time: 25 minutes

2 tablespoons olive oil
1 large onion, peeled and chopped
1 level teaspoon dried rosemary
1/4 level teaspoon caraway
    seeds (optional)
1/2 level teaspoon salt
2 tablespoons chopped
    fresh parsley
340 g (12 oz) cooked mixed
    vegetables (such as broccoli,
    cabbage, carrots or cauliflower),
    roughly chopped
225 g (8 oz) cooked roast beef,
    roughly chopped
340 g (12 oz) cooked potatoes,
    finely diced
1 tablespoon milk

Per serving
Calories 270 Protein 19 g
Total fat 14 g (saturated fat 3.9 g)
Carbohydrates 19 g (added sugar 0)
Fibre 2.9 g Sodium 286 mg

Leftover roast beef is lightly fried with aromatic rosemary and mixed vegetables to make a crisp patty. This versatile recipe tastes just as good with cooked ham or lamb in place of the beef, and you can use any type of vegetables that are to hand.

1 Heat the oil in a large nonstick frying pan. Add the onion, rosemary and, if using, caraway seeds, then cook over a moderate heat, stirring thoroughly, until the onions are softened.

2 Mix in the salt, parsley, mixed vegetables, beef, potatoes and milk, then flatten the mixture with a fish slice. Reduce the heat to low and cook for 15 minutes.

3 Carefully turn the mixture over (see p.284) and flatten again. Cook over a moderate heat for 5 minutes, or until the base of the patty is crisp and browned.

4 Loosen the mixture round the edge, then cover the pan with a large, warmed serving plate. Protecting your hands with oven gloves, turn pan and plate over together to turn out the patty. Cut into wedges and serve.

RICE MEATBALLS WITH SAUERKRAUT

Serves 4
Preparation time: 20 minutes
Cooking time: 20 minutes

- 225 g (8 oz) minced pork
- 225 g (8 oz) uncooked minced turkey
- 115 g (4 oz) easy-cook long-grain white rice
- 1 egg, size 3, beaten
- 30 g (1 oz) fresh white breadcrumbs
- 2 tablespoons milk
- ½ level teaspoon dried marjoram
- ½ level teaspoon salt
- Freshly ground black pepper
- 450 g (1 lb) sauerkraut, rinsed and drained
- 800 g (1¾ lb) canned tomatoes
- 340 g (12 oz) yellow or green courgettes, trimmed and thickly sliced
- Sprigs of fresh parsley to garnish

Per serving
Calories 356 Protein 34 g
Total fat 7.9 g (saturated fat 2.7 g)
Carbohydrates 40 g (added sugar 0)
Fibre 2.7 g Sodium 1142 mg

Soft pork, turkey and rice meatballs are cooked with piquant sauerkraut (pickled cabbage). Pork minced at home is a healthier option than supermarket-bought mince, which often contains added fat.

1 Mix together the minced pork, minced turkey, rice, beaten egg, breadcrumbs, milk, marjoram, salt and some pepper in a large bowl. Divide the mixture into 24 portions of roughly equal size and shape each one into a ball with wetted hands. Put the balls on a flat plate, then cover and chill in the refrigerator.

2 Put the sauerkraut and tomatoes in a large, wide saucepan and bring to the boil. Reduce the heat and add the meatballs and courgettes, then cover the pan and simmer for 15-20 minutes, or until the meatballs are cooked through. Garnish and serve with french bread.

The less common yellow variety of courgette will add colour to this wholesome casserole of meatballs in a thick and tasty tomato sauce.

QUICK BEEF AND MACARONI WITH THREE CHEESES

Serves 4
Preparation time: 10 minutes
Cooking time: 25 minutes

....

175 g (6 oz) fast-cooking macaroni
1 tablespoon olive oil
1 medium onion, peeled and
    finely chopped
450 g (1 lb) lean minced beef
450 g (1 lb) ready-prepared
    Napoletana tomato sauce
340 g (12 oz) fine green beans,
    trimmed and cut into short lengths
115 g (4 oz) ricotta cheese
115 g (4 oz) mozzarella
    cheese, grated
3 tablespoons grated
    Parmesan cheese
Tomato slices and finely shredded
    basil leaves to garnish

....

Per serving
Calories 664 Protein 45 g
Total fat 34 g (saturated fat 14 g)
Carbohydrates 47 g (added sugar 0)
Fibre 7.2 g Sodium 761 mg

....

Ricotta, mozzarella and Parmesan cheeses make a luxurious topping for a healthy blend of lean minced beef, green beans and onion in a thick tomato sauce. Serve piping hot immediately after finishing cooking, when the cheeses have just melted.

1 Cook the macaroni (see p.202), then drain and rinse it in a colander under cold water. Heat the oil in a large frying pan and soften the onion in it.

2 Add the minced beef and brown it for 5 minutes, stirring frequently. Drain off the fat, then mix in the Napoletana sauce and bring to a simmer. Stir in the green beans, reduce the heat to low and simmer for 10 minutes.

3 Add the macaroni, then put spoonfuls of ricotta evenly on top, and sprinkle the mozzarella between them. Cover the saucepan and cook over a high heat for about 10 minutes, or until the mozzarella melts. Sprinkle with the Parmesan, garnish with the tomato and fresh basil and serve immediately with a green salad.

SALAMI AND POTATO SAUTÉ

Serves 4
Preparation time: 15 minutes
Cooking time: 30 minutes

....

450 g (1 lb) salami in one piece, cut
    into small cubes
1 medium onion, peeled
    and chopped
2 large peppers, 1 green, 1 red,
    de-seeded and cut into
    small squares
550 g (1¼ lb) new potatoes,
    scrubbed and cut into small cubes
225 ml (8 fl oz) chicken stock
    (see p.8)
Freshly ground black pepper
1 tablespoon chopped
    fresh oregano

....

Per serving
Calories 669 Protein 25 g
Total fat 52 g (saturated fat 20 g)
Carbohydrates 28 g (added sugar 0)
Fibre 3.7 g Sodium 2100 mg

....

Sweet peppers and new potatoes combine with salami pieces in a tasty chicken stock. You can use smoked pork sausage or cooked ham in place of the salami, if you prefer.

1 Heat a large, nonstick frying pan over a moderate heat for 1 minute, then cook the salami in it for 10 minutes, stirring. Drain off all but 1 tablespoon of the fat.

2 Add the onion, peppers and potatoes to the pan and fry for 5 minutes. Stir in the stock and reduce the heat to low.

3 Cover and cook for 15 minutes, or until the potatoes are just soft, adding a little extra stock or water if necessary to prevent the potatoes from sticking. Sprinkle with the oregano and serve with a green salad and crusty bread.

CHICKEN WITH RICE AND WALNUTS

Serves 6
Preparation time: 20 minutes
Cooking time: 30 minutes

6 boneless chicken breasts, each about 175 g (6 oz), skinned
½ level teaspoon salt
Coarsely ground black pepper
2 tablespoons olive oil
570 ml (1 pint) chicken stock (see p.8)
225 g (8 oz) easy-cook mixed long-grain and wild rice
1 tablespoon finely grated orange rind
340 g (12 oz) curly kale, washed and torn into small pieces, or baby spinach leaves
60 g (2 oz) walnuts, roughly chopped
Orange segments and a thin strip of orange peel to garnish

This wholesome chicken risotto can be made with any sort of rice, but the wild rice mixture gives it a varied texture and enhances its nutty flavour.

1 Season the chicken breasts with the salt and pepper. Heat the olive oil in a large frying pan and cook the chicken breasts in it over a moderate heat for 5 minutes. Drain them on kitchen paper.

Per serving
Calories 465 Protein 44 g
Total fat 18 g
(saturated fat 3.2 g)
Carbohydrates 34 g
(added sugar 0)
Fibre 3.3 g
Sodium 315 mg

2 Discard any oil remaining in the frying pan, then pour in the stock. Add the rice and the grated orange rind, return the chicken to the pan and bring to the boil. Reduce the heat, cover and simmer for 20 minutes, or until the rice is almost tender and the chicken is just cooked (see p.117).

3 Take the chicken out of the pan and put it on a large heated serving plate. Cover and keep hot. Stir the kale or spinach and the walnuts into the rice, then cover and cook for 5 minutes, or until the vegetables are tender and all the stock has been absorbed.

4 Spoon the rice and greens around the chicken pieces, garnish with the orange segments and peel and serve at once.

Grated orange rind brings a lively citrus tang to this succulent blend of chicken, rice and greens cooked in a hearty stock, while walnuts add a tasty crunch.

STIR-FRIED RICE WITH TURKEY

Tender turkey strips steeped in a soy sauce and sherry marinade combine with rice, mangetout and spring onions in this exuberant stir-fry. Asparagus and broccoli are both good alternatives to the mangetout.

Serves 4
Preparation time: 30 minutes
Cooking time: 15 minutes

2 level teaspoons cornflour
4 tablespoons soy sauce
1 tablespoon dry sherry
450 g (1 lb) turkey fillets, cut into wide strips
2 tablespoons groundnut oil
400 g (14 oz) cooked rice
Finely grated rind and strained juice of 1 large orange
1 clove garlic, peeled and crushed
6 spring onions, trimmed and cut diagonally into short lengths
225 g (8 oz) mangetout, trimmed
175 g (6 oz) fresh baby sweetcorn, halved
1/4 level teaspoon dried chilli flakes, or 1/8 level teaspoon cayenne pepper
Chopped spring onions and finely shredded orange rind to garnish

Per serving
Calories 360 Protein 31 g
Total fat 10 g (saturated fat 1 g)
Carbohydrates 38 g (added sugar 0)
Fibre 3.2 g Sodium 917 mg

1 Mix together the cornflour, soy sauce and sherry in a bowl and toss the turkey strips in the mixture. Heat 1 tablespoon of the oil in a wok or large frying pan, and stir-fry the rice in it for 2-3 minutes, until pale golden in colour. Transfer the rice to a plate and leave to one side.

2 Heat the remaining oil in the wok or frying pan and stir-fry the orange rind and garlic for 1 minute. Mix in the spring onion lengths, mangetout and sweetcorn and stir-fry for 3-4 minutes, then remove and set aside on a plate.

3 Put the turkey and its marinade in the wok or pan and stir-fry over a moderate heat for 5 minutes, or until the turkey is cooked through. Stir in the orange juice and chilli flakes or cayenne, scraping up any brown bits from the base of the pan.

4 Return the vegetables to the wok or pan, stir in the rice and heat through for 2 minutes. Garnish with the spring onions and orange rind and serve.

SPICY CHICKEN TORTILLAS

Shredded chicken and black beans in a dressing of chilli, sweet pepper and cumin make a spicy filling for flour tortillas topped with soured cream, tomatoes and sliced avocado.

Serves 4
Preparation time: 20 minutes
Cooking time: 30 minutes

1 tablespoon olive oil
2 large peppers, 1 red, 1 green, de-seeded and chopped
2 green chillies, de-seeded and finely chopped
1 clove garlic, peeled and crushed
1/4 level teaspoon cumin seeds
2 cooked chicken breasts, each about 225 g (8 oz), skinned, boned and shredded
225 g (8 oz) mature Cheddar cheese, grated
425 g (15 oz) canned black beans, rinsed and drained
8 flour tortillas
285 ml (1/2 pint) soured cream
150 ml (1/4 pint) natural yoghurt
1/8 level teaspoon salt
Freshly ground black pepper
1 ripe avocado, halved, stoned, peeled and sliced
2 large tomatoes, sliced

Per serving
Calories 1096 Protein 68 g
Total fat 51 g (saturated fat 25 g)
Carbohydrates 96 g (added sugar 0)
Fibre 12 g Sodium 905 mg

1 Preheat the oven to 190°C (375°F, gas mark 5). Heat the oil in a frying pan for 1 minute, then cook the peppers, chillies and garlic in it over a moderate heat for 3-4 minutes. Sprinkle in the cumin seeds and cook for 1 minute. Remove from the heat.

2 Mix in the chicken, Cheddar and black beans. Spoon one-eighth of the mixture into the centre of each tortilla and then roll them up to enclose the filling. Arrange the tortillas seam-side down in a large, shallow, greased ovenproof dish.

3 Mix the soured cream with the yoghurt, season with the salt and some pepper and pour over the tortillas. Cover the dish with foil and bake in the centre of the oven for 15 minutes. Uncover and cook for a further 10 minutes, or until heated through. Arrange the sliced avocado and tomatoes on top of the tortillas and serve.

CHICKEN SCHNITZELS

Chicken breasts coated in breadcrumbs and topped with Italian cheeses are baked on a bed of thin ribbon pasta in this variant of the traditional German and Austrian dish. *Schnitzel* in German refers to a thin cutlet or escalope of any meat, usually coated in egg and breadcrumbs and fried in butter, but in restaurants the term is generally applied only to veal.

Serves 4
Preparation time: 20 minutes
Cooking time: 30 minutes

175 g (6 oz) spaghettini, spaghetti or other thin ribbon pasta
175 g (6 oz) each green and yellow courgettes, quartered lengthways and thickly sliced
4 boneless chicken breasts, each about 175 g (6 oz), skinned and beaten out thin
1 egg, size 3, beaten
60 g (2 oz) fine fresh white breadcrumbs
3 tablespoons olive oil
425 g (15 oz) bottled tomato sauce
60 g (2 oz) Parmesan cheese, grated
175 g (6 oz) mozzarella cheese, grated
Sprigs of fresh marjoram to garnish

Per serving
Calories 817   Protein 68 g
Total fat 38 g (saturated fat 14 g)
Carbohydrates 54 g (added sugar 0)
Fibre 5.1 g   Sodium 1055 mg

1 Preheat the oven to 200°C (400°F, gas mark 6). Cook the pasta (see p.202), adding the courgettes for the last 3 minutes of the cooking time.

2 In the meantime, dip the chicken breasts in the beaten egg, then coat both sides with the breadcrumbs, shaking off any excess. Heat 2 tablespoons of the oil in a large frying pan and brown the chicken breasts in it for 1 minute on each side.

3 Pour the pasta and courgettes into a colander, rinse under cold water and drain. Turn into a greased, shallow 33 cm x 23 cm (13 in x 9 in) baking dish and mix with the remaining oil.

4 Arrange the chicken on top of the pasta and cover with the sauce. Sprinkle with Parmesan, then bake in the centre of the oven for 15 minutes. Remove from the oven and sprinkle with the mozzarella. Bake for a further 5 minutes, until the mozzarella has melted, then garnish with the sprigs of marjoram and serve.

A topping of tomato sauce and melted mozzarella and Parmesan cheeses brings a touch of luxury to crisp chicken schnitzel. Chunks of green and yellow courgette add vitamins and colour to a bed of al dente spaghetti.

271

CHICKEN AND BLACK BEAN STIR-FRY

Serves 4
Preparation time: 20 minutes
Cooking time: 20 minutes

250 g (9 oz) Chinese fine
   egg noodles
3 tablespoons groundnut oil
450 g (1 lb) boneless chicken
   breasts, skinned and cut into
   thin strips
6-8 spring onions, trimmed and cut
   into fine strips
225 g (8 oz) courgettes, trimmed
   and cut into fine strips
2 medium peppers, 1 red and
   1 yellow, de-seeded and
   cut into strips
225 g (8 oz) canned water
   chestnuts, drained and sliced
250 g (9 oz) fresh beansprouts,
   rinsed and drained
4 tablespoons black bean sauce
Spring onion brushes (see p.311)
   to garnish, optional

Per serving
Calories 533 Protein 36 g
Total fat 19 g (saturated fat 1.4 g)
Carbohydrates 57 g (added sugar 0)
Fibre 9.3 g Sodium 206 mg

**Black bean sauce, which is
available in supermarkets and
oriental food shops, gives this
Chinese-style stir-fry its rich
and distinctive flavour.**

1 Cook the egg noodles
(see p.202) and drain. Heat
2 tablespoons of the oil in a wok
or large frying pan and stir-fry the
noodles in it over a high heat until
crispy. Drain on kitchen paper.

2 Put the chicken strips in the
wok or pan and stir-fry for
5 minutes, or until the chicken is
cooked (see p.117). Remove with
a slotted spoon and set aside.

*Chicken breasts and noodles,
courgettes and peppers,
water chestnuts and bean
sprouts, all stir-fried
with black bean sauce,
present an inviting
savoury dish with
a real relish of
the Orient.*

3 Add the remaining oil to the
wok or pan and heat for
1 minute. Mix in the spring
onions, courgettes and peppers
and stir-fry for 3 minutes.

4 Add the water chestnuts and
beansprouts and stir-fry for a
further 3 minutes.

5 Return the chicken to the
wok or pan and mix in the
black bean sauce. Stir-fry for
2-3 minutes, or until the chicken
is heated through and the sauce is
bubbling. Add the noodles and
toss gently with the chicken and
the sauce. Garnish with the spring
onion brushes, if using,
and serve.

CHICKEN POTATO CAKES

Serves 4
Preparation time: 15 minutes
Cooking time: 10 minutes

450 g (1 lb) cold mashed potato
340 g (12 oz) cooked chicken,
    finely chopped
250 g (9 oz) frozen mixed
    vegetables, thawed
    and drained
3 spring onions, trimmed
    and finely chopped
1 egg, size 1, lightly beaten
½ level teaspoon salt
Freshly ground black pepper
½ level teaspoon dried rosemary
85 g (3 oz) fine fresh white
    breadcrumbs
3 tablespoons olive oil
1 lemon, cut into thin wedges
    to garnish

Per serving
Calories 484 Protein 33 g
Total fat 23 g (saturated fat 5 g)
Carbohydrates 38 g (added sugar 0)
Fibre 2.7 g Sodium 610 mg

Chicken and mashed potato
leftovers in your fridge can be
turned into toothsome potato
cakes. This economical light
meal originated in Ireland.

1 Mix together the potato, chicken,
mixed vegetables, spring onions,
egg, salt, some pepper and the
rosemary. Divide the mixture into
12 portions and shape each piece
into a small cake or patty about
10 cm (4 in) across. Coat each cake
well with breadcrumbs.

2 Heat the oil in a large frying
pan for 1 minute, then fry the
cakes, in two batches, for about
2 minutes on each side or until
golden brown, adding a little
more oil if necessary. Keep the
first batch warm while frying the
rest. Garnish and serve hot with
a green salad or coleslaw.

LAST-MINUTE CHICKEN

Serves 4
Preparation time: 25 minutes
Cooking time: 30 minutes

115 g (4 oz) pepperoni sausage,
    thinly sliced
1 medium onion, peeled
    and finely chopped
1 clove garlic, peeled
    and crushed
340 g (12 oz) green cabbage,
    shredded
225 g (8 oz) frozen sliced carrots,
    thawed and drained
425 g (15 oz) canned black or
    red kidney beans, rinsed
    and drained
425 g (15 oz) canned chickpeas,
    rinsed and drained
400 g (14 oz) canned tomatoes
Freshly ground black pepper
4 roasted chicken breasts, skinned
    and boned

Per serving
Calories 650 Protein 64 g
Total fat 22 g (saturated fat 7.6 g)
Carbohydrates 51 g (added sugar 0)
Fibre 18 g Sodium 718 mg

Italian pepperoni sausage adds a
spicy flavour to this wholesome
fried dish of vegetables and
chickpeas, with ready-cooked
chicken the final ingredient.

1 Heat a large nonstick frying pan
over moderate heat for 1 minute,
then add the pepperoni sausage
and cook for 5 minutes, stirring.
Remove with a slotted spoon and
drain on kitchen paper.

2 Add the onion to the pan
and cook for 3 minutes, stirring
occasionally. Stir in the garlic and
cook for 3 minutes or until the
onion is softened, then stir in the
cabbage, carrots, beans, chickpeas,
tomatoes and some black pepper
and bring to the boil.

3 Place the chicken breasts on
top of the bean and vegetable
mixture. Cover and cook over a
low heat for 15 minutes, or until
the chicken is heated through.
Stir in the pepperoni and heat
for a further 3 minutes. Serve with
fresh granary bread.

SAUSAGE AND BEAN STEW

Serves 4
Preparation time: 10 minutes
Cooking time: 30 minutes

2 tablespoons olive oil
450 g (1 lb) Mediterranean-style
   pork sausages
1 onion, peeled and chopped
2 cloves garlic, peeled and crushed
1 level tablespoon plain flour
150 ml (¼ pint) chicken stock
   (see p.8)
400 g (14 oz) canned chopped
   tomatoes with basil
340 g (12 oz) frozen broad beans
1 level teaspoon dried marjoram
½ level teaspoon salt
Freshly ground black pepper
400 g (14 oz) canned flageolet
   beans, rinsed and drained
225 g (8 oz) frozen or canned
   sweetcorn kernels

Per serving
Calories 714 Protein 26 g
Total fat 45 g (saturated fat 15 g)
Carbohydrates 56 g
(added sugar 0)
Fibre 14 g
Sodium 1322 mg

This substantial, tasty sausage stew containing broad and flageolet beans, sweetcorn and tomatoes is reminiscent of succotash, a native American dish of sweetcorn and beans.

1 Heat the oil in a large frying pan and brown the sausages in it for 8 minutes, turning occasionally. Move them to a plate covered with kitchen paper to drain.

2 Pour off any excess oil from the pan, then add the onion and soften it over a moderate heat for 3 minutes. Then mix in the garlic and fry for 1 minute.

3 Stir in the flour, pour in the stock and tomatoes and bring to the boil, stirring. Add the broad beans, marjoram, salt and some pepper and bring back to the boil. Cover and simmer for 10 minutes.

4 Cut the sausages into thick pieces and stir them into the pan with the flageolet beans and sweetcorn. Bring to the boil, cover and simmer for 5 minutes more or until the sausages are cooked through completely, then serve.

Mediterranean-style pork sausages stewed with beans and sweetcorn combine the flavours of the American West and southern Europe.

FISH AND POTATO BAKE

A layer of crisp breadcrumbs tops fillets of fresh white fish baked on a bed of spinach and potatoes. It is a quick and satisfying meal that can also be made with any leftover cold potatoes in the refrigerator.

Serves 4
Preparation time: 20 minutes
Cooking time: 25 minutes

30 g (1 oz) butter
1 medium onion, peeled and
   finely chopped
1 clove garlic, peeled and crushed
800 g (1¾ lb) canned new
   potatoes, drained and quartered
1 level teaspoon oregano
450 g (1 lb) frozen leaf spinach,
   thawed, well drained and
   roughly chopped
¼ level teaspoon freshly
   grated nutmeg
½ level teaspoon salt
Freshly ground black pepper
8 large whiting or plaice fillets, each
   about 85 g (3 oz), skinned
1 tablespoon lemon juice
45 g (1½ oz) fresh white or
   brown breadcrumbs
2 tablespoons olive oil

1 Preheat the oven to 220°C (425°F, gas mark 7). Heat the butter in a frying pan and soften the onion in it over a moderate heat. Then add the garlic and cook for 1 minute more.

2 Stir in the potatoes and the oregano, then spread the mixture in the bottom of a shallow baking dish. Cover with the spinach and season with the nutmeg, salt and some pepper.

3 Fold the fish fillets in half, then arrange them on top of the spinach. Pour the lemon juice over the fish and season with some pepper. Sprinkle with the breadcrumbs and drizzle the oil over the top.

4 Cover the dish with foil and bake in the centre of the oven for 15 minutes. Uncover and cook for a further 6-8 minutes, until the fish is opaque and flakes easily with a fork and the breadcrumbs are golden. Serve straight from the oven.

Per serving
Calories 411 Protein 43 g
Total fat 13 g (saturated fat 1.7 g)
Carbohydrates 34 g (added sugar 0)
Fibre 7.9 g Sodium 943 mg

PASTA IN PRAWN AND PEANUT SAUCE

Crunchy peanuts add bite to the softness of the prawns and pasta and accentuate the taste of the sweet but spicy sauce in this exuberant dish.

Serves 4
Preparation time: 20 minutes
Cooking time: 10 minutes

4 tablespoons tomato ketchup
3 tablespoons light soy sauce
2 tablespoons fish stock (see p.8)
   or water
¼ teaspoon hot red pepper sauce
340 g (12 oz) spaghettini, vermicelli
   or capellini pasta
1 tablespoon olive oil
1 large red pepper, de-seeded
   and cut into small squares
225 g (8 oz) carrots, peeled and
   coarsely grated
2 cloves garlic, peeled and crushed
450 g (1 lb) frozen, cooked and
   peeled prawns
4 spring onions, trimmed and
   finely chopped
60 g (2 oz) unsalted dry
   roasted peanuts
2 tablespoons flaked or
   shredded coconut

1 Whisk together the ketchup, soy sauce, fish stock or water and the red pepper sauce in a small bowl, and then set aside.

2 Cook the pasta (see p.202), then put it in a colander and rinse under cold water. Drain well and set aside. Meanwhile, heat the oil in a large frying pan and cook the red pepper, carrots and garlic in it for 5 minutes, or until soft. Then stir in the prawns and cook for a further 3 minutes.

3 Add the ketchup mixture and the spring onions, peanuts and cooked pasta. Cook, stirring frequently, for another 3 minutes. Sprinkle with the flaked or shredded coconut and serve.

Per serving
Calories 613 Protein 42 g
Total fat 17 g (saturated fat 4.8 g)
Carbohydrates 77 g (added sugar 0)
Fibre 8.7 g Sodium 1978 mg

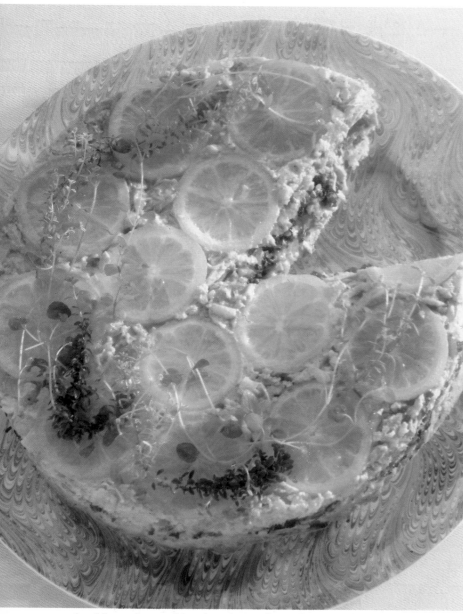

A soft but substantial cornbread crust forms the base of this decorative summer flan, in which a succulent strip of spinach is sandwiched between layers of filling tuna and egg.

TUNA AND SPINACH FLAN

The unusual cornbread base for this creamy, nutritious tart is made with cornmeal, which is available in health food shops and larger supermarkets.

Serves 6
Preparation time: 20 minutes
Cooking time: 30 minutes

1 large lemon, scrubbed and thinly sliced
3 eggs, size 3
225 ml (8 fl oz) milk
400 g (14 oz) canned tuna in oil, drained and flaked
80 g (3 oz) country stuffing mix
1 small onion, peeled and finely chopped
275 g (10 oz) canned cream of chicken, mushroom or celery soup
450 g (1 lb) frozen chopped spinach, thawed and well drained
115 g (4 oz) cornmeal
60 g (2 oz) plain flour
1/2 level teaspoon salt
1 1/2 level teaspoons baking powder
85 g (3 oz) butter, melted
Mustard and cress and sprigs of thyme to garnish

Per serving
Calories 476 Protein 30 g
Total fat 27 g (saturated fat 11 g)
Carbohydrates 30 g (added sugar 0)
Fibre 4 g Sodium 951 mg

1 Preheat the oven to 200°C (400°F, gas mark 6). Grease an expanding 25 cm (10 in) cake tin and line the bottom with a round of nonstick baking paper. Arrange the lemon slices on the paper.

2 Whisk two of the eggs with 115 ml (4 fl oz) of the milk in a large bowl, then stir in the tuna, stuffing mix, onion and soup.

3 Carefully spoon half the tuna mixture over the lemon slices in the cake tin, then cover with the chopped spinach. Spread the spinach evenly to the sides of the tin, then spoon the remaining tuna mixture over the top.

4 Sift the cornmeal, flour, salt and baking powder into a bowl and make a well in the centre. Add the remaining egg and milk, pour in the melted butter and beat together thoroughly. Spread the batter evenly over the tuna mixture and bake in the centre of the oven for 30 minutes, or until golden brown and firm in the centre.

5 Loosen the edges of the flan with a palette knife. Put a large, flat plate on top of the tin and carefully turn both the tin and plate upside-down. Lift off the tin and remove the baking paper, then garnish the flan with the mustard and cress and sprigs of thyme. Serve with a green salad.

CRAB AND PASTA BAKE

Lobster or prawn soup provides a rich and creamy seafood sauce coating crabmeat, macaroni and vegetables in this instant gratin.

Serves 4
Preparation time: 15 minutes
Cooking time: 30 minutes

225 g (8 oz) elbow macaroni
340 g (12 oz) frozen mixed vegetables
Freshly ground black pepper
175 g (6 oz) fresh or canned white crabmeat, drained
400 g (14 oz) canned lobster or prawn soup
285 ml (½ pint) single cream
60 g (2 oz) Gruyère or Parmesan cheese, grated
Slices of lime to garnish

Per serving
Calories 547 Protein 26 g
Total fat 26 g (saturated fat 12 g)
Carbohydrates 56 g (added sugar 0)
Fibre 2.8 g Sodium 845 mg

1 Preheat the oven to 200°C (400°F, gas mark 6). Cook the macaroni (see p.202), adding the frozen mixed vegetables for the last 2 minutes of cooking. Drain and rinse well.

2 Pour the macaroni and mixed vegetables into a large, greased gratin or pie dish. Season with some pepper, then spoon the crabmeat on top.

3 Pour the soup and cream into a saucepan and bring them to the boil over a moderate heat, stirring. Reduce the heat to low and simmer for 1 minute, then pour the sauce over the crabmeat. Sprinkle the Gruyère or Parmesan evenly over the top.

4 Bake the crab, pasta and vegetables in the centre of the oven for 20-30 minutes, or until bubbling hot and brown. Garnish with the lime slices and serve.

SLICED POTATOES WITH COD AND CHEESE SOUFFLÉ TOPPING

The tender chunks of cod or haddock in this delicate and impressive spur-of-the-moment supper can be replaced by any firm white fish.

Serves 4
Preparation time: 30 minutes
Cooking time: 25 minutes

675 g (1½ lb) potatoes, peeled and sliced
340 g (12 oz) frozen mixed vegetables, cooked and drained
1 level teaspoon salt
2 level tablespoons plain flour
2 level teaspoons soft light brown sugar
Freshly ground black pepper
675 g (1½ lb) cod or haddock, skinned, boned (see p.145) and cut into cubes
30 g (1 oz) butter, melted
6 level tablespoons mayonnaise
175 g (6 oz) Cheddar cheese, finely grated
1 level teaspoon mustard powder
⅛ level teaspoon cayenne pepper
2 eggs, size 1, separated

Per serving
Calories 799 Protein 51 g
Total fat 49 g (saturated fat 18 g)
Carbohydrates 40 g (added sugar 1.2 g)
Fibre 2.9 g Sodium 993 mg

1 Preheat the oven to 200°C (400°F, gas mark 6). Boil the potato slices for 10-15 minutes, until just cooked. Drain the potatoes and arrange them in the bottom of a shallow ovenproof dish. Scatter the cooked vegetables over the potatoes.

2 Put the salt, flour, sugar and pepper in a polythene bag and shake to combine. Add the fish and shake gently until the cubes are evenly coated. Take them out of the bag, shaking off any excess flour, and arrange them on top of the vegetables. Pour the melted butter over the fish and bake in the centre of the oven for 10 minutes.

3 In the meantime, mix together the mayonnaise, cheese, mustard, cayenne pepper and egg yolks. In a separate bowl, whisk the egg whites until they hold soft peaks, then gently fold them into the mayonnaise mixture.

4 Take the dish out of the oven and evenly cover the fish with the soufflé mixture. Return the dish to the oven and bake for 15 minutes, or until the top is puffed up and golden brown. Serve with a crisp green salad.

CREAMY SALMON AND FETTUCINE

Serves 4
Preparation time: 10 minutes
Cooking time: 15 minutes

225 g (8 oz) fettucine or tagliatelle
2 tablespoons olive oil
4 spring onions, trimmed and
    finely chopped
340 g (12 oz) fresh or frozen
    asparagus spears, trimmed
    and cut into short pieces
400 g (14 oz) canned red salmon,
    drained, skinned, boned
    and flaked
1 tablespoon capers, finely chopped
Freshly ground black pepper
285 ml (½ pint) double cream
1 lemon, cut into 4 wedges

Per serving
Calories 752 Protein 31 g
Total fat 51 g (saturated fat 25 g)
Carbohydrates 46 g (added sugar 0)
Fibre 4.3 g Sodium 600 mg

This quick but luxurious pasta meal makes an elegant dinner for unexpected guests. Use canned asparagus if you can't find fresh and add it to the sauce at the end of cooking.

1 Cook the pasta (see p.202). In the meantime, heat the oil in a large frying pan and cook the spring onions and asparagus in it over a moderate heat, covered, for 5 minutes.

2 Stir the salmon, capers, pepper and cream into the asparagus and onion mixture and heat through for 5 minutes, stirring.

Capers add sharpness to a thick, creamy sauce containing delicate asparagus and soft, flaky salmon.

3 Drain the pasta and toss it gently in the asparagus and salmon mixture to coat it evenly. Turn into a heated serving dish and serve with the lemon wedges and a green salad.

SPINACH AND EGG MUFFINS

Toasted muffins form a healthy wholemeal base for a buttery spinach and egg mixture flavoured with cream of mushroom soup and topped with tangy Gruyère cheese.

Serves 4
Preparation time: 15 minutes
Cooking time: 30 minutes

4 wholemeal muffins, split
  and toasted
60 g (2 oz) unsalted butter
1 small onion, peeled and
  finely chopped
225 g (8 oz) frozen chopped
  spinach, thawed, drained and
  squeezed dry
6 eggs, size 2
¼ level teaspoon salt
Freshly ground black pepper
300 g (11 oz) canned condensed
  cream of mushroom soup
115 ml (4 fl oz) milk
2 level teaspoons Dijon mustard
60 g (2 oz) Gruyère cheese, grated
1 level tablespoon chopped
  fresh parsley

Per serving
Calories 576 Protein 26 g
Total fat 35 g (saturated fat 14 g)
Carbohydrates 41 g (added sugar 0)
Fibre 4 g Sodium 934 mg

1 Preheat the oven to 200°C (400°F, gas mark 6). Arrange the muffins, cut-side up, in a single layer in a shallow ovenproof dish.

2 Melt half the butter in a frying pan and cook the onion in it over a moderate heat until soft. Add the spinach and cook, stirring, for 2-3 minutes. Spoon the mixture over the muffins.

3 Whisk together the eggs, salt and some pepper in a small bowl. Melt the remaining butter in the frying pan and cook the egg mixture in it, stirring, for 2-3 minutes or until softly set. Spoon over the top of the spinach.

4 Pour the soup and milk into the frying pan and slowly bring them to the boil, stirring. Remove from the heat and stir in the mustard and all but 2 tablespoons of the Gruyère. Pour this mixture over the eggs, then sprinkle with the remaining cheese.

5 Cook in the centre of the oven for 10-15 minutes or under a moderately hot grill for about 10 minutes, then sprinkle the parsley on and serve at once.

GRANARY TOAST WITH MUSHROOM SOUFFLÉ TOPPING

Dijon mustard adds a mild aromatic flavour to this simple version of the classic French soufflé. It is a versatile recipe that can be adapted to taste – try adding canned tuna to the soufflé mix, or using peppers in place of mushrooms.

Serves 4
Preparation time: 10 minutes
Cooking time: 5 minutes

60 g (2 oz) butter
225 g (8 oz) mushrooms, wiped
  and sliced
30 g (1 oz) plain flour
200 ml (7 fl oz) milk
2 level teaspoons Dijon mustard
Freshly ground black pepper
2 eggs, size 3, separated
1 large, round granary loaf, cut
  into 4 thick horizontal slices, top
  and bottom crusts discarded
90 g (3¼ oz) watercress, trimmed
  and washed

Per serving
Calories 450 Protein 17 g
Total fat 20 g (saturated fat 9.7 g)
Carbohydrates 55 g (added sugar 0)
Fibre 8.7 g Sodium 776 mg

1 Melt the butter in a saucepan and fry the mushrooms in it for 2 minutes. Mix in the flour, then add the milk and bring to the boil over a moderate heat, stirring until thickened. Add the mustard and season with some pepper, then simmer for 1 minute, stirring.

2 Take the saucepan off the heat and stir in the egg yolks. Whisk the egg whites until they form soft peaks, then gently fold them into the sauce with a metal spoon.

3 Put the bread slices on a baking tray and toast one side only under a moderately hot grill. Turn the bread over and cover the untoasted sides with the mushroom soufflé mixture.

4 Place under the grill for 1-2 minutes, or until puffed and browned. (If you need to, turn the baking tray round halfway through cooking to make sure the slices brown evenly.) Transfer the toast to four plates and serve with a garnish of watercress.

BAKED EGGS WITH RE-FRIED BEANS

Hot taco sauce and thick re-fried beans give an exciting Mexican flavour to this unusual egg, spinach and spring onion bake. Canned re-fried beans are stocked in most supermarkets.

Serves 4
Preparation time: 15 minutes
Cooking time: 20 minutes

450 g (1 lb) canned re-fried beans
3 tablespoons water
225 g (8 oz) frozen chopped
    spinach, thawed, drained and
    squeezed dry
5 large spring onions, trimmed and
    finely chopped
6 tablespoons soured cream
115 g (4 oz) Cheddar
    cheese, grated
4 eggs, size 2
6 tablespoons tomato and chilli
    taco sauce
Freshly ground black pepper

Per serving
Calories 376 Protein 23 g
Total fat 26 g (saturated fat 11 g)
Carbohydrates 14 g (added sugar 0)
Fibre 2 g Sodium 657 mg

1 Preheat the oven to 200°C (400°F, gas mark 6). Mix the beans and water and spread over the bottom of a shallow ovenproof dish. Combine the spinach with all but 2 tablespoons of the spring onions and spread the mixture over the beans. Top with the soured cream and Cheddar.

2 Make four hollows in the mixture and carefully break a whole egg into each one. Spoon the taco sauce around the eggs, then place in the centre of the oven and bake for 20 minutes, or until the eggs are set.

3 Sprinkle with some pepper and the remaining spring onions and then serve either with warm flour tortillas, guacamole and soured cream or simply with warm crusty bread.

CHEESE AND HAM SOUFFLÉ

Whisked eggs combine with cooked ham and Cheddar cheese in this delicate, airy dish. To ensure that your soufflé rises as it should, take care not to overbeat the egg whites.

Serves 4
Preparation time: 25 minutes
Cooking time: 25 minutes

15 g (½ oz) Parmesan
    cheese, grated
60 g (2 oz) butter
1 small onion, peeled and
    finely chopped
60 g (2 oz) plain flour
285 ml (½ pint) milk
4 eggs, size 2, separated
175 g (6 oz) cooked ham, chopped
115 g (4 oz) Cheddar
    cheese, grated
Freshly ground black pepper

Per serving
Calories 477 Protein 28 g
Total fat 33 g (saturated fat 18 g)
Carbohydrates 17 g (added sugar 0)
Fibre 0.8 g Sodium 1017 mg

1 Preheat the oven to 200°C (400°F, gas mark 6). Coat the inside of a well-greased, shallow ovenproof dish with the Parmesan.

2 Melt the butter in a saucepan and cook the onion in it until softened but not browned. Stir in the flour and cook for 1 minute, then gradually add the milk and bring to the boil, stirring until very thick. Cook gently for 1 minute, then take the pan off the heat and leave the sauce to cool slightly.

3 Beat in the egg yolks and then add the chopped ham, three-quarters of the grated Cheddar and some black pepper.

4 Whisk the egg whites until they form soft peaks. Fold a quarter of the egg whites into the sauce using a metal spoon, then gently fold in the remainder. Pour the mixture into the prepared dish and sprinkle with the remaining Cheddar. Bake in the centre of the oven for 25 minutes, or until well risen and lightly set. Serve immediately with warm french bread and a tossed green salad.

TORTELLINI PRIMAVERA

Serves 4
Preparation time: 15 minutes
Cooking time: 10 minutes

450 g (1 lb) fresh cheese-filled
   tortellini
225 g (8 oz) carrots, peeled
   and sliced
225 g (8 oz) broccoli florets
30 g (1 oz) fresh basil leaves
115 g (4 oz) pine nuts or
   blanched almonds
60 g (2 oz) Parmesan cheese, grated
1 large clove garlic, peeled
   and crushed
Freshly ground black pepper
150 ml (¼ pint) olive oil
225 g (8 oz) cherry tomatoes,
   halved
Sprigs of fresh basil to garnish

Per serving
Calories 853 Protein 22 g
Total fat 67 g (saturated fat 12 g)
Carbohydrates 40 g (added sugar 0)
Fibre 4.4 g Sodium 413 mg

Carrots and broccoli florets give a light, fresh taste to a dish of cheese-stuffed pasta pillows, which takes its name from the Italian word for springtime, *primavera*. Cooking the pasta in stock rather than water will give the meal even more flavour.

1 Boil the tortellini for 10 minutes, adding the carrots to the water after 5 minutes and the broccoli for the last 2 minutes of cooking.

2 Meanwhile, blend the basil leaves, pine nuts or almonds, Parmesan, garlic and some pepper in a food processor until smooth. Add the oil in a fine stream (while the motor is running) and continue to blend until thickened.

3 Drain the tortellini, carrots and broccoli and then transfer them to a large, heated serving bowl. Mix in the tomatoes, pour over the basil sauce and toss well. Garnish with the sprigs of basil and serve hot or cold.

A homemade pesto sauce – fresh basil leaves blended with pine nuts or almonds, Parmesan, garlic, olive oil and a touch of pepper – coats a combination of pasta, juicy cherry tomatoes and spring vegetables.

BROCCOLI AND HAM QUICHE

Serves 4
Preparation time: 30 minutes
Cooking time: 25 minutes

300 g (11 oz) shortcrust pastry
    (see p.9)
2 tablespoons olive oil
1 medium onion, peeled, halved
    and thinly sliced
225 g (8 oz) broccoli, trimmed and
    cut into small florets, stalks peeled
    and thinly sliced
3 eggs, size 2
200 ml (7 fl oz) milk
1/4 level teaspoon salt
Freshly ground black pepper
1/4 level teaspoon freshly grated or
    ground nutmeg
100 g (3 1/2 oz) sliced ham, cut into
    thin strips
100 g (3 1/2 oz) red Leicester cheese,
    coarsely grated

Per serving
Calories 599 Protein 25 g
Total fat 41 g (saturated fat 11 g)
Carbohydrates 35 g (added sugar 0)
Fibre 2.1 g Sodium 943 mg

To turn this simple quiche into a vegetarian dish, replace the ham with 100 g (3 1/2 oz) chopped walnuts, hazelnuts or cashews, or a mixture of all three.

1 Preheat the oven to 220°C (425°F, gas mark 7). On a floured surface, roll out the pastry to make a round large enough to line a 23 cm (9 in) flan dish. Fit the pastry into the dish and trim the edge. Refrigerate the case while you make the filling.

2 Heat the oil in a large frying pan. Add the onion and broccoli to it and stir over a moderate heat for 5 minutes, or until just tender. Remove the pan from the heat and leave the vegetables to cool slightly.

3 In a large bowl, whisk the eggs and milk together with the salt, some pepper and the nutmeg. Stir in the ham, red Leicester and the onion and broccoli mixture.

4 Put the chilled pastry case on a baking tray, then pour in the broccoli and ham filling. Bake in the centre of the oven for 25-30 minutes, or until risen, browned and set. Serve hot or cold with salad and french bread.

Mild and flaky red Leicester cheese makes a colourful and tasty topping for this savoury broccoli and ham quiche, which is delicious either hot or cold.

ASPARAGUS QUICHE

Serves 4
Preparation time: 20 minutes
Cooking time: 30 minutes

300 g (11 oz) shortcrust pastry
  (see p.9)
250 g (9 oz) ricotta cheese
225 ml (8 fl oz) soured cream
3 eggs, size 2
60 g (2 oz) Parmesan
  cheese, grated
4 spring onions, trimmed
  and finely chopped
2 level teaspoons Dijon mustard
½ level teaspoon salt
⅛ level teaspoon cayenne pepper
225 g (8 oz) fine asparagus spears,
  cooked, or frozen asparagus,
  thawed and drained

Per serving
Calories 690 Protein 25 g
Total fat 49 g (saturated fat 24 g)
Carbohydrates 39 g (added sugar 0)
Fibre 2.6 g Sodium 863 mg

Cayenne pepper, Dijon mustard and spring onions add spice to the subtle flavours of the asparagus and soft ricotta cheese. Use a small round onion if spring onions are not available.

1 Preheat the oven to 220°C (425°F, gas mark 7). Roll out the pastry to a round large enough to line a 25 cm (10 in) flan dish. Fit into the dish, pressing well into the flutes and trim the edge. Stand the lined dish on a baking tray.

2 Put the ricotta, soured cream, eggs, half the Parmesan, the spring onions, mustard, salt and cayenne into a food processor. Blend for around 10 seconds or until smooth.

3 Arrange the asparagus spears in the bottom of the lined flan dish. Pour over the ricotta mixture and sprinkle with the rest of the Parmesan. Bake for 30 minutes or until set. Serve with salad and crusty farmhouse bread.

TUNA FILO FLAN

Serves 4
Preparation time: 20 minutes
Cooking time: 20 minutes

3 tablespoons olive oil
8 sheets filo pastry, each
  30 cm x 19 cm (12 in x 7½ in)
30 g (1 oz) butter or margarine
30 g (1 oz) plain flour
250 ml (9 fl oz) milk
150 g (5 oz) mayonnaise
200 g (7 oz) canned tuna in oil,
  drained and flaked
2 eggs, size 1, hard-boiled, shelled
  and chopped
1 tablespoon capers
¼ level teaspoon salt
Freshly ground black pepper
30 g (1 oz) Parmesan or Gruyère
  cheese, grated

Per serving
Calories 884 Protein 27 g
Total fat 63 g (saturated fat 15 g)
Carbohydrates 56 g (added sugar 0)
Fibre 2.4 g Sodium 721 mg

Leaf-thin filo pastry, which originally came from Greece but is now available in many shops, makes an unusual crust for this egg and tuna flan.

1 Preheat the oven to 190°C (375°F, gas mark 5). Brush a 23 cm (9 in) flan dish with a little of the oil, then brush both sides of the pastry sheets with the rest. Arrange the sheets of pastry in the flan dish, partly overlapping so that the points are evenly spaced round the rim. Gently ease the pastry into the shape of the dish with the pastry brush. Bake the pastry case for 10 minutes, or until lightly browned.

2 Meanwhile, melt the butter or margarine in a saucepan. Stir in the flour and cook for 1 minute, then gradually add the milk and bring to the boil, stirring continuously until the sauce thickens. Reduce the heat and simmer for 1 minute.

3 Remove the sauce from the heat and stir in the mayonnaise, tuna, eggs, capers, salt and some pepper. Pour the mixture into the pastry case and sprinkle with the Parmesan or grated Gruyère.

4 Return to the oven and bake for 20 minutes, or until golden brown. (If the pastry edges brown too quickly, cover them with foil.) Serve with wholemeal rolls.

283

Making the most of limited cooking time

Versatile, basic ingredients are vital for producing wholesome meals at a moment's notice. A stock of essentials quickly to hand in the kitchen takes you halfway to solving the problem, while time-saving tricks can further ease the path to instant one-dish meals.

WHEN YOU ARE short of time, there are steps you can take to make sure that cooking a meal is quick and easy.

Read through the recipe two or three times to familiarise yourself with it, checking that you have all the ingredients listed. Get all the ingredients out before you start cooking, and keep them close to hand. Make sure that you take anything which needs thawing out of the freezer well ahead of time.

When time allows, prepare any of the ingredients ahead of cooking, or ask other people to help with the preparation. Ready-prepared salads and vegetables, although expensive, can be helpful here. Sharp knives makes chopping easier, quicker and safer.

Make use of any time-saving kitchen equipment, such as a food processor, blender, electric whisk or microwave (see pp.258-9).

Keeping a good stock

Rustling up a tasty and healthy meal in no more than 30 minutes is easy if you have, for example, pasta and canned tomatoes in the cupboard, salad and Parmesan cheese in the refrigerator and ready-to-bake bread in the freezer. The quantity and variety of foodstuffs in your kitchen is determined by personal preference, budget and storage space, but where possible a minimum stock of dried, canned and frozen foods should be kept (see panel).

Replenish stocks when necessary and make a note of 'use-by' dates, so that older products are used before the newer replacements.

Staple foods to keep in store

For the store cupboard
Salt and pepper; dried herbs; oils, vinegars and mustards, especially English, Dijon and whole-grain (see pp.12-13); dried spices (see pp.14-15); potatoes and onions; garlic; bottled dressings, tomato sauce, soy sauce and Tabasco sauce; stock cubes; plain flour; sugar; honey; long-life milk; pickles; relishes; capers; olives; dried pasta (see p.202); long-grain rice; canned foods, including soups, beans, chickpeas, sweetcorn, tomatoes, fish (tuna, salmon and crab) and meats, (ham and corned beef).

For the refrigerator
Milk, cream, yoghurt and soured cream; eggs; butter and margarine; cheeses, such as Cheddar, Parmesan, mozzarella and Gruyère; salad ingredients, such as lettuce, tomatoes, cucumber, peppers and spring onions (see p.232); fresh herbs (see p.12); carrots, broccoli, mangetout, fine green beans and asparagus; vacuum-packed meats and sausages, such as ham, salami, bratwurst and pepperoni; leftover food, such as cooked vegetables, meat, poultry, rice and pasta (these must be used within 48 hours of cooking).

For the freezer
Frozen broccoli, spinach, sweetcorn kernels, carrots, green beans and peas (see p.340); cooked peeled prawns; frozen cooked rice; pastry cases; bread; pizza bases (see p.203); pancakes (see p.9); sauces.

Quick and easy cooking techniques

Lining a flan tin, turning over a hash (a pan-sized potato cake) and whisking egg whites for soufflés and soufflé toppings are not difficult tasks, but they can slow down the preparation of a dish. If they are carried out incorrectly, particularly in the case of whisking egg whites, they may even ruin the dish. The steps below illustrate the best way to tackle each task.

Hashes need to be fried on both sides, which involves turning the hash over halfway through cooking, without breaking it. The task becomes much easier if you use a flat dinner plate or flat saucepan lid of about the same dimensions as the hash, and follow the simple steps below. Protect your hands with thick oven gloves.

Turning a hash

1 To turn a hash over, put a flat plate or flat saucepan lid on top of the frying pan. Hold the plate and pan firmly together with gloved hands and turn completely over so that the hash falls out of the pan onto the plate.

2 Slide the hash off the plate and back into the frying pan, using a fish slice or palette knife. Cook until the underneath is brown and crusty, then serve.

Pastry-making can be a trial, especially when the pastry crumbles or sticks. Ready-prepared, frozen or chilled pastry or filo pastry sheets make good alternatives. To make a flan case, using shortcrust pastry, you can roll the pastry around the rolling pin to transfer it into a flan tin, as shown right.

Ready-made filo pastry can be just as easily used to make a flan case, although the delicate tissue-thin sheets must be handled with care. Frozen filo must be thawed out completely before using. Different makes come in different sizes so you may need to cut the sheets into smaller squares to fit the dish.

Lining a dish with filo pastry

1 Use sheets of filo that are large enough to cover the bottom of the flan dish and stand 2.5-5 cm (1-2 in) above the side. Trim off any excess pastry, then brush each sheet and the bottom and side of the flan dish with a little olive oil or melted butter.

2 Place one of the sheets in the dish so that the corners stand upright at the edge. Ease the pastry into the dish with a soft pastry brush. Place the second sheet at a 45° angle to the first. Repeat with the remaining sheets, placing each one at a 45° angle to the one before, until the dish is completely lined.

Lining with shortcrust pastry

1 Roll out the pastry on a lightly floured surface to a neat round 5 cm (2 in) larger than the flan tin.

2 Carefully roll the pastry around the rolling pin. Lift it over the edge of the flan tin, then slowly unroll and lower the pastry into the tin.

3 Gently press the pastry into position over the bottom and up the sides of the tin, pressing it well into the flutes.

4 Roll the rolling pin across the top of the tin to trim off any excess pastry.

Soufflés become light and fluffy when the air bubbles in the whisked egg whites expand under heat and raise the mixture. The egg whites should be whisked until stiff enough to hold soft peaks, but not dry.

Whisking egg whites

1 Crack the egg in half down the centre by tapping it firmly on the edge of a bowl. Carefully separate the two halves and let the white fall into the bowl. Gently tip the yolk from one half of the shell to the other until it is completely separated from the white. Save the yolk and pour the white into a grease-free bowl.

2 Whisk the whites vigorously with a balloon whisk or electric beater until they become stiff but are not dry.

3 Don't overwhisk; overwhisked egg whites are dry and difficult to fold in. They will break down when mixed into the sauce or purée and cause the air to be expelled.

285

HOLIDAY MEALS

Holidays are a time for relaxation, but this can be in short supply for the cook. Here self-catering is made easy, with one-pot wonders to prepare with the simplest facilities at a holiday home, in a caravan or on a boat.

❖

Making the most of holiday cooking 318-19

A sweet, tangy cider and honey marinade keeps meat, fruit and vegetable chunks juicy and tender in Pork, Apple and Squash Brochettes (left) – an ideal recipe for summer entertaining or for a campsite barbecue (see p.293).

MARINATED BEEF KEBABS

In this simple but tasty kebab dish, a dry marinade of thyme, garlic and marjoram brings out the flavour of the beef. You will need four long metal skewers.

Serves 4
Preparation time: 20 minutes
Chilling time: 2 hours
Cooking time: 20 minutes

½ level teaspoon salt
1 level teaspoon each dried thyme and dried marjoram
Freshly ground black pepper
2 cloves garlic, peeled and crushed (see p.11)

450 g (1 lb) rump steak, trimmed of fat, cut into 12 cubes (see p.79)
550 g (1¼ lb) small new potatoes, scrubbed
2 small red peppers, de-seeded and each cut into 12 pieces
2 medium courgettes, trimmed and each cut into 6 thick slices
1 tablespoon olive oil
Long sprigs of fresh thyme

Per serving
Calories 315 Protein 31 g
Total fat 9.8 g (saturated fat 3.1 g)
Carbohydrates 28 g (added sugar 0)
Fibre 3.2 g Sodium 314 mg

1 Combine half the salt with the thyme, marjoram, some pepper and the garlic in a bowl. Toss the steak in the mixture until well coated, then cover and refrigerate for 2 hours.

2 Meanwhile, boil the potatoes until just cooked, then drain and rinse under cold water. Mix with the peppers, courgettes, the remaining salt and the oil.

3 Thread the marinated steak onto four long metal skewers, with the courgettes, potatoes and red peppers threaded in between.

4 Set the barbecue rack about 15 cm (6 in) above white-hot coals. Twist the sprigs of thyme around each kebab and cook for 10 minutes, turning, until the meat is browned on the outside but juicy inside. Serve with warm, crusty bread and a green salad.

Fresh thyme sprigs give a warm, earthy scent to beef and vegetable chunks.

STEAK TERIYAKI

The Japanese word *teriyaki* means 'shining grill', and in this barbecue recipe, cubes of steak marinated in soy sauce, rice wine, garlic and light brown sugar are grilled with kebabs of potato and red onion. You will need eight metal skewers in all.

Serves 4
Preparation time: 10 minutes
Marinating time: 2 hours
Cooking time: 20 minutes

3 tablespoons Japanese soy sauce
2 tablespoons rice wine or
   dry sherry
2 cloves garlic, peeled and crushed
   (see p.11)
1 tablespoon soft, light brown sugar
675 g (1½ lb) sirloin steak, trimmed
   of fat, cut into 24 cubes
450 g (1lb) new potatoes, halved
2 small red onions, peeled and
   each cut into 6 wedges
2 tablespoons sesame oil

Per serving
Calories 447 Protein 43 g
Total fat 20 g (saturated fat 5.6 g)
Carbohydrates 26 g (added sugar 4 g)
Fibre 2 g Sodium 849 mg

1 Mix the soy sauce, rice wine or sherry, garlic and sugar in a bowl, then toss the steak in the mixture. Cover and refrigerate for 2 hours.

2 Meanwhile, boil the potatoes for 5 minutes, then add the onions and cook for 3 minutes. Drain well, then gently toss the vegetables in the sesame oil.

3 Thread the meat onto four metal skewers, and the onions and potatoes alternately onto four other metal skewers.

4 Set the barbecue rack about 15 cm (6 in) above white-hot coals. Cook the kebabs on the rack, turning frequently, for 10 minutes for rare meat, or for 12 minutes for medium. Cook the vegetables for 8 minutes, turning and basting them with any of the remaining marinade. Serve the kebabs from the grill with salad and granary bread.

Rice wine, more commonly known as sake, is typically combined with soy sauce in a teriyaki marinade. It gives the steak a delicately sweet flavour.

STEAK WITH POTATO SALAD

The popular combination of steak and potatoes makes this salad a hearty meal to satisfy the healthiest of appetites.

Serves 4
Preparation time: 20 minutes
Marinating time: 1 hour
Cooking time: 15 minutes

225 g (8 oz) bottled salsa sauce
2 tablespoons cider vinegar
1 tablespoon Worcestershire sauce
1 level tablespoon soft light
   brown sugar
1 clove garlic, peeled and crushed
   (see p.11)
450 g (1 lb) fillet or rump steak, in
   one piece
3 tablespoons olive oil
450 g (1 lb) small new potatoes,
   scrubbed
3 medium peppers, 1 green, 1 red,
   1 yellow, de-seeded and cut
   into thin strips
Flat-leaf parsley to garnish

Per serving
Calories 448   Protein 36 g
Total fat 20 g (saturated fat 5.2 g)
Carbohydrates 32 g (added sugar 4 g)
Fibre 4.6 g   Sodium 271 mg

1 Mix together the salsa sauce, vinegar, Worcestershire sauce, sugar and garlic in a bowl. Toss the steak in the mixture until well coated, then cover and leave to marinate for 1 hour.

2 Meanwhile, boil the potatoes for 5 minutes, drain and leave to cool. Cut into thin slices and set aside.

3 Remove the steak from the marinade and pat dry with kitchen paper. Save the marinade. Heat the oil in a large frying pan and fry the steak in it for 3-4 minutes on each side, then lift onto a board.

4 Meanwhile, cook the potatoes and peppers in the pan for 5 minutes, then stir in the marinade and cook until the vegetables are tender. Take the pan off the heat.

5 Slice the steak at an angle across the grain and arrange the slices on a large platter. Spoon the potato and pepper mixture round the steak and pour over the pan juices. Garnish and serve with crusty bread rolls.

Green, red and yellow peppers make a colourful contribution to this attractive, full-flavoured salad. Salsa sauce adds a pleasing piquancy.

BARBECUED SPARE RIBS

The tangy sauce used to baste these ribs after cooking them in foil parcels is equally good with barbecued steaks, chicken and burgers. For more than four people, increase the ingredients accordingly. You can substitute a mixture of canned kidney or cannellini beans for baked beans; heat them through with a small amount of the sauce.

Serves 4
Preparation time: 15 minutes
Cooking time: 1 hour 25 minutes

12 pork spare ribs, about
　　1.6 kg (3½ lb) in total
8 tablespoons water
2 spring onions, trimmed and
　　finely chopped
4 tablespoons tomato ketchup
Juice of 1 large orange
1 tablespoon cider vinegar
1 level tablespoon soft light
　　brown sugar
2 tablespoons Worcestershire sauce
1 clove garlic, peeled and crushed
　　(see p.11)
400 g (14 oz) canned baked beans
225 g (8 oz) fine green beans,
　　trimmed, cut into short lengths
　　and cooked
1 level teaspoon ready-made
　　English mustard

Per serving
Calories 1159 Protein 95 g
Total fat 76 g (saturated fat 30 g)
Carbohydrates 25 g (added sugar 4 g)
Fibre 8.2 g Sodium 984 mg

1 Set the barbecue rack about 15 cm (6 in) above white-hot coals. Divide the spare ribs between four squares of heavy-duty foil. Sprinkle each one with 2 tablespoons of the water and wrap the foil tightly around the ribs, sealing the edges. Cook the parcels on the grill for 45 minutes, turning them over halfway through cooking without piercing the foil.

2 Mix together the spring onions, tomato ketchup, orange juice, vinegar, brown sugar, 1 tablespoon of the Worcestershire sauce and the garlic. Open the foil parcels and brush the ribs on all sides with the mixture. Cook with the foil open for 10 minutes.

3 Remove the ribs from the foil parcels and brush with the juices left in the foil. Cook the ribs on the grill for 15 minutes more, turning frequently, until tender and browned.

4 Meanwhile, mix together the baked beans, green beans, remaining Worcestershire sauce and the mustard in a large, shallow fireproof dish or frying pan. Cover and heat through on the barbecue for 15 minutes, stirring occasionally. Push the beans to the sides of the dish and arrange the ribs in the centre, then serve.

Brushing the pork spare ribs with the hot and fruity barbecue sauce keeps the meat moist inside and crisps the outsides to a deep golden brown.

ORIENTAL SHORT RIBS

Barbecued short ribs of pork make a tasty combination with sliced potatoes and carrot strips.

Serves 4
Preparation time: 1 hour 10 minutes
Marinating time: 4 hours
Cooking time: 20 minutes

450 g (1 lb) potatoes, scrubbed and cut into thick slices
4 large carrots, peeled and halved lengthways
1.4 kg (3 lb) pork short ribs, trimmed of fat and cut into four portions
4 tablespoons light soy sauce
2 tablespoons each dry sherry and sesame oil
¼ teaspoon hot red pepper sauce
1 tablespoon peeled and grated root ginger
2 level tablespoons soft dark brown sugar
2 cloves garlic, peeled and crushed (see p.11)
¼ level teaspoon ground cloves
Sprigs of fresh parsley to garnish

1 Boil the potatoes and carrots in a large saucepan until just cooked. Using a slotted spoon, lift them out of the pan and into a bowl and leave to cool. Cover the bowl and put it in the fridge.

2 Add the pork ribs to the pan, making sure they are covered with water. Simmer the ribs for 40 minutes, then drain well.

3 Mix the soy sauce, sherry, oil, hot red pepper sauce, ginger, sugar, garlic and cloves in a bowl. Coat the ribs in the mixture and then leave to cool. Cover and leave

Per serving
Calories 552 Protein 51 g
Total fat 24 g (saturated fat 6.3 g)
Carbohydrates 33 g (added sugar 7.5 g)
Fibre 3.4 g Sodium 1007 mg

in the fridge for at least 4 hours, or overnight if preferred, turning the ribs three or four times.

4 Set the barbecue rack about 15 cm (6 in) above white-hot coals. Sear the ribs on both sides, then cook for 10 minutes, brushing frequently with the marinade and turning occasionally.

5 Arrange the potatoes and carrots round the ribs, brush with the marinade and then grill for 5-10 minutes, or until the ribs are completely cooked (see p.81) and the vegetables are lightly browned. Transfer the ribs and vegetables to one or two serving platters, garnish with the parsley and serve with salad.

A spicy marinade gives these short ribs their oriental flavour and turns into a sweet, sticky coating on the barbecue, keeping the pork moist and tender.

MARINATED PORK KEBABS

Serves 4
Preparation time: 20 minutes
Marinating time: 30 minutes
Cooking time: 30 minutes

- 1-3 teaspoons chilli sauce or
  2 tablespoons tomato ketchup
- 2 tablespoons redcurrant jelly
- 1 tablespoon olive oil
- 1/4 level teaspoon ground allspice
- 1/8 level teaspoon cayenne pepper
- 1 clove garlic, peeled and crushed
  (see p.11)
- 450 g (1 lb) boneless loin of pork,
  trimmed of fat and cut into
  24 cubes
- 675 g (1 1/2 lb) sweet potatoes,
  washed and cut into quarters
- 4 large courgettes, trimmed and
  each cut into 8 pieces
- 2 large red onions, peeled and
  each cut into 12 wedges

Per serving
Calories 485 Protein 41 g
Total fat 16 g (saturated fat 5 g)
Carbohydrates 47 g (added sugar 5 g)
Fibre 4.7 g Sodium 165 mg

Sweet potatoes, courgettes and red onions pair well with the sweet and spicy flavour of pork in this simple recipe, but vegetables such as peppers, squash and cherry tomatoes are good alternative choices. The flavour of the marinade varies with the amount of chilli sauce you use – for a milder taste use ketchup. You will need 12 metal skewers for the kebabs.

1 Mix the chilli sauce or ketchup, redcurrant jelly, olive oil, allspice, cayenne pepper and garlic in a shallow dish, then toss the pork in the mixture. Cover and leave to marinate in the fridge for at least 30 minutes or overnight.

2 Boil the sweet potatoes for 12-15 minutes, until almost cooked, then drain and set aside. Thread the courgettes and red onions alternately onto eight metal skewers and the marinated pork cubes onto four metal skewers.

3 Set the barbecue grill 15 cm (6 in) above white-hot coals. Cook the sweet potatoes skin-side up on the grill rack for 3 minutes, then turn over. Brush the skewers of pork and vegetables with the marinade, then cook on the grill for 12 minutes, turning every 4 minutes and basting with the marinade, until the pork is cooked (see p.81). Serve straight from the grill with warm crusty bread.

PORK, APPLE AND SQUASH BROCHETTES

Serves 4
Preparation time: 30 minutes
Marinating time: 1 hour
Cooking time: 20 minutes

- 150 ml (1/4 pint) dry cider
- 1 tablespoon clear honey
- 1 clove garlic, peeled and crushed
  (see p.11)
- 1 tablespoon olive oil
- Freshly ground black pepper
- 450 g (1 lb) pork tenderloin,
  trimmed of fat and cut into cubes
- 2 green dessert apples, cored and
  each cut into 8 wedges
- 450 g (1 lb) butternut squash,
  peeled, de-seeded and cut
  into cubes
- 30 g (1 oz) butter
- 1 small onion, peeled and
  finely chopped
- 340 g (12 oz) cooked rice
  (see p.9)
- 45 g (1 1/2 oz) lightly toasted
  hazelnuts, roughly chopped
- 1/2 level teaspoon salt
- 24 fresh sage leaves
- Lemon and lime wedges to garnish

Per serving
Calories 488 Protein 23 g
Total fat 23 g (saturated fat 7.5 g)
Carbohydrates 47 g (added sugar 5 g)
Fibre 2.9 g Sodium 377 mg

Cider and honey highlight the fragrant flavour of these pork, apple and squash brochettes, and keep the meat moist and sweet during barbecuing. You will need heavy-duty foil, squares about 25 cm (10 in) each, for the rice, and eight skewers for the brochettes.

1 Mix the cider, honey, garlic, oil and some pepper in a shallow dish and toss the pork, apples and butternut squash in it. Cover and leave to marinate for 1 hour.

2 Melt the butter in a frying pan and soften the onion in it over a moderate heat. Stir in the rice, hazelnuts, salt and some pepper, then divide the mixture equally between the foil squares (see p.319), folding the sides to enclose the rice and sealing well.

3 Thread the pork, apple, squash and sage alternately onto the skewers – bamboo skewers need to be soaked for 30 minutes before use – and reserve the marinade.

4 Place the foil parcels and the brochettes on a grill rack set 15 cm (6 in) above white-hot coals. Cook for 15-20 minutes, turning the brochettes frequently and brushing them with the marinade. Turn the foil parcels halfway through cooking time. Garnish with the lemon and lime wedges and serve.

CHICKEN WITH CORN AND SWEET PEPPERS

Chicken breasts and wings, well seasoned and then brushed with barbecue sauce, are cooked with corn cobs and juicy red peppers.

Serves 4
Preparation time: 50 minutes
Cooking time: 45 minutes

4 medium corn cobs
2 cloves garlic, peeled and crushed (see p.11)
½ level teaspoon salt
Freshly ground black pepper
6 tablespoons olive oil
4 chicken breasts with wings, each about 225 g (8 oz)
4 medium red peppers, halved and de-seeded
1 teaspoon dried rosemary
6 tablespoons bottled barbecue sauce
1 french loaf, cut in half, then split lengthways

Per serving
Calories 772 Protein 61 g
Total fat 31 g (saturated fat 5.8 g)
Carbohydrates 65 g (added sugar 0)
Fibre 8 g Sodium 1016 mg

I Peel back the green husks from the corn and remove the silks, then smooth the husks back into place and tie the tops with string. To prevent the corn cobs catching fire, soak them in cold water for 30 minutes (see p.319).

2 Mix together the garlic, salt, some pepper and oil and set aside 2 tablespoons of the mixture. Brush the rest of it over both sides of each piece of chicken, the corn cobs and the red peppers. Sprinkle the chicken with the rosemary.

3 Wrap each of the corn cobs in foil and seal well, then set the barbecue grill about 15 cm (6 in) above white-hot coals. Cook the corn parcels and the chicken skin-side down on the grill for 20 minutes. Carefully unwrap the corn cobs and put them on the grill, then turn the chicken over. Grill for 10 minutes, then brush both sides of the chicken with the barbecue sauce.

4 Add the peppers to the grill and cook, turning frequently, until the peppers and the corn are cooked and slightly charred and the chicken is done (see p.117). Brush the reserved garlic and oil mixture over the cut sides of the french bread, then toast it on the grill for 1 minute until golden brown. Skin the peppers, if desired, then cut them into strips and arrange on a large heated serving plate with the chicken, corn and bread and serve.

Roasting whole cobs of corn in their husks on the barbecue keeps the kernels moist and tender and makes a sweet accompaniment to crisp chicken pieces and grilled red peppers.

POUSSINS WITH RICE AND PAWPAW

Rice, avocado and spring onions accompany barbecued poussins and fruity pawpaw kebabs. You will need 12 skewers altogether.

Serves 4
Preparation time: 30 minutes
Marinating time: 2 hours
Cooking time: 30 minutes

4 oven-ready poussins, each about 400 g (14 oz)
4 spring onions, trimmed and thinly sliced, white and green parts kept separately
2 teaspoons peeled and very finely diced fresh root ginger
Finely grated rind and strained juice of 1 lemon or lime
2 tablespoons each clear honey, soy sauce and olive oil
3/4 level teaspoon salt
Freshly ground black pepper
1/4 level teaspoon ground turmeric
450 g (1 lb) cooked brown rice (see p.9)
1 medium red pepper, de-seeded and diced
1 medium avocado, halved, stoned, peeled and diced
30 g (1 oz) butter, melted
1/4 level teaspoon ground nutmeg
1 large ripe but firm pawpaw, halved, de-seeded, peeled and cut into large cubes

Per serving
Calories 802 Protein 67 g
Total fat 35 g (saturated fat 11 g)
Carbohydrates 58 g (added sugar 10 g)
Fibre 5.3 g Sodium 1058 mg

1 Spatchcock the poussins (see p.116) but do not skewer them yet. In a large dish mix the white spring onion with the ginger, lemon or lime juice and rind, honey, soy sauce, olive oil, 1/4 level teaspoon of the salt, some pepper and the turmeric. Toss the poussins in the marinade until well coated, then cover and leave to marinate for at least 2 hours or overnight in the fridge, basting and turning occasionally (see p.319).

2 Mix the rice with the green spring onion, the red pepper, avocado, 1/4 level teaspoon of the salt and some pepper. Divide the mixture equally between four large pieces of heavy-duty foil, then seal well (see p.319).

3 Mix the melted butter with the nutmeg and the remaining salt, and gently toss the pawpaw cubes in it. Thread onto four skewers and cover temporarily.

4 Take the poussins from the marinade, skewer (see p.319) and arrange on a barbecue grill set 15 cm (6 in) above white-hot coals. Place the rice parcels round the edge. Cook for 20 minutes, turning the poussins once or twice and basting them frequently with the marinade. Uncover the skewered pawpaws and add to the grill rack. Cook, turning carefully, until they are heated through and the poussins are done (see p.117).

TURKEY BURGER PARCELS

Smoked back bacon and peppers give these substantial turkey burgers a warm, smoky flavour and chunky texture. The beans and sweetcorn cook with the burgers, wrapped in foil, on the barbecue. You will need four 30 cm (12 in) squares of heavy-duty foil for this recipe.

Serves 4
Preparation time: 20 minutes
Cooking time: 45 minutes

450 g (1 lb) minced turkey
4 rashers smoked back bacon, rinds removed, finely chopped
2 small peppers, 1 green and 1 red, de-seeded and finely chopped
1 small onion, peeled and finely chopped
2 tablespoons chopped fresh coriander
2 tablespoons tomato relish
1/2 level teaspoon salt
Freshly ground black pepper
225 g (8 oz) each frozen broad beans and frozen or canned sweetcorn kernels

Per serving
Calories 400 Protein 36 g
Total fat 16 g (saturated fat 6.1 g)
Carbohydrates 30 g (added sugar 0)
Fibre 4 g Sodium 916 mg

1 Mix the minced turkey, bacon, peppers, onion, coriander, tomato relish, half the salt and some pepper in a bowl. Divide the mixture into four and shape each portion into an oval burger.

2 Lightly butter the foil squares, then put a burger in the centre of each one. Mix the broad beans with the sweetcorn and the remaining salt and some pepper, then spoon the mixture round the edge of each burger. Fold the foil over to enclose the burgers and vegetables, and seal well.

3 Cook the parcels on a barbecue grill set 15 cm (6 in) above white-hot coals for 25 minutes. Turn over and cook for another 20 minutes. Serve the burgers and vegetables straight from the foil parcels with warm crusty bread.

295

MARINATED CHICKEN KEBABS

Aromatic cubes of chicken are grilled with courgettes, potatoes and tomatoes and served with mixed salad. Use a soured cream dressing to complement the succulence of the chicken. To thread the kebabs you will need four long metal skewers or eight soaked bamboo skewers.

Serves 4
Preparation time: 20 minutes
Marinating time: 1 hour
Cooking time: 30 minutes

2 tablespoons light soy sauce
1 tablespoon sesame oil
1 tablespoon dry sherry
1 level teaspoon ground ginger
1 clove garlic, peeled and crushed (see p.11)
Freshly ground black pepper
450 g (1 lb) boneless chicken breasts, skinned and cut into 24 cubes
12 medium new potatoes, about 340 g (12 oz), scrubbed
2 medium courgettes, trimmed and cut into thick slices
12 cherry tomatoes

Per serving
Calories 276 Protein 29 g
Total fat 6.2 g (saturated fat 1.5 g)
Carbohydrates 28 g (added sugar 0)
Fibre 2.9 g Sodium 528 mg

1 Combine the soy sauce, sesame oil, sherry, ginger, garlic and some pepper in a medium-sized bowl, add the chicken and toss it well. Cover and refrigerate for 1 hour, stirring occasionally. In the meantime, boil the potatoes for 10 minutes, drain and leave them to cool.

2 Take four long metal skewers, or eight bamboo skewers well soaked in water. Thread each skewer with the cooled potatoes, and alternate chicken cubes, courgette slices and cherry tomatoes with the potatoes.

3 Set the barbecue rack about 15 cm (6 in) above white-hot coals and put the kebabs on it. Cook for 15 minutes, turning them every 5 minutes, until the chicken is cooked through. Serve the kebabs with poppy seed rolls and a mixed lettuce salad.

GRILLED CHICKEN FAJITAS

In these barbecued Mexican pancakes, a spicy mashed avocado and tomato mixture combines with slices of tender chicken in a lime juice sauce.

Serves 4
Preparation time: 40 minutes
Marinating time: 2 hours
Cooking time: 10 minutes

2 tablespoons olive oil
4 tablespoons lime juice
2 cloves garlic, peeled and crushed (see p.11)
1 level teaspoon ground cumin
1 level teaspoon dried oregano
Freshly ground black pepper
450 g (1 lb) boneless chicken breasts, skinned
1 ripe avocado, halved, stoned and peeled
2 ripe tomatoes, de-seeded and chopped
1 small onion, peeled and finely chopped
2 tablespoons chopped fresh coriander
1 small green chilli, de-seeded and finely chopped
8 flour tortillas wrapped in foil
225 g (8 oz) taco (salsa) sauce
150 ml (¼ pint) soured cream
60 g (2 oz) Cheddar cheese, grated
½ small iceberg lettuce, shredded

Per serving
Calories 754 Protein 40 g
Total fat 35 g (saturated fat 13 g)
Carbohydrates 76 g (added sugar 0)
Fibre 5.1 g Sodium 704 mg

1 Combine the olive oil with 2 tablespoons of the lime juice, the garlic, cumin, oregano and some pepper in a shallow glass or china bowl. Coat the chicken with the mixture, then cover and refrigerate for at least 2 hours (or overnight, if you prefer).

2 Just before cooking the chicken, mash the avocado with the remaining lime juice and mix in the chopped tomatoes, onion, coriander and chilli. Smooth a piece of nontoxic food wrap over the surface to prevent the mixture from darkening, and refrigerate until required.

3 Set the barbecue grill 15 cm (6 in) above white-hot coals. Put the chicken breasts on the grill and cook for 10 minutes or until done (see p.117), turning over halfway through cooking. Place the foil-wrapped tortillas on the barbecue for the last 5 minutes.

4 Take both chicken and tortillas off the barbecue, and cut the chicken breasts into thin slices. Unwrap the tortillas and spread each one with the avocado mixture, then top it with the taco sauce, soured cream and the sliced chicken. Sprinkle on the grated Cheddar cheese and lettuce, fold over each tortilla to enclose the filling and serve.

MARINATED PRAWN BARBECUE

Serves 4
Preparation time: 20 minutes
Marinating time: 45 minutes
Cooking time: 25 minutes

2 tablespoons dry white wine
Finely grated rind and strained juice
    of 1 lemon
4 tablespoons olive oil
4 cloves garlic, peeled and crushed
    (see p.11)
4 tablespoons chopped
    fresh parsley
1/4 teaspoon hot red pepper sauce
3/4 level teaspoon salt
48 medium-sized uncooked prawns,
    about 550 g (1 1/4 lb) in all,
    shelled and de-veined
2 medium courgettes, trimmed,
    halved lengthways and cut
    into quarters
2 medium red peppers, de-seeded
    and cut into wide strips

Per serving
Calories 277 Protein 26 g
Total fat 15 g (saturated fat 2 g)
Carbohydrates 7.2 g (added sugar 0)
Fibre 2.2 g Sodium 631 mg

This tasty and refreshing dish is even quicker to prepare if you buy uncooked prawns already on skewers, as available in many large supermarkets. Otherwise, as well as heavy-duty foil – four rectangles each 30 cm x 10 cm (12 in x 4 in) – for wrapping the vegetables, you will need eight long wooden or metal skewers.

1 Pour the wine, the lemon rind and juice, half the oil, half the garlic, half the parsley, half the pepper sauce and 1/4 teaspoon of the salt into a large, shallow dish and stir. Add the prawns, turning them in the mixture until coated, cover and stand for 45 minutes. Meanwhile soak the wooden skewers in cold water, if using.

2 Mix the courgette and red pepper strips with the remaining parsley, olive oil, garlic, pepper sauce and salt. Then divide the vegetable mixture between the sheets of heavy-duty foil, fold the foil in half to form narrow parcels and seal the edges.

3 Put the parcels on a barbecue grill set 15 cm (6 in) above white-hot coals and cook for 15 minutes. Meanwhile, thread six prawns onto each of the eight skewers, reserving the marinade.

4 Place the prawns on the grill and cook for 6 minutes, brushing frequently with the reserved marinade and turning once halfway through cooking.

5 Remove the prawns and vegetable parcels from the grill. Open out the parcels and place one parcel and two skewers of prawns on each plate. Serve with crusty white bread and any remaining marinade.

Prawns marinated in white wine sauce are grilled together with foil-wrapped courgettes and red peppers.

MEDITERRANEAN GRILLED FISH AND VEGETABLES

Serves 4
Preparation time: 20 minutes
Cooking time: 40 minutes

1 tablespoon chopped fresh
   tarragon, or 2 level teaspoons
   dried tarragon
6 tablespoons olive oil
4 halibut, salmon or cod steaks,
   each about 175 g (6 oz)
4 small whole garlic bulbs, papery
   outer skins removed
2 tablespoons chopped
   fresh parsley
Freshly ground black pepper
450 g (1 lb) aubergines, trimmed
   and thickly sliced
4 medium tomatoes, halved
8 thick slices french bread

Per serving
Calories 709 Protein 50 g
Total fat 27 g (saturated fat 4.1 g)
Carbohydrates 71 g (added sugar 0)
Fibre 9.6 g Sodium 799 mg

Whole bulbs of garlic roasted in foil parcels on a barbecue rack taste delicious. Here they add a lively tang to a tasty, nutritious dish of grilled salmon or cod.

1 Mix together the tarragon and 2 tablespoons of the olive oil. Spoon the mixture over the fish steaks and set aside.

2 Place each garlic bulb on a piece of heavy-duty foil and sprinkle with a little of the remaining oil and 2 teaspoons of the chopped parsley. Fold the foil round the bulbs, then seal well.

3 Put a barbecue rack 15 cm (6 in) above white-hot coals. Place the foil-wrapped garlic in the centre of the rack and cook for 20 minutes, turning frequently.

4 Mix the remaining oil with the rest of the parsley and some pepper, and brush it over the slices of aubergine. Add the aubergines to the grill and cook for 10-15 minutes, brushing

Aubergines and tomatoes grilled with a succulent salmon steak are served with roasted garlic and toasted french bread.

them with the oil and parsley, and turning them occasionally. Place the fish steaks and tomatoes on the grill and cook for 5-7 minutes, until the fish flakes easily. Turn the fish and tomatoes halfway through cooking and brush them with the oil and parsley when necessary.

5 Shortly before the end of cooking, toast the french bread on the grill until lightly browned.

6 Unwrap the garlic bulbs and arrange them on a large platter with the fish steaks, aubergines, tomatoes and bread, then serve.

PAN-FRIED TROUT

Serves 4
Preparation time: 10 minutes
Cooking time: 20 minutes

225 g (8 oz) couscous
570 ml (1 pint) lukewarm water
4 trout, each about 340 g (12 oz),
    gutted, cleaned and dried with
    kitchen paper
½ level teaspoon salt
Freshly ground black pepper
4 sprigs of rosemary
4 large ripe tomatoes, halved
2 tablespoons olive oil
30 g (1 oz) butter
2 tablespoons chopped
    fresh parsley
1 lemon, cut into 4 wedges

Per serving
Calories 561 Protein 57 g
Total fat 24 g (saturated fat 5.1 g)
Carbohydrates 32 g (added sugar 0)
    Fibre 1.3 g Sodium 505 mg

Trout flavoured with rosemary, fried with tomatoes and served on a bed of couscous makes a simple but appetising meal.

1 Soak the couscous in the lukewarm water for 10 minutes, then drain the couscous and steam in a large metal sieve over a pan of simmering water for 10 minutes. Transfer to a large serving platter and keep warm.

2 Season the trout with half the salt and some pepper. Tuck a sprig of rosemary inside each fish. Sprinkle the tomatoes with the remaining salt and some pepper.

3 Heat half the oil and half the butter in a large frying pan for 2 minutes until golden brown. Add two of the trout and four tomato halves, cut sides down, and fry them for 4-5 minutes on each side until cooked through. Arrange on top of the couscous and keep warm. Repeat with the remaining trout and tomatoes. Sprinkle with the chopped parsley, garnish and serve hot.

FISH AND VEGETABLE PARCELS

Serves 4
Preparation time: 20 minutes
Cooking time: 20 minutes

4 thick halibut or cod steaks, each
    about 175 g (6 oz)
2 medium carrots, peeled and
    thinly sliced
2 medium courgettes, trimmed and
    thinly sliced
225 g (8 oz) medium open-cup
    mushrooms, wiped and
    thinly sliced
8 spring onions, trimmed and
    finely chopped
3 tablespoons fresh lemon juice
Freshly ground black pepper
2 tablespoons olive oil
2 tablespoons sesame seeds,
    lightly toasted
30 g (1 oz) lemon, garlic or
    herb butter
1 ciabatta or loose-textured loaf,
    thickly sliced

Per serving
Calories 412 Protein 37 g
Total fat 21 g (saturated fat 6 g)
Carbohydrates 20 g
(added sugar 0)
Fibre 3.6 g Sodium 386 mg

Fish and vegetables wrapped in foil and roasted over white-hot coals provide a juicy treat. You will need four pieces of heavy-duty foil, each about 40 cm x 20 cm (16 in x 8 in).

1 Place a fish steak on each piece of foil and spoon a quarter of the carrots, courgettes, mushrooms and spring onions over each one. Sprinkle with the lemon juice, pepper, oil and sesame seeds, then fold the sides of the foil over the fish and seal well.

2 Set the barbecue grill 15 cm (6 in) above white-hot coals. Put the foil parcels on the grill and cook for 15-20 minutes, or until the fish flakes easily with a fork and the vegetables are tender.

3 Just before the end of cooking, butter the bread and then toast it lightly on both sides on the grill. Open the foil packets and spoon the cooking juices over the fish and vegetables. Serve with the toasted bread.

BUBBLE AND SQUEAK

Serves 4
Preparation time: 15 minutes
Cooking time: 15 minutes

2 tablespoons olive oil
1 large onion, peeled and
  coarsely chopped
340 g (12 oz) cabbage, coarsely
  shredded (see p.11) and
  blanched for 3 minutes (see p.10)
¼ level teaspoon salt

½ level teaspoon dried
  marjoram
340 g (12 oz) cold roast beef or
  lamb, roughly chopped
675 g (1½ lb) mashed potatoes

Per serving
Calories 402 Protein 30 g
Total fat 18 g (saturated fat 4.1 g)
Carbohydrates 33 g (added sugar 0)
Fibre 5.2 g Sodium 256 mg

*Sizzling mashed potatoes and cabbage
fried with chunks of cold roast
meat are flavoured with
onion and marjoram.*

Named after the sounds made by the ingredients during cooking, bubble and squeak originated in the 18th century as a dish of cold meat and cabbage fried together. Nowadays potatoes are often used in place of the meat, but this wholesome version uses all three ingredients.

1 Heat 1 tablespoon of the oil in a frying pan and soften the onion in it over a moderate heat. Mix in the cabbage, salt and marjoram and stir-fry for 2-3 minutes.

2 Add the meat and potatoes and cook for 5 minutes. Carefully turn the mixture over and cook for another 5 minutes, until crisp and brown underneath, then serve with a carrot, celery, spring onion and radish salad.

CURRIED TURKEY WITH APPLES AND RICE

Serves 4
Preparation time: 15 minutes
Cooking time: 30 minutes

2 tablespoons olive oil
1 large onion, peeled and
    thinly sliced
175 g (6 oz) mangetout, trimmed
    and halved widthways
2 dessert apples, cored and cut into
    large chunks
1 level tablespoon medium
    curry powder
2 level tablespoons plain flour
1/4 level teaspoon salt
285 ml (1/2 pint) chicken stock
    (see p.8)
285 ml (1/2 pint) milk
1 tablespoon lemon juice
Freshly ground black pepper
225 g (8 oz) cooked turkey or
    chicken, diced
400 g (14 oz) cooked long-grain
    rice (see p.9)
60 g (2 oz) dry roasted
    peanuts, chopped

Per serving
Calories 447 Protein 27 g
Total fat 17 g (saturated fat 3.6 g)
Carbohydrates 49 g (added sugar 0)
Fibre 3.2 g Sodium 322 mg

Mangetout and large chunks of apple add a crispness and juiciness to this full-flavoured curry made with long-grain rice, turkey and peanuts.

1 Heat the oil in a large frying pan and soften the onion in it over a moderate heat. Mix in the mangetout and apples and stir-fry for 1 minute.

2 Add the curry powder, sprinkle with the flour and salt and cook, stirring, for 2 minutes. Gradually mix in the stock and milk, then bring to the boil, stirring, until thickened.

3 Stir in the lemon juice, some pepper, the turkey or chicken and the rice and bring back to the boil. Reduce the heat and simmer for 15 minutes. Sprinkle with the chopped peanuts and serve.

LAMB AND BARLEY PILAFF

Serves 4
Preparation time: 30 minutes
Cooking time: 45 minutes

2 tablespoons olive oil
1 large onion, peeled and chopped
4 medium carrots, peeled and
    thinly sliced
3 medium sticks celery, trimmed
    and thinly sliced
2 cloves garlic, peeled and crushed
    (see p.11)
550 g (1 1/4 lb) lean minced lamb
225 g (8 oz) pearl barley
1 level teaspoon dried thyme
1 bay leaf
1 level teaspoon ground cinnamon
1/2 level teaspoon ground nutmeg
850 ml (1 1/2 pints) beef stock
    (see p.8)
285 ml (1/2 pint) red wine
340 g (12 oz) chestnut mushrooms,
    wiped and thinly sliced
60 g (2 oz) sun-dried tomatoes,
    drained and chopped
1 level teaspoon salt
Freshly ground black pepper
2 tablespoons chopped fresh
    coriander or parsley

Per serving
Calories 591 Protein 36 g
Total fat 21 g (saturated fat 7.3 g)
Carbohydrates 56 g (added sugar 0)
Fibre 8.2 g Sodium 655 mg

Pearl barley, a much-underrated and nutritious staple, is used to thicken this unusual lamb dish. The barley is cooked in the same way as rice in a Turkish pilaff – by slow absorption of the cooking liquid during simmering. Sun-dried tomatoes, chestnut mushrooms and a garnish of chopped fresh herbs give the lamb and barley combination a robust flavour.

1 Heat the oil in a large flameproof casserole and soften the onion, carrots, celery and garlic in it, stirring occasionally. Add the lamb and cook, stirring, over a high heat for 2-3 minutes. Mix in the barley, thyme, bay leaf, cinnamon and nutmeg, and cook for 2 minutes.

2 Pour in the stock and wine and add the mushrooms, tomatoes, salt and some pepper. Bring to the boil, then reduce the heat to low, cover and simmer for 30 minutes, stirring occasionally.

3 Take the lid off the casserole and continue cooking for 10-15 minutes, or until the barley is tender and most of the liquid has been absorbed. Remove the bay leaf, stir in the coriander or parsley and serve.

Pot-roasted Beef

Time-saving pot roasts are even tastier when made the day before serving, as the flavours have had time to mature and develop.

Serves 6
Preparation time: 25 minutes
Cooking time: 3 hours 15 minutes

115 g (4 oz) streaky bacon, chopped and with rind removed
1.6 kg (3½ lb) topside beef, wiped
Freshly ground black pepper
2 tablespoons olive oil
2 medium onions, peeled, sliced and separated into rings
2 cloves garlic, peeled and crushed (see p.11)
2 sticks celery, trimmed and sliced
285 ml (½ pint) red wine
150 ml (¼ pint) beef stock (see p.8)
2 level tablespoons tomato purée
1 bay leaf
2 sprigs fresh rosemary
½ level teaspoon salt
450 g (1 lb) new potatoes, scrubbed
225 g (8 oz) baby carrots, trimmed and scrubbed
2 courgettes, trimmed and thickly sliced
225 g (8 oz) fine green beans, trimmed and halved
2 level tablespoons cornflour, blended with 3 tablespoons of cold water

Per serving
Calories 739 Protein 59 g
Total fat 43 g (saturated fat 16 g)
Carbohydrates 24 g (added sugar 0)
Fibre 3.7 g Sodium 615 mg

1 Heat the bacon in a large, flameproof casserole until the fat runs. Meanwhile, season the beef with some pepper.

2 Add the oil to the casserole and brown the beef on all sides over a moderate heat for 10 minutes, turning frequently. Take out the beef and set aside.

3 Add the onions, garlic and celery to the casserole and cook for 5 minutes, or until softened. Return the beef to the casserole, then pour in the wine and stock. Stir in the tomato purée, herbs, salt and some pepper and bring to the boil. Reduce the heat, cover and simmer gently for 2 hours, basting the meat occasionally.

4 Arrange the potatoes, carrots, courgettes and beans round the beef so that they are covered with the liquid. Cook for 45 minutes.

5 Move the beef from the casserole to a large, heated serving dish, cover and keep hot. Discard the bay leaf. Stir the cornflour into the casserole and bring to the boil, stirring, until it thickens. Reduce the heat and simmer for 5 minutes.

6 Slice the beef and arrange round the sides or down the centre of the serving dish. Spoon on the vegetables and sauce and serve.

Mixed Meat Potjie with Spiced Peaches

Serves 6
Preparation time: 30 minutes
Cooking time: 2 hours 15 minutes

250 g (9 oz) dried peaches
60 g (2 oz) soft dark brown sugar
2 cinnamon sticks
8 black peppercorns
2 cloves
1 long strip thinly pared lemon rind
2 tablespoons lemon juice
2 tablespoons olive oil
450 g (1 lb) blade or spare rib of pork, trimmed of fat and cut into cubes (see p.79)
450 g (1 lb) braising steak, trimmed of fat and cut into cubes
30 g (1 oz) plain flour
425 ml (¾ pint) strong pale ale
2 medium onions, peeled
6 medium carrots, peeled and cut into large chunks
1 bay leaf
2 cloves garlic, peeled and crushed (see p.11)
⅛ level teaspoon ground allspice
½ level teaspoon salt
Freshly ground black pepper
115 g (4 oz) smoked pork sausage, thickly sliced

Per serving
Calories 525 Protein 34 g
Total fat 19 g (saturated fat 6.2 g)
Carbohydrates 50 g (added sugar 10 g)
Fibre 7.7 g Sodium 414 mg

Peaches simmered with cloves and cinnamon add a rich and scented flavour to this delicious South African casserole: *potjie* is Afrikaans for 'little pot'.

1 Put the peaches in a large, flameproof casserole. Cover with cold water to a level 2.5 cm (1 in) above the fruit. Add the sugar, cinnamon, peppercorns, cloves, lemon rind and lemon juice. Bring to the boil, then reduce the heat and simmer for 20 minutes or until the peaches are tender. Pour into a bowl, cover and set aside. Rinse and dry the casserole.

2 Heat the oil in the casserole and lightly brown the pork and steak cubes in it for 6-8 minutes. Stir in the flour and cook for 1 minute. Pour in the pale ale and bring to the boil, stirring, until thickened.

3 Mix in the onions, carrots, bay leaf, garlic, allspice, salt and some pepper. Cover tightly and simmer gently for 2 hours.

4 Drain the peaches and add them to the casserole, then stir in the smoked pork sausage slices. Heat gently for 15 minutes, remove the bay leaf and serve with light rye bread.

BAKED HAM AND CHEESE WITH MUSHROOMS

This savoury bread pudding can be adapted to suit your tastes – try using broccoli florets in place of spinach.

Serves 4
Preparation time: 20 minutes
Cooking time: 50 minutes

30 g (1 oz) unsalted butter
1 medium onion, peeled and finely chopped
225 g (8 oz) mushrooms, wiped and thinly sliced
225 g (8 oz) fresh spinach, blanched (see p.10), squeezed and roughly shredded
2 cloves garlic, peeled and crushed (see p.11)
Freshly ground black pepper
285 ml (½ pint) milk
3 eggs, size 2
2 level teaspoons Dijon mustard
250 g (9 oz) ricotta cheese
30 g (1 oz) Parmesan cheese, grated
175 g (6 oz) cooked ham, diced
225 g (8 oz) white or wholemeal bread, crusts removed, cut into small cubes

1 Preheat the oven to 190°C (375°F, gas mark 5). Melt the butter in a large frying pan and soften the onion in it over a moderate heat.

2 Add the mushrooms and cook, stirring, for 2-3 minutes. Mix in the spinach, garlic and some pepper and cook, stirring, for 1-2 minutes, or until most of the liquid has evaporated.

3 In a large bowl whisk together the milk, eggs, mustard, ricotta and half the Parmesan. Then mix in the diced ham, bread cubes and the fried mushroom, garlic and spinach mixture.

4 Pour into a lightly greased, shallow ovenproof dish and sprinkle the remaining Parmesan over the top.

5 Cover the dish with foil and bake in the centre of the oven for 20 minutes. Uncover and continue cooking for another 20 minutes, or until set and golden brown. Serve hot.

Per serving
Calories 493 Protein 33 g
Total fat 26 g (saturated fat 13 g)
Carbohydrates 36 g (added sugar 0)
Fibre 6 g Sodium 1224 mg

Creamy ricotta cheese, Dijon mustard and garlic flavour this substantial supper.

303

MEXICAN POT-ROASTED PORK

Serves 6
Preparation time: 35 minutes
Cooking time: 2 hours 10 minutes

1 tablespoon olive oil
2 level teaspoons sugar
1.4 kg (3 lb) boneless spare rib,
  blade or leg of pork
450 g (1 lb) shallots or button
  onions, peeled
2 medium sticks celery, trimmed
  and chopped
85 ml (3 fl oz) beef stock
  (see p.8) or red wine
2 cloves garlic, peeled and crushed
  (see p.11)
2 level tablespoons mild
  chilli seasoning
½ level teaspoon ground cinnamon
400 g (14 oz) canned
  chopped tomatoes
½ level teaspoon salt
Freshly ground black pepper
1 large red pepper, de-seeded
  and cut into strips
115 g (4 oz) baby sweetcorn,
  halved lengthways
340 g (12 oz) canned red kidney
  beans, rinsed and drained
  (see p.172)
30 g (1 oz) butter, softened
2 level tablespoons plain flour
Fresh coriander to garnish

Per serving
Calories 472 Protein 57 g
Total fat 18 g
(saturated fat 7.6 g)
Carbohydrates 21 g
(added sugar 3 g)
Fibre 5.4 g
Sodium 592 mg

A slightly sweet, spicy gravy brings a taste of Mexico to this succulent pork dish. It makes an excellent substitute for a Sunday roast when you are restricted to using one cooking ring.

1 Heat the oil and sugar in a large flameproof casserole until the sugar dissolves and starts to turn golden brown. Add the pork and cook for about 10 minutes, turning, until evenly browned all over, then set aside.

2 Pour off all but 1 tablespoon of the fat from the casserole, add the shallots and celery and cook for 5 minutes. Stir in the stock or wine, scraping the juices from the bottom of the pot, then add the garlic, chilli seasoning, cinnamon, tomatoes, salt and some pepper.

Tender baby sweetcorn, shallots, juicy pieces of red pepper and chopped celery add colour and body to a rich, luxurious sauce seasoned with garlic, chilli and aromatic cinnamon.

3 Return the pork to the casserole and bring to the boil. Reduce the heat, cover the casserole and simmer for 1½ hours, turning the meat after 45 minutes.

4 Add the red pepper and sweetcorn and cook, covered, for 15 minutes. Turn the pork again, mix in the beans and cook for a further 15 minutes, or until the pork is done (see p.81) and the vegetables are tender.

5 Lift the pork from the casserole onto a large heated serving dish, cover with foil and allow to stand. Mix the butter and flour together in a small bowl to make a paste and gradually stir it into the casserole. Bring the sauce to the boil, stirring, and cook for 3 minutes, or until it thickens.

6 Remove the string from the pork, then spoon the vegetables and sauce around the meat. Garnish with the sprig of fresh coriander and serve.

CHICKEN POTJIE

Serves 6
Preparation time: 25 minutes
Marinating time: 2-3 hours
Cooking time: 1 hour 30 minutes

340 ml (12 fl oz) dry red wine
2 cloves garlic, peeled and crushed (see p.11)
1 level teaspoon dried marjoram
6 boneless chicken breasts and 6 chicken thighs, each about 115 g (4 oz), skinned
3 level tablespoons plain flour
2 tablespoons olive oil
115 ml (4 fl oz) brandy
1 level teaspoon dried mixed herbs or 1 tablespoon chopped fresh herbs
10 button onions, peeled
340 g (12 oz) button mushrooms, wiped
2 sticks celery, trimmed and chopped
½ level teaspoon salt
Freshly ground black pepper
340 g (12 oz) thickly sliced bacon rashers, rinds removed, cut into strips

Per serving
Calories 705 Protein 58 g
Total fat 38 g (saturated fat 13 g)
Carbohydrates 13 g (added sugar 0)
Fibre 3 g Sodium 1198 mg

This fortifying stew of chicken, bacon and mushrooms is based on the traditional South African potjie (see p.302), a variety of casserole cooked in a cast-iron pot, usually over an open fire.

1 Pour the wine into a bowl and stir in the garlic and marjoram. Add the chicken, cover and leave to marinate for 2-3 hours.

2 Remove the chicken, reserving the marinade, and pat dry with kitchen paper. Toss the chicken pieces in the flour until evenly coated. Heat the oil in a large flameproof casserole and brown the chicken in it on all sides for 8-10 minutes. Pour off all the excess fat from the casserole.

3 Heat the brandy in the casserole for a few seconds, then light it. When the flames have died down, stir in the herbs, onions, mushrooms and celery and cook the mixture for 1-2 minutes.

4 Pour the reserved marinade into the casserole and season with the salt and some pepper. Mix in the bacon pieces and bring to the boil. Reduce the heat and cover tightly. Simmer gently for about 1½ hours, or until the chicken is tender (see p.117), then serve with crusty french bread.

SAUSAGE HOT POT

This warming meal of sausages and vegetables in a rich cider sauce fortified with chicken stock can be cooked on the hob or over a camping stove.

Serves 4
Preparation time: 20 minutes
Cooking time: 35 minutes

1 tablespoon olive oil
450 g (1 lb) spicy or herb
  pork sausages
1 large onion, peeled and chopped
2 medium sticks celery, trimmed
  and sliced
1 clove garlic, peeled and crushed
  (see p.11)
225 g (8 oz) dessert apples, cored,
  quartered and sliced

Cider and apples infuse this hearty sausage casserole with a fruity tartness, while sweetcorn and celery add a light crispness and delicate colour.

285 ml (½ pint) chicken stock
  (see p.8)
150 ml (¼ pint) medium-dry cider
1 level teaspoon dried thyme
¼ level teaspoon salt
Freshly ground black pepper
340 g (12 oz) potatoes, peeled
  and cut into cubes
115 g (4 oz) baby sweetcorn
2 medium courgettes, trimmed
  and sliced
2 tablespoons chopped fresh
  parsley to garnish

Per serving
Calories 564 Protein 16 g
Total fat 40 g (saturated fat 15 g)
Carbohydrates 35 g (added sugar 0)
Fibre 3.7 g Sodium 1329 mg

1 Heat the oil in a large saucepan and brown the sausages in it for 10 minutes. Set aside on a plate.

2 Pour off all but 1 tablespoon of the fat from the pan. Soften the onion and celery in the remaining fat over a moderate heat, then stir in the garlic and apples and cook for 3 minutes.

3 Cut the sausages into large chunks and add to the pan with the stock, cider, thyme, salt, some pepper and the potatoes. Bring to the boil, reduce the heat, cover and simmer for 10 minutes.

4 Stir in the baby sweetcorn and courgettes, cover and simmer for 8 minutes more, or until all the vegetables are just softened. Garnish with the parsley and serve with warm poppyseed rolls.

LENTIL AND SAUSAGE STEW

Serves 4
Preparation time: 20 minutes
Cooking time: 1 hour

2 teaspoons olive oil
450 g (1 lb) fresh Italian
   spicy sausages
115 g (4 oz) smoked back bacon,
   rinds removed and cut into strips
1 large red onion, peeled
   and chopped
1 clove garlic, peeled and crushed
   (see p.11)
1 green pepper, de-seeded
   and chopped
1 medium stick celery, trimmed
   and chopped
2 small carrots, peeled and sliced
225 g (8 oz) green lentils, cleaned
   of grit and rinsed
1 level teaspoon each ground
   coriander and ground cumin
150 ml (¼ pint) red wine
425 ml (¾ pint) chicken stock
   (see p.8)
400 g (14 oz) canned tomatoes
½ level teaspoon salt
Freshly ground black pepper
Fresh coriander leaves to garnish

Lentils absorb the smoky, spicy flavours of sausage and bacon in this filling family meal. If you are unable to find fresh Italian sausages in a delicatessen, you can use 340 g (12 oz) of sliced pepperoni instead and add it at the same time as the lentils.

1 Heat the oil in a large saucepan and cook the sausages and bacon in it over a moderate heat for 5 minutes. Stir in the onion, garlic, green pepper, celery and carrots and cook gently for 10 minutes.

2 Add the lentils, coriander and cumin and cook for 1 minute, stirring. Stir in the wine, stock, tomatoes, salt and some pepper and bring to the boil. Reduce the heat, cover and simmer for about 45 minutes, or until the lentils are just cooked and not broken up. Garnish with the coriander leaves and serve with warm crusty bread.

Per serving
Calories 721 Protein 31 g
Total fat 43 g (saturated fat 17 g)
Carbohydrates 50 g (added sugar 0)
Fibre 3.5 g Sodium 1641 mg

FRANKFURTERS WITH SPICY BEANS AND COURGETTES

Serves 4
Preparation time: 15 minutes
Cooking time: 25 minutes

1 tablespoon olive oil
1 medium onion, peeled and sliced
450 g (1 lb) frankfurter sausages
   or kielbasa, sliced
800 g (1¾ lb) canned
   baked beans
2 level tablespoons each tomato
   purée, Dijon mustard and
   barbecue sauce
150 ml (¼ pint) beef stock
   (see p.8) or cider
1 level tablespoon dried thyme
¼ level teaspoon salt
Freshly ground black pepper
2 medium courgettes, halved
   lengthways and sliced

Mustard and barbecue sauce give a hot, spicy edge to this tasty stew of sausages and beans cooked with fragrant thyme in wholesome beef stock or cider.

1 Heat the oil in a large saucepan and soften the onion in it, then stir in the sausages and cook for 2 minutes.

2 Mix in the baked beans, tomato purée, mustard, barbecue sauce, stock or cider, thyme, salt and some pepper. Bring to the boil, cover, reduce the heat and simmer for 5 minutes.

3 Stir in the courgettes, cover and simmer for 8-10 minutes, or until just tender, then serve.

Per serving
Calories 555 Protein 22 g
Total fat 32 g (saturated fat 12 g)
Carbohydrates 48 g (added sugar 0)
Fibre 14 g Sodium 2217 mg

307

LAMB IN SHERRY

Serves 6
Preparation time: 25 minutes
Cooking time: 2 hours 30 minutes

....

1.6 kg (3½ lb) leg of lamb, trimmed
   of excess fat
3 cloves garlic, each peeled and
   cut into 2-3 pieces
Small sprigs fresh rosemary
2 tablespoons olive oil
16 shallots or button onions, peeled
285 ml (½ pint) medium dry or
   sweet sherry, warmed
340 g (12 oz) small carrots, peeled
1.4 kg (3 lb) medium potatoes,
   peeled and halved
4 tablespoons soy sauce
1 level tablespoon cornflour
2 tablespoons cold water
450 g (1 lb) courgettes, trimmed
   and thickly sliced diagonally
340 g (12 oz) chestnut mushrooms,
   wiped and sliced
Freshly ground black pepper

....

Per serving
Calories 741   Protein 68 g
Total fat 22 g (saturated fat 8.7 g)
Carbohydrates 58 g (added sugar 0)
Fibre 7.5 g   Sodium 751 mg

**Juicy whole carrots, thickly
sliced courgettes, chestnut
mushrooms and soft pieces of
potato accompany lean lamb
in a luxurious, fragrant stew.**

1 Make several small slits in the
lamb and insert a piece of garlic
and a rosemary sprig
in each one.

2 Heat the oil in a very large
flameproof casserole and brown
the lamb in it on all sides. Add the
shallots or onions and cook until
golden brown.

3 Pour the sherry over the lamb,
then cover the casserole with
a well-fitting lid and simmer
for 2 hours, adding more sherry
if necessary.

*Lamb on the bone, infused with rosemary and garlic, cooks slowly in a
rich sherry gravy with vegetables.*

4 Add the carrots and potatoes to the casserole and stir in the soy sauce. Cover and simmer for about 30 minutes.

5 Blend the cornflour with the water and stir into the cooking juices until thickened. Add the courgettes and mushrooms, then cover and cook for 10 minutes, or until all the vegetables are just tender. Season with some pepper.

6 Lift the lamb out of the casserole and onto a board. Carve into slices, then return the meat to the casserole and heat through with the vegetables, then serve.

CURRIED PORK AND BEANS

Serves 6
Preparation time: 15 minutes
Cooking time: 3 hours

2 tablespoons olive oil
1.4 kg (3 lb) spare rib pork chops
2 medium onions, peeled and thinly sliced
2 cloves garlic, peeled and crushed (see p.11)
2 level tablespoons medium curry powder
2 level teaspoons turmeric
340 g (12 oz) each cooked butter beans and haricot beans, rinsed and drained (see p.172)
1 small green chilli, de-seeded and finely chopped
1 bay leaf
3 tablespoons white wine vinegar
850 ml (1½ pints) beef stock (see p.8)
2 level tablespoons tomato pureé

Spare rib chops of pork are seasoned with curry powder, turmeric and fresh green chilli in this spicy casserole, which should bring cheer to downhearted holidaymakers in wet and chilly weather.

1 Heat the oil in a large flameproof casserole and brown the spare rib chops in it for 10-15 minutes. Remove from the casserole and set aside.

2 Soften the onions and garlic in the casserole, then stir in the curry powder and turmeric. Cook for 1-2 minutes, then remove from the casserole and put on a plate.

Per serving
Calories 769 Protein 60 g
Total fat 49 g (saturated fat 18 g)
Carbohydrates 23 g (added sugar 0)
Fibre 6.9 g Sodium 881 mg

3 Put half the spare rib chops in the casserole and cover with half the onion mixture, half the butter beans and half the haricot beans. Then cover this layer with the remaining chops and the rest of the onion mixture. Mix the remaining butter beans and haricot beans with the chilli and the bay leaf and spoon over the onions.

4 Mix together the vinegar, stock and tomato pureé and pour over the pork and beans. Bring to the boil, then reduce the heat, cover tightly and simmer gently for 2-2½ hours, or until the meat is tender. Take the bay leaf out of the casserole, stir gently and serve with crusty bread, sliced bananas and onion rings.

SAVOURY MINCE IN BUNS

Serves 4
Preparation time: 15 minutes
Cooking time: 25 minutes

2 tablespoons olive oil
1 large green pepper, de-seeded
   and chopped
6 spring onions, trimmed
   and chopped
340 g (12 oz) butternut squash,
   peeled and roughly chopped
450 g (1 lb) lean minced beef,
   pork or turkey
400 g (14 oz) canned
   chopped tomatoes
1-2 teaspoons brown sauce
60 g (2 oz) sultanas
2 tablespoons fresh orange juice
1/4 level teaspoon salt
Freshly ground black pepper
4 hamburger buns, cut in half
2 large carrots, peeled, halved
   and cut into long strips
4 sticks celery, washed

Per serving
Calories 506 Protein 31 g
Total fat 20 g (saturated fat 6.5 g)
Carbohydrates 54 g (added sugar 0)
Fibre 6.3 g Sodium 594 mg

A nutritious and hearty meal, where butternut squash, spring onions and green pepper are added to minced meat and served in hamburger buns – but watch out . . . it can get messy.

1 Heat the oil in a large frying pan and stir-fry the green pepper in it until just softened. Add the spring onions and squash and fry for 5 minutes, stirring occasionally.

2 Mix in the minced beef, pork or turkey and brown it for about 5 minutes, stirring occasionally, then stir in the tomatoes, brown sauce, sultanas, orange juice, salt and some pepper. Bring to the boil, then reduce the heat and simmer for 10 minutes, or until the meat is cooked and the sauce is thick.

3 Fill the halved buns with the mixture and serve with the carrot strips and celery sticks.

STIR-FRIED TURKEY IN PITTA BREAD

Serves 4
Preparation time: 20 minutes
Marinating time: 30 minutes
Cooking time: 15 minutes

3 tablespoons sesame oil
2 tablespoons each light soy sauce
   and dry sherry
1 clove garlic, peeled and crushed
   (see p.11)
1 tablespoon peeled and grated
   fresh root ginger
1 small green chilli, de-seeded
   and finely chopped
675 g (1 1/2 lb) boneless turkey,
   cut into thin strips
1 large red onion, peeled
   and chopped
1 large red pepper, de-seeded
   and chopped
175 g (6 oz) sugar snap peas
175 g (6 oz) mushrooms, wiped
   and sliced
115 g (4 oz) baby corn, sliced
   diagonally
225 g (8 oz) Chinese
   leaves, shredded
Freshly ground black pepper
4 pitta breads, lightly toasted and
   split open

Per serving
Calories 538 Protein 49 g
Total fat 15 g (saturated fat 1.4 g)
Carbohydrates 53 g (added sugar 0)
Fibre 5.2 g Sodium 820 mg

Chinese leaves, sugar snap peas, red onion and grated ginger make crunchy partners for turkey in this lively stir-fried filling for pitta bread pockets.

1 Mix together 2 tablespoons of the sesame oil, the soy sauce, sherry, garlic, ginger and chilli in a bowl, and toss the turkey in the mixture. Cover and leave to marinate for 30 minutes.

2 Heat the remaining oil in a wok or large frying pan and stir-fry the onion and red pepper in it for 3 minutes. Add the turkey strips and stir-fry for 3 minutes.

3 Mix in the sugar snap peas, mushrooms and baby corn, then cover and cook gently for 5 minutes. Add the Chinese leaves, cover and cook for a further 2 minutes, or until the leaves have wilted and the turkey is cooked (see p.117). Season with some pepper, then spoon the filling into the pitta breads and serve.

CRUNCHY FRIED RICE

Aromatic ginger, crunchy water chestnuts and spring onions are typically cooked with fried rice in China, where rice is eaten as a dish on its own, and not as a side dish. To garnish the fried rice with spring onion curls, make two or three long cuts down the tops of the onions and soak them in ice-cold water while the dish is being cooked.

Serves 4
Preparation time: 15 minutes
Cooking time: 10 minutes

3 tablespoons vegetable oil
2 sticks celery, trimmed and thinly sliced
1 large clove garlic, peeled and crushed (see p. 11)
1 teaspoon peeled and chopped fresh root ginger
450 g (1 lb) cooked rice (see p. 9)
250 g (9 oz) cooked chicken, diced
250 g (9 oz) frozen peas
225 g (8 oz) canned water chestnuts, drained and sliced
1 large carrot, peeled and thinly sliced
2 tablespoons soy sauce
2 eggs, size 2, lightly beaten
2 spring onions, trimmed and finely sliced
4 spring onion curls to garnish

Per serving
Calories 555 Protein 44 g
Total fat 22 g (saturated fat 3.9 g)
Carbohydrates 47 g (added sugar 0)
Fibre 7.6 g Sodium 664 mg

1 Heat the oil in a wok or large frying pan for 1 minute, then stir-fry the celery in it over a moderate heat for 2 minutes. Add the garlic and ginger and stir-fry for 1 minute more.

2 Mix in the cooked rice, chicken, frozen peas, water chestnuts, carrot and soy sauce and stir-fry for about 7 minutes, or until heated through.

3 Stir in the beaten eggs for 1 minute until just set, then mix in the sliced spring onions. Serve immediately, garnished with the spring onion curls.

Finely sliced celery, spring onions and whole water chestnuts add crunch and juiciness to tender fried rice. Authentic Chinese recipes use cold cooked rice because the grains remain separate during stir-frying.

CHICKEN AND MUSHROOM PASTIES

Serves 6
Preparation time: 45 minutes
Cooking time: 20 minutes

4 boneless chicken breasts, each
    about 175 g (6 oz), skinned
1 tablespoon lemon juice
150 ml (¼ pint) chicken stock
    (see p.8) or dry white wine
¼ level teaspoon salt
Freshly ground black pepper
15 g (½ oz) butter
1 medium onion, peeled
    and chopped
175 g (6 oz) mushrooms, wiped
    and sliced
1 tablespoon chopped fresh parsley
    or coriander
115 g (4 oz) Camembert cheese, cut
    into small cubes
600 g (1 lb 5 oz) shortcrust pastry
    (see p.9)
1 egg, size 2, beaten
1 tablespoon sesame seeds
Whole radishes to garnish

Per serving
Calories 695 Protein 37 g
Total fat 40 g (saturated fat 16 g)
Carbohydrates 48 g (added sugar 0)
Fibre 3.2 g
Sodium 738 mg

Marie Harel, an 18th-century Normandy farmer's wife, is thought to have perfected the recipe for the soft, creamy and mild-flavoured cheese that is now known as Camembert. Its creaminess enriches the tasty chicken, onion and mushroom filling in these picnic pasties.

1 Put the chicken breasts in a saucepan, pour over the lemon juice and stock or wine, and season with the salt and some pepper. Bring to the boil, then reduce the heat, cover and simmer for about 20 minutes, turning the breasts over halfway through cooking, until the chicken is done (see p.117).

2 Remove the chicken from the pan and set aside on a plate. Boil the cooking juices for about 10 minutes, or until reduced by half. Add the butter, onion and mushrooms and simmer for about 8 minutes, until softened. Take the pan off the heat and leave to cool.

3 Preheat the oven to 220°C (425°F, gas mark 7). Cut the chicken into small pieces, then mix into the onion and mushroom mixture with the parsley or coriander and the Camembert.

4 Divide the pastry into six and roll out each piece on a lightly floured surface to a circle 18 cm (7 in) across. Spoon one-sixth of the chicken mixture onto one half of each pastry round, leaving a 1.3 cm (½ in) border round the edge. Brush the edges with a little of the beaten egg and fold each pastry round in half, pressing the edges together to seal in the filling. Decorate the edge of each pasty, then put them on a baking tray.

5 Brush the pasties with the remaining egg and sprinkle with the sesame seeds. Bake in the centre of the oven for 20 minutes, or until crisp and golden brown. Cool on a wire rack, or wrap for a picnic, then garnish and serve with a green salad and french bread.

These sesame-seed coated pasties make neat individual meals for picnics. Wrap them in a clean cloth before packing in a basket so that they remain oven-warm for as long as possible.

Chicken, Mushroom and Vegetable Pie

Serves 4
Preparation time: 45 minutes
Cooking time: 1 hour 40 minutes

1.4 kg (3 lb) oven-ready chicken
1 medium onion, peeled
    and quartered
1 large carrot, peeled and sliced
2 sprigs each fresh rosemary
    and thyme
¾ level teaspoon salt
Freshly ground black pepper
285 ml (½ pint) chicken stock
    (see p.8)
1 tablespoon olive oil
30 g (1 oz) butter

115 g (4 oz) button mushrooms,
    wiped
115 g (4 oz) chestnut mushrooms,
    wiped and sliced
1 clove garlic, peeled and crushed
    (see p.11)
2½ level tablespoons plain flour
115 g (4 oz) canned
    sweetcorn kernels
1 level teaspoon fresh thyme leaves
3 tablespoons soured cream
600 g (1 lb 5 oz) shortcrust pastry
    (see p.9)
1 small egg, beaten, or
    2 tablespoons of milk to glaze

Per serving
Calories 555 Protein 22 g
Total fat 32 g (saturated fat 12 g)
Carbohydrates 48 g (added sugar 0)
Fibre 14 g Sodium 2217 mg

Button and chestnut mushrooms make a rich, nutty foil for the lightly simmered chicken in this substantial pie. If you are planning a special outdoor meal, you can make the pie in advance. Follow the recipe to the end of step 6, then refrigerate the pie, unbaked, overnight. Preheat the oven the following day and bake as directed in the final step.

1 Put the chicken, onion, carrot, rosemary, thyme, ½ teaspoon of the salt, some pepper and the stock in a saucepan and bring to the boil. Reduce the heat, cover and simmer for 1 hour, or until the chicken is cooked (see p.117).

2 Lift the chicken out of the pan and set aside on a plate until cool enough to handle. Strain the cooking liquid through a sieve into a measuring jug. Discard the skin and bones from the chicken and cut the meat into small pieces.

3 Heat the oil and butter in a saucepan and cook the button and chestnut mushrooms in it for 5 minutes. Stir in the garlic and flour and cook, stirring, for 1 minute. Gradually blend in 285 ml (½ pint) of the saved cooking liquid, then bring to the boil, stirring, until thickened.

4 Take the pan off the heat and stir in the chicken, sweetcorn, thyme, soured cream, remaining salt and some more pepper. Cover and leave to cool completely.

5 Preheat the oven to 220°C (425°F, gas mark 7). Roll out two-thirds of the pastry to a circle large enough to line a 23 cm (9 in) pie plate. Line the plate with the pastry, then fill with the chicken and mushroom mixture.

6 Roll out the remaining pastry to a circle large enough to cover the pie. Brush the pastry edge of the pie base with cold water and lay the pastry lid on top. Press the edges together and trim. Roll out the trimmings, cut into leaves and arrange on top of the pie.

7 Brush the top of the pie with the beaten egg or milk, then place it on a baking tray. Bake in the centre of the oven for 35-40 minutes, or until golden brown. Take the pie out of the oven and leave to cool, then refrigerate overnight.

Colourful strips of sweet pepper decorate the top of this attractive layered meatloaf, which combines a highly seasoned sausagemeat with tender, nutty bulgur wheat.

MEATLOAF WITH BULGUR WHEAT

Bulgur wheat adds fibre and texture to this chunky meatloaf, which is simple to prepare for a picnic or for your first meal on a self-catering holiday.

Serves 4
Preparation time: 35 minutes
Cooking time: 1 hour 30 minutes

115 g (4 oz) bulgur wheat
2 tablespoons chopped
   fresh parsley
285 ml (½ pint) boiling chicken
   stock (see p.8)
3 medium peppers, 1 red, 1 green,
   1 yellow, de-seeded and two
   rings cut from each, the rest
   finely chopped
1 tablespoon olive oil
1 clove garlic, peeled and crushed
   (see p.11)
1 medium onion, peeled and
   finely chopped
1 egg, size 3, lightly beaten
450 g (1 lb) pork sausagemeat
2 level tablespoons tomato purée

Per serving
Calories 616 Protein 18 g
Total fat 42 g (saturated fat 15 g)
Carbohydrates 43 g (added sugar 0)
Fibre 3 g Sodium 901 mg

I Put the bulgur wheat in a bowl with the parsley, then pour over the boiling stock. Soak for 15-20 minutes, or until all the liquid is absorbed.

2 Meanwhile, cut the pepper rings in half and arrange them in the base of a greased, nonstick, 23 cm x 13 cm (9 in x 5 in) loaf tin, overlapping slightly.

3 Preheat the oven to 180°C (350°F, gas mark 4). Heat the oil in a frying pan and soften the chopped peppers, garlic and onion in it for 10 minutes.

4 Stir half the beaten egg into the bulgur wheat, then mix the rest with the sausagemeat, the tomato purée and the pepper mixture in a separate bowl.

5 Carefully spoon one-third of the sausagemeat mixture over the pepper rings, and smooth it into the corners. Spread half of the bulgur wheat mixture on top. Repeat the layers, finishing with a layer of the sausagemeat. Level the top and cover with foil.

6 Stand the loaf tin in a roasting tin holding enough hot water to come halfway up the tin. Bake in the centre of the oven for 1½ hours, or until firmly set and cooked through. Drain off any excess fat. Allow the meat loaf to cool in the tin, then cover and refrigerate overnight. Serve the meatloaf cut into thick slices with tomatoes, celery, pickles and crusty bread.

Country Meatloaf Sandwiches

Serves 4
Preparation time: 20 minutes
Cooking time: 1 hour

1 tablespoon olive oil
1 medium onion, peeled and
   finely chopped
2 small peppers, 1 red, 1 green,
   de-seeded and finely chopped
1 clove garlic, peeled and crushed
   (see p.11)
½ level teaspoon each dried basil
   and thyme
1 egg, size 1
450 g (1 lb) lean minced beef
250 g (9 oz) minced veal or pork
200 g (7 oz) canned sweetcorn
   kernels, drained
60 g (2 oz) rolled oats
100 g (3½ oz) mozzarella cheese,
   cut into small cubes
30 g (1 oz) Parmesan
   cheese, grated
½ level teaspoon salt
Freshly ground black pepper
1 large french loaf or other
   bread or 8 rolls
1 small lettuce, separated into
   leaves, washed and dried
4 tablespoons tomato ketchup
   (optional)
8 large dill pickled cucumbers

Per serving
Calories 821 Protein 58 g
Total fat 28 g (saturated fat 9.9 g)
Carbohydrates 90 g (added sugar 0)
Fibre 11 g Sodium 1725 mg

Pickled cucumbers add the final touch to these substantial picnic sandwiches, which should be wrapped in waxed paper and then foil for transporting.

1 Preheat the oven to 190°C (375°F, gas mark 5). Heat the oil in a frying pan and soften the onion in it. Add the peppers, garlic, basil and thyme and cook for 7-10 minutes, stirring occasionally, until softened.

2 Beat the egg in a large bowl until slightly frothy, then mix in the minced meats, sweetcorn, oats, mozzarella, Parmesan, salt, some pepper and the onion mixture. Spoon into a greased, nonstick 23 cm x 13 cm (9 in x 5 in) loaf tin and level the top.

3 Bake uncovered in the oven for 1 hour, or until no longer pink inside. Take the meatloaf out of the oven, leave to cool, then cover and refrigerate overnight.

4 If using bread, cut it into eight, then cut each piece, or each roll if using, in half horizontally. Arrange the lettuce leaves on the bottom half of each piece of bread. Turn out the meat loaf and cut it into eight equal slices. Arrange the slices on top of the lettuce, spread with some ketchup, if using, and cover with the top pieces of bread. Serve with the pickled cucumbers.

Pan Bagnat

Basil, anchovies, grilled peppers and tomatoes provide the rich flavour in this traditional Provençal picnic dish, which improves with keeping. Its name translates as 'bathed bread', which refers to the sprinkling of the close-textured country bread with the vinaigrette dressing.

Serves 6
Preparation time: 30 minutes
Standing time: 2-3 hours

150 ml (¼ pint) extra virgin olive oil
5 tablespoons red wine vinegar
2 cloves garlic, peeled and crushed
   (see p.11)
¼ level teaspoon salt
Freshly ground black pepper
4 medium peppers, 2 red and
   2 green, grilled, de-seeded and
   sliced, juices reserved
2 French country loaves, each about
   400 g (14 oz)
100 g (3½ oz) canned anchovy
   fillets, drained and chopped
340 g (12 oz) beefsteak
   tomatoes, sliced
24 fresh basil leaves
1 large red onion, peeled and
   thinly sliced
16 pitted black olives, sliced

Per serving
Calories 644 Protein 17 g
Total fat 32 g (saturated fat 4.3 g)
Carbohydrates 76 g (added sugar 0)
Fibre 8.4 g Sodium 1622 mg

1 Whisk the oil with the vinegar, garlic, salt, some pepper and the reserved pepper juices to make up the dressing.

2 Cut each loaf into three equal slices horizontally. Take one loaf and remove the top two slices. Sprinkle 2 tablespoons of the dressing over the bottom slice of the loaf, then arrange a quarter of the peppers, anchovy fillets, tomatoes, basil leaves, onion and olives in layers on top.

3 Sprinkle another 2 tablespoons of the dressing over the top of the centre slice of bread, then lay it dressing-side down on the salad ingredients. Sprinkle a further 2 tablespoons of the dressing over the other side, and then arrange another quarter of the salad ingredients on top.

4 Sprinkle 2 tablespoons of dressing over the crumb side of the top slice of bread and lay it, dressing-side down, on top of the loaf. Press gently together, then wrap the loaf in greaseproof paper and then in foil. Repeat with the second loaf.

5 Leave to stand for at least 2-3 hours, but preferably overnight, to allow the loaves to absorb all the flavours. Cut into thick wedges and serve.

315

CREAMY CHICKEN AND POTATO PLATTER

Serves 4
Preparation time: 40 minutes
Cooking time: 10 minutes

450 g (1 lb) small new
   potatoes, scrubbed
3 tablespoons olive oil
2 tablespoons white wine vinegar
1 level tablespoon whole-grain
   mustard
1 tablespoon freshly snipped chives
¼ level teaspoon salt
Freshly ground black pepper
4 tablespoons mayonnaise
4 tablespoons soured cream
1 level tablespoon chopped
   fresh parsley
675 g (1½ lb) cooked chicken, cut
   into small pieces
2 sticks celery, trimmed and sliced
4 spring onions, trimmed
   and chopped
1 tablespoon capers, drained
   and chopped
2 eggs, size 2, hard-boiled, shelled
   and cut into wedges

Per serving
Calories 764 Protein 56 g
Total fat 51 g (saturated fat 12 g)
Carbohydrates 20 g (added sugar 0)
Fibre 1.9 g Sodium 471 mg

Chopped capers add a tangy
background taste to this light
summer salad combining
chicken, in a cool blend of
mayonnaise and soured cream,
with new potatoes tossed in a
mustard vinaigrette dressing.

1 Boil the potatoes until just
tender. Meanwhile, mix together
the oil, vinegar, mustard, chives,
salt and some pepper in a bowl.

2 Drain the potatoes and, when
cool enough to handle, cut
them into thick slices. Mix the
potato slices into the mustard
dressing and leave to cool.

3 Combine the mayonnaise with
the soured cream and parsley
in another large bowl. Stir in
the cooked chicken, celery, spring
onions and capers, then cover and
leave to stand for 20 minutes.

4 Spoon the cooled potato salad
around the edge of a serving
platter and pile the chicken
mixture into the centre. Garnish
with the egg wedges and serve.

CHICKEN AND FRUIT SALAD

Serves 6
Preparation time: 30 minutes

150 ml (¼ pint) low-fat
   natural yoghurt
150 g (5 oz) mayonnaise
3 tablespoons lemon juice
2 level teaspoons medium
   curry powder
½ level teaspoon salt
Freshly ground black pepper
2 level tablespoons chopped fresh
   coriander or flat-leaf parsley
200 g (7 oz) sugar snap peas,
   trimmed and blanched for
   1 minute (see p.10)
175 g (6 oz) cooked long-grain
   brown rice
450 g (1 lb) cooked chicken, diced
4 spring onions, trimmed and
   finely chopped
2 small Cantaloupe or Galia
   melons, quartered and de-seeded,
   flesh removed and cut into cubes
425 g (15 oz) canned, unsweetened
   pineapple pieces, well drained

Per serving
Calories 499 Protein 28 g
Total fat 26 g (saturated fat 4.7 g)
Carbohydrates 42 g (added sugar 0)
Fibre 2.9 g Sodium 370 mg

Tender cooked chicken comes
together with long-grain brown
rice, sugar snap peas, juicy
melon chunks and pineapple in a
refreshing, lightly spiced salad.

1 Whisk together the yoghurt,
mayonnaise, lemon juice, curry
powder, salt, some pepper and the
coriander or parsley in a bowl.

2 Cut the sugar snap peas into
strips and mix them into the
yoghurt dressing with the rice,
chicken, spring onions, melon
and pineapple. Transfer the salad
to a plastic container, then cover
and refrigerate until needed.

RIGATONI WITH TUNA, TOMATOES AND BROCCOLI

Serves 4
Preparation time: 20 minutes
Cooking time: 15 minutes

340 g (12 oz) rigatoni, or other
  medium-sized pasta shells
340 g (12 oz) broccoli, trimmed and
  cut into small florets, stalks
  peeled and sliced
4 tablespoons olive oil
2 tablespoons balsamic or
  red wine vinegar
1 level tablespoon Dijon mustard
Freshly ground black pepper
50 g (1¾ oz) canned anchovy
  fillets, drained and finely
  chopped, oil reserved
200 g (7 oz) canned tuna in oil,
  drained and flaked, oil reserved
3 spring onions, trimmed
  and chopped
2 ripe medium tomatoes, de-seeded
  and cut into wedges
2 level tablespoons chopped
  fresh parsley

Per serving
Calories 631 Protein 29 g
Total fat 29 g (saturated fat 4.2 g)
Carbohydrates 68 g (added sugar 0)
Fibre 5.1 g Sodium 723 mg

The green-headed broccoli that
is most common today is called
Calabrese, after the province
of Calabria, in Italy, where it
was first cultivated. Its lightly
cooked, peeled stalks add a
wonderfully crunchy texture to
this appetising pasta salad.

1 Cook the pasta (see p.202),
adding the broccoli for the
last 4 minutes of cooking. In
the meantime, whisk together the
oil, vinegar, mustard and some
pepper in a large bowl. Add the
anchovy and tuna oils and mix in
the anchovies, tuna, spring onions,
tomatoes and chopped parsley.

2 Drain the pasta and broccoli,
then toss them with the tuna
dressing. Serve warm or cold with
ciabatta or any other Italian bread.

Meaty flakes of tuna fish and finely chopped anchovy fillets – classic salad ingredients in Mediterranean countries – combine with al dente pasta quills, thick tomato wedges and spring onions. Adding the oils reserved from the canned fish fortifies a traditional olive oil, vinegar and mustard dressing.

Making the most of holiday cooking

Don't let anxiety about all the meals that have to be prepared mar your relaxation and enjoyment on a self-catering holiday. In a cottage or caravan, at home or abroad, a little forethought and improvisation make light of confined space and meagre cooking facilities.

WORKING OUT A menu plan before you go away can contribute to a carefree holiday, although it is important to allow for impromptu whims and the chance of sampling local specialities. If you plan to take food with you, restrict yourself to dried and canned items and buy fresh vegetables, fruits, eggs and bread from the local shops when you need them.

Unless you are certain there will be a freezer at your destination, there is no point in carrying frozen foods with you. If you have a cool box, however, taking a ready-made frozen meal to equip you for your first evening can give you an anxiety-free start. You can use the box later for keeping butter, yoghurt, cream and salad ingredients cool.

Tips for self-catering holidays

When the available cooking equipment is limited, you may well need to improvise.

Use strong polythene bags for marinating meat, poultry or fish and for mixing. Put the bag inside a saucepan or cardboard box for extra support, and fold the top of the bag down over the side. This saves on washing-up too.

Use a glass bottle filled with cold water if you need a rolling pin. The water inside the bottle will help to keep the pastry cool.

To crush garlic, if you have no garlic crusher, flatten the cloves with the blade of a knife (see p.11). It is always a good idea to take your own knives, as these will no doubt be sharper than any that are provided in your holiday kitchen, and remember to take a can and bottle opener with you. Take large pans rather than small ones – you can use a large plate or some foil as a substitute lid, if you need one.

If you do not have a fridge, keep bottles of water, milk or wine cool by standing them in a bucket of cold water, covered with a wet towel.

If you have space, take a nonstick wok, preferably one with a lid. You can use it for stir-frying and boiling, and it is easily cleaned. Without a measuring jug, save food cans and pots, wash them out and use the chart below.

The easy way to weigh things up

LIQUID MEASURES

Baked bean can 150 g (5 oz) holds .... 175 ml (6 fl oz)
Baked bean can 420 g (14¾ oz) holds .... 450 ml (16 fl oz)
Milk bottle holds .... 570 ml (1 pint)
Tuna can 200 g (7 oz) holds .... 225 ml (8 fl oz)
Yoghurt carton 150 g (5 oz) holds .... 175 ml (6 fl oz)

DRY INGREDIENTS	Yoghurt carton holds 150 g (5 oz)	Tuna can holds 200 g (7 oz)
Flour*	100 g (3½ oz)	150 g (5 oz)
Sugar*	150 g (5 oz)	200 g (7 oz)
Rice*	150 g (5 oz)	175 g (6 oz)
Couscous*	115 g (4 oz)	175 g (6 oz)
Bulgur wheat*	115 g (4 oz)	175 g (6 oz)
Lentils*	150 g (5 oz)	200 g (7 oz)
Barley*	150 g (5 oz)	200 g (7 oz)
Grated cheese*	60 g (2 oz)	115 g (4 oz)
Breadcrumbs*	45 g (1½ oz)	60 g (2 oz)
Pasta**	60 g (2 oz)	85 g (3 oz)
Almonds and hazelnuts	100 g (3½ oz)	150 g (5 oz)
Walnuts	70 g (2½ oz)	100 g (3½ oz)

 * Fill to the top, tap lightly and level with a knife
** Slightly rounded

Lighting a barbecue

A barbecue beside your caravan or in the garden of your holiday cottage is a wonderful way of cooking on a summer evening.

To cook evenly and thoroughly without burning the food, it is important that the coals are heated until they are glowing, with a coat of white ash, but with no flames.

Charcoal is the easiest fuel to use, and is readily available from many garages and DIY stores as either briquettes or lumpwood. Briquettes burn for longer as they are denser, but lumpwood gives the food a better flavour. Logs or branches from the garden can also be used, and those from fruit trees and vines add a distinctive aroma of their own to the food.

There are many ways to light a barbecue: one of the most reliable is shown below. Gas barbecue lighters work well, but try to avoid using lighting fluid, as this can give off an odour which will taint the food.

Lighting the barbecue

Spread a flat bed of charcoal in the bottom of the barbecue, large enough to cover the area over which the food will be cooked, then pile the charcoal into a pyramid. Make paper spills of tightly rolled newspaper and place them between the charcoal. Light the spills, which will then ignite the charcoal.

Preparing food for the barbecue

Meat, fish and vegetables benefit from being seasoned with salt, pepper and a sprinkling of herbs, or better still, from being marinated, even for just a short time while the barbecue heats up. Marinating in an aromatic blend of oil, herbs and spices will bring out the flavour, and an acid-based marinade will help tenderise tough cuts of meat (see p.81).

Prepare and marinate foods as far in advance as possible – preferably overnight in the fridge, or at least somewhere cool if there is no fridge – and always before you light the barbecue. If you are threading the food onto skewers, use either the long metal type or the shorter wooden ones. These need to be soaked in cold water for at least 20 minutes.

The recipe illustrated below is for poussins with rice and pawpaw (see p.295), but the principle is the same for all foods.

Marinating

Prepare the marinade in a large china or glass dish as instructed in the recipe. Do not use a metal dish as it could taint the food. Turn the poussins in the marinade until evenly coated, then cover and leave for at least 1 hour, turning them from time to time.

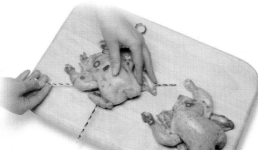

Skewering

When the coals are almost ready, remove the food from the marinade and thread it onto skewers. To hold open the spatchcocked poussins (see p.116) insert two skewers into each, diagonally across through the thigh, leg and then wing. Reserve the marinade.

Serving cooked rice mixtures or packets of mixed vegetables is an excellent way of extending the barbecue into a complete, one-dish meal. You can prepare the food mixtures ahead of time and wrap them in squares of heavy-duty foil. Heat the parcels through on the barbecue with the other food for the last 15-20 minutes of cooking time.

Foil vegetable packets

Brush a sheet of heavy-duty foil with olive oil and spoon the vegetables or rice into the centre. Bring the opposite sides of the square to the centre and fold over two or three times, then fold in each end to seal the parcel.

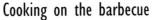

Cooking on the barbecue

Once the coals are white-hot, use a metal rake to spread them out into a compact layer. Place the grill rack on the barbecue, setting it about 15 cm (6 in) above the coals, and heat for 2-3 minutes before beginning to cook. Cook the food for the time specified, keeping the heat of the fire under control. A barbecue with vents can help you to do this – open vents increase the heat, and partially or completely closed ones reduce it – and a water spray, such as the type used for spraying house plants, is useful for dousing any fierce flames.

Using the barbecue

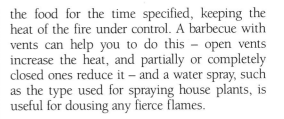

Turn foods frequently to prevent burning, and brush with the marinade to keep it moist. If the fire is too hot, spread out the coals; if it is not hot enough, push them into a pile together.

Roasting corn on the cob

1 Carefully peel back the green husks which cover the outside of the corn, but do not remove them. Pull off the fine silks underneath and discard.

2 Smooth the green husks back into place, then secure them with thin, clean string. Soak the tied cobs in a bowl of cold water for 30 minutes, then shake off any excess water – do not dry them – and cook as instructed.

MAKE AHEAD AND FREEZE

The freezer is a great boon to those who need a meal in a hurry, as well as to the cook who likes to be prepared ahead of time. Each of these tasty meals is prepared to the point where it simply needs to defrost overnight before the finishing touches are added. Nourishing stews, crusty pies and tasty soups are among an appetising selection of recipes that are ideal for entertaining and well worth making in advance.

❖

In Vegetable Curry (left), cauliflower florets, green beans, peas and chickpeas take on the warm flavours of authentic Indian curry spices. Once defrosted, this richly flavoured, creamy dish is ready to serve after just 45 minutes in the oven (see p.337).

LEMON SOUP WITH LAMB

This sumptuous soup combines the delicate flavour of lamb with the distinctive tang of lemon.

Serves 6
Preparation time: 25 minutes
Cooking time: 45 minutes

900 g (2 lb) very lean lamb,
  cut into small cubes
1 large onion, peeled and chopped
2 medium sticks celery, trimmed
  and chopped
1 small carrot, peeled and chopped
1.4 litres (2½ pints) chicken stock
  (see p.8)
285 ml (½ pint) water
1 teaspoon chopped fresh
  rosemary, or ½ level teaspoon
  dried rosemary
1 teaspoon chopped fresh thyme,
  or ½ level teaspoon dried thyme
½ level teaspoon salt
Freshly ground black pepper
175 g (6 oz) orzo or other small
  pasta shapes
175 g (6 oz) fresh spring greens,
  rinsed and finely shredded
3 eggs, size 3
Strained juice of 2 lemons
2 tablespoons chopped fresh dill
150 ml (¼ pint) double cream
  (optional)

Per serving
Calories 309 Protein 2.7 g
Total fat 12 g (saturated fat 5 g)
Carbohydrates 25 g (added sugar 0)
Fibre 3.3 g Sodium 306 mg

1 Put the lamb, onion, celery, carrot, stock, water, herbs, salt and some pepper into a large saucepan and bring to the boil. Reduce the heat and use a ladle to skim off any surface scum. Partially cover the saucepan and simmer for 30 minutes, skimming and stirring occasionally.

2 Bring the soup back to the boil and stir in the orzo or pasta shapes and the spring greens. Reduce the heat and simmer, uncovered, for 10 minutes, stirring occasionally. To freeze, remove from the heat and cool quickly (see p.341) – the other ingredients are added when serving, as they would separate during reheating. Pour the cooled soup into a rigid container, cover, label and freeze. Store for up to 2 months.

3 To serve, reheat from frozen. Whisk the eggs until frothy, then add the lemon juice. Ladle out 200 ml (7 fl oz) of the hot stock and whisk it into the eggs and lemon juice. Slowly stir the mixture back into the soup and cook over a low heat, stirring, for about 2 minutes, until it thickens.

4 Stir in the dill and the cream and heat the soup through for 1 minute. Ladle into hot bowls and serve piping hot with thick slices of olive bread.

Lean lamb and spring greens are the main ingredients of this inviting soup, thickened just before serving with eggs, lemon juice and cream.

GARDEN VEGETABLE SOUP

Serves 6
Preparation time: 20 minutes
Cooking time: 30 minutes

1.15 litres (2 pints) vegetable stock
  (see p.9)
2 medium potatoes, peeled
  and diced (see p.10)
2 medium carrots, peeled and sliced
1 medium onion, peeled
  and chopped
1 level teaspoon salt
340 g (12 oz) cooked cannellini
  beans, drained (see p.172)
225 g (8 oz) green beans, trimmed
  and cut into short lengths
2 medium courgettes, trimmed
  and diced
400 g (14 oz) canned
  chopped tomatoes
115 g (4 oz) small soup pasta
3 cloves garlic, peeled and
  crushed (see p.11)
15 g ($\frac{1}{2}$ oz) finely chopped fresh
  basil or parsley, or some of both
Freshly ground black pepper
150 g (5 oz) grated
  Parmesan cheese
3 tablespoons extra virgin olive oil
Fresh basil sprigs to garnish

Per serving
Calories 403 Protein 20 g
Total fat 16 g (saturated fat 6.3 g)
Carbohydrates 48 g (added sugar 0)
Fibre 11 g Sodium 673 mg

Any combination of vegetables is suitable for making this simple soup. Small white beans such as cannellini add both taste and bulk, but no cholesterol.

1 Combine the stock, potatoes, carrots, onion and salt in a large saucepan and bring to the boil. Reduce the heat to low, partially cover the saucepan and cook for about 20 minutes until the potatoes are tender.

2 Mix in the cannellini beans, green beans, courgettes, tomatoes and their juice and pasta. Cover and simmer, stirring from time to time, for about 10 minutes until the pasta is cooked. Remove the pan from the heat.

3 To freeze the soup, cool it quickly (see p.341), then pour into a rigid container. Cover, label and freeze for up to 2 months.

4 To serve, reheat the soup from frozen in a large saucepan. Remove from the heat and stir in the garlic, basil or parsley and some pepper, then ladle into six bowls, sprinkle each one with some of the grated Parmesan cheese and drizzle olive oil over it. Garnish with fresh basil sprigs and serve with warm Greek wholemeal bread. Pass round the remaining Parmesan separately.

CHICKEN MULLIGATAWNY SOUP

Serves 4
Preparation time: 30 minutes
Cooking time: 35 minutes

30 g (1 oz) butter
1 tablespoon olive oil
1 large Granny Smith apple, cored,
  peeled and diced
450 g (1 lb) boneless chicken
  breasts, skinned and cut into
  small cubes
1 level tablespoon mild curry paste
850 ml (1½ pints) chicken stock
  (see p.8)
2 medium carrots, peeled and
  thinly sliced
2 medium sticks celery, trimmed
  and thinly sliced
1 large onion, peeled and
  thinly sliced
60 g (2 oz) basmati rice
1 level tablespoon cornflour
2 tablespoons cold water
285 ml ($\frac{1}{2}$ pint) double cream
$\frac{1}{2}$ teaspoon finely grated
  lemon rind
$\frac{1}{2}$ level teaspoon salt
Freshly ground black pepper
2 tablespoons chopped
  fresh coriander

Per serving
Calories 655 Protein 28 g
Total fat 49 g (saturated fat 28 g)
Carbohydrates 27 g (added sugar 0)
Fibre 2.4 g Sodium 422 mg

The name mulligatawny, from the Tamil for 'pepper water', was given to a spicy soup adopted by the British Raj in India. Chicken, carrots, celery, basmati rice and double cream combine in this rich and tasty variation.

1 Heat the butter and oil in a large saucepan and cook the apple and chicken in it over a moderate heat for about 10 minutes or until golden brown. Stir in the curry paste and cook for 1 minute.

2 Pour in the stock, then stir in the carrots, celery, onion and rice and bring to the boil. Reduce the heat, cover and simmer for 20 minutes or until the chicken and vegetables are tender.

3 Meanwhile, blend the cornflour with the water, stir in the cream, lemon rind and salt, and add them to the simmering soup. Increase the heat and stir until the soup thickens. Reduce the heat, simmer for 2-3 minutes, add some pepper and stir in the coriander. Remove from the heat and cool quickly (see p.341). Pour into a rigid container, cover, label and freeze for up to 2 months.

4 To serve, reheat the soup slowly in a large saucepan, stirring frequently. Bring to a rolling boil, then serve with some warm naan bread.

323

BEEF STEW WITH BEER

Stout beer contributes a dark colour and nutty flavour to a filling and wholesome beef stew, which improves with keeping.

Serves 4
Preparation time: 35 minutes
Cooking time: 2 hours 30 minutes

900 g (2 lb) lean beef skirt, trimmed of fat and cut into cubes (see p.79)
1/2 level teaspoon salt
Freshly ground black pepper
2 tablespoons vegetable oil
2 medium onions, peeled and thickly sliced
1 level teaspoon sugar
285 ml (1/2 pint) stout
425 ml (3/4 pint) beef stock (see p.8)
1 1/2 level teaspoons dried thyme
1 bay leaf
8 medium carrots, peeled and thickly sliced
675 g (1 1/2 lb) small new potatoes, scrubbed
2 level tablespoons cornflour or arrowroot, blended with a little cold water
1 1/2 tablespoons white wine vinegar
Chopped fresh parsley to garnish

Per serving
Calories 510 Protein 40 g
Total fat 16 g (saturated fat 4.3 g)
Carbohydrates 52 g (added sugar 1.3 g)
Fibre 6.1 g Sodium 420 mg

1 Season the beef with half the salt and some black pepper. Heat the oil in a large flameproof casserole, and brown the beef on all sides for 8-10 minutes. Move the beef to a plate and set aside.

2 Add the onions to the casserole, and season with the remaining salt and some pepper. Cook over a moderate heat, stirring, for about 10 minutes until golden brown, then stir in the sugar.

3 Return the beef to the casserole. Pour in the stout and stock, add the thyme and bay leaf and bring to the boil. Reduce the heat, cover, and simmer gently for about 1 1/2 hours until the beef is tender. Stir in the carrots and potatoes, cover, and simmer for 20-30 minutes until cooked, then remove from the heat.

4 To freeze, cool as quickly as possible (see p.341) and then transfer to a foil-lined container. Cover the container with non-toxic plastic film and freeze. Once frozen, wrap completely in foil and store for up to 2 months.

5 To serve, thaw overnight in the refrigerator, or reheat slowly from frozen. Stir in the blended cornflour and cook, stirring, for 2-3 minutes until the sauce thickens. Discard the bay leaf and stir in the wine vinegar. Garnish with the parsley and serve.

Cubes of lean beef, new potatoes, carrots and onions are stewed in stock and stout beer, then garnished with chopped fresh parsley.

BEEF WITH LENTILS AND RICE

Using green lentils rather than the softer red variety will give extra body to this hearty stew.

Serves 6
Preparation time: 30 minutes
Cooking time: 2 hours 20 minutes

2 tablespoons olive oil
1.4 kg (3 lb) stewing steak, trimmed of fat and cut into cubes (see p.79)
2 large onions, peeled and chopped
2 cloves garlic, peeled and crushed (see p.11)
3 peppers, 1 red, 1 green, 1 yellow, de-seeded and diced
1 bay leaf
½ level teaspoon salt
1 level teaspoon dried thyme
½ level teaspoon dried rosemary, crushed
Freshly ground black pepper
1 litre (1¾ pints) beef stock (see p.8)
225 g (8 oz) green lentils, cleaned of grit and rinsed
85 g (3 oz) long-grain white rice
400 g (14 oz) canned chopped tomatoes
2 tablespoons chopped fresh parsley
Sprigs of fresh rosemary and thyme to garnish

1 Heat the olive oil in a large, flameproof casserole, and brown the beef in it in three batches for 5 minutes each. Spoon the beef onto a plate and set aside.

2 Stir in the onions and garlic, and cook for 10 minutes or until softened. Return the beef to the casserole and stir in the peppers, bay leaf, salt, thyme, rosemary, some pepper and the stock. Bring slowly to the boil. Reduce the heat, cover the casserole, and simmer for 1 hour, stirring occasionally.

3 Stir in the lentils, cover and simmer for 30 minutes. Mix in the rice and tomatoes, cover again and cook for another 25 minutes or until the rice, lentils and beef are cooked and the stew has thickened slightly.

4 To freeze the stew, cool it quickly (see p.341), then pour it into a rigid container, cover, label and freeze for up to 2 months.

5 To serve, thaw the stew overnight in the fridge, then reheat in a flameproof casserole or saucepan over a moderate heat, stirring frequently. Garnish with the fresh herbs and serve.

Per serving
Calories 529 Protein 60 g
Total fat 16 g (saturated fat 4.9 g)
Carbohydrates 40 g (added sugar 0)
Fibre 3 g Sodium 292 mg

CHUNKY CHILLI

This substantial variation on chilli con carne combines chunks of beef cooked in a spicy chilli sauce with kidney beans, peppers and sweetcorn.

Serves 6
Preparation time: 35 minutes
Cooking time: 1 hour 20 minutes

2 tablespoons olive oil
675 g (1½ lb) stewing steak, trimmed of fat and cut into small cubes (see p.79)
3 large peppers, 1 red, 1 green, 1 yellow, de-seeded and chopped
1 large onion, peeled and chopped
1 clove garlic, peeled and crushed (see p.11)
570 ml (1 pint) passata (sieved tomatoes)
4 tablespoons tomato purée
225 ml (8 fl oz) beef stock (see p.8)
225 g (8 oz) frozen sweetcorn kernels
225 g (8 oz) cooked red kidney beans, rinsed and drained (see p.172)
1 level tablespoon chilli powder
½ level teaspoon ground cumin
¼ level teaspoon salt
⅛ level teaspoon cayenne pepper
Soured cream, paprika and fresh green chillies, chopped, to garnish

1 Heat 1 tablespoon of the oil in a large saucepan and brown the beef in it in two batches. Spoon the beef onto a plate and set aside.

2 Add the remaining oil to the pan and sauté the peppers, onion and garlic over a moderate heat for about 10 minutes or until soft. Stir in the passata, tomato purée, stock, sweetcorn, kidney beans, chilli powder, cumin, salt and cayenne pepper. Bring to the boil, stirring continuously.

3 Return the beef and any juices on the plate to the pan and mix well into the sauce. Reduce the heat to low, cover the saucepan, and simmer gently for about 1 hour, stirring occasionally, or until the meat is tender.

4 To freeze, cool the chilli quickly (see p.341) and pour into a rigid container. Cover, label and freeze for up to 2 months.

5 To serve, thaw overnight in the fridge or reheat slowly from frozen in a flameproof casserole. Once it is heated through, top with the soured cream, green chillies and a little paprika. Serve with crusty bread and salad.

Per serving
Calories 415 Protein 42 g
Total fat 18 g (saturated fat 6.1 g)
Carbohydrates 23 g (added sugar 0)
Fibre 7 g Sodium 554 mg

PORK PATTIES IN PASTRY

Moist sage, onion and pork patties wrapped in shortcrust pastry conceal a soft and creamy centre of Stilton cheese.

Serves 8
Preparation time: 35 minutes
Cooking time: 40 minutes

550 g (1¼ lb) minced pork
1 small onion, peeled and
   finely chopped
1 level tablespoon chopped fresh
   sage, or 1 level teaspoon
   dried sage
85 g (3 oz) fresh brown or white
   breadcrumbs
1 egg, size 3, beaten
½ level teaspoon salt
Freshly ground black pepper
115 g (4 oz) Stilton cheese,
   cut into 8 cubes
600 g (1 lb 5 oz) shortcrust pastry
   (see p.9)

Per pattie
Calories 550 Protein 24 g
Total fat 32 g (saturated fat 13 g)
Carbohydrates 44 g (added sugar 0)
Fibre 2.4 g Sodium 706 mg

1 Mix together the minced pork, onion, sage, breadcrumbs, egg, salt and some pepper in a bowl. Divide the mixture into eight. Place a Stilton cube in the centre of each portion, then fold the meat over to enclose the cheese and shape into neat patties.

2 Roll out the pastry on a lightly floured surface and cut out eight rounds, each 20 cm (8 in) across. Place a meat patty in the centre of each pastry round. Brush the pastry edges with water, then wrap around the meat, pinching the join firmly together to seal. Place the pastry-wrapped patties join-side down on a baking tray lined with non-toxic plastic film.

3 Roll out the pastry trimmings and cut into leaves. Brush with cold water and arrange on the patty tops. Leave on the baking tray and open-freeze (see p.341) overnight. Put into a rigid container or freezer bags and store for up to 2 months.

4 To cook, preheat the oven to 220°C (425°F, gas mark 7). Remove as many patties as required from the freezer, place join-side down on a baking tray and brush with beaten egg or milk. Bake in the oven for 20 minutes, then reduce the heat to 190°C (375°F, gas mark 5) and cook for a further 15-20 minutes. Serve with a tossed mixed salad.

MOZZARELLA MEATLOAF PIE

In this unusual variation on a meatloaf, a meat crust is filled with layers of sliced tomatoes, spinach and cheese and topped with mashed potatoes. Be sure to make the pie with fresh meat rather than meat that has previously been frozen.

Serves 4
Preparation time: 25 minutes
Cooking time: 30 minutes

450 g (1 lb) potatoes, peeled
   and quartered
4 tablespoons milk
30 g (1 oz) butter
½ level teaspoon salt
Freshly ground black pepper
400 g (14 oz) fresh spinach,
   trimmed, washed and
   blanched (see p.10)
¼ level teaspoon freshly
   grated nutmeg
450 g (1 lb) very lean minced beef
3 tablespoons fine dry breadcrumbs
1 egg, size 2, lightly beaten
1 clove garlic, peeled and
   crushed (see p.11)
1 level teaspoon dried oregano
225 g (8 oz) tomatoes, sliced
175 g (6 oz) mozzarella or Cheddar
   cheese, grated
4 cherry tomatoes, halved, and fresh
   oregano leaves to garnish

Per serving
Calories 545 Protein 44 g
Total fat 24 g (saturated fat 13 g)
Carbohydrates 40 g (added sugar 0)
Fibre 8.1 g Sodium 883 mg

1 Preheat the oven to 180°C (350°F, gas mark 4). Cook the potatoes and drain well. Add the milk, butter, half the salt and plenty of pepper. Mash the potatoes until smooth.

2 Squeeze the blanched spinach dry, chop it roughly, put it in a bowl and mix with the nutmeg. In another bowl, combine the beef, breadcrumbs, egg, garlic, oregano and the remaining salt. Use the beef mixture to form a crust across the base and up the sides of a greased 23 cm (9 in) flan dish.

3 Layer the crust with the tomatoes, grated cheese and spinach, and then top with the mashed potatoes. Smooth the surface and then swirl with a fork.

4 Open-freeze the pie (see p.341), then place in a freezer bag or over-wrap with non-toxic plastic film and foil. Store in the freezer for up to 1 month.

5 Thaw the pie overnight in the refrigerator. Preheat the oven to 180°C (350°F, gas mark 4). Place the pie in the centre of the oven and bake, uncovered, for 30-40 minutes, or until the meat crust shrinks away from the sides of the dish and the top is lightly browned. Garnish with the cherry tomatoes and oregano and serve with a crisp green salad.

BEEF GOULASH

Serves 4
Preparation time: 45 minutes
Cooking time: 1 hour 45 minutes

2 tablespoons olive oil
675 g (1½ lb) chuck steak, trimmed
    of fat and cut into cubes
¼ level teaspoon salt
3 medium onions, peeled
    and chopped
2 cloves garlic, peeled and
    crushed (see p.11)
2 level tablespoons paprika
1½ level teaspoons caraway seeds
225 ml (8 fl oz) dry red wine
3 medium carrots, peeled and sliced
3 level tablespoons tomato purée
285 ml (½ pint) beef stock
    (see p.8)
450 g (1 lb) potatoes, peeled
    and diced
2 green peppers, de-seeded
    and sliced
150 g (5 oz) soured cream
¼ level teaspoon paprika and
    2 tablespoons chopped fresh
    parsley to garnish

Per serving
Calories 480 Protein 35 g
Total fat 21 g (saturated fat 8.4 g)
Carbohydrates 30 g (added sugar 0)
    Fibre 4.4 g Sodium 275 mg

This rich, full-flavoured beef stew is one of many Hungarian goulash recipes. An essential ingredient of these is paprika, a ground seasoning made from a variety of sweet red pepper.

1 Preheat the oven to 180°C (350°F, gas mark 4). Heat the oil in a large, flameproof casserole and brown the beef in it in three batches over a moderate heat. Transfer the meat to a plate, sprinkle with salt and reserve.

Soured cream adds a luxurious finishing touch to this typical red wine stew from Hungary, which is seasoned with caraway seeds and spicy paprika.

2 Add the onions and the garlic to the casserole and soften over a low heat. Turn up the heat and continue cooking until the onions are pale golden. Stir in the paprika and caraway seeds and cook for 1 minute. Add the wine, bring to the boil and cook for 3 minutes, until the liquid has reduced slightly.

3 Mix in the carrots, tomato purée and stock, and return the beef to the casserole. Bring to the boil, cover and place in the centre of the oven. Cook for 1 hour 10 minutes, or until the beef is almost tender.

4 Take the casserole out of the oven and stir in the potatoes and green peppers. Cover and cook for another 30-35 minutes, or until the potatoes are done.

5 Cool the goulash quickly (see p.341), then pour into a rigid container. Cover and freeze.

6 Thaw the goulash overnight in the refrigerator, then reheat in a flameproof casserole on top of the stove, stirring frequently. Spoon the soured cream on top of the goulash, sprinkle with the paprika and parsley, and serve.

TAJINE OF LAMB

A tajine is a North African dish of varied ingredients cooked together slowly in a special pot. This lamb tajine is stewed with dried fruits, which you can buy in many supermarkets.

Serves 4
Preparation time: 20 minutes
Cooking time: 1 hour 45 minutes

250 g (9 oz) dried fruit salad, soaked overnight in cold water
900 g (2 lb) boneless leg of lamb, trimmed of fat, cubed (see p. 79)
450 g (1 lb) onions, peeled and chopped
1 level teaspoon ground coriander
½ level teaspoon ground ginger
1 stick cinnamon
½ lemon
½ level teaspoon salt
Freshly ground black pepper
175 g (6 oz) couscous, soaked in 425 ml (¾ pint) lukewarm water, or 675 g (1½ lb) cooked rice

Per serving
Calories 642 Protein 57 g
Total fat 15 g (saturated fat 6.9 g)
Carbohydrates 74 g (added sugar 0)
Fibre 5.2 g Sodium 393 mg

Pour the liquid from the soaked dried fruit into a measuring jug, make it up to 570 ml (1 pint) with water and set the fruit aside. Pour the liquid into a large saucepan and add the lamb, chopped onions, coriander, ginger and cinnamon. Pare off a large strip of rind from the lemon and add to the pan with 1 tablespoon of the lemon juice. Add the salt and some pepper and stir well.

2 Bring to the boil, then reduce the heat, cover and simmer gently, stirring occasionally, for 1 hour. Stir in the dried fruit, cover and simmer for 45 minutes more, or until the fruit is soft and the lamb very tender. Cool, then put into a suitable container for freezing. Cover, label (see p.340) and freeze for up to 2 months.

3 Thaw overnight at room temperature until completely defrosted, then pour into a saucepan and bring slowly to the boil, stirring frequently.

4 Fit a steamer pan or a large metal sieve above the lamb. Put the couscous or rice in it and cover with a well-fitting lid or foil. Simmer for 15 minutes or until the lamb is heated through and the steamed couscous or rice is light and fluffy. Stir the lamb occasionally so that it does not stick to the pan. Serve garnished with a twist of lemon rind.

A full-flavoured North African broth of spiced lamb and dried fruit cooked in dried-fruit stock is served with couscous – or rice if you prefer.

Moussaka

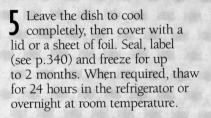

Serves 6
Preparation time: 1 hour 45 minutes
Cooking time: 1 hour 30 minutes

1.1 kg (2½ lb) aubergines, trimmed and sliced lengthways
3½ level teaspoons salt
175 ml (6 fl oz) olive oil
1.8 kg (4 lb) leg of lamb, boned, trimmed of fat and cut into very small dice (see p.79)
1 large onion, peeled and chopped
450 g (1 lb) beefsteak tomatoes, skinned, de-seeded and chopped
3 tablespoons chopped fresh parsley
½ level teaspoon cinnamon
½ level teaspoon freshly grated nutmeg
175 ml (6 fl oz) red wine
Freshly ground black pepper
60 g (2 oz) Parmesan cheese, grated

For the soufflé topping
570 ml (1 pint) milk
1 bay leaf
6 black peppercorns
1 sprig of parsley
1 small onion, peeled and quartered
2 cloves
60 g (2 oz) butter
60 g (2 oz) plain flour
2 eggs, size 2, separated
30 g (1 oz) Parmesan cheese, grated
Sprigs of flat-leaf parsley to garnish

Per serving
Calories 801 Protein 65 g
Total fat 49 g (saturated fat 19 g)
Carbohydrates 22 g (added sugar 0)
Fibre 7.1 g Sodium 1087 mg

The popular Greek dish of lamb, tomato and aubergine freezes well, and is an excellent standby for when you have to entertain at rather short notice. This version of moussaka is topped with a soufflé, added after defrosting.

1 Put the aubergines in a large colander and sprinkle with 3 teaspoons of the salt, then leave to stand on a plate for 30 minutes. Meanwhile, heat 2 tablespoons of the oil in a large saucepan and cook the lamb and onion in it over a high heat for 8-10 minutes, or until the lamb is lightly browned.

2 Mix in the tomatoes, parsley, spices, red wine, remaining salt and some pepper and bring to the boil. Reduce the heat and simmer uncovered for 30 minutes.

3 Meanwhile, rinse the aubergine slices under cold running water, drain and pat dry with kitchen paper. Fry in batches in the rest of the oil until lightly browned, then drain on kitchen paper.

4 Assemble the moussaka in a large 4 litre (7 pint) ovenproof dish, preferably only 6 cm (2½ in) deep, as a shallow dish will allow faster thawing. Cover the bottom with a quarter of the aubergine slices, add a third of the lamb mixture and sprinkle with a third of the Parmesan. Repeat the layers, finishing with aubergines.

5 Leave the dish to cool completely, then cover with a lid or a sheet of foil. Seal, label (see p.340) and freeze for up to 2 months. When required, thaw for 24 hours in the refrigerator or overnight at room temperature.

6 Preheat the oven to 190°C (375°F, gas mark 5). To prepare the soufflé topping, put the milk and the bay leaf, peppercorns, parsley, onion and cloves in a saucepan and bring to the boil. Remove from the heat, cover and leave to stand. Meanwhile, reheat the moussaka, covered with a lid or foil, in the oven for 1 hour.

7 To complete the topping, strain the milk, then melt the butter in a saucepan, stir in the flour and cook over a moderate heat for 1 minute. Gradually stir in the milk and bring to the boil, stirring, until the sauce thickens. Reduce the heat and simmer for 3 minutes, stirring frequently.

8 Remove the pan from the heat and beat in the egg yolks. In a bowl, whisk the egg whites until they hold soft peaks. Fold a quarter of the whites into the sauce, then fold in the rest.

9 Uncover the moussaka and pour over the topping. Sprinkle with the Parmesan cheese and return to the oven for 30 minutes, or until the soufflé topping is well risen and golden brown. Garnish with the parsley sprigs and serve with some Greek-style bread or warm pitta bread and green salad.

PIQUANT LAMB STEW

This tasty lamb and courgette stew, spiced with garlic and green chillies, can be made with yoghurt if you want a slightly sharper flavour, or soured cream if you prefer a softer taste.

Serves 6
Preparation time: 45 minutes
Cooking time: 1 hour 30 minutes

2 tablespoons olive oil
1 large onion, peeled and chopped
2 large green chillies, de-seeded and finely chopped
1 clove garlic, peeled and crushed (see p.11)
1/2 level teaspoon salt
Freshly ground black pepper
1/2 level teaspoon cinnamon
1/4 level teaspoon ground cloves
1.1 kg (2 1/2 lb) boned shoulder of lamb, trimmed of fat and cut into large cubes (see p.79)
425 ml (15 fl oz) beef stock (see p.8)
450 g (1 lb) small new potatoes, scrubbed
450 g (1 lb) courgettes, trimmed and thickly sliced
1 level tablespoon cornflour
150 ml (1/4 pint) low-fat natural yoghurt or soured cream
2 tablespoons chopped fresh coriander

Per serving
Calories 331 Protein 28 g
Total fat 16 g (saturated fat 6.3 g)
Carbohydrates 19 g (added sugar 0)
Fibre 1.2 g Sodium 260 mg

1 Heat the olive oil in a large, flameproof casserole or large saucepan and cook the onion in it, stirring occasionally, for 5 minutes or until just softened.

2 Add the chillies, garlic, salt, some pepper, cinnamon and cloves. Cook, stirring, for 5 minutes, then add the lamb. Cook for another 10 minutes, stirring occasionally, until the meat is browned.

3 Stir in the stock, bring to the boil, cover, and simmer for 1 hour 15 minutes. Add the potatoes, cover and simmer for 10 minutes, then stir in the courgettes and cook for a further 7 minutes, or until the vegetables and meat are tender.

4 Cool the stew quickly, pour it into a rigid container, cover and label (see p.340). Freeze for up to 2 months. To serve, reheat from frozen in a large saucepan over a low heat, stirring from time to time, then bring to the boil.

5 Blend the cornflour with 2 tablespoons of the yoghurt or soured cream and stir it quickly into the reheated stew. Add the remaining yoghurt or soured cream and cook over a moderate heat for 5 minutes, stirring to make sure that the stew thickens smoothly. Sprinkle with the coriander and serve immediately.

POTATO-TOPPED LAMB PIE

Home-made stock or canned consommé gives a rich, meaty flavour to this warming lamb and vegetable pie.

Serves 4
Preparation time: 25 minutes
Cooking time: 15 minutes

285 ml (1/2 pint) canned chicken or beef consommé or stock (see p.8)
1/4 level teaspoon each dried thyme and marjoram
340 g (12 oz) frozen mixed vegetables
1 level tablespoon cornflour
2 tablespoons cold water
340 g (12 oz) cold roast lamb, diced (see p.79)
900 g (2 lb) potatoes, peeled and quartered
30 g (1 oz) butter or margarine
3 tablespoons milk
1/4 level teaspoon salt
1/4 level teaspoon paprika
Sprigs of parsley to garnish

Per serving
Calories 445 Protein 28 g
Total fat 17 g (saturated fat 8.8 g)
Carbohydrates 48 g (added sugar 0)
Fibre 2.9 g Sodium 343 mg

1 Pour the consommé or stock into a large saucepan, add the thyme and marjoram and bring to the boil. Stir in the frozen mixed vegetables and bring back to the boil. Reduce the heat and simmer for 3 minutes.

2 Blend the cornflour with the cold water and then stir it into the pan. Cook, stirring, until thickened, then reduce the heat and simmer for 1 minute. Remove the pan from the heat and leave until cold, then mix in the lamb.

3 Meanwhile, boil and then mash the potatoes, adding the butter or margarine, milk and salt.

4 Pour the lamb mixture into a pie dish and spread the mashed potato over the top, using a fork or small palette knife to mark it with swirls. Leave the dish to cool, then cover the top with non-toxic plastic film, wrap it completely in foil and label (see p.340). Freeze for up to 2 months.

5 To thaw the pie, remove the foil and defrost at room temperature overnight. To serve, preheat the oven to 200°C (400°F, gas mark 6). Take off the plastic film and sprinkle the pie with the paprika. Bake in the oven for 30 minutes or until heated through and the potato topping is golden brown. Garnish and serve.

STUFFED CABBAGE LEAVES

Crisp savoy cabbage leaves are stuffed with a spicy beef mixture and served with rice.

Serves 4
Preparation time: 1 hour 10 minutes
Cooking time: 55 minutes

1 tablespoon olive oil
450 g (1 lb) lean minced beef
1 medium onion, peeled and
   finely chopped
1 clove garlic, peeled and
   crushed (see p.11)
½ level teaspoon ground cumin
1 level teaspoon ground coriander
1 small green chilli, de-seeded
   and finely chopped
115 g (4 oz) long-grain white rice
285 ml (½ pint) beef stock
   (see p.8)
8 large savoy cabbage leaves,
   trimmed and blanched
   (see p.10)
225 g (8 oz) cooked easy-cook
   long-grain and wild rice (see p.9)

For the sauce
30 g (1 oz) butter
6-8 spring onions, trimmed
   and finely chopped
1 clove garlic, peeled and crushed
1 large carrot, peeled and
   finely diced (see p.10)
400 g (14 oz) canned
   chopped tomatoes
1 level tablespoon tomato purée
1 whole clove
¼ level teaspoon sugar
¼ level teaspoon salt
Freshly ground black pepper

Per serving
Calories 542 Protein 30 g
Total fat 25 g (saturated fat 10 g)
Carbohydrates 54 g (added sugar 0)
Fibre 5.6 g Sodium 329 mg

1 Heat the olive oil in a frying pan and brown the beef in it over a high heat for 5 minutes. Add the onion and garlic and cook for 5 minutes, then stir in the cumin and coriander and cook over a high heat, stirring, for 1 minute.

2 Stir in the chilli and white rice and pour in the stock. Bring to the boil, stirring occasionally. Reduce the heat, cover and simmer for 30 minutes, or until the rice is cooked and the mixture thickened. Remove the pan from the heat and leave to cool.

3 To make the sauce, melt the butter in a large saucepan and fry the onions, garlic and carrot in it for 10 minutes. Stir in the tomatoes, tomato purée, clove, sugar, salt and some black pepper. Bring to the boil, then reduce the heat, cover and simmer for 15 minutes, stirring occasionally. Take the sauce off the heat, discard the clove, and leave to cool.

4 Pat the blanched cabbage leaves dry with kitchen paper, and lay them vein-side up on a board. Trim the centre stalks if they are very thick. Spoon one-eighth of the beef filling onto each cabbage leaf. Fold the left and right-hand sides of each leaf over its filling and roll up tightly.

5 Spoon the cooked rice mixture onto a shallow ovenproof dish and arrange the stuffed cabbage leaves on it. Pour the cooled sauce over the stuffed cabbage leaves.

6 To freeze, cover the top of the dish with non-toxic plastic film, then wrap it completely in foil and label (see p.340). Freeze for up to 2 months.

7 To thaw, remove the foil covering, then leave overnight in the refrigerator. To serve, preheat the oven to 180°C (350°F, gas mark 4). Remove the plastic film and cover the top of the dish with foil. Cook in the centre of the oven for 40 minutes or until the sauce is bubbling hot and the stuffed cabbage leaves are heated through, then serve.

A piquant and slightly sweet sauce of tomatoes, carrot and spring onions with a hint of cloves makes a colourful topping for cabbage leaves and rice.

CHICKEN IN RED WINE CASSEROLE

Lean bacon, mushrooms, button onions and sugarsnap peas complete a tasty, full-bodied chicken and red wine stew.

Serves 4
Preparation time: 1 hour
Cooking time: 1 hour 15 minutes

2 tablespoons olive oil
4 rashers lean back bacon, trimmed of fat and cut into pieces
1.6 kg (3½ lb) chicken, cut into eight pieces (see p.115)
½ level teaspoon salt
Freshly ground black pepper
450 g (1 lb) button onions, peeled
225 g (8 oz) small new potatoes, scrubbed
225 g (8 oz) button mushrooms, wiped and sliced
2 medium carrots, peeled and thickly sliced
225 ml (8 fl oz) dry red wine
400 g (14 oz) canned tomatoes
2 cloves garlic, peeled and crushed (see p.11)
½ level teaspoon each dried rosemary and thyme
1 bay leaf
225 g (8 oz) sugarsnap peas, trimmed
2 tablespoons chopped fresh parsley
Parsley, rosemary, thyme to garnish

Per serving
Calories 642 Protein 74 g
Total fat 23 g (saturated fat 6.9 g)
Carbohydrates 27 g (added sugar 0)
Fibre 5.3 g Sodium 958 mg

1 Heat 1 tablespoon of the oil in a large saucepan, add the bacon and cook until crisp. Use a slotted spoon to lift it onto kitchen paper to drain. Cover and set aside.

2 Sprinkle the chicken with the salt and some pepper. Heat the remaining oil in the saucepan and fry the chicken pieces, four at a time, for about 7 minutes or until evenly golden. Set aside.

3 In the same pan, sauté the onions, potatoes, mushrooms and carrots for 5 minutes. Pour in the wine, bring to the boil, and boil uncovered for about 1 minute. Return the chicken to the pan and stir in the tomatoes, their juice, the garlic, herbs and bay leaf.

4 Bring back to the boil, then reduce the heat, cover and simmer for about 45 minutes, or until the vegetables and chicken are cooked through (see p.117). Stir in the sugarsnap peas, parsley and bacon pieces and cook for 5 minutes. Discard the bay leaf.

5 To freeze, cool the stew as quickly as possible (see p.341). Skim off any fat from the surface, pour into a rigid container, cover and freeze for up to 2 months. Before serving, thaw overnight in the fridge and then reheat. Garnish with the fresh herbs and serve with garlic french bread.

PORK AND MUSTARD POTATO GRATIN

Whole-grain mustard gives this dish a deep flavour that goes well with the pork. You can freeze the gratin in one large dish or in individual portions.

Serves 4
Preparation time: 40 minutes
Cooking time: 40 minutes

675 g (1½ lb) potatoes, peeled and diced
30 g (1 oz) butter
1 medium onion, peeled and chopped
3 level tablespoons cornflour
570 ml (1 pint) milk
2 tablespoons whole-grain mustard
340 g (12 oz) cooked pork, diced
60 g (2 oz) Gruyère cheese, grated
30 g (1 oz) toasted chopped hazelnuts
60 g (2 oz) wholemeal breadcrumbs
Thin slices of red apple and sage leaves to garnish

Per serving
Calories 721 Protein 39 g
Total fat 40 g (saturated fat 17 g)
Carbohydrates 55 g (added sugar 0)
Fibre 4.9 g Sodium 408 mg

1 Boil the potatoes for 10-15 minutes until just cooked. Drain and leave to cool.

2 Meanwhile, melt the butter in a saucepan and soften the onion in it over a low heat. In a bowl, blend the cornflour with 6 tablespoons of the milk.

3 Pour the remaining milk onto the onion and bring to the boil, then quickly stir in the cornflour mixture. Cook over a moderate heat, stirring, until the sauce thickens. Stir for 2 minutes more, then remove from the heat, stir in the mustard and leave to cool, stirring frequently to prevent a skin forming on the top.

4 Spread a third of the potatoes over the bottom of an ovenproof dish, cover with a third of the sauce, then spoon on half of the pork. Repeat the layers then top with the remaining potatoes and cover with the rest of the sauce. Mix together the cheese, hazelnuts and breadcrumbs and scatter them evenly over the top.

5 To freeze, cover the top of the dish with non-toxic plastic film, then wrap in foil, label (see p.340) and freeze for up to 2 months.

6 To thaw, remove the foil and leave to stand at room temperature for 4 hours, or overnight in the refrigerator. To reheat the dish, preheat the oven to 200°C (400°F, gas mark 6). Remove the plastic film, cover the top of the dish with foil and cook in the centre of the oven for 25 minutes. Remove the foil and cook for a further 15 minutes or until the topping is crisp and golden. Serve garnished with the apple slices and sage leaves.

PORK AND APPLE PIE

The cider base of this tasty pie highlights the hearty flavours of its pork and apple filling.

Serves 4
Preparation time: 30 minutes
Cooking time: 1 hour 30 minutes

1 tablespoon olive oil
3 rashers lean back bacon, rind removed and diced
675 g (1½ lb) lean pork spare rib, boned and cut into small cubes
½ level teaspoon salt
1 large onion, peeled and chopped
2 medium carrots, peeled, halved lengthways and sliced
2 medium turnips, peeled and diced
1 large dessert apple, peeled, cored and diced
1 level tablespoon plain flour
½ level teaspoon each dried sage and rosemary
Freshly ground black pepper
225 ml (8 fl oz) dry cider
300 g (11 oz) shortcrust pastry (see p.9)
1 egg, size 3, lightly beaten

Per serving
Calories 673 Protein 30 g
Total fat 39 g (saturated fat 14 g)
Carbohydrates 49 g (added sugar 0)
Fibre 4.6 g Sodium 888 mg

1 Heat the oil in a large frying pan and fry the bacon for 3-4 minutes until crisp, then put it on kitchen paper to drain. Season the pork with half the salt and fry in the pan until browned all over. Remove and drain with the bacon.

2 Toss the onion, carrots, turnips and apple in the cooking juices left in the pan, then stir in the flour, sage, rosemary and the remaining salt. Season with black pepper, pour in the cider and bring to the boil, stirring continuously.

3 Return the pork and bacon to the pan and mix with the vegetables. Bring back to the boil, then reduce the heat, cover and simmer for 1½ hours until the pork is tender. Take the pan off the heat and leave the filling to cool.

4 On a lightly floured surface, roll the pastry to a round 5 cm (2 in) larger than a 20 cm (8 in) pie plate. Cut a 2.5 cm (1 in) wide strip from round the pastry edge, brush the plate rim with water and press the strip firmly round it. Spoon the pork mixture into the pie plate, then brush the pastry strip with water and cover the pie with the pastry round. Press the edges together with a fork and trim the pie. Use the trimmings to make leaves, then arrange them in the centre of the pie and make a small escape hole for the steam.

5 To freeze, loosely wrap the pie in non-toxic plastic film or foil, then label (see p.340) and freeze for up to 2 months. To thaw, leave for 5-6 hours at room temperature or overnight in the fridge.

6 Preheat the oven to 220°C (425°F, gas mark 7). Brush the pie with the beaten egg, put in the centre of the oven and cook for 40-45 minutes. Serve with salad and warm crusty bread.

A traditional blend of lean pork and apple is cooked with back bacon, onion, carrots and turnips in this mouth-watering pie.

CHICKEN AND ONION CASSEROLE

Serves 4
Preparation time: 30 minutes
Cooking time: 35 minutes

4 boneless chicken breasts, each
   about 175 g (6 oz), skinned
1/2 level teaspoon salt
Freshly ground black pepper
30 g (1 oz) plain flour
4 tablespoons olive oil
225 g (8 oz) button onions, peeled
225 g (8 oz) button mushrooms,
   wiped and halved
425 ml (3/4 pint) chicken stock
   (see p.8)
1 clove garlic, peeled and
   crushed (see p.11)
2 level teaspoons tomato purée
1/4 level teaspoon each dried
   rosemary and fennel seeds
450 g (1 lb) baking potatoes,
   peeled and cut into dice
115 g (4 oz) thickly sliced back
   bacon, trimmed of fat and cut
   into wide strips
225 g (8 oz) asparagus, cut into
   short lengths, or broccoli florets
2 tablespoons chopped
   fresh parsley
Sprigs of fresh rosemary to garnish

Per serving
Calories 515 Protein 50 g
Total fat 22 g (saturated fat 4.5 g)
Carbohydrates 31 g (added sugar 0)
Fibre 5.2 g Sodium 926 mg

Onions heighten the flavour of
this tasty casserole. Use medium
onions, peeled and quartered, if
button onions are not available.

1 Sprinkle the chicken breasts with
the salt and some pepper, and
then lightly coat them with flour.

*Mushrooms and asparagus
complement seasoned chicken
breasts and
lean strips
of bacon.*

2 Heat 2 tablespoons of the oil in
a large, flameproof casserole
and cook the chicken in it over a
moderate heat for 2-3 minutes on
each side, or until golden brown.
Set the chicken aside on a plate.

3 Put the onions and mushrooms
into the casserole and cook for
about 7 minutes, or until softened.
Stir in the stock, garlic, tomato
purée, rosemary and fennel seeds.

4 Return the chicken to the
casserole and bring to the boil.
Reduce the heat, cover and simmer
for 15 minutes. While the
chicken is simmering, heat a

teaspoon of oil in a frying pan and
cook the bacon in it until crisp.
Drain it on kitchen paper. At the
same time, gently boil the diced
potatoes for 10-15 minutes, until
just cooked, then drain well and
mix with the remaining olive oil.

5 Stir the asparagus or
broccoli and the bacon into
the casserole and cook for
8 minutes. Take
the dish
off the

334

heat and spread the potatoes evenly over the top of the casserole. Leave to cool, cover, label (see p.340) and freeze for up to 2 months.

6 Thaw overnight at room temperature. Heat the oven to 200°C (400°F, gas mark 6). Uncover the casserole and reheat in the oven for 30-35 minutes, or until bubbling hot.
Sprinkle with the parsley, garnish and serve.

TURKEY LASAGNE

Serves 4
Preparation time: 45 minutes
Cooking time: 1 hour

570 ml (1 pint) milk
1 bay leaf
6 black peppercorns
1 small onion, peeled
2 tablespoons olive oil
1 large onion, peeled and chopped
60 g (2 oz) streaky bacon, rinds removed, chopped
1 clove garlic, peeled and crushed (see p.11)
115 g (4 oz) mushrooms, wiped and sliced
675 g (1½ lb) minced turkey
60 g (2 oz) plain flour
1 level teaspoon dried oregano
400 g (14 oz) canned chopped tomatoes
150 ml (¼ pint) dry white wine or chicken stock (see p.8)
30 g (1 oz) pitted black olives, sliced
½ level teaspoon salt
Freshly ground black pepper
200 g (7 oz) fresh lasagne
45 g (1½ oz) butter or margarine
¼ level teaspoon ground nutmeg
30 g (1 oz) Parmesan cheese, grated
Black olives and tomato slices to garnish

Minced turkey flavoured with garlic, onion, bacon, mushrooms and tomatoes is the basis for this low-fat poultry lasagne, which is ideal for freezing and makes a tasty supper.

1 Put the milk, bay leaf, peppercorns and whole onion in a pan and bring to the boil. Remove from the heat and cover.

2 Heat the oil in a large saucepan and fry the onion and bacon in it for 3 minutes. Stir in the garlic and mushrooms and fry for 2 minutes, then add the minced turkey. Fry, stirring, for 3 minutes, until the meat changes colour, then stir in 2 level tablespoons of the flour, oregano, tomatoes, wine or stock and olives. Season with half the salt and some pepper and bring to the boil, stirring. Reduce the heat and simmer gently, uncovered, for 20 minutes, or until the mixture thickens slightly.

Per serving
Calories 635   Protein 53 g
Total fat 25 g (saturated fat 13 g)
Carbohydrates 46 g (added sugar 0)
Fibre 4 g   Sodium 1016 mg

3 Cook the pasta (see p.202) and drain well. Meanwhile, strain the milk, discarding the bay leaf, onion and peppercorns. Melt the butter or margarine in a saucepan, stir in the flour and cook over a low heat for 1 minute. Gradually stir in the milk and bring to the boil, stirring, until smooth and thick. Add the rest of the salt, some pepper and the nutmeg and simmer for 2 minutes.

4 Grease a large, shallow, ovenproof dish. Place a third of the lasagne sheets, overlapping slightly, over the base. Spread half the turkey sauce over the lasagne, then drizzle over a third of the white sauce. Repeat the layers, finishing with white sauce. Cover with the remaining lasagne and sprinkle with Parmesan. Allow to cool. Cover with non-toxic plastic film, wrap in foil, label (see p.340) and freeze for up to 2 months.

5 To thaw, unwrap the foil and place in the refrigerator bottom for 24 hours, or for 12 hours at room temperature, then uncover. Heat the oven to 180°C (350°F, gas mark 4), put the dish in the centre and bake for 1 hour, or until golden and bubbling. Garnish and serve.

SEAFOOD LASAGNE

Cod, prawns and mussels combine with pasta and white sauce to make this tasty lasagne.

Serves 4
Preparation time: 45 minutes
Cooking time: 1 hour

450 g (1 lb) cod fillet
570 ml (1 pint) water
1 bay leaf
Finely grated rind of ½ lemon
¼ level teaspoon salt
Freshly ground black pepper
60 g (2 oz) butter
2 spring onions, trimmed and
    finely chopped
60 g (2 oz) plain flour
150 ml (¼ pint) single cream
¼ level teaspoon ground nutmeg
1 tablespoon lemon juice
1 teaspoon anchovy essence
1 teaspoon tomato purée
115 g (4 oz) frozen cooked
    peeled prawns
115 g (4 oz) frozen cooked
    shelled mussels
200 g (7 oz) fresh egg lasagne
30 g (1 oz) fresh white breadcrumbs
30 g (1 oz) Parmesan cheese, grated
1 tablespoon chopped fresh parsley

Per serving
Calories 560 Protein 40 g
Total fat 25 g (saturated fat 15 g)
Carbohydrates 48 g (added sugar 0)
Fibre 2.8 g Sodium 997 mg

1 Cut the cod into two or three pieces, put them in a saucepan and cover with the water. Add the bay leaf, lemon rind, salt and some pepper and bring to the boil. Cover the pan, remove from the heat and leave to stand for 10 minutes. Then strain and reserve the cooking liquid. Flake the cod, discarding the skin and bones.

2 Melt the butter in a saucepan and sauté the spring onions in it for 1 minute. Stir in the flour and cook over a low heat for 1 minute, then gradually stir in 570 ml (1 pint) of the reserved cooking liquid. Bring to the boil, stirring, until thickened and smooth, then mix in the cream and nutmeg.

3 Pour off 285 ml (½ pint) of the sauce and set aside. Stir the lemon juice, anchovy essence and tomato purée into the remaining sauce and allow to cool, then mix in the cod, prawns and mussels.

4 Cook the lasagne (see p.202) and drain well. Grease a large shallow, 2 litre (3½ pint) ovenproof dish and arrange a third of the pasta in the bottom, with the sheets slightly overlapping. Spread half the seafood sauce evenly over the lasagne, then

repeat the layers, finishing with lasagne. Cover the top with the remaining pasta.

5 Stir the reserved white sauce and then spread it evenly over the top. Mix together the breadcrumbs, Parmesan and parsley and then sprinkle over the sauce.

6 Cover the top of the lasagne with non-toxic plastic film. Wrap the dish entirely in foil, label (see p.340) and freeze for up to 2 months.

7 To thaw the lasagne, remove the foil and leave it in the bottom of the refrigerator for 24 hours, or leave it to stand at room temperature for 12 hours.

8 Heat the oven to 180°C (350°F, gas mark 4). Remove the plastic film, place the lasagne in the centre of the oven, and bake for 1 hour or until golden brown and bubbling hot. (If the lasagne has not thawed completely in the centre, you may need to allow a little more baking time.)

Prawns, mussels and flaky cod baked with creamy sauce and lasagne make a light but sumptuous treat.

VEGETABLE CURRY

Serves 4
Preparation time: 45 minutes
Cooking time: 45 minutes

2 tablespoons olive oil
225 g (8 oz) onions, peeled and chopped
1 large clove garlic, peeled and crushed (see p.11)
2 teaspoons peeled and finely chopped fresh root ginger
½ level teaspoon chilli powder
1 level teaspoon each turmeric, ground cumin, ground coriander and paprika
4 cardamom pods
570 ml (1 pint) vegetable stock (see p.9) or water
1 tablespoon lemon juice
30 g (1 oz) creamed coconut, coarsely grated or chopped
250 g (9 oz) cooked chickpeas, rinsed and drained (see p.172)
115 g (4 oz) green lentils, sorted and rinsed
1.15 litres (2 pints) water
115 g (4 oz) long-grain brown rice
1 medium cauliflower, about 600 g (1 lb 5 oz), cut into small florets
115 g (4 oz) fine green beans, cut into short lengths
115 g (4 oz) frozen peas
1 tablespoon chopped fresh coriander to garnish

Cauliflower florets, fine green beans and peas are baked with long-grain brown rice, lentils and a spicy coconut sauce.

1 Heat the oil in a large saucepan and soften the onions in it over a moderate heat for 3 minutes. Add the garlic and ginger and fry for 2 minutes, stirring. Mix in the chilli powder, turmeric, cumin, coriander, paprika and cardamom pods, and fry gently, stirring, for 3 minutes.

2 Pour in the stock and add the lemon juice and creamed coconut. Bring to the boil, stirring, until slightly thickened. Mix in the cooked chickpeas, cover and simmer gently for 20 minutes.

3 Meanwhile, put the lentils and water in a saucepan, bring to the boil, and boil rapidly for 10 minutes. Stir in the rice, reduce

the heat, cover and simmer for 20 minutes, or until the rice and lentils are cooked. Drain well and allow to cool.

4 Add the cauliflower, beans and peas to the chickpeas, stirring until well coated with curry sauce. Cover and simmer for 5 minutes, then remove from the heat and leave to cool.

5 To freeze, arrange the rice and lentil mixture diagonally across the centre of a large, shallow, ovenproof dish and spoon the curry along either side. Cover with non-toxic plastic film. Wrap the dish in foil, label (see p.340) and freeze for up to 2 months.

6 To thaw, remove the foil from the dish and leave overnight at room temperature until completely defrosted. Preheat the oven to 180°C (350°F, gas mark 4). Remove the plastic film, cover the dish with foil and bake in the centre of the oven for 45 minutes, or until the rice and curry are heated through. Sprinkle with the coriander and serve.

Per serving
Calories 453 Protein 21 g
Total fat 16 g (saturated fat 5.8 g)
Carbohydrates 60 g (added sugar 0)
Fibre 10 g Sodium 22 mg

RATATOUILLE CRÊPES

Serves 4
Preparation time: 1 hour 45 minutes
Cooking time: 30 minutes

- 115 g (4 oz) plain flour
- ¼ level teaspoon salt
- 3 eggs, size 2, beaten
- 285 ml (½ pint) milk
- 450 g (1 lb) aubergines, trimmed and diced
- 1 level tablespoon salt
- 1 tablespoon olive oil
- 1 medium red onion, peeled and chopped
- 1 clove garlic, peeled and crushed
- 1 red pepper, de-seeded and chopped
- 3 medium plum tomatoes, skinned, de-seeded and chopped
- 2-3 level tablespoons chopped fresh coriander
- Freshly ground black pepper
- 2-3 tablespoons vegetable oil
- 175 g (6 oz) fine fresh white breadcrumbs
- Fresh watercress to garnish

Per serving
Calories 495 Protein 18 g
Total fat 19 g (saturated fat 3 g)
Carbohydrates 68 g (added sugar 0)
Fibre 7.8 g Sodium 814 mg

Wafer-thin pancakes are known as crêpes in France. They are served for dessert, or, as here, with a light savoury filling.

1 To make the crêpe batter, sift the flour and salt into a bowl. Make a well in the centre and beat in one egg and the milk to form a smooth batter. Pour into a jug, cover and leave for 1 hour.

2 Meanwhile, put the aubergine pieces in a large colander and sprinkle with the salt. Leave to stand on a plate for 30 minutes, then rinse under cold water, drain and pat dry with kitchen paper.

3 Heat the olive oil in a saucepan and cook the onion in it until softened. Stir in the garlic, red pepper, tomatoes, coriander and aubergines and season with pepper. Cook, uncovered,

Crispy breadcrumbs add crunch to lightly fried, stuffed pancakes.

over a moderate heat for about 30 minutes, or until almost all the liquid has evaporated. Remove from the heat and allow to cool.

4 In the meantime, cook 12 pancakes (see p.9) using the vegetable oil. Stack them between sheets of kitchen paper.

5 Spoon one-twelfth of the ratatouille mixture onto the centre of each pancake. Fold the sides to the middle, then fold in the ends to enclose the filling.

6 Beat the remaining eggs in a deep plate, then coat the pancakes, first with the egg and then with the breadcrumbs. Line a baking tray with foil and lay the pancakes in a single layer in the bottom of the tray.

7 Open-freeze the pancakes (see p.341), then transfer them to a rigid container. Cover, label and freeze for up to 3 months.

8 To serve, preheat the oven to 200°C (400°F, gas mark 6). Put the frozen pancakes on a greased baking tray and bake in the centre of the oven for 25-30 minutes, or until they are golden brown and the filling is thoroughly heated through. Garnish with watercress and serve hot with salad.

Broccoli and Ricotta Lasagne

Creamy ricotta cheese joins with broccoli, mushrooms, fresh lasagne and cashew nuts in a luxurious pasta bake.

Serves 4
Preparation time: 45 minutes
Cooking time: 1 hour

---

60 g (2 oz) butter
1 medium onion, peeled and chopped
60 g (2 oz) plain flour
425 ml (¾ pint) chicken or vegetable stock (see pp.8-9)
285 ml (½ pint) milk
¼ level teaspoon salt
Freshly ground black pepper
¼ level teaspoon ground nutmeg
1 level tablespoon Dijon mustard
115 g (4 oz) Gruyère cheese, grated
200 g (7 oz) fresh lasagne
2 tablespoons olive oil
100 g (3½ oz) cashew nuts
340 g (12 oz) broccoli, trimmed into small florets with stalks peeled and cut into matchstick strips
115 g (4 oz) mushrooms, wiped and sliced
1 large clove garlic, peeled and crushed (see p.11)
250 g (9 oz) ricotta cheese
30 g (1 oz) Parmesan cheese, grated
Fresh basil leaves to garnish

Per serving
Calories 809 Protein 34 g
Total fat 53 g (saturated fat 24 g)
Carbohydrates 53 g (added sugar 0)
Fibre 3.5 g Sodium 632 mg

1 Melt the butter in a saucepan and fry the onion in it over a moderate heat until softened but not browned. Stir in the flour and cook for 1 minute, then gradually add the stock and milk. Bring to the boil, stirring, until thickened and smooth. Add the salt, some pepper, the nutmeg and mustard and simmer for 2 minutes. Remove from the heat and stir in the grated Gruyère until melted, then cover the pan and set aside.

2 Cook the lasagne (see p.202) and drain well. Meanwhile, heat the oil in a frying pan and fry the cashew nuts in it until golden brown. Transfer the cashews onto a plate and then add the broccoli to the pan. Fry over a high heat for 2-3 minutes, then mix in the mushrooms and garlic and stir-fry for a further 2 minutes. Add the nuts, then remove from the heat.

3 Grease a shallow 2 litre (3½ pint) ovenproof dish and arrange one-third of the lasagne on the bottom, the sheets slightly overlapping. Spread with half the ricotta, then spoon half the broccoli mixture evenly on top. Cover with one-third of the cheese sauce, then repeat the layers, finishing with lasagne. Spread the rest of the sauce over the top and sprinkle with the Parmesan.

4 Leave the lasagne to cool, then cover the top with non-toxic plastic film. Wrap the dish entirely in foil, label (see p.340) and freeze for up to 2 months. To thaw the lasagne, remove the foil and leave it in the bottom of the refrigerator for 24 hours, or at room temperature for 12 hours.

5 Heat the oven to 180°C (350°F, gas mark 4). Remove the plastic film and place the lasagne in the centre of the oven. Bake for 1 hour, until golden brown and bubbling – it may be necessary to allow a little more baking time if the lasagne has not thawed out completely in the centre. Garnish with the basil and serve with pugliese or other Italian bread.

Making the most of the freezer

Freezing eases the planning and provision of meals, especially if you cook for a busy family or entertain a great deal. Careful preparation of raw and cooked food for the freezer and safe thawing will ensure that food looks and tastes as fresh as it did when put in to freeze.

MEAT, FISH, VEGETABLES and basic foodstuffs such as bread and butter can be stored in a freezer alongside a good stock of complete, precooked meals. Dishes that require lengthy preparation, such as moussaka or lasagne, can be made in advance, when you have the time, then frozen, ready for use when you entertain. Using the freezer to its full potential reduces the stress of planning and preparing meals – but there are several precautions to bear in mind to ensure that food is frozen safely.

To freeze fresh foods, only use freezers marked with a 4-star symbol. The temperature inside the freezer should be kept at –18 to –23°C (0 to –10°F) and checked regularly with a freezer thermometer. Allow food to cool completely before freezing. Hot or warm food will raise the internal temperature of the freezer and slow down freezing, and may also affect other frozen dishes.

Preparing food for the freezer

Pack or wrap food in moisture proof materials before freezing, and remove as much air as possible to prevent drying out and 'freezer burn' (discoloured patches). All items should be labelled – use a waterproof pen to write on the name, date and weight or number of servings, where appropriate.

Polythene freezer bags are suitable for wrapping all types of food, although rigid plastic or waxed containers are best for liquids. Only bags marked 'suitable for freezing' are thick enough to protect food.

Heavy-duty foil can be used for small portions of foods, or to overwrap joints of meat, poultry or fresh fish which have already been wrapped in freezer film. Thinner foil is not suitable for the freezer as it splits easily. Foil should not be used to wrap acid food, such as tomatoes or fruit as it reacts with the acid.

Foods which are to be stored for long periods or which have protruding bones, need extra protection from their wrappings splitting open and from drying out. After wrapping, put them in polythene freezer bags before freezing.

Wrapping a joint of meat

1 Wrap joints of meat closely with non-toxic plastic film.

2 Overwrap the joint with heavy-duty foil, seal well and label clearly. Put large joints with protruding bones inside a large, polythene freezer bag for extra protection.

Vegetables need to be blanched in boiling water for 1-2 minutes before being frozen to destroy the enzymes that would cause the gradual deterioration of their colour, flavour and texture while frozen.

Once the vegetables have been blanched, cooled and dried, they should be packed into polythene freezer bags and frozen, or open-frozen (see below) and transferred to polythene freezer bags for storage in the freezer.

Blanching broccoli

1 Plunge the broccoli florets into a saucepan of boiling water for 1-2 minutes, then remove from the pan and immediately plunge the broccoli in a bowl of ice-cold water to cool.

2 Once the broccoli has cooled, shake off any excess water. Spread the broccoli out on kitchen paper and leave to dry for about 5 minutes.

3 Transfer the vegetables to polythene freezer bags, extract the air, tie and label, or open-freeze them (see right) before packing.

Open freezing is a good way of freezing blanched vegetables and fruits to keep them free-flowing, and also for small, individual items such as pasties and fish cakes (see below). Cooked rice can be frozen this way, then added to soups, stews, casseroles and stir-fries from frozen.

Open-freezing pasties

Arrange the pasties in a single layer on a tray lined with plastic film. Cover loosely with more film and freeze. Once frozen, transfer to a rigid plastic container. To exclude as much air as possible, fill any space left at the top of the container with crumpled plastic film, then cover with the lid, label clearly and return to the freezer.

Cooked dishes must be cooled and frozen as quickly as possible to prevent attack by bacteria and to stop the activity of organisms which cause food to deteriorate. If you forget to freeze a dish the same day as making it, use it up rather than freeze it the next day.

To cool food quickly to room temperature, leave it in the coldest part of the kitchen and cover it with a net food umbrella to keep the flies off and allow the steam to escape. Stand deeper dishes containing casseroles or stews in a bowl of iced water. As soon as the food is cool, chill it in the fridge for 1-2 hours before freezing.

Freezing meals could mean that many of your ovenproof dishes end up in the freezer. To avoid this problem, freeze cooked dishes by following the steps (below).

Freezing in a foil-lined dish

1 Line an ovenproof dish with heavy-duty foil, then pour the cooled stew into it. Cover with freezer film and freeze.

2 Turn the block of frozen stew out of the dish, then wrap with heavy-duty foil and secure with freezer tape. Label and return to the freezer. If the stew is to be frozen for a long period, then put it in a strong polythene freezer bag first for extra protection.

3 Remove the frozen stew from the freezer and take off the wrappings. Put the stew back in the same dish in which it was frozen, cover with a lid or foil, then thaw and/or reheat as instructed in the recipe.

Thawing food from the freezer

When food is frozen, the water content turns to crystals and damages the cell structure of the ingredients. As a result, frozen foods are consequently more vulnerable to being attacked by bacteria during and after thawing than are fresh foods; they should therefore be cooked as quickly as possible once thawed, or reheated or cooked from frozen.

Uncooked meat, poultry and fish should be left to thaw on a rack or upturned saucer on a large plate, covered with a large bowl or foil tent which allows the air to circulate. They should not be left to sit in their own juices, because these can contain bacteria. Cooked dishes, such as stews or soups, should be left to thaw as directed in the recipes – generally overnight in the fridge.

Every recipe in this chapter gives an approximate thawing time for the dish, but **thawing times vary** for a number of reasons. These include the size of the dish, its thickness and composition (a cast-iron dish will remain colder for a longer time than an ovenproof glass casserole); the temperature of the dish when it was taken out of the freezer; the depth of the cooked food (the same lasagne assembled in a deep dish will take longer to thaw than in a shallow dish); the temperature of the room and larder – these in turn can be affected by the time of year; and the temperature of the fridge.

Reheating food from frozen

Soups and stews can be reheated slowly in a saucepan, and must be stirred occasionally.

Casseroles that can be thawed and reheated in the oven must be frozen in suitable dishes (most ovenproof dishes will crack if put into a hot oven from a freezer) or wrapped. Bear in mind that dishes reheated from frozen will take 1-1½ hours longer than the reheating time given in the recipes in this chapter.

Glossary

The entries in this A-Z glossary define cookery terms and some of the techniques and more unusual ingredients used in the recipes in this book, to enhance your understanding and enjoyment of the food you cook. The illustrations help you to identify many of the ingredients you will be using.

akee Oval or oblong Caribbean fruit with cream-coloured flesh, shiny black seeds and a woody shell. It has the taste and texture of scrambled eggs. It is cooked like a vegetable and typically served with salted cod.

al dente Term used to describe the tender, yet firm to the bite texture of cooked pasta. The words are Italian for 'to the tooth'.

au gratin Term used to describe a dish covered in a sauce and topped with breadcrumbs or grated cheese, or both, then browned under the grill or baked in the oven.

bake blind To bake a pastry case without a filling. The pastry is usually covered with a circle of greaseproof paper and some dried beans to prevent it rising while cooking.

baste To spoon or pour melted fat or liquid over food during cooking to keep it moist.

blanch To immerse food briefly in boiling water, then plunge it into cold water to cool it. Blanching is used to soften vegetables, loosen the skin of nuts, fruits and vegetables, remove strong, bitter or salty flavours or kill enzymes and set the colour of food before freezing. See pp.10 and 340.

bouquet garni Bunch of herbs which usually includes parsley, thyme, marjoram and bay leaves and is used to flavour soups and stews.

bratwurst Fine-textured, delicately seasoned sausage made of minced veal or pork.

bulgur wheat Whole grains of wheat which are boiled and baked before being cracked. After soaking in water, the mild nutty grains can be eaten boiled or steamed, in FALAFEL or in salads such as TABBOULEH. When bulgur wheat is used to make a PILAFF it does not need to be soaked first.

cajun cooking Culinary style from the southern United States which employs many of the ingredients and cooking techniques of French cooking, but with African, Indian and Spanish influences. Seafood, game birds, spicy sausages, sweet potatoes, aubergines, peppers, tomatoes, OKRA, hot spices and rice are typically used. GUMBO and jambalaya are typical of this style of cooking. Creole cooking is virtually the same as cajun cooking but it is slightly less rustic and hearty in character, and more influenced by the cooking of other ethnic groups.

callalloo Caribbean soup made with callalloo greens – the young leaves of the dasheen or taro plant – and crab. Callalloo greens have a faintly bitter flavour reminiscent of spinach, Swiss chard or PAK CHOI.

Camembert Soft, creamy yellow French cheese, similar to Brie but with a more pronounced flavour.

capers Small, olive-green flower buds which are pickled in brine. Their salty, piquant flavour enlivens bland poultry, fish or egg dishes.

caponata Sicilian speciality which includes aubergines, tomatoes, onion, capers, tomato purée, vinegar, olives and anchovies. It is served as an hors d'oeuvre, used to make pasta sauces or served with CROSTINI or crackers.

cassoulet Traditional French country stew of dried haricot beans, pork, lamb, goose or duck, sausage, herbs and vegetables.

Bread contributes starch, fibre, minerals, vitamins and a welcome texture as an accompaniment to many one-dish meals. Italian focaccia, ciabatta and pugliese and Spanish pan gallego are shown among the more familiar varieties of bread.

Seeded light rye · Light rye · Naan · Pan gallego · Focaccia · Walnut · Olive · French bread · Grissini stick · Pugliese · Ciabatta · Pitta bread · Tortilla · Baguette · Pumpernickel · Poppy seed roll · Large bap · Baton · Granary cottage roll · Farmhouse

chickpeas Small, round dried peas which are pale tan or dark brown in colour. They need soaking and gentle simmering to become soft. Chickpeas are eaten in salads, soups, stews and with pasta. They are used extensively in Middle Eastern cookery to make dishes such as FALAFEL. They are also known by the Spanish name *garbanzo*.

Chinese egg noodles Soft, thin noodles made from wheat flour and used in hot and cold oriental dishes. See p.202.

Chinese greens Member of the chard family with long white stems topped by rich green leaves. The crisp leaves and stems are good in stir-fried dishes. The Cantonese name is pak choi, meaning 'white vegetable'.

chorizo Coarse-textured, smoked Spanish sausage made from pork and seasoned with garlic, herbs, paprika and other spices. Chorizo come in many regional varieties and are eaten raw, grilled or added to stews.

chowder Thick, creamy soup or stew made with fish or shellfish, especially clams, and vegetables.

ciabatta Open-textured Italian bread, made with olive oil.

cocotte Small ovenproof ramekin dish in which eggs, soufflés and mousses are cooked and served. The method of cooking in one is known as *en cocotte*.

cornflour Fine white powdery flour which is made from corn and used to thicken gravies, sauces and puddings, and in baking.

cornmeal Coarse or medium ground white or yellow corn used with wheat flour to make cakes and breads. In Italy it is used to make POLENTA.

couscous Tiny round grains made from semolina, the golden heart of

durum wheat which has a buttery flavour that pairs well with spicy foods. See p.173.

creamed coconut Concentrated coconut milk, which is sold in blocks and used to flavour stews, curries and rice. It is widely used in Caribbean and South-east Asian cookery.

creole cooking See CAJUN COOKING.

crostini Slices of fried or toasted bread used as a garnish. See p.47.

croutons Small cubes of bread, fried in oil or butter until crunchy and used as a garnish for soups and salads. Croutes are larger cubes or shapes of bread that are fried in the same way.

curry paste Ground curry spices which are fried, then mixed with oil, and tend to give a fresher, more fragrant flavour than curry powder.

de-beard To remove the stringy 'beard' from mussels before cooking them.

de-vein To remove the fine, bitter-tasting black vein from shellfish, particularly from the backs of prawns, using the tip of a small, sharp knife or a cocktail stick.

drizzle To moisten food with a very fine, steady stream of oil, dressing or liquid, without coating it completely.

Emmenthal Pale yellow, Swiss cheese with large holes, which has a sweet, musky flavour. Emmenthal is a good cooking cheese because it melts easily.

falafel Middle Eastern rissole, cake, or other small shape made from ground, dried CHICKPEAS mixed with spices, and sometimes BULGUR WHEAT. Falafel is served with salad, used as a filling in pitta bread or baked in a casserole.

feta Crumbly Greek white cheese of sheep or goat's milk which is ripened in brine, giving it a piquant flavour.

Semolina
Polenta
Couscous
Bulgur wheat
Wild rice
Basmati rice
Arborio rice
White long-grain rice
Whole-grain barley
Cornmeal
Pearl barley
Brown long-grain rice
Wild rice and long-grain mixture

Grains are rich in minerals and form the basis of many vegetarian dishes and many national dishes, such as the polenta of Italy and the couscous of North Africa.

filo pastry Tissue-thin sheets of a wheat flour pastry, which are brushed with butter or oil and then layered. Filo is used in Greek, Turkish and Middle Eastern cookery. See p.285.

flambé Term used to describe food tossed in warm alcohol which has been set alight in a pan. Flambéing flavours a dish and burns off any fat it may contain.

flameproof Term used to describe cookery utensils which can safely be used over a gas flame or electric ring.

focaccia Flat, Italian bread which can be plain or flavoured with olives or sun-dried tomatoes.

frittata Flat, Italian omelette cake made of eggs and vegetables, which is served hot, warm or cold.

fromage frais Soft, light curd cheese which has the consistency of thick yoghurt. Low-fat varieties are healthy substitutes for cream.

gazpacho Cold Spanish soup of puréed tomatoes, peppers, cucumber, garlic, olive oil and vinegar. Recipes vary throughout Spain, but the original recipe comes from Andalusia.

gnocchi Small dumplings made from flour, potatoes, choux pastry, semolina or maize flour.

goulash Hungarian soup or stew of beef, onions and tomatoes seasoned with paprika.

grains Seeds or fruits of cereal grasses, such as wheat, barley and corn, which are invariably staple foods. See illustration (above) and pp.172-3.

grissini Long, crisp Italian bread sticks. See illustration on p.342.

groundnut Another name for the peanut. Groundnuts produce a bland, versatile oil, which is suitable for cooking and salad dressings.

Gruyère Smooth, yellow Swiss cheese with small holes and a nutty flavour. It is an excellent cooking cheese for sauces, quiches and fondues because it melts easily and smoothly.

gumbo Thick stew of fish or poultry, or both together, with tomatoes and OKRA, the juice of which gives the stew its thick, gelatinous consistency.

hash Flat, pan-sized cake of chopped meat, potatoes and other vegetables which are mixed together and fried until crisp and browned.

heatproof Term used to describe cookery equipment (including handles) that can withstand high oven temperatures. Heatproof equipment cannot always be used over a flame or under the grill: compare FLAMEPROOF.

julienne Term used to describe vegetables cut into uniform fine strips, which are cooked and served as an accompaniment or garnish to a dish, or in clear soups. See p.10.

kale Coarse-textured, dark green winter cabbage which can be either crinkly or smooth-leaved and has a strong but sweet flavour.

knackwurst Sausage made of minced pork and fresh pork fat, which is flavoured with salt, cumin and garlic. Knackwurst sausages are sold in pairs or in long links, and are similar to frankfurters. See BRATWURST.

marinate To soak food, particularly meat, poultry and game in a marinade, or seasoned liquid, paste or dry blend of herbs and spices, to tenderise and flavour it. See p.81.

microwave-safe Term used to describe cookware made of glass or ceramic with a non-metallic glaze, or HEATPROOF plastic, which is marked as suitable for use in a microwave oven.

Monterey Jack Yellow American cheese with a flavour similar to Cheddar but a softer texture. Like Cheddar, Monterey Jack ranges in flavour from mild to mature.

mozzarella Rubbery, moist, white cheese originally made from buffalo's milk, but now more often from cow's milk. It stretches into strings when hot and is a traditional ingredient in pizza.

mushrooms The common white mushroom is sold at three stages of growth – button (closed) when young, cup (good for stuffing), and flat (open) when older. The more mature the mushroom the deeper the flavour. Wild European porcini (ceps) and the dark brown oriental shiitake are sold fresh and dried. Their meaty, rich flavour and chewy texture combine well with other mushrooms. Oysters have a milder flavour and softer texture than shiitake, and shrink to half their original size during cooking. Dried mushrooms can be found in delicatessens and some of the larger supermarkets. See illustration (left).

okra Soft tapering green pods of an African plant of the cotton family. They have an earthy flavour that pairs well with spicy dishes, and ooze a sticky juice when cut. Okra is used to make GUMBO, Indian vegetable curries, and Caribbean, Greek and Turkish dishes. Okra is also known as lady's finger and by its Indian name, *bhindi*.

ovenproof Term describing plates, dishes and pots that can withstand the heat of a conventional oven.

pak choi See CHINESE GREENS.

parboil To boil vegetables briefly until they are partially cooked.

Parma ham Raw, salted Italian ham which is cured by air-drying in the hills of the Parma region.

Parmesan Hard, yellow, Italian cooking cheese which has a tangy, fruity flavour and is best eaten fresh.

passata Thick, concentrated sauce of sieved tomatoes used to flavour Italian pasta and pizza dishes.

pasta Italian speciality which can be bought fresh or dried. It is mostly made from durum wheat semolina mixed with water, or with eggs and olive oil, to make a dough which is then rolled or extruded into hundreds of different shapes. See p.202.

paupiettes Thin slices of meat, fish or poultry, rolled around a savoury filling and served with a sauce.

pawpaw Large, pear-shaped fruit of a West Indian tree with a thin, smooth orange skin, sweet, fragrant flesh and many small black seeds. Pawpaw makes a refreshing accompaniment for smoked meats and spicy food. It is also known as papaw or papaya.

pesto Paste made by grinding together fresh basil, PINE NUTS, garlic, Parmesan and olive oil. Pesto has a fresh, pungent flavour and aroma, and is used as a base for sauces or served on its own with pasta.

pilaff Eastern Mediterranean rice dish that is prepared by simmering rice, COUSCOUS or BULGUR WHEAT, without stirring, until all the liquid has been absorbed. Cooked meat or fish and vegetables are then added to the rice.

pine nuts Small blanched edible seeds of the stone pine, having a sweetly resinous taste and a plump chewiness that are intensified when the seeds are lightly toasted, grilled or fried.

plantain Fruit of the banana family, similar in appearance to a banana but larger and not as sweet. It is often used under-ripe, and must be cooked before being eaten.

Flat   Chestnut   Porcini (ceps)

Dried shiitake   Fresh shiitake

Oyster

Yellow oyster

Cup

Button

Mushrooms are sold fresh, dried and at various stages of growth. Combinations of varieties bring out the best in flavour and texture.

Black turtle beans

Black kidney beans

Aduki beans

Brown lentils

Green lentils

Puy

Cannellini beans

Red kidney beans

Black-eyed beans

Flageolet beans

Red lentils

Yellow split peas

Broth mix

Haricot beans

Chickpeas

Green split peas

Pinto beans

Pulses *are rich in carbohydrates, proteins and minerals, and often replace meat in a vegetarian diet.*

Butter beans

Broad beans

Borlotti beans

polenta Italian dish made by boiling ground CORNMEAL until thick, cooling the mixture until set, then steaming, grilling or frying it.

prosciutto Italian name for ham, used in Italy for the uncooked, cooked and smoked varieties, but in Britain it usually refers to raw smoked ham, which is served finely sliced.

provençal, à la Food cooked with garlic and tomatoes.

pugliese Close-textured Italian bread which is made with olive oil.

pulses Plants that yield edible seeds in a pod, often eaten after drying, such as lentils, dried beans and peas. Pulses always require cleaning, and usually soaking, before cooking. See illustration (above) and pp.172-3.

purée To reduce food to a thick liquid or paste by passing it through a sieve or food mill, or in an electric blender or food processor. See p.46.

reduce To boil a liquid rapidly until its volume reduces by evaporation. This action usually thickens the liquid and concentrates its flavour. To reduce by a third means to boil until a third of the liquid has evaporated.

rice wine Slightly sweet wine made from rice, which is used in oriental recipes to impart a delicate, almost flowery flavour. It is also known as *sake*. Dry sherry is a good substitute.

ricotta Dry, creamy Italian cheese made from leftover whey from other cheeses made with sheep's milk. It is especially good mixed with Parmesan and spinach in ravioli.

sake See RICE WINE.

salad greens and leaves Lettuces, cabbages, sprouts, edible leaves and edible flowers, which range from soft to crisp in texture and sweet to bitter in flavour. See p.232.

salsa sauce Thick sauce made with tomatoes, onions, spices and chilli and served with TORTILLAS. Salsa is the Italian and Spanish word for sauce.

salted cod Dried, salted cod with a pungent flavour. It needs to be soaked at least overnight, or for up to 48 hours, before cooking, and the soaking water has to be changed regularly to remove the salt. There are several types of salted cod which vary in saltiness and dryness, and it is available whole or cut into pieces. See p.146.

sauerkraut Shredded, salted and fermented white cabbage which traditionally accompanies smoked meats and sausages and boiled potatoes. The Austrians gave sauerkraut its name, which means 'sour plant', and passed it to the Germans and French, who call it *choucroute*.

sauté To toss and turn food in shallow, hot fat in an uncovered pan until evenly browned.

seitan Meat substitute made from wheat gluten, which has a similar texture and appearance to chunks of stewed beef. It is rich in protein and amino acids and is suitable for vegans.

shallots Small nut-brown onions that grow in clusters similar to garlic. Shallots taste less harsh than onions, less pungent than garlic, yet subtly combine the fragrances of both.

shellfish The two main groups of shellfish are crustaceans, such as lobster, crab, shrimps and prawns and crayfish, and molluscs, which include oysters, mussels, scallops and clams. Some confusion can arise over the names of crustaceans, particularly concerning prawns, shrimps and crayfish. Prawns come from all over the world, from cold seas and from warm seas. Common prawns come mainly from cold seas and vary in size from 2.5-10 cm (1-4 in) long. These are sold cooked, shelled and unshelled, either fresh or frozen. Dublin Bay prawns are also known as langoustines, and when they are peeled and cooked, their tails are known as scampi. Tiger prawns and crevettes are warm water prawns and can be bought cooked or uncooked. King prawns are very large prawns which are caught in warm seas. Small prawns from warm seas do not have the same flavour as common prawns from cold seas, and can be bought quite cheaply, already cooked, peeled and frozen – these are often labelled cooking prawns. Crayfish, also known as *écrevisse*, are small freshwater crustaceans similar to lobster. See illustration (right).

simmer To keep a liquid just below boiling point, when small bubbles form at the edges only. Also, to cook food in a simmering liquid.

skim To remove fat, foam or scum from the surface of soup, stock or pan drippings with a spoon or ladle.

soufflé Light, airy, sweet or savoury baked dish. It is made by folding stiffly beaten egg whites into a thick sauce or purée. Cooking the mixture in a straight-sided, circular soufflé dish helps it to rise successfully.

soya bean curd See TOFU.

spatchcock Old English method of cooking a chicken by splitting it down the back, laying it out flat and grilling or frying it. The method is suitable for small game birds, which do not require hanging, and oven-ready poussins. The name comes from dispatch-cock, and was used in the 18th century when a chicken might be hurriedly killed and cooked for unexpected guests. See p.116.

stir-fry To cook small, uniform pieces of food quickly in hot oil in a wok or deep frying pan over high heat, tossing and turning them constantly.

tabbouleh Middle Eastern salad made with BULGUR WHEAT, diced tomato, cucumber and onion and chopped herbs, bound together with lemon juice and olive oil.

taco Crisp corn TORTILLA, fried in oil and folded and filled with minced beef, chicken or pork, an avocado and

tomato sauce and shredded lettuce. In America, grated cheese and hot chilli sauce are added.

tahini Thick, creamy, nutty paste made from crushed sesame seeds.

tapas Small cooked and uncooked appetisers, which are traditionally served in Spanish bars. They include shellfish, vegetables, meat, sausages, such as CHORIZO, and TORTILLAS.

tempeh Solid frozen block of fermented soya beans or whole grains, which is thawed, then cut into cubes or slices and cooked as a substitute for meat. Tempeh should be stored in the refrigerator, wrapped in non-toxic plastic film, and used within 3-4 days.

textured vegetable protein (TVP) Dehydrated product made primarily from de-fatted soya beans, but also from wheat flour and pulses. It is available in plain or flavoured chunks or minced. After water or stock is added, it has a fibrous, meat-like texture which is suitable for stews, casseroles, pies, curries, burgers or rissoles. It will keep for up to 12 months in an air-tight container.

tofu Bland, cream-coloured soya bean curd with the same protein content as chicken. It is made from soya milk by a process which is similar to that used for cheese making. Tofu is low in fat, high in protein and cholesterol-free. It is also a good source of calcium, vitamins and minerals, and quickly absorbs other flavours, such as marinades. Firm tofu has a smooth texture which makes it easy to cut it into cubes or slices before grilling, frying or stir-fying. The silken variety is softer and good for blending and making dips and sauces. Smoked and ready-marinated tofu is also available.

tortilla Spanish omelette cake which is made with eggs, sliced potatoes and onions, and served hot or cold as a main part of TAPAS. Flour tortillas are flat, round Mexican breads or pancakes. Tortilla chips are spicy, triangular corn crisps, usually eaten as a snack with dips or crushed and sprinkled over food as a garnish.

truss To draw the legs of a bird tightly together with string or skewers, then tuck the wings under the body so that the bird is compact, holds its shape, and roasts more evenly. See p.117.

vinaigrette Salad dressing made from oil, vinegar and seasonings. It is sometimes referred to as French dressing. See p.233.

water chestnuts Small, round, dark-skinned tubers with a crisp, white flesh inside. They grow under water and are often used in Chinese cookery, such as in stir-fries. Water chestnuts have a crunchy texture and a delicate nut flavour. They are sold fresh or in cans, whole or sliced.

yam Long tuberous root with a texture similar to the potato. The flesh may be white, yellow or red and is sweet and moist. Yams are usually lightly boiled and served with butter, nutmeg, and other spices, or with some fruits and nuts. The term yam is sometimes wrongly applied to the soft, orange-coloured sweet potato.

zest Thin, outer rind of an orange or lemon which is removed with a grater or paring knife. Zest contains aromatic oils used to flavour foods.

Venus clams

Amande clams

Common prawn

Lobster

Scallop

Brown shrimps

Pink shrimps

Oysters

Cooked mussel

Uncooked mussel

Crab

Cooked tiger prawns

Uncooked tiger prawn

Shellfish have the best flavour when bought live in their shells, although lobsters are mostly sold freshly cooked. The best prawns are those sold unpeeled – cooked or uncooked.

Index

Acknowledgments

The publishers express their thanks to:
Meat and Livestock Commission
Sharp Electronics (UK) Limited

Some of the photographs in this book were taken from 'One Dish Meals', published in 1991 by Reader's Digest, USA (photographer Michael Molkenthin); from 'One Dish Meals', published in 1992 by Reader's Digest, South Africa (photographer Roger Bell); and from 'Piatto unico!', published in 1991 by Selezione dal Reader's Digest, Italy (photographer Umberto Torromacco). Photographs of cuts of beef, lamb and pork on pp.78-79 supplied by Meat and Livestock Commission. All of the photographs in this book are Reader's Digest copyright.

The editors are grateful to the following organisations for their courtesy in providing the following items for the photography in this book:
26-27 Soup bowl and dinner plate: Villeroy & Boch Tableware Ltd. **30** Soup bowl: Wedgwood. **36** Soup cup and saucer: Eigen Arts Inc. **39** Napkin: Le Jacquard Français; tray: The Museum of Modern Art Design Store. **41** Soup bowl and dinner plate: Hutschenreuther. **46-47** Napkin: Le Jacquard Français; soup bowl and dinner plate: Villeroy & Boch Tableware Ltd. **51** Platter, salt and pepper shakers, and wineglasses: Royal Copenhagen/Georg Jensen Silversmiths. **58-59** Napkin: Le Jacquard Français; plate: Eigen Arts Inc. **60-61** Trivet: Dansk International Designs Ltd; small bowl: Eigen Arts Inc. **66-67** Tablecloth surface and dinner plate: Spode; fork and flatware: Jean Couzon Inc; tablecloth: Le Jacquard Français. **75** Platter: Hutschenreuther. **88-89** Platter: Hutschenreuther. **95** Platter and glasses: Dansk International Designs Ltd; tablecloth: The Bebe Winkler Collection. **99** Plate: Dansk International Designs Ltd. **100** Condiment bowls: Eigen Arts Inc.; platter: Wedgwood. **112** Plate: Dansk International Designs Ltd.

Cover photograph Vernon Morgan
Home Economist Kathy Man

Retouching Ian Atkinson and Paragon Studios
Separations Saxon Photo Litho Ltd, Norwich
Printing and binding Grafica Editoriale Srl, Bologna

40-379-1